"N. T. Wright's thesis that most Second Temple Jews believed that they were in a protracted state of punitive exile, despite the fact that many Judeans had returned to the land from Babylon, is one of the most exciting and controversial proposals in biblical scholarship. In this volume, James Scott has assembled a wonderful cast of scholars to prod, evaluate, critique, and engage Wright's thesis about exile in biblical theology, Jewish literature, and as a theological idea in the New Testament. It's the best exploration to date of what it meant for the Jewish people, including the early church, to look forward to the day when 'many will come from the east and west to recline in the company of Abraham.'"

Michael F. Bird, lecturer in theology, Ridley College, Melbourne, Australia

"For some New Testament scholars, the notion of exiled Israel awaiting return is a powerful explanatory paradigm for a range of biblical texts. For others, it is a vague impulse that may or may not have been 'in the air' in the first century but in any case does little interpretive work for reading the Gospels and Paul. This fresh engagement with N. T. Wright's thesis and his restatement of it and response to critics brings the discussion up to date and provides scholars and students with an excellent survey of the state of the question."

Timothy Gombis, Grand Rapids Theological Seminary

"Editor James Scott suggests that many scholars think Tom Wright's thesis of ongoing exile in Second Temple Judaism and its role in the visions of Jesus and Paul is either his 'greatest accomplishment' or his 'most serious weakness.' This collection of perceptive essays engages Wright's thesis in a dialogical manner, generally affirming but also refining, developing, and challenging aspects of it. A book not to be missed by anyone interested in this important topic."

Michael J. Gorman, Raymond E. Brown Professor of Biblical Studies and Theology, St. Mary's Seminary & University, Baltimore

"Over the course of his remarkable career, N. T. Wright has somehow managed to ignite contemporary biblical scholarship's most burning questions. Of these, one of the hottest revolves around Wright's thesis of ongoing exile. Now James Scott and company do us a great service by providing some important illumination on an issue that for too long has been dominated by reactive smoke and heat."

Nicholas Perrin, Franklin S. Dyrness Chair of Biblical Studies, dean, Wheaton Graduate School

"The idea of the end of Israel's exile is one of the most distinctive features of N. T. Wright's ambitious construction of a theology of Jesus and Paul. It has also proved controversial. Most of the essays in this volume are broadly favorable toward Wright's project but probe the idea of 'exile' from various perspectives. The arguments they advance and the responses Wright gives are full of interest. Both fans and critics of Wright's work will find themselves entering a fruitful conversation."

Richard Bauckham, emeritus professor of New Testament studies, University of St. Andrews, Scotland

EXILE

A Conversation with

N. T. WRIGHT

Edited by
JAMES M. SCOTT

IVP Academic

An imprint of InterVarsity Press
Downers Grove, Illinois

InterVarsity Press
P.O. Box 1400, Downers Grove, IL 60515-1426
ivpress.com
email@ivpress.com

InterVarsity Press® is the book-publishing division of InterVarsity Christian Fellowship/USA®, a movement of students and faculty active on campus at hundreds of universities, colleges, and schools of nursing in the United States of America, and a member movement of the International Fellowship of Evangelical Students. For information about local and regional activities, visit intervarsity.org.

Cover design: Cindy Kiple
Interior design: Daniel van Loon
Images: Jerusalem: The City of Jerusalem and surrounding area, detail from the Ma'daba mosaic map,
  Byzantine, 6th century (mosaic), Byzantine School at Church of Saint Gaorge, Ma'daba,
  Jordan / Bridgeman Images
    Grunge paper: © asimetric/iStockphoto

ISBN 978-0-8308-5183-6 (print)
ISBN 978-0-8308-9000-2 (digital)

Printed in the United States of America ∞

Library of Congress Cataloging-in-Publication Data
A catalog record for this book is available from the Library of Congress.
Names: Scott, James M., 1955- editor.
Title: Exile : a conversation with N.T. Wright / edited by James M. Scott.
Description: Downers Grove : InterVarsity Press, 2017. | Includes index.
Identifiers: LCCN 2017019259 (print) | LCCN 2017021561 (ebook) | ISBN 9780830890002 (eBook) | ISBN 9780830851836 (hardcover : alk. paper)
Subjects: LCSH: Wright, N. T. (Nicholas Thomas)–Philosophy. | Jews–History–586 B.C.-70 A.D. | Exile (Punishment)–Biblical teaching. | Bible–Criticism, interpretation, etc.
Classification: LCC DS122 (ebook) | LCC DS122 .E95 2017 (print) | DDC 933–dc23
LC record available at https://lccn.loc.gov/2017019259

| P | 25 | 24 | 23 | 22 | 21 | 20 | 19 | 18 | 17 | 16 | 15 | 14 | 13 | 12 | 11 | 10 | 9 | 8 | 7 | 6 | 5 | 4 | 3 | 2 | 1 |
| Y | 34 | 33 | 32 | 31 | 30 | 29 | 28 | 27 | 26 | 25 | 24 | 23 | 22 | 21 | 20 | 19 | | 18 | | 17 |

For Sylvie Vandekerkhove

Visionary, Benefactor, Friend

CONTENTS

PREFACE

In November of 2010, N. T. Wright came to Trinity Western University as the speaker for the University's annual Distinguished Lecturer Series. In order to take full advantage of his visit to the university, I organized a symposium on exile in collaboration with the MA program in biblical studies and the Department of Religious Studies at TWU. The idea was to provide an opportunity for Wright to rearticulate his controversial thesis about a continuing exile (more on that later) and then to invite scholars from a variety of academic disciplines to interact with that thesis from their own unique vantage points. Many of the essays that are included in this volume originated as papers read at the symposium, although they were revised—often quite substantially—for publication. The rest were commissioned in order to provide additional coverage of the subject from other perspectives.

I am grateful to N. T. Wright for agreeing to expand the original scope of his visit to TWU in order to include the symposium on exile. My sincere thanks go to the Reid Trust for funding both the symposium itself and the subsequent preparation of this volume for publication. I wish to thank Dan Reid at InterVarsity Press for shepherding the publication of this project from the beginning and for exercising supreme patience as we anxiously waited for all the contributors to submit their essays. Tony Cummins has been an invaluable sounding board and faithful partner in this endeavor at every stage, and Spencer Jones has been of enormous help in bringing this volume into final form. I would like to express my heartfelt appreciation to them both.

This book is dedicated in profound gratitude to Sylvie Vandekerkhove, who not only hosted an exquisite dinner for the participants at the conclusion of the symposium but also for many years has been a staunch supporter of the Department of Religious Studies.

ABBREVIATIONS

General

DSS	Dead Sea Scrolls
LXX	Septuagint
MT	Masoretic Text

Deuterocanonical Works and Septuagint

1 Esdr	1 Esdras
1 Macc	1 Maccabees
2 Macc	2 Maccabees
3 Macc	3 Maccabees
Bar	Baruch
Jdt	Judith
Sir	Sirach (Ecclesiasticus)
Tob	Tobit

Old Testament Pseudepigrapha

Pss. Sol.	Psalms of Solomon
T. Ab.	Testament of Abraham
T. Benj.	Testament of Benjamin
T. Jud.	Testament of Judah

Mishnah, Talmud, and Related Literature

m. 'Abot	Mishnah 'Abot
Tg. Song	Targum Song of Songs
y. Ta'an	Jerusalem Ta'anit

Other

Apoc. Jas.	Apocalypse of James

| Gos. Thom. | Gospel of Thomas |
| P. Oxy. | Oxyrhynchus Papyri |

GREEK AND LATIN WORKS

Ep.	*Epistula* (Letter)
Josephus, *Ant.*	*Jewish Antiquities*
Josephus, *J.W.*	*Jewish Wars*
Philo, *Her.*	*Quis rerum divinarum heres sit* (*Who Is the Heir?*)
Philo, *Hypoth.*	*Hypothetica*
Philo, *Mos.*	*De vita Moses* (*On the Life of Moses*)
Philo, *Praem.*	*De praemiis et poenis* (*On Rewards and Punishments*)
Philo, *Prob.*	*Quod omnis probus liber sit* (*That Every Good Person Is Free*)
Plutarch, *Tranq. an.*	*De tranquillitate animi*
Seneca, *Ben.*	*De beneficiis*

DEAD SEA SCROLLS

1QH[a]	Hodayot[a] or Thanksgiving Hymns[a]
1QM	Milḥamah or War Scroll
1QpHab	Pesher Habakkuk
1QS	Serek Hayaḥad or Rule of the Community
1QSa	Rule of the Congregation (appendix a to 1QS)
4Q159	Ordinances[a]
4Q161	pIsa[a]
4Q164	pIsa[d]
4Q166	pHos[a]
4Q171	pPs[a]
4Q174	Florilegium, also Midrash on Eschatology[a]
4Q177	Catena[a], also Midrash on Eschatology[b]
4Q212	Letter of Enoch
4Q259	S[e]
4Q266	Damascus Document[a]
4Q267	D[b]
4Q372	apocrJoseph[a]
4Q385a	aporJer C[a]

4Q387	Apocryphon of Joshua[a]
4Q388a	Jer C[c]
4Q389	Jer C[d]
4Q390	apocrJer E
4Q504	Dibre Hame'orot[a] or Words of the Luminaries[a]
4Q505	papDibHam[a]
4Q506	papDibHam[b]
4QD[a]	Damascus Document[a]
4QMMT	Miqṣat Ma'aśê ha-Torah[a]
11Q13	Melchizedek
11Q19	Temple Scroll[a]
CD	Cairo Genizah copy of the Damascus Document

SECONDARY SOURCES

AB	Anchor Bible
ABD	*Anchor Bible Dictionary*. Edited by David Noel Freedman. 6 vols. New York: Doubleday, 1992
ABG	Arbeiten zur Bibel und ihrer Geschichte
AGJU	Arbeiten zur Geschichte des antiken Judentums und des Urchristentums
ANRW	*Aufstieg und Niedergang der römischen Welt: Geschichte und Kultur Roms im Spiegel der neueren Forschung*. Part 2, *Principat*. Edited by Hildegard Temporini and Wolfgang Haase. Berlin: de Gruyter, 1972–
BDB	Francis Brown, S. R. Driver, and Charles A. Briggs. *A Hebrew and English Lexicon of the Old Testament*
BHS	*Biblia Hebraica Stuttgartensia*. Edited by Karl Elliger and Wilhelm Rudolph. Stuttgart: Deutsche Bibelgesellschaft, 1983
BJS	Brown Judaic Studies
BZAW	Beihefte zur Zeitschrift für die alttestamentliche Wissenschaft
BZNW	Beihefte zur Zeitschrift für die neutestamentliche Wissenschaft
CBQ	*Catholic Biblical Quarterly*

CSCO	Corpos Scriptorum Christianorum Orientalium. Edited by Jean Baptiste Chabot et al. Paris, 1903
CurBS	*Currents in Research: Biblical Studies*
DJD	Discoveries in the Judaean Desert
DSD	*Dead Sea Discoveries*
ECDSS	Eerdmans Commentary on the Dead Sea Scrolls
EJL	Early Judaism and Its Literature
EvT	*Evangelische Theologie*
HALOT	*The Hebrew and Aramaic Lexicon of the Old Testament.* Ludwig Koehler, Walter Baumgartner, and Johann J. Stamm. Translated and edited under the supervision of Mervyn E. J. Richardson. 4 vols. Leiden: Brill, 1994–1999
HeyJ	*Heythrop Journal*
JBL	*Journal of Biblical Literature*
JETS	*Journal of the Evangelical Theological Society*
JSHRZ	Jüdische Schriften aus hellenistiche-römischer Zeit
JSJ	*Journal for the Study of Judaism in the Persian, Hellenistic, and Roman Periods*
JSJSup	Journal for the Study of Judaism Supplement Series
JSNT	*Journal for the Study of the New Testament*
JSNTSup	Journal for the Study of the New Testament Supplement Series
JSOT	*Journal for the Study of the Old Testament*
JSOTSup	Journal for the Study of the Old Testament Supplement Series
JTS	*Journal of Theological Studies*
LSJ	Henry George Liddell, Robert Scott, and Henry Stuart Jones. *A Greek-English Lexicon.* 9th ed. with revised supplement. Oxford: Clarendon, 1996
NovTSup	Supplements to Novum Testamentum
NPNF[2]	*Nicene and Post-Nicene Fathers*, Series 2
PL	Patrologia Latina [= *Patrologiae Cursus Completus*: Series Latina]. Edited by Jacques-Paul Migne. 217 vols. Paris, 1844–1864

PTMS	Pittsburgh Theological Monograph Series
PTSDSSP	Princeton Theological Seminary Dead Sea Scrolls Project
RevQ	*Revue de Qumran*
SBLEJL	SBL Early Judaism and Its Literature Series
SBLSCS	SBL Septuagint and Cognate Studies Series
SBLSP	Society of Biblical Literature Seminar Papers
SNTSMS	Society for New Testament Studies Monograph Series
STDJ	Studies on the Texts of the Desert of Judah
TRE	*Theologische Realenzyklopädie.* Edited by Gerhard Krause and Gerhard Müller. Berlin: de Gruyter, 1977–
TSAJ	Texte und Studien zum antiken Judentum
TynBul	*Tyndale Bulletin*
VTSup	Supplements to Vetus Testamentum
WMANT	Wissenschaftliche Monographien zum Alten und Neuen Testament
WUNT	Wissenschaftliche Untersuchungen zum Neuen Testament

INTRODUCTION

N. T. WRIGHT'S HYPOTHESIS OF AN "ONGOING EXILE"

Issues and Answers

*I knew that God was at the same time near and far, magnanimous
and severe, rigorous and merciful. I knew that I belonged to his
chosen people—people chosen to serve him by suffering as well as
by hope. I knew that I was in exile and that the exile was total,
universal, even cosmic. I knew as well that the exile would not last,
that it would end in redemption.*

ELIE WIESEL, "Making Ghosts Speak"

THE CONTROLLING NARRATIVE

Perhaps the following modern analogy will help readers relate to the subject
of the present volume—the notion of exile in the Second Temple period. In
my adopted country of Canada, there is a national mythology of

---

Elie Wiesel, "Making Ghosts Speak," in *From the Kingdom of Memory* (New York: Summit Books,
1990), 135-45 (137). The notion of an ongoing exile is something of a theme in Wiesel's work. See,
e.g., Wiesel, *Souls on Fire: Portraits and Legends of Hasidic Masters* (New York: Simon & Schuster,
1972), 3-39 (3), which refers to a legendary tale of Rebbe Israel Baal Shem Tov: "He had tried many
times before—and failed. Burning with impatience, he wanted to end the ordeals of exile forcibly;
and this time he was but one step away from success. The gates were ajar; the Messiah was about
to appear and console the children and old men awaiting him, awaiting no one else but him. The
Diaspora had lasted long enough; now men everywhere would gather and rejoice." I am grateful
to Spencer Jones for the latter quote.

immigration.[1] The traditional story we tell ourselves is that we are a nation of immigrants, welcoming people from around the world who want to come and start a better life. Around this feel-good story, slogans abound: "Canada is a patchwork quilt," "Canada is a mosaic," and "Immigration is what drives our multiculturalism forward." This powerful narrative captivates the national imagination and therefore has adherents right across the political spectrum. On the one hand, those who are left-leaning advocates of immigration adhere to the immigration mythology story because it says that migrants are very grateful for the opportunity to come here, will make enormous sacrifices, and will end up making Canada a better place. It is all about the next generation: the immigrants are really here for their children, and they're going to do anything they can to fit into the Canadian story.

On the other hand, those who are right-leaning opponents to a lot of immigration, those who are very concerned about the way immigration works at the moment, nonetheless adhere to the old mythology, because it serves as a story against which the new migrants are measured and found to be failing. From this perspective, the newcomers are not as successful at integrating into the Canadian landscape as previous generations of immigrants were. "We have all these PhDs driving taxis. Why are we letting people into the country like this?"

Meanwhile, during the past few decades, the Canadian government has subtly changed the rules of immigration. These days, most people who come to Canada are economic migrants, entering the country under programs such as Express Entry, which allows Canadian employers to influence which immigrants get to come and when they get to come. These are not people risking life and limb to become Canadians, but people who are good at making money in their home country whom the Canadian government wants to make money here instead. Nevertheless, the old narrative of immigration serves the government really well. It says, "We are opening our

---

[1]The opening analogy is based on comments by Catherine Dauvergne, Dean of the Allard School of Law at the University of British Columbia, in a recent CBC Radio interview about her new book, *The New Politics of Immigration and the End of Settler Societies* (Cambridge: Cambridge University Press, 2016), "Canada Needs a New Immigration Policy, Says UBC Law Dean," CBC Radio, www.cbc.ca/radio/the180/vancouver-recovers-from-jane-jacobs-women-on-banknotes-and-the-politics-of-climate-change-and-wildfires-1.3570513/canada-needs-a-new-immigration-policy-says-ubc-law-dean-1.3570610.

door to migrants because this is our tradition. We're not really changing anything fundamentally; we're just tweaking a few things at the edges." And if the new immigration policy does not work, the old narrative provides a strong basis on which the newcomer can be blamed for not living up to the mythology.

Hence, no matter what the lived reality is on the ground, no matter what one's political perspective is, the robust national mythology of immigration can be pressed into service in a variety of ways as support.

Canada, of course, is not the only country with a national mythology of migration. The present volume deals with Israel's national narrative of "forced migration," a term that is now often preferred instead of *exile*.[2] The question we are asking is whether, in various and sundry ways, the traumatic national experience of forced migration had a profound and lasting effect on the way the Jewish people understood their ongoing plight during the Second Temple period and, if so, whether that helps us to contextualize some aspects of the early Jesus movement. In other words, is this another situation in which, regardless of the actual circumstances on the ground, a controlling national narrative shapes thinking in a variety of ways?

Israel and Judah experienced several major forced migrations or exiles at the hands of foreign superpowers. The ten northern tribes of Israel were exiled from their land by the Assyrians in 722 BCE. As a consequence, the northerners were so thoroughly assimilated into the surrounding Mesopotamian culture that in subsequent tradition they became "the ten lost tribes of Israel."[3] A century and a quarter later, the southern kingdom of Judah

---

[2]See, e.g., Mark J. Boda et al., eds., *The Prophets Speak on Forced Migration*, Ancient Israel and Its Literature (Atlanta: Society of Biblical Literature, 2015). The basis for this change of term is the observation that the Hebrew word *golah*, commonly translated as "exile" or "captivity," can in fact be translated as "emigration." This move allows the infusion of modern migration studies into the discussion. This new emphasis on forced migration moves the discussion away from exile as punishment for sins and toward a more constructive approach to the subject. See also John J. Ahn, *Exile as Forced Migrations: A Sociological, Literary, and Theological Approach on the Displacement and Resettlement of the Southern Kingdom of Judah*, BZAW 417 (Berlin: de Gruyter, 2011). See further Stanley E. Porter, ed., *Rejection: God's Refugees in Biblical and Contemporary Perspective* (Eugene, OR: Pickwick, 2015).

[3]See Zvi Ben-Dor Benite, *The Ten Lost Tribes: A World History* (Oxford: Oxford University Press, 2013). On 4 Ezra 13:39-46, a passage that refers to the ten lost tribes, see Florentino García Martínez, "The Authority of 4 Ezra and the Jewish Origin of (Native) American Indians," in *Between Philology and Theology: Contributions to the Study of Ancient Jewish Interpretation*, JSJSup 162 (Leiden: Brill, 2013), 175-89.

experienced the exile of its elites by the Babylonians in 597 BCE. Then, a decade after that, when the temple was destroyed by the Babylonians, a new wave of Judean exiles were forced to migrate to Babylon, although many Judeans remained behind.

From one perspective, the Babylonian exile ended in 538 BCE when Cyrus, the Persian king, permitted the exiled Jews to return to Jerusalem and rebuild their city and their temple (2 Chron 36:23; Ezra 1:1-4; 6:3-5). Although many Jews chose to remain in Babylon (cf. Josephus, *Ant.* 11.8), the return under Cyrus could be viewed as a fulfillment of Jeremiah's prophecy that the exile would end after seventy years (Jer 25:11-12; 29:10; cf. 2 Chron 36:20-22; Ezra 1:1; Josephus, *Ant.* 11.1-2). From another perspective, however, "exile" could be seen as a chronic spiritual condition that the partial return under Cyrus did not remedy.[4] Same reality, different interpretation. Thus, a number of early Jewish writings, such as Daniel and 2 Baruch, understood the condition of exile to persist for centuries and looked forward a more complete restoration at the end of exile in the future. In Daniel 9, for instance, the seventy years of Jeremiah's prophecy is famously reinterpreted as seventy "weeks" of years, or 490 years.[5]

It seems, then, that the rupture that was brought on by the succession of exilic experiences under Assyria and Babylon continued to be felt in the self-understanding of the Jewish people long after their partial return from Babylonian exile in the sixth century BCE. Indeed, there was a sense in which even Jews in the land understood themselves to be still in exile. Was this self-understanding bolstered by the fact that most Jews still lived in the Diaspora? What about the ten northern tribes that were driven into exile under the

---

[4]See Martien A. Halvorson-Taylor, *Enduring Exile: The Metaphorization of Exile in the Hebrew Bible*, VTSup 141 (Leiden: Brill, 2011), who argues that the extension of exile's meaning, which allowed it to function as a metaphor, is not an exilic or postexilic innovation but is in fact rooted in preexilic thinking about the threat of exile.

[5]See, however, John S. Bergsma, "The Persian Period as Penitential Era: The 'Exegetical Logic' of Daniel 9.1-27," in *Exile and Restoration Revisited: Essays on the Babylonian and Persian Periods in Memory of Peter R. Ackroyd*, ed. Gary N. Knoppers, Lester L. Grabbe, and Deirdre Fulton. Library of Second Temple Studies (London: T&T Clark, 2009), 50-64 (60 [author's emphasis]): "It would be better to recognize that Dan. 9.24 announces a 70-week penitential period that does not start with Jeremiah's prophecy of '70 years,' but rather is *subsequent* to the Jeremianic period. *Cyrus' decree—the 'word to restore and build Jerusalem' of Dan. 9.25—terminates the '70 weeks' of years of Daniel.* Jeremiah's 70 years were unsuccessful in producing repentance, so a seven-fold longer penitential period is to begin at their termination."

Assyrians? Were they thought to be lost irrevocably, despite the fact that the prophets expected the reunification of all twelve tribes in a restored nation?

There is no reason to assume that all Jews of the first century CE thought the same way about these matters. Indeed, the paucity of the extant sources and the diversity of Judaism during this period precludes all-encompassing generalizations. Nevertheless, there is a substantial body of evidence that the narrative of an ongoing exile had taken root in early Jewish writings. Take, for example, 2 Baruch. If this pseudepigraphon was written toward the end of the first century in response to the destruction of Jerusalem and the temple under the Romans in 70 CE, why is it set in the context of the Babylonian invasion of Jerusalem in 587 BCE? Matthias Henze comments on the anomaly:

> By choosing the Babylonian invasion of Jerusalem as the setting for his book, the author of *2Bar* suggests, albeit implicitly, that the root cause for Israel's demise under the Romans dates back to 587 BCE. The real break between Israel and her god, the main caesura in their relationship and the true reason why God delivered Israel into the hands of her enemies, is to be found in the sixth century BCE, not in the first century CE. In a way, Israel never completely overcame the blow she suffered from the hand of Nebuchadnezzar, so that Titus's devastating advances should be interpreted as a recrudescence of the old wounds, wounds that never healed. Cyrus's edict allowed some exiles to return home, to be sure, and the rebuilding of Jerusalem included the physical reconstruction of the temple, but this never led to a complete restoration of Israel. Israel never fully recovered from the shock and disruption inflicted upon her by the Babylonians and, in a sense, had always remained in "exile." Devastation and exile had become permanent aspects of Israel's existence and could only be overcome through divine intervention and the inauguration of the end of time. And so it is only plausible that the author of *2Bar* would choose to return to that crucial moment, to the original manifestation of the problem, the moment that was so decisive for the fate of Israel.[6]

Here, we are dealing not simply with an analogy between the two historic events, but rather with the ongoing effects of the earlier incursion.

---

[6]Matthias Henze, *Jewish Apocalypticism in Late First Century Israel: Reading Second Baruch in Context*, TSAJ 142 (Tübingen: Mohr Siebeck, 2011), 119. See also Philip S. Alexander, "Was the Ninth of Av Observed in the Second Temple Period? Reflections on the Concept of the Continuing Exile in Early Judaism," in *Envisioning Judaism: Studies in Honor of Peter Schäfer on the Occasion of His Seventieth Birthday*, ed. Ra'anan S. Boustan et al. (Tübingen: Mohr Siebeck, 2013), 1:23-38.

Moreover, as Henze notes, in this respect 2 Baruch "resembles a number of other texts from the Second Temple period that assume an ongoing state of 'exile.'"[7] The fundamental conception is that Israel's exile, at least *theologically* speaking, will not come to an end until the eschaton, when God intervenes in this world and establishes his rule.

N. T. Wright does not cite Henze's book on 2 Baruch for his thesis of an ongoing exile, but he well could have. For it is precisely within this sort of first-century Jewish tradition that Wright seeks to situate the "controlling narrative," "grand story," "metanarrative," that fundamentally shaped Jesus' and Paul's thinking.[8] According to this narrative, Israel had fallen into grievous sin and indeed national apostasy for which the people had come under divine judgment in the form of exile. Moreover, that condition of the ongoing exile was brought to an end through the person and work of Jesus Christ, who constitutes the climax of the salvation-historical story of Israel.

---

[7]Ibid., 119n162. On the notion of an ongoing exile in the book of Daniel, see James L. Kugel, *How to Read the Bible: A Guide to Scripture, Then and Now* (New York: Free Press, 2007), 654-58. For discussion of other early Jewish literature of the Second Temple period that envisions an ongoing exile, see Michael E. Fuller, *The Restoration of Israel: Israel's Re-gathering and the Fate of the Nations in Early Jewish Literature and Luke-Acts*, BZNW 138 (Berlin: de Gruyter, 2006); Jörn Kiefer, *Exil und Diaspora: Begrifflichkeit und Deutungen im antiken Judentum und in der Hebräischen Bibel*, Arbeiten zur Bibel und ihrer Geschichte 19 (Leipzig: Evangelische Verlagsanstalt, 2005); Lutz Doering, *Ancient Jewish Letters and the Beginnings of Christian Epistolography*, WUNT 298 (Tübingen: Mohr Siebeck, 2012), esp. 154-58 (on the Epistle of Jeremiah). Hindy Najman repeatedly refers to the idea of an ongoing exile during the whole Second Temple period. See., e.g., Hindy Najman, *Past Renewals: Interpretative Authority, Renewed Revelation and the Quest for Perfection in Jewish Antiquity*, JSJSup 53 (Leiden: Brill, 2010), 147, 148, 151, 193, 235; here, 177: "By emphasizing the way in which the Second Temple period was considered incomplete, we can better understand much later Second Temple claims—found, notably, in the Dead Sea Scrolls—that deny or even challenge the Second Temple, and instead claim that their community is still in exile (never having returned from Babylon)."

[8]See, e.g., N. T. Wright, *Paul and the Faithfulness of God*, 2 vols., Christian Origins and the Question of God 4 (Minneapolis: Fortress, 2013), 103-5, 107-8, 114 ("continuing exile"), 115n153, 117-18 ("the extended exile"), 119-27, 129, 132, 135-36 ("extended exile"), 139-63 ("the continuing exile"), 170, 173n385, 178 ("continuing exile"), 182, 185, 188, 278, 345, 346, 380n107, 416, 501-4, 514-16, 526-27, 622 ("continuing exile"), 629, 633, 653, 655, 656, 679, 703-4, 714, 716n300, 724, 741, 744, 761, 772, 775, 782, 787-88, 792, 800, 802, 815, 823, 846n210, 867, 911, 923, 929, 931, 996, 999-1000, 1008, 1010, 1036, 1050-52, 1054-55, 1058, 1059n73 ("present age" = "a time of sorrow and exile" to be succeeded by an "age to come"), 1071, 1073, 1130, 1137-41, 1159, 1164-68, 1172, 1173n504, 1179, 1184n526, 1185, 1191-93, 1227, 1247, 1259n727, 1274, 1279, 1284, 1298-99, 1301, 1322-23, 1358, 1412, 1415, 1433, 1454-55, 1463-64 ("continuing exile"), 1465, 1479, 1481, 1512.

SCHOLARLY REACTION TO WRIGHT'S THESIS

How have scholars responded to Wright's thesis of an ongoing exile?[9] There is no need here to give a full *Forschungsbericht*, for an extensive, up-to-date review of the issue is provided by Nicholas G. Piotrowski.[10] Moreover, in *God and the Faithfulness of Paul* (2016), Christoph Heilig, J. Thomas Hewitt, and Michael F. Bird have edited a full-scale, 832-page assessment of Wright's recent two-volume, 1,660-page magnum opus, *Paul and the Faithfulness of God* (2013), which includes further reactions to Wright's thesis of an ongoing exile.[11] Wright himself has countered some of his critics on this point both in his *Paul and His Recent Interpreters: Some Contemporary Debates* (2015)[12] and in an epilogue to *God and the Faithfulness of Paul.*[13] What remains for us to do in this section is to outline the broad contours of the debate as a prelude to the present volume.

---

[9]My own interest in exile was originally independent of N. T. Wright; it stemmed from my 1989 Tübingen dissertation, in which I interpreted Gal 4:1-7 and Rom 8:15, 23 (cf. Rom 9:4) as reflecting the Old Testament and Jewish concept of the new exodus. See J. M. Scott, *Adoption as Sons of God*, WUNT 2.48 (Tübingen: Mohr Siebeck, 1992). This interpretation has been widely adopted, but it has also been criticized. On the debate, see J. M. Scott, "Heir," in *Encyclopedia of the Bible and Its Reception*, ed. Christine Helmer et al. (Berlin: de Gruyter, 2015), 11:727-30. On the relationship between the "new exodus" and the concept of exile, see Daniel L. Smith, "The Uses of 'New Exodus' in New Testament Scholarship: Preparing a Way Through the Wilderness," *Currents in Biblical Research* 14 (2016): 207-43.

[10]Nicholas G. Piotrowski, "The Concept of Exile in Late Second Temple Judaism: A Review of Recent Scholarship," *Currents in Biblical Research*, 15, no. 2 (2017): 214-47. At the conclusion of his study, Piotrowski writes, "Such scholarly diversity notwithstanding, recognition of the crucial place of 'exile' in the late Second Temple Judaism thought-world is clearly rising" (ibid., 239). A few lines later he continues: "Even if scholars cannot currently agree upon a specific working definition of 'exile' in late Second Temple Judaism, it must nonetheless be conceded that surely *something* was in the air. Any NT author, therefore, can reasonably be expected both to employ (at least a general semblance of) the 'idea of exile' and also to develop it in a unique way altogether."

[11]Christoph Heilig, J. Thomas Hewitt, and Michael F. Bird, eds., *God and the Faithfulness of Paul: A Critical Examination of the Pauline Theology of N. T. Wright*, WUNT 2.413 (Tübingen: Mohr Siebeck, 2016). See also Michael F. Bird's important study "Jesus and the Continuing Exile of Israel in the Writings of N. T. Wright," *Journal for the Study of the Historical Jesus* 13 (2015): 209-31. Bird defends a "chastened view of Wright's thesis that return-from-exile remains a useful category for understanding Judaism and Jesus even if it does not necessarily carry the metanarratival freight that Wright attributes to it" (ibid., 209).

[12]N. T. Wright, *Paul and His Recent Interpreters: Some Contemporary Debates* (Minneapolis: Fortress, 2015), 40, 98n32, 139, 151, 159-60, 180. See also Wright, *The Paul Debate: Critical Questions for Understanding the Apostle* (Waco, TX: Baylor University Press, 2015), 57, 80-81, 83.

[13]See also N. T. Wright, "The Challenge of Dialogue: A Partial and Preliminary Response," in *Paul and the Faithfulness of God*, 712-68 (739-41).

On the one hand, Wright has convinced many scholars that his thesis is correct.[14] Joel R. Wright provides a salient example: "I regard Wright's identification of a controlling 'ongoing exile' narrative as the expression of dominant Jewish worldview of the NT era as his major and, as I think it will prove to be, most enduring scholarly accomplishment."[15] Nicholas Perrin has also been persuaded: "Skimming the surface of the NT, we would not be going too far to say that the motif of exile is quietly rampant."[16] To be sure, some scholars accept part of Wright's thesis about an ongoing exile but object to other aspects. For example, Richard B. Hays accepts that the Gospels of Matthew and Luke do have the concept of an ongoing exile, but he denies that this necessarily goes back to the historical Jesus, as Wright himself maintains.[17] Brant Pitre accepts Wright's point that the historical

---

[14]See, e.g., many of the essays in Carey C. Newman, ed., *Jesus and the Restoration of Israel: A Critical Assessment of N. T. Wright's Jesus and the Victory of God* (Downers Grove, IL: InterVarsity Press, 1999).

[15]Joel R. White, "N. T. Wright's Narrative Approach," in *God and the Faithfulness of Paul*, 180-204 (195). See further White, "Führt der Messias sein Volk aus dem Exil? Eine kritische Auseinandersetzung mit N. T. Wrights Thesen eines impliziten Metanarrativs hinter dem paulinischen Evangelium," in *Der jüdische Messias Jesus und sein jüdischer Apostel Paulus*, ed. Armin D. Baum, Detlef Häußer, and Emmanuel L. Rehfeld, WUNT 2.425 (Tübingen: Mohr Siebeck, 2016), 227-42. I am grateful to Joel White for providing me with a prepublication copy of his article.

[16]Nicholas Perrin, "Exile," in *The World of the New Testament: Cultural, Social, and Historical Contexts*, ed. Joel B. Green and Lee Martin McDonald (Grand Rapids: Baker Academic, 2013), 25-37 (26). In his conclusion, Perrin summarizes: "Notions of exile were as variegated as Judaism itself. This neither proves nor disproves the assumption that exile and return were fundamental categories for the NT writers. However, precisely because exile was put to such a widespread and wide-ranging use in Second Temple Jewish texts, we have some reason to expect something similar in the texts of the NT. Each NT book should be understood on its own terms and with its own unique theology of exile. At the same time, since the authors of the NT held certain core convictions in common, there is reasonable warrant for teasing out family resemblances between these exilic theologies. One such family resemblance, difficult to dispute, is the sense in some NT texts that return from exile has already occurred in Christ even as, paradoxically, a condition of exile still endures. Much like the kingdom of God (at least as it is now commonly though not universally understood), exile retains an already-but-not-yet aspect. This makes sense inasmuch as return from exile is a highly allusive and rich way of describing the coming of the kingdom; it provides not only an eschatological framework but also conceptual handles for coming to terms with the 'present evil age' (Gal. 1:4), the existence from which believers have been redeemed."

[17]Richard B. Hays, *Reading Backwards: Figural Christology and the Fourfold Gospel Witness* (Waco, TX: Baylor University Press, 2014), 7, 12, 15-16, 20, 31, 40-43, 49-50, 63, 97, 98, 106. See esp. ibid., 41n19: "Readers conversant with current debates in NT scholarship will recognize that the themes summarized here (Israel's return from exile, and Jesus as the one who enacts and leads the return) resonate strongly with the characteristic emphases of N. T. Wright's interpretation of Jesus' activity (*Jesus and the Victory of God*). Should such theological ideas be ascribed, as Wright argues, to Jesus' own conscious self-conception and purposes? Or do these ideas belong to the secondary level of Matthew's interpretation of the significance of Jesus? The latter is fairly certain, on the basis of explicit narrative features of Matthew's text. The former is a far more speculative matter."

Jesus did have a concept of ongoing exile, but he criticizes Wright for limiting *exile* to a theological concept rather than applying it to the actual ongoing exile of the northern tribes of Israel.[18] As Pitre cleverly puts it, "Wright
has the *right insight* but the *wrong exile*."[19]

On the other hand, Wright's thesis has provoked some staunch criticism.
Seyoon Kim, for example, objects to Wright's interpretation of Galatians 3:10-14,
which sees Paul's use of Deuteronomy 27:26 in Galatians 3:10 as presupposing
the ongoing covenantal curse of exile.[20] And after calling into question Wright's
interpretation of several key passages in Paul's letters relating to the theme of a
continuing exile and Paul's use of Scripture, Steve Moyise concludes,

> It is beyond the scope of this essay to evaluate whether the Deuteronomy-
> inspired "end of exile" theme was as prevalent as Wright claims, but it is
> worth asking whether such a general theme could ever exert the sort of spe-
> cific influence that Wright claims. It is rather like appealing to the theory of
> gravity in order to explain why I slipped on the pavement last week. It is of
> course true but not really the sort of explanation that is required. In fact, the
> north of England was covered in snow last week and I should have chosen
> more suitable footwear.[21]

---

[18]Brant Pitre, "The 'Ransom for Many,' the New Exodus, and the End of Exile: Redemption as the
Restoration of All Israel (Mark 10:35-45)," *Letter & Spirit* 1 (2005): 41–68 (esp. 42n5, 66); Pitre,
Jesus, the Tribulation, and the End of Exile: Restoration Eschatology and the Origin of the Atonement
(Tübingen: Mohr Siebeck; Grand Rapids: Baker Academic, 2005), 31-40. White ("Wright's Narrative Approach," 195) raises this point as well with respect to Paul: "Until they [the ten northern
tribes of Israel] returned, exile would continue to be a stark and undeniable reality, not simply
a sense of disappointment, however profound, with life in the Promised Land. Brant Pitre
pointed to this over a decade ago as the strongest argument in favor of the 'ongoing exile' thesis,
but Wright seems not to have recognized the force it adds to his argument." For an argument
that Jesus' gathering of the twelve disciples implies the eschatological homecoming of the ten
northern tribes of Israel, see Dale C. Allison Jr., *Constructing Jesus: Memory, Imagination, and
History* (Grand Rapids: Baker Academic, 2010), 71-76, who relates this to Jesus' expectation in
"Q" (Matt 19:28//Luke 22:28-30) that the twelve disciples will rule/judge the twelve tribes of
Israel, which again presupposes the return of the northern tribes (ibid., 42-43, 186).

[19]Pitre, *Jesus, the Tribulation, and the End of Exile*, 35 (author's emphasis). Pitre continues: "The Jews of
the first century were certainly waiting for 'the End of the Exile'—but not the Babylonian Exile. Rather,
they were waiting for the end of the Assyrian Exile, as we saw with the quote from Josephus [*Ant.*
11.133]. For it was only with the end of the Assyrian Exile that *all twelve tribes* could be restored to Zion."

[20]Seyoon Kim, "Paul, the Spirit, and the Law: Galatians 3:10-14 as a Test Case," in *Paul and the New
Perspective: Second Thoughts on the Origin of Paul's Gospel* (Grand Rapids: Eerdmans, 2002),
128-64 (131-46). See also Gregory Tatum, "Law and Covenant in *Paul and the Faithfulness of God*,"
in *God and the Faithfulness of Paul*, 311-27 (317).

[21]Steve Moyise, "Wright's Understanding of Paul's Use of Scripture," in *God and the Faithfulness of
Paul*, 165-80 (179). Theresa Heilig and Christoph Heilig cite Moyise's point approvingly ("Historical Methodology," in *God and the Faithfulness of Paul*, 115-50 [122]).

Markus Bockmuehl objects to Wright's whole approach for a variety of reasons:

> The attempt to find a single overarching theme of biblical theology has too often floundered on its apparent inability to account for the diversity in Scripture—whether that theme be "salvation history" (Oscar Cullmann and Gerhard von Rad), "the mighty acts of God" (G. Ernest Wright), or more recently "the end of exile" and "the return of Yahweh to Zion" (N. T. Wright). Such reconstructions are perhaps too often wedded to contingent claims of historicity and original meanings that are rarely verifiable, and they cannot readily support the interpretive theological weight imposed upon them. This is quite apart from the fact that many of these grand objective visions have classically failed to acknowledge their own perspectival location and thus fall foul of the postmodern deconstructive project. (Is it significant that no one has ever seen this or that supposedly central theme before?)[22]

Perhaps the most vociferous opponent of Wright's view of an ongoing exile has been James D. G. Dunn. In discussing Wright's notion of a grand narrative,[23] Dunn argues in *Jesus Remembered*,

> The most serious weakness of Wright's grand hypothesis is his inability to demonstrate that the narrative of return from exile was a controlling factor in Jesus' own teaching. It will not do simply to insert passages into the assumed narrative framework or to read tradition . . . through spectacles provided by the controlling story, as though by invocation of the mantra "end of exile," "return from exile" the interpretation of these traditions becomes clear. "Serious verification" requires demonstration of at least a fair number of plausible echoes and allusions to return from exile within the Jesus tradition itself. The most plausible is the parable of the prodigal son, who repents and returns from "a far country" (Luke 15.11–24). But the grand narrative of return from exile proves inadequate to explain the second half of the parable, where the refusal of the elder brother to accept the younger clearly works with the different motif of contrasting pairs. And Wright hardly strengthens his case by giving a pivotal place to the parable of the sower (Mark 4.2–8 par.). The problem is not that an allusion to the idea of the returnees from exile as seed being sown (again) in the land is farfetched. It is rather that planting and

---

[22]Markus Bockmuehl, *Seeing the Word: Refocusing New Testament Study*, Studies in Theological Interpretation (Grand Rapids: Baker Academic, 2006), 114.

[23]James D. G. Dunn, *Christianity in the Making*, vol. 1, *Jesus Remembered* (Grand Rapids: Eerdmans, 2003), 472-77.

fruitful growth are metaphors of much more diverse application and that the parable's imagery of different soils and outcomes more naturally invites a different line of thought and application from that of the return from exile. The calling of the twelve disciples certainly evokes thought of eschatological restoration or renewal of Israel (the twelve tribes), but if "return-from-exile theology" was a prominent feature of the rationale, it is surprising that so little is made of it. And the first petition of the Lord's Prayer ("May your name be sanctified") could evoke the prophecy of Ezek. 36.22–28. For the most part, however, Wright is content to read the Jesus tradition through the lens of his grand narrative without further attempt at justification. But in squeezing the diversity of Jesus' proclamation of the kingdom into conformity with that single controlling story he misses much that is of central significance within that proclamation—not least Jesus' own critique of Israel's current leadership and concern for the "poor" and "sinners."[24]

Wright's view of an ongoing exile in Paul fares little better in the hands of Dunn. In "An Insider's Perspective on Wright's Version of the New Perspective," Dunn comments on Wright's recent two-volume Pauline theology:

> Wright's role as a third partner with [E. P.] Sanders and Dunn on "New Perspective" issues is somewhat spoiled by his criticizing both of us for failing to recognize that "the idea of continuing exile" was, or should have been, seen to be part of that "revolution." To be fair, Wright may well be justified in highlighting the thought of continuing exile in pre-NT writers (*PFG* 162), but his insistence that such was a continuing factor in shaping Paul's (as also Jesus's) teaching has hardly been demonstrated. His apparent determination to restate his "continuing exile" thesis (*PFG* 114–63), despite the many criticisms it has received, and without making any real attempt to demonstrate that Paul was influenced by it or responded to it is one of the less attractive features of the two volumes. He seems here to ignore his own stated principle in his recent *Surprised by Scripture*, namely "to allow the biblical writers to set the agenda rather than forcing on them a scheme that does not do them justice."[25]

Based on what we have seen in the foregoing, Wright's thesis of an ongoing exile is either his "greatest accomplishment" or his "most serious

---

[24]Ibid., 475-77.

[25]James D. G. Dunn, "An Insider's Perspective on Wright's Version of the New Perspective," in *God and the Faithfulness of Paul*, 347-58 (350). See also Dunn, *The Theology of Paul the Apostle* (Grand Rapids: Eerdmans, 1998), 145n90.

weakness."[26] There is clearly a need for further discussion of the matter. Hence, the present volume aims to extend the conversation in order to seek further clarification of this contentious issue.

THE CONVERSATION CONTINUES

The essays in this volume are divided into four main sections and are framed by contributions from N. T. Wright. In his lead essay, Wright reasserts his thesis about the ongoing exile with renewed vigor and fresh insight, marshaling additional evidence in support of his case. Thereupon follows a series of responses to this essay from specialists in various fields: part one contains essays with a focus on aspects of Wright's thesis relating to the Old Testament/Hebrew Bible and the Septuagint; part two pertains to early Judaism; part three concentrates on the New Testament; and part four on theology. The goal in each case is not simply to applaud Wright's approach but to assess it critically from a particular vantage point and, if possible, even to go beyond it in some way. Finally, Wright receives the last word in an essay that provides a rejoinder to the foregoing scholarly responses to his thesis.

Thus, with this structure of the book in view, we turn now to the subject at hand. The Targum Song of Songs opens with the midrash of the Ten Songs, a listing of songs recited from the creation of the world up to the final song that will be recited at the culmination of history when Israel shall return from its exiles:

> Songs and praises which Solomon, the prophet, the king of Israel, recited in the Holy Spirit before the Sovereign of all the World, the Lord.

> Ten songs were recited in this world; this song is the most excellent of them all.

> The first song was recited by Adam when his sin was forgiven him and the Sabbath day came and protected him. He opened his mouth and said: "A psalm, a song for the Sabbath day" (Ps 92:1).

> The second song was recited by Moses, together with the Children of Israel, on the day when the Lord of the World divided for them the Red Sea. They

---

[26]For a methodological critique of Wright's historiography, see Samuel V. Adams, *The Reality of God and Historical Method: Apocalyptic Theology in Conversation with N. T. Wright*, New Explorations in Theology (Downers Grove, IL: IVP Academic, 2015). This has implications for Wright's use of exile to explain the perspectives of Jesus and Paul.

all opened their mouths in unison and recited a song, as it is written: "Then sang Moses and the Children of Israel this song" (Exod 15:1).

The third song was recited by the Children of Israel when the well of water was given to them, as it is written, "Then sang Israel this song" (Num 21:17).

The fourth song was recited by Moses the prophet when his time had come to depart from the world, and he reproved with it the people of the house of Israel, as it is written: "Give ear, O heavens, and I will speak" (Deut 32:1).

The fifth song was recited by Joshua the son of Nun, when he waged war against Gibeon and the sun and the moon stood still for him for thirty-six hours. They ceased reciting [their] song, and he opened his mouth and recited [his] song, as it is written: "Then sang Joshua before the Lord" (Josh 10:12).

The sixth song was recited by Barak and Deborah on the day when the Lord delivered Sisera and his host into the hand of the Children of Israel, as it is written: "And Deborah and Barak the son of Abinoam sang" (Judg 5:1).

The seventh song was recited by Hannah, when a son was granted her from before the Lord, as it is written: "Hannah prayed in prophecy and said" (1 Sam 2:1).

The eighth song was recited by David, king of Israel, concerning all the wonders which the Lord wrought for him. He opened his mouth and recited the song, as it is written: "David sang in prophecy before the Lord" (2 Sam 22:1).

The ninth song was recited by Solomon, the king of Israel, in the Holy Spirit before the Sovereign of all the World, the Lord.

The tenth song will be recited by the children of the exile when they depart from their exiles, as is clearly written by Isaiah the prophet: "You shall have this song of joy, as on the night when the festival of Passover is sanctified, and [you shall have] gladness of heart, like the people who go to appear before the Lord three times in the year with all kinds of musical instruments and [with] the sound of the pipe, [who go] ascend into the Mountain of the Lord, and to worship before the Mighty One of Israel" (Is 30:29).[27]

---

[27]The translation is from Philip S. Alexander, *The Targum of Canticles*, The Aramaic Bible 17A (Collegeville, MN: Liturgical Press, 2003), 75-78. On the theme of exile in Tg. Song, see ibid., 19-20, 77: "The analogy between the Exodus from Egypt and the final exodus of the Jews from the exile at the beginning of the Messianic redemption is picked up again and again in Tg. Cant." See further Christian M. M. Brady, "The Use of Eschatological Lists in the Targumim of the Megilloth," *JSJ* 40 (2009): 493-509 (497-507).

According to this list, the story of Israel—and indeed that of the whole world—will culminate in the establishment of God's order, characterized by the return of Israel from the nations to worship the Lord in Jerusalem.[28] May the chorus of different voices brought together in the present volume— certainly not a four-part harmony—contribute to the ongoing discussion of this important topos.

---

[28]Paul has a similar conception in Romans, which traces the history of humankind from its initial failure to honor the Creator as God or to give him thanks (Rom 1:21) all the way to its unified praise of God by Israel and the nations in the eschaton (Rom 15:9-12). A separate study would be needed to explore all the ways in which this theme is developed in Romans. See, e.g., Rom 1:8, 21; 6:17; 7:25; 9:5, 15 (alluding to golden calf incident); Rom 11:2-4 (referring to the worship of Baal by the northern kingdom of Israel), Rom 11:33-36; 12:1; 14:6; 15:6, 9-11; 16:4. On Paul's catena of scriptural citations in Rom 15:9-12, which aligns passages from Torah (Deut 32:43), Prophets (Is 11:10), and Psalms (Ps 17:50 LXX; Ps 116:1 LXX) to testify that the divine purpose of the Messiah's ministry is the creation of a community of Israel and the nations glorifying God together, see further J. Ross Wagner, *Heralds of the Good News: Isaiah and Paul in Concert in the Letter to the Romans* (Leiden: Brill, 2003), 310-27. These citations should be seen in light of the Old Testament expectations that in connection with the ingathering of the exiles, the nations would worship God with restored Israel in Zion. See also Paula Fredriksen, "The Question of Worship: Gods, Pagans, and the Redemption of Israel," in *Paul Within Judaism: Restoring the First-Century Context to the Apostle*, ed. Mark D. Nanos and Magnus Zetterholm (Minneapolis: Fortress, 2015), 175-201 (187 with n32); James M. Scott, *Paul and the Nations: The Old Testament and Jewish Background of Paul's Mission to the Nations with Special Reference to the Destination of Galatians*, WUNT 84 (Tübingen: Mohr Siebeck, 1995), 146-47. On exile in Romans 9–11, see Ross, *Heralds of Good News*, 30n105, 358n46: "My claim that Paul figuratively places his contemporaries 'in exile' should be distinguished from the *historical* argument advanced by [J. M.] Scott, [N. T.] Wright, and others that many Second Temple Jews considered themselves in fact *to be* 'in exile.'"

LEAD ESSAY

YET THE SUN WILL RISE AGAIN

Reflections on the Exile and Restoration in Second Temple Judaism, Jesus, Paul, and the Church Today

N. T. WRIGHT

THIS CHAPTER ATTEMPTS TO TRACE ONE PARTICULAR THEME, that of a continuing "exile," from Second Temple Judaism through early Christianity, and to indicate some of the challenges this seems to pose in the present day. The treatment will of course be selective, focusing on pre-Christian Jewish views, on Jesus, and on Paul. Even in those areas it will naturally have to concentrate on highlights. My argument, in line with previous forays into the same area, is that the majority of Second Temple Jews saw themselves as living within an ongoing exile. Both Jesus and Paul drew on this theme. Jesus believed that he himself was bringing this state to an end; Paul believed that Jesus had indeed accomplished it. If we today are to understand their work we need to grasp the whole concept, what it meant and what it means.[1]

---

[1]The main exposition of the Second Temple material is borrowed from chapter two of my *Paul and the Faithfulness of God*, 2 vols. Christian Origins and the Question of God 4 (Minneapolis: Fortress, 2013). The discussion of Jesus himself draws partly on published and partly on unpublished material; the treatment of Paul summarizes material that is set out much more fully both in that new work and in my previous writings. See *Jesus and the Victory of God* (Minneapolis: Fortress, 1996); "The Historical Jesus and Christian Theology," *Sewanee Theology Review* 39, no. 4 (Michaelmas 1996): 404-12; "Jesus, Israel, and the Cross," in *SBL 1985 Seminar Papers*, ed. Kent H. Richards (Chico, CA: Scholars Press, 1985), 75-95; "Jerusalem in the New Testament," in *Jerusalem Past and Present in the Purposes of God*, ed. Peter W. L. Walker (Cambridge: Cambridge

Israel and the Unending Dusk: The Continuing Exile

Whatever the underlying causes of resistance to the idea of continuing exile, it remains the case that previous attempts, by myself and several others, have not yet convinced the doubters. Let us then assemble the argument one more time.[2]

The fundamental study remains that of O. H. Steck. I suspect from some of the reactions to this theme of a continuing exile that his book has remained unread. "All Israel," he wrote, summarizing the widespread Second Temple viewpoint, "is still in Exile just as before, whether she now finds herself in the Land, which others rule, or in the Diaspora."[3] There is more support for this overall hypothesis of a continuing exile, seen as a political and theological state rather than just a geographical one, than I had realized in earlier publications.[4]

University Press: 1994), 53-77; "Redemption from the New Perspective? Towards a Multi-Layered Theology of the Cross," in *The Redemption*, ed. Stephen. T. Davis, Daniel Kendall, and Gerald O'Collins (Oxford: Oxford University Press, 2006), 69-100; "Paul and Caesar: A New Reading of Romans," in *A Royal Priesthood: The Use of the Bible Ethically and Politically*, ed. Craig Bartholomew (Carlisle, UK: Paternoster, 2002), 173-93. Unless otherwise specified, scripture quotations in this chapter come from the NRSV.

[2]Against, e.g., D. A. Carson, introduction to *Justification and Variegated Nomism*, vol. 1, *The Complexities of Second Temple Judaism*, ed. D. A. Carson, Peter T. O'Brien, and Mark A. Seifrid (Tübingen: Mohr Siebeck, 2001), 5; D. A. Carson, "Summaries and Conclusions," in ibid., 546. Interestingly, in both cases Carson cites me without referring to any actual writings. My previous statements include N. T. Wright, *The Climax of the Covenant: Christ and the Law in Pauline Theology* (Minneapolis: Fortress, 1992), 140-41; Wright, *The New Testament and the People of God* (Minneapolis: Fortress, 1992), 268-70; Wright, *Jesus and the Victory of God* (Minneapolis: Fortress, 1996), xvii-xviii, 126-27, 203-4; Wright, "In Grateful Dialogue: A Response," in *Jesus and the Restoration of Israel: A Critical Assessment of N. T. Wright's* Jesus and the Victory of God, ed. Carey C. Newman (Downers Grove, IL: InterVarsity Press), 244-77 (252-61); Wright, *Paul: In Fresh Perspective* (Minneapolis: Fortress, 2005), 138-40; Wright, *Justification: God's Plan and Paul's Vision* (Downers Grove, IL: InterVarsity Press, 2009), 57-62. I realize, in listing these discussions, that none of them is very long. I had thought the biblical passages noted there would have been sufficient. Clearly I was wrong (and clearly those lists effectively oversimplify the quite complex evidence).

[3]Odil Hannes Steck, "Das Problem theologischer Strömungen in nachexilischer," *EvT* 28 (1968): 454; see also Steck, *Israel und das gewaltsame Geschick der Propheten: Untersuchungen zur Überlieferung des deuteronomistischen Geschichtsbildes im Alten Testament, Spätjudentum und Urchristentum*, WMANT 23 (Neukirchen-Vluyn: Neukirchener Verlag, 1967). Cf. George W. E. Nickelsburg, *Jewish Literature Between the Bible and the Mishnah* (London: SCM Press; Philadelphia: Fortress, 1981), 18.

[4]James M. Scott, "Restoration of Israel," in *Dictionary of Paul and His Letters*, ed. Gerald F. Hawthorne, Ralph P. Martin, and Daniel G. Reid (Downers Grove, IL: InterVarsity Press, 1993), 796-805; Scott, "Paul's Use of Deuteronomic Tradition," *JBL* 112, no. 4 (1993): 645-65; Scott, "For as Many as Are of Works of the Law Are Under a Curse," in *Paul and the Scriptures of Israel*, ed. Craig A. Evans and James A. Sanders, JSNTSup 83 (Sheffield: JSOT Press, 1993), 187-220,

This cuts clean across those who, reading what I and others have said, have spoken of this notion of continuing exile as an image or metaphor, an idea from the miscellaneous Jewish past picked up here to illuminate a different situation.[5] It can of course be used that way, and obviously was and indeed still is, but that is not the basic point. The basic point I, and others, have made is that within the *continuing narrative* that a great many Jews believed themselves to be living in, many Second Temple Jews interpreted *that part of the continuing narrative in which they were living* in terms of the so-called Deuteronomic scheme of sin—exile—restoration. They understood their place as still somewhere in the middle stage of exile looking forward to the restoration but being shackled at the ankles by their past sins—both corporately and individually. This remains true whether, for

---

suggesting (201) that the point is now "widely recognized" and speaking (213) of a "growing consensus," which is I fear overoptimistic; Scott, "Exile and the Self-Understanding of Diaspora Jews in the Greco-Roman Period," in *Exile: Old Testament, Jewish, and Christian Conceptions*, ed. James M. Scott, JSJSup 56 (Leiden: Brill, 1997), 173-218, at 189; the whole volume is important; e.g., Craig A. Evans, "Aspects of Exile and Restoration in the Proclamation of Jesus and the Gospels," in ibid., 305-12. See too, e.g., Frank Thielman, *Theology of the New Testament: A Canonical and Synthetic Approach* (Grand Rapids: Zondervan, 2005), 369; Thielman, *Paul and the Law: A Contextual Approach* (Downers Grove, IL: InterVarsity Press, 1994), 49-55; Thielman, *From Plight to Solution: A Jewish Framework for Understanding Paul's View of the Law in Galatians and Romans*, NovTSup 61 (Leiden: Brill, 1989), 28-45; Thielman, "The Story of Israel and the Theology of Romans 5–8," in *Pauline Theology*, vol. 3, *Romans*, ed. David M. Hay and Elizabeth E. Johnson (Minneapolis: Fortress, 1995), 172-76 Robert P. Carroll, "Israel, History of (Post-Monarch Period)," *ABD* 3:567-76 (575): "Much of the literature of the Second Temple period recognizes a category of exile after the destruction of Jerusalem in 587/86, but it does not recognize any return in subsequent centuries. This literature . . . represents Israel as being in exile for centuries; virtually in permanent exile. . . . Exile becomes a symbol in this literature; a symbol for the alienation of the group (or sect) from power in Jerusalem, or one related to messianic expectations which alone would restore the people to their land." (I owe this reference to James Scott.) Among older writers not previously noted by me is Peter R. Ackroyd, *Exile and Restoration: A Study of Hebrew Thought of the Sixth Century BC* (London: SCM Press, 1968), 232-47, making it crystal clear that exile quickly becomes not simply a geographical reality but "the symbol for the bondage from which release is to be found" (247); Rudolf Schmidt, "Exil I. Altes und Neues Testament," *TRE* 10 (1982), quoted in Scott, "Exile and the Self-Understanding of Diaspora Jews," 188-89.
[5]E.g., Darrell L. Bock, "The Trial and Death of Jesus in N. T. Wright's *Jesus and the Victory of God*," in *Jesus and the Restoration of Israel: A Critical Assessment of N. T. Wright's* Jesus and the Victory of God, ed. Carey C. Newman (Downers Grove, IL: InterVarsity Press, 1999), 309n15. Far worse is the apparently deliberate misunderstanding of the position by Maurice P. Casey, "Review of *Jesus and the Victory of God*," *JSNT* 69 (1998): 95-103, ridiculing the idea that Jews could be "in exile" when they were living in Jerusalem. This shows merely that Casey has not heard the point being made. The same is true in a different way of Robert H. Stein, "Review of *Jesus and the Victory of God*," *JETS* 44 (2001): 207-18. Stein writes as if I have replaced "kingdom of God" in Jesus' teaching with "return from exile." Of course not; I simply interpreted "kingdom" in terms of a widespread expectation of the time.

them, exile was in fact a geographical reality, as for many in the Diaspora (though we recognize that many Jews were quite comfortable away from the land and did not see distance as a destitution in need of a reconstitution), whether they were aware of the continuing theological and cultural oppression of foreign nations as indicating that Daniel 9 had not yet been fulfilled (which we shall see to be true for a great many), or whether they believed that in some sense they themselves were the advance guard of the "real return from exile," indicating that it had been going on right up to their time and still was for everyone except themselves (as in Qumran). Whichever of these viewpoints is true, the point remains that *the theological awareness of being at a particular stage within the overall continuing narrative*, coupled with *the exegetical awareness of a large-scale Deuteronomic prophecy being worked out* was at the heart of the worldview of many Second Temple Jews (if their literature is allowed to speak for them, that is).

    While no doubt we can go on fine-tuning the details of what kind of exile people thought they were living in, the greatest resistance to the overall construal I and others have put forward is not, I think, to do with those details but rather with the sense of the overall narrative itself.

    The seventy weeks of Daniel 9. The proper starting point is Daniel 9. Within the fictive scenario of the book, the exiled Daniel has poured out his heart and soul in prayer, insisting that it must be time for the exile to end, because Jeremiah predicted that it would last for seventy years, and that time is now up.[6] The prayer retells the sorry story in terms of the law of Moses, strongly echoing Deuteronomy 28–29:

> All Israel has transgressed your law and turned aside, refusing to obey your
> voice. So the curse and the oath written in the law of Moses, the servant of
> God, have been poured out upon us, because we have sinned against you. He
> has confirmed his words, which he spoke against us and against our rulers,
> by bringing upon us a calamity so great that what has been done against Je
> rusalem has never before been done under the whole heaven. Just as it is
> written in the law of Moses, all this calamity has come upon us. (Dan 9:11-13)[7]

---

[6]Dan 9:2, citing Jer 25:11-12; cf. too Jer 29:10; 2 Chron 36:21-22; Zech 1:12; 7:5; 1 Esdr 1:57-58; Josephus, *Ant.* 11:1-2, citing also Is 44:28. Cf. too Is 23:15 (the fate of Tyre, forgotten for seventy years).
[7]Direct reference is made here to Deut 28:15-68; 29:20-28 (the curse); Deut 29:12, 14, 19 (the oath) (the two seem almost interchangeable; the LXX for "oath" is *ara*, for "curse" *katara*); in Deut 29:20, 21 the MT and LXX (Deut 29:19, 20) speak of God bringing "all the oaths" of "this book" or "of

"Daniel" is thus positioning himself and his people within the continuous narrative promised by Moses. It is not that Deuteronomy promised, in general terms, that "disobedience would bring exile," as though this were something that might just happen every so often in a miscellaneous fashion, unconnected with any larger narrative. Rather, Deuteronomy set out, briefly in Deuteronomy 4, fully in Deuteronomy 27–30, and then again in the great poem of Deuteronomy 32 and its flanking chapters of Deuteronomy 31; 33, a *single historical sequence*, which—though it has taken hundreds of years!— has eventually come to pass.[8] The prayer of Daniel 9 takes its stand within this single narrative at the point of transition from the end of Deuteronomy 29 to the start of Deuteronomy 30. All these things have happened to us, says Daniel, because we were unfaithful, and God did what he said he would do. But now we appeal to that same covenantal faithfulness of his to bring us through and out the other side. If we return with all our heart and soul, calling the blessings and the curses to mind in the lands to which we have been driven, then Deuteronomy tells us what ought to happen next:

> The LORD your God will restore your fortunes and have compassion on you, gathering you again from all the people among whom the LORD your God has scattered you. Even if you are exiled to the ends of the world, from there the LORD your God will gather you, and from there he will bring you back. The LORD your God will bring you into the land that your ancestors possessed, and you will possess it. (Deut 30:3-5)[9]

---

the covenant" upon them. In Deut 29:27 (MT/LXX 29:26) the Hebrew speaks of "all the curses in this book," and a variant in the A version of LXX speaks of "all the oaths of the covenant." Deut 30:7 speaks of God putting "all the oaths" on Israel's enemies as part of the great reversal (see further below).

[8]It is not, either in Deut 27–30 or Deut 31–33, a "repeated pattern," as suggested by, e.g., Robert A. Kugler, "Testaments," in *Justification and Variegated Nomism,* 1:194n19; however, in later Jewish thought exile becomes just such a pattern, as seen rightly, e.g., by Jacob Neusner, William S. Green, and Ernest Frerichs, eds., *Judaisms and Their Messiahs at the Turn of the Christian Era* (Cambridge: Cambridge University Press, 1987), 1-3. Gerhard von Rad, *Old Testament Theology: The Theology of Israel's Historical Traditions,* trans. D. Stalker (Edinburgh and London: Oliver and Boyd, 1962), 346, suggests that Deut 30 is offering "what is at bottom a simple religious message." Note 1 Enoch 103: in this poem, it appears that both the elite and the nonelite are claiming the narrative of Deut 28-30 for themselves (I owe this point to Loren Stuckenbruck).

[9]Michael Fishbane, *Biblical Interpretation in Ancient Israel* (Oxford: Oxford University Press, 1988), 198, 541, suggests that Deut 29:29, the last verse of the chapter, which speaks of "the secret things" as belonging to YHWH but "the revealed things" as belonging to "us and our children," is meant to function as a warning to subsequent readers not to try to probe too exactly into the timings of when these prophecies will be fulfilled—a warning that Jeremiah and Daniel failed to heed.

That is what "Daniel" is now hoping for. Deuteronomy promised it; Jeremiah said it would come in seventy years; so please, God willing, may it happen right now:

> And now, O Lord our God, who brought your people out of the land of Egypt with a mighty hand and made your name renowned even to this day—we have sinned, we have done wickedly. O Lord, in view of all your righteous acts, let your anger and wrath, we pray, turn away from your city Jerusalem, your holy mountain; because of our sins and the iniquities of our ancestors, Jerusalem and your people have become a disgrace among all our neighbors. Now therefore, O our God, listen to the prayer of your servant and to his supplication, and for your own sake, Lord, let your face shine upon your desolated sanctuary. Incline your ear, O my God, and hear. Open your eyes and look at our desolation and the city that bears your name. We do not present our supplication before you on the ground of our righteousness, but on the ground of your great mercies. O Lord, hear; O Lord, forgive; O Lord, listen and act and do not delay! For your own sake, O my God, because your city and your people bear your name! (Dan 9:15-19)[10]

It is one of the greatest prayers in the biblical tradition. And, like another that would press such a claim, it doesn't receive the hoped-for answer. The cup does not pass from Jesus in Gethsemane; and the time is not yet for Daniel and his friends to receive the full blessing of restoration promised in Deuteronomy 30. Yes, Jeremiah had said seventy years; but actually there is a greater time still in prospect, seventy times seven:

> [The man Gabriel] came and said to me, "Daniel, I have now come out to give you wisdom and understanding. At the beginning of your supplications a word went out, and I have come to declare it, for you are greatly beloved. So consider the word and understand the vision:
> "Seventy weeks are decreed for your people and your holy city: to finish the transgression, to put an end to sin, and to atone for iniquity, to bring in everlasting righteousness, to seal both vision and prophet, and to anoint a most holy place. Know therefore and understand: from the time that the word went out to restore and rebuild Jerusalem until the time of an anointed prince, there shall be

---

"The revealed things" is then a reference to Torah: you know what you have to do, don't worry about when future events will happen!

[10]Scott, "For as Many as Are of Works of the Law Are Under a Curse," 199n35, points out that this prayer "is saturated with the Deuteronomic covenantal tradition," citing many other scholars on the point.

seven weeks; and for sixty-two weeks it shall be built again with streets and moat, but in a troubled time. After the sixty-two weeks, an anointed one shall be cut off and shall have nothing, and the troops of the prince who is to come shall destroy the city and the sanctuary. Its end shall come with a flood, and to the end there shall be war. Desolations are decreed. He shall make a strong covenant with many for one week, and for half of the week he shall make sacrifice and offering cease; and in their place shall be an abomination that desolates, until the decreed end is poured out upon the desolator." (Dan 9:22-27)

This is neither what "Daniel" wants nor when he wants it. Instead of seventy years, four hundred and ninety. Instead of the restoration he had imagined, a flurry of frightening events, with wars and devastations and only a hint, at the very end, that a "decreed end" will finish for good those who have been oppressing God's people.

Now it is of course regularly understood that the actual setting for this book, and this prayer, is the time of the Maccabean revolt. The author of 1 Maccabees refers specifically to this passage when he speaks of Antiochus Epiphanes setting up an "abomination that desolates" in the holy place (1 Macc 1:54). How the calculation is then worked out, however, is not clear: four hundred and ninety years before 167 BCE is 657 BCE, a full sixty years before Nebuchadnezzar took the city in 597, and seventy before he destroyed it in 587. But it was precisely that sort of calculation that Daniel 9 set in motion, teasing pious Jews for the next three hundred years with the challenge to work out a riddle. Somehow those 490 years must mean something . . .

And calculate they did. As several scholars have shown, such calculations were a significant feature of the period.[11] Roger Beckwith showed in a pair of articles many years ago—and this is evidence not only that many Jews of the

---

[11]See, e.g., Ben Zion Wacholder, *Essays on Jewish Chronology and Chronography* (New York: Ktav, 1975); Lester L. Grabbe, "Chronography in Hellenistic Jewish Historiography," in *SBL Seminar Papers* (Missoula, MT: 1979), 2:43-68; Adela Yarbro Collins, "Early Christian Apocalyptic Literature," *ANRW* II.25.6 (1988): 4665-4711; Gabriele Boccaccini, *Beyond the Essene Hypothesis: The Parting of the Ways Between Qumran and Enochic Judaism* (Grand Rapids: Eerdmans, 1989); James M. Scott, *On Earth as in Heaven: The Restoration of Sacred Time and Sacred Space in the Book of Jubilees* (Leiden: Brill, 2005), e.g., 94: "Calculating the end of the protracted exile—and especially its end—seems to have been one of the main impulses for the development of sabbatical chronologies expressed in terms of sabbatical and jubilee language," i.e., esp. Jubilees itself, and the Qumran literature; and particularly Roger T. Beckwith, *Calendar and Chronology, Jewish and Christian: Biblical, Intertestamental and Patristic Studies*, AGJU 33 (Leiden: Brill, 1996); Beckwith, "The Significance of the Calendar for Interpreting Essene Chronology and Eschatology," *RevQ* 38 (1980): 167-202; Beckwith, "Daniel 9 and the Date of Messiah's Coming in Essene,

time believed in a continuing exile but also that they were indeed thinking in terms of a continuous history—that many of the debates between different schools of thought, including inner-Pharisaic debates, concerned precisely the question of chronology: Have you done your sums right? Do you know when the 490 begins, and hence when it will end? One of the arguments against Akiba's hailing of Bar-Kokhba as Messiah was that *his calculations were wrong*. "Grass will be growing from between your jaws, Akiba," declared Yohanan ben Torta, "before the Son of David comes."[12] But the point, however you calculated it, was this: *Jeremiah said that the exile would last seventy years, and Daniel was told that this had to be interpreted as "seventy times seven."* That's what the text said, and there is abundant evidence that after the time of Daniel—certainly from the mid-second century onwards, through at least to the second century of the Common Era—people were calculating exactly that. Thus, as Beckwith summarizes the situation (and it is remarkable how many people have written about Second Temple Judaism in recent years without showing any recognition of this vital element),

> There is strong evidence to show that the Essenes, the Pharisees and the Zealots all thought that they could date, at least approximately, the time when the Son of David would come, and that in each case their calculations were based upon Daniel's prophecy of the 70 Weeks (Dan 9:24–27), understood as 70 weeks of years. The later attempts of the Christian Fathers to show that this prophecy was fulfilled by the coming of Jesus, and accords with the time at which he came, had therefore a considerable tradition behind them.[13]

The reason for these calculations can be stated simply and sharply. These different groups of Jews were anxiously trying to work out when Daniel's "seventy weeks" would be over, not simply because that was when the Messiah would come, but because, as Daniel 9 indicates, that was when the long exile, seventy times longer than Jeremiah had foretold, would finally be complete. In other words, *they knew that, despite the geographical "return" in*

Hellenistic, Pharisaic, Zelot and Early Christian Computation," *RevQ* 40 (1981): 521-42; so Scott, "For as Many as Are of Works of the Law Are Under a Curse," 200n39.

[12]y. Ta'an 4:6, 68d; see Beckwith, "Significance of the Calendar"; Beckwith, "Daniel 9 and the Date of Messiah's Coming," esp. 536-39 (now combined in Beckwith, *Calendar and Chronology*, chap. 8), and the discussion in Wright, *New Testament and the People of God*, 198n156. Even if the legend is much later, it shows what was at stake: Dan 9 put a date on the coming of Messiah, but nobody could be sure what that date was.

[13]Beckwith, *Calendar and Chronology*, 217.

the late sixth century and on to the time of Ezra and Nehemiah in the mid-fifth century BCE, something they still regarded as "exile" was not yet over. And they were reading their own situation, again and again, within the single flow of national narrative they found in Deuteronomy 27–30.[14]

This is the heart of what I take to be common knowledge both among first-century Jews and among the great majority of scholars of first-century Judaism. This is confirmed time and again by those closest to the texts under discussion: so, for instance, James VanderKam of Notre Dame University: "A common portrait of exile in the apocalyptic literature envisages it as a state of affairs that began at some point near the end of the kingdom of Judah and continued to the author's day and even beyond."[15]

A Qumran passage which appears to develop the same sequence of thought, though in this case is complicated by the interweaving of the "messianic" prophecy of 2 Samuel 7, is 11QTemple 59. The passage opens with a description of the curses that shall come upon Israel: they will find themselves crying and screaming for help "in the lands of their enemies," but God will not come to their rescue, "for they broke my covenant and their soul loathed my law." But that will not be the last stage in the narrative. The promise of Deuteronomy is to be blended with biblical promises about the coming Davidic king:

> Afterwards they shall come back to me with all their heart and with all their soul, in agreement with all the words of this law, and I will save them from the hand of their enemies and redeem them from the hand of those who hate them, and bring them into the land of their fathers, and I shall redeem them, and multiply them, and rejoice in them. And I shall be their God and they shall be my people. And the king who prostitutes his heart and his eyes (removing them) from my commandments, shall have no-one who will sit on the throne of his fathers, never, because I shall prevent for ever his descendants from governing again in Israel. But if he walks according to my precepts and keeps my commandments and does what is right and good before me, he shall not lack one of his sons to sit on the throne of the kingdom of Israel for ever. And I shall be with him and free him from the hand of those who hate him and from the hand of those who seek to destroy his life; and I

---

[14]See too Deut 4:25-31 as precursor of this theme.
[15]James C. VanderKam, "Exile in Apocalyptic Jewish Literature," in *Exile: Old Testament, Jewish, and Christian Conceptions*, 94.

shall give to him all his enemies and he shall rule them at his will but they
shall not rule him. And I shall place him above and not below, at the head
and not the tail, and he will extend his kingdom for many days, he and his
sons after him.[16]

This blend of the Deuteronomic historical sequence with royal promise,
making the prophecy about being "the head and not the tail" specific to the
king, is, to my knowledge, unique in Second Temple literature, though the
elements it thus combines are woven separately into many other passages,
as we have seen.

Before we proceed further, we should note that Deuteronomy 27–30 is not
the only Pentateuchal passage to carry the promise of a historical sequence
culminating in a continuing exile and an ultimate return.[17] At the climax of
the ordering of Israel's festivals in Leviticus 23–24 we find Leviticus 25, with
its detailed commandment about the sabbatical year, and with that the year
of Jubilee, the multiplication of seven by seven, so that the fiftieth year is the
time to proclaim liberty throughout the land.[18] That is then spelled out in
terms of agriculture, property, and the release of slaves. Leviticus 26 picks up
this theme with a sudden, and to many readers quite unexpected, burst of
what can only be called historical prophecy, in which we find ourselves in
the world of the late chapters of Deuteronomy: if you follow my

---

[16]11QT [11Q19] 59 (= 4Q524.6-13), 5-9; 9-21, trans. F. García-Martínez and E. J. C. Tigchelaar, *The Dead Sea Scrolls Study Edition* (Leiden: Brill, 1998), 1281.

[17]Willem Cornelis van Unnik, *Das Selbstverständnis der jüdischen Diaspora in der hellenistisch-römischen Zeit*, ed. Pieter Willem van der Horst, AGJU 17 (Leiden: Brill, 1993), presents an overall thesis about the Diaspora, arguing that Diaspora itself was seen by many within it as the fulfillment of the punishment promised in Lev 26 and Deut 28. See too Paul R. Trebilco, *Jewish Communities in Asia Minor* (Cambridge: Cambridge University Press, 1991), 60-69, on the curses inscribed on some Jewish tombstones in Asia Minor, referring to "the curses in Deuteronomy" in a way that indicates that (1) these were well known, (2) they were interpreted in terms of the present ongoing situation of Jews in the Diaspora, and (3) they were looking ahead to a future fulfillment of Deut 30:7 when "the curses" would be put instead on the heads of the persecutors.

[18]Lev 25:10. Philo, *Praem.*, in the remarkable passage that concludes the book (127-72), gives a lengthy combined exposition of Deuteronomy and Leviticus, finishing with a prediction of a great return yet to be accomplished (163-72). He includes a meditation (see below) on the sabbatical year, or rather the shame of its not being kept (153-61). On this see esp. Trebilco, *Jewish Communities*, 214n38; though Trebilco's interpretation has been disputed (see Scott, "Exile and the Self-Understanding of Diaspora Jews," 199), it remains suggestive; van Unnik, *Das Selbstverständnis*, 127-37. On Philo's reading of Deut 30 see John M. G. Barclay, "By the Grace of God I Am What I Am: Grace and Agency in Philo and Paul," in *Divine and Human Agency in Paul and His Cultural Environment*, ed. John M. G. Barclay and Simon J. Gathercole (London: T&T Clark, 2008), 145.

commandments, all will go well (Lev 26:1-13), but if you will not, you will be punished (Lev 26:14-33). And the end of that punishment will be exile: "I will scatter you among the nations, and I will unsheathe the sword against you; your land shall be a desolation, and your cities a waste" (Lev 26:33).

What has this got to do with Israel's appointed festivals, particularly the great Jubilee that forms the main subject of the previous chapter in Leviticus? Just this, says the writer: that, when you are languishing in exile, *the land will enjoy its Sabbaths*, making up as it were for lost time (Lev 26:34–35). But—another great biblical "but"—"if they confess their iniquity . . ." then God will remember his covenant with Abraham, Isaac and Jacob; he will remember the covenant he made at the exodus; and—this is not said, but it is surely implied—he will rescue them from their continuing exile (Lev 26:40–45).[19] There we have a strong parallel with Deuteronomy 26–30, and this time it contains a new element: the land will enjoy its Sabbaths. How many Sabbaths? Well, a Sabbath is seven years; a jubilee comes after seven times seven; for a jubilee of jubilees, the moment of ultimate freedom, suppose we say . . . seventy times seven? And with that, we find ourselves back in Daniel 9. If the God who made the world in six days and rested on the seventh, commanding his people to follow suit, were to liberate his people at last, an ultimate jubilee might make the point exactly.[20]

What then does "exile" mean, in this continuing sense? Answer: the time of the curse spoken of in Deuteronomy and Leviticus, a curse that lasts as long as Israel is "the tail and not the head," still subject to the rule, and often the abusive treatment, of foreign nations with their blasphemous and wicked idolatry and immorality. As long (in other words) as the condition of Israel is much like that in Egypt, they will be waiting for the new exodus. As long as Persia, Egypt, Greece, Syria, or Rome are in charge, the exile is not really over. And as long as that exile is not over, we are still in Deuteronomy 29, hoping and praying that Daniel's 490 years will soon be complete, that the Messiah

---

[19]What is promised is that God "will not spurn them, or abhor them so as to destroy them utterly and break my covenant with them; for I am the Lord their God; but I will remember in their favor the covenant" (Lev 26:44-45). Leviticus seems to me here to adopt the principle we see so often in the rabbis: when you can see to the end of an argument, you do not need to spell it out further. The chess game stops three or four moves short, since both players can see that the winning move is inevitable. So here: "God will remember the covenant . . ." and the reader, knowing that up to that point Israel was in exile, can draw the right conclusion.

[20]See esp. Fishbane, *Biblical Interpretation*, 482-83.

will come at last, and that—in Daniel's majestic language—Israel's God will act in accordance with his righteousness, his faithfulness to the covenant.

The question then is, how do you know when it's happening? What are the signs? And what if—as the Scrolls in particular strongly imply—the real "return from exile" is happening at last, but secretly and with a small group whose interpretation of key elements of the Torah is the sign that at last Israel is being faithful? I and others have quoted and discussed the relevant Scrolls elsewhere and do not need to repeat that discussion here.[21]

Ezra 9 and Nehemiah 9. Long before the time of Qumran, though, the same point emerges in texts from the so-called postexilic period. As is noted often enough, both Ezra and Nehemiah, in their great prayers, very similar to the prayer in Daniel 9, speak of a continuing state that is hardly the great liberation the prophets had promised. We are still guilty, confesses Ezra: yes, a remnant has returned, but this is so that God may "brighten our eyes and grant us a little sustenance in our slavery. For we are slaves; yet our God has not forsaken us in our slavery" (Ezra 9:8-9).[22] But we are still sinful and guilty. This is hardly the language of forgiveness, of the new covenant promised in Jeremiah 31, of

---

[21]See Wright, *New Testament and the People of God*, 269-70, quoting CD 1:3-11; see too, e.g., CD 3:10-14, where the sect are the remnant with whom Israel's God has secretly reestablished the covenant; on CD see now, e.g., Michael E. Fuller, *The Restoration of Israel: Israel's Re-gathering and the Fate of the Nations in Early Jewish Literature and Luke–Acts*, BZNW 138 (Berlin: de Gruyter, 2006), 52-60. Evans, "Aspects of Exile and Restoration in the Proclamation of Jesus and the Gospels," 308-9, suggests that almost the whole of 4Q504-506 could be cited to make the same point; so too Paul Garnet, *Salvation and Atonement in the Qumran Scrolls*, WUNT 2.3 (Tübingen: Mohr Siebeck, 1977). It is worth quoting again S. Talmon, "Waiting for the Messiah: The Spiritual Universe of the Covenanters," in *Judaisms and Their Messiahs at the Turn of the Christian Era*, ed. J. Neusner et al. (Cambridge: Cambridge University Press, 1987), 116-17: the writers of the Scrolls "intended to obliterate it [i.e., the 'return from exile' as normally understood] entirely from their conception of Israel's history, and to claim for themselves the distinction of being the first returnees after the destruction." One of the first to draw attention to this whole theme in Qumran was Michael A. Knibb, "The Exile in the Literature of the Intertestamental Period," *HeyJ* (1976): 253-79; Knibb, *The Qumran Community*, Cambridge Commentaries on Writings of the Jewish and Christian World, 200 BC to AD 200 (Cambridge: Cambridge University Press, 1987). See too David Moessner, *Lord of the Banquet: The Literary and Theological Significance of the Lukan Travel Narrative* (Harrisburg, PA: Trinity Press International, 1989), 88-91, citing, e.g., 1QpHab 2:5-10; also VanderKam, "Exile in Apocalyptic Jewish Literature," e.g., 90. See the fuller presentation in Wright, *Paul and the Faithfulness of God*, chap. 2.

[22]Evans, "Aspects of Exile," 309, quotes H. G. M. Williamson, *Ezra, Nehemiah* (Dallas: Word, 1985), 136, on the passage: "The final consummation is by no means yet reached." See Donald E. Gowan, "The Exile in Jewish Apocalyptic," in *Scripture in History and Theology: Essays in Honor of J. Coert Rylaarsdam*, ed. A. E. Merrill and T. W. Overholt, PTMS 17 (Pittsburgh: Pickwick, 1977), 219, suggesting this situation as a reason for the rise of "apocalyptic": the people were "without security, living in an alien world, even though it was their own country."

the incredulous delight of Isaiah 54 or Psalm 126. We are back in the land, but we might as well still be with Daniel in Babylon (to put it anachronistically in terms of the probable date of the books in question). So too in the longer prayer of Ezra in Nehemiah 9. The prayer moves from creation to Abraham, on to the exodus and, despite rebellion, into the Promised Land at last; then on to the continuing rebellion that produced the exile, just as had been warned; and now, at last, "here we are, slaves to this day— slaves in the land that you gave to our ancestors to enjoy its fruit and its good gifts" (Neh 9:36). Here is the dilemma: the prophecies have let us down, and though we are back in our own land the promises about being blessed in that land have not come to pass. Instead, "its rich yield goes to the kings whom you have set over us" (Neh 9:37; this is a direct reference to Deut 28:33, 51; in other words, the prayer is locating "us" still firmly on the exilic time sequence in the key prophetic passage). These kings "have power also over our bodies and over our livestock and their pleasure, and we are in great distress" (Neh 9:37). This cannot be the time that Isaiah 40–55 had in mind, or the great renewal spoken of in the last twenty or so chapters of Ezekiel. "We are still slaves"; and slaves need an exodus, a fresh act of liberation, a new Moses, a victory over the pagan tyrants who still oppress them.[23]

Exceptions to the rule? What might count as exceptions to the rule? My case, after all, is certainly not that *all Jews throughout the period* understood themselves to be living in a state of continuing exile, only that such an understanding was widespread and was particularly likely to be true, generally speaking, of Second Temple Jews, and particularly of Pharisees and Essenes. One might say the same, interestingly, about belief in the bodily resurrection.

Ben Sira might be thought an obvious exception: the great scene in Sirach 50, with Simon son of Onias appearing in the temple, can be read as a sort of fulfillment of the promise of divine splendor being once again displayed, and hence as a sign that the exile is well and truly over.[24] That, of course, is what we should expect from an aristocrat writing in the early years

---

[23]See esp., e.g., Steck, "Das Problem," 454-55. The "irony" of which Steven M. Bryan, *Jesus and Israel's Traditions of Judgment and Restoration* (Cambridge: Cambridge University Press, 2002), 12, accuses me (of using an idea which connotes removal from the land to describe the situation of Jews living in the land) is thus not mine, but Ezra's.

[24]So, e.g., James D. G. Dunn, review of N. T. Wright, *Jesus and the Victory of God*, *JTS* 49 (1998): 730; Mark A. Seifrid, "Blind Alleys in the Controversy over the Paul of History," *TynBul* 45 (1994): 86-87. Steck, *Israel und das gewaltsame Geschick der Propheten*, 146-47, appears to concede this.

of the second century BC, before the trouble with Syria really began. But even in Ben Sira there are signs of an expectation that reaches out toward a fulfillment of prophecy yet to be realized:

> Have mercy upon us, O God of all,
>> and put all the nations in fear of you. . . .
> Give new signs, and work other wonders;
>> make your hand and right arm glorious. . . .
> Hasten the day, and remember the appointed time,
>> and let people recount your mighty deeds. . . .
> Gather all the tribes of Jacob,
>> and give them their inheritance, as at the beginning.
> Have mercy, O Lord, on the people called by your name,
>> on Israel, whom you have named your firstborn;
> Have pity on the city of your sanctuary,
>> Jerusalem, the place of your dwelling [so Hebrew:
>>> Greek has "your rest"].
> Fill Zion with your majesty,
>> and your temple with your glory.
> Bear witness to those whom you created in the beginning,
>> and fulfill the prophecies spoken in your name.
> Reward those who wait for you
>> and let your prophets be found trustworthy.
>> (Sir 36:1-2, 6, 10, 13-21)[25]

What is especially striking about this passage is the repeated sense toward the end that there are unfulfilled prophecies still outstanding. It is important to the writer that the prophets (presumably including Isaiah, Jeremiah, and Ezekiel) should be proved right in a way that has not yet happened. However splendid the high priest may be, therefore, we should not regard Ben Sira as offering anything like a fully realized eschatology, a claim

---

[25]Seifrid, "Blind Alleys," 88, discounts this passage and insists that Sirach is an exception to my rule. I might have been happy to grant the point (though being then still puzzled as to what that prayer is doing) had it not been for the remarkable treatment by Fuller, *Restoration of Israel*, 33-42, making it quite clear that Sirach (1) saw the exile as having continued to the time of Simon II, who has at last properly restored the temple, and (2) very much envisaged a further, more glorious restoration still to come. See too Gowan, "Exile in Jewish Apocalyptic," 207.

that prophecy has been fulfilled and the people no longer need to be "gathered."[26]

The book of Judith can be cited as another counterexample. The book describes how Nebuchadnezzar's general Holofernes had struck terror into the hearts of the Judeans, since they had only just returned from exile and reconsecrated the temple and its vessels (Jdt 4:3). When Holofernes makes enquiry about Jerusalem, the Ammonite leader tells him Israel's story, culminating in the exile that was the result of Israel's sin, and then says, echoing Deuteronomy (not bad for an Ammonite, though the words are of course put in his mouth by the pious author), "But now they have returned to their God, and have come back from the places where they were scattered, and have occupied Jerusalem, where their sanctuary is" (Jdt 5:19). Fair enough: though we note that the rhetorical force of the book, if indeed it was composed (as is normally thought) in the mid-second century BC, is to place Holofernes in parallel with the new persecutors such as Antiochus Epiphanes. We do not imagine that the book was simply a tale of a heroine from centuries before, without relevance to the continuing pagan threat. But Judith can happily be allowed as a clear apparent exception to the larger pattern.[27]

What about the books of the Maccabees? It is true that 1 Maccabees uses such exalted language about the results of Simon's rule (140–134 BCE) that we might well think the promised last days had arrived (1 Macc 14:4-15).[28] But the book ends with Simon and his sons getting drunk and being murdered, with the remaining son, John, succeeding him. No sign of the glorious eschaton there. And in 2 Maccabees there is the same strong sense we have seen elsewhere that, despite the dazzling victories of Judas and the establishment of the Hasmonean dynasty, more remains to be done. The "more" in question is once again explicitly linked to Deuteronomy 30:3-5: "We have hope in God

[26]So Evans, "Aspects of Exile," 305-6.

[27]Frank Thielman, *Paul and the Law: A Contextual Approach* (Downers Grove, IL: InterVarsity Press, 1994), 50-51, notes that even though Judith is thus part of "the literature of the establishment," the book bears witness to the same basic Deuteronomic pattern of sin/punishment (Jdt 8:18-19). To this extent, the perspective of Judith may be seen in a kind of parallel with that of Qumran (exile was indeed prolonged, but it is now over), with the difference that in Qumran the "real return" was a secret, small-scale movement, whereas for Judith it seems to be a public and political settlement (i.e., presumably the Hasmonean regime).

[28]See Wright, *New Testament and the People of God*, 429.

that he will soon have mercy on us and will gather us from everywhere under heaven into his holy place, for he has rescued us from great evils and has purified the place" (2 Macc 2:18).[29] God *has* rescued us and purified the place; and he *will soon* gather us from everywhere and have mercy on us. This sounds very like the "double return" found in Tobit and 1 Enoch.

What about Josephus? Was he not an aristocrat who might have been satisfied with how things had been, at least until those wretched revolutionaries went and ruined it all? By no means: the period of life under Rome was a time of *douleia*, "slavery," and it was all Israel's own fault.[30] But there may be a further deliverance yet to come, precisely in line with the prophecies at the end of Deuteronomy.

We may end this survey by picking up from James Scott and Jonathan Goldstein the discussion of the remarkable wall paintings in the synagogue at Dura-Europos, out on the eastern edge of Syria.[31] These paintings, from the second and third centuries of the Common Era, include, it is claimed, a depiction of the defeat of the Roman Empire and the rescue of Israel from exile. A second Moses (the Messiah) leads the people to victory over Rome. The paintings look as if they were carefully designed so as not to arouse suspicions; but, like African American spirituals with a deep double

---

[29]It has been suggested (Seifrid, "Blind Alleys," 88) that the end of the book, with Jerusalem rescued and "in the possession of the Hebrews" (2 Macc 15:37), indicates that the "plight" of 2 Macc 2:18 has been fully dealt with. Evans, "Aspects of Exile," 307, however, follows J. A. Goldstein "How the Authors of 1 and 2 Maccabees Treated the 'Messianic' Promises," in *Judaisms and Their Messiahs at the Turn of the Christian Era*, 81-85, in concluding that the author believed "that the Jewish people were still experiencing the Age of Wrath, with many Jews still in exile." See too Fuller, *Restoration of Israel*, 44n113, who sees the ending of the book as "signify[ing] once more God's protection of Israel and Jerusalem," not an ultimate restoration, which he sees as yet to come.

[30]*Jewish War* 5.395, part of Josephus's own reported speech (as having already gone over to the attackers) to the implacable defenders on the ramparts of Jerusalem. Granted, he places the start of the present mode of "slavery" at the time of the Roman conquest in 63 BCE. But Josephus is careful not to cash out too clearly the longer narratives with their antipagan denouement. This, I think, is the reason for his silence about covenant (see Lester L. Grabbe, "Did All Jews Think Alike? 'Covenant' in Philo and Josephus in the Context of Second Temple Judaic Religion," in *The Concept of the Covenant in the Second Temple Period*, ed. Stanley E. Porter and J. C. R. de Roo [Leiden: Brill, 2003], 257-58 [266]), cognate with his sudden silence about the meaning of the stone in Dan 2 and the devastating imagery of Dan 7. See the discussion in Wright, *New Testament and the People of God*, 303-14, with full references.

[31]Scott, "Exile," 193-94; Jonathan A. Goldstein, "The Judaism of the Synagogues (Focusing on the Synagogue of Dura-Europas)," in *Judaism in Late Antiquity, Part 2: Historical Syntheses*, ed. Jacob Neusner, Handbuch der Orientalistik 1.17 (Leiden: Brill, 1995), 109-60.

meaning, what might have looked like paintings of biblical scenes from long ago should be read as a promise of final restoration after exile.

The objections to this reading of a fairly substantial body of evidence are not strong and seem to me to stem from the usual problem, "we never saw it this way before," underneath which is the more serious problem, "this might force us to reread some favorite texts." (It will indeed.) "It is difficult to imagine that in the heady days of Hasmonean success, people still widely perceived themselves to be in exile."[32] Well, imagination has to be educated by evidence; and the evidence points to a very brief time of exhilaration at the Hasmonean success, in which indeed some may have supposed that the promised time of full blessing had virtually arrived. People were eager for signs that the bad times of pagan oppression were over and the good times of freedom, promised so long ago, were here at last. I would ask critics to face the question: Would any serious-thinking first-century Jew claim that the promises of Isaiah 40–66, or of Jeremiah, Ezekiel, or Zechariah, had been fulfilled? That the power and domination of paganism had been broken? That YHWH had already returned to Zion? That the covenant had been renewed and Israel's sins forgiven? That the long-awaited "new exodus" had happened? That the second temple was the true, final, and perfect one? Or—in other words—that the exile was really over? Various books of the period explicitly question or challenge the adequacy, or even the God-givenness, of the second temple.[33] That is why the writings at Qumran see the sect as *the secret advance guard* of the real return from exile, which of course implies that the rest of Israel is exiled still.

---

[32]Bryan, *Jesus and Israel's Traditions*, 15. Seifrid, "Blind Alleys," 86-87, suggests that there were many periods when the returned exiles were happy and content, e.g., at the rebuilding of the temple (but what about Malachi's disaffected priests who needed to be reassured that YHWH would indeed come back one day soon?), the Maccabaean victories (yes indeed, but the joy was short-lived), the Hasmonean rule (nice work for the new aristocrats, not so good for the rest, which is precisely why the Essenes and the Pharisees either start up or are freshly energized in that period), and those who enjoyed the status quo under Rome (again, nice work for Rome's appointed henchmen such as Herod, and for tax collectors and a few others; but the majority, if Josephus and the Psalms of Solomon are to be believed, were far from content).

[33]E.g., 1 Enoch 89:73-77; Assumption of Moses 4:5–6:9; 1QpHab 9:3-7; 12:7-9; 4QTest 25-30. Cf., e.g., Christopher Rowland, "The Second Temple: Focus of Ideological Struggle?," in *Templum Amicitiae: Essays on the Second Temple Presented to Ernst Bammel*, ed. William Horbury (Sheffield: JSOT Press, 1991), 175-98.

The point of all this is not that the exile functioned in this period as an *example*, an illustration from the past of the way in which YHWH might perhaps work; nor was it just an *idea*, a type or image that might have been useful in formulating a soteriology that "really" consisted in something else. The point is that Jewish eschatology in the Second Temple period focused on the hope that that which had happened in the Babylonian exile, the triumph of paganism over Israel because of its sins, was still the dominant state of affairs but would at last be undone.

The Temple in the Continuing Exile

The temple in Jerusalem was the focus of the whole Jewish life and way of life. A good deal of Torah was about what to do in the temple, and the practice of Torah in the Diaspora itself could be thought of in terms of gaining, at a distance, the blessings you would gain if you were actually there—the blessing, in other words, of the sacred presence itself, the Shekinah, the glory which dwelt in the temple but would also dwell "where two or three study Torah."[34] An equivalent move was undertaken in Qumran: the sect was to be seen as "a human temple" in which "works of law" are to be offered.[35] Synagogues were often built so that they pointed toward the temple or otherwise indicated their relation to it.[36] Far-off Jews collected temple tax and transported it to Jerusalem so that they might take

---

[34]m. 'Abot 3:2, going on to say that this is true even if only one person is "occupying himself in the Law."

[35]E.g., 1QS 9:3-7; 4Q174 (= 4QFlor) 1:1-7, on which see, e.g., David Flusser, *Judaism and the Origins of Christianity* (Jerusalem: Magnes, 1988), 88-98; Flusser, "Die Gesetzeswerke in Qumran und bei Paulus," in *Geschichte—Tradition—Reflexion: Festschrift für Martin Hengel zum 70. Geburtstag. Bd 1: Judentum*, ed. H. Cancick et al. (Tübingen: Mohr Siebeck, 1996), 398-99; Bertil Gärtner, *The Temple and the Community in Qumran and the New Testament*, SNTSMS 1 (Cambridge: Cambridge University Press, 1965); Markus Bockmuehl, "1QS and Salvation at Qumran," in *Justification and Variegated Nomism*, 1:401n71, with other references. "Works of law" in 1:7 presupposes a text of *ma'se torah*, as, e.g., Geza Vermes, *The Complete Dead Sea Scrolls in English* (Harmondsworth, UK: Penguin, 1997), 493, following J. M. Allegro, *Qumran Cave 4.I (4Q158–4Q186)*, DJD V (Oxford: Clarendon, 1968), 53, with Plate XIX, where the letter in question, though indistinct, does indeed look like a *resh* rather than a *dalet*; others (e.g., Florentino García Martínez and Eibert J. C. Tigchelaar, *The Dead Sea Scrolls* [Grand Rapids: Eerdmans, 1999], 1:352) assume *todah* ("thanksgiving") for *torah* ("law"), perhaps as being the more natural thing to expect. In favor of *torah* we note that 1:11 speaks in the same way of the coming "interpreter of the law," *doresh hatorah*. See the similar questions in relation to 1QS 5:21; 6:18.

[36]On synagogues see S. Fine and J. D. Brolley, "Synagogue," in *The New Interpreter's Dictionary of the Bible*, ed. Katharine Doob Sakenfeld (Nashville, TN: Abingdon, 2009), 5:416-27.

part in the sacrificial cult personally, albeit at a distance.[37] Long centuries after the temple had been destroyed, some continued to regard the activity of studying the laws concerning temple worship as the functional equivalent of taking part in the long-defunct liturgy.[38] It would be a mistake to suppose that just because Pharisees developed strong temple substitutes (in part, no doubt, because of their frustration with the Sadducees who were actually running the temple) they therefore disregarded the institution itself. Far from it. Like Philo, they could produce (as it were) allegorical equivalents of the concrete reality, but the concrete reality still mattered. The wrong people might be in charge of it, but the temple was still the temple.

The temple as God's dwelling. The point of the temple—and this is where I want to develop considerably further what was said in my earlier works—is that it was the meeting point of heaven and earth, the place where Israel's God, YHWH, had long ago promised to put his name, to make his glory present. The temple, and before it the wilderness tabernacle, were thus heirs, within the biblical narrative, to moments like Jacob's vision, the discovery that a particular spot on earth could intersect with, and be the gateway into, heaven itself (Gen 28:10-22). In the later period, even synagogues could sometimes be thought of as meeting places between heaven and earth; how much more the temple itself.[39] The temple was not simply a convenient place to meet for worship. It was not even just the "single sanctuary," the one place where the One God was to be worshiped with sacrifice.[40] It was the place above all where the twin halves of the good creation intersected. When you went up to the temple, it was not *as though* you were "in heaven." You were actually there. That was the point. Israel's God did not have to leave heaven in order to come down and dwell in the wilderness tabernacle or the

[37]See Oskar Skarsaune, *In the Shadow of the Temple: Jewish Influences on Early Christianity* (Downers Grove, IL: InterVarsity Press, 2002), 83.

[38]David Instone-Brewer, *Techniques and Assumptions in Jewish Exegesis Before 70 CE* (Tübingen: Mohr Siebeck, 2004), 35.

[39]Jack N. Lightstone, *Commerce of the Sacred: Mediation of the Divine Among Jews in the Greco-Roman Diaspora* (New York: Columbia University Press, 2006), 99.

[40]Deut 12:5; 14:23; 16:2; 17:8; 18:6; 26:2; 1 Kings 11:13; 14:21; 1 Chron 22:1; 2 Chron 7:12; 12:13; Neh 1:9; 1 Macc 7:37. For the earlier "single sanctuary" at Shiloh see Josh 18:1; 19:51; 21:2; 22:9; Judg 18:31; 1 Sam 1:3, 24; 3:21; 4:3; 1 Kings 14:2; Ps 78:60 (explaining YHWH's change of residence); Jer 7:12; 26:6.

Jerusalem temple. In fact, however surprising it may be for modern Westerners to hear it, within the worldview formed by the ancient Scriptures heaven and earth were always made to work together, to interlock and overlap. There might in principle be many places and ways in which this could happen, but the Jewish people had believed, throughout the millennium prior to Jesus, that the Jerusalem temple was the place and the means par excellence of this strange and powerful mystery.[41]

The roots of this temple belief go back to the very heart of the great controlling narrative: passover, exodus, freedom, Sinai, covenant, and homecoming.[42] Within the book of Exodus, no sooner had the children of Israel come out of Egypt and been given the law on Mount Sinai than Moses was given instructions on how to construct the tabernacle. This, he was told, was the point of bringing them out in the first place:

> And they shall know that I am YHWH their God, the one who brought them out from the land of Egypt *so that I might dwell in their midst*. I am YHWH their God." (Ex 29:46 NRSV, altered)[43]

"That I might dwell in their midst"; the Hebrew for "dwell" is *shkn*, from the same root as *mshkn*, "tabernacle."[44] That was the aim of the whole thing: that the people rescued from slavery and formed by Torah might be the people in whose midst the living God would pitch his tabernacle, would "dwell" (an apparently insignificant word that, in its early Christian reappropriation, needs to be heard as resonating with this entire harmony). There was, of course, an unfortunate digression. Israel's sin with the golden calf, a ghastly parody of the presence of the true God with his people, caused YHWH to threaten not to dwell in their midst after all, nor to go with them into the Promised Land. This provoked the great crisis, and Moses' great

---

[41]On the temple in ancient Israel and its continuing significance in biblical theology, see, e.g., R. E. Clements, *God and Temple* (Oxford: Blackwell, 1965); Samuel L. Terrien, *The Elusive Presence: Toward a New Biblical Theology* (Eugene, OR: Wipf and Stock, 1978).

[42]The "covenant" motif is all over the place even when the word *berith* is not used, as Sanders argued in relation to the rabbis (see N. T. Wright, *Paul and His Recent Interpreters* [Minneapolis: Fortress, 2015], 71). See, e.g., J. S. Kaminsky, *Yet I Loved Jacob: Reclaiming the Biblical Concept of Election* (Nashville, TN: Abingdon, 2007), 137: Amos is "covenantal" despite the absence of the word.

[43]For "dwell," the LXX has *epiklēthēnai*, "to be invoked"; the word *epikaleō* has as a primary meaning the idea of summoning or invoking a god (LSJ, s.v.).

[44]E.g., Ex 26:1; the LXX translation of *mishkan* is *skēnē*, "tent."

prayer, recorded in Exodus 32–34. But the tabernacle was eventually constructed according to plan—even though it now had to be placed outside the camp. There is something of a sigh of relief as the book of Exodus then reaches its climax:

> The cloud covered the tent of meeting, and the glory of YHWH filled the tabernacle. Moses was not able to enter the tent of meeting because the cloud settled upon it, and the glory of YHWH filled the tabernacle. Whenever the cloud was taken up from the tabernacle, the Israelites would set out on each stage of their journey; but if the cloud was not taken up, then they did not set out until the day that it was taken up. For the cloud of YHWH was on the tabernacle by day, and fire was in the cloud by night, before the eyes of all the house of Israel at each stage of their journey. (Ex 40:34-38 NRSV, altered)

The cloud and fire had been present before, of course, leading them out of Egypt, but now these strange symbols of YHWH's presence had found a permanent residence.

This in turn was basic to the understanding of Solomon's temple in Jerusalem. At its dedication, this temple, like the tabernacle before it, was filled with the sign of YHWH's presence:

> When the priests came out of the holy place, a cloud filled the house of YHWH, so that the priests could not stand to minister because of the cloud; for the glory of YHWH filled the house of YHWH. (1 Kings 8:10-11 NRSV, altered)[45]

This is then repeated in the famous scene of Isaiah's vision:

> In the year that King Uzziah died, I saw the Lord, sitting on a throne, high and lifted up; and the hem of his robe filled the temple. Seraphs were in attendance above him, each with six wings. With two they covered their faces, with two they covered their feet, and with two they flew. And they were crying to one another,
>
> > "Holy, holy, holy is YHWH Sebaoth;
> > the whole earth is full of his glory."
>
> The pivots on the thresholds shook at the voices of those who called, and the house filled with smoke. And I said, "Woe is me . . ." (Is 6:1-5 NRSV, altered)

---

[45]This picture remained potent in Israel's memory, to be invoked much later when the second temple was in distress: e.g., 3 Macc 2:16.

These are the scenes that provide a backdrop for all the language in the Psalms about YHWH choosing Zion, and the temple, as the place to dwell, to "place his name there," to "let his glory dwell there," to have as "his inheritance":

> For YHWH has chosen Zion;
>> he has desired it for his habitation:
> "This is my resting place forever;
>> here I will dwell, for I have desired it." (Ps 132:13-14 NRSV, altered) [46]

Again, stressing that the "name" of YHWH will be in the temple, we find Solomon's speech immediately after that filling of the house with the power and the glory of YHWH:

> Blessed be YHWH, the God of Israel, who with his hand has fulfilled what he promised with his mouth to my father David, saying, "Since the day that I brought my people Israel out of Egypt, I have not chosen a city from any of the tribes of Israel in which to build a house, that my name might be there; but I chose David to be over my people Israel." My father David had it in mind to build a house for the name of YHWH, the God of Israel. But YHWH said to my father David, "You did well to consider building a house for my name; nevertheless, you shall not build the house, but your son who shall be born to you shall build the house for my name." Now YHWH has upheld the promise that he made; for I have risen in the place of my father David; I sit on the throne of Israel, as YHWH promised, and have built the house for the name of YHWH, the God of Israel. There I have provided a place for the ark, in which is the covenant of YHWH that he made with our ancestors when he brought them out of the land of Egypt. (1 Kings 8:15-21 NRSV, altered)[47]

It would be hard to overestimate the lasting power of this combination of ideas—and not just ideas, either, but literally facts on the ground. Here

---

[46]Ps 132:13-14 draws together the theme of the whole psalm, which itself draws together much of the Zion/temple theology here described; cf. Deut 12:5, 11; 14:23; 16:2; 17:8; 18:6; 26:2; 1 Kings 11:13; 14:21; Ps 9:11; 26:8; 43:3; 46:4-5; 48:1-3; 68:16-18 (indicating as it were YHWH's moving house from Sinai to Zion); Ps 74:2; 76:2; 78:68; 79:1; 87:2; 122 *passim*; Ps 135:21; Joel 3:21. For the continuance of this theme in the Second Temple period see D. A. Renwick, *Paul, the Temple, and the Presence of God*, BJS 224 (Atlanta: Scholars Press, 1991), 33-41, citing e.g., Sirach 50:5-7; Jubilees 1:27-28; 1 Enoch 14:13-24; 90:29-33; Psalms of Solomon 7:1, 6; 1QS 8, 5-10; 11QTemple (noting, as many do, that the Qumran community saw itself as a kind of new temple; see above), and other literature ancient and modern.

[47]Many of the references to the "single sanctuary" (above) specify that this is the place where YHWH will make "his name" to dwell.

is David's son Solomon, fulfilling the promises made about the house that
David would make for God and the house that God would make for
David, a combined promise that echoed down through Second Temple
Judaism and on into the New Testament.[48] Here is the temple itself, filled
with the powerful glory, that is, the personal presence in power and glory,
of YHWH himself.[49] This is the place that will now be the place of sacrifice, the place toward which prayer will be offered, even from far away,[50]
the place of wisdom,[51] the place from which blessing or deliverance
will come.[52]

The temple and cosmos. The temple was a microcosm of the whole creation. We do not have many artifacts from the Second Temple period with
which to form an impression of the visual symbolic world of the day, but we
have enough descriptions of the temple to know that it was quite deliberately
constructed so as to reflect the whole creation, the stars in the heavens on
the one hand and the multiplicity of beautiful vegetation on the other. As
one recent writer has summarized it:

> The rest of the iconography that filled the Temple from its very beginning—
> the carvings of cherubim, palm trees, and open flowers in the inner shrine,
> the central hall, and on the doors leading into both rooms, the lily work, the
> lattice work, and the pomegranates on the bronze pillars, the bronze oxen
> under the molten sea, and the cherubim, lions, palm trees, oxen, and wreaths
> on the moveable basin frames, and at some point the pole-mounted
> seraphim—all had a symbolic significance.[53]

---

[48]2 Sam 7:1-17, focused on 2 Sam 7:12-14: "When your days are fulfilled and you lie down with
your ancestors, I will raise up your seed after you, who shall come forth from your body, and
I will establish his kingdom. He shall build a house for my name, and I will establish the
throne of his kingdom for ever. I will be his father, and he shall be a son to me." This is then
reflected in Ps 2:7, immediately following the promise: "I have set my king on Zion, my holy
hill" (Ps 2:6).

[49]See Ps 24:7-10; 29:9; 63:2; 99:2; 68:35 (the psalm brings together in a very striking manner the
sovereignty of Israel's God over all creation and his awesome presence in the temple).

[50]See Ps 3:4; 18:6; 28:2; 63:2: "So I have looked upon you in the sanctuary, beholding your power
and glory"; Ps 65:1-2; 116:4, 18-19; and, expressing that distant longing, Ps 42–43 *passim*.

[51]Ps 73:17.

[52]See Ps 14:7; 20:2-3; 53:6; 97:8; 110:2; 134:3; Is 26:21; Mic 1:2-3. When the psalmist says that God
will send "from heaven" to save him (e.g., Ps 57:3), this should probably be seen as another way
of saying the same thing (so Jimmy Jack McBee Roberts, "Temple, Jerusalem," in *New Interpreter's Dictionary of the Bible*, 5:502, citing Ps 18:7, 10).

[53]Roberts, "Temple," 5:501.

Thus the throne of cherubs on which YHWH's presence was supposed to rest was designed to indicate his rule as divine king, lord of the whole world, with cherubim and seraphim expressing the awesome power of his presence. Josephus describes the curtain in the second temple that represented an image of the universe, covered with symbolic colored embroidery and mystical figures. In the Holy of Holies itself were three wonderful works of art: the lampstand, whose seven branches represented the seven planets; the table, on which the twelve loaves represented the circle of the Zodiac and the year; and the altar of incense, on which were thirteen spices, from every part of land and sea, signifying, Josephus declares, that "all things are of God and for God."[54] Likewise, the Wisdom of Solomon describes the robe of Aaron, the first high priest, as depicting "the whole world" (*holos ho kosmos*).[55]

The temple and king. If the cosmic significance of the temple is the first main point to be made about Israel's central symbol, the second is much more sharply focused. The temple was inextricably bound up, in Jewish thought from a thousand years before Paul, with the royal house of David. It was David who conceived the idea of the temple, even though it was Solomon who built it; Chronicles in particular emphasizes that David had the entire scheme laid out for Solomon to implement, rather like God showing Moses the plan of the tabernacle on the mountain so that he could go down and get to work. There is here an echo, perhaps, of the figure of wisdom in Proverbs 8, being at the right hand of the Creator and bringing his plans to birth: Moses, like Solomon, is the truly wise man, and indeed both Moses and Solomon enlist, for the construction of their respective buildings, the services of men who are said to be especially equipped with

---

[54]Josephus, *J.W.* 5.212-18, here at 218: the Greek, reminding us of, e.g., Rom 11:36, is *hoti tou theou panta kai tō theō.* The thirteen spices are further explained in Thackeray's note in the Loeb (*Josephus*, trans. H. St. J. Thackeray, 9 vols. [Cambridge, MA: Harvard University Press, 1927]), 266. For Josephus's other interpretations of the cosmic meaning of the tabernacle, etc., see *Ant.* 3.179-87; *J.W.* 4.324; and for Philo, similarly, *Her.* 197 (the four parts of the incense representing the four elements); *Mos.* 2.117 (the high priest's robe representing the cosmos and its parts).

[55]Wisdom 18:24, describing Aaron's intervention during the plague in Num 16:41-30. (Sir 45:7-12; 50:11, we note, omits this, emphasizing only the robe's beauty and its representation of the people of Israel.) As R. D. Chesnutt, "Covenant and Cosmos in Wisdom of Solomon 10–19," in *Concept of the Covenant in the Second Temple Period*, 225-26, points out, this constitutes a fascinating moment in which the strongly nationalist claim of Wisdom 10–19 overlaps with a feature held in common with many pagan philosophers of the time, namely the Stoic and Cynic idea of the whole world as the divine temple: Heraclitus, *Ep.* 4; Seneca, *Ben.* 7.7.3; *Ep.* 90.29; Plutarch, *Tranq. an.* 20, etc.

the divine spirit and wisdom.[56] Indeed, Solomon's prayer for wisdom is intimately connected to his building of the temple. That project appears in the narrative as the primary, or at least the first, answer his prayer receives.[57]

For the next thousand years the question of kingship and the question of temple are tied closely together.[58] The division of the kingdom in the generation after Solomon created a major problem for the split Israelite world that resulted, as the northern tribes had to create a replacement for the single sanctuary as part of their breaking away from David's house. Threats to the temple were threats to the king, and vice versa; conversely, the two kings seen as heroic by the Deuteronomic historian are Hezekiah and Josiah, who reform the temple, its worship, and its central place in the life of Judah.[59] The destruction of the temple by the Babylonians goes hand in hand with the overthrow of the monarchy, and the rebuilding after the partial return from Babylonian exile is entrusted to Zerubbabel—though the puzzle of the second temple, to which we shall return presently, was part of the problem that meant that the Davidic house was not restored to its former glory.[60]

There was then a hiatus until the second century BCE, when Judas Maccabaeus cleansed and restored the temple after its desecration by Antiochus Epiphanes. This at one fell swoop legitimated his family as rulers, indeed priests as well as kings, for the next hundred years, despite the fact of their belonging neither to the royal tribe of Judah nor the high-priestly family of Zadok. Arguably, one of the motives of Herod the Great in rebuilding the temple to be the most stunning piece of architecture in the ancient world was the hope that, despite even less auspicious ancestry, he might legitimate at least his successors as the true kings of the Jews.[61] The question of kingship

---

[56]Prov 8:22-31; 1 Kings 3:9-12 (cf. 2 Chron 1:7-13; Wis 7:7–9:18); 2 Sam 7:12-13; 1 Chron 28:1–29:22; 2 Chron 2–7; Ex 31:1-11 with 2 Chron 2:13-16 (12-15 MT/LXX). Translations sometimes obscure the primary quality of "wisdom" here, by translating *sophia* as "ability," etc., in Ex 31:2; 2 Chron 2:12.

[57]Prayer for wisdom: 1 Kings 3:5-14. Solomon at once (1 Kings 3:15) goes to Jerusalem and offers sacrifices before the ark of the covenant. There then follows the famous story of the two women disputing over a live and a dead child, with Solomon's wise judgment (1 Kings 3:16-28). First Kings 4 gives a general survey of Solomon's administration, magnificence, and fame, and then with 1 Kings 5 we get down to work on the temple itself.

[58]See previous notes in Wright, *New Testament and the People of God*, etc.

[59]The Chronicler describes a largely unsuccessful attempt by Hezekiah to persuade the northern kingdom to come to the Passover in Jerusalem: 2 Chron 30:1-12.

[60]Zerubbabel is still hailed by Ben Sira as the rebuilder: Sir 49:11-12.

[61]For the combination of themes, see, e.g., CD 7:15-16, where "the books of the Law are the Tabernacle of the King" (quoting Amos 5:26-27) but where "the King" in the Amos text "means 'the

hung ominously over the first century along with the question of the temple, which was scarcely completed in its new magnificence before the Romans finally burned it down once and for all. But the memory of the royal vocation of temple building continued.

All this is reflected in many texts of the relevant periods and would have been as well known—common coin, one might say—among Jews of the day, especially biblically literate ones, as it is relatively unknown and unreflected on by today's Western world, including much of today's biblical scholarship. It is highly significant for our understanding of Jesus and Paul, and their reuse of the temple motif at various key points, that temple and (Davidic) messiahship go together.

The temple and new creation. The two themes so far noted—temple and cosmos, temple and king—are both implicated in the third theme, of special importance for the study of the whole Second Temple period and, not least, the rise and self-understanding of the early Christian movement. What happens to the worldview that was focused on the temple when the king was killed and the temple destroyed? Answer: it threatens to fall apart: YHWH has abandoned the temple to its fate, thereby removing his presence from Israel and leaving nation and king to their fate. The worldview can be put back together again only with the help of prophecies about the coming new temple—which will, of course, mean both the work of the true king and the restoration of the true cosmos. New temple, new king, new creation: that is the combined promise of the exilic prophets. Israel's God will return to his temple at last, the temple that the coming king will build. Then, and only then, the new Genesis will come about.[62] That is the promise, too, of the so-called postexilic prophets.

The point of all this, for our present purposes, is to say: all this would, again, be common coin, second nature, to Jews of the period who were soaked in Scripture and who were living as it were within the implicit narrative of the temple. To those who pored over Torah night and day, looking for the consolation of Israel, this combination of motifs—temple, presence,

---

congregation'"—not to the exclusion of a messiah, but rather as his setting, because at once the text speaks of the coming "scepter" and "star" in accordance with Num 24:17. Clearly it was second nature for a Jew of this period to combine temple, Torah, community, and messiah.

[62]Jeremiah (e.g., Jer 3:17); Ezekiel (Ezek 8–11, etc.); Isaiah (Is 2:2-3; 11:1-11; 31:4-5). See especially Wright, *Jesus and the Victory of God*, 615-24, with Old Testament and postbiblical passages.

glory, kingship, wisdom, creation, exile, rebuilding, and unfulfilled promise—
would be part of their mental and emotional furniture. Touch one and you
touch them all. Torah itself intersected with them all, being the true repos-
itory of wisdom; wisdom itself was the secret of creation, and both together
constituted the divine presence.[63]

All the other symbols of ancient Israel and Second Temple Judaism
gathered around this majestic, potent building, and from it they took their
meaning and power. And this was where the great narratives clustered, the
stories upon which the Jewish people had already been living for centuries
before Jesus of Nazareth or Saul of Tarsus came along, narratives that had
developed fresh resonances in the years immediately before their day and
would, through their agency, develop significantly new ones as they radically
altered it and rebuilt it.

JESUS AND THE BREAK OF DAWN: THE VICTORY OF GOD

Nobody in Jesus' day would have claimed that the visions of Isaiah, Jeremiah, or Ezekiel had been fulfilled. The Babylons of this world had not
been defeated, and Israel was not free. This real "return from exile"—that
is, this complete liberation—would, of course, involve the return of YHWH
to Zion. Prophet after prophet says so; nowhere in Second Temple literature,
as I have demonstrated, this time hopefully convincingly, does anyone
claim that it has actually happened. The Maccabees cleansed the temple, but
it remained an empty, albeit restored, temple. The prophets, moreover, interpreted the exile as the punishment for Israel's sin; the end of exile would,
therefore, be "the forgiveness of sins." It would mean Israel's redemption,
evil's defeat, and YHWH's return.

Kingdom stories of exile and restoration. Exile and restoration was the
central drama that Israel believed itself to be acting out. Jesus belongs exactly within that drama. He fittingly told stories about the kingdom of God,
centered on himself, bent on putting to rights all that Israel's sins had torn
asunder. For Jesus to say "the kingdom of God is at hand" (Mt 4:17 ESV) was
to supply the missing line in the story that Second Temple Jews wanted to

---

[63]Sir 24. (On lawkeeping in Sirach see further Sir 19:20.) We have no reason to think that post-
Maccabean Jews of whatever variety would substantially disagree with this pre-Maccabean
perspective.

hear. One of the main kingdom themes informing Jesus' stories was his belief that the real return from exile for the people, and the real return of YHWH to Zion, were happening in and through his own work.[64] In his parables, Jesus invited his hearers to become part of that story. His radical narrative summoned all and sundry to celebrate with him the real return from exile, the real forgiveness of sins. He was offering the latter precisely because he was enacting the former.

Jesus' stories, along with the rest of his teaching, warned his contemporaries that failure to come his way would result in ruin. He stood in the great tradition of Israel's prophets, notably Elijah and Jeremiah. His story had two possible endings, between which his hearers had to choose. If they followed his way, the way of peace, they would be the light of the world, the city set on a hill that could not be hidden. This, after all, was Israel's original calling, its true vocation, to be for God a kingdom of priests (Ex 19). If they went the other way, as Jesus saw many of his contemporaries eager to do, they would call down on themselves the wrath of Rome. Jesus, like Amos or Jeremiah, warned that Rome's wrath would constitute God's wrath. To follow his teachings, his subversive wisdom, would be the only way to build the house on the rock. To follow the would-be prophets who were leading Israel into nationalist revolution would cause the house to fall with a great crash.

As a case in point of what I am proposing, consider a son who goes off in disgrace into a far country and then comes back, only to find the welcome challenged by another son who has stayed put (Lk 15:11-32). The overtones are so strong that we surely cannot ignore them. This is the story of Israel, in particular of exile and restoration. It corresponds closely to the narrative grammar which underlies the exilic prophets, and the books of Ezra and Nehemiah, and a good deal of subsequent Jewish literature, and which must therefore be seen as formative for Second Temple Judaism. The exodus itself is the *ultimate backdrop*: Israel goes off into a pagan country, becomes a slave, and then is brought back to its own land. But exile and restoration is the *main theme*.

As we saw above, in Jesus' day many, if not most, Jews regarded the exile as still continuing. What was Israel to do? Why, to repent of the sin that had

---

[64]Wright, *Jesus and the Victory of God*, chaps. 5–8.

driven it into exile, and to return to YHWH with all its heart.[65] Who would stand in its way, to prevent its return? The mixed multitude, not least the Samaritans, who had remained in the land while the people were in exile.[66] But Israel would return, humbled and redeemed: sins would be forgiven, the covenant renewed, the temple rebuilt, and the dead raised. What its God had done for it in the exodus—always the crucial backdrop for Jewish expectation—he would at last do again, even more gloriously. YHWH would finally become king, and would do for Israel, in covenant love, what the prophets had foretold.[67]

And the story of the prodigal says, quite simply: this hope is now being fulfilled—but it does not look like what was expected. Israel went into exile because of its own folly and disobedience, and is now returning simply because of the fantastically generous, indeed prodigal, love of its God. But this is a highly subversive retelling. The real return from exile, including the real resurrection from the dead, is taking place, in an extremely paradoxical fashion, in Jesus' own ministry. Those who grumble at what is happening are cast in the role of the Jews who did not go into exile and who opposed the returning people. They are, in effect, virtually Samaritans. The true Israel is coming to its senses, and returning to its father, as Jeremiah had foretold (Jer 31:18-20); and those who oppose this great movement of divine love and grace are defining themselves as outside the true people. These give to the story a sense of depth and resonance. But the main line remains clear. Israel's history is turning its long-awaited corner; this is happening within the ministry of Jesus himself; and those who oppose it are the enemies of the true people of God.

Reconstructed symbols. Jesus not only told stories that indicated that in and through his work Israel's God was restoring his people. He also reworked the key symbols of Second Temple Judaism. Jesus did not, in other words, invent new symbols out of thin air, as though he were detached from Judaism. He took the already existing symbols and reconstructed them to embody his vision of the long-awaited redemption he believed God was at

---

[65]See Deut 30:1-10; Ezra 9:5–10:5; Neh 1:4-11; 9:6-38; Jer 3:11-15, 19-25; 24:4-7; 29:10-14; Dan 9:3-19; Hos 5:15–6:2; 13:14; 14:1-7; etc.

[66]See 2 Kings 17:24-41; Ezra 4:1-24; 9:1-2; Neh 4:1-8; 6:1-19; 13:23-29; etc.

[67]See Wright, *New Testament and the People of God*, 268-338; and cf. Ezek 36–37; Hos 11:1-9, Is 40–55, etc.

last bringing about. These symbols focus on how Jesus redefined who Israel is, what the land and Torah are, and where the temple really is.

Israel. There is now growing agreement that the category of "the Twelve" goes back to Jesus himself, and that it signifies his intention to remake the people of God.[68] The fact of their being twelve carries an implicit meaning about the place of Jesus himself in the whole system. He is not himself one of the Twelve, not even *primus inter pares.* He stands over against them, calling them into being; they are the beginnings of the reconstituted Israel insofar as they are his followers. It is important not to read too much into this, but equally important not to read too little. I suggest that the natural implication is that they are "Israel" *because he is Israel.*[69] The call of the Twelve is undoubtedly saying that this is where YHWH was at last restoring his people.

Thus, when Jesus called the Twelve, took them up into the hills, and told them that they were his special, close followers, through whom he wished to operate, anyone hearing about such an event would most naturally have interpreted it, not as a foretaste of what the church thinks of as "ordination," but on the model of other groups that collected up in the hills of Galilee to plan their strategy. We know about such groups from Josephus: holy brigands bent on assisting God in the bringing of his kingdom.

For example, the table fellowship he celebrated could not have been offensive to anyone if he had been simply acting as a private individual. The reason it caused a stir was that his whole ministry presented itself as a national movement of renewal. Instead of eating in strict ritual purity, his table fellowship implied that purity came as a result of eating with him. "Who are my mother and my brothers? . . . Whoever does the will of God" (Mk 3:33, 35): Israel was being redefined around him. Jesus restores to membership in Israel those who had been on the margins of the holy society, whether through physical defects (compare 1QSa 2:4-9) or moral or social blemishes. Jesus' physical contact with lepers, with the woman suffering from the hemorrhage, with corpses, and so on, rendered him technically unclean, just as

---

[68]See E. P. Sanders, *Jesus and Judaism* (Philadelphia: Fortress, 1985), 95-106. See also Evans, "Jesus and the Continuing Exile of Israel," 91-92.

[69]See the careful, but ultimately inconclusive, discussions in Sanders, *Jesus and Judaism*, 321-25, 333, etc.

did his eating with Matthew, or with Zacchaeus. Those two stories, in fact, could be seen as paradigmatic for this aspect of the ministry. Jesus *identifies himself with sinful Israel* and thus contracts its uncleanness: nevertheless, when he emerges from Zacchaeus's house to face the accusing crowd, it is not he who is unclean but Zacchaeus who is "a son of Abraham." The miracles and the welcome to outcasts thus invite the same interpretation as I have given to the call of the Twelve. They only make sense if Jesus, who eats with the sinners, is himself the center-point of the reconstituted Israel that is being called into existence.

Land and Torah. Jesus also redefined the symbol of land. Jesus urged his followers to abandon their possessions, which in his world mostly meant land. A rich ruler comes to him and asks, "What must I do to inherit eternal life?" (Lk 18:18). The rich landowner asked the question in light of Deuteronomy 30:19-20 (NRSV, altered):

> I call heaven and earth to witness against you today that I have set before you life and death, blessings and curses. Choose life so that you and your descendants may live, *loving YHWH your God, obeying him, and holding fast to him; for that means life to you and length of days, so that you may live in the land that YHWH swore to give to your ancestors*, to Abraham, to Isaac, and to Jacob.

The rich ruler is ultimately concerned with acquiring and retaining his land holdings. Consider Deuteronomy 30:3-6 (NRSV, altered):

> Then *YHWH your God will restore your fortunes* and have compassion on you, gathering you again from all the peoples among whom YHWH your God has scattered you. Even if you are exiled to the ends of the world, from there YHWH your God will gather you, and from there he will bring you back. YHWH your God will bring you into *the land that your ancestors possessed, and you will possess it*; he *will make you more prosperous* and numerous than your ancestors.
>
> Moreover, YHWH your God will circumcise your heart and the heart of your descendants, so that you will love YHWH your God with all your heart and with all your soul, *in order that you may live.*

Obedience to the law results in God's favor. God's favor results in a return from exile and the regathering of all who were scattered, of whom the young ruler may have counted himself among, and the repossession of the land

along with a greater prosperity. "What must I do to inherit eternal life?" the
young ruler asks, and Jesus tells him to sell everything he owns and give it
to the poor (Lk 18:22). The very thing the young ruler tried to retain, namely
his land, and the very reward for being obedient to God's law, apart from
long life, Jesus instructed him to give up and to give to the poor. Here as
elsewhere Jesus has redefined what the symbol of land is. The focus of land
was being transferred, it seems, to restored human beings. Jesus offered an
"inheritance," and greater possessions than they would have abandoned; but
he construed this in terms of human lives and communities that were being
renewed through the coming of the kingdom. The pearl of great price was
available for those who sold everything else (Mt 13:45-46); among the things
that would have to be sold was the symbol of sacred land itself. It was swallowed up in the eschatological promise that YHWH was now to be king of
all the earth. Here we see what Paul saw, that the inheritance of the land has
now, through the Messiah Jesus, been extended to all the earth.

This points across to the similar question asked by a lawyer, to which
Jesus answers with the parable of the "good Samaritan." The commands to
love God and to love one's neighbor echo, of course, both the Shema of
Deuteronomy 6 and the command about neighbors in Leviticus 19:

> Speak to all the congregation of the people of Israel and say to them: You shall
> be holy, for I YHWH your God am holy. You shall each revere your mother
> and father, and you shall keep my sabbaths: I am YHWH your God. Do not
> turn to idols or make cast images for yourselves: I am YHWH your God. . . .
> You shall not steal; you shall not deal falsely; and you shall not lie to one
> another. And you shall not swear falsely by my name, profaning the name of
> your God: I am YHWH. . . . You shall not hate in your heart anyone of your
> kin; you shall reprove your neighbor, or you will incur guilt yourself.
> (Lev 19:2-4, 11-12, 17 NRSV, altered)

At the heart of Leviticus 19 are the commandments. What Jesus did with the
lawyer was to redefine what "neighbor" was. Consider Leviticus 19:9-18
(NRSV, altered):

> When you reap the harvest of your land, you shall not reap to the very edges
> of your field, or gather the gleanings of your harvest. You shall not strip your
> vineyard bare, or gather the fallen grapes of your vineyard; *you shall leave
> them for the poor and the alien:* I am YHWH your God.

You shall not steal; you shall not deal falsely; and you shall not lie to one another. And you shall not swear falsely by my name, profaning the name of your God: I am YHWH.

You shall not defraud your neighbor; you shall not steal; and *you shall not keep for yourself the wages of a laborer until morning.* You shall not revile the deaf or put a stumbling block before the blind; you shall fear your God: I am YHWH.

You shall not render an unjust judgment; *you shall not be partial to the poor or defer to the great: with justice you shall judge your neighbor.* You shall not go around as a slanderer among your people, and you shall not profit by the blood of your neighbor: I am YHWH.

You shall not hate in your heart anyone of your kin; you shall reprove your neighbor, or you will incur guilt yourself. You shall not take vengeance or bear a grudge against any of your people, but you shall love your neighbor as yourself: I am YHWH.

The lawyer answered correctly that the law was to be read with Deuteronomy 6 and Leviticus 19 as the chief principles, but by implication he was defining "neighbor" narrowly, as a fellow kinsman (which might claim some support from Lev 19). In line with his redefinition of the land, and the notions of kinsfolk and neighbors, Jesus told the parable of the good Samaritan to demonstrate that a neighbor was every fellow human being, precisely because the eschatological promise was that YHWH was becoming king of the entire world.

Torah, of course, was one of the central ways in which Israel was defined. The works of Torah functioned as symbolic praxis, as the set of badges that demonstrated both to observant Jews and to their neighbors that they were indeed people of the covenant. For Jesus, the symbolic praxis that would mark out his followers, and which can therefore be classified as, in that sense, redefined Torah, is set out in such places as the Sermon on the Mount. Forgiveness, itself a telltale sign of covenant renewal (as in Jer 31), lay at the heart of the praxis that was to characterize his redefined Israel.[70] This belongs closely with the redefinition of "neighbor." Jesus envisaged the renewed people of God as being at last a light to the nations, rather than a people to be defined in perpetuity over against the rest of the world.

---

[70]See Mt 18:21-35.

Temple. All these redefined symbols came together, not surprisingly, in Jesus' alternative temple symbolism. Until 70 CE the Torah remained firmly in second place, dependent on the temple. Loyalty to temple in Judea functioned in parallel to loyalty to Torah in Galilee and, not least, in the Diaspora.

Jesus' actions and words in the temple thus functioned symbolically in more or less the same way as his actions and words concerning the Torah. In neither case was he denying that the institution was good, given by Israel's God, and to be respected. In both cases he was, as it were, pointing to a fulfillment beyond previous imaginings. In that light, the way the systems were operating in his day was bound to come under scrutiny: if the new day was dawning through the work of Jesus himself, things could no longer operate as they had done up to now. There is a straight line here forward to Paul's wrestling with the law in Galatians 3 and elsewhere. It is vital to realize that neither for Jesus nor for Paul was this a matter of suggesting that there was something "wrong" with temple or Torah. In both cases, it was a critique from within, generated not by a negative analysis of "Judaism" as a "system" or "religion," but by the basic eschatological claim that Israel's God was now at last doing what he had promised. The new wine needed new wineskins.

Jesus' action in the temple (Mk 11) provides the sharp focal point of his redefinition of the temple symbol around himself. It will help to examine first the echoes of Isaiah 56:7 (and Jer 7:11) in Mark 11:17 and its parallels,[71] and then the wider echoes of Zechariah in the whole incident.

Mark 11:15-18 describes the scene:

> Then they came to Jerusalem. And he entered the temple and began to drive out those who were selling and those who were buying in the temple, and he overturned the tables of the money changers and the seats of those who sold doves; and he would not allow anyone to carry anything through the temple. He was teaching and saying, "Is it not written,
>
> 'My house shall be called a house of prayer for all the nations'?
>   But you have made it a den of robbers."

---

[71]On which see Bruce Chilton and Craig A. Evans, eds., *Studying the Historical Jesus: Evaluations of the State of Current Research*, New Testament Tools and Studies 19 (Leiden: Brill, 1994), 288-89 (319-20). They note that the quotations are linked together, in typical Jewish style, by the catchword *house*, which occurs in the part of Jer 7:11 not quoted ("Has *my house*, which is called by my name, become a den of robbers in your eyes?").

And when the chief priests and the scribes heard it, they kept looking for a way to kill him; for they were afraid of him, because the whole crowd was spellbound by his teaching.

The context of the Isaiah passage is the prediction of the full return from exile and all that it would mean:

> And the foreigners who join themselves to YHWH,
> > to minister to him, to love the name of YHWH,
> > and to be his servants . . .
> these will I bring to my holy mountain,
> > and make them joyful in my house of prayer;
> their burnt offerings and their sacrifices
> > will be accepted on my altar;
> *for my house shall be called a house of prayer*
> > *for all peoples.*
> Thus says YHWH,
> > the God who gathers the outcasts of Israel,
> I will gather others to them
> > besides those already gathered. (Is 56:6-8 NRSV, altered)

This passage belongs with those that predict, as one aspect of Israel's eventual blessing, the ingathering of the Gentiles into the one people of YHWH.[72] It is followed at once, however, by passages strongly critical of the present condition of Israel (Is 56:9-12; 57:1-21). Gentiles are to be welcomed in, but the present people of Israel, especially their supposed leaders and guardians (Is 56:10-11), are under judgment. This offers a natural link into the passage from Jeremiah, which forms part of the sermon denouncing the temple and warning against an unthinking trust in it:

> Thus says YHWH of hosts, the God of Israel: Amend your ways and your doings, and let me dwell with you in this place. Do not trust in these deceptive

---

[72]See Wright, *New Testament and the People of God*, 267-68. Why do Matthew (Mt 21:13) and Luke (Lk 19:46) omit "for all the nations"? Possibly because, writing after 70 CE, there was no prospect of this (see Marcus J. Borg, *Conflict, Holiness and Politics in the Teachings of Jesus* [Lewiston, NY: Mellen Press, 1984], 349n67, with other references)? But there was no chance then of its being a house of prayer, either. Perhaps it was because Matthew and Luke had already begun the process of transforming the event from an acted parable of judgment into a purely economic protest?

words: "This is the temple of YHWH, the temple of YHWH, the temple of YHWH."

For if you truly amend your ways and your doings, if you truly act justly one with another, if you do not oppress the alien, the orphan, and the widow, or shed innocent blood in this place, and if you do not go after other gods to your own hurt, then I will dwell with you in this place, in the land that I gave of old to your ancestors forever and ever.

Here you are, trusting in deceptive words to no avail. Will you steal, murder, commit adultery, swear falsely, make offerings to Baal, and go after other gods that you have not known, and then come and stand before me in this house, which is called by my name, and say, "We are safe!"—only to go on doing all these abominations? *Has this house, which is called by my name, become a den of robbers in your sight?* You know, I too am watching, says YHWH. Go now to my place that was in Shiloh, where I made my name dwell at first, and see what I did to it for the wickedness of my people Israel. And now, because you have done all these things, says YHWH, and when I spoke to you persistently, you did not listen, and when I called you, you did not answer, therefore I will do to the house that is called by my name, in which you trust, and to the place that I gave to you and to your ancestors, just what I did to Shiloh. And I will cast you out of my sight, just as I cast out all your kinsfolk, all the offspring of Ephraim. (Jer 7:3-15 NRSV, altered)[73]

There can be no question about the thrust of this passage. On the one hand, it is a devastating critique of corruption within Jewish society in general. On the other, it is an obvious warning that, as a result, the temple is to be destroyed.[74]

Jesus' announcement of the kingdom, and the warnings that went with this announcement, were thus sharply and concretely focused in his echoing of Jeremiah's warning of coming destruction. This saying gave the most immediate and direct explanation for the symbolic prophetic action that had just taken place, which otherwise might have remained opaque. The present grievous distortion (from Jesus' point of view) of Israel's national vocation could lead to only one thing: a destruction of the temple for which the Babylonian invasion, as predicted by Jeremiah, would be the most natural historical backdrop.

---

[73]The passage goes on to warn that the valley of Hinnom (= "Gehenna") will become a mass grave (Jer 7:31-32).

[74]See Wright, *Jesus and the Victory of God*, 419-20, for arguments for *lēstēs* to be seen as denoting destruction as opposed to a mere cleansing.

Another angle on Jesus' view of the temple can be seen in his statements about fasting, found in all three Synoptic Gospels.[75] Fasting in this period was not, for Jews, simply an ascetic discipline, part of the general practice of piety. It had to do with Israel's present condition: it was still in exile. More specifically, it had to do with commemorating the destruction of the temple.[76] Zechariah's promise that the fasts would turn into feasts could come true only when YHWH restored the fortunes of his people (Zech 8:19). That, of course, was precisely what Jesus' cryptic comments implied:

> The wedding guests cannot fast while the bridegroom is with them, can they? As long as they have the bridegroom with them, they cannot fast. . . .
>
> No one sews a piece of unshrunk cloth on an old cloak; otherwise, the patch pulls away from it, the new from the old, and a worse tear is made. And no one puts new wine into old wineskins; otherwise, the wine will burst the skins, and the wine is lost, and so are the skins; but one puts new wine into fresh skins.[77]

In other words, the party is in full swing, and nobody wants glum faces at a wedding. This is not a piece of "teaching" about "religion" or "morality"; nor is it the dissemination of a timeless truth. It is a claim about eschatology. The time is fulfilled; the exile is over; the bridegroom is at hand. Jesus' acted symbol, feasting rather than fasting, brings into public visibility his controversial claim, that in his work Israel's hope was being realized; more specifically, that in his work *the temple was being rebuilt*.

The same was true about Jesus' claim to be able to provide forgiveness.[78] This "forgiveness" should not be thought of as a detached, ahistorical blessing, such as might be offered by anyone at any time. Jesus' offer is not to be construed, as it has been so often, as an attempt to play at "being God"; nor is it to be rejected as unhistorical on the grounds that such an attempt is unthinkable. Forgiveness was an eschatological blessing. If Israel went into exile because of its sins, then forgiveness consists in its returning: returning

---

[75]Mk 2:18-22 // Mt 9:14-17 // Lk 5:33-39 // Gos. Thom. 47:1-5; 104:1.

[76]See Wright, *New Testament and the People of God*, 234-35, with references to both primary and secondary sources.

[77]Mk 2:19, 21-22 // Mt 9:15, 16 // Lk 5:34, 36-37. Luke describes the latter double saying as a "parable"; it has become a detached aphorism in Gos. Thom. 47:4-5 (see too Gos. Thom. 104:1-3).

[78]Mk 2:1-13 // Mt 9:1-8 // Lk 5:17-26; 7:36-50; see too Lk 19:1-10.

to YHWH, returning from exile.[79] Jesus' action and claim indicated that this symbol of return was now becoming a reality. If the authors of the Scrolls believed that their group, being the real returned-from-exile people, had received forgiveness of sins,[80] it is not a large step to think of an eschatological prophet, such as John the Baptist or Jesus, offering his followers the same thing.

This brings us to the heart of Jesus' countertemple movement:

> The scribe said, "You are right, teacher: you have said truly that he is one, and that there is none beside him; and that to love him with all the heart and with all the understanding and with all the strength, and to love one's neighbor as oneself, is more than all burnt-offerings and sacrifices." And when Jesus saw that he had answered intelligently, he said to him: "You are not far from the kingdom of God." (Mk 12:32-34)[81]

In context, this can mean only one thing: the kingdom behavior in which Israel's basic confession of faith is truly fulfilled *is worth more than the temple and its sacrificial system*. And, since Jesus was claiming to offer the renewed heart, the blessing of the new covenant through which people would at last be able to keep the Shema by loving their God and neighbor, this conversation resonates symbolically with the rest of the evidence. It indicates that, for Jesus, part of the point of the kingdom he was claiming to inaugurate would be that it would bring with it all that the temple offered, thereby redefining what Israel's greatest symbol was.

Jesus' practice jumps suddenly into startling and symbolic focus when seen in this light. "My child, your sins are forgiven":[82] that sentence has the effect of a private individual approaching you on the street and offering to issue you with a passport or driver's license—or, perhaps more appropriately in this case, a private individual approaching a prisoner in jail and offering him a royal pardon, personally signed. From the twentieth-century, late-deist, Western-individual perception, it looks simply as if Jesus is behaving as "God," dispensing forgiveness from a great metaphysical height. That gives a spurious perception of why such symbolic behavior was shocking. In

---

[79]See especially Is 40:1-2; Lam 4:22; Dan 9:1-19; etc.
[80]E.g., 1QH 4:11-12; 5:4; 15:30-31 (García-Martinez and Tigchelaar, *Dead Sea Scrolls*, 317, 319, 344).
[81]Cf. Mt 9:13; 12:7, quoting Hos 6:6.
[82]Mk 2:5 // Mt 9:2 // Lk 5:20.

first-century Jewish reality, the way YHWH forgave sins, as we saw, was ultimately through the officially established and authorized channels of temple and priesthood.[83] Jesus was claiming, as Sanders has argued, to be in that sense "speaking for God," claiming by strong implication that he carried in himself the authority normally vested elsewhere.[84]

The vindication of the Son of Man. Jesus' action in the temple constitutes the most obvious act of messianic praxis within the Gospel narratives.[85] Jesus was claiming some kind of authority over the temple and its life. Though the chief priests ruled the temple de facto in this period, the scriptural pattern, which we know to have been alive and well in this period not only from texts but from historical movements, spoke of the temple's ruler being the true Davidic king.

The triumphal entry was not so much a matter of *teaching* as of *symbolic action*. Jesus, as we have seen often enough, was as capable as any of his contemporaries of deliberately performing actions that had rich symbolic value. Within his own time and culture, his riding on a donkey over the Mount of Olives, across Kidron, and up to the temple mount spoke more powerfully than words could have done of a royal claim.[86] The allusion to Zechariah (and, with that, several other passages) is obvious:

Rejoice greatly, O daughter Zion!
Shout aloud, O daughter Jerusalem!
Lo, your king comes to you;
triumphant and victorious is he,
humble and riding on a donkey,
on a colt, the foal of a donkey.
He will cut off the chariot from Ephraim
and the war horse from Jerusalem;

---

[83]Paula Fredriksen, "What You See Is What You Get: Context and Content in Current Research on the Historical Jesus," *Theology Today* 52 (1995): 75-97, suggests that forgiveness was available anywhere, at any time, within Judaism, whenever someone repented. This is true at one level, but as Sanders makes clear (*Judaism: Practice and Belief, 63 BCE-66 CE* [Philadelphia: Trinity Press International, 1992], 103-18) the transaction was not complete without sacrifice. Fredriksen, it seems, is looking at the question from an essentially post–70 CE perspective.

[84]E.g. Sanders, *Jesus and Judaism*, 240, 273; Sanders, *The Historical Figure of Jesus* (London: Penguin, 1993), 239.

[85]See Wright, *Jesus and the Victory of God*, chap. 9.

[86]Mt 21:1-9 // Mk 11:1-10 // Lk 19:28-40 // Jn 12:12-19. Cf. 2 Sam 15:23-32.

and the battle bow shall be cut off,

>and he shall command peace to the nations;

his dominion shall be from sea to sea,

>and from the River to the ends of the earth. (Zech 9:9-10)[87]

The triumphal entry was thus clearly messianic. Jesus believed that he was Israel's Messiah, the one through whom YHWH would restore the fortunes of his people. Anyone doing and saying what Jesus did and said must have faced the question: Will I be the one through whom the liberation will come? All the evidence—not least the temple action and the title on the cross—suggests that Jesus answered, "Yes."

What happens when we integrate this picture with Jesus' prophetic warnings against the temple in Mark 11:15-19, and his prophetic action against the temple in Mark 11:1-11? The answer is, more or less, Mark 13 and its parallels. Jesus' temple action is here, too, explained in terms of his messiahship. So closely do they belong together, in fact, that the destruction of the temple—predicted already in symbolic action, and here in Mark 13 as a prophetic oracle—is bound up with Jesus' own vindication, as prophet and also as Messiah. When his prophecy of its destruction comes true, that event will demonstrate that he was indeed the Messiah who had the authority over it. Jesus, like some other Jewish sectarians, was inviting his hearers to join him in the establishment of the true temple. The Jerusalem temple was under judgment, a judgment that would fall before too long. It is in this context that Jesus' dramatic action in the temple makes perfect sense: it was an acted parable of judgment, of destruction. The "house" had become a den of *lestai*, brigands. Jesus, like Jeremiah, whom he quoted, was declaring divine judgment on it.[88]

The same conclusion is reached by a different route when we consider other sayings that implicitly declare the temple redundant. Jesus quotes Hosea to the effect that what Israel's God desires is "mercy, not sacrifice."[89] The same point is implied, as we just saw, in the conversation with the scribe

---

[87]Behind this passage may be echoes of Gen 49:8-12, of which, in turn, Gen 49:11 may be echoed by Is 63:2-3. The last couplet of Zech 9:10 is a quotation from a "messianic"—by which I mean "ideally royal"—psalm (Ps 72:8). The Mount of Olives location evokes Zech 14:4.

[88]Mt 21:13 // Mk 11:17 // Lk 19:46; cf. Jer 7:11 and, indeed, Jer 7 as a whole. See especially Borg, *Conflict, Holiness and Politics in the Teachings of Jesus*, chap. 7, e.g., 174.

[89]Mt 9:13; 12:7; cf. Hos 6:6.

in Mark 12:28-34: Jesus was inaugurating a way of life that had no further need of the temple. This remarkable assertion coheres completely with the theme that emerges steadily at the center of Jesus' story. He was claiming prophetic and messianic authority to pronounce judgment on the temple.

Throughout his public career, Jesus told a story, very much like the implicit narrative of the Scrolls, in which the judgment usually associated with YHWH's action against the pagan nations would fall on those Jews who were refusing to follow in the new way now being announced. And the judgment which was to come was conceived in classic scriptural terms: invasion and destruction by foreign armies. YHWH, having warned his people beyond patience and beyond hope, has deliberately abandoned them to their fate. Assyria and Babylon had been the instruments of YHWH's wrath before; now it would be the turn of Rome.

At the same time, the emphasis of Jesus' announcement of the kingdom was that Israel's God certainly would vindicate his people, his elect who cried to him day and night. If this were not so, the charge that Jesus' proclamation (as we have expounded it) was overthrowing the foundations of all things Jewish might seem, despite everything, to have some weight. This, after all, was the basic hope of Israel: that the enemies of the chosen people would be destroyed, and the chosen themselves vindicated. Jesus seems to have been reaffirming this expectation, even though radically redrawing it. How then would the fulfillment come? What form would it take? How would the story proceed to its resolution?

The constant emphasis we find here is that those who had followed Jesus (and, by implication, those who would follow his way in the future) would escape the great coming disaster and would themselves receive the vindication that had been promised to Israel. They would be the ones who would inherit the promise, who would experience the real release from exile. Not only would they be preserved and protected in and through tribulation and persecution; they would be given positions of responsibility, so that in the *palingenesia*, the great time of renewal, they would sit on twelve thrones judging the twelve tribes.[90] Those who had abandoned all in order to follow Jesus would receive back far more than they had lost.[91] Israel's God would

---

[90]Mt 19:28 // Lk 22:30.
[91]Mt 19:29 // Mk 10:29-30 // Lk 18:29-30; cf. Apoc. Jas. 4.1.

speedily vindicate his elect; those who acknowledged Jesus would themselves be acknowledged on the great and terrible day.[92]

Thus, if Jesus had pronounced judgment on the temple, we should
expect a balancing assertion. Jesus would build the new temple; it would
consist of his followers.[93] The whole of the story, of judgment for those who
had not followed Jesus and vindication for those who had, is summed up
in the cryptic but frequently repeated saying: the first shall be last, and the
last first.[94]

The so-called Apocalyptic Discourse of Mark 13 and parallels needs to
be read in this light. Jesus is not speaking here about a supernatural figure
floating downwards on a cloud to bring the space-time world to an end.
Rather, he is speaking, as his use of Danielic imagery should have made
clear, about the "beasts" that make war on the "people of the saints of the
most high," and about the "son of man" who will be exalted and vindicated
over them. The "coming" of the Son of Man is not, therefore, his "coming"
from heaven to earth but his coming from earth to heaven, in vindication
and exaltation over his enemies. Moreover, just as no interpreter would
imagine that Daniel, Jesus, or indeed the author of Revelation envisaged
real "beasts" emerging from the Mediterranean, so no interpreter ought to
imagine that the "Son of Man" can be interpreted "literally" as a human
figure floating on a cloud. The image speaks clearly, to anyone with ears
attuned to the first century, of the vindication of the true Israel over
its enemies.

It is, then, from Jerusalem that the true Israel must now flee, lest they
partake in its destruction (Mk 13:14). It is Jerusalem whose destruction will
be the sign that the God whom Jesus has proclaimed is now indeed manifestly the king of the whole earth. According to Jesus, therefore, the real
referent of Daniel 7 is the destruction of Jerusalem: the Son of Man will be
vindicated, but the fourth beast (the present temple and its hierarchy) will
be destroyed. Jerusalem and its leaders have taken on the role of Babylon,

---

[92]Lk 17:1-10; Mt 10:32 // Lk 12:8-9; and especially Mt 16:24-28 // Mk 8:34–9:1 // Lk 9:23-27, which
Luke insists is a saying to do with the kingdom.

[93]Mt 16:17-19; 18:15-20. See especially Ben F. Meyer, *The Aims of Jesus* (London: SCM Press, 1979),
185-97, with 302-3; Meyer, *Christus Faber: The Master-Builder and the House of God* (Allison Park,
PA: Pickwick, 1992), 258-62.

[94]Mt 19:30 // Mk 10:31 // Lk 13:30, cf. Mt 20:16; P. Oxy. 654.4; Gos. Thom. 4.

Edom, and Antiochus Epiphanes. They are the city whose fall spells the vindication of the true people of Israel's God. The prophecies of rescue from the tyrant have come true in and for Jesus and in his people. When this city falls they must leave quickly; this is their moment of salvation and vindication.[95]

Conclusion by way of the cross. So Jesus went to his death, convinced within his own first-century Jewish worldview that Israel's destiny had devolved on him and that he represented the true Israel in the eyes of God. His death would therefore be the means of drawing to its climax the wrath of God against the nation, forging a way through that wrath and out the other side. All who followed him, who constituted his people, would find rescue from the great and imminent disaster. Those who chose to stick to the path of nationalistic militarism would find that such a route led to death.

Jesus' understanding of his own death and vindication must be seen in this light. He was drawing together the threads of Israel's destiny and acting them out in pursuit of one of Israel's oldest goals and vocations, long forgotten in the dark years of foreign oppression: it was to be the "light to the nations" (Is 42:6). God's house in Jerusalem was meant to be a "place of prayer for all the nations" (Is 56:7; Mk 11:17); but God would now achieve this though the new temple, which was Jesus himself and his people. As Jesus made clear at the Last Supper, his own death was to be the true and ultimate sacrifice: he would embody in himself the coming destruction (the death of the rebel, at the hands of the occupying forces) that he had predicted for Israel, so that his fellow countrymen might have a way by which to avoid it. Thus the resurrection would be seen as the launch of the real return from exile, the ultimate liberation of the people of God, from the exile that lay deeper than the exile of Egypt or Babylon. Jesus' disciples were not in the least expecting this kind of fulfillment. A messiah, after all, was supposed to defeat the pagans, not die at their hands. But Jesus had believed all along that he was fighting a different enemy. The resurrection demonstrated that the battle had been won.

---

[95]Cf. Jer 51:26 with Mk 13:2; Is 13:10; 34:4 with Mk 13:24; Is 52:11-12; Jer 51:6, 45 with Mk 13:14-17; Jer 51:46 with Mk 13:7-8; Zech 2–6 (in context) with Mk 13:27; and Dan 7:13-14 with Mk 13:26.

Paul and the Undying Dawn: Living in the New World of the Cross and Resurrection

Paul's Christian theological reflection begins, I suggest, from within exactly this matrix of thought, with the realization that *what the Creator/covenant God was supposed to do for Israel at the end of history, this God had done for Jesus in the middle of history.* Jesus himself, as one person in the middle of ongoing "exilic" history, had been vindicated, raised from the dead, after suffering at the hands of the pagans. God had done for him, in the midst of time, what Saul of Tarsus had thought he would do for Israel at the end of time.

This by itself would have been enough, I think, to propel a Jewish thinker to the conclusion that Jesus had somehow borne Israel's destiny by himself, was somehow its representative. When we add to this the early Christian belief in Jesus' messiahship, and Paul's own exposition of this theme, there is every reason to suppose that Paul made exactly this connection, and indeed made it central to his whole theology. The Creator/covenant God has brought his covenant purpose for Israel to fruition *in Israel's representative, the Messiah, Jesus. Therefore, now, a new world has dawned.* The new day promised by the prophets, and by Moses himself in Deuteronomy, has arrived. For Paul, the period of exile has ended in Christ.[96]

Paul's view of the story. Paul's thought, like that of many Second Temple Jews, has a complex narrative structure. But one of its most obvious reference points is the story of the exodus. Romans 8 uses exodus language in relation to the whole creation, speaking of the people of God traveling through the wilderness toward their "inheritance." Similarly, Galatians 4 speaks of God's people as being enslaved, and then, at the right time (the time for the Abrahamic promises of Gen 15 to be fulfilled, which Paul has been expounding in the previous chapter), God sending forth his Son and his Spirit to rescue those who are "under the law." This is of course heavily ironic in that, in the original exodus story, the law is God's good gift to the newly redeemed people, whereas here it is a force or power from whose enslavement people need to be freed. Paul speaks of baptism in 1 Corinthians 10:2 in terms of the crossing of the Red Sea, and, so it seems to me, he

---

[96]Thielman, *Theology of the New Testament*, 369.

echoes this in Romans 6: the slaves (slaves to sin) are freed by sharing the death and resurrection of the Messiah.

The story of the exodus is reused in various ways both in the Old Testament and New Testament. In the latter, as in some other Second Temple contexts, it gives shape in particular to stories and prophecies about the "return from exile," as discussed above. Paul draws on exilic themes in passages such as Romans 2:17-24, where he quotes Isaiah 52:5 and Ezekiel 36:20, indicating that Israel now needs a new act of divine covenant faithfulness to bring about "redemption" (Rom 3:21, 24). This would be the true answer to a prayer like Daniel 9:16, bringing Israel and now also the whole world through to the long-promised and long-awaited state of renewal, restoration, and redemption.

If exile is the problem, the answer given in Isaiah 40–55 is the "Servant." Paul made extensive though subtle use of the Servant Songs at several places in his writings. An obvious example is Romans 4:24-25, where the entire train of thought of Romans 3:21–4:25 is summed up in a formulaic sentence that clearly evokes Isaiah 53 and to which Paul refers in his statements about the "obedience of the one man" in Romans 5:12-21. Not that Paul has removed the Servant from his wider context in Isaiah. Isaiah 40–55 are all about the righteousness of God, through which the powers of the world are defeated and God's people in consequence rescued; and that is of course the main theme of Romans, stated in Romans 1:16-17 and expounded in Romans 3:21–4:25 and Romans 9:30–10:13.

Paul's symbols in the light of the cross. Near the center of Paul's thought is his belief that Jesus is Israel's Messiah, the one in whom God's promises to Israel are fulfilled, and hence the one who will lead Israel to be the light to the world. (This belief nests alongside his belief that in Jesus Israel's God himself had returned to rescue his people.) The motif of Jesus-as-Israel functions as the vital turning point in at least *four* interlocking narratives that we can trace in his writings. And this composite narrative points to the newly symbolic world of the people of God, as Paul conceived it. For him, the people of God were no longer in exile: they were living under the rule of the one God, as free citizens of his kingdom. It was a world of new daylight, with the sun forever rising to cast its light and warmth throughout the world.

Creation and new creation. The *first story* Paul tells, by implication throughout, is that of creation and new creation. A consistently Jewish thinker, Paul never imagines that creation is evil. It is the good creation of the good God, and to be enjoyed as such. But, in line with much apocalyptic thought, Paul believes that God is planning to renew creation, to bring it out of its present state of decay and death and into the new world, where it would find its true fulfillment. The classic passage for this is of course Romans 8:18-27, which offers one of the rare occurrences of the word *redemption* itself.

Paul does not mention the cross in this passage. Here the focus is on the sufferings of Christians, which are, for Paul, the sharing of Christ's sufferings as they are conformed to his "image" (Rom 8:17, 29). They hold the key to the current state of affairs, through which the world must pass to attain its final deliverance from decay (Rom 8:18-26).

This explains why, at the end of Galatians (Gal 6:14-15), Paul can suddenly broaden the horizon of what has been up till then a sharply focused discussion:

> May I never boast of anything except the cross of our Lord Jesus Christ, by which the world has been crucified to me, and I to the world. For neither circumcision nor uncircumcision is anything; but a new creation is everything!

The "to me" is clearly important. The "new creation" has begun with the call of a new people, created through the gospel in the power of the Spirit, and defined by "faith" rather than by the badges of ethnic Israel. But Paul's claim here is that this human "new creation" is a signpost to a much larger reality. The landscape itself has decisively changed. The world as a whole has been crucified in the crucifixion of the Messiah, and a new world has been brought to birth. This is presumably why he can say in Colossians 1:23 that the gospel has already been proclaimed to every creature under heaven. When Jesus died and rose again, the cosmos as a whole became a different place! This is also closely linked to the famous 2 Corinthians 5:17: "Anyone in Christ is new creation—the old things have gone, and look, new things have come into being" (author's translation). That passage, too, belongs closely with a sustained exposition of the meaning of the cross, and of the way the cross has worked its way through Paul's apostolic ministry, as we shall see later. Paul understands the death of Jesus, and the continuing resonances of that death in the suffering of the apostles and the church, as the hinge on which the door of world history turns. From that moment, the forces of decay and death have suffered their major defeat. From now on, new creation is under way, with its first signs being the new life of those who believe the gospel. "New creation" thus refers in the first instance to the actual people concerned; but they are, for Paul, the sign of the new life that will one day flood the entire creation.

Israel. The *second great narrative* that Paul has in mind throughout his writing is the story of Israel. This is more complicated. Paul sees Israel, in good biblical terms, as the people called to bear God's solution to the problem of the world; but Israel itself, he sees, is part of the problem. Paul wrestles with this puzzle in the same way that many other Second Temple writers had done, with the all-important difference that he believes the crucified and risen Jesus really is Israel's Messiah. In him, therefore, the ultimate "solution" has been provided. The Abrahamic promises were indeed God's solution to the problem of the world; the exodus was the first great fulfillment of those promises; the Torah was God's good gift to his redeemed people, designed to stop them going to the bad until the final fulfillment . . . and the catastrophe of exile, with Torah itself turning against Israel and condemning it, was all part of the strange divine plan as foretold in the great covenant document, Deuteronomy itself. So what did the one God have to do to bring about redemption, renewal, and the fulfillment of the promises? How was God to be faithful to the plan to bless the whole world through Israel?

This is exactly the way Paul sets up the problem in two classic passages, Romans 2:17–3:9 and Galatians 3:6-12. The answer, in both cases, is the death of Jesus, bursting through the blockage and enabling the promises to be fulfilled despite the failure of Israel. In Romans, Jesus appears as the Messiah, the faithful Israelite (Rom 3:22 with Rom 3:2), whose redeeming death (Rom 3:24-26) is the means of God's now declaring that all who share this faith are "righteous," that is, members of the sin-forgiven family (Rom 3:27-31). That is how God has fulfilled the Abrahamic promises (Rom 4:1-25). Paul envisages the entire story of Israel as a single narrative that, having threatened to run out of steam entirely in the exile, has now been rescued from that oblivion and given its proper fulfillment.

The prophetic judgments quoted by Paul in Romans 2:17-24 are not, then, a matter of "proving that all Jews are sinful." The point is that the Old Testament itself declares that things had not worked out the way Israel might have hoped. The single-plan-through-Israel-for-the-world had run into the sand. Ah, but, says someone, Isaiah 52 and Ezekiel 36 are texts that go on to speak of God's rescue operation for Israel, of a new work that will deliver Israel from the awful situation of . . . yes, exile. Well, precisely. Exile is the massive demonstration, carved in the granite rock of Israel's history, that the promise-bearing people are themselves in need of the same redemption that they were supposed to bring to the world. Isaiah 52 leads straight into the promise of the Servant who will be "handed over for our transgression," and Ezekiel 36 goes on to speak of God's new work, transforming the heart by the Spirit, so Israel will be able to keep his commandments, and so that the nations will know that he has done it (Ezek 36:24-36).

And that is precisely what Paul is talking about in Romans 2:25-29. What we see here, looming up from a close reading of what Paul actually says (as opposed to the misleading summaries of those who think Romans 2 is *only* about "proving all people sinful"), is the prospect of a new ecclesiology, a mission-oriented people, a people based on the work of the Servant and the work of the Spirit, who now carry God's light, truth and teaching to the waiting nations. This theology is rooted in Ezekiel: it is, in fact, return-from-exile theology. That is what Paul thinks has happened, at last, after Daniel 9's putative 490 years, in the covenant renewal effected by the Messiah and the Spirit. That is the foundation, in particular, for Romans 8 and Romans 10, though you would never know it from the de-Judaized and decovenant-alized readings of Paul in the Western tradition.

In Galatians, more specifically, the curse of exile that had bottled up the promises and prevented them from getting through to the Gentiles, leaving Israel itself under condemnation, is dealt with by the death of Jesus. He takes Israel's curse on himself (and thus the world's curse, though this is not what is in view in this passage, despite efforts to employ it as a generalized statement of "atonement theology"). He thus makes it possible at last for "the blessing of Abraham to come on the Gentiles" and also that "we" (Jews who had been under the very specific "curse" of Deuteronomy) might receive the promise of the Spirit through faith. In other words, the covenant has been renewed at last—through the death of Jesus as Israel's representative Messiah. The exile is over.

I do not think, in other words, that Paul's train of thought ran the way so many have suggested: (1) Jesus was crucified, (2) therefore he was cursed by the law, (3) but God raised him from the dead, (4) therefore the law was shown to be wrong, (5) therefore justification must be by faith alone because (6) his death was redemptive. There are several flaws with that popular account. Paul is quite clear that Jesus *did* bear the curse: the law was right to pronounce it on Israel and the world, and in his death he liberated Israel from that curse, the curse that in Deuteronomy 28–29 reaches its height in exile. As he says in 2 Corinthians 5:21, God "made him to be sin for us who knew no sin" (KJV).

This explains, among many other things, why Paul says at the start of Galatians (the point in the letter when we might expect a thematic statement) that "our Lord Jesus the Messiah gave himself for our sins, to deliver us from the present evil age according to the will of God our Father" (Gal 1:3-4, author's translation). This in turn brings into view the central statement of the common early creed quoted by Paul in 1 Corinthians 15:3: the Messiah "died for our sins in accordance with the scriptures." Galatians 1:4 shows very clearly what this means, offering once more a historical understanding rather than a dehistoricized atonement theory. For a Second Temple Jew soaked in passages such as Daniel 9, the present parlous state of Israel, which I have shown earlier as "continuing exile," was the result of Israel's sins. The ancient Israelites had sinned and had gone into exile; now their successors, even those living back in the land, had continued to sin, and as a result the final redemption, the real "return from exile," was delayed.

The problem of "sin" in this picture is not, then, simply that it separates the individual from God in his or her existential spirituality (true though that is as well). The problem is that Israel's sins had sent Israel into exile and were keeping it there. Conversely, if somehow Israel's sins were to be dealt with, finished with, and blotted out, then exile could be undone and the people could go free, and with them the whole world, waiting for Israel to be redeemed. That is the train of thought that dominates Isaiah 40–55 as a whole—the passage, of course, in which the vital role is taken by the Servant.

Saul of Tarsus would have believed that Israel, right up to his own day, had been languishing in "the present evil age," waiting for "the age to come" to arrive, the time of redemption and forgiveness. This forgiveness would not mean simply that individuals could now enter a happy and intimate relationship with their heavenly Father, true again though that would be. The point was that, if sins were forgiven, the exile would be over, the rule of the evil powers would be broken, and Israel—and the rest of the world— would be summoned to enjoy, and to take part in, God's renewed world. And *this is what Paul believes has happened with the death of Jesus.* Neither in Galatians 1 nor in 1 Corinthians 15:3 does he explain how it is that the death of Jesus delivers us from the evil age. The equation depends on two other things, which he supplies plentifully elsewhere, not least in 1 Corinthians 15 itself. First, Jesus was and is Israel's representative Messiah; second, God raised him from the dead (note 1 Cor 15:17: if the Messiah is not raised, your faith is futile, *and you are still in your sins*; in other words, the new age has not begun). Thus in his very person the exile reached its climax and the true "return" began.

The story of the crucified Messiah is thus at the heart of Paul's way of telling the story of how Israel has been brought to the very depth of exile and has now been rescued to live as God's new creation. The sharpest statement of this comes at the end of Galatians 2:19-21:

> I through the Torah died to Torah, that I might live to God. I have been crucified with the Messiah; however, I am alive, yet it is not me, but the Messiah lives in me. And the life I now live in the flesh, I live by faith in the Son of God, who loved me and gave himself for me. I do not nullify God's grace; for if covenant membership came by Torah, then the Messiah died for no reason. (author's translation)

Paul's point, in other words, is that through the faithful death of the Messiah God has acted to *transform the category of "the righteous,"* so that it now denotes not those who are defined by Torah but those who are defined by the Messiah. And "those who are defined by the Messiah" means those who have died and come to life in and with him; those, in other words, who have been co-crucified with him (Gal 2:19). Here the cross determines the death of the old identity: the Messiah, Israel's representative, dies, therefore Israel dies according to the flesh. And, by implication, the resurrection determines the new life of the new identity: the Messiah, Israel's representative, "lives to God" (cf. Rom 6:10), and those who are "in him" possess this same new life. That which was said in the plural in Galatians 1:3-4 is now brought into the sharp singular: "The Son of God loved . . . *me* and gave himself for me" (Gal 2:20). The final verse (Gal 2:21) sums up the effect of the cross on the story of Israel: if Torah could have defined covenant membership, the Messiah would not have needed to die, but (so Paul clearly implies) the fact that the Messiah *did* need to die indicates that Israel, as defined by Torah, needed to die and to come through to a new sort of life, a life in which the promises would at last be fulfilled.

Torah. The *third great narrative* that Paul offers is embedded within the second, as the second is in the first: it is the story of Torah. Torah is almost personified in some Pauline passages, and its multiple ambiguities have precipitated a huge secondary literature. The crucial passages are again in Galatians and Romans.

In Galatians 4:1-7, Paul tells the story of Israel being redeemed from Torah as though Torah were a new sort of Pharaoh, an enslaving power. Torah has now been linked up with the *stoicheia tou kosmou*, the "elements" of earth, air, fire, and water that make up the world, so that all Torah can do is to produce regulations for adjusting those elements rather than what is really required, a way of escaping their grip and moving the world, and God's people, towards the intended new-creational fulfillment. This explains how Paul can say that in their former state the ex-Gentile Galatians had been enslaved to beings that by nature were not divine, but had now been set free by God's "knowing" of them (Gal 4:8-9). Paul can then chide them with turning *back* to the "elements" once more (Gal 4:9), when what they were seeking to do was to embrace Torah, presumably in the hope of getting "further in" within the people of the true God than they had been able to do by believing in Jesus and being baptized. The only way we can make sense of this is to remind ourselves, from Galatians 3:21-25, that the God-given Torah had a *deliberately negative purpose*, to shut up Israel under a new kind of slavery until the ultimate redemption, which has now been accomplished through "the son of God," his sending, his birth, and his "being under Torah" (Gal 4:4). Though Paul does not mention Jesus' death at this point we should surely infer it.

We should do so not least in the light of the parallel in Romans 7:1–8:11.[97] The main point to be drawn out here is found in two seminal statements:

---

[97]See my commentary on Romans in the *New Interpreters Bible Commentary.*

Romans 7:4 and Romans 8:3-4. Paul's advance summary in Romans 7:4 is very close to Galatians 2:16-21: "You died to the law through the body of the Messiah, so that you could belong to another, to the one who was raised from the dead, so that you could bear fruit for God" (author's translation). Briefly, the point is this: Torah had bound Israel, not to God as had been thought, but to Adam.[98] The death of the Messiah is then to be counted as the death of his people; so those who, formerly under Torah, die with the Messiah to the Torah are set free from the bond that binds them to Adam (the "former husband" of Rom 7:1-3, like the "old man" of Rom 6:6). As a result, they are free for a new life, a life in the risen Christ, a life in the new undying dawn of the new day, a life of "being fruitful" as Adam had originally been commanded. This points the way forwards into the exposition of Romans 7, where Torah demonstrates that Israel is indeed in Adam (Rom 7:7-12), and that Israel, even though possessing Torah as God's gift and rejoicing in it as such, finds that all Torah can do is condemn and kill, not because there is anything wrong with Torah but because there is something right about Torah; it must point out sin and condemn it. That is what it is there for. Israel's ultimate problem is not the fact of possessing Torah, but the fact of possessing it *while being a sinful people, a people in Adam*. The result is *captivity* (Rom 7:23); in other words, exile.

Torah, however, has throughout this process had an important and God-given negative purpose: to draw sin onto one place, luring it forward to concentrate all its efforts at one spot. That is the meaning of the otherwise puzzling Romans 5:20: "But law came in, with the result that the trespass multiplied; but where sin increased, grace abounded all the more." When this has been done—when "sin" has "increased"—then the trap can be sprung: sin, the real culprit, must be condemned. That is the line of thought that runs through Romans 7 to the explosive conclusion in Romans 8:3. This is the closest Paul comes to saying in so many words what so many of his interpreters have attributed to him: that the death of Jesus was the ultimate moment of judicial condemnation, of God's punishment; "God, sending his own son in the likeness of sinful flesh and as a sin-offering, condemned sin in the flesh" (author's translation). This is strongly penal language. The point

---

[98]See Rom 5:20; 6:14; 7:1-3.

within this third story is that Torah, God's agent in the necessarily negative period between Moses and Jesus, was used to draw sin onto one place—Israel, and thence to Israel's representative, the Messiah—so that in his crucifixion, it could be punished at last as it deserved. And in that punishment "there is therefore now no condemnation for those who are in Christ Jesus" (Rom 8:1). No condemnation for Christ's people because God has condemned sin in the flesh of Christ: that is the Pauline point underneath the substitutionary language that has proved so powerful for some and so problematic for others.

Humanity. This leads us to the *fourth story*, which is that of the human race. For Paul, the Creator's purposes always focused on the call of image-bearing humanity to be the stewards of creation. The problem with the whole world, as we see in Romans 8:18-24, is that humans are not yet capable of exercising that stewardship. Paul therefore offers an account, focused on the transforming work of the gospel and the Spirit, of how humans will at last regain their noble status, their "glory" (Rom 5:2; 8:17, 21, 30). We may glimpse here Paul's own retrieval of a motif that was certainly in the minds of those who edited and studied the early chapters of Genesis in the "exilic" period: the expulsion of Adam and Eve from the garden, and the garden's bringing forth thorns and thistles, is the equivalent in terms of the whole human race of the expulsion of Israel from the land. When, therefore, Israel's Messiah completes Israel's redemptive task as its faithful representative, this means that the "exile" *of the whole human* race has at last been dealt with. Paul's entire theology of justification is moving toward this goal: humans are put right by divine grace in order that they may be "glorified" (Rom 8:30). The divine "glory" that would return to live in the temple has indeed returned—to live, now, within faithful human beings (Rom 8:9-11; 2 Cor 3:7; 4:6). Israel's "return from exile" in the Messiah is therefore the sign and the means of the "return from exile" of the whole human race, and with it the cosmos that has longed for humans to be restored to their proper glory in order that it, too, might be set free from its "slavery to decay" (Rom 8:21).

Conclusion. The inner logic of all this must be clear. For the Second Temple Jew, Israel was carrying God's purposes for the world; Israel's stewardship of the land, and God's blessing on that stewardship, was the advance sign of that eventual purpose, which Paul has expounded in Romans 8:18-26. Exile was not an arbitrary punishment for disobedience. It was the inevitable consequence of Israel's idolatry and rebellion. Israel recapitulated the primal sin of Adam and Eve. Creation was designed to flourish under wise human stewardship, reflecting the love of God the Creator. When the humans rebelled, creation suffered too. The humans must therefore be put out of the garden. So, as Genesis opened with the vision of created blessing and vocation turning into disaster and tragedy, so Deuteronomy, drawing toward the close of the five-book Torah, envisaged Israel going through the same exile-from-the-garden, only now with the promise of redemption, of covenant renewal. Abraham's people would indeed inherit the land, but they would in the end have to go into exile. If they were still to carry the long promises of God (Rom 3:1-8), it would be necessary for that exile to be undone, for the story to reach the point Moses had predicted in Deuteronomy 30, the point to which prophets like Jeremiah and Ezekiel had looked back in order to gain fresh hope. That is why Paul expounds Deuteronomy 30 in Romans 10, having just declared that the Messiah was where the long story of Torah had been going all along. This whole complex but coherent narrative is what, according to Paul, was accomplished through the cross and resurrection of the Messiah and the gift of the Spirit.

THEOLOGICAL REFLECTIONS ON THE CONTINUING EXILE

History is not the handmaid of theology, nor theology of history. If we understand Jesus and Paul in the way I have suggested, history and theology turn out to be mutually interdependent ways of talking about the same thing. Thus far, we have been exploring what some might call a "theology *of* history": this is how (in other words) Second Temple Jews and early Christians, and indeed Jesus himself, envisaged that the Creator God was at work both *in and through* the events of history and as *sovereign over* those events. This leads me, in conclusion, to some wider remarks, again about history and theology.

What, for a start, are we saying about the historical Jesus himself and "Christian theology"? We are taking Hermann Reimarus's challenge seriously: investigate Jesus and see whether Christianity is not based on a mistake.[99] We are taking Albert Schweitzer's challenge seriously: put Jesus

---

[99]See Charles H. Talbert, ed., *Reimarus: Fragments*, trans. Ralph S. Fraser (London: SCM Press, 1971), 146-51. It provides two extracts from Hermann Samuel Reimarus's *Apologie oder*

within apocalyptic Judaism and watch bland, unthinking dogma shiver in its shoes.[100] Some, a century ago, found this too dangerous and proposed escape routes. First, Wilhelm Wrede: Mark is theological fiction, and Jesus is a non-apocalpytic, teasing teacher.[101] This view is alive and well over one hundred years later. Second, Martin Kähler: the true Christ is a Christ of faith detached from the Jesus of history.[102] This, too, is alive and well today. The church may urge this latter escape route; part of the academic guild may urge the former. Both should be resisted. Instead, we should accept both Reimarus's challenge and Schweitzer's proposal. Locating Jesus within his historical context, once we do the serious homework and discover more about what that context really was, will not get in the way of the church's proclamation. After all, one of the things that *does* hinder that proclamation, in many Western countries at least, is the sneer that the church has invented a "Jesus" who is quite unlike the one who really existed. It will not do, in response, to say "Ah, but we know the Christ of the church's faith." If the "Christ" is not the same as the one and only "Jesus," we are whistling in the dark. And that is where an account of exile can help—despite the nervous protests of those who have not considered how Second Temple Judaism actually worked, or what Jesus' contemporaries would have thought as they saw and heard him in action.

All this means that Schweitzer's account of apocalyptic must be seriously modified. First-century Jewish apocalyptic was not about the actual "end of the world." Instead, it invested major events within history with their theological significance. It looked, specifically, for the unique and climactic moment in—not the abolition of—Israel's long historical story.

Schutzschrift für die vernünftigen Verehrer Gottes. Reimarus (1694–1768) refrained from publishing the *Apologie* during his lifetime, but after his death these and other parts of it were published in 1774–1778 by G. E. Lessing under the general title *Wolfenbüttel Fragments.*

[100]Albert Schweitzer, *The Quest of the Historical Jesus: A Critical Study of Its Progress from Reimarus to Wrede,* trans. W. Montgomery (New York: Macmillan, 1910, 1960), 330-403. Originally published as *Von Reimarus zu Wrede: Eine Geschichte der Leben Jesu-Forschung* (Tübingen: J. C. B. Mohr, 1906).

[101]Wilhelm Wrede, *The Messianic Secret,* trans. J. C. G. Grieg (Cambridge: James Clarke, 1971). Originally published as *Das Messiasgeheimnis in den Evangelien: Zugleich ein Beitrag zum Verständnis des Markusevangeliums* (Göttingen: Vandenhoeck & Ruprecht, 1901).

[102]Martin Kähler, *The So-Called Historical Jesus and the Historical Biblical Christ,* trans. Carl E. Braaten (Philadelphia: Fortress, 1964). Originally published as *Der sogenannte historische Jesus und der geschichtliche, biblische Christus* (Leipzig: A. Deichart, 1892).

Where Schweitzer (or at least his followers—there is some debate about "the historical Schweitzer"!) saw the end of the *world*, Jesus was announcing the end of *exile*—in the sense we have explored. We must, then, renounce literalism, whether fundamentalist or scholarly. "Apocalyptic" was the symbolic and richly charged language of protest, affirming that God would do the new thing, that his kingdom would come on earth as in heaven—not in some imagined heavenly realm to be created after the present world had been destroyed. In particular, "apocalyptic" was the language of revolution: not that YHWH would destroy the world, but that he would act dramatically within it, to bring Israel's long night of suffering to an end, to usher in the new day in which peace and justice would reign. Telling Israel's story that way encouraged people to sign on and be part of the coming new world. All of that was contained within the longing for "return from exile."[103]

Schweitzer, then, was right to see that his eschatological Jesus would shake comfortable Western orthodoxy to its foundations. I have modified his scheme by interpreting apocalyptic historically, but the Jesus that I discover remains shocking. Western orthodoxy has for too long had an overly lofty, detached, and oppressive view of God. It has approached Christology by assuming this view of God and has tried to fit Jesus into it. Hardly surprisingly, the result has been a Docetic Jesus offering an escapist salvation. That, in turn, was the sort of thing that generated Reimarus's protest, not least because of the social and cultural nonsense that the combination of deism, Docetism, and escapism reinforced. That combination remains powerful and still needs to be challenged. My proposal, then, is not that we assume that we know what the word *God* means and somehow manage to fit Jesus into that. Instead, I suggest that we think historically about a young Jew, possessed of a desperately risky—indeed, apparently crazy—vocation, riding into Jerusalem in tears, denouncing the temple, dining once more with his friends, and dying on a Roman cross, and that we somehow allow our meaning for the word *God* to be recentered around that point. Place Jesus within his genuine first-century context—Christian dogma has, after all, insisted that he was fully human as well as fully divine—and all this makes

---

[103]See the seminal discussion in G. B. Caird, *The Language and Imagery of the Bible* (London: Duckworth, 1980), 243-71; see further Wright, *New Testament and the People of God*, 280-338.

sense. God's kingdom was indeed coming "on earth as in heaven"—even though it did not look like what Jesus' contemporaries were expecting, and does not look like what ours are expecting either.

I and others who have written about Israel's extended exile, and who have made that thematic for an understanding of the New Testament, have sometimes been accused of importing this large, global narrative into the text. I return the charge with interest: much Western Christianity has assumed a large implicit narrative, that of "humans trying to find a gracious God," or "sinners wanting to go to heaven," and have used that as a Procrustean bed on which to fit the New Testament, cutting off, or stretching, the bits that do not fit. Of course, grace, sin, and the glories of the new creation remain important. But it will not do to say that a historical account, focusing on the strongly implicit narratives of Second Temple Jews, must be ruled out because it does not sit comfortably with our dehistoricized assumptions. After all, when we look at Scripture as a whole it does indeed offer a clear overall narrative: the Creator and the cosmos, the place of humans, the calling of Abraham and his family, and all finding resolution and renewal in Jesus. *The point of the covenant with Israel, in the whole of Scripture, is that it was the means by which God was rescuing the children of Adam and so restoring the world.* And this entire narrative had to pass through the narrow door of exile, and ultimately of the cross of Jesus. This is not a side issue or a different point. It is the key to everything else.

I have been accused (in particular at the symposium on exile at Trinity Western University where some of this material was presented and discussed) of presenting a novelty: a view of exile that nobody in the Christian tradition had thought of before. That was, of course, what people in the sixteenth century said to Luther, Calvin, and their friends. As the Reformers all believed, God may well have more light to break out of his holy Word. Again and again that has happened through fresh study of the sources themselves; and that includes, and focuses on, fresh *historical* study. We cannot assume that first-century Jews (or for that matter pagans) carried the same implicit narratives in their heads that post-Enlightenment Western humans do. All the evidence suggests they did not. Tradition matters; but tradition is, as Aquinas said, the story of how the church has read Scripture, not a separate "source." And the result of this fresh reading is to highlight once again that central Reformational principle that is often obscured or even erased in the eagerness to detect a "universal," and instantly "applicable," message in the New Testament. The achievement of Jesus the Messiah was unique, one-off, unrepeatable. To highlight exile in the way I have done is to see all of history focused on the cross, not flattened out into a set of general truths that just happened to be exemplified in Jesus.

For many systematic theologians, it would seem, the very idea of the Abrahamic covenant and its outworking in Deuteronomy 26–30, as then lived out in the long years of Israel's history, remain strangely foreign and alien, and certainly do not form a grid within which early Christian theology can be understood. There are various reasons for this, no doubt. I suspect that among them are two things in particular. First, the long Western tradition, both Catholic and Protestant, has focused attention on "going to heaven" in strictly otherworldly terms, so that any view that seems to speak of a redemption and renewal *within* the present order is drastically counterintuitive. Second, most Protestantism has lived for so long with a "broken" narrative—church history lapsing into the darkness of the Middle Ages and God then doing a new thing in the Reformation, and many variations on that theme—that the idea of a *single* narrative, albeit with radical new things happening within it, is anathema. In fact, it is often the subject of caricatures, as though the sort of thing I have been talking about here were the same sort of thing as was offered by nineteenth-century German idealism: a smooth development or progression. Nobody who takes the Messiah's cross seriously could propose such a thing, and I certainly would not and have not—though, equally, nobody who takes the Messiah's resurrection seriously could imagine that the fresh divine work accomplished in Jesus meant that the Creator was saying no to the world and doing something entirely different. The cross is God's judgment on the corruption that has infected his world, not on the creation itself; the resurrection is God's reaffirmation of that good creation, his launching of the project of creation's renewal that will be complete with the coming together of heaven and earth (Eph 1:10) and the resurrection of the renewed humans (1 Cor 15:20-28).

Within this context, it appears that the proposal of "continuing exile," and its resolution in Jesus, touches certain nerves in theology and the church. We need to look, in conclusion, at three of these. Each could of course be set out much more fully. I hope this brief treatment will at least serve to raise the issues.

Otherworldly or this-worldly? What was the hope of a first-century Jew? The obvious answer might be "salvation." But what did salvation actually mean? A good deal of the secondary literature on the hope of Second Temple Judaism has assumed a model of otherworldly salvation. This passes unquestioned in many circles: you do not look *at* your spectacles until looking *through* them becomes problematic. This assumed otherworldly salvation, "going to heaven when you die," has then contextualized and conditioned the ways in which scholars and preachers alike have handled the questions, and biblical texts, that swirl around salvation: questions, not least, of justification, the law, "works," "grace," and so on.

But the Second Temple texts themselves tell strongly against an otherworldly salvation, against the notion that the ultimate aim of humans in general and Jews in particular was the escape of saved souls from their present embodiment and indeed from space, time, and matter altogether. In the texts we have studied, and in particular in the continuous story we have been examining, the aim and goal does not have to do with the abolition of the universe of space, time, and matter, or the escape of humans from such a wreckage, but with its rescue, its renewal, its consummation.[104]

Participatory or escapist? Salvation is not, then, about escape. It is about finding oneself a member of the family who are promised resurrection. (*Salvation*, after all, means "rescue"; and the ultimate power from which we seek rescue is death itself.) God, through the gospel and in the power of the Spirit, summons people into the covenant, to be his people, to share the "sonship" of the Messiah himself, and to be part of his work of bringing all things to renewal. When we read passages that raise the question "What must I do to inherit eternal life?" (cf. Mt 19:16//Mk 10:17//

---

[104]See especially Wright, *New Testament and the People of God*, chap. 10, 15.6; Wright, *Jesus and the Victory of God*, chap. 6, 8; Wright, *The Resurrection of the Son of God* (Minneapolis: Fortress, 2003), chap. 4; and Wright, *Surprised by Hope: Rethinking Heaven, the Resurrection, and the Mission of the Church* (New York: HarperOne, 2008).

Lk 10:25; 18:18), we should know that the modern Western understanding ("How can I go to heaven when I die") is radically anachronistic. The question means, rather, "How can I be part of the Coming Age, the Age to Come, *ha'olam ha-ba'*?"[105]

As all the texts we have mentioned make clear, this "age to come" was not much like the heaven of medieval and postmedieval Western imagination, and much more like the liberated Israel, and also the liberated creation, of biblical and Second Temple hope. If we insist on projecting onto the texts the questions of individual salvation, in a classic Western heaven-or-hell scheme, trying to discern where they fit in terms of the "qualifications" people might have for the one or the other, and how (either through God's grace or human merit or some combination of the two) some might attain such a salvation, we will miss the entire story within which the writers of those texts were living. And in doing this we will almost certainly distort quite radically the other terms that cluster around the larger notion of salvation. The question of Second Temple "exile," then, is not a matter of a single curious motif that we might or might not factor into our thought about Jesus, Paul, and the early church. It is one focal point of an entire vision of what the Creator God has promised to do in his great work of "salvation." It is, above all, woven into the very fabric of the biblical texts themselves to which the church has always declared allegiance.

Individual or corporate? This relatively modern approach to the texts, understanding them in terms of a non-spatiotemporal "salvation," is basically *telling the wrong story*. It collapses Israel's story, the main theme of book after book of the Bible itself and much Second Temple writing, into "my story," the story of the individual soul on the way to heaven or hell. In the modern world, "my story" is then contextualized, by implication, within a larger implicit narrative: either the modern dream of personal fulfillment, or the Platonic one of leaving this world and going to a disembodied one instead; or some combination of the two. But to tell the story like this is arguably to take a large step away from the basic Jewish worldview and

---

[105]Mk 10:18; Mt 19:16; Lk 18:18; Wright, *Jesus and the Victory of God*, 301. On biblical visions of salvation and eternal life, see Wright, *Resurrection of the Son of God*, and Wright, *Surprised by Hope*.

toward an essentially pagan one. Such an approach is widespread both in academic and in popular circles.[106]

Let us, though, be clear: *this is not to say that personal "salvation" is not at issue* or is deemed unimportant. That is a regular slur against fresh interpretations of Jesus and Paul, but it misses the point entirely. Of course "salvation" matters. What is being said, however, is that "salvation" does not mean what the Western tradition has often taken it to mean (escaping to a disembodied "heaven"), and that it is not the main narrative that they are trying to explicate. In the New Testament the rescue of human beings from sin and death, which remains vital throughout, serves a much larger purpose, namely that of God's restorative justice for the whole creation.[107] And to understand that properly we need to understand the ancient Jewish perception not only of Israel's exile but of the "exile" of the whole human race. That is the context within which Paul's vision of justification and salvation mean what they mean. It is also, as I have argued here and elsewhere, the context within which Jesus' own announcement of God's kingdom, and his dying on the cross to bring that about, mean what they mean.

CONCLUSION

The theme of continuing exile, then, is well attested in the Second Temple literature. The perception of most Jews in that period was of a long night, with the promised dawn seemingly indefinitely postponed. There were hints that the sun might be about to rise, but those hopes would be dashed as the sun would, once again, sink back below the horizon. This was how Israel understood their lot in life: waiting for the sun to rise, for the break of dawn.

---

[106]An obvious recent example: C. VanLandingham, *Judgment and Justification in Early Judaism and the Apostle Paul* (Peabody, MA: Hendrickson, 2006). His central chapter on "the last judgment according to deeds," etc., opens by quoting Mk 10:18, meaning it clearly in its usual late Western sense, and insists that "the texts surveyed below respond to" this question (66). This criticism applies only partially, in my view, to K. L. Yinger, *Paul, Judaism and Justification According to Deeds* (Cambridge: Cambridge University Press, 1999), who emphasizes that what is at issue is the membership of the individual in the group that is being considered (94). He rightly, in my view, follows M. Reiser, *Jesus and Judgment: The Eschatological Proclamation in Its Jewish Context*, trans. L. M. Maloney (Minneapolis: Fortress, 1997), 161, in seeing that individual appearance at a last judgment is a tannaitic innovation (94n142), more like what we find in paganism than in classic Judaism (139-40), and stresses that at Qumran at least (I think elsewhere too) what is in view is what he calls a "historical eschatology" (135-36).

[107]Outside Paul, obvious passages include Rev 5:9-10; in Paul, one naturally thinks, e.g., of Rom 8:17-25.

When Jesus is understood in this light, his kingdom stories become clear, and the overall aim of his entire public career, and indeed his death, becomes clear as well. Jesus told "kingdom stories" about the return from exile, and in his own ministry he understood himself to be bringing about that return and restoration of Israel, in order to fulfill the ancient divine plan. Jesus redefined the central Second Temple Jewish symbols around his own presence and work. Paul belongs, and thought of himself as belonging, in the same story—though of course at a new moment within it, the moment that had been unveiled precisely in Jesus' death and resurrection. As a Pharisee, Saul of Tarsus had been longing for the promises to come true: for the "return from exile," the rebuilding or cleansing of the temple, and ultimately for the return of YHWH to Zion. Paul the apostle believed that YHWH had indeed returned—in and as Jesus himself. He believed that the "exile" had been brought to an end—by Jesus' death on the cross. He believed that the postexilic covenant renewal had been launched—in Jesus' resurrection and the gift of the Spirit. That is what Romans 10:1-13 is about, focusing on Deuteronomy 30, the great promise of restoration after exile. The multiple narratives and symbols that come together in Paul's coherent worldview can all be seen to great advantage from this perspective. For Paul, Jesus' death and resurrection has inaugurated the dawn of new creation, the first day of the undying dawn. Israel's God had promised that one day the sun would rise at last. He had been faithful to the covenant in which those promises were central. In Jesus, crucified, vindicated in the resurrection, and now already reigning (1 Cor 15:20-28), Paul believed that the Creator had done what he said he would. Once we understand how "exile" actually works, in Second Temple Judaism and the New Testament, Paul's gospel shines out as good news for the whole creation, and for all individual humans within it. The sun had risen at last, and Paul instructed his hearers to live in the light of that new day.

PART ONE

OLD TESTAMENT/
HEBREW BIBLE/
SEPTUAGINT

CHAPTER ONE

WRIGHT ON EXILE

A Response

WALTER BRUEGGEMANN

N. T. WRIGHT'S PROGRAMMATIC essay on exile is a delight to read. As always, Wright brings to his work a combination of erudition and mastery of the critical apparatus and an agile imagination that permits him to make interpretive connections in rich and compelling ways. I find the main claim of his paper—that the narrative of exile and restoration is the key to ongoing Judaism (and derivatively of early Christianity)—to be evocative and rich in possibility. My reflections are inside this affirmation. His claim, however, is so comprehensive and far-reaching that he allows ample room for critical engagement.

There is no doubt much merit in his governing judgment that the theological mindset of Deuteronomy, particularly Deuteronomy 30–31, is definitive, and that Judaism read its historical context not only concerning "exile and restoration" but also "guilt and penitence." Thus the hoped-for alternative to exile is geographical and concerns return to the security and well-being of the homeland. It is also theological and requires reconciliation with God, whether by ritual acts of atonement or by performance of Torah, or both.

WRIGHT'S DELIBERATE USE OF LANGUAGE

At the outset one may wonder about some of the terms Wright employs to begin his case:

(1) He concedes that his treatment of texts is "selective" and concentrates on "highlights" (p. 19). That might mean that there is too much material to cover and so he must choose the best representative texts. But it may also

mean that he has tilted the evidence by the choices he has made, so that other selections might have led to other conclusions. By the time he finishes very strongly with the "victory" of Jesus, in fact the data from the Old Testament to which he appeals is quite limited in making the case for exile and restoration as the dominant narrative of Judaism.

(2) He asserts that a "majority" of "Second Temple Jews saw themselves as living within an ongoing exile" (p. 19). Perhaps; but perhaps not. Perhaps this is a view established by elite opinion makers who created the normative tradition. And while this narrative account may have dominated the world that they managed, it does not necessarily follow that the majority perceived their own lives in this way. Erich Voegelin, and after him Jacob Neusner, have written of a "paradigmatic history," and paradigms are impositions and interpretive lenses.[1] The matter of elite imposition is important in Old Testament study, and I will return to it.

(3) Wright eschews the thought that the "continuing exile" could be an "image" or a "metaphor" (p. 21). He insists that exile was not "just an idea, a type or image," but an act of hope:

> The point is that Jewish eschatology in the Second Temple focused on the hope that that which had happened in the Babylonian exile, the triumph of paganism over Israel because of its sins, was still the dominant state of affairs, but would at last be undone. (p. 36)

But such hope is exactly an act of imagination, even if, as he says, "imagination has to be educated by evidence" (p. 35). I do not quite understand why Wright refuses the notion of "image, metaphor, or idea," possibly because such terms would indicate an intentional constructivism that would perhaps point to the reality of a deliberate act of interpretation by those who generated the paradigm. After all, the paradigm is not "just there." It is generated, advocated, and sponsored, and one can imagine

---

[1]Eric Voegelin, *Israel and Revelation* (Baton Rouge: Louisiana State University Press, 2000); Jacob Neusner, *Understanding Seeking Faith: Essays on the Case of Judaism,* vol. 1, *Debates on Methods, Report of Results* (Atlanta: Scholars Press, 1986), 126-41. See also David Weiss Halivni, *Revelation Restored: Divine Writ and Critical Responses* (Boulder, CO: Westview Press, 1997). On the latter I have found helpful the commentary by Peter Ochs, "Talmudic Scholarship as Textual Reasoning; Halivni's Pragmatic Historiography," in *Textual Reasonings: Jewish Philosophy and Text Study at the End of the Twentieth Century,* ed. Peter Ochs and Nancy Levene (Grand Rapids: Eerdmans, 2002), 120-43.

(or at least this one can imagine) that such generativity is never completely innocent but reflects certain interests, even if many others have signed on to it against their own interest.[2] Thus I am inclined to be more suspicious than is Wright about the emergence and maintenance of the notion of continuing exile, a notion perhaps reflective of a certain claim to the land by those who do not now have land but who fully intend to have the land in time to come. Restoration is aimed at land and city, and such a hope is never disinterested. It is rather an act of quite interested imagination. Clearly the notion of "image" or "metaphor" tends to problematize the dominant narrative.

A Few Central Texts

I am struck by the fact that the actual texts of the Hebrew Bible to which Wright appeals are relatively few in number. He does, to be sure, fill out the argument with other texts, notably Ben Sira, Judith, the Maccabees, evidence from Qumran, and Josephus. But from the Hebrew Bible itself he moves from Deuteronomy 30–31 (surely a correct beginning point) and then focuses on the three great prayers in Daniel 9; Ezra 9; and Nehemiah 9. His central case is from Daniel 9 with its speculation about "seventy" and all that that may mean for the festival calendar of Judaism. It may be that these prayers merit such a privileged place, but it is to be noted that they reflect a learned historiography that is intensely didactic! The elites who framed such prayers were fully and centrally informed by Deuteronomy, and are occupied with a Deuteronomic theology of sin-punishment-repentance. They take into account a recognition that "we are still slaves in our own land" (Neh 9:36). But the didactic tone of the prayers may suggest a determined effort to invite others into this paradigm; it may be that they required many recruits in order to become "the majority" with the normative narrative. We do not know; but I wonder whether Wright's focus on these few texts, central as they appear to be, will support the huge claims he makes for his paradigm.

---

[2]A contemporary example of recruitment of others to share a paradigm that is against their own interest is suggested by Thomas Frank, *What's the Matter with Kansas: How Conservatives Won the Heart of America* (New York: Henry Holt, 2005).

THE TEMPLE ALONGSIDE OTHER REFERENCE POINTS

Wright invests a great deal in the temple and takes it as the single focal point for Judaism. Much of what he claims for the temple is fully reflective of something like a scholarly consensus, thus, the temple as God's dwelling place, the temple as the offer of a cosmos, the temple as alternative creation as the old creation is so marked by chaos and so the temple as "new creation."[3] I think, however, that his argument runs the risk of being so all-inclusive of the temple that it fails to reckon with claims, practices, and traditions that fall outside the temple. It is evident, for example, that the "name theology" of Deuteronomy does not regard the temple as the dwelling place of God (see Deut 26:15; 1 Kings 8:27). One cannot simply elide the traditions so that they all fit under the single reference point. Thus I suggest that Wright himself is busy, as were the generators of the great paradigm of exile and restoration, offering a paradigm that encourages us as his readers to assess the data according to his temple paradigm. His belated paradigm echoes the force of the ancient paradigm that he is expositing. But it cannot be so all-inclusive.

In Old Testament studies, a very different paradigm is worth considering. Frank Cross has proposed (another paradigm!), in his "history of the priesthood" in ancient Israel (concretely evident in the time of David in the dual priesthood of Abiathar and Zadok), that there was a "Mushite" tradition of priesthood from Moses that focused on the Torah that eventuated in the work of the Levites.[4] Conversely Aaron stands at the head of a competing tradition, represented by Zadok, that focused on the temple. One can trace the two trajectories of Levites who interpret Torah and Aaronide priests who champion the temple, a tension voiced in the provision of Ezekiel 44 from an Aaronide perspective. Wright is ready to subsume Torah and all else under the temple, but I wonder whether one has to allow for an unsettled interface whereby the Torah tradition cannot simply be

---

[3]See Jon D. Levenson, *Creation and the Persistence of Evil: The Jewish Drama of Omnipotence* (San Francisco: Harper & Row, 1988), 53-127; Kevin J. Madigan and Jon D. Levenson, *Resurrection: The Power of God for Christians and Jews* (New Haven, CT: Yale University Press, 2008), chap. 5; Samuel Terrien, *The Elusive Presence: Toward a New Biblical Theology* (San Francisco: Harper & Row, 1978), chap. 4.

[4]Frank Moore Cross, *Canaanite Myth and Hebrew Epic: Essays in the History of the Religion of Israel* (Cambridge, MA: Harvard University Press, 1973), 195-215.

subsumed under the rubric of the temple but stands as a counterpoint and alternative accent to the temple. As a side issue, I am unconvinced that the role of king so readily goes with the temple, a point long ago mapped out by Ben Ollenburger.[5]

MULTIDIMENSIONAL HOPE

When Wright comes to Paul's testimony, he is able to identify four notions that are crucial for Paul's interpretation. The first of these is "creation and new creation." The second is the story of Israel, with particular reference to Abraham. The third is the story of the Torah, and the fourth is the nature of the human race with an assurance of justification for all (pp. 63-71). I have no special competence about the Pauline tradition, but such a summary seems fair enough to me.

But if Paul can appeal to all of the traditions, he clearly did not invent them. He appeals to old known and treasured traditions and sees in each one a particular and important accent for faith and for theological interpretation. But that inventory to which Paul appeals and that he reworks has been there all along. The generative inventiveness of Paul, propelled by his sense of and passion for Jesus as the awaited Messiah, is based on the generative inventiveness of the tradition. I think that Wright has perhaps poorly appreciated that generative inventiveness in the tradition, because he has, in what strikes me as a reductionist way, subsumed everything under the temple in the tradition to which Paul appealed. In fact such matters as Torah, land, king, and father Abraham are quite distinct traditions and cannot, in Judaism prior to Paul, be so readily absorbed by the theme of temple.

Most specifically Jeremiah is an heir to Moses and the "Mushite" tradition. (See the sequence of texts concerning that line of priests from 1 Sam 2:33 to 1 Kings 2:26-27 to Jer 1:1). His core anticipation for the future of Israel, albeit with "a scattering and a gathering" (Jer 31:10), is a new covenant based on Torah, not on temple-grounded theology (Jer 31:31-34). As Jeremiah lines it out, moreover, Israel's future from God breaks out beyond the Deuteronomic structure of sin-repentance. The interpretive tradition, already from the sixth century, is not enthralled by the codes of Deuteronomy.

---

[5]Ben C. Ollenburger, *Zion, the City of the Great King: A Theological Symbol of the Jerusalem Cult*, JSOTSup 41 (Sheffield: Sheffield Academic Press, 1987).

In Jeremiah, as in Ezekiel, the future does not come from repentance but from a leap of generative newness on God's part.[6] In Jeremiah the grounding is in divine forgiveness (Jer 31:34; 33:8). In Ezekiel it is a "new spirit and a heart of flesh" (Ezek 36:26). Already in the exilic period there is a deep and radical break with the Deuteronomic fix on which Wright focuses. Thus it seems to me that there is more energy for new possibility in these traditions than can be accounted for either from the temple or from the Deuteronomic structure. The reduction of the "problem" to Deuteronomy and the "resolution" to the temple in Judaism does not, I think, take into account the rich and thick pluralism of the text as it ponders that "problem" and anticipates the "resolution."

Thus I suggest that the accents that Wright identifies in Paul's exposition are, in the "Second Temple" period, already important and generative in Judaism, even without reference to the temple. Perhaps they are so important that we might playfully consider the reidentification of the period of Persian, Hellenistic, and early Roman hegemony not as the "Second Temple" period but as the "Second Torah" period. The difference that makes of course is that one does not need to "return from exile" in order to be a faithful and blessed Jew. Thus I am struck by how much of Israel's hope can do without a temple focus. I am resistant to the notion that "exile" is "the key to everything" (p. 75), as the tradition is complex and restless enough to defy such a one-dimensional settlement.

As a confessing Christian, I have no wish to detract from the truth claims for Jesus that Wright so well exposits. Thus he can say of the Synoptic traditions that they concern an eschatological claim: "It is a claim about eschatology. The time is fulfilled; the exile is over; the bridegroom is at hand" (p. 55). That claim is partly utterance in the Gospel narrative; it is partly performance. It seems to me, however, that allowance must be made for the recognition that this combination of utterance and performance is exactly what goes on in the prophetic tradition all through the "Second Temple" period. Paul Hanson's contrast and interface of "pragmatist" and "visionary" is to the point.[7] The visionary part of the tradition concerns recovery and

---

[6]See Jacqueline E. Lapsley, *Can These Bones Live? The Problem of the Moral Self in the Book of Ezekiel*, BZAW 301 (Berlin: de Gruyter, 2000).

[7]Paul D. Hanson, *The Dawn of Apocalyptic* (Philadelphia: Fortress, 1975).

homecoming. But the pragmatist part concerns the more immediate daily reality of life without awaiting the interruption of miracle. The endless interpretive negotiation in Judaism is richer and more variegated than simply a single theme, even one that merits much airtime. Of course Judaism probes in generic ways a "resolution" to its historic "problem." But that is only to say that Judaism is a "religion of redemption." That redemption may take many forms, not all of which concern homecoming and not all of which are temple based.

LIVELY MINORITY REPORTS

I want to return to Wright's opening judgment about the self-understanding of the "majority" of Jews in the Second Temple period. In Old Testament study, there is now a broad awareness that operative faith in Judaism was a sociologically layered and differentiated phenomenon. Erhard Gerstenberger has in many places proposed that alongside official "state" religion we can identify the religion of clan and family that stood quite apart from the establishment movement that produced the "authorized" picture of Judaism. That religion resists the categories and control of centralized elitist religious authority, a resistance that is perhaps reflected in the contrasts of Luke 19:47-48. As Gerstenberger states:

> What remains of the pre-exilic prophetic movement is, first, a diversity of mediator activities in the sphere of manticism and healing and, secondly, the sporadic opposition of marginal group mediators to the growing injustices and violations of clan solidarity in a bureaucratic and centralized society.[8]

In an earlier study of the Psalms, Gerstenberger proposed that many of the Psalms reflect local rituals of "rehabilitation" that were clearly apart from temple practices.[9] And Rainer Albertz has made a compelling contrast between official religion and personal piety.[10] Most recently Albertz, along with Ruediger Schmitt, has explored household religion quite apart from

---

[8]Erhard Gerstenberger, *Theologies of the Old Testament* (Minneapolis: Fortress, 2002), 197.

[9]Erhard Gerstenberger, *Der bittende Mensch*, WMANT 51 (Neukirchen-Vluyn: Neukirchener Verlag, 1980).

[10]Rainer Albertz, *A History of Israelite Religion in the Old Testament Period* (Louisville, KY: Westminster John Knox, 1994), 2:437-533.

the temple.[11] A most remarkable part of their analysis is the data concerning proper names assigned to children. They conclude that almost none of the names assigned to children are linked to YHWH, the Lord of the temple and the primary agent in the narrative of exile and return; but a great many of the names allude to the "lesser" gods who are not participants in the large narrative of YHWH. The judgment Albertz and Schmitt draw is that family religion was not at all preoccupied with the great paradigms of Yahwism that characterize the Hebrew Bible; they were concerned with daily matters of birth and death, of sowing and reaping, rather than the narrative drama of exile and return. That is, they were embedded in a very different notion that lives below the radar of official religion.

Given this preoccupation with the dailyness of life, I wonder whether the quite domestic matters that Jesus utilizes in some of his teaching might reflect a focus on the daily tribulations and possibilities of life without regard to the great paradigmatic narratives sponsored by the elites. This I take it is evidence that may tell against the way Wright claims the "majority" understood itself. I could imagine that on great festival occasions such peasants could participate in the great dramatic performance of exile and return, but in fact their self-understanding was rooted in more immediate mundane realities that had an acute religious dimension to them. In any case the tradition is in fact much more complex than a single claim. I doubt that here or anywhere is there "a key to everything else."

AMID HEGEMONY

Finally I want to comment on the "church today" in Wright's subtitle. The conclusion of his paper offers a welcome agenda with which we must continue to struggle in our time and place:

- otherworldly or this-worldly;
- participatory or escapist;
- individual or corporate.

Surely Wright is correct in his tilt on these matters. But his articulation still lingers in a rather abstract way. He leaves us much more work to do about

---

[11]Rainer Albertz and Ruediger Schmitt, *Family and Household Religion in Ancient Israel and the Levant* (Winona Lake, IN: Eisenbrauns, 2012).

the matter of exile in contemporary life. Of course he writes from Britain, and I respond from the United States. But if we can permit the image of exile to have leverage for our imagination, then we must join issue with the Babylon (or the Rome) of our day that surely takes the form of corporate capitalism in which all are "left behind" except the well connected who control the flow of capital.

More might usefully be said about the maintenance of covenantal identity (baptismal identity) in the face of such a systemically hostile environment that resists and does not welcome the claims of Torah. I dare to imagine that such hegemonic ideology does not in principle resist the claims of temple, for who can seriously object to the presence of the transcendent God of the temple, especially one who has signed on with a commitment to the exceptionalism of the dominant system? If we are to entertain a resilient identity rooted in alternative, then we might think of Daniel, the one given in the narrative of Daniel 1. This Daniel is a very different Daniel from the voice cited by Wright in Daniel 9. The Daniel of the first chapter is situated amid the Babylonian empire. He is recruited for civil service in the empire, and he succeeds in that role. Amid his training program, which includes rich imperial food, however, he engaged in a bold act of resistance. He refused the food of the empire (on which see Mk 8:15). He defied, but he stayed. This Daniel is not going home. He is not a candidate for restoration. He will dwell in the empire, benefit from it, and serve it. But he will keep Torah and thereby keep Torah identity, refusing the "defilement" of the empire. In the narratives that follow concerning him, the appeal is not to restoration; rather, the narrative pivots on his piety, his learning, and his courage, all rooted in his Torah identity.

It is useful to see the power arrangements (with totems of legitimacy) in our society as a context of exile. But "homecoming" is not an especially useful image for us. In fact the summons of faith is much more of the kind voiced in Jeremiah's letter to the exiles in Jeremiah 29 that pivots on a note of historical realism ("educated by evidence"). The counsel of the prophet to the exiles is to settle in, make a life, and engage Babylon. In the Daniel narrative there is a refusal to bow down (Dan 3:16-18). But that resolve is rooted not in a resolve to return, but in a resolve to remain, and to remain faithful.

It will be clear to the reader that Wright's essay has evoked for me quite fresh thinking, and I am grateful to him. I am much instructed by his paper. And even while I resist what strikes me as a kind of reductionism in his argument, I am glad to find myself on the same page with Wright on the main issues. Wright models for us a readiness to continue to engage the tradition with our best imagination. He rightly insists that our imagination must be educated by evidence. But all the evidence we can muster is not given mastery over our imagination.

It is imagination, and finally not evidence, that sustains those who must inescapably find their home in alien territory. Finding one's home there may still permit a refusal of despair. It is a refusal to conform either to the hegemony of empire or to the authority of the elites who are not disinterested in their advocacy for a master paradigm. Hope, that interruptive act of imagination, cannot finally be about flight to a more perfect home. It more likely concerns the grind that is daily—sowing and reaping, birthing and dying.

CHAPTER TWO

EXILE AND RESTORATION TERMINOLOGY IN THE SEPTUAGINT AND THE NEW TESTAMENT

ROBERT J. V. HIEBERT

I BEGIN THIS CONTRIBUTION TO THE PRESENT COLLECTION OF ESSAYS on the theme of exile in the Jewish and Christian Scriptures by expressing my sincere thanks to Professor N. T. Wright for his stimulating and substantive work over the years in the fields of biblical and theological scholarship. I also appreciate his ability to communicate the results of his research in such a lucid fashion, whether to an audience of academics or to the general populace, as is evident in the remarkable range of his publications. This is a gift—to be acknowledged and duly celebrated—that not many in the scholarly guild possess.

The first of Wright's books I read was *Jesus and the Victory of God*. This was some years ago, but one part of the book that I remember giving me pause was the beginning of chapter four, titled "Prodigals and Paradigms." Wright quotes the text of the so-called parable of the prodigal son (Lk 15:11-32), and in the ensuing discussion regarding what he considers to be the significance of that parable, he says the following:

> Years of scholarship have produced many commentaries on Luke, and many books on the parables. But none that I have been able to consult has noted the feature which seems to me most striking and obvious. Consider: here is a son who goes off in disgrace into a far country and then comes back, only to find the welcome challenged by another son who has stayed

put. The overtones are so strong that we surely cannot ignore them. This is the story of Israel, in particular of exile and restoration. It corresponds more or less exactly to the narrative grammar which underlies the exilic prophets, and the books of Ezra and Nehemiah, and a good deal of subsequent Jewish literature, and which must therefore be seen as formative for second-Temple Judaism. The exodus itself is the ultimate backdrop: Israel goes off into a pagan country, becomes a slave, and then is brought back to her own land. But exile and restoration is the main theme. This is what the parable is about.

Exile and restoration: this is the central drama that Israel believed herself to be acting out. And the story of the prodigal says, quite simply: this hope is now being fulfilled—but it does not look like what was expected. Israel went into exile because of her own folly and disobedience, and is now returning simply because of the fantastically generous, indeed prodigal, love of her god. But this is a highly subversive retelling. The real return from exile, including the real resurrection from the dead, is taking place, in an extremely paradoxical fashion, in Jesus' own ministry. Those who grumble at what is happening are cast in the role of the Jews who did not go into exile, and who opposed the returning people. They are, in effect, virtually Samaritans. The true Israel is coming to its senses, and returning to its father, as Jeremiah had foretold; and those who oppose this great movement of divine love and grace are defining themselves as outside the true family. . . . Israel's history is turning its long-awaited corner; this is happening within the ministry of Jesus himself; and those who oppose it are the enemies of the true people of god.[1]

As I recall, my reaction to this reading of the parable was mixed. On the one hand, I was intrigued by Wright's interpretation of it—one that is, to borrow his terminology, somewhat subversive. On the other hand, I was not entirely convinced by it and wondered whether he was not reading into the parable a meaning that was not inherent in it. Since then, as I have thought about the theme of exile and a related one, exodus, I have, however, come to appreciate their importance for the shaping of the canon and of biblical theology.

[1]N. T. Wright, *Jesus and the Victory of God*, Christian Origins and the Question of God 2 (Minneapolis: Fortress, 1996), 126-27.

EXILE TERMINOLOGY IN THE NEW TESTAMENT

A variety of terms in the New Testament that connote spending time away from home or living somewhere as an alien could be mentioned in this connection: παροικέω (*paroikeō*; reside as a foreigner/stranger), παροικία (*paroikia*; residing as a foreigner/stranger), πάροικος (*paroikos*; foreigner, stranger); παρεπίδημος (*parepidēmos*; sojourner); ξένος (*xenos*; stranger). My focus here, however, is on clusters of interrelated terms in this corpus that have to do with various senses of captivity, deportation, and exile.

A. αἰχμαλωσία (*aichmalōsia*), αἰχμαλωτεύω (*aichmalōteuō*), αἰχμαλωτίζω (*aichmalōtizō*), αἰχμάλωτος (*aichmalōtos*).

> The Spirit of the Lord is upon me,
>> because he has anointed me
>>> to bring good news to the poor.
> He has sent me to proclaim release to the captives (αἰχμαλώτοις
>> *aichmalōtois*)
> and recovery of sight to the blind,
>> to let the oppressed go free. (Lk 4:18)

They will fall by the edge of the sword and be taken away as captives (αἰχμαλωτισθήσονται *aichmalōtisthēsontai*) among all nations; and Jerusalem will be trampled on by the Gentiles, until the times of the Gentiles are fulfilled. (Lk 21:24)

But I see in my members another law at war with the law of my mind, making me captive (αἰχμαλωτίζοντα *aichmalōtizonta*) to the law of sin that dwells in my members. (Rom 7:23)

We take every thought captive (αἰχμαλωτίζοντες *aichmalōtizontes*) to obey Christ. (2 Cor 10:5)

Therefore it is said,
> "When he ascended on high he made captivity itself a captive
>> (ἠχμαλώτευσεν αἰχμαλωσίαν, *ēchmalōteusen aichmalōsian*);
> he gave gifts to his people." (Eph 4:8)

For among them are those who make their way into households and captivate (αἰχμαλωτίζοντες *aichmalōtizontes*) silly women, overwhelmed by their sins and swayed by all kinds of desires. (2 Tim 3:6)

If someone is to be taken captive (αἰχμαλωσίαν *aichmalōsian*),

　　into captivity (αἰχμαλωσίαν *aichmalōsian*) that one goes;

if someone is killed with the sword,

　　with the sword that one [the killer] must be killed.

Here is a call for the endurance and faith of the saints. (Rev 13:10)[2]

B. μετοικεσία (*metoikesia*), μετοικίζω (*metoikizō*).

At the time of the deportation (μετοικεσίας *metoikesias*) to Babylon. (Mt 1:11)

And after the deportation (μετοικεσίαν *metoikesian*) to Babylon. (Mt 1:12)

And from David to the deportation (μετοικεσίας *metoikesias*) to Babylon, fourteen generations; and from the deportation (μετοικεσίας *metoikesias*) to Babylon to the Messiah, fourteen generations. (Mt 1:17)

After his father died, God had him move (μετῴκισεν *metōkisen*) from there to this country in which you are now living. (Acts 7:4)

You took along the tent of Moloch,

　　and the star of your god Rephan,

　　　　the images that you made to worship;

so I will remove (μετοικιῶ *metoikiō*) you beyond Babylon. (Acts 7:43)

C. διασπείρω (*diaspeirō*), διασπορά (*diaspora*).

Where does this man intend to go that we will not find him? Does he intend to go to the Dispersion (διασποράν *diasporan*) among the Greeks and teach the Greeks? (Jn 7:35)

All except the apostles were scattered (διεσπάρησαν *diesparēsan*) throughout the countryside of Judea and Samaria. (Acts 8:1)

Now those who were scattered (διασπαρέντες *diasparentes*) went from place to place, proclaiming the word. (Acts 8:4)

Now those who were scattered (διασπαρέντες *diasparentes*) because of the persecution that took place over Stephen traveled as far as Phoenicia, Cyprus, and Antioch. (Acts 11:19)

James, a servant of God and of the Lord Jesus Christ,

　　To the twelve tribes in the Dispersion (διασπορᾷ *diaspora*): Greetings. (Jas 1:1)

---

[2]This is my translation, reflecting the Greek text more closely than does the NRSV, which unless otherwise stated is reproduced in this chapter.

Peter, an apostle of Jesus Christ,
To the exiles of the Dispersion (διασπορᾶς *diasporas*). (1 Pet 1:1)

A number of observations may be made regarding the usage of these terms in the preceding contexts. First, several of the preceding passages contain quotations from, or paraphrases of, the Jewish Scriptures: Luke 4:18 is a composite of parts of Isaiah 61:1; 58:6; Ephesians 4:8 contains an adapted version of Psalm 67(68):19(18);[3] Revelation 13:10 consists of modified excerpts of Jeremiah 15:2; and Acts 7:43 cites a slightly divergent form of Amos 5:26-27 in which the mention of the deportation of people beyond Damascus has been extended to beyond Babylon. Second, the featured terms in these texts are employed in a variety of senses in the New Testament. On the one hand, passages such as Matthew 1:11, 12, 17; Luke 21:24; Acts 7:43; and Revelation 13:10 refer to situations of literal captivity at the hands of imperialist forces, and texts such as John 7:35; Acts 11:19; James 1:1; and 1 Peter 1:1 make mention of what was known as the Diaspora—namely, regions in the Greco-Roman empire outside Palestine where Jewish people lived. On the other hand, the captivity language of Romans 7:23; 2 Timothy 3:6; and 2 Corinthians 10:5 is metaphorical and theological in nature, with the first two passages addressing the issue of bondage in sin and the third the matter of disciplining oneself (taking "every thought captive") in obedience to Christ. Similarly, references to the scattering (διασπείρω *diaspeirō*) of Christians from Jerusalem during the persecution that broke out following the martyrdom of Stephen (Acts 8:1, 4) are part of the narrative about the growth of the fledgling church to include non-Jews (Samaritans, the Ethiopian eunuch)—a narrative that is set, however, within the region known as Palestine and thus technically not in the Diaspora as it is traditionally understood (Acts 8:5-40). Third, some kind of captivity or exilic state appears to be the reality at the time in which these words are written in the first century (Lk 4:16-21; 21:20-24; Rom 7:21-24). Indeed, that sense of exile or diaspora is evidently regarded to persist even after Jesus' earthly ministry (Jas 1:1; 1 Pet 1:1), which is supposed to have effected a release from captivity.

---

[3]In Psalms, verse numbering in the Septuagint and the Hebrew Bible is often different. In this case, the Septuagint numbering is 67:19(18) (depending on whether or not one gives the inscription the number 1), and the Hebrew numbering is 68:19.

Exile Terminology in the Septuagint

The three clusters of Greek terms that are identified in the New Testament passages cited above are well represented in the Septuagint version of the Jewish Scriptures, which embraces both the so-called Old Testament and the Apocrypha. These terms serve as the counterparts to a range of Hebrew and Aramaic terms in the Masoretic Text, which is usually, but not always, equivalent to the source text for the relevant Septuagint translators.[4] As will be argued below, the terms chosen by these translators in the rendering of their Semitic exemplars appear, in at least some cases, to reflect their sense of living in a state of continuing exile.

A.1. αἰχμαλωσία (*aichmalōsia*; 124x).[5] גְּאֻלָּה (*ge'ullah*; redemption), גּוֹלָה (*golah*; exile), גָּלָה (*galah*; go into exile), גָּלוּ Aramaic (*galu*; exile), גָּלוּת (*galuth*; exile, exiles), מִשְׁכָּן (*mishkan*; dwelling), שָׂב Aramaic (*sav*; elder), שְׁבָאִים (*sheva'im*; Sabeans), שְׁבוּת (*shevuth*; fortunes, captivity)[6]; שְׁבִי (*shevi*; captivity, captives), שִׁבְיָה (*shivyah*; captivity, captives), שֶׁבֶר / שֵׁבֶר (*shever*; breaking, destruction), שׁוּב (*shuv*; return, repent), שִׁיבָה (*shivah*; restoration).

---

[4]Another sizable cluster of terms that falls within the same semantic domain (captivity, deportation, exile) is found in the Septuagint but does not occur in the New Testament, though it can be considered to provide background for the theme of exile as it is developed in the Jewish and Christian canons: ἀποικίζω *apoikizō* (גָּלָא, גָּלָה, גְּ *gela', gelah* Aramaic *haphel*, גָּלוּת *galuth*, שָׁבָה *shavah*), ἀποικεσία *apoikesia* (וֹלָה *golah*, גָּל *gal*, גָּלוּ *galu* Aramaic, גָּלוּת *galuth*), ἀποικία *apoikia* (גּוֹלָה)% *golah*, גָּלָה *galah*, גָּלוּת *galuth*, שְׁבוּת *shevuth*), ἀποικισμός *apoikismos* (גּוֹלָה *golah*, שְׁבִי *shevi*).

[5]Counterparts in the MT: גְּאֻלָּה *ge'ullah*: Ezek 11:15; גּוֹלָה *golah*: Amos 1:15; Zech 6:10; 14:2; Ezek 1:1; 3:11, 15; 11:24, 25; 12:3, 4, 7; 25:3; גָּלָה *galah*: Jer 1:3; גָּלוּ *galu* (Aramaic): Dan 2:25; גָּלוּת *galuth*: Amos 1:6, 9; Is 45:13; Ezek 1:2; 33:21; 40:1; מִשְׁכָּן *mishkan*: Jer 37(30):18; שָׂב *sav* (Aramaic): Ezra 5:5; שְׁבָאִים *sheva'im*: Joel 4(3):8; שְׁבוּת *shevuth*: Ps 13(14):7; 52(53):7; 84(85):2(1); 125(126):4; Hos 6:11; Amos 9:14; Joel 4(3):1; Zeph 2:7; 3:20; Jer 25:19(49:39); Jer 38(31):23; Lam 2:14; Ezek 29:14; 39:25; שְׁבִי *shevi*: Num 21:1; 31:12, 19, 26; Deut 21:13; 28:41; Judg 5:12; 2 Chron 6:37; 28:17; 29:9; Ezra 2:1; 3:8; 8:35; 9:7; Neh 1:2, 3; 7:6; 8:17; Ps 67(68):19(18); 77(78):61; Amos 4:10; 9:4; Hab 1:9; Is 20:4; Jer 15:2 (2x); 20:6; 22:22; 26(46):27; Lam 1:5, 18; Ezek 12:11; 30:17; Dan 11:8, 33; שִׁבְיָה *shivyah*: Deut 32:42; 2 Chron 28:5, 11, 13, 14, 15; Neh 3:36; שֶׁבֶר / שֵׁבֶר *shever*: Ezek 32:9; שׁוּב *shuv*: Is 1:27; Jer 38(31):19; שִׁיבָה *shivah*: Ps 125(126):1; no MT counterpart: 2 Kings 24:14; 1 Esdr 2:11; 5:7, 54, 64; 6:5, 8, 27; 7:6, 10, 11, 12, 13; 8:63, 74; 9:3, 4, 15; Esther 11:4(A.3); Jdt 2:9; 4:3; 8:22; 9:4; Tob 3:4, 15; 13:8; 14:5; 1 Macc 9:70, 72; 14:7; 2 Macc 8:10, 36; Ps 95(96):1; Pss. Sol. 2:6; Bar 4:10, 14, 24; Lam 2:21; Dan 5:10; 8:11.

[6]Lexicographers debate as to whether the noun שְׁבוּת *shevuth* / שְׁבִית *shevith* derives from שׁוּב (*shuv*) "turn back, return" or שָׁבָה (*shavah*) "take captive." In *HALOT*, the expression שְׁבוּת שׁוּב (*shuv shevuth*) is translated literally as "to turn a turning" and more idiomatically as "to restore the situation which prevailed earlier"—i.e., restore the fortunes of—because it is concluded that the noun is derived from שׁוּב (*shuv*). In BDB, the conclusion is that the noun is derived from שָׁבָה (*shavah*) and the above expression is rendered "restore the captivity of." As the editors of *HALOT* correctly point out, however, the translations in the versions (Septuagint, Vulgate, Targum, Peshitta) are based on the assumption that the noun is cognate to שָׁבָה (*shavah*).

A.2. αἰχμαλωτεύω (*aichmalōteuō*; 39x).[7] גָּלָה (*galah*; go into exile), לָקַח (*laqakh*; take), שְׁבָא (*sheva'*; Sabeans), שָׁבָה (*shavah*; take captive), שְׁבִי (*shevi*; captivity, captives).

A.3. αἰχμαλωτίζω (*aichmalōtizō*; 18x).[8] גָּלָה (*galah*; go into exile), שָׁבָה (*shavah*; take captive).

A.4. αἰχμάλωτος (*aichmalōtos*; 24x).[9] גּוֹלָה (*golah*; exile), גָּלָה (*galah*; go into exile), שֵׂיבָה (*sevah*; gray-/white-haired), שָׁבָה (*shavah*; take captive), שְׁבִי (*shevi*; captivity, captives), שָׁבִי (*shavi*; captive), שְׁבִית (*shevith*; captivity, captives), שׁוֹלָל (*sholal*; barefoot, stripped).

B.1. μετοικεσία (*metoikesia*; 8x).[10] גָּלָה (*galah*; go into exile), גּוֹלָה (*golah*; exile), גָּלוּת (*galuth*; exile, exiles).

B.2. μετοικίζω (*metoikizō*; 10x).[11] גָּלָה (*galah*; go into exile), גָּרַשׁ (*garash*; drive out).

C.1. διασπείρω (*diaspeirō*; 65x).[12] אֱוִיל (*'evil*; fool), זָרָה (*zarah*; scatter, winnow), נָדַח (*nadakh*; be scattered/banished), נָכָה (*nakhah*; smite), נָפַץ (*napats*; disperse), פָּאָה (*pa'ah*; cut in pieces), פּוּץ (*puts*; spread, disperse), פָּזַר (*pazar*; scatter), פָּרַד (*parad*; separate), פְּרָזִי (*perazi*; village dweller), פָּרַשׂ (*paras*; scatter), רִיק (*riq*; make/leave empty), שָׁגָה (*shagah*; go astray).

---

[7]Counterparts in the MT: גָּלָה *galah*: Esther 2:6; Amos 1:5, 6; 5:5 (2x); Mic 1:16; Ezek 12:3; 39:23; לָקַח *laqakh*: Job 1:15, 17; שְׁבָא *sheva'*: Job 1:15; שָׁבָה *shavah*: Gen 14:14; 34:29; Num 24:22; 1 Sam 30:2, 3, 5; 1 Kings 8:50; 2 Kings 5:2; 6:22; 1 Chron 5:21; 2 Chron 6:36 (2x); 28:5, 11; Ps 67(68):19(18); 136(137):3; Obad 11; Is 14:2; Jer 27(50):33; Ezek 6:9; שְׁבִי *shevi*: 2 Chron 6:38; Is 49:24, 25; no MT counterpart: 1 Esd 6:15; Esther 11:4(A.3); Jdt 5:18; Tob 1:2; 1 Macc 9:72.

[8]Counterparts in the MT: גָּלָה *galah*: 2 Kings 24:14; 2 Chron 28:8; שָׁבָה *shavah*: Judg 5:12; 1 Kings 8:46 (2x); 2 Chron 28:17; 30:9; Ps 105(106):46; no MT counterpart: Jdt 16:9; Tob 1:10; 14:15; 1 Macc 1:32; 5:13; 8:10; 10:33; 15:40; Ps 70(71):1; Lam 1:1.

[9]Counterparts in the MT: גּוֹלָה *golah*: Ezek 12:4; גָּלָה *galah*: Esther 2:6; Amos 6:7; 7:11, 17; Is 5:13; 23:1; שֵׂיבָה *sevah*: Job 41:24; שָׁבָה *shavah*: Ex 22:9; Is 14:2; 61:1; שְׁבִי *shevi*: Nahum 3:10; Is 46:2; Ezek 30:18; שָׁבִי *shavi*: Is 52:2; שְׁבִית *shevith*: Num 21:29; שׁוֹלָל *sholal*: Job 12:17, 19; no MT counterpart: Ex 22:13; Tob 7:3; 13:12; 1 Macc 2:9; Ep Jer Prol (Bar 6:1), 1(2).

[10]Counterparts in the MT: גָּלָה *galah*: Judg 18:30; גּוֹלָה *golah*: 2 Kings 24:16; 1 Chron 5:22; Nahum 3:10; Ezek 12:11; גָּלוּת *galuth*: Obad 20 (2x).

[11]Counterparts in the MT: גָּלָה *galah*: 1 Chron 5:6, 26; 8:6; Hos 10:5; Amos 5:27; Jer 20:4; 22:12; Lam 1:3; גָּרַשׁ *garash*: Judg 2:3; no MT counterpart: 1 Esdr 5:7.

[12]Counterparts in the MT: אֱוִיל *'evil*: Is 35:8; זָרָה *zarah*: Lev 26:33; Ps 43:12(11)(44:12[11]); Jer 15:7; 25:16(36)(49:36); Ezek 12:14, 15; 20:23; 22:15; נָדַח *nadakh*: Is 56:8; Jer 30:21(16[27])(49:5); 39(32):37; נָכָה *nakhah*: Ezek 32:15; נָפַץ *napats*: Gen 9:19; 1 Sam 13:11; Is 33:3; פָּאָה *pa'ah*: Deut 32:26; פּוּץ *puts*: Gen 10:18; 11:4, 8, 9; 49:7; Ex 5:12; Deut 4:27; 28:64; 1 Sam 11:11; 13:8; 14:34; 2 Sam 18:8; 20:22; 1 Kings 22:17; 2 Kings 25:5; 2 Chron 18:16; Is 11:12; 24:1; 41:16; Jer 13:24; 18:17; 47(40):15; 52:8; Ezek 11:17; 29:12; 30:23, 26; 34:5, 6, 12; 36:19; פָּזַר *pazar*: Esther 3:8; Joel 4(3):2; פָּרַד *parad*: Gen 10:32; Deut 32:8; פְּרָזִי *perazi*: Esther 9:19; פָּרַשׂ *paras*: Ezek 17:21; רִיק *riq*: Is 32:6; שָׁגָה *shagah*: Ezek 34:6; no MT counterpart: 1 Sam 14:23; 1 Kings 12:24u; Jdt 5:19; Tob 13:3; 1 Macc 11:47; Bar 2:4, 13, 29; 3:8.

C.2. διασπορά (*diaspora*; 12x).[13] דְּרָאוֹן (*derảon*; abhorrence), זְוָעָה (*zeva'ah*; trembling, terror), זַעֲוָה (*za'avah*; trembling, terror), מִזְרֶה (*mizreh*; winnowing fork), נָדַח (*nadakh*; be scattered/banished), נָצַר (*natsar*; spare, preserve).

What becomes immediately evident when perusing the data from the Septuagint is that this terminology is to be found in all parts of the corpus, and that various Greek translators have engaged in semantic leveling in employing a few clusters of cognate forms to render a broader spectrum of Hebrew and Aramaic terms. This is true particularly of the αἰχμαλ- (*aichmal-*) and διασπ- (*diasp-*) groups. The μετοικ- (*metoik-*) group is, apart from one instance of גָּרַשׁ (*garash*; drive out), employed to translate primarily a single Semitic root with cognates, גָּלָה (*galah*; go into exile).

While in many cases there is semantic overlap between the Greek terms and their Semitic counterparts, in some instances that is not the case:

αἰχμαλωσία (*aichmalōsia*)—גְּאֻלָּה (*ge'ullah*; redemption) (Ezek 11:15), מִשְׁכָּן (*mishkan*; dwelling) (Jer 37[30]:18), שָׂב Aramaic (*sav*; elder) (Ezra 5:5), שְׁבָאִים (*sheva'im*; Sabeans) (Joel 4[3]:8), שֶׁבֶר / שֵׁבֶר (*shever*; breaking, destruction) (Ezek 32:9), שׁוּב (*shuv*; return, repent) (Is 1:27; Jer 38[31]:19).

αἰχμαλωτεύω (*aichmalōteuō*)—לָקַח (*laqakh*; take) (Job 1:15, 17), שְׁבָא (*sheva*'; Sabeans) (Job 1:15).

αἰχμάλωτος (*aichmalōtos*)—שֵׂיבָה (*sevah*; gray-/white-haired) (Job 41:24), שׁוֹלָל (*sholal*; barefoot, stripped) (Job 12:17, 19).

διασπείρω (*diaspeirō*)—אֱוִיל (*'evil*; fool) (Is 35:8), זָרָה (*zarah*; winnow) (Jer 15:7), נָכָה (*nakhah*; strike) (Ezek 32:15), פָּאָה (*pa'ah*; cut in pieces) (Deut 32:26), פְּרָזִי (*perazi*; village dweller) (Esther 9:19), ריק hiphil (*riq*; make/leave empty) (Is 32:6), שָׁגָה (*shagah*; go astray) (Ezek 34:6).

διασπορά (*diaspora*)—דְּרָאוֹן (*dera'on*; abhorrence) (Dan 12:2), זְוָעָה (*zeva'ah*; trembling, terror) (Jer 41[34]:17), זַעֲוָה (*za'avah*; trembling, terror) (Deut 28:25), מִזְרֶה (*mizreh*; winnowing fork) (Jer 15:7), נָצַר (*natsar*; spare, preserve) (Is 49:6).

---

[13]Counterparts in the MT: דְּרָאוֹן *dera'on*: Dan 12:2; זְוָעָה *zeva'ah*: Jer 41(34):17; זַעֲוָה *za'avah*: Deut 28:25; מִזְרֶה *mizreh*: Jer 15:7; נָדַח *nadakh*: Deut 30:4; Neh 1:9; Ps 146(147):2; נָצַר *natsar*: Is 49:6; no MT counterpart: Jdt 5:19; 2 Macc 1:27; Pss Sol 8:28; 9:2.

In some of the preceding examples, it would appear that the Septuagint translators either worked from a source text that differed from the Masoretic Text, or simply construed the same consonantal text differently than the Masoretes did. In these contexts, a translator would have intended to function as an *interpres* (a literal translator) rather than as an *expositor* (an interpretative translator).[14] This is likely the case in situations in which Semitic terms denoting exile or captivity are similar or identical to other words.

Ezekiel 11:15. גְּאֻלָּה (*ge'ullah*; redemption)—גָּלוּת (*galuth*; exile, exiles).

> NETS: Son of man, your brothers and the men of your captivity (τῆς αἰχμαλωσίας σου *tēs aichmalōsias sou* // גָּלוּתֶךָ *galuthekha*) and the entire house of Israel have been finished off . . .

> NRSV: Mortal, your kinsfolk, your own kin, your fellow exiles (גָּלוּתֶךָ *galuthekha*—גָּאֻלָּתֶךָ *ge'ullathekha*),[15] the whole house of Israel, all of them . . .

Jeremiah 15:7. מִזְרֶה (*mizreh*; winnowing fork) / זָרָה (*zarah*; winnow)—מזרה (*mzrh*; dispersion) / זָרָה (*zarah*; disperse).

> NETS: And I will disperse them (καὶ διασπερῶ αὐτούς *kai diasperō autous* // וְאֶזְרֵם *ve'ezrem*) in a dispersion (ἐν διασπορᾷ *en diaspora* // בְּמזרה *bemzrh*)[16]

---

[14]This is a distinction made in the preface to the Latin translator's version of the writings of Dionysius the Areopagite (Sebastian Brock, "To Revise or Not to Revise: Attitudes to Jewish Biblical Translation," in *Septuagint, Scrolls and Cognate Writings: Papers Presented to the International Symposium on the Septuagint and Its Relations to the Dead Sea Scrolls and Other Writings (Manchester 1990)*, ed. George J. Brooke and Barnabas Lindars, SBLSCS 33 [Atlanta: Scholars Press, 1992], 311-12).

[15]The NRSV adopts the Septuagint reading, and in footnote renders גָּאֻלָּתֶךָ (*ge'ullathekha*) as "people of your kindred."

[16]In this case, the translator has quite plausibly interpreted the cognate pair זָרָה (*zarah*)/מִזְרֶה (*mizreh*)—which has to do with the action of scattering grain in the wind by means of a winnowing implement as a metaphor for Yahweh's response to the rejection of him by the inhabitants of Jerusalem—in terms of sending the people into exile (see Jer 15:5-9). The consonantal texts of the translator's source text and the MT would have been the same. In both cases, the same verbal root זרה (*zrh*)—denoting "scatter, disperse, winnow" (*HALOT*, BDB)—and a derivative cognate noun מזרה (*mzrh*) are involved. The Greek phrase καὶ διασπερῶ αὐτούς (*kai diasperō autous*) would, however, be equivalent to וְאֶזְרֵם (*ve'ezrem*; vav conjunction + qal imperfect + pronominal suffix) understood as "And I will disperse them," rather than to וָאֶזְרֵם (*va'ezrem*; vav consecutive + qal preterite + pronominal suffix) meaning "I have winnowed them." Likewise, διασπορά (*diaspora*) seems to have been the result of the translator's construal of מזרה (*mzrh*) as semantically cognate to זָרָה (*zarah*) in the sense of "scatter" rather than that of "winnow," which presupposes an otherwise unattested homograph of מִזְרֶה (*mizreh*) "winnowing fork" meaning "dispersion."

in the gates of my people.
I was made childless;
I destroyed my people because of their evils.

NRSV: I have winnowed them (וָאֶזְרֵם *ve'ezrem*) with a winnowing fork (בְּמִזְרֶה *bemizreh*)
in the gates of the land;
I have bereaved them, I have destroyed my people;
they did not turn from their ways.

Esther 9:19. פרז *prz* (הַפְּרוֹזִים[17] [*happerazim*; village dwellers])—פָּזַר *pazar* (הַפְּזוּרִים [*happezurim*; scattered ones]).

NETS: Therefore for this reason, the Judeans who are scattered (οἱ διεσπαρμένοι *hoi diesparmenoi* // הַפְּזוּרִים *happezurim*) in every land outside . . .

NRSV: Therefore the Jews of the villages (הַפְּרוֹזִים *happerazim*), who live in the open towns . . .

Ezra 5:5. שָׂבֵי (*save*; elders)—שְׁבִי (*shevi*; captivity).

NETS: And the eyes of God were upon the captivity (τὴν αἰχμαλωσίαν *tēn aichmalōsian* // שְׁבִי *shevi*) of Iouda

NRSV: But the eye of their God was upon the elders (שָׂבֵי *save*) of the Jews

Job 41:32. שֵׂיבָה (*sevah*; white-haired)—שִׁבְיָה (*shivyah*; captivity, captive) / שְׁבִיָּה (*sheviyyah*; captive).

NETS: . . . and Tartarus *of the deep as a captive* (αἰχμάλωτον *aichmalōton* // שִׁבְיָה *shivyah* / שְׁבִיָּה *sheviyyah*).

NRSV: . . . one would think the deep to be white-haired (שֵׂיבָה *sevah*).

Ezekiel 32:9. שֶׁבֶר / שֵׁבֶר (*shever*; destruction)—שְׁבִי (*shevi*; captivity).

NETS: And I will provoke the heart of many peoples,
when I take your captivity (αἰχμαλωσίαν σου *aichmalōsian sou* // שִׁבְיְךָ *shivyekha*) into the nations

---

[17]*Kethiv* הַפְּרוֹזִים *happerozim* (פְּרוֹזִים *perozim* is marked as a hypothetical form in *HALOT*); *qere* הַפְּרָזִים *happerazim*. The fact that פֻּזַר *pzr* (*pual* participle, rendered by a perfect medio-passive participle of διασπείρω *diaspeirō*) occurs in Esther 3:8 in reference to the Jews who have been "scattered" throughout the empire of King Ahasuerus/Artaxerxes may account for the Septuagint translator's choice of the perfect medio-passive participle of διασπείρω (*diaspeirō*) here in Esther 9:19.

NRSV: I will trouble the hearts of many peoples,

  as I carry you captive (שִׁבְיֶךָ *shivyekha* –שִׁבְרֵךְ *shivrekha*)[18] among
  the nations

Isaiah 1:27. שׁוּב (*shuv*; return, repent)— שְׁבִי (*shevi*; captivity).

NETS: For her [sc. Sion's] captivity (ἡ αἰχμαλωσία αὐτῆς *hē aichmalōsia
  autēs* // שִׁבְיָה *shivyah*) shall be saved
  with judgment and with mercy.

NRSV: Zion shall be redeemed by justice,
  and those in her who repent (שָׁבֶיהָ *shaveha*), by righteousness.

Jeremiah 38(31):19. שׁוּב (*shuv*; turn)— שְׁבִי (*shevi*; captivity).

NETS: Because later than my captivity (αἰχμαλωσίας μου *aichmalōsias mou*
  // שִׁבְיִי *shivyi*) I repented (μετενόησα *metenoēsa*) . . .

NRSV: For after I had turned away (שׁוּבִי *shuvi*) I repented (נִחַמְתִּי *nikhamti*) . . .

It is possible that contexts that speak about the Sabeans have also been transformed into statements about exile by virtue of the similarity of the orthography for the Hebrew terms for Sabean (שְׁבָא *sheva'* [Job 1:15], שְׁבָאִים *sheva'im* [Joel 4(3):8]), and captivity (שְׁבִי *shevi*, etc.).

In other cases, a given Septuagint translator seemingly went beyond the *interpres* mode to take up the task of an *expositor*.

Jeremiah 37(30):18. αἰχμαλωσία (*aichmalōsia*; captivity)—מִשְׁכָּן (*mishkan*; dwelling).

NETS: Thus did the Lord say:
  Behold, I am bringing back the exile (ἀποικίαν *apoikian*) of Iakob
  and will have mercy on his captivity (αἰχμαλωσίαν *aichmalōsian*) . . .

NRSV: Thus says the LORD:
  I am going to restore the fortunes (שְׁבוּת *shevuth*) of the tents of Jacob,
  and have compassion on his dwellings (מִשְׁכְּנֹתָיו *mishkenothav*) . . .

The counterpart in the Septuagint to the Masoretic Text's וּמִשְׁכְּנֹתָיו (*umishkenothav*) is καὶ αἰχμαλωσίαν αὐτοῦ (*kai aichmalōsian autou*), which is in fact semantically equivalent to וּשְׁבִתוֹ (*ushevitho*).[19] It seems

---

[18]The NRSV adopts the Septuagint reading, and in a footnote שִׁבְרֵךְ (*shivrekha*) is rendered as "your destruction."

[19]As noted by the *BHS* editor.

unlikely that the translator's version here can be attributed to the mis-reading of a source text that equals the Masoretic Text. One is therefore left to conclude either that the translator's Hebrew text differed from the Masoretic Text, or more likely that, in expositing a source text that was identical to it, he intentionally recast its message of restoration from exile and in the process made more explicit than did the original Hebrew author the state of banishment from which rescue was promised. This was achieved, not only by dropping the reference to Jacob's tents and by ren-dering שְׁבוּת (*shevuth*; fortunes, captivity) as ἀποικία (*apoikia*; settlement far from home, exile), but also by replacing the mention of dwellings מִשְׁכְּנֹת (*mishkenoth*) with one for captivity αἰχμαλωσία (*aichmalōsia*).

Job 1:15. αἰχμαλωτεύω (*aichmalōteuō*; take captive)—שְׁבָא (*sheva'*; Sa-beans) / לָקַח (*laqakh*; take).

> NETS: . . . and marauders (αἰχμαλωτεύοντες *aichmalōteuontes*) came and
> carried them off (ἠχμαλώτευσαν *ēchmalōteusan*) . . .

> NRSV: . . . and the Sabeans (שְׁבָא *sheva'*) fell on them and carried them off
> (וַתִּקָּחֵם *vattiqqakhem*) . . .

Job 1:17. αἰχμαλωτεύω (*aichmalōteuō*; take captive)—לָקַח (*laqakh*; take).

> NETS: Horsemen formed three columns against us, and they encircled the
> camels and carried them off (ἠχμαλώτευσαν *ēchmalōteusan*) . . .

> NRSV: The Chaldeans formed three columns, made a raid on the camels and
> carried them off (וַיִּקָּחוּם *vayyiqqakhum*) . . .

The choice of αἰχμαλωτεύω (*aichmalōteuō*) to render both שְׁבָא (*sheva'*) and לָקַח (*laqakh*) makes it explicit that the fate of Job's livestock was captivity.

Job 12:17. αἰχμάλωτος (*aichmalōtos*; captive)—שׁוֹלָל (*sholal*; barefoot, stripped).

> NETS: Leading counselors away captive (αἰχμαλώτους *aichmalōtous*) . . .

> NRSV: He leads counselors away stripped (שׁוֹלָל *sholal*) . . .

Job 12:19. αἰχμάλωτος (*aichmalōtos* captive)—שׁוֹלָל (*sholal*; barefoot, stripped).

> NETS: . . . sending away priests captive (αἰχμαλώτους *aichmalōtous*) . . .

> NRSV: He leads priests away stripped (שׁוֹלָל *sholal*) . . .

In both of the preceding verses, faced with the causative *hiphil* stem of הָלַךְ *halakh* "go" and an adjective שׁוֹלָל *sholal* "barefoot, stripped" that he may have associated with the verb שָׁלַל *shalal* and its cognate noun שָׁלָל *shalal* "spoil, plunder," the Septuagint translator chose to describe the fate of the leaders mentioned in these two verses in terms of captivity. That scenario could be what the original Hebrew author had in mind, but the Hebrew wording admits of other possibilities as well. It is noteworthy that the same *hiphil* verb is rendered by different Greek verbs: διάγω (*diagō*; Job 12: 17), which in the sense that it is used here suggests God's accompaniment of the counselors as he conducts them into captivity, and ἐξαποστέλλω (*exapostellō*; Job 12:19), which does not connote accompaniment.

Isaiah 35:8. διασπείρω (*diaspeirō*; scatter, disperse)—אֱוִיל ('*evil*; fool).

NETS: A pure way shall be there,
  and it shall be called a holy way;
  and the unclean shall not pass by there,
  nor shall be there an unclean way,
  but those who have been dispersed (διεσπαρμένοι *diesparmenoi*)
   shall walk on it,
  and they shall not go astray.

NRSV: A highway shall be there,
  and it shall be called the Holy Way;
  the unclean shall not travel on it,
   but it shall be for God's people;
  no traveler, not even fools (אֱוִילִים '*evilim*), shall go astray.

There is no obvious orthographic or etymological connection between אֱוִילִים '*evilim* "fools" and whatever might have been the Hebrew source text for οἱ διεσπαρμένοι *hoi diesparmenoi* "the dispersed," so one might speculate that the translator as *expositor* made a connection between the folly of Israel and the consequence of exile.

Ezekiel 32:15. διασπείρω (*diaspeirō*; scatter, disperse)—נָכָה (*nakhah*; strike).

NETS: When I give Egypt into destruction
  and the land is made desolate together with its plenty,
  when I disperse (διασπείρω *diaspeirō*) all the inhabitants in it,
  then they shall know that I am the Lord.

NRSV: When I make the land of Egypt desolate
    and when the land is stripped of all that fills it,
        when I strike down (בְּהַכּוֹתִי *behakkothi*) all who live in it,
            then they shall know that I am the LORD.

ὅταν διασπείρω (*hotan diaspeirō*) is equivalent to בְּזָרוֹתִי (*bezarothi*)[20] rather than to בְּהַכּוֹתִי (*behakhothi*). It appears that the translator deliberately chose in the second protasis of this temporal sentence to describe the fate of the inhabitants of Egypt in terms of dispersion rather than of smiting or striking down, in order to prevent the possibility of interpreting this as a fatal blow. The rationale might have been that only those who would survive the judgment that the Lord had in store for the Egyptians could be expected to acknowledge what is said in the accompanying apodosis: "They shall know that I am the LORD."

Deuteronomy 32:26. διασπείρω (*diaspeirō*; scatter, disperse)—פָּאָה (*pa'ah*; cut in pieces).

NETS: I said, I will disperse (διασπείρω *diaspeirō*) them;
    indeed, I will cause their memory to cease from among humans . . .

NRSV: I thought to scatter[21] (אַפְאֵיהֶם *'ap'ehem*) them
    and blot out the memory of them from humankind . . .

The words διασπερῶ αὐτούς (*diaspeirō autous*) seem to reflect the Hebrew אֲפִיצֵם (*'apitsem*),[22] namely a *hiphil* imperfect form of the root פּוּץ (*puts*) "disperse, be scattered" with a pronominal suffix, rather than a *hiphil* imperfect form of the *hapax legomenon* פָּאָה (*pa'ah*) "cut in pieces"[23] that appears in the Masoretic Text. Several options with regard to how the Septuagint translator's rendering came about might be suggested: (1) אֲפִיצֵם (*'apitsem*) was, in fact, in the translator's source text, which he then rendered faithfully; (2) אַפְאֵיהֶם (*'ap'ehem*) was originally in his source text, which he misread as אֲפִיצֵם (*'apitsem*) either due to physical damage of some sort in his *Vorlage* or because he confused similarly shaped letters; (3) אַפְאֵיהֶם (*'ap'ehem*) was in his source text, but he deliberately chose to exposit this rare word in terms of a

---

[20]As suggested by the *BHS* editor.
[21]The NRSV adopts the Septuagint reading, and in a footnote it is stated that the meaning of the Hebrew is uncertain.
[22]As suggested by the *BHS* editor.
[23]BDB.

description of dispersion, based on the context of the following line. The last option seems most likely.[24]

Ezekiel 34:6. διασπείρω (*diaspeirō*; scatter, disperse)—פּוּץ (*puts*; be scattered/dispersed).

> NETS: And my sheep were scattered (διεσπάρη *diesparē*) on every mountain and upon every lofty hill, and they were scattered (διεσπάρη *diesparē*) upon the surface of every land

> NRSV: My sheep were scattered (וַתְּפוּצֶינָה *vatteputsenah*), they wandered over all the mountains and on every high hill; my sheep were scattered (נָפֹצוּ *napotsu*) over all the face of the earth

It seems that the Septuagint translation here presupposes the linkage of the last word of Ezekiel 34:5 in the Masoretic Text (וַתְּפוּצֶינָה *vatteputsenah*) with Ezekiel 34:6 and the absence of an explicit counterpart for יִשְׁגּוּ (*yishgu*),[25] with the result that the subject of the former verb is צֹאנִי *tso'ni* "my sheep" (וַתְּפוּצֶינָה צֹאנִי *vattephutsenah tso'ni* = καὶ διεσπάρη τὰ πρόβατά μου *kai diesparē ta probata mou*). The same verbal equivalence occurs later in Ezekiel 34:6 (נָפֹצוּ *naphotsu* = διεσπάρη *diesparē*) where the Old Greek reflects the Masoretic Text.

Isaiah 49:6. διασπορά (*diaspora*; dispersion)—נָצַר (*natsar*; spare, preserve).

> NETS: And he said to me,
>> "It is a great thing for you to be called my servant
>>> so that you may set up the tribes of Iakob
>>> and turn back the dispersion (διασποράν *diasporan*) of Israel.

> NRSV: He says,
>> "It is too light a thing that you should be my servant
>>> to raise up the tribes of Jacob
>>> and to restore the survivors (וּנְצִירֵי *unetsre*) of Israel;"

In this second of the so-called Servant Songs in the book of Isaiah, the Septuagint translator evidently exposits the clause containing a derivative form of the verb נָצַר *natsar* "preserve, spare"—whether the *kethiv* נְצִירֵי (*netsire*; masculine plural construct adjective/substantive)[26] or the *qere* נְצוּרֵי

---

[24]John William Wevers, *Notes on the Greek Text of Deuteronomy*, ed. Bernard A. Taylor, SBLSCS 39 (Atlanta: Scholars Press, 1995), 524.

[25]שָׁגָה *shagah* means "stray, err" (*HALOT*, BDB).

[26]BDB, s.v. נציר= *ntsyr*.

(*netsure*; *qal* passive participle construct)[27]—in terms of the reversal of the exile event. The Masoretic Text, however, seems to focus on the return of the original exiles and/or their descendants.

Deuteronomy 28:25. διασπορά (*diaspora*; dispersion)—זַעֲוָה (*za'avah*; trembling, terror).

> NETS: And you shall be in dispersion (ἐν διασπορᾷ *en diaspora*) in all the kingdoms of the earth.

> NRSV: You shall become an object of horror (לְזַעֲוָה *leza'avah*) to all the kingdoms of the earth.

Jeremiah 41(34):17. διασπορά (*diaspora*; dispersion)—זְעָוָה (*ze'avah*; trembling, terror).

> NETS: Therefore, thus did the Lord say: You have not obeyed me by calling for a release, each pertaining to his fellow. Behold, I am calling for a release for you to the dagger and to death and to the famine, and I will give you as a dispersion (εἰς διασποράν *eis diasporan*) to all the kingdoms of the earth.

> NRSV: Therefore, thus says the LORD: You have not obeyed me by granting a release to your neighbors and friends; I am going to grant a release to you, says the LORD—a release to the sword, to pestilence, and to famine. I will make you a horror (לְזַעֲוָה *leza'avah*) to all the kingdoms of the earth.

The term זַעֲוָה (*za'avah*) in the preceding Deuteronomy passage is derived, via the transposition of the letters ו and ע, from זְוָעָה (*zeva'ah*),[28] which is the *kethiv* form in the Jeremiah passage. One wonders whether the choice of equivalent by these Greek translators is conditioned by a linkage to the verbal root זוּעַ (*zua'*), with its connotation of movement in the form of trembling or quaking,[29] and that kind of characterization of the state of those who are destined for exile (Deut 28:64-67; Jer 15:1-4). Whatever the case, this rendering seems expository in nature.

Isaiah 32:6. διασπείρω (*diaspeirō*; scatter, disperse)—רִיק *hiphil* (*riq*; make/leave empty).

---

[27]BDB, s.v. נָצַר *natsar*; HALOT, s.v. נצר *ntsr*.
[28]BDB, s.v. זְוָעָה *zeva'ah*.
[29]BDB, s.v. זוּעַ *zua'*.

NETS: For the fool will speak folly,
>> and his heart will devise vain things
> in order to accomplish lawless things
> and to speak error against the Lord,
>> in order to scatter (τοῦ διασπεῖραι *tou diaspeirai*) hungry souls
>> and to make empty the souls that thirst.

NRSV: For fools speak folly,
>> and their minds plot iniquity:
> to practice ungodliness,
>> to utter error concerning the LORD,
> to leave the craving of the hungry unsatisfied (לְהָרִיק *lehariq*),
>> and to deprive the thirsty of drink.

This appears to be an instance of the translator interpreting a Hebrew word—in this case, the *hiphil* form of רִיק *riq* "empty out, leave empty"[30]—in terms of a reference to the dispersion or scattering of those whose lives are characterized as profane/ungodly and who misrepresent Yahweh.

Daniel 12:2. διασπορά (*diaspora*; dispersion)—דְּרָאוֹן (*deraʾon*; abhorrence)

NETS: And many of those who sleep in the flat of the earth will arise, some to everlasting life but others to shame and others to dispersion (εἰς διασποράν *eis diasporan*) [and contempt] everlasting.

NRSV: Many of those who sleep in the dust of the earth shall awake, some to everlasting life, and some to shame and everlasting contempt (לְדִרְאוֹן *ledirʾon*).

The Septuagint translator's expository choice of διασπορά (*diaspora*) as the counterpart to the rare term דְּרָאוֹן *deraʾon* "abhorrence"[31] is a striking one, inasmuch as the subject being discussed is the destiny of some following their resurrection.

All things considered, then, the various translators of the Septuagint corpus made rather frequent use of terminology that is commonly associated with the idea of exile, even in situations in which that concept was not explicit in the underlying Hebrew source text, nor in which the context in fact pertained to one or another of Israel's national dispersions. Given that the translators of the Pentateuch and of at least parts of the rest of the Septuagint were likely living

---

[30]*HALOT.*
[31]*HALOT.* The only other place in which it is found in the Hebrew Bible is Is 66:24.

outside the Promised Land, long after the deportations of Israelites during the neo-Assyrian and neo-Babylonian periods and following other migrations of Jews to various parts of the Near East early in the Hellenistic era, the frequent reiteration of the themes of captivity and exile throughout this corpus is perhaps not too surprising. As Wright has pointed out, however, it was not just among the many Jews who lived outside their ancestral homeland that a feeling of dislocation persisted. Among their compatriots situated within the borders of the Promised Land were those who expressed a chronic sense of unsettledness within their own country and disillusionment with the state of their existence (Ezra 9:7-9, 15; Hag 1:1-11; 2:1-3; Mal 2:13, 17; 3:13-15). As clear an indication of this frame of mind as any is articulated in Ezra's prayer recorded in Nehemiah 9:36-37: "Here we are, slaves to this day—slaves in the land that you gave to our ancestors to enjoy its fruit and its good gifts. Its rich yield goes to the kings whom you have set over us because of our sins; they have power also over our bodies and over our livestock at their pleasure, and we are in great distress."[32]

The Hope of Restoration

The malaise that settled on those who, after the Babylonian exile, sought to rebuild their lives in the land that their forebears had occupied was engendered by a failure to experience what the prophets of old had anticipated in terms of a glorious future in a fully restored and optimally functioning covenant community (e.g., Is 2:1-4; 54:7-14; 65:17-25; Jer 33:4-26; Ezek 37:1-14; Hag 2:6-9). Thus even in the so-called postexilic period, the hope that continued to be expressed involved completion of the process of regathering those who had been scattered and establishing them in the life of God's kingdom on earth, predicated on the forgiveness of sins and the formation of a community characterized by true justice, equity, and acceptable worship of their covenant God. Among the assorted texts that articulate various components of this vision are the following:

> Gather (συνάγαγε *synagage*) all the tribes of Iakob,
>   and give them an inheritance, as from the beginning.
>   (Sir 36[33]:13, [36]:16)

---

[32]N. T. Wright, *The New Testament and the People of God*, Christian Origins and the Question of God 1 (Minneapolis: Fortress, 1992), 268-70; Wright, *Jesus and the Victory of God*, 271.

Gather together (συνάγαγε *synagage*) the dispersion of Israel (τὴν διασπορὰν Ισραηλ *tēn diasporan Israēl*) with pity and kindness, for your faithfulness is with us. (Pss Sol 8:28)

We therefore have hope (ἐλπίζομεν *elpizomen*) in God that he will soon have mercy on us and will gather (ἐπισυνάξει *episynaxei*) us from everywhere under heaven to his holy place, for he has rescued us from great evils and has cleansed the place. (2 Macc 2:18)

Seventy weeks are decreed for your people and your holy city: to finish the transgression, to put an end to sin, and to atone for iniquity, to bring in everlasting righteousness, to seal both vision and prophet, and to anoint a most holy place. (Dan 9:24)

But again God will have mercy on them, and God will bring them back into the land of Israel, and again they will build the house, but not like the first one, until the time when the time of the appointed times will be completed. Then after this they all will return from their captivity (ἐκ τῶν αἰχμαλωσιῶν *ek tōn aichmalōsiōn*), and they will build Ierousalem honorably. And the house of God will be built in it, just as the prophets of Israel said concerning it. . . . All the sons of Israel who are saved in those days, mindful of God in truth, will be gathered together. And they will go into Ierousalem and live forever in the land of Abraam with security, and it will be given over to them. And those who love God in truth will rejoice, but those who commit sin and injustice will vanish from all the earth. (Tob 14:5, 7)

When one reads various texts that talk about both the reasons for exile and what would be necessary for restoration from an exilic state, it becomes evident that Israel's sins constituted a significant factor that had to be addressed. As indicated in a number of the passages cited above, it was because of Israel's unfaithfulness to, and transgressions against, its covenant God that judgment came in the form of deportation from its homeland, and dealing with that matter would be key to bringing an end to the exile. Some passages make it clear that the forgiveness of Israel's sins was a function simply of God's initiative and grace (e.g., Ezek 36:22-32). In other texts, Israel's time spent in exile itself was counted as payment for its sins (e.g., Is 40:2). In still other ones, the suffering of a certain member or of some members of the covenant community was interpreted as having ransoming/atoning/propitiatory efficacy for the nation as a whole (e.g., Is 53:4-12).

A. ἱλαστήριον (*hilastērion*). With regard to this last perspective, there are certain striking parallels in texts pertaining to the Maccabean martyrs— the aged priest ἱερεύς (*hiereus*) and lawyer νομικός (*nomikos*), Eleazar (4 Macc 5:4), along with seven brothers and their elderly mother—who are portrayed as staying true to their ancestral faith in the face of unspeakable torture and ultimate death at the hands of the tyrant, Antiochus IV Epiphanes. But more than that, the author of this treatise that combines Jewish theology with Greek philosophy asserts that the martyrs' deaths had a profound significance for the nation as a whole:

> And through the blood of those pious people and the propitiatory (ἱλαστηρίου *hilastēriou*) of their death, divine Providence preserved Israel, though before it had been afflicted. (4 Macc 17:22)

For twenty of the twenty-eight occurrences of ἱλαστήριον (*hilastērion*) in the Septuagint—always translated "propitiatory" in NETS—it is the counterpart to כַּפֹּרֶת (*kapporeth*), rendered "mercy seat" in the NRSV, "propitiatory" in BDB.[33] As these contexts indicate, this was the golden cover that was placed on the ark and that was identified as the locus at which the Lord would make his appearance in a cloud (Lev 16:2), from above which the Lord would communicate to Moses his commands for the Israelites (Ex 25:20[21]-21[22]), and on which the high priest Aaron would sprinkle blood as part of atonement rituals (Lev 16:11-16).[34]

The Greek term ἱλαστήριον (*hilastērion*), which first occurs in the Septuagint, and its verbal cognate ἱλάσκομαι (*hilaskomai*), which is attested as early as the writings attributed to Homer, are often associated with the concept of appeasement/propitiation.[35] The NETS translation "propitiatory" in 4 Maccabees 17:22 reflects this association. What is debated, however, is

---

[33]Ex 25:16(17), 17(18), 18(19), 19(20) (2x), 20(21), 21(22); 31:7; 35:11(12); 38:5(37:6), 7(8), 8(9); Lev 16:2 (2x), 13, 1 4 (2x), 15 (2x); Num 7:89.

[34]In five other cases, ἱλαστήριον *hilastērion* is employed to translate עֲזָרָה *'azarah* "ledge" (of the altar and altar hearth) (Ex 43:14[3x], 17, 20), and once its Hebrew counterpart is כַּפְתּוֹר *kaptor* "capitals" (of the sanctuary) (Amos 9:1). In another place besides the passage in 4 Macc 17:22 cited above, there is no Hebrew equivalent (Ex 38:7[37:8]).

[35]LSJ, s.vv. ἱλάσκομαι *hilaskomai*, ἱλαστήριον *hilastērion*. See also Dirk Büchner, "Ἐξιλάσασθαι: Appeasing God in the Septuagint Pentateuch," *JBL* 129 (2010): 237-60.

the original wording of the phrase in which the term is found. In the Göttingen Septuagint originally edited by Alfred Rahlfs, the reading is τοῦ ἱλαστηρίου τοῦ θανάτου αὐτῶν (*tou hilastēriou tou thanatou autōn*),[36] whereas in the Cambridge Septuagint prepared by Henry Swete, the second τοῦ (*tou*) is lacking.[37] The former reading makes ἱλαστηρίου (*hilastēriou*) a noun ("the propitiatory of their death"), while the latter one makes it an attributive adjective ("their propitiatory death").[38]

As the one assigned to prepare the critical edition of this book for the Göttingen Septuaginta series, I have had occasion to examine the relevant manuscript evidence. The Göttingen text is attested by S *m-m2-62* 577, while the Cambridge text appears in A′ V L *q-ql-q2 m1* 46 52 340 668 690 741 771.[39] Although one could argue that it is easier to account for the originality of the longer reading than for the shorter one on the grounds that the latter could have arisen due to homoioteleuton on ου (*ou*) in the contiguous words ἱλαστηρίου τοῦ (*hilastēriou tou*), the diversity—not to mention the numerical superiority—of the manuscript evidence for the shorter reading would seem to point to its originality.[40] Furthermore, since ἱλαστήριον

---

[36]*Septuaginta: id est Vetus Testamentum graece iuxta LXX interpretes*, ed. Alfred Rahlfs, rev. and emended by Robert Hanhart (Stuttgart: Deutsche Bibelgesellschaft, 2006).

[37]*The Old Testament in Greek According to the Septuagint*, ed. Henry B. Swete (Cambridge: Cambridge University Press, 1909).

[38]David A. deSilva, *4 Maccabees: Introduction and Commentary on the Greek Text in Codex Sinaiticus*, Septuagint Commentary Series (Boston: Brill, 2006), 59, 250; H.-J. Klauck, *4 Makkabäerbuch*, JSHRZ 3.6 (Gütersloh: Gerd Mohn, 1989), 753.

[39]The manuscript groups for 4 Maccabees are the following:
Uncials: A S V
A′ = A-542 (11:5—fin libri)
L: 236 534
q: 74 120 370 452 731 3002
ql: 44 107 610
q2: 55 747
m: 316 317 322 325 391 397 446 457 467 472 473 586 591 592 594 595 596 597 607 617 639 640 656 677 682 683 686 699 713 714 778 782 789
m1: 455 585
m2: 587 738
m3 (init libri—11:4): 62 542 747[c/mg]
m groups 11:5—fin libri: *m m1 m2* 62 747[c/mg]
Codices mixti: 46 52 340 577 668 690 741 771

[40]The shorter reading is favored by Klauck (*4 Makkabäerbuch*, 753) and J. W. van Henten ("The Tradition-Historical Background of Romans 3.25: A Search for Pagan and Jewish Parallels," in *From Jesus to John: Essays on Jesus and New Testament Christology in Honor of Marinus de Jonge*, ed. M. C. De Boer, JSNTSup 84 [Sheffield: Sheffield Academic Press, 1993], 123).

(*hilastērion*) as a substantive occurs much more frequently in extant Greek literature than ἱλαστήριος (*hilastērios*) as an adjective, the latter would appear to be the *lectio difficilior* and therefore, on that count as well, the shorter reading is to be preferred.

The term ἱλαστήριον (*hilastērion*) occurs twice in the New Testament.

> Above it [the ark of the covenant] were the cherubim of glory overshadowing the mercy seat (ἱλαστήριον *hilastērion*). (Heb 9:5)

> They are now justified by his grace as a gift, through the redemption that is in Christ Jesus, whom God put forward as a sacrifice of atonement (ἱλαστήριον *hilastērion*) by his blood, effective through faith. He did this to show his righteousness, because in his divine forbearance he had passed over the sins previously committed. (Rom 3:24-25)

The translation of ἱλαστήριον (*hilastērion*) as "a sacrifice of atonement" in the Romans passage has been challenged by Daniel P. Bailey, who argues that the evidence from ancient sources outside the Bible shows that this term is used of "only concrete, inanimate referents"; it is "always a thing—never an idea or an action or an animal."[41] The NRSV rendering seems to represent an instance of theological considerations overriding lexicology. In this case, it presumably comes about as a result of the assumption that the mention of blood in the same context is what determines the meaning of ἱλαστήριον (*hilastērion*), whereas in fact it never signifies an animal victim, nor does it have to do with the act of sacrifice.[42] A footnote in the NRSV provides an alternative rendering of "a place of atonement," which, as in Wright's translation of Romans 3:24-25, lines up with the Pentateuchal uses of the term that connote a specific location.

> By God's grace they are freely declared to be in the right, to be members of the covenant, through the redemption which is found in the Messiah, Jesus. God put Jesus forth as the place of mercy (ἱλαστήριον *hilastērion*), through his faithfulness, by means of his blood. He did this to demonstrate his covenant justice through the passing over (in the divine forbearance) of sins committed beforehand.[43]

---

[41]Daniel P. Bailey, "Jesus as the Mercy Seat: The Semantics and Theology of Paul's Use of *Hilastērion* in Romans 3:25," *TynBul* 5, no. 1 (2000): 155.
[42]Ibid. 155-58.
[43]N. T. Wright, *Paul for Everyone. Romans: Part 1, Chapters 1–8* (Louisville, KY: Westminster John Knox, 2004), 51, 55.

If it is a particular place, or an object associated with that place, rather than an atoning sacrifice that is being referred to in the above-mentioned passages in the Pentateuch and the New Testament, the question remains as to whether what occurs at that place is appeasement, atonement, or the extension of mercy. In the final analysis, the answer may be that these terms represent different aspects of the same overarching reality since, as noted above, the process by which the covenant relationship between God and his people is restored is portrayed in different ways in various biblical and extrabiblical texts.[44]

B. ἀντίψυχον (*antipsychon*). Another term that the author of 4 Maccabees uses in his characterization of the significance of the Maccabean martyrs' suffering and ultimate deaths occurs only twice in the Septuagint but not at all in the New Testament. In 4 Maccabees 6:27-29, Eleazar makes the following appeal to God before he dies: "You know, O God, that though it is within my power to save myself, I die in fiery tortures for the sake of the law. Be merciful to your people, and be satisfied with our punishment on their behalf. Make my blood their purification, and take my life in exchange (ἀντίψυχον *antipsychon*) for theirs." Near the end of the book, in speaking about Eleazar and the others whom Antiochus IV Epiphanes so cruelly put to death, the author says the following:

> And these who have been divinely sanctified are honored not only with this honor, but also in that, thanks to them, our enemies did not prevail over our nation; the tyrant was punished, and the homeland was purified, since they became, as it were, a ransom (ἀντίψυχον *antipsychon*) for the sin of the nation. (4 Macc 17:20-21)

Attested only once in Greek literature prior to these occurrences in 4 Maccabees, ἀντίψυχος,-ον (*antipsychos, -on*) connotes the giving of something to spare a life, and thus a ransom. The terminology associated with giving up one's life for others as it pertains to the description of Jesus' self-sacrifice in the New Testament involves the verb λυτρόω (*lytroō*; 1 Pet 1:18) and the cognate nouns λύτρον (*lytron*; Mt 20:28; Mk 10:45) and ἀντίλυτρον

---

[44]David deSilva comments, "The effect of the propitiatory gift is . . . fundamentally the same as the sacrifice of atonement: on the basis of the martyrs' loyalty to God unto death, God's anger turns away from Israel, and God turns again to Israel with a favorable disposition so as to deliver her from her enemies" (*4 Maccabees: Introduction and Commentary*, 251).

(*antilytron*; 1 Tim 2:6). The concept is similar, however, to that which is expressed by means of ἀντίψυχον (*antipsychon*) in connection with the offering up of their lives for their nation by the Maccabean martyrs.

Wright's summary of the "strands of belief" that undergird the story of these martyrs as it is recounted in both 2 Maccabees and 4 Maccabees points out how those traditions are part of theological foundation of the story of Jesus, whose mission was to bring Israel's exile to an end as part of the divine plan that would culminate in covenant renewal and ultimately a new creation:

> First, the fate of the martyrs is bound up with the fate of the nation as a whole. Second, as a result, their suffering forms as it were the focal point of the suffering of the nation, continuing the theme of exile-as-the-punishment-for-sin which we find in the great prophetic writings such as Jeremiah, Ezekiel, Isaiah 40–55 and Daniel, but now giving it more precise focus. Third, this representative exilic suffering functions *redemptively*: not only will the martyrs themselves enjoy subsequent heavenly blessing and/or resurrection life, but their sufferings will have the effect of drawing on to themselves the sufferings of the nation as a whole, *so that the nation may somehow escape.*[45]

As he suggests, the body of tradition of which the Maccabean martyr story is a part provides "substantial clues as to the world of thought within which a prophet and would-be Messiah, in the first third of the first century, might find his own vocation being decisively shaped."[46]

CONCLUSION

The focus of this essay has been on some of the terminology in the Septuagint and the New Testament that is used in connection with the concepts of exile and the return from exile. I have shown that Septuagint translators employed terms that connote captivity and displacement even in some contexts in which their Hebrew/Aramaic source texts did not. There were undoubtedly various reasons for this, but one possibility to consider in explaining this phenomenon is that these translators were reflecting in their work their perception of themselves as living in a state

---

[45]Wright, *Jesus and the Victory of God*, 583.
[46]Ibid., 584.

of continuing exile. That sense of dislocation and unfulfilled expectations during the so-called postexilic era, in turn, gave rise to soul searching and reflection on what would need to occur in order for this situation to be remedied and the new order of things envisioned by the prophets to become a reality.

CHAPTER THREE

NOT ALL GLOOM AND DOOM

Positive Interpretations of Exile and Diaspora in the Hebrew Bible and Early Judaism

JÖRN KIEFER

THE GERMAN WORD FOR MISERY IS *ELEND*. Etymologically, it means "to be outside the homeland" and was understood in that way up until the beginning of modern times. This is evident, for example, in quite a lot of Lutheran chorales. Is there some connection between exile and misery? The very terminology we use to describe a matter often includes interpretation. In this case, with regard to the word *exile*, it would seem to have a negative connotation. As far as the evaluation of Israel's exile in the theological historiography is concerned, it did not simply remain a matter of a negative aftertaste but the development of robust prejudices and clichés that are no longer questioned since they belong to the basic lessons of some theological primer.

It is widely assumed that ancient Jews considered life outside Israel-Palestine to be inferior to life in the land of their ancestors. Most interpreters read the descriptions of exile in the Hebrew Bible primarily, if not exclusively, in terms of God's punishment of his people for their sins. As a result, life for the Jews in exile is often equated to life under God's wrath. Moreover, Jews in the "dispersion" are said to have considered themselves homeless, yearning to return to the land in order to reestablish preexilic ideals. In later times, as the evidence available to us shows the Diaspora Jews more fully embracing their life outside the land, interpreters have too easily dismissed that acceptance as assimilation to the pagan culture of the nations, assuming that the Diaspora Jews were so enamored with their new surroundings that they willingly abandoned their national inheritance.

But as we will see, ancient Jews who lived in exile and in the Diaspora did not view their situation in such simplistic ways. Rather, each of these assumptions grows out of the mistaken notion that exile is inherently negative and has always been viewed that way.

Where did this mistaken notion come from? Contemporary historical-critical theology is in many ways a product of the nineteenth century. In effect, we have unwittingly imposed certain modern political ideals onto the ancient Jewish texts. The ideal of a national state was particularly important for the nineteenth century. The idea was that a nation needs its own state, and that the life of an individual can only be fully validated in one's native country. Thus, in the categories of the nineteenth century, exile and diaspora could be nothing more than inferior forms of existence. However, if such judgments are exposed as prejudices that impose completely inappropriate criteria on the Old Testament, we are then able to turn our attention to a more useful question: How did the large number of Jews who lived outside their homeland during the biblical era understand their situation?

Several key Old Testament texts suggest that the Diaspora situation was accepted as a given condition even as early as the Babylonian exile. Jeremiah 29:7 reads, "And seek the welfare [*shalom*] of the city where I have sent you [into exile], and pray to YHWH on its behalf, for in its welfare [you will find] your welfare."[1] This verse obviously does not see the exile in Babylon as an entirely negative situation. Admittedly, scholars have given such verses a fair amount of attention, but the literature tends to leave the impression this is merely an exception and that the Bible more often describes the Babylonian exile as a punishment that would come to an end with the return to Jerusalem. I have demonstrated elsewhere that the attitude adopted in this verse is not a special case but is part of a broader trend.[2]

It is crucial that we do not confuse our own presuppositions about Israel's exile and diaspora with the self-understanding of the biblical authors. Of course, there is no way to be completely neutral, but we can attempt to be

---

[1] All translations of primary sources are my own.

[2] Jörn Kiefer, *Exil und Diaspora: Begrifflichkeit und Deutungen im antiken Judentum und in der hebräischen Bibel*, ABG 19 (Leipzig: Evangelische Verlagsanstalt, 2005).

aware of our own biases and aim to examine the evidence on its own terms. Just as Old Testament theology in the nineteenth century was influenced by the ideal of a national state, one might suspect that the positive approach to exile and diaspora presented here may similarly be a product of its time. Has the pendulum swung to the opposite extreme in an age of multicultural societies and globalization?

The best approach would be to evaluate the biblical statements in light of similar written sources from the same time period. However, such reference material is almost completely lacking from the Neo-Assyrian, Neo-Babylonian, and Persian periods. Fortunately, a plentiful corpus of material exists from the Hellenistic-Roman period that is filled with multifaceted conceptions of exile and diaspora. As a working hypothesis, we assume that conceptions from these periods might have been valid even in the preceding era (i.e., the biblical period), since there are no notable paradigm shifts between the Persian (539–332 BCE) and the Hellenistic period (from 332 BCE). We will thus reduce the historical gap by far more than we could ever afford by reading the texts through the lenses of nineteenth-century ideology.

For example, it can be demonstrated that Jews in Hellenistic Alexandria called themselves "Alexandrians" and had no intentions of immigrating to Israel-Palestine. In view of that fact, it is reasonable to ask whether similar trends may already have existed in the Old Testament. Indeed, if one reads biblical books such as Esther or Daniel 1–7 from this point of view, they do seem to contain parallel tendencies. Similarly, in the books of Ezekiel and Jeremiah there are many indications that the Israelite-Jewish faith was not limited by geopolitical boundaries.

We may also take into consideration the self-conception of Jewish expatriate communities around the Mediterranean. According to estimates, Jews constituted around 7 to 10 percent of the total population,[3] and they were described as "colonies" of the mother country Israel, as outposts of Judaism. Perhaps, then, it is conceivable that the Jewish exiles of the Old Testament were likewise capable of making a positive impact on their pagan environment. Once again, when read from this perspective, a universalistic

---

[3]See Willem Cornelis van Unnik, *Das Selbstverständnis der jüdischen Diaspora in der hellenistisch-römischen Zeit*, Arbeiten zur Geschichte des Antiken Judentums und des Urchristentums 17 (Leiden: Brill, 1993), 54.

aspect is discernible in many of the Old Testament texts that address the dispersion of God's people. In other words, due to the Diaspora Jewish faith becomes a matter for all humankind.

The vocabulary that the biblical texts use to describe exile and diaspora is equally instructive. The language of modern Bible versions has also been affected by the above-mentioned presupposition of a negative outlook on exile. For example, our Bible translations often talk about captives who are led away. However, the vast majority of passages actually refer to a deportation of people as the plunder of war (Hebrew root *shbh*). The status of these "captives" is not comparable to that of incarcerated criminals or even modern prisoners of war. In Old Testament times, "prisoners of war" always included civilians, who were considered valuable loot and treated accordingly. They were neither put into chains nor locked up but resettled for strategic and politico-economic reasons.[4]

Our Bible translations also render another common Old Testament term, Hebrew root *glh*, usually in the *hiphil*, with the phrase "leading away captive." However, the basic *qal* form of this verb can describe several distinct types of going away, including a flight or an emigration for economic purposes. In such cases, the departure into exile served as a life-saving means of escape (e.g., 2 Sam 15:19; Lam 1:3).

The Septuagint renders the Hebrew root *glh* with *apoikia* ("emigration" or "domicile far from home") or with *metoikia* ("cohabitation as foreigner") and the appropriate derivatives.[5] It would seem, then, that the Hellenistic Bible translators found in these passages quite positive connotations.[6] They described Israel's moving abroad either as the settlement of a colony (*apoikia*), the way Philo also did in his writings,[7] or they compared the situation of the Jews in the diaspora with the legally defined status of metics (*metoikoi*).[8]

---

[4]See Bustenay Oded, *Mass Deportations and Deportees in the Neo-Assyrian Empire* (Wiesbaden: Reichert, 1979).

[5]On these terms in the Septuagint, see also Robert Hiebert's contribution in the present volume.

[6]See Joseph Mélèze Modrzejewski, "How to Be a Jew in Hellenistic Egypt," in *Diasporas in Antiquity*, ed. Shaye J. D. Cohen and Ernest S. Frerichs, Brown Judaic Studies 288 (Atlanta: Scholars Press, 1993), 47-92 (68-70).

[7]See James M. Scott, "Exile and the Self-Understanding of Diaspora Jews in the Greco-Roman Period," in *Exile: Old Testament, Jewish, and Christian Conceptions*, ed. James M. Scott, JSJSup 56 (Leiden: Brill 1997), 173-218 (556-62); Kiefer, *Exil*, 404-7.

[8]E.g., Josephus, *J.W.* 2:479, 487. See Kiefer, *Exil*, 427-29.

It should be noted that there is no fixed term like *exile* in the Old Testament. Neither *golah* nor *galut*, both of which are nouns derived from the Hebrew verb *glh*, describe a situation or condition of exile. Rather, *golah* refers to a group of people who are either in exile or are about to leave for exile, and *galut* refers to the act of migration, for whatever reasons. Neither term implies any sort of valuation. Where our Bible translations render *golah* or *galut* with "exile" or "captivity," they introduce nuances that are not present in the original language.

Where the Old Testament refers to dispersion, that terminology especially tends to have positive overtones. To disperse something has to do with spreading. This progressing effect is already present in theological background of Genesis 9–11, but unfortunately it is often overlooked even there.[9]

The scholarly literature is incorrect when it speaks of "*the* exile," meaning specifically the Babylonian one. In fact, the Old Testament does not differentiate between exile and diaspora in terms of its vocabulary. Descriptions of Israelites and Judeans living outside the Palestinian heartland are very familiar and not at all confined to the Babylonian exile community. Rather, the Old Testament tells of numerous distinct emigration movements at various times and under differing circumstances. The possibility that there were already outposts abroad at the time of the monarchy, which functioned to represent the interests of the king, cannot be ruled out (cf. 1 Kings 20:34). Minorities of Israelites or Judeans very likely already lived in the areas between the Euphrates and the "Wadi of Egypt," which temporarily belonged to Israel and Judah at various times (cf. Is 27:12-13). Economic refugees apparently sometimes settled in the neighboring regions in order to survive famine or other hardships (cf. Ruth 1:1). Particularly in times of war, refugees from Israel and Judah emigrated to Moab, Ammon, and Edom (Jer 40:11-12; cf. Is 16:4).

Long before the disaster of 587 BCE, Egypt was the destination of Judean emigrants (cf. Jer 42:14), because it provided better economic and political security for people who needed asylum (1 Kings 11:40; Is 20:6; 30:6; 31:1; Jer 26:20-24). The beginnings of an Israelite-Judean exile community in Egypt

---

[9]See Benno Jacob, *Das Buch Genesis* (Berlin: Schocken, 1934; reprint ed., Stuttgart: Calwer Verlag, 2000), 297-304; Thomas Willi, "Die Funktion der Schlußsequenzen in der Komposition der jahwistischen Urgeschichte," in *Prophetie und geschichtliche Wirklichkeit im alten Israel. Festschrift für Siegfried Herrmann zum 65. Geburtstag,* ed. Rüdiger Liwak and Siegfried Wagner (Stuttgart: Kohlhammer, 1991), 429-44.

go back to the twenty-sixth dynasty (672–525 BCE). The Letter of Aristeas (§13) tells of Jewish mercenaries under Psammetichus I (664–610 BCE) or Psammetichus II (595–589 BCE), and the origin of the Judean military colony in Elephantine, on Egypt's southern border with Nubia, might be connected with the Nubian wars of this period. Elephantine later flourished under Persian rule (525–399 BCE).

Thus, taking into account the neo-Assyrian mass deportations of Israelites (732 and 722–720 BCE) and Judeans (701 BCE) as well as the mass exodus that such military actions regularly caused (cf. Jer 40:11-12), it is quite possible to speak of a "diaspora" even before 587 BCE.

The Babylonian campaigns of 597 and 587 BCE were accompanied by additional emigration waves. The refugees set out for the eastern neighbor states (Jer 40:11-12) and also for Egypt (Jer 24:8; 40:9; 41:16-18; 43:7). The exiles settled there in places where there were already Judean colonies (Jer 43:7; 44:1).

Against the background of this historical and lexicographical information, I would now like to illustrate, by means of some selected examples, how the aforementioned method of drawing conclusions by working backwards from later to former times can provide us with a new perspective on some controversial passages. As we will see, sometimes the evaluation of a familiar biblical statement regarding exile and diaspora depends on the viewpoint from which one looks.

It will be demonstrated that in the Hebrew Bible exile and diaspora are not necessarily and primarily a story of gloom and doom. Of course, there is no uniform conception. But, besides the well-known assessment as divine punishment, there are clear signs of rethinking the status of exile long before the Hellenistic era. These remarkable points of view do not represent merely a sporadic silver lining to the dark clouds of an allegedly cursed exile but rather the actual dawn of a new era in which the Jewish Diaspora is treated as an accepted reality.

GOD'S PRESENCE IN THE EXILE

The *Mekhilta*, a rabbinic Bible commentary edited in the second century CE but surely containing older traditions, makes the bold claim that when the Israelites had to leave their homeland, God himself went into exile with them. The *Mekhilta* to Exodus 12:41 reads: "At each place, to which the Israelites immigrated, the *Shekhina* [a periphrasis for the divine presence], so to speak, emigrated with them. They immigrated to Egypt; the *Shekhina* with them . . . [1 Sam 2:27 follows as scriptural proof]. They immigrated to Babel; the *Shekhina* with them . . . [Is 43:14 follows as scriptural proof, but with a passive reading of the verb: "I was sent"]. They immigrated to Elam; the *Shekhina* with them . . . [Jer 49:38 follows as scriptural proof]. They immigrated to Edom; the *Shekhina* with them." Exile, therefore, does not mean that God abandoned Israel. On the contrary, his presence is emphasized all the more because of the exile. This may shed new light on some biblical texts that have often been interpreted quite differently.

One notable example is found in Ezekiel 11:16: "So said the Lord, YHWH: Indeed, I sent them far away among the nations and, indeed, I dispersed them in the countries; but I became a sanctuary for them, to some extent, in the countries to which they came." The Hebrew idiom that I rendered with "to some extent" is, for the sake of simplicity, usually translated either adverbially as "for a little while" (cf. NRSV) or attributively, relating to "sanctuary," as "little" (cf. NKJV). However, with the above interpretation in mind, we can determine what a more exact linguistic-syntactic investigation of the Hebrew text suggests: here the prophet notes with wonder and awe God's presence in exile. The distance from their former home should not be equated with distance from God. God goes with the ones who belong to him into exile; he himself becomes a meeting place for them on foreign ground. Thus, the banished priest Ezekiel formulates this totally new message hesitantly, almost stammeringly: "I became a sanctuary for them, to some extent, so to speak." The peculiar adverbial idiom "to some extent, so to speak" gives the impression of an expression added as an afterthought. It is the distant echo of a tremendous message that the prophet may have only been able to pronounce haltingly.

We come across a similar figure of speech in Ezekiel 1:28. There the prophet describes an overwhelming vision: YHWH appears at the river Kebar in the heart of the Gentile Babylonia. To describe this, the prophet uses the long-winded expression: "It was the view of the image of the glory of YHWH," another stammering attempt to express something inexpressible.[10]

---

[10]See Paul M. Joyce, "Dislocation and Adaption in the Exilic Age and After," in *After the Exile: Essays in Honour of Rex Mason*, ed. John Barton and David J. Reimer (Macon, GA: Mercer University Press, 1996), 45-58 (57-58).

God himself in his transboundary power becomes "the sanctuary, to some extent" for his people in the middle of the exile. Here we discover the beginnings of a theology that ensured the Jews would retain their identity through the centuries even without their own national state and without the temple.

The composition Ezekiel 8–11 is permeated by the topic of proximity and distance between God and his people, a topic that became a burning issue particularly after the events of 597 BCE. As is well known, this topic was controversially discussed between the exiles in Babylon and those who remained at home. The inhabitants of Jerusalem raised the claim that they were the only legitimate heirs to the material and spiritual blessings on God's people. After all, only they remained in the Promised Land and thus in close proximity to God. Ezekiel declares just the opposite, claiming that the inhabitants of Jerusalem were the ones who were distant from God because of their idolatry. He thus distinguishes between spatial and relational proximity and argues that the latter is more important with God. Even though God caused a deportation of his people into Babylon, it remained within his power to forge a relationship with them while they were in exile. Thus, Ezekiel argues that distance from home certainly does not equal distance from God. Even Ezekiel's changes of location, which were effected by God's spirit (Ezek 8:3; 11:24) and which frame the vision in Ezekiel 8–11, as well as the divine revelations to the prophet in Babylon (cf. Ezek 1:3; 3:22), demonstrate that from God's perspective spatial distance is insignificant.

According to the context of Ezekiel 8–11, the people who stayed behind in the homeland were the truly godforsaken ones. The section is filled with statements that describe a turning away of the "glory of YHWH" from the temple and Jerusalem (cf. Ezek 8:4; 9:3; 10:4, 18-19; 11:22-23) and indicate a turn toward the exiles in Babylon (cf. the recourse of Ezek 8:4 to Ezek 1:28; 3:12, 23).

EXILE AND DIASPORA AS AN OPPORTUNITY TO BEAR WITNESS TO THE JEWISH FAITH

The hymn in the apocryphal book of Tobit 13 is more than a prayer. It exhorts the Jews in the Diaspora to join in Tobit's praise and to bear witness to God under the watchful eyes of their non-Jewish neighbors: "Profess (your faith) in him, you children of Israel, before the nations, for he has scattered us among them. There demonstrate his greatness. Exalt him before all the living; for he is our Lord and he is God, our Father in all eternity" (Tob 13:3-4).

The causal subordinate clause in Tobit 13:3 ("for he has scattered us among them") cannot refer to the action of the main clause, since scattering is hardly a reason to praise. Therefore the connecting factor can be seen in the specific local reference: Israel has to bear witness to their God before the Gentiles, because that is the very reason they were scattered among them. The Greek text, using a verbal root related to *diaspora*, thus implies a positive function of the dispersion. Tobit is a shining example in his testimony: his public praise of God is at the same time a call to the Gentiles to turn to this magnificent and merciful God (cf. Tob 13:8). Praise, as the most intimate expression of a relationship with God, is therefore possible for Tobit even in exile. Indeed, life among foreign peoples with its testimonial character therefore has a positive sense.

Another Old Testament text on the positive effects of the Judean exile is found in Jeremiah 24. Jeremiah 24:5 describes a vision in which baskets of figs appear, one with good fruits, the other with rotten ones. Both sorts of figs are compared to groups of Judeans. The good figs are part of the population that was deported to Babylon in 597 BCE (Jer 24:1), and the bad figs are the people who escaped this deportation. Jeremiah 24:5-7 reads,

> Thus YHWH, the God of Israel, said: "Like these good figs, so I acknowledge for good the [group of] exiles from Judah, whom I have sent away from this place to the land of the Chaldeans. And I will set my eyes upon them for good and let them come back to this land and build them up, and not tear them down and plant them, and not pluck them out. And I will give them a heart, so that they know that I am YHWH. And they shall be my people and I myself will be their God, for they shall return to me with their whole heart."

This statement is significant. By kindly treating the Judeans who were led away to Babylon, YHWH chooses to acknowledge the very people whose deportation was thought to be a punishment from God. Considering the word order of the idiom "for good"; it may be read as part of the subordinate clause. The verse would then speak of "sending away for a good purpose." Nearly all translators and commentators avoid this pointed emphasis. Is it the force of habit that prevents them from acknowledging such a positive view of the exile? In light of the numerous texts from the Hellenistic-Roman era, that is no longer inconceivable. The harsh reality of being deported as war booty into a faraway country serves a positive purpose in these texts. A true conversion to YHWH seems to become possible only after being uprooted and brought far from the homeland. Many statements in the books of Jeremiah and Ezekiel point in this direction.

Still another text portraying exile in a positive way is found in Micah 5:6-7:

> And it will happen: the remnant of Jacob in the midst of many peoples [shall be] like dew from YHWH, like rain showers on the grass, which do not [have to] hope for any man, nor wait for any human being. And it will happen: the remnant of Jacob among the nations, in the midst of many peoples [shall be] like a lion among the packs of the forest, like a young lion among the flocks of sheep, which, when it goes through, treads down and tears in pieces, and no one is there who wrests [them from it].

These two statements about Israel's role among the nations deliberately parallel each other, yet contrast in significant ways. In Micah 5:6, Israel's status as exiles is described as a benefit to the nations. Israel imbues the peoples with its faith in YHWH and does not depend on any human impetus, expectation, or assistance. In Micah 5:7, Micah borrows the frequently used metaphorical depiction of Israel as a scattered flock, threatened by predators (cf. Ezek 34:5; Jer 50:7, 17) but deliberately reverses the roles. The remnant that was once thought to be poor, unprotected, and even insignificant as plunder suddenly emerges as a predator baring its teeth.

It is conceivable that this contrast portrays the various circumstances in which the Israelites and Judeans found themselves as part of their diaspora situation. If so, these verses seemingly aim to encompass the entire reality of life in the Diaspora at different times and in different places. Therefore, the possibility of a positive interpretation of the Diaspora existence shows up here once again.

ENDURING EXILE

N. T. Wright convincingly suggests that the motif of an enduring exile condition continued beyond the so-called postexilic period. It is even possible to trace this line of tradition back into the Old Testament. In Hellenistic times this motif appears in different texts in distinctive forms. One example may be found in the "Damascus Document" (CD), known inter alia from Qumran.

The section in CD 1:5-11 (cf. CD 20:13-5) is inspired by Ezekiel 4:4-8. Ezekiel announced 390 years of exile, referring specifically to the *northern* kingdom, but CD applies that same prophecy to the Israel of its day, i.e., the Jews. After this period, according to CD, a new branch would sprout in Israel, namely the pious Hasidim. Twenty years later "the teacher of righteousness" would start his instruction, leading to the break with the Jerusalem priesthood, whereupon his disciples would go again into "exile." Meanwhile, the forty years of *Judah's* captivity mentioned in Ezekiel 4 symbolize the exile of this community of the pious, the Qumran community, and this period is then understood as the "end time" before the eschatological intervention of God.

Thus, the biblical exilic era did not come to an end, according to CD, until 390 years had passed, because only then, after the "teacher of righteousness" arose, was there a chance for a radical new beginning. The intervening years did not seem to include any noteworthy development in the eyes of the author of CD. In particular, the return of the exiles during the Persian period and the temple restoration are not even mentioned at all.

Whether the community immigrated to Jerusalem at this point, or suffered an enduring "Babylonian exile" in the land of Israel, the God-effected turn begins "in the land of Damascus" (CD 19:34). The "new covenant" is established, not *after*, but *during* this "exile" (cf. CD 19:33-34; 20:12). The question of residence is clearly subordinate to the decision for or against the new covenant. The holy city and the holy land do not guarantee holy life. Moreover, the men of the community preferred life consecrated to God in Damascus to the bad compromises of the Jews ruling in Jerusalem. For them, life as "strangers" in the world (cf. CD 4:6; 6:5) seemed to be an appropriate lifestyle for the "end time."

A similar enduring exile condition is presupposed in some of the postexilic texts of the Old Testament. The prayer in Daniel 9 accepts the present situation of the God's people as a result of Israel's transgressions and God's fair punishment (Dan 9:5-7, 9-14). Daniel 9:7 reads: "To you, Lord, [belongs] righteousness, but to us the shame [written all over] the face, as at this day, to the men of Judah, to the inhabitants of Jerusalem, and to all Israel, those who are near and those who are far away, in all the lands to which you have scattered them, because of the unfaithfulness that they have committed against you." There is fundamentally no distinction between the exiles and those who remained in the land of Israel. Whether they are far off or near, both have to suffer the consequences of God's judgment. The "great calamity" in Dan 9:12, moreover, is apparently not the scattering but the destruction of Jerusalem and the temple (cf. Dan 9:18).

For Daniel, the truth of the Scripture shows up in the disaster. It is the fulfillment of the curses announced by Moses (Dan 9:11-13; cf. Deut 28:15-68), but Daniel also appeals to God on the basis of the promises of the Scripture, particularly those in Jeremiah, in which Jerusalem would be desolated for seventy years (cf. Jer 25:11-12). He thus places his hope squarely on the reliability of the word of God.

It is remarkable that neither a homecoming of the exiles nor a gathering of the scattered comes into Daniel's focus even though the period of seventy years in Jeremiah 29:10 relates specifically to the deportees. Obviously, what was regarded as crucial for the Jews, whether near or far, in Israel-Palestine or abroad, was the existence and the function of the "holy city" (Dan 9:24) and the temple. This point of reference was substantial also for Daniel, a Diaspora Jew, who oriented the time and direction of his prayers to the daily sacrifices in the temple of Jerusalem (Dan 9:21; cf. Dan 6:11, 14).

Considering the given dating, the impact of the seventy years in the context of the narrative is immediately clear: depending on the dating of Darius mentioned in Dan 9:1, the merciful intervention of God was either about to happen or had just happened. But the angel Gabriel slows down these expectations with a reinterpretation of the seventy years in "seventy weeks (of years)" (Dan 9:24).

This all comes together in an amazing statement: a total of 490 years after the destruction of Jerusalem, the city would still not be completely rebuilt, the sin would still not be dismissed, the guilt would still not be expiated, and both the "eternal justice" and the anointing of the Holy of Holies (Dan 9:24) would still be pending. In other words, Israel had not yet received its promised blessings. The historical events in the intervening time, including the rededication of the temple, the return of some exiles, and the relative religious and political autonomy in Judea, did not change the fact that the Jews living in Judea together with the Jews of the Diaspora in some sense remained "in exile."

The final chapter of the book of Chronicles, which begins with a report of the conquest of Jerusalem by Nebuchadnezzar, is of great importance for the Chronicler's view on exile. The seventy-year-long "era of exile" is discussed in only one verse, albeit a significant one (2 Chron 36:21). It states that the seventy years during which Israel remained desolate correspond to the seventy sabbatical years that were neglected during the reign of several kings and are necessary for the healing of the country. The exile thus becomes an integral part of God's plan, rather than some regrettable, devastating loss.

If the "exile era" was a theologically necessary time of rest, it is understandable that there would be no detailed description of it here. However, the fact that the restoration at the end of the seventy years is also glossed over seems puzzling. The book of Chronicles ends with an outlook at the opportunities, which provides the edict of Cyrus in which he invites all Jews to the restoration of the temple (2 Chron 36:22-23). However, there is no mention of the actual revival of the Judean province. Considering that Chronicles was created in the late Persian or Hellenistic period, that it was written with a very specific conception of exile in mind, and that it places Cyrus's edict at such a prominent place in the text, the absence of an account of the restoration is no coincidence.

The Chronicler is apparently using a literary device, deliberately leaving the conclusion of the book open in order to express his view that the actual restoration still lies before them as a task.[11] The work of the Chronicler was very likely understood in this way when it was moved to the end of the Hebrew canon. The Hebrew Bible thus concludes with a request to implement Cyrus's edict with all of its implications in order to bring about true restoration.

Conclusion

These are only a few of the many parallels between the Jewish literature from Hellenistic-Roman times and the Hebrew Bible. We have seen that

---

[11]Cf. Sara Japhet, "Exile and Restoration in the Book of Chronicles," in *The Crisis of Israelite Religion: Transformation of Religious Tradition in Exilic and Post-Exilic Times*, ed. Bob Becking and Marjo C. A. Korpel, Oudtestamentische Studiën 42 (Leiden: Brill, 1999), 33-44.

positive interpretations of the exile and widespread acceptance of the Diaspora existence are not at all alien to the Hebrew Bible.

The books of Esther, Daniel, Ezra-Nehemiah, and Zechariah all talk about Israel in the Diaspora. Ezra and Nehemiah are introduced as Diaspora Jews. Daniel and his companions, as well as Esther and Mordecai, established their careers in foreign royal courts. Like Joseph in Egypt, they experienced endangerment as well as preservation. Even as foreigners in an alien environment, they were able to experience God's presence in specific ways. In the lives of these Jewish representatives, God's intervention in favor of his people always came in the form of salvation *in* the exile, never *from* the exile.

The Hebrew Bible does not theologically disparage Israel's existence in exile. On the contrary, the Judean exiles were able to find YHWH (e.g., Deut 4:27), pray (e.g., 1 Kings 8:47), adhere to God's law (e.g., Esther 3:8; Dan 6:14), celebrate religious festivals, and even establish such festivals (Esther 9:19). Some were able to receive revelations from God (Ezek 1:1), and the truth of God itself was confirmed through the dispersion (e.g., Ezek 12:15). The welfare (*shalom*, Jer 29:7) of the people was attainable in exile. It was not bound to any holy place or chosen land but to prayer and a relationship with God, which is possible everywhere, because YHWH has universal power.

Even the numerous promises of return or regathering do not inevitably imply a negative view of the geographical dispersion in the sense of an undesirable status that has to be revised as soon as possible. First, in many cases the mentioned return is explicitly regarded as an event at the end of times. Thus, one has to consider Israel's current Diaspora existence as a God-given and therefore purposeful reality (cf. particularly Jer 28–29). Moreover, in light of our findings from Hellenistic-Roman times, it should be evident that a great number of those promises do not refer to some literal migration to Jerusalem but rather to a spiritual "homecoming." If one interprets the motif of return and regathering in the context of an eschatological transformation of the world, the main focus of that motif moves from the geographical dimension of homecoming to a theological "change of location": the return of Israel to their God and the regathering of the flock around their shepherd (e.g., Jer 50:4-7; Mic 4:6-8).

When preservation in exile or God's renewed devotion to his people is mentioned, it does not always refer to a return to the homeland. Even Ezra and Nehemiah made no attempt to abolish the status of dispersion. Instead, they aimed to revitalize Jerusalem as religious center of a dispersed people. The building of the temple would have been inconceivable without the support of pilgrims from the Mesopotamian exile community, yet it is telling that Nehemiah returned to Persian Susa after completing his mission. Even those who defend the idea that the primary role of exile was to be a fair punishment of God's sinful people do not deny that exile was seen as an opportunity for survival and was therefore a positive challenge for Israel.

Furthermore, exile motifs in the Hebrew Bible refer not only to the historical events of the Assyrian and Babylonian deportations but also to a continuous situation of oppression. That status of oppression included the land of Israel itself, as is evident in numerous texts from Hellenistic-Roman times as well as in Ezekiel 20; Zechariah 1–8; Daniel 9; Ezra 9; Nehemiah 1; and 2 Chronicles 36. Lack of freedom, dependence, and even homelessness thus do not distinguish the life abroad from an allegedly desirable life in Israel-Palestine.

The Hebrew Bible's assessment of the Diaspora situation is neutral for the most part, but it also contains early indications of a distinctly positive assessment. For instance, several passages take it for granted that it is easier to learn and achieve complete dependence on God in exile than in the homeland (cf. Lev 26:40-41; Deut 4:30; 30:2; 1 Kings 8:47-48; Ezek 20:33-38). Positive evaluations can also be seen where the exile is described as an educational measure (e.g., Jer 30:11; 46:28).

Similarly, as expressly documented by Philo and Josephus,[12] there are tendencies in the Hebrew Bible to attribute a universal meaning to exile and return. Specifically, this means that exile is less like a catastrophic punishment and more like a revelation with salvific implications. Not only do exile and Diaspora reveal God's truth and truthfulness toward Israel (e.g., Ezek 12:15-16, 20), but the nations that encountered Israel were influenced by them (cf. Is 49:6; Jer 29:7; Zeph 3:9-10; and the idiom "before the eyes of the peoples" throughout Ezekiel).

---

[12]See James M. Scott, "Philo and the Restoration of Israel," *Society of Biblical Literature Seminar Papers* 34 (1995): 553-75; See also Louis H. Feldman, "The Concept of Exile in Josephus," in *Exile: Old Testament, Jewish, and Christian Conceptions,* ed. James M. Scott, JSJSup 56 (Leiden: Brill, 1997), 145-72.

Thus, it should be noted that, according to the Hebrew Bible, life in exile is by no means a life under the wrath of God. The Jewish acceptance of their Diaspora situation, well-known in Jewish literature of the Hellenistic-Roman era, should not be ascribed merely to their assimilation to a pagan environment. To the contrary, the "theology of exile" of the Hebrew Bible already supports acceptance of their Diaspora situation as normative.

The phenomenon of diaspora became a characteristic feature of Judaism no later than the Persian period, and eventually became a fundamental element of it. The Hebrew Bible took shape during the same time. Therefore, it can be assumed that the emphasis of certain motifs in the canon, such as migration, expulsion, sojourn abroad, and the promise of land, may be connected with the special Diaspora situation, in which those who collected and edited the Scriptures considered it important to offer the "dispersed people" some model they could identify with. These considerations had some influence on their editorial work. The canon of the Hebrew Bible can be deemed as evidence of the theological processing of the Diaspora situation. Israel evokes in its stories the God who met Abraham in Mesopotamia, Joseph in Egypt, and Moses in Midian. They and their God were familiar with life in foreign lands. For this people, exile and diaspora do not at all mean the end of their story with God.

PART TWO

EARLY JUDAISM

▒▒

JEWISH NATIONALISM FROM JUDAH THE MACCABEE TO JUDAH THE PRINCE AND THE PROBLEM OF "CONTINUING EXILE"

PHILIP ALEXANDER

THE QUESTION OF WHETHER or not some Jews in Palestine in the time
of Jesus believed that the exile had never truly ended has been discussed
largely in terms of *testimonia*—proof-texts from the period that state or
suggest that this was the case (e.g., Tom Wright's piece in the present
volume). This is the obvious place to start, but equally important are actual
political events. Exile and return are fundamentally political ideas that cry
out for implementation in the political sphere. Implicit in them is a political
program. Is there any evidence that the implications were drawn? Did these
ideas motivate political activity? Was anyone, feeling they were still in
"exile," inspired to attempt a "return"?

These questions need to be handled with care. They relate to the problem
of the relationship between ideology and politics. On the whole this relationship is not well handled in the modern historiography of our period. Political history and religious history tend to be written side by side. This is in
part due to a reluctance of political historians to see ideas as real, historical
causes. The standard approach is reductive, predicated on the assumption that
although people may look like—indeed may even say that—they are behaving

in certain political ways because they hold certain political beliefs, in reality it is always about something else—about basic power plays and the gaining of material advantage. And so in analyzing what was really going on we can disregard ideologies and concentrate on uncovering the power struggles between the parties. Ideologies, on this view, are only ways *post factum* of disguising and justifying the primal urge to power. Ancient histories are not much better, because they tend to concentrate simply on events and seldom relate those events to the worldviews of the actors on the historical stage.

I cannot attempt here a critique of this approach. Suffice to say that the present essay is predicated on the assumption that although it can be difficult to know what truly drives people to act as they do, and although a simple, single motive seldom lies behind any act (actions are often overdetermined), worldview *is* a significant factor. People live out a story that makes sense of the world for them and defines their place within it, and this is especially true when they band together into ideologically shaped communities such as religious sects or political parties. This means that there must be a nexus between ideology and politics. This nexus is particularly strong and particularly relevant to understanding political history in periods of high ideological awareness. Few societies, I would suggest, in few periods of history can have been more ideologically aware than Jewish society in Palestine in the period under review. Jews at this time seem intoxicated by ideas, ideas that, as I have said, are fraught with political consequences. We can, if we wish, confine ourselves to ideological statements in ideological texts, but if we do, we will miss a trick. My approach in this paper will be to start basically from political events and see to what extent they can be explained by the political ideologies of the day. In this way we will be able to assess the impact of different ideologies on society and life.

THE CONCEPTS OF "EXILE" AND "RETURN/RESTORATION"

But before we look at events we need to clarify a basic term. What does *exile* mean in early Jewish political discourse? The term *exile* (Hebrew *golah*, *galut*) is widely used already in the Hebrew Bible, and that biblical usage continued into our period.[1] It denotes a condition of living outside the

---

[1] One would assume that the Greek equivalent would be *diaspora*, but, in fact, the LXX uses a variety of other words for *golah*, *galut*: *aichmalōsia*, *apoikia*, *apoikismos*, *metoikesia*, *paroikia*.

homeland, a condition resulting from forcible removal. Being outside the land is not necessarily experienced as negative. Not all Jews were expelled from their ancient land. Some may have been economic migrants, who saw a chance of a better life abroad. Some living abroad flourished materially and even culturally, and for them to have returned would have meant a diminution in their quality of life. Experiencing living outside the land as *galut* is subjective; it is a state of mind: it is not primarily determined by material circumstances, and, indeed, it is sometimes among the better off that it seems most acutely felt. The feeling arises, fundamentally, from internalizing a theological understanding of exile as divine punishment for sins committed by the people. The feeling is *theologically* constructed. It occurs within the context of the idea that Israel is a covenant people. They had made a covenant with their God, a key stipulation of which was that, if they kept its terms—if they obeyed God's laws—they would be given their own land in which to dwell in peace and safety, and would enjoy his presence in their midst. But if they failed to keep the covenant he would exile them from their land. The sense of exile manifests itself in a longing for return, most movingly expressed by Psalm 137, or at least in a continuing emotional attachment to or orientation toward Zion.

So far so good. But we need to nuance this a little. The experience of living outside the land did not have to be seen even theologically in a totally negative light. More neutral or even positive positions are possible. Let me begin to explore this by quoting an early modern Reform Jewish view. It comes from the principles adopted at the Philadelphia Conference in 1869:

> We look upon the destruction of the second Jewish commonwealth not as a punishment for the sinfulness of Israel, but as a result of the divine purpose revealed to Abraham, which, as has become ever clearer in the course of the world's history, consists in the dispersion of the Jews to all parts of the earth, for the realization of their high priestly mission, to lead the nations to the true knowledge and worship of God.

Where *diaspora* occurs in the LXX it usually represents the Hebrew *ndḥ* ("to banish, expel"), where there is an identifiable equivalent in the Masoretic Text. *Diaspora* in Greek has a more neutral feel to it than *galut* in Hebrew, and its equivalent in Modern Hebrew, *tefutzah*, is sometimes used precisely to avoid the negative connotations of *galut*. On the Septuagintal usage of Greek terms, see further Rob Hiebert's essay in the present volume.

Now this is a nineteenth-century statement, and the historian's instinct is to see it as inextricably embedded in nineteenth-century discourse. Its historical context is Jewish emancipation, the grateful acceptance by Jews of their place as citizens enjoying equal rights in the countries where they lived, and their consequent downplaying of a return to Zion, to avoid a charge of dual loyalty. The statement neatly positions itself not only as a negation of traditional Jewish Zionism but of the traditional Christian view, going back at least to Eusebius,[2] that the destruction of the Second Temple was not just God's punishment of the Jewish people but his very public demonstration of his final rejection of the old covenant. It also, probably, plays to a minority Christian view, one I do not think attested before modern times, that the Jewish Diaspora prepared the way, under God, for the spread of the gospel, by suggesting that that providential role for the Jewish people has not, as Christian supersessionism would have it, come to an end. So the statement is thoroughly tangled up in the political and religious discourse of its time. And yet it points to the existence of theological resources, *deep within Jewish tradition*, that would allow a more positive view of "exile" to be developed.

Is there any evidence for such a view in antiquity? Not, perhaps, in so many words, but we do have models of exile, especially from the Diaspora, that, on the face of it, are less negatively charged.[3] Take, for example, Philo's description of the Diaspora in his *Legatio ad Gaium*, where he sees the scattered Jewish communities as colonies (*apoikiai*) of the mother city (the *mētropolis*) of Jerusalem.[4] The analogy here, of course, is with the expansion of the mainland Greek cities oversees, their sending out of colonies to the far-flung shores of the Mediterranean—as Corinth and Tenea did in the case of Syracuse. Many of those colonies flourished and became independent of the mother city. Their citizens had no desire to return to their ancient homeland. Now Philo undoubtedly had a certain emotional attachment to Jerusalem, but it was essentially nostalgic and romantic. He draws from it

---

[2]Eusebius, *Ecclesiastical History* 2.6.
[3]On this, see Jörn Kiefer's contribution in the present volume.
[4]Philo, *Embassy to Gaius* 281: "As for the holy city, I must say what befits me to say. While she, as I have said, is my native city [*patris*], she is also the mother city not just of one country Judea, but of most of the others in virtue of the colonies she has sent out at divers times to the neighbouring lands" (*Philo*, trans. F. H. Colson, Loeb Classical Library [Cambridge, MA: Harvard University Press, 1962], 10:143).

no political discourse advocating a return: on the contrary, he is proud of the Jewish Diaspora.[5] And this would be in keeping with the general tenor of Egyptian Greek-speaking Judaism, which, by and large, to judge by its extensive surviving literature, had effectively denationalized and universalized Judaism. It is for this very reason that Alexandrian Judaism was regarded by some modern Reform Jewish thinkers as a forerunner of Reform.[6] I cannot pursue this complex question further here. Suffice to say that I see it as a shot across the bows not to overplay the negative view of "exile" as universal among Jews in antiquity, nor overplay the centrality of the land in Second Temple Jewish thought—a mistake that some Christian scholars, under the influence of modern Zionism, have tended to make.[7]

Let us return to the thread of our argument. In a certain theological context exile is a negative experience that can only be erased by a return to the land. *Return* is the obvious antonym of *exile*. But is return in and of itself sufficient to negate the exile? The answer has to be no. Return is a necessary but not in itself sufficient condition. The reason for this is simple. Exile is bad because it means the loss of independence, of statehood. Exiles are subservient to a foreign power. They are not masters of their own destiny and able to worship their God in freedom. If that subservience continues after the return to the ancient homeland, then the exile cannot be deemed to be fully ended. This idea is poignantly expressed in Nehemiah 9:36, in which the people sorrowfully say: "Here we are, slaves to this day—slaves in the land that you gave to our ancestors to enjoy its fruit and its good gifts." Behind this surely lies the deuteronomic paradigm, which envisages the

---

[5]See further Sîan Jones and Sarah Pearce, eds., *Jewish Local Patriotism and Self-Identification in the Graeco-Roman Period* (Sheffield: Sheffield Academic Press, 1998).

[6]Samuel Sandmel draws some interesting parallels between Alexandrian Jewry in the Greco-Roman period and American Jewry in his own day: see his "'The Clew to Survival,'" *The Central Conference of American Rabbis Yearbook* 63 (1953): 199-208. He claims that "[Alexandrian Jewry] regarded itself as not in exile, but at home; and it expressed its will loyally to maintain and propagate its Judaism in the very center of the then cosmopolitan culture" (203). My thanks to Francesca Frazer for drawing my attention to this interesting essay.

[7]This is true particularly of W. D. Davies's two influential books, *The Gospel and the Land* (Berkeley: University of California Press, 1974), and *The Territorial Dimension of Judaism, with a Symposium and Further Reflections* (Minneapolis: Fortress, 1991). Davies, who was notably friendly toward Jews and the state of Israel, accepted more or less without question the modern Zionist insistence on the centrality of the land, and was then puzzled why early Christianity was able so casually to ignore it. For an important corrective to Davies's position see Isaiah Gafni, *Land, Centre, Diaspora: Jewish Constructs in Late Antiquity* (Sheffield: Sheffield Academic Press, 1997).

supreme blessedness of the people as consisting of national independence. On this view of the matter the antonym of exile is not *return* but *restoration*—restoration of a sovereign Jewish state. What this analysis makes clear is that "exile" is part of the discourse of Jewish nationalism, of messianism conceived of as the restoration of the ancient, independent Jewish polity under the King Messiah, who, as God's supreme agent in history, inaugurates the rule of God, the kingdom of heaven. Though the phrase is not unknown in contemporary Zionist discourse,[8] I cannot find anywhere in the ancient sources where this intermediate condition of living in the land but still not living in the kingdom is called "continuing exile," but I am happy to accept it as a useful shorthand for this idea. The idea itself is unquestionably there. Anyone who looked for the coming of the Messiah or the messianic state, and there were surely many such in Second Temple times, was in one way or another buying into it.

But again we must nuance the picture. Does it make any sense to talk of Jewish *nationalism* in antiquity? Is nationalism not a modern construct that really only makes sense from the French Revolution onwards and the rise of the modern nation-state? Are we not in danger of reading a modern political concept back anachronistically into antiquity? There *is* a danger here, but it can be overstated. I would argue that there *was* a phenomenon in antiquity that can be meaningfully called, in terms of political discourse, Jewish *nationalism*. Jews shared a strong identity across the whole of the known world. This was evident not only to outsiders but to Jews themselves. Through most of the period under review here an element of that identity was a shared attachment to the old homeland, though the identity could, and did, survive the loss of the homeland. Jews saw themselves as an *ethnos*, and some believed that their ethnicity could only be fully expressed if they ruled

---

[8] I have heard the phrase *galut nimshekhet* used in this sense in Israel, but the idea is more sharply and precisely expressed by the oxymoron *galut ba'aretz* ("exile within the land"), or *galut be'eretz Yisra'el* ("exile in the land of Israel"): see Aviezer Ravitzky, "Exile in the Holy Land—The Dilemma of Haredi Jewry," in *Israel—State and Society, 1948–88*, ed. Peter Medding, Studies in Contemporary Jewry V (New York: Oxford University Press, 1989), 89-121. The idea is found not only on the religious right but also, in a somewhat ironic sense, on the secular political left: see Amnon Raz-Krakotzkin, "Exile Through Sovereignty: A Critique of the 'Negation of Exile' in Israel Culture," part 1, *Theory and Criticism* 4 (1993): 23-55; part 2, *Theory and Criticism* 5 (1994): 113-32 [Hebrew]. See also Israel Bartal, "'Exile in the Land': A Study of the Historiography of the Pre-Zionist Jewish Settlement in the Land of Israel," in *Proceedings of the World Congress of Jewish Studies*, X B, vol. 1 (1989), 269-304 [Hebrew]. The phrase "continuing Nakba" is sometimes used to describe the continuing state of exile of the Palestinian people.

as sovereign in their own land. This was a direct result of them accepting that they were party to the covenant at Sinai. The key text here, as many have seen, is Deuteronomy—the canon within the canon, as far as Torah was concerned. The arc traced by the deuteronomic paradigm from late biblical through Second Temple to rabbinic thought is the closest we get to a normative line in Judaism at this period. Jewish nationhood was one of the most strongly and clearly defined of any *ethnos* in antiquity, based as it was on a sense of "chosenness," on the idea that Jews had uniquely entered into a covenant with God and had been assigned by him a land and a manifest national destiny in his purposes.[9]

This traditional Jewish religious nationalism was to have profound consequences in our own times. Modern Zionism in its origins was a deeply secular phenomenon, which set itself strongly against religion. It saw itself as a Jewish manifestation of the powerful nationalist movements that swept across Europe in the later part of the nineteenth century, and it argued the case for an independent Jewish state in ways that made sense in terms of modern nationalism. But, as some perceptive Jewish thinkers saw, it was only a matter of time before this secular Zionism would collide with the older religious Zionism of Judaism. That collision has now taken place, and the consequences have been dramatic. Interestingly it looks as if the older, religious Zionism will prove to be the more dynamic and resilient of the two Zionisms. Whether that turns out in the end to be the case remains to be seen. I would simply here make the point that the relative ease with which modern secular and premodern religious Zionism can be politically merged suggests a deep structural congruence between them, and that, in turn, reinforces my point that premodern Zionism can be legitimately seen as a form of nationalism.

JEWISH NATIONALISM IN LATE ANTIQUITY: A BRIEF HISTORY[10]

The Maccabean revolt. Now let us turn to political events and pose the question: To what extent can we see in the history of our period the

---

[9]See the important study by Doron Mendels, *The Rise and Fall of Jewish Nationalism: Jewish and Christian Ethnicity in Ancient Palestine* (Grand Rapids: Eerdmans, 1997). Also relevant is his earlier study, *The Land of Israel as a Political Concept in Hasmonean Literature: Recourse to History in Second Century BC Claims to the Holy Land* (Tübingen: Mohr Siebeck, 1987).

[10]The best overall historical narrative for the period from the Maccabees to Bar Kokhba remains vol. 1 of Emil Schürer, *The History of the Jewish People in the Age of Jesus Christ*, rev. ed., ed.

outworking of a theology of exile and return? I begin with the definitive upsurge of Jewish nationalism in antiquity—the Maccabean revolt. First and Second Maccabees say remarkably little about the ideology that drove this revolt, but that it was ideologically driven can be in little doubt. Judah and his followers clearly opposed the Hellenizing policies of Antiochus Epiphanes and his Jewish supporters. This was evidently motivated, as they saw it, by loyalty to Jewish tradition and law. The rebels were prepared to die rather than violate their ancestral ways. But was there more to it than this? Arguably there was. A very revealing moment occurred in 162–161 BCE when there was, apparently, a chance of reaching a negotiated settlement. The king (Antiochus V) offered the Jews religious freedom, though they would still remain his subjects and part of the Seleucid Empire. He would allow them "to live by their laws as they did before," if they gave up armed rebellion. Many Jews accepted. A little later, Demetrius, after overthrowing Antiochus and assuming the throne, appointed Alcimus high priest. Alcimus arrived in Jerusalem to assume office and was accepted by many Jews, including the Hasidim, whose support had been crucial to Judah in the early phases of the uprising. But Judah would have none of this. He would settle for nothing less than complete independence, even though it meant he lost important allies and was knocked back almost to "square one."[11] Suddenly the issues at stake were clarified. Was the revolt about *religious* freedom or about *political* freedom? Judah made it abundantly clear that in his view it was fundamentally about the latter, though, of course, he wanted religious freedom as well.

Now why would he have taken this line? All sorts of possibilities come to mind, starting with sheer cussedness, but the possibility should not be ruled out that he was trying to realize a restoration of Israel in line with the

G. Vermes, F. Millar, and M. Goodman, 3 vols. (Edinburgh: T&T Clark, 1973–1989). A well-organized and judicious overview of the problems is Lester Grabbe, *Judaism from Cyrus to Hadrian* (London: SCM Press, 1994). For the period from Bar Kokhba to Judah the Prince see: Seth Schwarz, *Imperialism and Jewish Society 200 B.C.E. to 640 C.E.* (Princeton, NJ: Princeton University Press, 2001); Marc Hirshman, *The Stabilization of Rabbinic Culture, 100 C.E.–350 C.E.: Texts on Education in their Late Antique Context* (Oxford: Oxford University Press, 2009); and Hayim Lapin, *Rabbis as Romans: The Rabbinic Movement in Palestine, 100–400 CE* (Oxford: Oxford University Press, 2012).
[11]See 1 Macc 6:55–7:18. Needless to say the explanation given above involves reading between the lines of the highly partisan account to 1 Maccabees but, I would argue, it offers a plausible explanation of what actually happened.

promises of the Sinai covenant, and that demanded sovereignty. It seems extraordinary that this possibility is not one that commends itself much to modern historians. All sorts of subtle reasons are given as to why the revolt broke out, but one as simple as this is seldom considered. Though 1 and 2 Maccabees say little about the ideology that drove the revolt, there is one contemporary document that arguably does, Daniel 7–12. The scholarly consensus is that this section of Daniel was composed right at the start of the revolt, and it clearly envisages that the defeat of the Seleucids will inaugurate the kingdom of God (see, e.g., Dan 7:13-14). It can be seen as a manifesto of the revolt, and it makes perfect sense if Judah and his party cast themselves in the role of God's agents who would bring in the rule of the saints. Daniel 7–12 sees the revolt as a messianic war, and it is perfectly feasible that the Maccabees saw it in a similar light.

Once, however, the main political goal of the rebellion was reached, and the Jews had won independence, it was inevitable that the Hasmoneans would have regarded national restoration as achieved. They assumed first the high priesthood and then the kingship, though they had no traditional entitlement to either. Kingship is interesting, because at first sight it might be taken to imply precisely that they did not have *messianic* pretensions: the Messiah was supposed to be from the house of David, and they could not claim that. Whatever kind of kingship they exercised, it was not messianic. But not all messianic scenarios presupposed a *Davidic* messiah: the main eschatological agent does not have to be a scion of the house of David. The Hasmoneans instituted a festival, Hanukkah—a major, eight-day festival no less; only Passover was as long!—that glorified them as the restorers of Israel, and they tried to promote its observance even in the Diaspora. They posed as the leaders not only of the Palestinian Jewish community but of Jews worldwide. Against this backdrop there can surely be little doubt that they would have taken a dim view of anyone who, under their rule, stirred up the people to look for a messiah, because it would have raised awkward questions about their own legitimacy and invited unflattering comparisons between conditions under their rule and the glories of the messianic age.

We know for certain of one group who, though probably descended from the Hasidim, and so broadly within the nationalist camp, vehemently opposed the Hasmoneans and looked forward to the imminent

coming of the true Messiah. I mean the community of the Dead Sea
Scrolls. For the Qumran covenanters the restoration for sure had not
taken place.[12] They ended up demonizing their Jewish opponents, including, presumably, the Hasmoneans.[13] They and nations oppressing
Israel were Sons of Darkness, who would have to be defeated by the Sons
of Light in the eschatological war.

Any claim that the Hasmoneans may have made that they had restored
Israel lost any credibility in the civil war that raged 67–63 BCE between
Hyrcanus and Aristobulus, the sons of Queen Alexandra Salome. Both sides
appealed to Pompey, who moved in swiftly and annexed the Hasmonean
state to the Roman Empire. He had to storm the temple to evict Aristobulus
and his supporters, and, in the process, he violated its sanctity by entering
the Holy of Holies.[14]

We have an interesting contemporary view of these events in Psalms of
Solomon 17, one of the major surviving messianic texts of the Second
Temple period. It seems to have been composed shortly after Pompey's
capture of Jerusalem in 63 BCE. He is clearly "the man alien to our race" who
is used by God as an instrument of judgment on those who had wickedly
usurped the throne of David, the Hasmoneans. The Hasmonean state is
implicitly described as pseudo-messianic, which by its usurpation had prevented the coming of the true Davidic kingdom. The author refers to his own
community as "the pious." The Greek *hosioi* is possibly a translation of the
Hebrew *ḥasidim*. This is suggestive. He may have belonged to the

---

[12]Note, for example, the evidence that they were still mourning the destruction of the temple by
Nebuchadnezzar—a clear indication, I would argue, that they did not think it had ever been
restored. See my essay "Was the Ninth of Av Observed in the Second Temple Period? Reflections
on the Concept of Continuing Exile in Early Judaism," in *Envisioning Judaism: Studies in Honor
of Peter Schäfer on the Occasion of His Seventieth Birthday*, ed. Ra'anan Boustan et al. (Tübingen:
Mohr Siebeck, 2013), 2:23-39.

[13]One might be tempted to suppose that the Sons of Darkness language belongs to a late, more
"Zealot," phase of the community's development, were it not for the fact that it is clearly adum-
brated in what I regard as one of the community's founding documents—the so-called Sermon
on the Two Spirits (1QS). See my essay "Predestination and Free Will in the Theology of the
Dead Sea Scrolls," in *Divine and Human Agency in Paul and His Environment*, ed. John Barclay
and Simon Gathercole (London: Continuum/T&T Clark, 2006), 27-49. It should also be noted,
however, that there was a strong sense of realized eschatology at Qumran, as, e.g., in the Songs
of the Sabbath Sacrifice. See my *Companions to the Dead Sea Scrolls: The Mystical Texts* (London:
Continuum, 2005).

[14]Josephus, *J.W.* 1.138-58.

traditionalist Hasidim who had once formed a political alliance with the Maccabees but were now bitterly disillusioned with them.

Particularly pertinent to our present theme are the frequent and very pointed references to exile in the psalm. There is an ongoing implicit comparison between the condition that the Jewish people are now in and the condition they were in after Nebuchadnezzar laid waste the land and destroyed the temple. The meter of the original text may have been the *qinah*, the traditional meter of lament. Echoes of the book of Lamentations can be heard. All this seems a little over the top. Our historical sources do not suggest that the devastation and damage inflicted by Pompey was that great, or anything like that perpetrated by Nebuchadnezzar. Certainly the temple was not destroyed. But it is a matter of perception, and the point is clear: the Jewish people are back in a state of exile—exile both outside and inside the land. They are in need of restoration, and that will come about only through the King Messiah. Maccabean propaganda had used a rather similar ploy to promote the Maccabean revolution. It had exaggerated the devastation of the temple perpetrated by Antiochus, with hints that he was a new Nebuchadnezzar, in order to throw into greater relief the restoration effected by the Maccabees.[15] Though Psalms of Solomon 17 is a deeply political, nationalist document, it does not advocate any political activity beyond passive resistance, and waiting on God to send the redeemer.

The First War against Rome. Over the next hundred years there was no concerted effort to throw off the Roman yoke, however much some people may have wanted to do so. Jewish politics was dominated in the period by a power struggle between the remnants of the Hasmonean house and the house of the upstart Herod, a struggle that the Herodians comprehensively won. But this is best seen as an *internal* power struggle that has little light to throw on our theme. For by far the greater part of this period the Jews in Palestine were governed by their own rulers, whether Hasmonean or Herodian, rather than as direct subjects of Rome. True, Herod was widely disliked by his Jewish subjects, and his Idumean ancestry long remembered, but he married into Jewish aristocracy, and

---

[15]See my article "Was the Ninth of Av Observed in the Second Temple Period?" for a discussion of the evidence.

his refurbishment of the temple must have won him some favor, not least by providing work and transforming the economy of Jerusalem. And he and his successors unquestionably shielded the Jews from direct Roman rule. A significant moment came in 44, when Herod Agrippa died, and his kingdom, which was by then more or less coterminous with Herod the Great's, came under procuratorial administration. Relations between the Jews in Palestine and their Roman rulers deteriorated rapidly, till finally open and widespread revolt broke out in 66 CE—a revolt that took eight years to crush.

The causes of the First War against Rome are as contested among historians as the causes of the Maccabean revolt, but we must again reckon with an ideological component.[16] Josephus makes it clear that it was the wing of Judaism that he calls the Fourth Philosophy that played a major role in fanning the flames of rebellion and keeping the conflagration going, even when all seemed lost. He links the founding of the Fourth Philosophy with the annexation in 6 CE of the territories of Archelaus (Samaria, Judea, and Idumea). When Quirinius the Roman governor of Syria undertook a census of the newly acquired territory for tax purposes, Judas the Galilean urged the Jews to resist. Paying taxes to Rome, he argued, was a mark of slavery. The people should unite to assert their liberty, acknowledging God alone as their leader and master.[17] What Judas seemed to have stirred into life was a dormant revolutionary movement, which grew in strength over the following decades, and fragmented, as such revolutionary movements are prone to do, into different, sometimes warring, factions. Two of these factions are singled out by Josephus as playing a particularly active part in the rebellion—the Sicarii and the Zealots. He first mentions the Sicarii in connection with the procuratorship of Felix (52–59 CE). They engaged in political assassination (usually of their Jewish opponents!), carried on guerrilla warfare against the Romans, and kidnapped high officials to hold as hostage against the release of political prisoners. They remained loyal to the family of Judas that gave them their leadership down to the time of

---

[16]See the important study by Martin Goodman, *The Ruling Class of Judea: The Origins of the Jewish Revolt Against Rome, A.D. 66–70* (Cambridge: Cambridge University Press, 1987), which stresses social factors.

[17]Josephus, *Ant.* 18.4, 23.

Eleazar ben Yair, who urged them to make their famous last stand at Masada in 64.

Josephus first mentions the Zealots as a separate party only after the outbreak of the war in 66, though there is good reason to think that they existed before then. He depicts them as one of the rebel groups in Jerusalem, led by the priest Eleazar ben Simon. The Galilean rebel leader John of Gischala joined them after he came to Jerusalem in late 67, but he and Eleazar quarreled and for a time headed up opposing Zealot factions. Josephus is by and large consistent in treating the Zealots and the Sicarii as distinct. The Zealots were based in Jerusalem, and there they perished or were captured and sold into slavery when Titus finally took the city. The Sicarii, having played a part in Jerusalem at the beginning of the war, withdrew from there after the assassination of their leader Menaḥem (a descendant of Judas the Galilean) to Masada, which remained their center and stronghold until the end of the war. Just what the differences between the Sicarii and the Zealots were is now hard to say. The Zealots may have been much more class warriors, out to settle old scores with the Jerusalem priestly aristocracy, but both parties were united in their implacable hatred of Rome.

Josephus is often accused of spinning his account of the war for apologetic ends. He wanted to suggest to his Roman audience that the rebellion was caused by a small group of hotheads and was not supported by the people at large. But this aspect of his account rings broadly true to me. It is not unlikely that in the aftermath of the initial rebel successes various elements of the ruling classes, and, indeed, the more general population, opportunistically supported the revolt, but as soon as the going got tough these fell away, leaving only the diehards to carry on the fight. It goes almost without saying that this group must have been highly motivated by ideology: there is no other reasonable explanation for their fanatical behavior; but what ideology drove them on? Here Josephus does, I think, introduce a bit of spin, but only a little. He constantly stresses the rebels' desire for "freedom (*eleutheria*)": they were prepared to die rather than be slaves. Now a Roman audience would have heard "freedom" here as *libertas*—a virtue every Roman admired: Josephus was casting the rebels in the role of noble foe. But the freedom the *rebels* themselves would have desired was not *libertas* but *ḥerut*—freedom from foreign oppression so that they could worship their

God and follow his Torah.[18] They wanted to be able to acknowledge God alone as their leader and master: they were bent on introducing a theocracy. It is surely not unreasonable to flesh out their ideology from the kind of messianism we noted in Psalms of Solomon 17—the only difference being that the nationalists who espoused the Fourth Philosophy, unlike the author of the psalm, were prepared to take up arms to bring the kingdom in by force.[19]

The war(s) of Qitos and the Second War against Rome. The period immediately after the end of the First Revolt is shrouded in obscurity. It is safe to assume that the Jews of Palestine had no capacity and little appetite left to continue armed resistance, and yet there is clear evidence that the messianic ideologies that probably had fueled the First Revolt continued to flourish. If texts such as 2 Baruch and 4 Ezra are anything to go by, then there was actually an *upsurge* of messianic apocalypticism.[20] We have only to wait till 115–117 CE to hear again about Jewish rebellion against Rome, during Trajan's Parthian campaign. This happened, however, in the Diaspora, in Mesopotamia, Cyprus, and Cyrenaica. There is no clear evidence that Judea was affected. The uprisings were, apparently, brutally suppressed—a suppression in which Trajan's Berber cavalry commander Lusius Quietus seems to have played a role, and it is for this reason that they are known in rabbinic literature as "the war(s) of Qitos." We simply know too little about these events to know what caused them, but the fact that they took place outside the land would, on the face of it, make it somewhat unlikely that nationalism was a major factor.[21]

However, in 132 another major revolt against Rome broke out on Palestinian soil. Our evidence for the Second Revolt is sparse, and almost

---

[18]See the classic study by Chaim Wirszubski, *Libertas as a Political Idea at Rome During the Late Republic and Early Principate* (Cambridge: Cambridge University Press, 1968). On the Hebrew term ḥerut see n25 below.

[19]The fundamental study of the philosophy of the Fourth Philosophy remains Martin Hengel's *The Zealots: Investigations into the Jewish Freedom Movement in the Period from Herod I to 70 AD* (Edinburgh: T&T Clark, 1997).

[20]See Martin Goodman, "Messianism and Politics in the Land of Israel, 66–135 C.E.," in *Redemption and Resistance: The Messianic Hopes of Jews and Christians in Antiquity*, ed. Markus Bockmuehl and James Carleton Paget (London: T&T Clark, 2007), 149-57.

[21]Further, William Horbury, "The Beginnings of the Jewish Revolt Under Trajan," in *Geschichte— Tradition—Reflexion: Festschrift für Martin Hengel zum. 70. Geburtstag*, ed. H. Cancik et al. (Tübingen: Mohr Siebeck, 1996), 1:283-304.

everything about it is hotly disputed, but we have some hints as to its possible ideological makeup.[22] Its leader Shimʿon bar Kosiba seems to have been regarded at least by some as Messiah and given the messianic title Bar Kokhba ("Son of the Star"). The primary evidence for this comes from rabbinic sources,[23] which also claim that Rabbi Aqiva accepted his messiahship, though his colleague Yoḥanan b. Torta sharply disagreed. Though this tradition is recorded much later, I can see no good grounds for questioning its basic claims, viz., that Bar Kokhba was hailed by some—including some in the rabbinic movement—as Messiah, especially as this may receive some indirect support from writings emanating from the Jewish Christian community of the period, which Bar Kokhba seems to have persecuted.[24]

Date formulae and inscriptions on the coins and in the documents of the Bar Kokhba period are also suggestive, because of the ideologically charged terms they use: "Year One of the *Redemption* (*geʾullah*) of Israel," "Year Two of the *Freedom* (*ḥerut*) of Israel," and "For the *Freedom* (*ḥerut*) of Jerusalem." One coin depicts a monumental building with a star above its pediment, and the name "Shimʿon" wrapped round it in paleo-Hebrew script—presumably a reference to the temple that the messiah Shimʿon hoped to restore.[25] There can be no doubt that the Second Revolt was a full-blown nationalist rebellion

---

[22]Fundamental studies are Peter Schäfer, *Der Bar Kokhba-Aufstand; Studien zum zweiten jüdischen Krieg gegen Rom* (Tübingen: Mohr Siebeck, 1981), and Schäfer, ed., *The Bar Kokhba War Reconsidered: New Perspectives on the Second Jewish Revolt Against Rome* (Tübingen: Mohr Siebeck, 2003). See now William Horbury, *Jewish War Under Trajan and Hadrian* (Cambridge: Cambridge University Press, 2014).

[23]y. Taʿan 4.8, 68a.

[24]See Richard Bauckham, "The Apocalypse of Peter: A Jewish-Christian Apocalypse from the Time of Bar Kokhba," in *The Fate of the Dead: Studies in Jewish and Christian Apocalypses*, ed. Richard Bauckham (Leiden: Brill, 1998), 160-258; Bauckham, "Jews and Jewish Christians in the Land of Israel at the Time of the Bar Kokhba War, with Special Reference to the *Apocalypse of Peter*," in *Tolerance and Intolerance in Early Judaism and Christianity*, ed. G. N. Stanton and G. G. Stroumsa (Cambridge: Cambridge University Press, 1998), 228-38.

[25]Though we cannot be sure of the wording of the ʿAmidah in the second century, it is at least suggestive that the two terms *geʾullah* and *ḥerut* appear so prominently in it, and in a context that resonates strongly with the Bar Kokhba period usage. Benediction 1: "You [God] . . . in love will bring a redeemer (*goʾel*)"; Benediction 7: "Redeem us (*geʾalenu*) swiftly for you are a mighty Redeemer (*goʾel*)"; Benediction 10: "Sound the great horn for our freedom (*le-ḥerutenu*)." See Hanan Eshel, "The Dates Used During the Bar Kokhba Revolt," in *Bar Kokhba War Reconsidered*, 93-106; L. Mildenberg, *The Coinage of the Bar Kokhba War* (Frankfurt am Main and Salzburg: Aarau, 1984); Martin Goodman, "Coinage and Identity: The Jewish Evidence," in *Coinage and Identity in the Roman Provinces*, ed. Christopher Howgego et al. (Oxford: Oxford University Press, 2007), 163-66. The ideological implications of Bar Kokhba calling himself in a letter *Nesi Yisraʾel* rather than *Melekh Yisraʾel*, as one might expect if he is messiah, are not clear.

that was brutally suppressed. The building of a pagan city, Aelia Capitolina, on the site of the old national capital, a city from which, it seems, Jews were barred, was, surely, intended once and for all, to erase the *political* identity of the Jewish people. The Romans were happy for them to exist as a religious community, but not as a *nation*.

The rabbinic settlement. Jewish politics in Palestine in the aftermath of the Bar Kokhba revolt was dominated by the gradual rise of the rabbinic movement, till, under Judah the Prince at the end of the second century, it found itself at last allied to real political power. It seemed to be a period of steady recovery, social and economic, and of growing acceptance of Roman rule. The old apocalyptic fires had not entirely died. Certainly if Jews continued to recite the ʿAmidah in anything like its current form they were regularly reciting a fiercely nationalist, messianic prayer. We hear also of a group known as the Mourners for Zion, who seemed to have lived a life of extreme asceticism and penitence for the destruction of the temple. This mourning for the past must have been tinged with longing for the future: it was, presumably, aimed at moving God to restore his people. The Mourners would, for sure, have agreed that the exile had not ended.[26] The general drift of rabbinic thinking, however, seems to have been to play down messianism and stress the importance of studying and obeying the commandments in the here and now: that brought its own reward, which was enough. They moved toward a strongly realized eschatology.[27] This is expressed in passages such as Mishnah Pirqei ʾAbot 3.6, which opens with the claim that "if ten men sit together and occupy themselves with Torah, the Shekhinah rests among them, for it is written, *God stands in the congregation of God* (Ps 82:1)." The text then goes on to ask whether the Shekinah rests also on five who study Torah, or even on only one, and answers in both cases in the affirmative. We are so used to this famous dictum that we fail

---

[26]On the Mourners for Zion see my *Targum of Lamentations Translated, with a Critical Introduction, Apparatus, and Notes* (Collegeville, MN: Liturgical Press, 2008), 78-86, and my essay, "The Mourners for Zion and the Suffering Messiah: Pesiqta Rabbati 34—Structure, Theology, and Context," in *Midrash Unbound: Transformations and Innovations*, ed. Michael Fishbane and Joanna Weinberg (Oxford: Littman Library, 2013), 137-57.

[27]See my essays "The King Messiah in Rabbinic Judaism," in *King and Messiah in Israel and the Ancient Near East*, ed. John Day (Sheffield: Sheffield Academic Press, 1998), 456-73, and "The Rabbis and Messianism," in *Redemption and Resistance: The Messianic Hopes of Jews and Christians*, ed. Markus Bockmuehl and James Carleton Paget (London: Continuum, 2007), 227-44.

to register how extraordinary it is. Experiencing the divine presence (the Shekinah) is surely the ultimate description of the redeemed state. The Shekinah traditionally was God's indwelling in the temple, and it was experienced collectively by Israel. Here the claim is boldly made that, through the everyday study of Torah, it can be experienced here and now even by an individual. There is no need to wait till the end time, when the temple will be rebuilt. The stress on inwardness, on the individual, on the here and now is startling. It raises the obvious question of what an end-time redemption can add to this.[28]

This stress on a realized eschatology may have been accompanied by a reassessment in some quarters of Roman rule, and an assigning to it of a rather more positive role in the purposes of God—precisely to keep the peace and allow people to flourish.[29] There may have been an attempt to bolster the authority of Judah by suggesting that he was of Davidic descent.[30] This may have been some sort of nod in the direction of nationalist sentiment, but what is striking here is that if Davidic ancestry was claimed for

---

[28]Note how it resonates with the 'Amidah Benediction 17, "Blessed are you, O Lord, who brings back his Shekinah to Zion." This is in the context of rebuilding the temple at the end of days ("restore the service to the sanctuary of your House"). Here we have the traditional view: the Shekinah is the eschatological presence of God with his people in the restored temple. In Pirqei 'Abot it denotes his presence with an individual here and now.

[29]Jewish attitudes toward Rome were, to say the least, mixed, but rabbinic literature of the third century records one strikingly positive assessment in Mishnah Pirqei 'Abot 3.2: "Rabbi Hanina [read: Hananiah] the Prefect of the Priests said: Pray for the peace of the kingdom (*malkhut*), since but for fear of it men would have swallowed each other alive." Hananiah must have been a pre-70 figure, but it is interesting that this dictum of his should have been recovered in the third century. Contrast the petition to God in the *Birkat Ha-Minim* "to uproot, smash, overthrow and humble swiftly in our days the arrogant kingdom (*malkhut zadon*)"—though once again it is impossible to be sure what the ancient text of this benediction might have been: see Ruth Langer, *Cursing the Christians? A History of the Birkat HaMinim* (New York: Oxford University Press, 2012). On what might be meant by *malkhut zadon* see Yaakov Y. Teppler, *Birkat HaMinim: Jews and Christians in Conflict in the Ancient World* (Tübingen: Mohr Siebeck, 2007), 135-48. The absence of the definite article before *malkhut* in Rabbi Hananiah's original statement suggests he was referring to government in general (note Danby's translation: "pray for the peace of the ruling power"), but by the third century the text would surely have been understood as referring to Rome. Cf. Mishnah Sotah 9.15, "R. Eliezer the Great says . . . when the Messiah is at hand, insolence will abound . . . and the Kingdom (*ha-malkhut*) will be turned to heresy (*minut*)." It is possible that from the time of Judah the Prince rabbinic attitudes to Rome may have been somewhat more favorable than those of the population at large. In general see Nicholas de Lange, "Jewish Attitudes to the Roman Empire," in *Imperialism in the Ancient World*, ed. P. D. A. Garnsey and C. R. Whittaker (Cambridge: Cambridge University Press, 1978), 225-81.

[30]See the important study by David Goodblatt, *The Monarchic Principle: Studies in Jewish Self-Government in Antiquity* (Tübingen: Mohr Siebeck, 1994), esp. 176-231.

the Prince, it laid no duty on him to take up arms against Rome and play the part of the warrior messiah. On the contrary, Judah's role was to foster good relations with Rome, while at the same time ruling his community and bringing them back to observance of the Torah. If a sense of continuing exile existed, it was to be negated by study and observance of the Torah.

In the broad narrative I have sketched I find it hard not to see this rabbinic position as a calculated move away from the nationalist messianism of earlier times, a messianism that had brought much pointless suffering on the Jewish people. But this analysis, if sound, strongly suggests that that nationalism was a significant factor in the politics of the earlier period.

This outline of Jewish politics in Palestine from Judah the Maccabee to Judah the Prince leaves many questions unanswered and makes many statements that I know will be disputed. It requires fuller argument and documentation than I can give it here, but I hope I have said enough to make a prima facie case that in these three and a half centuries there was a close correlation between ideology and politics. Events were to an unusual degree driven by ideas, and one of the most potent of these ideas was Jewish nationalism—the unshakable belief that the Jewish people had a divine destiny to live in freedom in their own land, worshiping their own God. It is surely not too big a leap to see that nationalism as being fed by the apocalyptic speculations that were so rife at this time. Jewish nationalism was deeply messianic. Not everyone would necessarily have subscribed to it, even passively and still less actively, but our analysis indicates that it would have been well known, well understood, and, at times, widely embraced. People fired up by this nationalism would have regarded themselves as "still slaves in their own land" so long as they were occupied by a foreign power. If that were the case, then they would surely have held as an inevitable corollary that the exile had not been totally ended, because Israel had not yet been fully restored.

ANALOGIES WITH MODERN ZIONISM?

Throughout this essay, sometimes explicitly, sometimes implicitly, I have made reference to modern Zionism. This has been deliberate, because the issues we are discussing here are of more than antiquarian interest. They resonate powerfully in our own world. Whether we like it or not, there is an elephant in the room—the present-day state of Israel—and this fact should

be acknowledged and addressed.[31] Debates about the exile and return of the
Jews *today* can play both a negative and a positive role in the present discussion. Our understanding of the past always starts from our experience
of the present and is achieved through analogies to it. Modern Zionism
offers, I would argue, on the one hand a resource for understanding
premodern attempts to return to Zion, but, on the other, poses a danger in
that it may lead us, wittingly or unwittingly, to project aspects of the current
situation back into the past in ways that are distorting and inappropriate.

Let me develop this latter point with reference to Shlomo Sand's controversial book, *The Invention of the Jewish People*.[32] Sand argues that the idea
of a Jewish exile from the land of Israel is a myth invented by Zionism to
justify the creation of the Jewish state—the myth that the Jewish people,
having been forcibly expelled from their land, had a right to return and reclaim it. Sand actually argues very specifically against the view, found more
commonly in older, popular Zionist historiography, that it was the *Romans*
who inaugurated the great exile, with the destruction of Jerusalem in 70.
Now that statement is patently wrong, at least in the sense that the exile
began in 70 (though we should not ignore the fact that the Romans may have

---

[31]The founding of the state of Israel, just as much as the Holocaust, challenges Christian theology
on many fronts. The church cannot be indifferent to the reality that is the state of Israel. There
are "pro" and "anti" Israel factions within the church. An example of the former would be the
movement increasingly known as Christian Zionism, which maintains that the modern state of
Israel is the fulfillment of biblical prophecy and part of the special purposes of God in history.
An example of the latter would be pro-Palestinian organizations such as the Sabeel Ecumenical
Liberation Theology Centre in Jerusalem, whose guiding spirit is Naim Ateek. Some members
of these pro-Palestinian groups campaign actively for churches to condemn Israeli policies and
to promote boycotts and disinvestment in Israel. I take no sides here. My point is simply that
the question of the exile and return of the Jewish people is a contested issue *within* the church:
it has become highly visible and highly politicized, and we need to be sensitive to the possibility
that this might intrude on and skew the debate around "continuing exile" in Second Temple
times. See Stephen Sizer, *Christian Zionism: Road Map to Armageddon?* (Leicester, UK: Inter-
Varsity Press, 2004); Sizer, *Zion's Christian Soldiers? The Bible, Israel and the Church* (Downers
Grove, IL: InterVarsity Press, 2007); Paul Wilkinson, *For Zion's Sake: Christian Zionism and the
Role of John Nelson Darby* (Milton Keynes, UK: Paternoster, 2007); Robert O. Smith, *More Desired
than Our Own Salvation: The Roots of Christian Zionism* (New York: Oxford University Press,
2013).
[32]Shlomo Sand, *The Invention of the Jewish People* (New York: Verso, 2007). Sand, of course, was
not by any means the first to attack as myth the idea of the Jewish people. Debate on the subject
has long raged within the academic discipline of biblical studies: see, for example Philip R.
Davies, *In Search of "Ancient Israel,"* 2nd ed. (Sheffield: Sheffield Academic Press, 1995); Keith
Whitelam, *The Invention of Ancient Israel* (London: Routledge, 1996); Thomas L. Thompson, *The
Mythic Past: Biblical Archaeology and the Myth of Israel* (London: Basic Books, 1999).

sold tens of thousands of Jews into slavery at the end of the First Revolt), and to knock it down is to knock down a straw man. Despite this, and despite the fact that, actually, the Zionist case does not stand or fall on whether or not 70 began the exile, Sand is widely regarded on the political left critical of Zionism as having destroyed one of the major planks of the Zionist historical justification of the state of Israel.[33]

This anti-Zionist argument is sometimes developed in the following way. It was the *Christians* who were keen, for their own polemical purposes, to stress the exiled, degraded condition of the Jewish people. As a punishment for the crucifixion of Jesus the Jews had been expelled from their land and compelled to wander homeless and rootless throughout the world. Jews, so the argument goes, in effect took over this essentially *Christian* idea of Jewish exile and absorbed it into their own theology. This is neither the time nor the place to debate these theses. Suffice to say that they clearly have implications for the matter in hand. If we follow Sand, then we will be strongly inclined to play down the significance of the fall of Jerusalem in 70 and to question whether nationhood, in any meaningful sense of the term, or the idea of exile and return, was central to early Jewish theology. And if it *was* central, then there was little historical reality behind it. It was largely self-delusion and myth. There are big, contemporary political agendas in play here, and we need to be aware of this fact.

Although we must be sensitive to how the hermeneutical standpoint in which history has placed us may impinge unhelpfully on our discussion of "continuing exile" in the time of Jesus, it would be wrong to ignore the fact that modern Zionism can, nevertheless, be a useful resource. Modern Zionist analysis of the condition of *galut* is extensive and penetrating[34] and can

---

[33]Note, for example, the endorsements by Tony Judt and Tom Segev on the dust jacket of Sand's book. Segev writes: "Israel's Declaration of Independence states that the Jewish people arose in the Land of Israel and was exiled from its homeland. Every Israeli schoolchild is taught that this happened during the period of the Roman rule, in 70 CE. The nation remained loyal to its land, to which it began to return after two millennia of exile. Wrong says the historian Shlomo Sand, in one of the most fascinating and challenging books published here in a long time. There never was a Jewish people, and the exile also never happened—hence there was no return."

[34]A convenient place to start is the entry by H. H. Ben-Sasson on "Galut," in the *Encyclopaedia Judaica* (Jerusalem: Keter, 1971), vol. 7, cols 275-94. Further, Yitzhak Baer, *Galut* (New York: Schocken Books, 1947); Arnold M. Eisen, *Galut: Modern Jewish Reflection on Homelessness and Homecoming* (Bloomington: Indiana University Press, 1986); Eliezer Don-Yehiya, "The Negation of Galut in Religious Zionism," *Modern Judaism* 12 (1992): 129-55; and the works cited in n8 above.

be suggestive, by way of comparison and contrast, when we try to work out what exile may have meant to Jews in the past. Much of the modern analysis is secular and political and does not rely on religious premises. The result is that many Zionist definitions of exile will differ in obvious ways from the theological concept that we find in biblical and postbiblical Judaism. And yet at a deeper level there are obvious links between the two, and a case can be made that modern secular Zionism offers an interesting "take" on the traditional religious idea.

The relationship between secular Zionism and Jewish tradition is highly complex. The founding fathers of modern political Zionism were aggressively secular and claimed that they were breaking radically with the Jewish past. And yet you do not have to read far in their writings before finding religious language cropping up. One might take the view that this use of religious language is cynical—a tug at the Jewish heartstrings to gain support. There may be some truth in this, but it is not the whole story. In fact modern secular Zionism *needs* traditional religious Zionism to establish its claim that Jews have always seen themselves as having a *national* identity and as aspiring to return to their ancient homeland and become a nation once again. Jews may have clothed their national aspirations in premodern times in religious garb, which is no longer appropriate to modernity, but the desire to return to statehood was very deep and very real, and secular Zionism is simply restating it in ways appropriate to a post-Enlightenment world.

It can also be instructive to compare the modern historical process of the return to the land with what may have happened in antiquity. The argument here is not just one of historical analogy, though historical analogy pure and simple, if carefully used, is a tool that the historian would be foolish to ignore. In this case the analogy is sharpened by the fact that the modern return has, arguably, happened within the same broad framework of assumptions as pertained back in antiquity. Observation of what is happening today under our very noses can be helpful in disclosing the political *potential* of that framework, in establishing what is *possible* within its parameters, and so it can suggestively help to fill in manifest gaps in our record of the past.

Early political Zionism put all its energies into "the negation of the exile" (*shelilat ha-galut*), and there was a sort of unspoken assumption that after independence was achieved within the old homeland that goal would be attained. The sense was that simply being in the land in freedom brought the exile to an end. But even before independence many secular Zionists were aware that that would not be enough. There was the question of *how* one should be in the land. What should be the *cultural* identity of the new Jewish state? And after independence, as Israeli Jewish society matured, it became increasingly clear even to many secular Zionists that that Jewish cultural identity would have to be based in some way on traditional Jewish *religious* sources and *religious* practices. There would have to be an accommodation, albeit at a cultural level, with *Judaism*. So even after independence was achieved, there were goals to be worked for, a process to be completed, before one can finally declare the end of exile.

This sense is found right across the political spectrum in Israel. Secular, socialist Zionism has tended strongly toward a utopian view of the state, and that utopianism from time to time gets expressed in traditional messianic language: Israel should not simply aspire to be "like all the nations" but to be "a light to the nations." A reasonable deduction from this is that the Zionist project is still not finished and will not be finished till the socialist "kingdom of heaven" (if I may speak paradoxically) is achieved.

The sense of "now but not yet" is even stronger in religious Zionism. The establishment of the state of Israel posed a massive theological problem for traditional religious Zionism. What is the relationship between the new political entity that has come into being and the messianic kingdom? For some the answer was "nothing at all." Indeed, because it is so secular and godless, because it is based on the cardinal sin of "forcing the redemption," it has to be rejected. It is a delusion to think that it marks the end of exile. Indeed some, speaking of it in apocalyptic terms as a demonic entity that by inhibiting the coming of the true kingdom is perpetuating the exile, work openly for its downfall. Most religious Zionists, however, have embraced the Zionist project and taken the line that the present state should be seen as the "beginning of the redemption." This allows them to enter the political arena and to work within it for the coming of the kingdom. In this case the implication is even stronger that simply being in the land, even in sovereignty, is not enough. The exile will not be truly ended till a Torah-observant theocracy is established in Israel, within the borders promised to the patriarchs.[35]

Religious Zionism has been increasingly successful in pushing its agenda in Israel, to the growing alarm of the secularists, some of whom speak of a *Kulturkampf* or even of a coup d'état, but in fact it can be argued that it was secular Zionism itself that opened the door for this religious upsurge, which actually grew from *inside* the political process—fundamentally from the fact, as noted earlier, that Israeli Jewish culture was compelled to draw on its traditional religious heritage to create an authentic Jewish identity. There was, to be sure, an attempt to build a Jewish culture exclusively on the ancient *biblical* past of the Jewish people, because at least that had been forged within the land, but it failed, because there was just not enough cultural content in the Bible to make it work.[36] Many secular Zionists have retained a "soft spot" for rabbinic Judaism, a nostalgic, romantic view that it possesses, despite being a product of a *galut* mentality, some sort of intrinsic Jewish authenticity that nothing else can quite match. It should not be forgotten that it was the secularists who passed the *Rabbinical Courts Jurisdiction (Marriage and Divorce) Law* of 1953, the purpose of which, openly expressed at the time, was to maximize the presence of Halakhah within the state legal system, and that the 1970 amendment of the *Law of Return* (1950/54), which created a *religious* definition of a Jew more stringent than that in Halakhah, had support right across the political spectrum.

AND FINALLY JESUS . . .

I conclude with some thoughts on Jesus' preaching on the kingdom. If, as I have argued, there is good evidence that a particular nationalist view of exile and restoration was prevalent in the Jewish community of Palestine in Jesus'

---

[35]See Aviezer Ravitzky, *Messianism, Zionism, and Jewish Religious Radicalism* (Chicago: University of Chicago Press, 1996).

[36]I refer here to the so-called Canaanite movement, which tried to create an Israeli culture based not just on the culture of the Bible but on the culture of the ancient Near East in biblical times, of which, following critical historical scholarship, it held biblical culture to be a part. The Canaanite experiment petered out, but for a while it alarmed the establishment, both secular and religious, and it was probably instrumental in persuading some secularists that traditional Judaism would have to be a part of Jewish identity, even though much of it was forged in conditions of *galut*. See James S. Diamond, *Homeland or Holy Land? The "Canaanite" Critique of Israel* (Bloomington, IN: Indiana University Press, 1986); Y'aakov Shavit, *The New Hebrew Nation: A Study in Israeli Heresy and Fantasy* (London: Cass, 1986).

day (as attested not only by texts but also by events), then we should try to read Jesus' teaching about the kingdom against it. It is unthinkable that he would not have known about it or had it in mind. But when we conduct this exercise, it becomes startlingly clear that Jesus' message would have come across *only as extreme paradox* to anyone holding, in any shape or form, the views we sketched above. There seems to be no point where his view meaningfully converges with theirs. It is not so much that Jesus stressed that the kingdom would come only when individuals repented and put themselves right with God. A religious nationalist could have accepted that, but his inevitable question would be, "Then what? What shape will the kingdom take? Will repentance lead to the throwing off of the Roman yoke? Sketch out for me, if you would, what you think the Jewish state will be like?"[37] The most disconcerting aspect of Jesus' teaching was that his relentless insistence on inner transformation and personal relationship to God could be read as implying that *that* was the coming of the kingdom. It was an end *in itself*—not a means to an end. True, his healing miracles taken as signs of the kingdom, his campaign for justice for the poor and the outcast, his overthrowing of the money-changers' tables in the temple, and other "messianic acts," could be seen as pointing to a view of the kingdom that goes beyond individualism and inwardness. And it is not impossible that toward the end of his ministry, he developed a sense that he personally had a role to play in bringing in the kingdom, over and above that of preaching repentance, and that that role somehow involved him embracing a martyr's death.

---

[37]One thinks of Joseph Klausner's assessment of Jesus as a fine religious teacher ("*the* Jewish moralist *par excellence*") but completely "unsound" on the national question. See Klausner, *Jesus of Nazareth: His Life, Times and Teaching*, trans. Herbert Danby (New York: Macmillan, 1925). The novelist Amos Oz, Klausner's grandnephew, recalls in his wonderful autobiography: "Once Uncle Joseph said to me: 'At your school, my dear, I imagine they teach you to loathe that tragic and wonderful Jew, and I only hope that they do not teach you to spit every time you go past his image or his cross. When you are older, my dear, read the New Testament, despite your teachers, and you will discover that this man was flesh of our flesh and bone of our bone, he was a kind of wonder-working Jewish pietist, and although he was indeed a dreamer, lacking any political understanding whatsoever, yet nevertheless he has, his place in the pantheon of great Jews, beside Baruch Spinoza, who was also excommunicated'" (Oz, *A Tale of Love and Darkness*, trans. Nicholas de Lange [London: Vintage, 2005], 58-59). As Oz notes, Herbert Danby got into hot water for translating Klausner's book: the Anglican establishment in Jerusalem demanded that he be dismissed from his post (he was a residentiary canon at St. George's, Jerusalem), because he had helped promote something "tainted with heresy, in that it portrays our Saviour as a kind of Reform rabbi, as a mortal, as a Jew who has nothing to do with the Church."

But his fundamental stress that everything begins in the heart of the individual remains utterly astonishing.

There can surely be no doubt that Jesus bequeathed to his followers only an embryonic, enigmatic doctrine of the kingdom that left much theological work to be done. That work evolved in two somewhat contradictory directions. Some were to insist that Jesus would come back to earth again to do some of the things that the Messiah was traditionally supposed to do. This can be seen as an attempt to key Jesus' deeply radical teaching on the kingdom back, at least partially, into standard Jewish apocalyptic scenarios. Others, however, were to take the line that it was through the banding together of those individuals reconciled to God into a redeemed community (the church), a community that grew out of the one Jesus himself had founded, and through their preaching and living out of his teaching in the world, that Israel and ultimately humanity would be brought back to God and the kingdom realized. The church was the shock-troops of the new spiritual order: the answer was ecclesiology. But it is hard to avoid the conclusion that Jesus himself was a lone, radical voice in the Jewish politics of his day. Some aspects of realized eschatology at Qumran perhaps edge toward his position, but at Qumran there remained a belief in a national, political redemption. The closest analogue to Jesus' own position, paradoxically, seems to be that developed by the rabbinic movement in the late second and third centuries.

CHAPTER FIVE

CONTINUING EXILE AMONG THE PEOPLE OF THE DEAD SEA SCROLLS

Nuancing N. T. Wright's Hypothesis

ROBERT KUGLER

THE BASIC IDEA BEHIND N. T. WRIGHT'S ARGUMENT—that many Jews at the turn of the eras thought themselves to be in enduring exile well after the end of Babylonian dominance—I regard as relatively uncontroversial: there is little doubt that first-century Jews, both BCE and CE, defined themselves in a very basic way by the loss of autonomy over the land of Israel (what I call a "negated" relationship to the land), regardless of their place of habitation—in the land itself or in Diaspora.[1] That being said, a close look at one of the bodies of evidence Wright calls on to make his argument, the Dead Sea Scrolls, proves that in at least one important respect

---

[1]For Wright's treatment of this theme, see, among others, *Paul and the Faithfulness of God, Book I, Parts I and II* (Minneapolis: Fortress, 2013), 139-63; Wright, "Yet the Sun Will Rise Again: Reflections on the Exile and Restoration in Second Temple Judaism, Jesus, Paul, and the Church Today," in this volume. Wright appropriately acknowledges that many others have made the same argument, some well before him and others after him, and often in different ways (e.g., *Paul and the Faithfulness of God*, 139). He acknowledges especially O. H. Steck, *Israel und das gewaltsame Geschick der Propheten. Untersuchungen zur Überlieferung des deuteronomistischen Geschichtsbildes im Alten Testament, Spätjudentum und Urchristentum*, WMANT 23 (Neukirchen-Vluyn: Neukirchener Verlag, 1967); Steck, "Das Problem theologischer Strömungen in nachexilischer Zeit," *EvT* 28 (1968): 445-58. One does not have to look far to see the degree to which the topic is well rehearsed among students of Jewish and Christian origins; see as but a pair of examples Martien Halvorson-Taylor, *Enduring Exile: The Metaphorization of Exile in the Hebrew Bible*, VTSup 141 (Leiden: Brill, 2010); James M. Scott, ed., *Exile: Old Testament, Jewish and Christian Conceptions*, JSJSup 56 (Leiden: Brill, 1997).

his understanding of this basic element of Jewish identity in the later Second Temple period can be refined. The way the exile theme is deployed in the Scrolls confirms a variety in the ways that Jews imagined the continuing exile would come to an end that Wright, it seems to me, has not elaborated, a variety that is present even among the texts he treats as foundational to the basic idea of continuing exile (Dan 9; Deut 27–30).[2] Taking account of this insight offers a degree of additional nuance to Wright's basic argument regarding exile and could have at least modest consequences for his larger project of investigating "Christian origins and the question of God."[3]

I begin with an overview of Wright's own argument for the importance of continuing exile to Jews at the turn of the eras (through which I also point out the variety of views regarding exile's end present in the key texts Wright uses to make his argument). From there I turn to demonstrate the presence of the same variety in the Scrolls. I close by commenting on the significance of these enhancements for Wright's emphasis on continuing exile and for his larger project.

N. T. WRIGHT AND THE THEME OF "CONTINUING EXILE" AMONG SECOND TEMPLE JEWS

Wright describes Israel's continuing exile as a "political and theological state rather than a geographical one,"[4] in recognition of the fact that Jews could view themselves in exile even if they dwelt in Judea itself.[5] Laying out the essential characteristics of his position, Wright says that

---

[2]To be sure, Wright does elaborate the character of the exile's end at length, and that is a critical part of his overall project. But the "why" of exile's end—what triggers it—he seems to have glossed over.

[3]Also worthy of note will be the implication of the Qumran evidence for Wright's insistence that that the continuing exile topos so consistently worked in Jewish imagination just as he says it did, as a *single historical sequence*. Below we evidence from the Scrolls that there were Jews around the turn of the eras who were able to posit the sequence as having repeated itself in the past and as repeating itself again in their present experience.

[4]Wright, *Paul and the Faithfulness of God*, 139; Wright, "Yet the Sun Will Rise Again," 20.

[5]That exile was a political state is easily understood, and whether Wright meant it as such or not, saying that it was also a "theological state" nicely captures its character as a feature of ethnic, not religious, identity among ancient peoples. On the contemporary debate as to whether we should speak of Judaism as a religion or an ethnicity in Greco-Roman antiquity, see, among others, Shaye Cohen, *The Beginnings of Jewishness: Boundaries, Varieties, Uncertainties* (Berkeley: University of California Press, 1999), a work that in many ways marks the beginning of the ongoing debate among scholars of early Judaism about the appropriate categories for analyzing and talking about Judaism before Late Antiquity. For the genealogy and details of the debate since Cohen, see now David M. Miller, "Ethnicity, Religion and the Meaning of *Ioudaios* in Ancient 'Judaism,'"

we can get at the heart of what I am saying like this: that, within the *continuing narrative* that virtually all Jews believed themselves to be living in . . . a great many second-temple Jews interpreted *that part of the continuing narrative in which they were living* in terms of the so-called Deuteronomic scheme of sin—exile—restoration, with themselves still somewhere in the middle stage, that of "exile."[6]

And while he acknowledges that there were "different perceptions of this at the time," he nonetheless insists on the consistency with which there was "the sense of living within the middle term of the Deuteronomic scheme," "the *theological* awareness of being at a particular stage within the overall continuing narrative, coupled with the *exegetical* awareness of the large-scale Deuteronomic prophecy being worked out."[7]

As for how the "overall construal" works, Wright argues that it begins with Daniel 9 and the central figure's petitionary prayer that Jeremiah's prophecy of seventy years has been fulfilled (Dan 9:2), and the angelic response that it is rather seventy-times-seven, a 490-year period that Israel must endure in exile (Dan 9:24-27). Between those two points in the prayer he points out the echoes of Deuteronomy 28–29 in Daniel 9:11-13, suggesting that

> "Daniel" is thus positioning himself and his people within the continuous narrative promised by Moses. It is not that Deuteronomy promised, in general terms, that "disobedience would bring exile," as though this were something that might just happen every so often in a miscellaneous fashion, unconnected with any larger narrative. Rather, Deuteronomy set out, briefly in Deuteronomy 4, fully in Deuteronomy 27–30, and then again in the great poem of Deuteronomy 32 and its flanking chapters of Deuteronomy 31–33, a *single historical sequence*, which—though it has taken hundreds of years!—has eventually come to pass. The prayer of Daniel 9 takes its stand within this single narrative at the point of transition from the end of Deuteronomy 29 to the start of Deuteronomy 30.[8]

CurBS 12 (2014): 216-65; see also Miller's two earlier essays that form the rest of his three-part series on key aspects of this debate: "The Meaning of *Ioudaios* and Its Relationship to Other Group Labels in Ancient 'Judaism,'" *CurBS* 9 (2010): 98-126; "Ethnicity Comes of Age: An Overview of Twentieth-Century Terms for *Ioudaios*," *CurBS* 10 (2012): 293-311. While the centrality of the theme of continuing exile in early Judaism (and the diversity of understandings of it) is, in fact, consequential for the debate as to whether Judaism was an ethnicity or religion in antiquity, I leave that question mostly aside in this essay. See, however, the concluding comments.

[6]Wright, *Paul and the Faithfulness of God*, 140; Wright, "Yet the Sun Will Rise Again," 21.

[7]Ibid.

[8]Wright, *Paul and the Faithfulness of God*, 139; Wright, "Yet the Sun Will Rise Again," 23. Notably, Wright inserts a footnote at the end of the penultimate sentence in this quote that criticizes me (and others) for suggesting that the SER cycle is "in [Deuteronomy] chs. 27–30 or 31–33, a

That is to say, Daniel calls on the promise to Israel in Deuteronomy 30:1-5 that if they returned to God with all their heart and soul from the lands to which they would be driven as punishment for their faithlessness, God would restore the people to the land and the holy city. Gabriel's response to Daniel, however, is to declare that the restoration would be delayed for the duration of seventy-times-seven and that afflictions would come to Israel in that period. Thus, according to Wright, "this combination of Daniel's revised prophecy about the 490 years and the Deuteronomic warning of the curse of the exile followed by the blessing of covenant renewal is . . . at the heart of the controlling story within the worldview not only of first-century Pharisees but also of a great many other second-temple Jews as well."[9] Understanding themselves in the decades and centuries following the "publication" of Daniel to be within the promised continuing exile, but also near its end, Jews were consumed with calculating the 490 years to determine the moment when restoration would be achieved and the continuing exile would conclude.[10]

'repeated pattern.'" In fact, I suggested that the pattern that repeats in Israel's history is one of "election, apostasy, punishment, and vindication by God" (Robert Kugler, "Testaments," in *Justification and Variegated Nomism*, vol. 1, *The Complexities of Second Temple Judaism*, ed. D. A. Carson et al. [Tübingen: Mohr Siebeck, 2001], 194n19), and I was referring specifically at that point to Deut 31–32 (inasmuch as the Song of Moses itself creates the sense of the repetition of the pattern—Moses provides it as a record of the past to describe what he sees to be the people's future so that they might sing it in that future to fulfill it again!). That said, I would also happily defend the view that it is repeated several times in the complex of traditions that appear in Deut 27–33. The pattern of election, apostasy, punishment, and vindication is manifestly repeated in those complex chapters, surely in part because of the chapters' editorial history, but also because it served the purposes of the writers of the chapters to reiterate the pattern. And that that is so does not mean that later readers could not treat the *literary* repetitions of a pattern of election, apostasy, punishment, and vindication as referring to one *continuing exile* (which some clearly did, as Wright's work and that of many others shows). Just so, though, other later readers could read the chapters to authorize an understanding of the people's history—past, present and future—as subject to several repetitions of the pattern (and why not, considering that in a few short chapters Deuteronomy gives way to the Deuteronomistic History, which records multiple episodes of sin-punishment-restoration within its own bounds!); see for instance the speech put in the mouth of Achior in Judith 5:5-21 (upon which Wright remarks with these words: "In the book of Judith, the Ammonite leader Achior tells the pagan king Holofernes the long story of the patriarchs, of Israel's slavery in Egypt, and of Israel's repeated sin, defeat and exile but also restoration under God's protection" [*Paul and the Faithfulness of God*, 121, and which he treats as a rare "exception" to the Deuteronomic scheme he thinks predominated, although he hedges a bit in this case; ibid., 158]).
[9]Wright, *Paul and the Faithfulness of God*, 146.
[10]Wright writes: "In other words, *they* [Jewish readers of Dan 9] *knew that, despite the geographical 'return' in the late sixth century and on to the time of Ezra and Nehemiah in the mid-fifth century*

As to *why* first-century Jews saw exile ending, Wright appears to hold strongly to the position that with few exceptions it was as Deuteronomy 30 "prophesied"—through the people's turn toward God in obedience and God's merciful restoration of them in response. Take, for example, his discussion of Baruch's wisdom poem in Baruch Deuteronomy 3:9–5:9. The wisdom, which Israel must rediscover to end its exile (Bar 3:14), Wright declares to be Deuteronomy 30, citing the rhetoric especially of Deuteronomy 3:29–4:4 and its echoes of Deuteronomy 30:11-14; from this he draws the conclusion that Baruch shares in the Deuteronomic scheme he thinks predominates in Jewish imagination about how the continuing exile would come to an end. The "insight that drives the prayer, the poem and the promise" is that if the people do what is pleasing to God—"take hold of Wisdom/Torah" according to the standards of Deuteronomy 30—"the promise of Deuteronomy 30 is going to come true."[11] A mark of his confidence in the consistency of this perspective across a variety of Jewish literature and ideological perspectives is his concluding remarks to his discussion of Baruch in this regard that anticipate my own brief discussion of 4QMMT below: "Baruch is a very, very different book from 4QMMT, but the underlying theological and exegetical point is exactly the same."[12]

Yet a close reading of the two texts at the crux of his argument, Deuteronomy 30:1-5 and Daniel 9:15-19, reveals a critical tension between them on the question of why the exile should come to an end, which suggests that, in Wright's own words, there were indeed "different perceptions of this at the time," at least with respect to what would bring the exile to an end. To begin with Deuteronomy 30:1-5, Wright correctly points out that it conditions the restoration on the people's return to God; indeed Deuteronomy 30:2 goes a step further to command the people to "obey him with all your heart and with all your soul, just as I am commanding you today"—to precipitate the end of exile they must accrue renewed righteousness by the standard of the law decreed to Israel by Moses. By sharp contrast, in Daniel 9:14-19, Daniel acknowledges that God brought calamity on Israel because the people

---

BC, *something they still regarded as 'exile' was not yet over.* And they were reading their own situation, again and again, within the single flow of national narrative which they found in Deuteronomy 27–30" (ibid., 146).

[11]Ibid., 153.

[12]Ibid.

"disobeyed his voice" (Dan 9:14), but he goes on to ask for Israel's restoration not on the basis of Israel's renewed righteousness but for the sake of God's own reputation. Daniel begins by observing that because God brought the people from Egypt God's name is "renowned even to this day" (Dan 9:15), but that Israel's sin has made God's people a disgrace among the peoples (Dan 9:16). Therefore, Daniel argues, God should listen to his prayer: "For your own sake, Lord [Heb, *lemaʿan ʾadonay*] let your face shine upon your desolated sanctuary" (Dan 9:17).[13] Daniel repeats that God should "look at our desolation and the city that bears your name," and declares that he does "not present . . . supplication before you on the ground of our righteousness, but on the ground of your great mercies," that God should hasten to forgive, to "act and . . . not delay" precisely for "for your own sake, O my God, because your city and your people bear your name" (Dan 9:18-19).[14] In short, while the version of the sequence in Deuteronomy 30 conditions Israel's restoration on its obedience to the law, Daniel's prayer argues that it is in God's reputational interest to restore Israel, quite (indeed, explicitly) apart from the people's righteousness or sinfulness.

It is worth noting that Daniel's prayer is not the only text cited by Wright in his discussion of the exile theme that supports this notion of why exile ends. In the article included in this volume, and in his book on Paul, Wright mentions Leviticus 26 as another "Pentateuchal passage to carry the promise of a historical sequence culminating in a continuing exile and an ultimate return."[15] He rightly observes that Leviticus 26:1-13 rehearses the benefits of God's covenant promises for the people in the land, Leviticus 26:14-33 explains the curses that will befall the people if they fail to heed God's commandments and break the covenant, climaxing with the exile of the people

---

[13]The Masoretic Text of the phrase given in the Hebrew is more properly translated "for the sake of my Lord." The NRSV and others assume an error here and follow the pre-Hexaplaric revision of the Greek translation ascribed to Theodotion, *heneken sou*, and rely on the clear occurrence of *lemaʿanka* in Dan 9:19 (but see the additional possibilities suggested by other ancient translations recorded in John J. Collins, *Daniel*, Hermeneia [Minneapolis: Fortress, 1993], 345n25). In any case, the sense is clear. What is notable for the purpose of the present essay is the use of *lemaʿan* + a pronominal suffix referring to God (or God's name) in this context. This proves to be a recurring construct in the tradition regarding the cause of exile's end.

[14]The repeated second-person singular possessive suffixes in Daniel's address to God underscore the emphasis on God's interest in ending the exile; see the comment in this regard by Sharon Pace, *Daniel* (Macon, GA: Smith & Helwys, 2008), 290.

[15]Wright, *Paul and the Faithfulness of God*, 149; Wright, "Yet the Sun Will Rise Again," 28.

from the land, and Leviticus 26:34-39 indicates that in the people's absence from it the land will enjoy the Sabbath years the people did not allow it.[16] Alluding to Leviticus 26:40-45, he then writes, "But—one of those great biblical 'but's!—'if they confess their iniquity . . .' then God will remember his covenant with Abraham, Isaac and Jacob; he will remember the covenant he made at the Exodus; and—this is not said, but it is surely implied—he will rescue them from their continuing exile."[17]

While it is not clear from his comments on the passage which side of the issue he would take on the matter, that this is a case of anticipating exile's end entirely thanks to God's covenant faithfulness—and not at all because of the people's renewed righteousness—is evident from a careful reading of Leviticus 26:40-41. The passage reads,

> But if they confess their iniquity and the iniquity of their ancestors—that they committed in their treachery against me, and in their hostility to me so that I, in turn, was hostile to them and brought them into the land of their enemies—if then their uncircumcised heart is humbled and they accept their iniquity (*yirtsu' et 'avonam*), then I will remember my covenant with Jacob, and I will remember my covenant with Isaac and also my covenant with Abraham, and I will remember the land. (Lev 26:40-42)

The key phrase in this passage comes at the end of Leviticus 26:41 and is given in Hebrew and English above. Most translations assign to *ratsah* its secondary meaning, "to make atonement for," "to make amends for."[18] The immediately preceding text, however, indicates that what is required is remorse, not self-redeeming action, a point well made by Jacob Milgrom in his defense of the translating *ratsah* with its primary meaning, "to accept," as I do here.[19] On this reading, exile's end is solely the work of

---

[16]Wright, *Paul and the Faithfulness of God*, 149-50.
[17]Wright, *Paul and the Faithfulness of God*, 150.
[18]E.g., the NRSV translates "make amends for." For a discussion of the ancient translational record, modern translations, and contemporary commentators on *ratsah* in Lev 26:41, see Robert Kugler, "A Note on Lev 26:41, 43; 4Q4343 1 II 3 and 4Q504 1–2 Recto 5–6; and 1QS 8:3 (par. 4Q259 2:12): On Human Agency in the Divine Economy at Qumran," in *Prayer and Poetry in the Dead Sea Scrolls and Related Literature: Essays in Honor of Eileen Schuller on the Occasion of Her 65th Birthday*, ed. Jeremey Penner et al., STDJ 98 (Leiden: Brill, 2012), 245-50, esp. 245-47.
[19]Jacob Milgrom, *Leviticus 22–27*, AB 3B (New York: Doubleday, 2001), 2333: "The renderings 'and they make amends for their guilt' (NAB), 'and they make amends for their iniquity' (NRSV), 'and they shall atone for their iniquity' (NJPS) cannot be correct because they impute to Israel a further activity to secure its redemption. This cannot be. One should not confuse Israel's

God, as in Daniel's prayer.[20] As we see below in the discussion of 4Q504, this is a reading of Leviticus 26 taken over fully in one of the Dead Sea Scrolls.

Last, that exile's end is the work of God or the result of renewed human righteousness are not the only two perspectives on the matter in the Hebrew Scriptures is already plain from Daniel 9 within its context. While Daniel's prayer takes the position we have just seen in Leviticus 26, the book of Daniel—indeed the angel's response to Daniel's prayer!—has a radically different view: the end of exile is predetermined by God's mastery of history from beginning to end; neither does it depend on the righteousness of the people, nor does it hang on the pride of God.

The Variety of Exile's End in the Dead Sea Scrolls

That the people of the Dead Sea Scrolls once considered themselves in particular to be enduring a continuing exile is a virtual commonplace among students of the Scrolls. That being said, just as the following discussion aims to add nuance to this general observation, other work on the topic in the past has also uncovered significant distinctions in the way the community deployed that theme, distinctions that are useful to recognize here. For example, in work devoted in particular to the theme in the Damascus Document, Michael Knibb distinguished two different uses of the exile—a theological use that argues that God initiated an authentic return from exile only with the establishment of the faithful community (e.g., CD 1:1–2:1; 3:9-20; 5:20–6:2; cf. 4Q372 1:10-15; 4Q390) and a community history use that speaks of the group's self-imposed exile from other Jews in Palestine (CD 7:14-19 and "Damascus" as the place of exile for an elect law studying group; cf. CD 4:2-3; 6:3-4; [par. 4QD^a 2 iii 20; 3 ii 11–12; 4QD^b 2:11–12]; 1QpHab 11:4-8; 1QHa 12:8-9; 4Q177 1:8-9).[21] Martin Abegg

---

confession and remorse with the prophetic doctrine of repentance. Here Israel is only required to change its heart, but not its ways. From this point on, all the activity stems from God: once the land has made up its neglected sabbaticals, God will recall the covenant and, presumably (it is not stated explicitly), restore Israel to its land."

[20]Still many other texts might be cited here, but see especially Is 43:14-25; 48:1-21, both of which return in the discussion of 4Q504 below.

[21]Michael Knibb, "Exile," in *Encyclopedia of the Dead Sea Scrolls*, ed. Lawrence Schiffman and James VanderKam (Oxford: Oxford University Press, 2000), 1:276-77; Knibb, "Exile in the Damascus Document," *JSOT* 25 (1983): 99-117.

demonstrated that the covenanters used the exile theme by invoking not only the Babylonian captivity but also the enslavement of the people in Egypt before the exodus and the dispersion of the tribes of Israel by the Assyrians.[22] Commenting in particular on the interpretation of Isaiah 40:3 in 1QS 8:13-16 (par. 4QS[e] III 3-6), Devorah Dimant brought to attention the degree to which exile is imagined as a "spiritual" rather than geographical experience among the covenanters.[23] George Brooke highlighted the ways in which coming out of exile was used in similar ways by the emerging and established Qumran community in the second and first centuries BCE to give space to prophetic experiences that facilitated the community's claims to be in special connection with God.[24] Aharon Shemesh has uncovered another nuanced use of the notion exile, whereby the Qumran penal codes reserve *kareth*, "expulsion," for those who err intentionally (*beyad ramah*) and assign only *galuth*, "exile," for those who sin without intent (*shogeg*).[25] And Noah Hacham has drawn attention to the similarities and differences between the Qumran community's self-understanding as a community in self-imposed, religiously significant exile within Palestine and the experience of Diaspora Jews of the time.[26]

Turning now to the evidence of the Scrolls on why exile ends, we see present among them all three of the notions of exile's end identified above in the Hebrew Scriptures. Return on the basis of the covenanters' righteousness and according to a plan prearranged by God are both unsurprising among the Scrolls, given the widely recognized focus of the community responsible for them on the effectual character of their own righteousness and on God's sovereign manipulation of time and events to

[22]Martin Abegg, "Exile in the Dead Sea Scrolls," in Scott, ed., *Exile*, 111-25.

[23]Devorah Dimant, "Not Exile in the Desert but Exile in Spirit: The *Pesher* of Is 40:3 in the *Rule of the Community*," *Megillot* 2 (2004): 21-36 (Hebrew).

[24]George Broke, "The Place of Prophecy in Coming Out of Exile: The Case of the Dead Sea Scrolls," in *Scripture in Transition: Essays on the Septuagint, Hebrew Bible, and Dead Sea Scrolls in Honour of Raija Sollamo*, ed. Anssi Voitila and Jutta Jokiranta, JSJSup 126 (Leiden: Brill, 2008), 535-50.

[25]Aharon Shemesh, "Expulsion and Exclusion in the Community Rule and the Damascus Document," *DSD* 9 (2002): 44-74.

[26]Noah Hacham, "Exile and Self-Identity in the Qumran Sect and in Hellenistic Judaism," in *New Perspectives on Old Texts: Proceedings of the Tenth International Symposium of the Orion Center for the Study of the Dead Sea Scrolls and Associated Literature, 9–11 January 2005*, ed. Esther Chazon et al., STDJ 88 (Leiden: Brill, 2010), 3-21.

prove them right. Especially in light of those emphases, less expected is the relatively vibrant presence of the perspective that God will end the exile chiefly out of concern for God's own reputation. Thus I cite only briefly one example of each of the first two perspectives to devote more attention to the third.

The view that exile would end through renewed righteousness on the part of at least some among God's people is well known in the Scrolls— indeed the group members view themselves as the true "repentants of Israel" (*shebe yisr'ael*), whose Torah piety will bring an end to Israel's exile. The phrase itself appears in a limited number of passages,[27] but the concept is widespread. For instance, one of the passages Wright leans on in his exposition of the theme in the Scrolls, 4QMMT C, the work's closing exhortation,[28] clearly presumes that Israel endured a continuing exile that was beginning to draw to a close precisely because of the Torah observance of the group associated with the document's author(s). From the perspective of the text's author(s), the exile brought on by the behaviors of (and sponsored by) the kings of the divided kingdom had lasted unabated since Babylon conquered Jerusalem (C 18–22), but had now begun to give way to a new phase because of the righteousness of the "we" associated with the text's author(s) (C 23–25).[29]

Closely related to and often intertwined with this tradition of the group's righteousness precipitating the end of the continuing exile is the view among the covenanters that it is also the inevitable outcome of God's plan for human history. A casual reading of 4QMMT C already signals that inclination among the covenanters, but its presence is most pronounced in the texts that offer a fully developed periodization of history at the end of which comes the conclusion of the continuing alienation from the land. An example of this that has received much attention in recent years is 4Q390, classified by its editor, Devorah Dimant, as a manuscript of Apocryphon of Jeremiah C.[30]

---

[27]See 4Q266 3 ii 12 [par. 4Q267 2:11; CD 6:5]; 4Q166 1 i 16; 4Q171 3–10 iv 24; 4Q266 5 i 15; see also CD 4:2; 8:16; 19:29.

[28]Wright, *Paul and the Faithfulness of God*, 146-48nn289-91.

[29]For 4QMMT C, see Elisha Qimron and John Strugnell, *Qumran Cave 4.V. Miqsat Ma'ase Ha-Torah*, DJD X (Oxford: Clarendon Press, 1994), 58-63.

[30]For the *edition princeps*, see Devorah Dimant, *Qumran Cave 4.XXI: Parabiblical Texts, Part 4: Pseudo-Prophetic Texts*, DJD XXX (Oxford: Clarendon Press, 2001), 235-54. Some argue that 4Q390 is, in fact, a separate work; see especially the discussion in C. J. Patrick Davis, "Torah

Whatever its proper assignment, it is a work that builds a temple- and priesthood-focused account of the 490 years of exile prophesied in Daniel 9:24-27. While we do not have the end of the work and therefore do not know precisely how it imagined exile ending, it clearly hews closely to the Danielic scheme. The first period is seventy years of exile in Babylon under apostate priests (1:1-5); the second period lasts until sometime in the seventh jubilee and features those who returned from Babylon to rebuild the temple and restore sacral order (1:5-7). Yet the restoration is disrupted by the third period, an era of renewed cultic apostasy that compels God to hand all the people, save a remnant, over to the angels of Mastemah (1:11) and Belial (2 i 4) for a period of seven years. The description of the final period of seventy years, also given over to the control of the angels of Mastemah, begins in 2 i 6 and is characterized by covenant violations and violent and unjust avarice.[31] Presumably the lost portion of the text narrates the end of the final period of tribulation and the corresponding end of exile. An indication of how it might have ended is possibly available in the combined testimony of the other manuscripts assigned by Dimant to the Apocryphon of Jeremiah C, especially if Kipp Davis's hypothesis regarding 4Q390 being a later exegetical development of the remaining manuscripts is accurate.[32] In that case, the conclusion would be associated with a renewed hunger and thirst for the Torah (or more probably a renewed cult and purified priesthood).

It is the third view in the Scrolls of why exile ends that holds most interest here, largely because it is so little observed. This approach conforms with the perspective that Daniel articulated in his prayer and that appears in traditions such as Leviticus 26. It turns up in texts as different as the War Scroll and the Words of the Heavenly Luminaries.

Performance in the *Golah*: Rewritten Bible of 'Re-Presentational' Authority in the *Apocryphon of Jeremiah C*," in *The Dead Sea Scrolls at Sixty Years: Canadian Scholarship in the Dead Sea Scrolls and Other Essays*, ed. Peter Flint et al., EJL (Atlanta: SBL Press, 2010), 467-95; Eibert Tigchelaar, "Classification of the Dead Sea Scrolls and the Case of *Apocryphon of Jeremiah C*," *JSJ* 43 (2012): 519-50.

[31]This instance of exile, punishment, restoration, followed by a repetition of the cycle is one of the instances from the Dead Sea Scrolls alluded to in n2 above that seems to undercut Wright's insistence that the experience of continuing exile was almost universally viewed as a *single historical sequence*.

[32]See 4Q385a, 4Q387, 4Q387a, 4Q388a, and 4Q389 in DJD 30.129-234, 255-60; see Davis, "Torah Performance in the *Golah*," *passim*; see also Cana Werman, "Epochs and End-Time: The 490-Year Scheme in Second Temple Literature," *DSD* 13 (2006): 229-55.

In association with the seventh engagement in the final battle of the war, 18:6b-8 of the War Scroll assigns to the priests and the fighters the saying of this blessing.[33]

> Blessed is your name, God of gods, for you have made great with your people
> to do wonders, and you have kept your covenant for us (*uberitkah shemartah*
> *lanu*) from old, and the gates of salvation you opened for us many times for
> the sake of your covenant (*lemaan beritkah*). And you lift up our affliction
> according to your goodness among us (*w[etis]a enenu ketobkah banu*), and
> you, God of righteousness, acted for the sake of your name (*lemaan shimkah*).

While direct mention of the exile is absent from the passage, the progress of the war between the Sons of Light and the Kittim entails the going up of "the exile of the Sons of Light (*golat bene or*) from the wilderness of the peoples (*mimidbar haamim*) to encamp in the wilderness of Jerusalem (*lekhanut bamidbar yerushalayim*)" (1QM 1:3), from where they set out to fight the Kittim until God gives them victory; and "after the war they go up from there" (*weakhar hamilkhamah yaalu misham*), an unmistakable reference to the end of continuing exile and the reoccupation of Jerusalem by the righteous. That this blessing related to the final engagement of the final battle emphasizes that God acts decisively on the side of the Sons of Light precisely for the sake of his covenant and his very name makes crystal clear this scroll's perspective on why the continuing exile comes to an end: God's pride and covenant obligations are controlling.[34]

A further instance of this that is remarkably well developed can be seen in 4Q504, a manuscript of the Words of the Heavenly Luminaries. Dating

---

[33]For the Hebrew text and a translation, see Jean Duhaime, "War Scroll," in *Damascus Document, War Scroll, and Related Documents*, ed. James H. Charlesworth, PTSDSSP 2 (Tübingen: Mohr Siebeck, 1995), 136-37.

[34]Note especially the recurring second-person possessive suffixes that stress this theme as a matter of grammar and meaning (and even sound in the hearing of the text read aloud). Brian Schultz, *Conquering the World: The War Scroll (1QM) Reconsidered*, STDJ 76 (Leiden: Brill, 2007), has convincingly demonstrated that 1QM 1 previews and summarizes the first phase of a two-phase eschatological war wherein the Sons of Light experience the end of their exile through the intervention of God, and columns 15–19 give an account of that phase of the war (while the second phase against the whole world, covered in columns 10–14, takes place *within* the messianic age); for a concise statement of his understanding of 1QM and the relationship between it and the related Cave 4 manuscripts, see Brian Schultz, "Compositional Layers in the War Scroll (1QM)," in *Qumran Cave 1 Revisited: Texts from Cave 1 Sixty Years After Their Discovery: Proceedings of the Sixth Meeting of the IOQS in Ljubljana*, ed. Sariana Metso et al., STDJ 91 (Leiden: Brill, 2010), 153-64.

to around 150 BCE, 4Q504 almost certainly predated the founding of the community site by the Dead Sea, but the community used the work as their own throughout the period of habitation there, as evidenced by the later copies of it among the scrolls (see 4Q505 [70–60 BCE] and 4Q506 [50 CE]).[35] The prayer for Friday, the sixth day, in fragment 1–2 v–vi, draws our attention.

While we lack both the beginning of the prayer and its conclusion, more than enough survives to understand its shape. Like the other prayers in the collection, it begins with a historical prologue (1–2 v 1–vi 10) that sets up the petition proper (1–2 vi 10–19). And like the other prayers in the collection it is redolent with echoes of Hebrew Scriptures,[36] in this case especially of Deuteronomy 30 and Leviticus 26, texts we saw above to be on opposite ends of the spectrum when it comes to the "why" of exile's end.[37] As the following comments on key portions of the prayer make clear, it calls on those two texts, among others, to tell the people reciting it that exile ends thanks only to God's willing (Lev 26), and in no way thanks to human will (Deut 30).

The historical prologue divides into two parts, 1–2 v 1–17a and 1–2 v 17b–21, vi 2–10a.[38] Both parts follow a similar pattern that begins with recollection

---

[35]The manuscripts appear in M. Baillet, *Qumran Grotte 4 III (4Q482–4Q520)*, DJD 7 (Oxford: Clarendon Press, 1982), 137-75. For the key studies of the Friday prayer referenced below, see Esther Chazon, "'Gather the Dispersed of Judah': Seeking a Return to the Land as a Factor in Jewish Identity in Late Antiquity," in *Heavenly Tablets: Interpretation, Identity and Tradition in Ancient Judaism*, ed. Lynn LiDonnici and Andrea Lieber, JSJSup 119 (Leiden: Brill, 2007), 159-75, esp. 167-71; Chazon, "Scripture and Prayer in 'The Words of the Luminaries,'" in *Prayers That Cite Scripture*, ed. James Kugel (Cambridge, MA: Harvard University Press, 2006), 25-41; Chazon, "*Dibre Hammeʾorot*: Prayer for the Sixth Day (4Q504 1-2 v–vi)," in *Prayer from Alexander to Constantine: A Critical Anthology*, ed. Mark Kiley (London: Routledge, 1997), 23-27; Bilhah Nitzan, "Traditional and Atypical Motifs in Penitential Prayers from Qumran," in *Seeking the Favor of God*, vol. 2, *The Development of Penitential Prayer in Second Temple Judaism*, ed. Mark Boda et al., EJL 22 (Atlanta: Society of Biblical Literature, 2007), 187-208, esp. 192-98; James Davila, *Liturgical Works*, ECDSS (Grand Rapids: Eerdmans, 2000), 239-65.

[36]Chazon, "Scripture and Prayer in 'The Words of the Luminaries,'" 34-38, uses *florilegium* to name the use of Scripture in the historical prologue for the sixth day, borrowing on the term's reference to linking a number of quotations together in a new composition (28). She views the petition proper, on the other hand, as a "free composition" that does not invoke particular Scripture passages, but rather deploys rather standard, ubiquitous rhetoric recognizable as such to the person reciting the prayer (38-41).

[37]Notably, it also differs from other prayers in the collection in that it deals with the "present state of the worshipers" (Nitzan, "Traditional and Atypical Motifs," 197) and not merely past events.

[38]For this division, see Chazon, "*Dibre Hammeʾorot*," 24. Note, though, that my own description of the sections within each iteration of the patterns differs from Chazon's in important respects; see further below.

of the people's sin and punishment, continues with an ode to God's faithfulness to the covenant nonetheless, and concludes in the first part with an
account of how God's mercy is the trigger for the people's return to God,
especially in prayer, and God's concomitant restoration of the people. The
second part, 1–2 v 17b–21, vi 2–10a, follows a similar progression but appears
to reflect on a contemporary experience of the cycle, and the final stage leads
not to the recollection of prayer poured out but to the petition proper in the
prayer for the sixth day.[39]

The pattern in the first part is as follows. Fragment 1–2 v 1–6a, using the
rhetoric of Leviticus 26:32-33, recalls the curses that befall Israel for dis-
loyalty to the covenant.[40] The following passage, 1–2 v 6b–11a, then invokes
Leviticus 26:44-45 to declare that in spite of Israel's apostasy, rather than
forsake them or the covenant promises, God remembered how he brought
the people out in the sight of the nations and did not leave them among the
goyim, the peoples, a reference surely to the exile and return.[41] The third
section of the pattern divides into two subsections, beginning with 1–2 v
11b–14. Deuteronomy 30:1-2 is used here, but it is also subverted by re-
phrasing.[42] The biblical passage uses the *hiphil* of *shub* in Deuteronomy 30:1
to speak of the addressee in exile taking to heart all the curses and blessings
spoken just before this by Moses, with the result being that he returns to the
Lord and obeys the commandments again. By contrast, the prayer begins by
noting that God shows mercy to his people in all the lands where he drove
them to *cause them* to take to mind (*hiphil* of *shub*) to return to God and to
obey God's voice according to all that God commanded them; the prayer
converted the entirely human action of returning and obeying conveyed in
Deuteronomy 30:1-2 into the result of God's initiating act of mercy—
God *caused* the people to take it in mind to return. The next subsection,

---

[39]Notably this repetition provides a clear instance where an interpreter of the sin-exile-return
pattern provided by the Hebrew Scriptures is viewed as repeated and repeatable in Israelite
experience.

[40]See also Josh 24:20 and Jer 5:19 for the phrase '*abad el nekar*, and Jer 2:13; 7:3 for *maqom mayim
khayyim*; cf. Davila, *Liturgical Works*, 261; Nitzan, "Traditional and Atypical Motifs," 193.

[41]Chazon, "'Gather the Dispersed of Judah,'" 16, concurs on this point.

[42]Nitzan, "Traditional and Atypical Motifs," 193; and Davila, *Liturgical Works*, 261, also connect
this section to Deut 30; Chazon, "Gather the Dispersed," 168; Chazon, "Scripture and Prayer,"
36, agrees that Deut 30:1-2 is tinkered with here but does not describe its use as a subversion of
its meaning.

1–2 v 15–17a, repeats this pattern of God's action that causes the human response of reaching out to God. As in Isaiah 44:3, God pours out his holy spirit upon the people (*yatsaktah ruakh qodshekah alenu*) to bring his blessings upon them (*lehebi birkotekah alenu*). Echoing Isaiah 26:16, the prayer says that as a consequence they seek him in their distress (*lifqodkah betsar lanu*) and pour out a prayer when his chastening was upon them (*lelakhesh beqatson musarkah*). While the passage depends on Isaiah 26:16, it uses the language of the verse solely to ascribe to God all action that brings restoration to Israel in its troubles, save prayer and petition.[43]

The second part of the historical prologue (which is particularly thick with scriptural echoes and allusions) repeats the pattern apparent in the first part. It begins with a section that appears to be a reference to the current situation: the people have entered into tribulation and punishment because they vexed God (1–2 v 17b–19; see Is 51:13 for 18–18a; Is 43:23-24 for 18b–19). The second section (on God's covenant faithfulness) argues, however, that even though they vexed God and have failed to heed the commandments, God has not compelled the people to serve God or to take a more profitable path (1–2 v 20–21; see Is 43:23-24; 48:17-18; cf. Neh 9:34; Job 21:15); [44] God even cast away their iniquity and purified them from their sin for his own sake (vi 2–3a; see Ezek 18:31; Lev 16:30; cf. Prov 20:9). This he did out of his righteousness and sovereignty over all things (vi 3b–4a). The third section of the second part returns to Leviticus 26, invoking especially Leviticus 26:40-45. Fragment 1–2 vi 4b–6a all but quotes Leviticus 26:40-41, and in keeping with the translation of it in the discussion of the Leviticus passage above, the verb *ratsah* should also be

---

[43]Here too commentators recognize the parallel, yet some overlook the way the prayer's author(s) seem to have deployed it; see, for example, Davila, *Liturgical Works*, 262. But see Nitzan, "Traditional and Atypical Motifs," 194, citing Chazon's unpublished dissertation: "Chazon states rightly that these phrases are based on Is 44:3b and 26:16, importing the promise of future blessings into the consciousness of the penitent worshippers that they are those who are blessed by God's holy spirit, which *enabled them* [italics mine] to seek God and to pour out prayer before him in time of tribulation" (who adds Is 44:3b); see also Chazon, "Scripture and Prayer," 36-37.

[44]Nitzan, "Traditional and Atypical Motifs," 195n31, does not accept the restoration of *lo* ("not") at the beginning of line 20 on the basis of the clear reliance on Is 43:23, saying that it is "not appropriate to the context." She suggests instead *weattah* ("and you"). Yet the context would seem to argue most strongly for a faithful use of the negative from Is 43:23, as the thrust of the prayer as a whole is God's faithfulness to his promises *for his own sake* and *in spite of the people's disobedience*.

read here in its primary sense "to accept," rather than in its secondary sense "to make atonement for"—the consistent theme of God determining the people's fate favorably and of the people not being asked, let alone being able, to act to save themselves from their iniquity requires it.[45] Then 1–2 vi 6b–10a builds on the communal acknowledgement of sin to invoke and rework Leviticus 26:44: the people thus accept their chastisement so that they do not break the covenant with God (6b–8a) but even that is owing to God having strengthened their heart so that they could recount God's mighty deeds for all eternity (8b–10a).[46]

The petition proper follows in fragment 1–2 vi 10b–19, and although it is, as Chazon argues, a free composition that echoes a panoply of "scriptural rhetoric" without quoting texts directly,[47] it does invoke Deuteronomy 30:1 (especially in lines 12–14), but in a way similar to the first use of Deuteronomy 30:1-2 in the early part of the historical prologue: it subverts the conditionality of the passage and turns it into a remark on divine unilateralism in restoring the people from the lands to which they had been dispersed, near and far. Whereas the deuteronomic source text stresses the requirement that the people renew their obedience to God's commandments, such language is absent here, giving way entirely to the passage's emphasis on God bringing the people back from their exile and out of their tribulation. One expects nothing less, given the relentless focus in the historical prologue on God's sovereign action in punishing and reclaiming the people for his own sake.[48]

---

[45]Nitzan, "Traditional and Atypical Motifs," 196; and Davila, *Liturgical Works*, 263, recognize Lev 26:41 and translate *ratsah* as "to atone," "to make amends for." Chazon, *"Dibre Hamme'orot,"* 25, also translates the verb in its transitive sense.

[46]Chazon, "Scripture and Prayer," 37-38, takes a very different view of the significance of the prayer's reworking of Lev 26:44; she writes, "In this radically revised quotation, the worshippers effectively declare that they have done even more than was required to ensure that God would answer their plea and prevent them from being destroyed."

[47]See note 36 above.

[48]Chazon, "Scripture and Prayer," 40, also remarks on the reappearance of Deut 30:1 in the midst of what is otherwise a "free composition." Indeed, she writes, "While the *florilegium* in the prologue openly quotes the deuteronomic promise and retains the biblical context, merely updating it to the time of its fulfillment, the petition now freely reuses this revised quotation, distancing the language further from its deuteronomic source." I would only add that it also separates it from its deuteronomic notion of God's justice, replacing it with the unilateralism that is otherwise so prevalent in the prayer.

CONSIDERING THE CONSEQUENCES OF DIVERSITY OF OPINION ON THE NATURE OF EXILE'S END IN THE DEAD SEA SCROLLS

We have seen now that among the people of the Dead Sea Scrolls there were at least three visions of the way exile ends. By the reckoning of some, the moment could come to pass through the cooperation of human and divine agency—human righteousness would precipitate divine action. Others figured that God had determined the timing and nature of exile's end, and agency for it coming to pass belonged only to the course of history. And still others viewed exile's end as God's doing alone, an act that depended solely on God, who would give it as pure gift to God's people.

To this summary we must add an observation left to this point only implicitly acknowledged. Already in the Scrolls we see these three views, which are rooted in distinct biblical traditions, beginning to overlap in single works. For evidence of this one must look only so far as some of the texts discussed above. 4QMMT certainly hints at the twinning of a divine timetable with human righteousness that precipitates the end of exile. Merging these two perspectives is even more evident in the *Apocryphon of Jeremiah C*, which gives restored zeal for Torah and for the temple's purity a role to play in its divinely determined chronology for the end of history (and exile).

It is also important to acknowledge the tension between the variety of ideas at Qumran about how exile ends and the otherwise tightly focused nature of the core of that community's thought regarding temple and priestly purity. Like the pluriformity of the scriptural texts found among the Scrolls, the penal codes that govern the community(ies), and the structural norms for the community(ies), this diversity of ideas on a single topic seems dissonant with what we rightly take to be a group that otherwise held some ideas to be nonnegotiable in nature. There is, I think, a clear explanation for this phenomenon that rests on understanding the people of Qumran not as a religious group but as a subgroup within the established Judean ethnicity of the ancient Mediterranean world. A hallmark of ancient ethnic groups was their openness to a diversity of views on matters inessential to a group's identity, counterbalanced by firmness on issues that were fundamentally constitutive of that identity. This apparent contradiction between a relaxed attitude toward inessentials and rigidity regarding core topics was especially true of subgroups engendered by conflict with their parent ethnic group over such central concerns.[49] As I have argued at length elsewhere, the latter form of this pattern characterizes the people of the Dead Sea Scrolls; understanding that explains the apparent incongruity of diversity among the covenanters regarding some topics and the relative immutability of their ideas regarding temple and priestly purity.[50]

These last two observations and the central insight of this essay regarding the diversity of views on exile's end in the Dead Sea Scrolls have consequences for Wright's larger project of investigating "Christian origins and the question of God."

First, inasmuch as the people of the Scrolls were a subgroup with a particularly intense commitment to their core ideas, it seems sensible to anticipate similar or even greater diversity of views on exile's end where it is also not a central concern for other groups and thinkers that were, nonetheless, less rigid at their core than the covenanters. Thus as Wright moves forward in his analysis of the key figures of Christian origins whose thought he strives to unveil for his readers—from Jesus' Jewish precursors and contemporaries to Jesus, from Paul to Paul's interpreters, and from the authors of the Gospels to the earliest Christians—he might be well served by openness to the variety of schemes for exile's end beyond the one he identifies with Deuteronomy 30, which he seems to favor.

Second, the discovery that different biblical notions of exile's end already began to merge in single works among the covenanters of Qumran suggests that the same can be expected, a fortiori, among the writings of later Jews and Christians. An illustration of this phenomenon, using the opening passage of 1 Peter, is useful.

First Peter is deeply concerned with the life and conduct of its addressees as they endure a sort of exile in anticipation of its end with Jesus' imminent return to complete God's salvation history (1 Pet 1:7, 13; 4:7). That the addressees live in the "in-between time" characteristic of the continuing exile Wright identifies across early Jewish and Christian literature is clear from the writer's rhetoric. The very first verse addresses the recipients as

---

[49]On the key aspects of this view of ancient ethnic identity, see Jonathan Hall, *Ethnic Identity in Greek Antiquity* (Cambridge: Cambridge University Press, 1997), 17-33, esp. 32-33.

[50]I have elaborated this theory at greater length in "Ethnicity: A Fresh Context for Locating the 'Religion' of the Dead Sea Scrolls," in *A Companion to the Dead Sea Scrolls*, ed. George J. Brooke and Charlotte Hempel (London: T&T Clark, forthcoming).

parepidēmois diasporas, "exiles of the Dispersion." In 1 Peter 1:17 the author exhorts his audience to conduct themselves with reverence for God *ton tēs paroikias hymōn chronon,* "during the time of your exile." And in 1 Peter 2:11 he urges them *hos paroikous kai parepidēmous,* "as aliens and exiles" to keep themselves from corporeal desires that distract from the cares of the soul. While the predilection to resort to the term *exile* for *paroikia, paroikos,* and *parepidēmos* attested in the NRSV can rightly be questioned,[51] it nonetheless captures the author's understanding of his audience's condition as corresponding to that of the Israel's exiles awaiting the fulfillment of God's promise of return. That the author has the exile as such in mind is underscored by his use of the classical language of exile to denote Rome—like so many other early Jewish and Christian writers, he dubs it Babylon (1 Pet 5:13).[52]

In this context, the salutation and thanksgiving make for striking reading on the question of how the audience's "exile" will come to an end. In the salutation alone, one could argue that two of the perspectives we found in the Scrolls already make an appearance. In 1 Peter 1:1-2 the writer salutes the "exiles of the Dispersion . . . who have been *chosen and destined by God the Father* and sanctified by the Spirit *to be obedient to Jesus Christ* and to be sprinkled with his blood."[53] By contrast, 1 Peter 1:3-5 ascribes the believer's new birth, hope, imperishable inheritance, and salvation to God's mercy—deliverance from the present sojourning in exile is due to God's direct, unconditioned gift. And as if to ensure that the nod toward the efficacy of human action in 1 Peter 1:2 is secure, 1 Peter 1:6-9 declares that the genuineness of the

---

[51]See especially the discussions of the terms offered by John H. Elliott, *1 Peter: A New Translation with Introduction and Commentary* (New York: Doubleday, 2000), 312-15, 366-69, 476-83, who argues strongly against translating any of them with the term *exile.*

[52]See ibid., 882-87, for a discussion of the term's appearance in 1 Pet 5:13 and elsewhere in the literature of the period. On the general importance of exile in the idea world projected by 1 Peter, see Andrew Mutua Mbuvi, *Temple, Exile and Identity in 1 Peter* (London: Continuum, 2007).

[53]To be sure, the syntax of the clause in 1 Pet 1:2 that permits the translation "to be obedient to Jesus Christ" is difficult, and it has been argued that it allows the alternative "because of the obedience and sprinkling of the blood of Jesus Christ" (see Francis Agnew, "1 Peter 1:2—An Alternative Translation," *CBQ* 45 [1983]: 68-73, accepted by Elliott, *1 Peter,* 319-21). However, even if Agnew's proposal is accepted—even though it has to rest on the highly unusual (and contested) translation of the preposition *eis* with a causative sense—Agnew himself argues that the *result* of Christ's obedience and the purpose the author has in mentioning it is encouragement of the audience's obedience in conformity with Christ (see esp. 72 and the passages in 1 Peter cited there). In light of Agnew's argument it is tempting to think that the author, in fact, intended a *double entendre,* evoking the obedience of Jesus and invoking the believer's response with the same clause.

believer's faith will bring "praise and glory and honor when Jesus Christ is revealed" (1 Pet 1:7; i.e., the present exile ends) and that the "outcome of your faith" will be "the salvation of your souls" (1 Pet 1:9). First Peter 1:10-12 closes the thanksgiving by further underscoring that salvation from alien status in a strange land was predetermined by God: the prophets investigated and determined that it was God's plan all along to give the elect exiles a deliverance that the angels could only "long to see" (1 Pet 1:12).

A few moments' reflection on this last passage lifts up a third potential consequence of this study for Wright's project, perhaps the most theologically significant one. Our look at the Scrolls shows that notions of God predetermining the moment of history's conclusion and active human participation in that can be made to live together, even if the fit might seem a bit uncomfortable to the modern reader (cf. Apocryphon of Jeremiah C). But 1 Peter brings all three schemes for "exile's end" into one text, highlighting a seemingly irreconcilable tension between two of them that I have thus far not explicitly acknowledged. If God liberates human beings from their alienation as a *sovereign act of divine mercy*, what logical role can *human obedience* contribute to that liberation?[54] And yet 1 Peter 1:1-12 would seem to allow precisely those two schemes to coexist. What this connotes— Is 1 Peter simply theologically inconsistent? Does 1 Peter demonstrate a way in which seemingly mutually exclusive theological notions are not, in fact, irreconcilable?—I cannot say here but must rather leave to the theologians to consider. But for Wright's ongoing project, at least, the implication is clear. As he continues his impressive journey through the history of Christian origins and the question of God, not only should he be on the lookout for the diverse modes of bringing exile's end identified in this study; he will also do his readers yet another good turn by identifying and wrestling with further instances of the theological tension apparent in 1 Peter.

---

[54]For the record, I would argue that while these two views do appear in the Scrolls, they do not occur together in a single text from Qumran as starkly as they do in 1 Peter. In that sense, their co-presence among the people of the Scrolls falls into the category of acceptable differences of opinion among members of a subgroup united in its opposition to its parent group on other core ideas. This has significant implications for how we understand the intensity of *theological* concerns among the people of the Scrolls, but the task of fleshing that out waits for another occasion.

CHAPTER SIX

THE DEAD SEA SCROLLS AND EXILE'S END

Sword and Word and the Execution of Judgment

DOROTHY M. PETERS

For the In[structor, the Rule of] the War.

The beginning of the dominion of the Sons of Light

shall be undertaken against the forces of the Sons of Darkness . . .

Supporting them are those who have violated the covenant.

The sons of Levi, the sons of Judah, and the sons of Benjamin,

those exiled to the wilderness,

shall fight against them . . .

when the exiles of the Sons of Light return from the Wilderness

of the Peoples

to camp in the Wilderness of Jerusalem.

EXCERPTED FROM THE WAR SCROLL

And I [Noah] atoned for all the land . . .

Again, I blessed the one who had compassion on the land,

because he removed and destroyed from upon it

Funding for this study was provided, in part, by the Social Sciences and Research Council of Canada under a postdoctoral fellowship carried out at Trinity Western University and subsequently, by the Harold Hyam Wingate Fellowship while the author was Visiting Fellow at the Oxford for Hebrew and Jewish Studies, University of Oxford.

War Scroll (1QM 1:1-3). English translations of the DSS adapted from Michael O. Wise, Martin G. Abegg Jr., and Edward M. Cook, *The Dead Sea Scrolls: A New Translation*, 2nd ed. (San Francisco: HarperSanFrancisco, 2005), with adaptation as necessary.

all who work violence and wickedness and deceit
but rescued the righteous man.

FROM THE GENESIS APOCRYPHON[1]

EXILE MUST END. Among those who agreed that they were still living in
exile were the Second Temple Jewish Essenes, a movement that included
those calling themselves the *Yahad* or "Community," some of whom dwelt
on the shores of the Dead Sea at Qumran.[2] For these Jews, Israel had never
fully returned from exile, had never been fully restored to the land. Return
from exile would happen only after God judged the nations. Understanding
that God had turned away from his sanctuary and given Israel up to the
sword because of unfaithfulness, the priestly Essenes viewed themselves as
"exiled" from the temple and their beloved founder, the Teacher of Righteousness, as driven into involuntary exile where the "Wicked Priest" (un-
named high priest in Jerusalem) pursued him.[3]

However, their theology was resilient, and they quickly found God's purposes, assuming a new identity as a remnant living on the margins, but who
would escape the utter destruction to come.[4] A confession in the Community Rule includes three verbs found in biblical prayers offered during
exile: "We have committed iniquity, we have transgressed, we have sinned,
we have been wicked, we and our fathers before us."[5] Now in wilderness exile,
they prepared for the eschatological war against the sons of Belial planned
for the next "thousand generations."[6]

---

[1]1Q20 10:13; 11:11-14.

[2]The *Yahad* at Qumran was likely just one of many settlements of a larger, diverse, and developing
Essene movement in ongoing conversation with unifying, codifying centers, such as Jerusalem. Each
settlement exhibited individual variations in thought and practice. Alison Schofield, *From Qumran
to* Yahad*: A New Paradigm of Textual Development for* The Community Rule, STDJ 77 (Leiden: Brill,
2009), 65. On the similarities between the internally, self-identified *Yahad* and the Essenes known
from the external, classical sources, see Joan E. Taylor, "The Classical Sources on the Essenes and
the Scrolls," in *The Oxford Handbook of the Dead Sea Scrolls*, ed. Timothy H. Lim and John J. Collins
(Oxford: Oxford University Press, 2010), 173-99: cf. Philo (*Hypoth.* 11.1) and Josephus (*J.W.* 2.124).

[3]Damascus Document (CD 1:3-4; cf. Lev 26:25); Thanksgiving Psalms (1QH³ 12:8-9); Catena A
(4Q171 1:5-10); 1QpHab 11:2-8.

[4]4QApocryphon of Jeremiah Cᵉ (4Q390 1:7b-10).

[5]1QS 1:24-26; cf. Ps 106:6; Dan 9:5; 2 Chron 6:37; 1 Kings 8:47. See George J. Brooke, "Psalms 105
and 106 at Qumran," *RevQ* 14 (1990): 267-92.

[6]The Rule of the Community (1QS 8:12-14; 9:18-20); 1QM 1:2-3; 4QpPsª (4Q171 frgs. 1–10 ii, 26–iii,
2). For the self-understanding of "exile" as a continuing state, see Martin G. Abegg Jr., "Exile and

Yet, even among the people of the Dead Sea Scrolls (DSS) who agreed that exile must end are found echoes of vigorous debates about the *means* to exile's end. They explored with apparent eagerness how they might participate with God in the execution of judgment—with "sword" sheathed and unsheathed—to bring about end of exile and true return to land and temple. This essay pieces together fragments of these ancient debates about the role of words and swords, about scripture and its interpretation, and how Jews believed they were meant to live as the people of God in the present and in the future when they hoped that exile would end.

VIOLENCE AND NONVIOLENCE: THE YAHAD AND THEIR CONTEMPORARIES

The ebb and flow of bloodshed between the third century BCE and 70 CE shaped scriptural interpretation and the debate about the sword and violence during the time that the Scrolls were being composed, copied, and collected at Qumran. Known to the Essenes were the Hasmoneans, sword-wielding priestly contemporaries resembling the later priestly, nationalistic, militaristic Zealots of Jesus' day. The priestly Hasmoneans (nicknamed Maccabees) adopted the "Phinehas model" for priestly roles in warfare.[7] A zealous, priestly, sword-brandishing Phinehas, known from the Scriptures for having killed a defiler with his sword, became the idealized archetype for the Maccabees and, later, the Zealots.[8] Positioning themselves on a "back-to-the-Bible" and "back-to-Hebrew" platform, the Maccabees revolted violently against Antiochus IV Epiphanes, putting both Hellenizing Seleucids and assimilated Jews to the sword, forcing circumcisions, cleansing

---

the Dead Sea Scrolls," in *Exile: Old Testament, Jewish, and Christian Conceptions*, ed. James M. Scott, JSJSup 56 (Leiden: Brill, 1997), 111-25. Abegg sees CD 7:9b-15 and 4QpsEzek^a (4Q385 frg. 16 i, 3–6) as a rehearsal of the Babylonian exile (Abegg, "Exile," 118). Cf. N. T. Wright's contribution to this volume, where he argues for and against "continuing exile" ("Yet the Sun Will Rise Again," n2 and n4; for the DSS and the real "return from exile," n24).

[7]So Christophe Batsch, "Priests in Warfare in Second Temple Judaism: 1QM, or the *Anti-Phinehas*," in *Qumran Cave I Revisited. Texts from Cave 1 Sixty Years After Their Discovery: Proceedings of the Sixth Meeting of the IOQS Ljubljana*, ed. Daniel K. Falk et al., STDJ 91 (Leiden: Brill, 2010), 165-78, here 172-73.

[8]Num 25:6-15; 1 Macc 2:23-68; 3:18-19; 2 Macc 5:1-4. On the violence of the Zealots (Josephan "Fourth Philosophy"), see *Ant.* 18.9-10, 23-25; *J.W.* 2.651. For an excellent overview of this period, see Hanan Eshel, *The Dead Sea Scrolls and the Hasmonean State* (Grand Rapids: Eerdmans, 2008). The priest elected by the Zealots was aptly named Phinehas (*J.W.* 4.154-155).

the temple in 164 BCE, and reestablishing worship until the Hasmonean dynasty ended in 37 BCE.

The way of life of most Essenes, in contrast, resembled the "way of peace" Wright describes as found in Jesus' teaching. In the descriptions of the Essenes in the external, classical sources, Philo and Josephus communicate that they did not make weapons of war;[9] instead, the Essenes were "ministers of peace" and swore to do no harm even while they hated the wicked.[10]

There were differences, however, between the Essenes and the early Jesus movement. Jesus' followers were instructed to love their enemies, to bless those who cursed them, and to pray for those who abused them (Lk 6:27-28); in contrast, the internal, sectarian Dead Sea Scrolls writings instructed those living according to the rule of the *Yahad* quite differently. Consistently with Josephus's description, the Community Rule of the *Yahad* did teach restraint from returning evil for evil and instructed its initiates to the pursuit of others, but only for good.[11] However, they were told to bless only those "foreordained to God," whereas those "foreordained to Belial" they were to curse.[12] As "Children of Light" they were to hate the "Children of Darkness," but their hatred for the "Men of the Pit" was to be concealed until a future, eschatological Day of Vengeance when they expected to "attack the wicked."[13]

Scholars such as David Flusser have attempted to resolve the apparently dissonant beliefs and practices of a movement known externally for its peaceful way of life and, internally, for instructing its adherents to hate and to curse, and for whom the purpose for nonretaliatory behavior was to hasten the keenly anticipated vengeance of God.[14] Some scholars have

---

[9]Philo, *Prob.* 78.

[10]Josephus, *J.W.* 2.135, 139, 142. However, Essenes did carry arms for protection against brigands (*J.W.* 2.125), and "John the Essene" was a military commander (*J.W.* 2.567; 3.11).

[11]1QS 10:17-20.

[12]1QS 2:1-5.

[13]1QS 1:9-10; 9:21-23. More so than the Hebrew DSS, some Aramaic texts represented in the DSS allow for the potential of carefully circumscribed but mutually beneficial relationships between Jews and their neighbors in the Diaspora (*ALD* 13.8-10; 1Q20 19:23-25). See James M. Scott, "Exile and Self-Understanding of Diaspora Jews in the Greco-Roman Period," in *Exile: Old Testament, Jewish, and Christian Conceptions*, ed. J.M. Scott, JSJSup 56 (Leiden: Brill, 1997), 173-218.

[14]David Flusser, "The Hatred Through the Love," in *The Spiritual History of the Dead Sea Sect* (Woodstock, VA: Jewish Lights Publishing, 1989), 76-82; cf. Hippolytus's documentation of Essenes who refused to hate their enemies and prayed for their persecutors (*Elenchus* 9.23); for evidence that Hippolytus was "Christianizing" Josephan sources, see, "Classical Sources," 186.

assumed that, at any given point in space and time, a group would have spoken with a unified voice. Therefore, some have attempted to assign different expressed ideologies to different subgroups or to different stages of the group's development. For example, J. T. Milik proposed that Essenes developed militaristic Zealot-like tendencies only at a *late* stage of their existence and that they became a "centre of military resistance."[15] Alternatively, Gordon Zerbe constructed a framework in which the "prohibition of retaliation" and a "sometimes passionate interest in vengeance" are held together in "eschatological tension."[16] Alex Jassen proposes that the "rhetoric of violence" effectively empowered those disempowered before Rome's military might and Jerusalem's powerful priesthood. He provocatively argues that the *infusion* of a violent worldview was simultaneously *defused* by the delay of all punishment until the legitimatized eschatological battle.[17]

However, if we do not insist that the Essenes spoke in a unified voice, then the DSS can be read more straightforwardly as a multivoiced recording of snatches of the conversations among the various Essene settlements and throughout the history of the movement concerning the means to exile's end. We now turn to a brief survey of the unsheathed sword, as it was authorized in the scriptural stories of the Jewish ancestors, and as the *Yahad* Essenes visualized it in their imagined *future*.

With Sword Unsheathed: Interpretation of Scriptural Past

Before the Bible became a book, when Scriptures were still written into scrolls, and when the books of Enoch and Jubilees were still authoritative for some Jews, the Essenes found within their Scriptures a generous range of exegetical possibilities concerning human participation in divine acts of judgment. Certainly, the people of the Dead Sea Scrolls were not

---

[15]J. T. Milik, *Ten Years of Discovery in the Wilderness of Judea*, trans. J. Strugnell (London: SCM Press, 1959), 95-97.

[16]Gordon M. Zerbe, *Non-Retaliation in Early Jewish and New Testament Texts: Ethical Themes in Social Contexts*, JSPSup 13 (Sheffield: Sheffield Academic Press, 1993), 135.

[17]Alex Jassen, "The Dead Sea Scrolls and Violence: Sectarian Formation and Eschatological Imagination," *Biblical Interpretation* 17, nos. 1–2 (2009): 12-44. However, the DSS *never* describe judgment acts by the righteous as "violence (*hamas*)," attributing "violence" only to others; e.g., a commentary on Habakkuk protests the violence of the "Wicked Priest," the principal adversary to the "Teacher of Righteousness" (1QpHab 8:1-13).

sword-carrying priestly Maccabees or Zealots! Yet, these questions they pondered as they searched their Scriptures: Under what conditions and by what means might they participate with God in the judgment that would precede the end of exile? *Who* should wield the metaphorical or literal two-edged sword (*herev*) of judgment?[18] *How* did God authorize it? Against *whom* would the sword be wielded? Finally, *when* would it happen?[19]

Interpreters of antiquity studying their scrolls of Genesis and Exodus would have noticed a God capable of performing acts of judgment all by himself. The flood upon the earth, the fire upon Sodom and Gomorrah, and the plagues upon Egypt required no help from Noah, Abram, or Moses. Second Temple Jews continually and diversely re-formed biblical characters into archetypes freighted with the differing theologies and ideologies of their interpreters. Noah, for example, became an appealing archetype for those who favored an ideology that left vengeance and judgment in the hands of God. A postexilic Noachic archetype had already been foreshadowed in Isaiah 54:9-10 ("For this is like the days of Noah to me"), with the flood becoming an archetypical exile and God's covenant with Noah an archetypical "covenant of peace." For his interpreters, therefore, Noah also embodied and prefigured their own experiences of exile, hoped-for judgment upon evildoers and return to the land and the place of worship.

While judgments by flood, fire, and plague could easily be imagined as sent directly from God, the two-edged sword normally had attached to it a human hand. In Genesis, Levi and Simeon had killed the Shechemites with their swords for defiling their sister, but this proved problematic. Jacob immediately censured his sons and later rebuked their swords as "weapons of violence" (Gen 34:25-31; 49:5). Therein lay the dilemma for Levi's priestly, purity-conscious Second Temple period descendants, especially those attempting to distance themselves from the kinds of priests who were wielding the sword willy-nilly in supposed defense of Jewish purity. For that reason, the sword of Levi had to undergo rehabilitation by means of creative

---

[18]Unless otherwise noted, the term *sword* in this essay represents the Hebrew חֶרֶב (*herev*).

[19]For more on the conversations around these specific questions, see Dorothy M. Peters, "The Sword in the Dead Sea Scrolls and Sixteenth-Century Anabaptism," in *Struggles for Shalom: Peace and Violence Across the Testaments*, ed. Laura Brenneman and Brad D. Schantz, Studies in Peace and Scripture: Institute of Mennonite Studies (Eugene, OR: Pickwick Publications, 2014), 125-37.

exegesis.[20] For example, in the second-century BCE book of Jubilees, it is explicitly God who delivers the Shechemites into the hands of Levi and Simeon so that the brothers could execute a divinely authorized judgment upon the defilers, destroying them with the sword.[21]

In Leviticus, in a passage Wright describes as "historical prophecy" pointing to the exile, the time is foretold when God would personally unsheathe his metaphorical sword of vengeance against his own people for covenant violations (Lev 26:25, 35-36).[22] The unsheathed sword was thus effectively preauthorized against covenant violators. This excited the imaginations of the exiled authors of the War Scroll liturgical drama. With hope, they anticipated a day of vengeance by the "sword of God" and fervently hoped to "do mightily" when God "called out a sword against all the nations."[23]

In the Bible, even within Deuteronomy and the Deuteronomistic history, there is ambivalence about the sword wielded in human hands. On one hand, upon the initial entry into the land following the exodus from Egypt, Moses communicates God's authorization of the Israelites to practice *herem* warfare. That is, all inhabitants of some cities—men, women, and children—were to be put to the sword and annihilated (Deut 13:12-15). Later, the *Temple Scroll*, a reworking and rewriting of some of the Torah, heightened the authority of this command by placing it into God's own mouth: "Concerning on[e of your cities that] *I* am giving you to in[dwell]"; now it was God who directly and explicitly authorized annihilation.[24]

On the other hand, the Deuteronomist records Gideon and company shouting, "A sword of the LORD and of Gideon!" but these warriors are holding only trumpets, jars, and torches. Ultimately, God set his metaphorical sword into the hands of the Midianites, who then used it against each other (Judg 7:19-22). David is another curiously conflicted figure when it comes to the sword. His military prowess is certainly praised: "Saul has

---

[20]See Dorothy M. Peters and Esther Eshel, "Cutting Off and Cutting Down Shechem: Levi and His Sword in the Rylands Genizah Fragment of the Aramaic Levi Document," in *The War Scroll, War and Peace in the Dead Sea Scrolls and Related Literature*, ed. Kipp Davis, Dorothy M. Peters, Kyung S. Baek, and Peter W. Flint, Studies in the Texts of the Desert of Judah 115 (Leiden: Brill, 2015), 237-59.
[21]Jub. 30:6.
[22]Wright, "Yet the Sun Will Rise Again," 28.
[23]1QM 15:3; 16:1.
[24]11QT 55:2-8.

killed his thousands, and David his ten thousands" (1 Sam 18:7). It is the
giant, Goliath, who comes with "sword and spear and javelin" while the nar-
rator emphasizes that David comes in the "name of the LORD of hosts," who
does not "save by sword and spear." No sword is found in David's hand until
he picks up Goliath's own sword to finish off the already fallen, dying giant
(1 Sam 17:45-51). Later, the priestly editorial disqualifies David from building
the temple because of the blood he has shed (1 Chron 28:3), preserving also
the story of a destroying angel who confronts David with the "sword of the
LORD" after David takes a census of sword-carrying males (1 Chron 21:1-30).
It seems as if the priestly authors of writings such as Leviticus and Chronicles were inclined to visualize the unsheathed sword in the hand of God
rather than in the hand of humans.[25]

WITH SWORD UNSHEATHED: ESCHATOLOGICAL FUTURE

In one of the Aramaic Dead Sea Scrolls, the sword is visualized in righteous
hands but in the imminent *future*.[26] The Apocalypse of Weeks, one of the
books of Enoch, records the expectation that the righteous would be given
the sword in order to "execute righteous judgment on all the wicked."[27] The
Yahad Essenes expected a "Last Days," militaristic "Branch of David" who
would control all the peoples with his sword. Their hope was that the wicked
would be handed over to the sword at the coming of the "Messiah of Aaron
and of Israel."[28]

Bloodshed normally occurs before a battle is won, and the War Scroll
seems to have anticipated this in its descriptions of the eschatological battles
between the exiled "Sons of Light" and the covenant violators and the "Sons
of Darkness." Following the battle, the land and the warriors themselves
were to be cleansed from corpse impurity.[29]

Anyone hoping, however, to find explicit details about the actual killing
by sword would be disappointed. The curious absence of the recording of
the actual act recalls a Jane Austen novel in which the gentle reader would

---

[25]Cf. Ezek 30:24-25; 39:23.
[26]On the themes of exile in apocalyptic literature, see James C. VanderKam, "Exile in Jewish
Apocalyptic Literature," in *Old Testament, Jewish, and Christian Conceptions*, 95-96.
[27]4Q212 frg. 1 iv 12–17; cf. 1 Enoch 91:11-12.
[28]4QIsaiah Pesher[a] (4Q161 frgs. 8–10 17–23; CD 19:6-11).
[29]1QM 1:1-3; 7:2-3; 14:2-3.

be hard-pressed to find any obvious linkage between the flowery speeches and letters, courtly dances, and chaste embraces (all of the preamble) and the birth of babies (anticipated outcome). Similarly, the War Scroll is filled with descriptions to the preamble to battle: speeches, trumpets, banners, priestly prayers, and intricate descriptions of artistically designed weaponry, including the shield, lance, and a sword-weapon called the *kidon*.[30] Those under the command of the "Prince of the Congregation" use spear and shield and *kidon* sword but, with echoes of David using the sword on an already-fallen giant, these warriors bring down the already "fatally wounded by the judgment of God."[31] In the War Scroll, God calls out a "sword against all the nations"; however, when the infantry comes within throwing range, it is not a sword (*herev*) that each one raises but his more generic "weapon of war."[32] Indeed, the nearest that any War Scroll warrior would get to the sword was the inscription on the dart he threw, which read, "The blade of a sword devours the slain of wickedness by the judgment of God."[33]

One wonders why this squeamishness about placing the sword in the hands of the sectarian War Scroll warriors when the presectarian Aramaic Apocalypse of Weeks had envisioned that this sword would be given to the righteous. There are several overlapping, possibly synonymously true, alternatives.

The sword may have been a problematic two-edged metaphor. On one hand, it may have been viewed as authorized only in the hand of God. On the other hand, in the view of the *Yahad* Essenes, their priestly adversaries, the Maccabees, had infamously and illegitimately wielded the sword. The term, therefore, may have been contaminated by "violence" and "bloodshed." Christophe Batsch has observed that the Torah had already provided a "pattern of double authority" and a "cleavage of function" between the Joshua and Moses, a pattern that applied until the Maccabean revolt.[34] Both priestly Zealot and Qumran Community priests believed they would have strategic and tactical command in war. In contrast to the Zealots, who expected to be

---

[30]1QM 5:3-7. Traditionally translated as the "javelin" in Goliath's hand (1 Sam 17:45); the measurements of the *kidon* in the War Scroll measures the *kidon* as 1.5 cubits long and four fingers wide.
[31]1QM V, 1; VI, 5. The term for "fatally wounded," sometimes translated "slain," is used in other contexts to connote "defiled." Perhaps, the author of this composition was indulging in a little wordplay; i.e., the slain ones are also the defiled ones.
[32]1QM 16:1-7; cf. 1QM 9:7-8; 15:2-3.
[33]1QM 6:1-3.
[34]So Batsch, "Priests in Warfare," 169.

"priests in the first line of battle, fighting with weapons in hand, like Phinehas," the *Yahad* Essenes believed that the actual fighting would be left to a Davidic Messiah or "Prince of the Congregation." Priests would direct war but without coming into contact with blood.[35]

The War Scroll, which would have circulated in various recensions for over 150 years, thus likely functioned simultaneously as a polemic against the priestly Hasmoneans and the Zealots, who wielded the sword illegitimately.[36] The sword was authorized only in the hands of legitimate princes and armies, not in the hands of priests.

Finally, the sectarian reticence about visualizing the details of hand-to-hand combat may have emanated from the regulations governing corpse impurity, an obstacle apparently overcome by the priestly Maccabees and Zealots. The *kidon* sword, understood from their scriptures as a javelin or dart, was a weapon that could be thrown from a distance and was thus an intriguing substitutionary term for the "sword" in the hands of the War Scroll warriors.[37] Perhaps the priestly sectarians—concerned about purity (and possibly inept with the sword!)—could nonetheless tolerate the hurling of darts and arrows from afar.

WITH SWORD SHEATHED: THE EXECUTION
OF JUDGMENT BY WORD

As Wright has pointed out in his lead essay in the present volume, Jesus believed that he was bringing about exile's end, and Paul believed he had already accomplished it.[38] It could be argued that much of what the Essenes did and said, from purifying rituals to prayers and liturgies, was done with the end of exile in view. Their relocation as a desert settlement at Qumran, in particular, served to reenact the exile by reliteralizing the Isaianic wilderness metaphor, "in the wilderness prepare the way of the LORD."[39]

---

[35]So ibid., 174-76. See 1QM 9:7-9.

[36]Batsch, "Priests in Warfare," 169-72.

[37]1QM 5:11-14 measures *kidon* within its scabbard as 1.5 cubits long and 4 fingers wide. While the language of javelin or dart, the *kidon* had the shape and dimensions of a two-edged sword. See 1QM 1:14-15; 11:11-12; 18:1-3; cf. Is 31:8.

[38]Wright, "Yet the Sun Will Rise Again," 19.

[39]1QS 8:12b-14; cf. 1QS 9:18-20; cf. Is 40:3. See George J. Brooke, "Isaiah 40:3 and the Wilderness Community," in *New Qumran Texts and Studies: Proceedings of the First Meeting of the Interna-*

As scribes and priests, the *Yahad* Essenes were likely inexperienced in swordplay while skilled in wordplay. For them, words were powerful implements and speech-acts of judgment. In their rewritings and reinterpretations of scriptural figures, an archetypical Enoch bore witness, in writing, to the wickedness of angels and humans until judgment day.[40] An archetypical "Jacob learned writing," while his nemesis "Esau . . . learned war."[41] These *Yahad* Essenes perceived their founding leader, the Teacher of Righteousness, as a latter-day Habakkuk who was recording divine revelations in anticipation of coming judgments.[42]

The *Yahad* Essenes obliterated those "foreordained to Belial" in a liturgy of curses, thereby correctly differentiating between the blessed and cursed, just as their priestly ancestors had done prior entering the land.[43] They create sobriquets such as "Man of the Lie" and "Men of Mockery" and "Children of Darkness" as pithy condemnatory expressions of judgment.[44]

Elsewhere, in one of their liturgical texts, the penitents confess, hoping that God would remember his covenant and their exile. Using language from the historical prophecy in Leviticus 26:40-45, they accepted this historical guilt of "paying off the debt" of their own iniquities and the iniquities of their ancestors.[45] Another scroll also uses the language of "paying off the debt of iniquity" within a description of the *Yahad's* self-identity: "They are to preserve faithfulness in the land with a sound inclination and a broken spirit and to pay off the debt of iniquity by executing judgment and by the travail of refining" (The Rule of the Community [1QS 8:2-4]).

In the Rule of the Community, the end of exile is anticipated in a writing replete with recognizable scriptural and priestly metaphors—eternal planting, holy house, Holy of Holies, tested wall, cornerstone—but it is not

---

tional Organization of Qumran Studies, Paris 1992, ed. George J. Brooke with Florentino García Martínez, STDJ 15 (Leiden: Brill, 1994), 117-32.

[40] *Jub.* 4:16-26.

[41] *Jub.* 19:14.

[42] 1QpHab 6:12–7:14.

[43] 1QS 2:4-18; cf. Deut 27–28.

[44] CD 20:11, 15; 1QS 1:9-10.

[45] *Words of Luminaries* (4Q504 frgs. 1–2R vi, 4–18). The *Yahad* accepted the "prescriptive programs" in Lev 26:40-41, atoning for the land by "daily communal rituals of confession of sin and penitential prayer." So Daniel K. Falk, "Religious Life at Qumran," in *Celebrating the Dead Sea Scrolls: A Canadian Collection*, ed. Peter W. Flint et al., SBLEJL 30 (Atlanta: Society of Biblical Literature, 2011), 253-85 (277).

the language of the Day of Atonement that is used. Instead, the *Yahad* expected to "atone for the land," terminology reinterpreted to include covenant and judgment:[46]

> Then shall the Council of the *Yahad* be established in truth as an "eternal planting"[47] as a holy house for Israel, and as an assembly, a Holy of Holies for Aaron; witnesses of truth for judgment, and chosen by God's favor in order to atone for the land and to recompense the wicked their retribution. They will be the tested wall, the precious cornerstone. . . . In all of their knowledge with respect to a covenant of judgment, they must bring a soothing aroma and be a blameless and true house in Israel, in order to uphold a covenant of eternal statutes. They will be an acceptable sacrifice in order to atone for the land and to decide judgment of wickedness so there will no longer be iniquity. (Excerpted from 1QS 8:5-10a)[48]

Already present in the Torah was the idea that the land (*'eretz*) defiled by bloodshed could be atoned for by the blood of the ones who had shed the blood: "You shall not pollute the land in which you live; for blood pollutes the land, and no atonement can be made for the land for the blood that is shed in it, except by the blood of the one who shed it" (Num 35:33).[49]

Theologically, the land could already have been atoned for its defilement by the offenders' death in the flood, especially if Numbers was read alongside the postdiluvian instructions to Noah requiring capital punishment for shedders of blood (Gen 9:6). However, an innovative and possibly subversively coded twist was added to new formations of a priestly archetype of the exile.

In the Genesis Apocryphon, Noah is re-formed as the divinely appointed "apportioner of the earth," and his authoritative role as a "new Adam" is extended to his lordship of "geographic features of the earth," including the seas and the mountains."[50] Prior to disembarking from the ark—traditionally

---

[46]Cf. a future Day of Atonement when a priestly Melchizedek would atone for the Sons of Light and deliver vengeance upon those predestined to Belial (11Q13 2:7-8, 12-13).

[47]Cf. variant "eternal judgment" (4Q259 2:14).

[48]1QS 9 adds that atonement of the land is required because of the "guilt of transgression" and the "rebellion of sin" and could happen apart from the flesh of burnt offerings.

[49]Cf. Deut 32:43. Here "land" is represented by a different Hebrew word, *'adamah*, and God himself initiates and enacts vengeance for the blood of his children, thereby atoning for the land.

[50]1Q20 1:8-9; 7:1-2. So Daniel Machiela, *The Dead Sea Genesis Apocryphon: A New Text and Translation with Introduction and Special Treatment of Columns 13–17*, STDJ 79 (Leiden: Brill, 2009), 91. In the Genesis Apocryphon, Noah's expanded role includes receiving and transmitting divine

the location of the altar of the Jerusalem temple—Noah offers a sacrifice "to atone for all the land."[51] After Noah exits the ark, he blesses God for destroying those who worked "violence, wickedness, and deceit" and for rescuing a "righteous man."[52]

The land, having suffered from morally defiling sin, would also need ritual purification. Although Noah's sacrifice purportedly atones for the "land," given the physical location of the sacrifice, this term may have been a subversive code for "temple." The people who were writing themselves into the retelling of Noah's story could identify with Noah as the "postexilic righteous" returning to land and temple. There, they hoped to be able to offer proper sacrifices of atonement for the defiled land and temple following the destruction of those who practiced "violence, wickedness, and deceit."

The priestly Noah found in the Genesis Apocryphon has an exegetically fraternal twin in the book of Jubilees.[53] The sins listed here as having precipitated the flood—fornication, impurity, and the shedding of blood—are sins that, according to Torah legislation, defiled and profaned the land.[54] Jubilees brings covenant and judgment into closer relationship with atonement. Moses receives Torah on Mount Sinai in the third month, the month of covenant renewal.[55] Noah's "atoning for the land" sacrifice follows disembarkation from the ark and is located in the third month, inaugurating the designated month for covenant renewal. In contrast to Genesis, where covenant making happens *after* promises, blessings, and prohibitions, God's covenant with Noah comes *before*, intensifying the importance and scope of the Noachic covenant.[56]

---

visions concerning the coming judgment upon the "sons of the earth" and the response to the "blood that the Nephilin had poured out," wrongful unions with daughters of men, and divinatory arts (1Q20 6:10–7:6).

[51]1Q20 10:13-17. See Daniel K. Falk, *The Parabiblical Texts: Strategies for Extending the Scriptures Among the Dead Sea Scrolls*, Companion to the Qumran Scrolls 8, Library of Second Temple Studies 63 (New York: T&T Clark, 2007), 59-60.

[52]1Q20 11:1, 13-14.

[53]For the variously formed archetypes of Noah, see Dorothy M. Peters, *Noah Traditions in the Dead Sea Scrolls: Conversations and Controversies of Antiquity*, SBLEJL 26 (Atlanta: Society of Biblical Literature, 2008).

[54]Jub. 7:21-25; see Ex 34:15; Lev 18:26-28; Num 35:33-34.

[55]Jub. 6:1; cf. 4Q266 frg. 11, 16b–17.

[56]Jub. 6:1-4; cf. Gen 8:20–9:17.

Although Noah's "atoning for the land" sacrifice does not happen during the month in which the Day of Atonement is observed—the seventh month—this day, while not mentioned explicitly, is described within the larger context of the narrative:

> Regarding the Israelites it has been written and ordained: "If they turn to him in the right way, he will forgive all their wickedness and will pardon all their sins." It has been written and ordained that he will have mercy on all who turn from all their errors once each year. To all who corrupted their ways and their plan(s) before the flood no favor was shown except to Noah alone. (Jub. 5:17-19a)[57]

Among other offerings, Noah sacrifices a goat, the animal that atones for the sanctuary on the Day of Atonement.[58] Atonement is linked also to judgment in Jubilees. Angels are bound for future judgment, their sons kill each other by the sword sent by God, and the floodwaters blot out all living beings except for Noah and his family. Judgment is executed by God upon everyone except for the archetypical righteous Noah and his family.[59]

If "atoning for the land" was being used as subversive, coded language, then the righteous and repentant people were—like the archetypical Noah formed in their image—the ones who would escape judgment, who believed they were in true covenant relationship with God, and who would be restored to land and temple, where they would make atoning sacrifices.

"Atoning for the land" appears also in the sectarian texts, such as the Rule of the Community cited above, detached from the archetypical Noah and attached to the *Yahad.* An odd conflation of ideas is found in 4QMiscellaneous Rules, where fifteen members *Yahad* are to atone for the land while anticipating judgment.[60] Immediately following are the purity regulations governing a postpartum woman's times of uncleanness following the birth of a male child (forty days) and a female child (eighty days). Following her time of purification, she comes with her burnt and sin offerings, and the priests

---

[57]Trans. James C. VanderKam, *The Book of Jubilees,* CSCO 511 (Leuven: Peeters, 1989).
[58]Lev 16:15-16.
[59]Jub. 5:6-20.
[60]Cf. the setting of "Last Days," during which the "Congregation of Israel" must live by the "judgment" of the "men of the Council" who have kept the covenant in the midst of wickedness, atoning for the land (1QSa 1:1-3).

make atonement for her.[61] This interpretation equates the "sanctuary," from which the woman is barred during her period of uncleanness in Leviticus 12, with the "Garden of Eden," adding that "Adam" (the male) could only come into the "Garden of Eden" after forty days of purification and "Eve" (the female) after eighty days.[62] Thus, these archetypical first humans represent the *Yahad* in its period of purification prior to return to the "sanctuary" in juxtaposition with the language of atoning for the land.

Marginalized priests, "exiled" from positions of priestly power in the temple, may not have wished to write openly about their hopes for the destruction of powerful priests whom they perceived to be violent, wicked, and deceitful. By hiding their criticisms within rewritten Bible stories, or a concept such as "atoning for the land," they were able communicate to insiders in coded language while maintaining the outward appearance of a people who were not a threat. Their survival may have depended on the use of words rather than the sword.

Finally, the War Scroll may not have been a true military manual for eschatological warfare, after all. Daniel K. Falk has found a "living liturgical context" by comparing the language of liturgical prayer found elsewhere in the Scrolls with the language employed in the War Scroll, Therefore, it may well be, as Falk suggests, that prayer was a military tactic, and the true function of the War Scroll was to promote "worship as spiritual warfare."[63]

CONCLUSIONS

The *Yahad* Essenes had the same hope as did most Second Temple Jews, that exile would end and that they would be restored to a purified land. They explored different *means* to exile's end. Not for them was a theology of the Jesus movement, of loving their enemies, blessing those who cursed them, or a dying, suffering servant Messiah. But neither did they accept a violent, nationalist militarism that required its priestly members to wield the sword like the Maccabees or the Zealots. For them, there was a third way. Executing judgment with the sword sheathed, they believed their words and deeds

---

[61] A variant version of this interpretation is found in Jub. 3:8–14.

[62] 4Q265 frg. 7, 12.

[63] Daniel K. Falk, "Prayer, Liturgy, and War," in *The War Scroll, War and Peace in the Dead Sea Scrolls and Related Literature: Essays in Honour of Martin G. Abegg on the Occasion of His 65th Birthday,* ed. Kyung Baek et al., STDJ 115 (Leiden, Brill, 2015), 275-94.

were actively achieving exile's end while living in the hope of the imminent unsheathing of the sword of the LORD.

They generally affirmed and legitimized the use of weapons in the hands of their scriptural ancestors. They hoped to participate with God in executing judgment in future. Unlike their priestly counterparts among the Maccabees and Zealots, they understood that the sword of vengeance and judgment belonged in the hand of God, who ultimately authorized and powered its use. They refused to pick up the sword prematurely, for this would simply delay the vengeance of God. The continual deferment of an active, physical role into the ever-receding eschatological future, and the practice of nonlethal alternatives for resolving conflict in the meantime, made for a de facto, if not ideological, "peace position" in the present.

In the meantime, they anticipated the end of exile while dwelling in a literal and metaphorical wilderness. A reinterpreted "atoning for the land" may have become a subversive and versatile technical term for these priestly, covenant-keeping Jews who saw themselves in continuing exile but were hoping for judgment of their adversaries and restoration to land and temple.

Although they did not wield *swords* in the execution of judgment, the members of the Essene *Yahad* did not hesitate to write and speak *words*. They retold their ancient stories and wrote themselves into the new narratives. Through skillful and subversive wielding of words as they reminded themselves of who they were, reciting their prayers, blessings, and curses, and creating their liturgical war dramas, they awaited the next step. Very soon, they believed, God would unsheathe his sword. The land would be atoned for in two ways: wickedness would be destroyed and the land and the temple cleansed of its defilement, and the righteous ones would return to land and temple. Then, exile would end.

PART THREE

NEW TESTAMENT

CHAPTER SEVEN

EXILED TO THE LAND

N. T. Wright's Exile Theory as Organic to Judaism

SCOT McKNIGHT

WHEN N. T. WRIGHT'S *JESUS and the Victory of God* appeared in 1996 I was one of his immediate readers. In part because his *New Testament and the People of God* had given me such a boost on pondering how best to teach seminary students the "context" for Jesus and the Gospels, and in part because I was now teaching college students an introductory course on Jesus, and big categories and themes were my immediate need. But then, too, I have always found Tom Wright's writing superior to the stodgy, pseudo-disinterested prose of so many in our field (footnotes omitted). One of my doctoral students, Mark Rapinchuk, wrote a dissertation on the theme of exile and restoration in the Gospel of Matthew, and on top of all this, two friends, Bruce Chilton and Craig Evans, had asked me to write a book on the teachings of Jesus in which I plotted to use exile and restoration.[1] What struck me in my first reading of *Jesus and the Victory of God* was how organic "exile," "return from exile," and "restoration" were to Judaism in comparison with the systematic categories so many (mostly evangelical) theologians use for eschatology. Indeed, if I had to choose between "exile and restoration"—two terms that belong together in the world of Judaism(s)[2]—or "millennium" or "heaven" or "rapture" or "tribulation" or

---

[1]Scot McKnight, *A New Vision for Israel: The Teachings of Jesus in National Context* (Grand Rapids: Eerdmans, 1999).

[2]E.g., as in Peter Ackroyd, *Exile and Restoration*, Old Testament Library (Philadelphia: Westminster, 1968). See also H. G. M. Williamson, "The Exile and After: Historical Study," in *The Face of Old Testament Study*, ed. B. T. Arnold and D. W. Baker (Grand Rapids: Baker, 1995), 236d D.

even "inaugurated eschatology," I would opt for "exile and restoration" every time. Wright's books then gave me new categories through which to begin thinking again about the sort of theology at work in my own interpreting of Jesus. I began to devise "concept maps" that I drew on our chalkboards and then revised over and over as I was teaching my Jesus classes.

When friends and teachers of mine got hung up on whether it was even possible for Jews at the time of Jesus to think they could both be dwelling in the land and still in exile, I found such concerns to be trivial to the overall usefulness and general accuracy of the organic categories Tom was using. So, for me, exile became a category through which I would think.[3] Scholarship has more than demonstrated that exile and restoration were both ongoing and the hope of Israel. One has to wonder at times whether a brilliant and pervasive scholarly contribution by one scholar, in this case by N. T. Wright, does not generate an ugly jealousy and envy to such a degree that other scholars must disagree to retain their honor. What I saw in Wright was a fresh but organic expression of how Jews were thinking and a set of categories that needed more exploitation for understanding Jesus and the apostolic explorations of Christology and eschatology. At some level one needs to ask what was promised and expected by Israel's and Judah's prophets when the "return" or "restoration" came about. One cannot reduce these expectations simply to returning to the land or dwelling in the land, but instead one must see any such return in the context of the larger expectations of what God will do, and this is where Wright's original theses—including ideas such as the return of YHWH to the temple, fullness of obedience to the Torah, a Messiah on the throne, and the vanquishing of Israel's Gentile enemies— simply carry the day. Until those events occur the exile is still on at some level. I call this an "organic" eschatology because it was how Israel's prophets and the many Jews between the prophets and the arrival of King Jesus (in the Christian sense) conceived of their condition. What is later called "the age to come" and "return from exile" then must be connected substantively. To press this further, Wright is not alone these days in Christian discussions

---

[3]The literature on exile and restoration is extensive, and James Scott, editor of this volume, might be considered the official librarian for this field. He has a splendid *Forschungsbericht*-like article for a good start; see "Exile and Restoration," in *Dictionary of Jesus and the Gospels*, ed. Joel B. Green et al., 2nd ed. (Downers Grove, IL: IVP Academic, 2013), 251-58.

about "heaven," but the far more important emphasis today is not the traditional disembodied "heaven" where souls go when they die but a far more realistic "place," the new heavens and the new earth. I would contend that Wright's exploration of the concrete realities of exile and restoration needs to be connected to the same kind of concrete, Jewish, early Christian reality called new heavens and the new earth.[4] In his study of the future kingdom of God in the earliest Christian literature, then, Wright and others have stripped away even more of Christian theology's penchant for dualism.

More importantly, Wright's proposal about the end of exile sets us off to explore how Israel's historiography and hermeneutics worked, and then how that historiography found a new approach in Jesus and the apostles. In responding then to N. T. Wright's proposals I shall offer a fresh reworking and reimagining of his end-of-exile hermeneutic, not by way of superseding but by way of fulfillment and expansion of what is there, or is perhaps there.

ISRAEL'S HISTORIOGRAPHY

The exile and restoration potently formed how Israel told its story, in fact, each of its stories. The northern kingdom's story ended with exile, the southern kingdom experienced both an exile and a restoration, and it is not without some merit that some see the exile in the expulsion of Adam and Eve from the Garden of Eden or even in the great fish's spitting out of Jonah. Exile and restoration are written into the fabric of Israel's historiography and hermeneutics.[5] One finds it in the Psalms (Ps 78; 105–106) and the Deuteronomic History (Deuteronomy–2 Kings) as well as the Chronicler's own version, and the Prophets (none more vital than Is 40–55), and it is

---

[4]See here N. T. Wright, *Jesus and the Victory of God*, Christian Origins and the Question of God 2 (Minneapolis: Fortress, 1996); Wright, *The Resurrection of the Son of God*, The New Testament and the Question of God 3 (Minneapolis: Fortress, 2003); Wright, *Surprised by Hope: Rethinking Heaven, the Resurrection, and the Mission of the Church* (New York: HarperOne, 2008). Also the exceptional study of J. Richard Middleton, *A New Heaven and a New Earth: Reclaiming Biblical Eschatology* (Grand Rapids: Baker Academic, 2014).

[5]There is a wonderful set of articles in B. T. Arnold and H. G. M. Williamson, eds., *The Dictionary of the Old Testament Historical Books* (Downers Grove, IL: InterVarsity Press, 2005), beginning with S. L. McKenzie, "Historiography, Old Testament," 418-25, but continuing with separate entries on every "period" in Israel's history (425-97). In this context, also see N. T. Wright, *The New Testament and the People of God*, Christian Origins and the Question of God 1 (Minneapolis: Fortress, 1992), 145-338; Wright, *Paul and the Faithfulness of God*, Christian Origins and the Question of God 4 (Minneapolis: Fortress, 2013), 108-79.

written back into the Pentateuch (Deut 28–30; Lev 26). To be sure, there is a simple pattern of obedience and blessing or disobedience and curse/exile, but the hermeneutic of Israel's historiography is more than a moral tale designed to spark covenant observance. There were exiles, and there was one notable restoration. There will be a final restoration. These are not then moral fables but Israel's concrete realities, both in history and eschatology. It really happened to the northern kingdom (2 Kings 17:7-23), and it really happened to the southern kingdom (2 Kings 25). The southern kingdom really did return (Ezra–Nehemiah). Inasmuch as the northern kingdom's restoration never occurred and inasmuch as the eschatological hope is the restoration of the *twelve* tribes (e.g., Ezek 37:15-22), the northern kingdom is still in exile, and the end of exile is yet to come. One can say until the twelve tribes are regathered in the land the exile is still on, and not a few texts in the Jewish world evince such a hope, and in these texts twelve is often connected to covenant establishment as well as covenant renewal (e.g., Josh 4:1, 3, 7, 9, 20).[6] Hence, twelve has an eschatological dimension, and it would not be mischievous to see the arrival of the twelve to coincide with the end of exile (cf. 4Q159, frgs. 2–4:3–4; 4Q164 4–6; 11Q19 57:11-14; T. Ab. 13:6; T. Jud. 25:1-2; T. Benj. 10:7). That Jesus called twelve apostles then is a claim on all Israel and at the same time an evocation of this classic theme in Israel's historiography and eschatology.

A notable example from the New Testament, revealing that the Jesus movement's historiographers had an end-of-exile hermeneutic at work, is the genealogy of Matthew 1:1-17. Here is a history of Israel from the days of Abraham to the days of the Messiah broken into three distinct periods: Abraham to David, David to the exile, the exile to the Messiah, Jesus. Emphasizing the point only repeats what is obvious: the Messiah's arrival in the Matthean genealogy is the end of the exile, and the whole genealogy is structured according to David's name—the number fourteen is what David's letters add up to (called *gematria* in Hebrew). A Davidic genealogy that is fulfilled in the Davidic Son, King Jesus, and the arrival of this King loudly declares "No more exile!"

---

[6]See E. P. Sanders, *Jesus and Judaism* (Philadelphia: Fortress, 1985), 95-98; Scot McKnight, "Jesus and the Twelve," *Bulletin for Biblical Research* 11 (2001): 203-31; Darrell L. Bock and Robert L. Webb, eds., *Key Events in the Life of the Historical Jesus*, WUNT 247 (Tübingen: Mohr Siebeck, 2009), 181-214.

While the expression "end of exile" might not appear in these texts, only a wooden historiography and linguistic reductionism would not observe that the motifs are all woven together into Israel's historiography and eschatology. Israel's future is one in which the twelve tribes will come together, the exile will be fully over for all twelve tribes, and God will return to Zion to flood the temple with his glory.

THE STORY REVISED WITH JESUS

The covenant, command, exile, and restoration motif running through Israel's historiography, however, is not the dominant narrative for Israel. The moment one even suggests there is such a thing as a "dominant" story one can see the postmodern finger pointing at such a colonialist, imperialist approach. So many back down, and one who has not is N. T. Wright. From the beginning, with sensitivity to the implications of colonizing a narrative, Wright has proposed a narrative for understanding the "context" of Jesus and the apostles and for how Judaism understood itself. Wright's "story" is essentially the kingdom story, and from time to time, especially in his early Paul studies and then in his Jesus book and now also in his magnum opus on Paul, he has emphasized the "end of exile."[7] I would contend that "end of exile" is a thread in the kingdom story, and I trust Tom would agree. Whether he does or not, I want to offer an alternative story that both sanctifies the end-of-exile story and places it in what I think is the most compelling narrative from the angle of Jesus and the apostles. In the history of historiographical hermeneutics and their attempt to frame a story that fits the evidence and that anticipates how eschatology works in Judaism, there have been a few major proposals. At one level is the brute historiography that is closer to chronicle than to theology, and in this the historian works away at the data and the facts and proposes little more than the evidence provides. Most importantly, no meaning making like the exile-and-restoration theory is offered. One can find this in many history-of-Israel books. What narrative meaning is attached to the facts has been shaped by the historian—and I mean here the Deuteronomist, the Chronicler, Josephus, or Tobit. But the

---

[7]On the notion of exile in Paul, see also now N. T. Wright, *Paul and the Faithfulness of God*, passim (the introduction [n9] to the present volume has a full listing of these pages). See further the essay by Tony Cummins in the present volume.

narrative that has shaped much discussion in the theological world, and one that reflects more Christian theology than Christian historians of Israel often admit, is the classic narrative with four chapters: creation, fall, redemption, and consummation. The narrative here is thoroughly soteriological, sometimes corporate, but far more often the narrative is profoundly individualistic and more a product of Augustine and the Reformers than ancient Israel. This C-F-R-C story deserves some explication so we can set up a narrative that develops what N. T. Wright has been proposing for a few decades.[8]

C-F-R-C

The C-F-R-C story is the story of salvation in the Bible, and its decisive impulse comes from 1 Corinthians 15:45-49 and Romans 5:12-21, and though rarely stated it is not a narrative found in preceding or contemporary Jewish texts. It goes like this: C: God is the author of *Creation* (the C), Adam and Eve are made in God's image and likeness, and they were placed by God in a probationary period in Eden. F: Adam and Eve sin by seeking to be like God, and in this fall narrative the doctrine of "original sin" now comes into play (regardless of anachronisms). But God, who is rich in mercy, acts to redeem those who have sinned. Hence, the R: the quest from Genesis 4–11 is for Genesis 12; 15; 17; 21—that is, for the redemption God establishes through covenant formation with Israel. But this covenant redemption grows in the story from the simple covenant of election in Genesis 12; 15 to the sacrificial system of Exodus, Leviticus, and Deuteronomy, and it all leads to the covenant redemption in the life, death, burial, resurrection and exaltation of Jesus the Messiah—Savior and Lord of all. This redemptive movement on God's part will be completed in the consummation of salvation. Thus, C: the consummation of redemption in the kingdom of God when God will be all in all, when justice and peace will flourish, and where the people of God will dwell with God. Now in many versions of the C-F-R-C this consummation is a disembodied heaven for souls, while for others it takes on more of a new heavens and new earth. Regardless, this is the C-F-R-C story that has shaped much of Christianity. In some ways, I suggest, the theme of "end of exile" fits into this C-F-R-C story as a more

---

[8]In what follows I adjust what is found in Scot McKnight, *Kingdom Conspiracy: Returning to the Radical Mission of the Local Church* (Grand Rapids: Brazos, 2014), 23-35.

organic story as well as a more expansive sense of salvation itself. N. T. Wright's own framing of this narrative, however, is not reducible to the end-of-exile theme, and neither can it be contained by the C-F-R-C narrative. He has a more expansive sense of the story.

Questioning this age-old way of reading the Bible is like sticking my finger into your coffee to see whether it is warm enough, knowing that I might get burned. Those who read the Bible solely through the C-F-R-C plot have an annoying propensity to read Genesis 1–3 to get their C and their F in place, but then leap to Romans 3 or to the crucifixion scenes in the Gospels to get to the R. This skips 99.5 percent of the Old Testament. Some, too, tend to omit any serious discussion of Israel or church or the people of God as the locus of what God is doing in this world. Why? Because the focus of the C-F-R-C story is on personal salvation, it is also a focus on the salvation of the *individual*. By all means, the Bible tells the story of redemption, and each of us needs to be saved, and the C-F-R-C tells us how that happens. That's good. But when the Bible's story is reduced to the redemption story, we lose the fabric of the story itself.

If it is not already clear, I want to make it clear. There is more than one way to tell Israel's story—and one sees versions of Israel's basic story in documents as diverse as Ben Sirach, the Psalms of Solomon, the Rule of the Community from Qumran, Philo, and Josephus—and we could go on. I contend that the *Jesus-based or apostle-based*—call it the Christian—narrative *tells the same story from a singular, compelling approach*. Namely, the Bible's story is fundamentally a christological story before it is a soteriological story. The standard C-F-R-C narrative, then, exploits the soteriological narrative of the Christian faith at the expense of the christological narrative, because in the C-F-R-C narrative Jesus is reduced to a *means of redemption*, and in so doing Jesus is not the point of the story. My contention is that the gospel statement of the apostles, recorded as a deposit of the tradition in 1 Corinthians 15:3-5,[9] tells a christological narrative that generates salvation for those who enter into that christological narrative. If the gospel deposit is the story of Jesus fulfilling the story of Israel, *then we need to create a narrative that prompts a christological reading first and foremost* before it tells the

---

[9]See my Scot McKnight, *The King Jesus Gospel: The Original Good News Revisited* (Grand Rapids: Zondervan, 2011).

soteriological narrative. So we need a story that swallows the C-F-R-C into a larger story, and a good example of someone who is doing this is N. T. Wright.

REFOCUSING THE STORY

For Jesus, Wright says, to "say 'the kingdom of god is at hand' makes sense only when the hearers know 'the story so far' and are waiting for it to be completed."[10] The story at work can be found in Tom's book *The New Testament and the People of God*.[11] There he did the important work of proving that the "story" at work with Jesus was not simply what happened in Israel's history, such as creation and the exodus and the exile, such as the figures of Abraham and Moses and David, and such as the comedies and tragedies of kings, prophets, invasions, captivities, economics, politics, family life, international relations, and times of peace. Those are elements in the story, but they are in turn part of a worldview—made of story, symbols, and praxis—that sets the people and events into a meaning-making story.

Tom's way of framing all this is worth a brief retelling because it anticipates our expansion. The story begins with the Creator God and the fall, then the calling of the patriarchs and the exodus redemption-as-liberation under Moses, a story that becomes the paradigm story in Israel. Then the conquest sets up the story of David. His successors failed, however, and their failure leads to the exile in Babylon. This sets up the hope for another (new) exodus and the return to the land, and yet—and this is foundational to Wright's understanding of the story—even that return does not seem to bring together all that was expected. Here is one way Tom puts it: "The great story of the Hebrew Scriptures was therefore inevitably read in the Second Temple period as a story in search of a conclusion."[12] Wright's magical expression of this is that Israel is still "living in exile," and what Jesus announces is the "end of exile." Kingdom and end of exile, then, are ways of telling the grand story. That Wright focuses on end of exile as the way to read the story at the time of Jesus has been criticized,[13] but I would contend that Wright's expression emerges organically from the expectations of Israel's

---

[10]Wright, *Jesus and the Victory of God*, 226.
[11]Wright, *New Testament and the People of God*, 215-43, with quotations from 214, 232, 243.
[12]Ibid., 217.
[13]Carey C. Newman, ed., *Jesus and the Restoration of Israel: A Critical Assessment of N. T. Wright's Jesus and the Victory of God* (Downers Grove, IL: InterVarsity Press, 1999).

prophets and leads us more directly to a storied understanding of kingdom. In some ways, then, "end of exile" means "kingdom has come" means "Messiah has come." What Wright's proposal does perhaps most is put before us a series of questions that were being asked at the time of Jesus, and he provides a series of answers first-century Jewish thinkers were no doubt giving. In this context, then, the kingdom story of Jesus flourishes. Here are Tom's questions and answers:

1. Who are we? We are Israel, the chosen people of the Creator God.

2. Where are we? We are in the holy land, focused on the temple; but, paradoxically, we are still in exile.

3. What is wrong? We have the wrong rulers; pagans on the one hand, compromised Jews on the other, or, halfway between, Herod and his family. We are all involved in a less-than-ideal situation.

4. What is the solution? Our God must act again to give us the true sort of rule, that is, his own kingship exercised through properly appointed officials (a true priesthood; possibly a true King); and in the meantime Israel must be faithful to his covenant charter.[14]

This set of questions, I think, reorients our "story" approaches, and it clearly surpasses the C-F-R-C approach. But I want to suggest that even Tom Wright's story could be focused less on the benefits of the story (exile is over) and more on the king of the story. I suggest the A-B-A' story does just that.

A-B-A'

When Jesus declared, "The time has come. The kingdom of God has come near. Repent and believe the good news," the average Jewish listener did not say, "Finally, someone to tell me how I can get saved personally." I propose that the following A-B-A' story will lead us squarely to focus on the gospel declaration that Jesus is Messiah, Lord, and Savior. In other words, it will lead us to a christological, which means royal and kingdom, story that entails the soteriological.

Plan A extends from Adam and Abraham to Samuel: *God rules the world through his elected people, but God is the one and only King.* God is the

[14]Wright, *New Testament and the People of God*, 243.

Creator—that is how the Bible's story begins. As Creator, God is King, but God does something amazingly radical: he shares his rule with Adam and Eve, or God creates Adam and Eve to represent his kingship. However, sharing royalty is not enough for them, as the fall story in Genesis 3 makes clear. This A-B-A' story asks us to adjust the *F* part of the C-F-R-C story. The problem to be solved by redemption is the *kind* of sin Adam and Eve committed *in light of their assignment*. The story of sin in the Bible is the story of God's elect people wanting to be God-like instead of god-ly, of ruling instead of subruling and being ruled.

To end the mutiny of humans against God, and at the same time to forgive and bond humans to God according to Plan A, God *elects* one solitary man and cuts a covenant of grace with him, calling him and his people to rule for God. This begins the *R* in the C-F-R-C story. That man's name is Abraham, and the principal texts of this part of the story can be found in Genesis 12; 15; 17. The story to Samuel is all about God ruling through Israel. There is no human king because a human king is, *by definition*, a usurper. In Plan A God remains the ruler.

Plan A has four characteristics:

- God alone is King.

- Humans, from Adam and Eve to Abraham, are to rule under God.

- Humans usurp God's rule.

- God forgives the usurpers and forms a covenant with Abraham.

Plan B has a most unusual development, one that is almost always neglected in kingdom discussions.[15] In fact, it is so neglected that I need to dust off the story so we can see it again. Samuel, who was not a king in name, toys with turning his own rule into a dynasty by appointing his own sons to rule after him (1 Sam 8:1). But his sons are moral failures as leaders. Samuel then comes to God in 1 Samuel 8 to announce that some arrogant Israelite "elders" would like to have a king (instead of his sons). Their request is the sin of

---

[15]But see John Bright, *The Kingdom of God: The Biblical Concept and Its Meaning for the Church* (Nashville, TN: Abingdon, 1981), 17-44. A more extensive study of the political theology that emerges from Genesis through 2 Kings, one that touches on the theme I am discussing in "Plan B," can be found in J. Gordon McConville, *God and Earthly Power: An Old Testament Political Theology (Genesis–Kings)* (New York: T&T Clark, 2008), esp. 133-47.

Adam and Eve and the option Gideon refused (Judg 8:23). The words of the arrogant elders to Samuel in 1 Samuel 8:5 concern his age and what will happen if his knucklehead sons rule when he is gone: "You are old, and your sons do not follow your ways; *now appoint a king to lead us, such as all the other nations have*" (1 Sam 8:5).[16]

Samuel's displeasure (1 Sam 8:6)[17] is met by a revelation from God that provides one of the secrets to understanding kingdom. In YHWH's revelation to Samuel, YHWH explains what is really going on in the minds and hearts of those who want a king like the other nations. We learn from YHWH that Israel does not want to rule *for* God in this world but wants to be like the world and rule *like* God.

> And the LORD told him: "Listen to all that the people are saying to you; it is not you they have rejected, *but they have rejected me as their king.* As they have done from the day I brought them up out of Egypt until this day, forsaking me and serving other gods, so they are doing to you. Now listen to them; but warn them solemnly and let them know what the king who will reign over them will claim as his rights." (1 Sam 8:7-9)[18]

From Adam and Abraham to Samuel, God is King. It is a theocracy. God rules Israel in a decentralized manner and often through a leader marked by nothing more than God's call. But from this event recorded in 1 Samuel 8— that is, from Saul forward—*a king* rules (1 Sam 8:10-18). *A human king for Israel is Plan B in God's eyes.*

Plan B is the story of David[19] and is emphasized by the Chronicler: David the good king over against the bad kings and the hope for a new Davidic king:

---

[16]Scripture quotations in this essay are taken from the NIV 2011.

[17]Another translation would be, "The matter was evil in Samuel's eyes." The word *king* is the problem here; Samuel, the last of the judges and the first of the prophets, is not, however, a king, and so his sons are not kings. That the elders want to replace his sons does not seem the issue to Samuel; his concern is their desire for a "king."

[18]1 Sam 8:5 has an interesting parallel in Deut 17:14-15, where, without disregarding the revelation of YHWH to Samuel, the author looks beyond this primal act of rebellion to the days of kings in the land and what the requirements will be for that king. Even within 1 Sam 8–13, there is some tension between favor and disfavor toward a monarchy.

[19]I am indebted to my friend Joel Willitts in this section. See further on the scholarship of David at William M. Schniedewind, *Society and the Promise to David: The Reception History of 2 Samuel 7:1-17* (New York: Oxford University Press, 1999); Steven L. McKenzie, *King David: A Biography* (New York: Oxford University Press, 2000); Baruch Halpern, *David's Secret Demons: Messiah,*

I will set him over my house and my kingdom forever; his throne will be established forever. (1 Chron 17:14)

Of all my sons—and the Lord has given me many—he has chosen my son Solomon to sit on the throne of the kingdom of the Lord over Israel. (1 Chron 28:5)

And now you plan to resist the kingdom of the Lord, which is in the hands of David's descendants. You are indeed a vast army and have with you the golden calves that Jeroboam made to be your gods. (2 Chron 13:8)

In Plan B God has focused his plan on David as the king whose descendants will be the rulers in Israel, and their "kingdom" is "the kingdom of God." So there are six elements in Plan B:

- God alone is (still) King.

- Israel is to rule God's created world under God.

- Israel wants to usurp God's rule.

- God accommodates Israel by granting it a human king.

- The story of the Old Testament becomes the story of David.

- God continues to forgive Israel of its sins through the temple system of sacrifice, purity, and forgiveness.

A human king on the throne, even David and even approved and blessed by God, was still Plan B. But that is the story of the Old Testament from the time of David on. God did not want a human king on Israel's throne, and lusty Solomon is but one good example of why. Kingship meant dynasty and empire and kings thinking they were God. Under a (bad) king Israel became a temple-state, and taxes blanketed the land like manna; theocracy, God's rule, was gone, and monarchy had arrived; treaties became vogue.[20] YHWH the King became a distant memory, yet the memory lingered of the days when YHWH alone ruled. That memory morphs into hope during Plan B,

---

Murderer, Traitor, King, The Bible in Its World (Grand Rapids: Eerdmans, 2001); Paul Borgman, *David, Saul, and God: Rediscovering an Ancient Story* (New York: Oxford University Press, 2008); Joseph Blenkinsopp, *David Remembered: Kingship and National Identity in Ancient Israel* (Grand Rapids: Eerdmans, 2013).

[20]See here Walter Brueggemann, *The Prophetic Imagination,* 2nd ed. (Minneapolis: Fortress, 2001).

hope that God will someday rule once again.[21] From Amos on there is hope for the right kind of king and kingdom, often expressed in the hope for a remnant (see Is 4:2-4; 10:20-22; 37:30-32). The southern tribe, Judah, was sent by God into exile to Babylon as discipline for unfaithfulness. In Babylon the ideas of ending their exile and returning to the land converged into a story of hope. Some seventy years later the exiles returned, but *not all of the promises were fulfilled* when they returned. So Wright argues that even though the children of Israel were back in the land, the exile had not yet completely ended.

The question then is this: When would it end? When *God* once again sat on the throne and ruled the land. The exile will only truly end when *God* rules, when the glowing words of Isaiah 40–66 are more than glimpsed in the realities in the land, when—in other words—*the damage of 1 Samuel 8 is undone and redeemed.* Until Jerusalem is ruled by God and God alone, the exile is still on. The template for how God will rule, it must be emphasized, is the rule of God through David, but the drive is for the elimination of the human king when it will be again the kingdom of *God.*

But there is more in the hope during exile. With exile is bound up a new development in the *R* portion of the C-F-R-C story: Israel's exile ends when Israel's sins are forgiven, and surely one of the most evocative sets of images is found in Isaiah 52:13–53:12. Here the Servant—a term that signifies at once Israel in exile, Israel's faithful leader, and Jesus as its anticipated Davidic and messianic king and redeemer—suffers on behalf of the whole nation in order that forgiveness can be granted following divine discipline, the exile can end, and the exiles can return to the land. The *R* now becomes a single representative person, the Servant King.[22] On the basis of these chapters in Isaiah, something prevalent everywhere in the work of N. T. Wright, Jesus builds

---

[21]The so-called King Yahweh psalms (e.g., Ps 89; 93; 96–99) are seen by many as the assertion of YHWH as king over against a human king; as such, they correspond to the Plan B element of our approach. See on this J. Gordon McConville, "Law and Monarchy in the Old Testament," in *A Royal Priesthood? The Use of the Bible Ethically and Politically; A Dialogue with Oliver O'Donovan*, Scripture and Hermeneutics 3 (Grand Rapids: Zondervan, 2002), 69-88.

[22]It is not possible here to engage atonement theory or even develop the soteriological dimension of the narrative, inasmuch as it is already prominent in the C-F-R-C narrative (which the A-B-A´ narrative engulfs but not does not delete) and would engage a conversation beyond the scope of this essay. For my own study, see Scot McKnight, *Jesus and His Death: Historiography, the Historical Jesus, and Atonement Theory* (Waco, TX: Baylor University Press, 2005); McKnight, *A Community Called Atonement* (Nashville, TN: Abingdon, 2007). N. T. Wright has himself

his kingdom vision—a vision that centrally entails an atoning death and resurrection.

PLAN A REVISED

Plan A was God ruling through Israel; Plan B was ideally David and then also an Israelite king ruling (and usually not very well because humans do not "do" God right). Under Jesus, Plan A takes on a new form as Plan A Revised. How so? In Jesus God now rules once again, but this time following a life, atoning death, and resurrection.[23] So when Jesus declares that the "kingdom of *God* has come near," we need to pause for a moment to see something very special in the "of God." This is not the kingdom of Moses or Samuel or David or Solomon or any other of the kings of Israel and Judah. This is the kingdom *of God* as it was before Samuel's fateful request and God's accommodation to Israel, and yet God rules in his Son, King Jesus, and he will be modeled on David.

Here, then, is Plan A Revised: in Jesus, who is called Messiah (which means king), who is also called Son of God (which also means anointed king), *God establishes his rule over Israel and the world one more time as under Plan A.* Here are the major elements:

- God alone is King.

- God is now ruling in King Jesus.

- Israel and the church live under the rule of King Jesus.

- Forgiveness is granted through King Jesus, the Savior.

- This rule of Jesus will be complete in the final kingdom.

So the A-B-A′ looks like this:

Plan A: God is king through his people.

Plan B: Human kings are kings, and God uses them.

Plan A Revised: God is king in King Jesus.

Jesus is all of Israel's major leaders and more: he is a new Moses and especially a new David and a new Solomon and a new Servant and a new Son of

---

touched on the atonement themes in a number of settings, none more suggestively than N. T. Wright, *Evil and the Justice of God* (Downers Grove, IL: InterVarsity Press, 2006).

[23]This theme is developed in N. T. Wright, *How God Became King: The Forgotten Story of the Gospels* (New York: HarperOne, 2012).

Man and a whole new redemptive order. Joseph and Mary name him *Yeshua* because he will "save his people from their sins" (Mt 1:21). The story is that in Jesus God now rules, and God's kind of ruling is saving, rescuing, atoning, justifying, and reconciling. The cross and the resurrection redefine kingdom in all directions: Israel is not the same, obedience is not the same, love is not the same, peace is not the same, and justice is not the same. In other words, to say the kingdom has drawn near is to make a christological claim; it is to say the kingdom is now present in Jesus. The always-worth-quoting Karl Barth says it well: "What is meant in the New Testament by the presence of the kingdom of God? . . . 'The kingdom of God is at hand' means 'the Word was made flesh and dwelt among us' (John 1:14)."[24]

When Jesus said "the kingdom of God has drawn near," he announced a new day in an old story, and that story, I propose, is the A-B-A' story that includes and modifies the C-F-R-C story into the kingdom story. Yes, the arrival of Jesus as God's King ends the exile and establishes the inauguration of the kingdom of God.

---

[24]Karl Barth, *The Christian Life*, Church Dogmatics 4.4 (Lecture Fragments) (Grand Rapids: Eerdmans, 1981), 248-49.

CHAPTER EIGHT

PAUL, EXILE, AND THE ECONOMY OF GOD

S. A. CUMMINS

EXILE IS AN EVOCATIVE WORD and can express in rich and resonant ways key aspects of the human experience. For N. T. Wright the term, as focused on Israel and closely tied to return and restoration, carries considerable weight as a key explanatory element in his extensive and influential work in biblical and cognate studies. This is evident in compressed fashion in his essay that appears in this volume, more fully in various earlier publications, and most expansively with respect to Paul in his recent and massive *Paul and the Faithfulness of God*.[1] While much might be said, this contribution will offer initial observations on the meaning and significance of the term *exile* as understood and employed by Wright; recognize that it functions within his notable narrative approach to Paul; and then consider aspects of his exposition of exile in certain select and pertinent passages in Paul's letters, followed by some brief concluding comments.

Wright's creative, if contested, treatment of this topic employs an interpretative approach that combines history, narrative, and covenantal theology, worked out in engaging and enlightening exegetical analysis. Together this serves to show that exile, integrated with other important related elements, is woven into and variously discernible at key points in Paul's writings.

---

[1]In what follows the extent of my indebtedness to N. T. (Tom) Wright will become readily apparent, and also the impossibility of adequately representing and critiquing in any detail the scope and significance of his contribution on this wide-ranging subject.

N. T. Wright, *Paul and the Faithfulness of God*, Christian Origins and the Question of God 4 (Minneapolis: Fortress, 2013).

And when viewed in relation to Paul's Jewish matrix as reworked in the light of Jesus and the Spirit, this informs his understanding of the gospel and the Christian life in important and instructive ways. Yet arguably, if paradoxically, exile might be seen as both less and more significant in Paul than even Wright's expansive and illuminating analysis allows. Less, in that exile is not explicitly evident everywhere; its existence and impact is deeply embedded within wider associations and serves the more obvious and pressing particularities of Paul's letters and their respective contexts.[2] More, in that all that is envisioned and entailed therein may invite an even more comprehensive theological approach. Wright's illuminating engagement with exile deserves to be further considered within a broader perspective on the unfolding economy (that is, plan and providence) of God.

Exile: Meaning and Significance

In common currency the word *exile* can often refer to geopolitical deportation or expatriation. Yet it can also evoke various wider associations, including estrangement of an existential and sociocultural nature. In his essay and elsewhere, Wright's Israel-centered use of the term operates with a certain range of interrelated elements in play, requiring discernment as to what is (and is not) entailed. It may, for example, be referred to as a "theme, concept, state, period," and, with restoration, be seen as the "central drama" in Israel's life.[3] It includes historical, geographic, political, cultural, narrative, theological, and ethical dimensions. This continuing exile is variously and widely attested in the literature of Israel, Second Temple Judaism, and early Christianity.[4] At times Wright places "exile" within quotation

---

[2]These considerations will not be directly developed at any length here. But they are ostensible factors in discussions between Wright and his interlocutors on the nature, extent, and significance of exile in the Bible and Second Temple Judaism, including its presence and role in Paul's thought and writings. On exile in recent biblical scholarship, with helpful bibliographies, see Nicholas Perrin, "Exile," in *The World of the New Testament: Cultural, Social, and Historical Contexts*, ed. Joel B. Green and Lee Martin McDonald (Grand Rapids: Baker Academic, 2013), 26-29; and J. M. Scott, "Exile and Restoration," in *Dictionary of Jesus and the Gospels*, 2nd ed., ed. Joel B. Green et al. (Downers Grove, IL: IVP Academic, 2013), 251-58.

[3]In Wright's essay, compare "theme" (19 [2x], 20, 27n14, 30n21, 46, 63, 79); "concept" (19); "state" (19, 20, 30, 31, 36, 67); "period" (25, 31, 36, 62, 71, 79); and "central drama" (45). Throughout page references to Wright's essay are given in parentheses.

[4]The fundamental reference point is the Deuteronomic "promise of a historical sequence culminating in a continuing exile and an ultimate return," 28. It is not that all Jews during this period saw themselves as living within this continuing exile, "only that such an understanding was

marks to indicate that he is well aware that "the geographical 'exile' ended, in a sense, when the captives returned from Babylon"; but since Israel is still under oppression and the great promises of Isaiah and Ezekiel remain unfulfilled, "the exile (the real exile, as opposed to the merely geographical exile in Babylon) is still continuing," with this experience to be seen as the ongoing outworking of the "covenantal curse" (Deut 27–29).[5]

Wright allows that this use of exile is metaphorical insofar as "its meaning transcends geographical exile," but maintains that exile is "a real period of actual human history."[6] In keeping with this, his reference to "end of exile" is shorthand for "the richly textured and many-layered second-Temple Jewish expectation that Israel's god would once again act *within her history*."[7] Thus, he insists on the enduring historical and experiential actuality of Israel's exile, even if this trying and protracted situation is such that it merits metaphorical depiction as "a long night, with the promised dawn seemingly indefinitely postponed" (79).[8]

Yet Wright also stresses that exile is not merely an "image" or a "metaphor" in the sense of an idea adopted from Israel's past to cast light on a later separate scenario (21).[9] Nor is it only an "example" or "illustration" of God's earlier actions in Israel. And it is not simply a "type" (or, again, "image"), meaning an idea taken up into a wider theological reflection (36). Rather, Israel was "living within" an ongoing historical reality, caught up as a participant in a debilitating condition whose end—real return and restoration— arrives in Jesus, as experienced and attested in Paul and the early church.

While Wright has in various places deliberately and helpfully delineated his understanding and use of the term *exile*, there is still a lot going on here: a number of evocative and interrelated referents and dimensions, capable of

---

widespread, and was particularly likely to be true generally speaking, of Second Temple Jews, and particularly of Pharisees and Essenes," 31.
[5]So N. T. Wright, *Justification: God's Plan & Paul's Vision* (Downers Grove, IL: IVP Academic, 2009), 60.
[6]N. T. Wright, "In Grateful Dialogue: A Response," in *Jesus & The Restoration of Israel: A Critical Assessment of N. T. Wright's Jesus and the Victory of God*, ed. Carey C. Newman (Downers Grove, IL: InterVarsity Press, 1999), 244-77 (260).
[7]N. T. Wright, *Jesus and the Victory of God*, Christian Origins and the Question of God 2 (Minneapolis: Fortress, 1996), xviii (italics original).
[8]Similarly, "*a long passage through a state of continuing 'exile'*" (Wright, *Justification*, 60, italics original); and "a long tunnel" (Wright, *Paul and the Faithfulness of God*, 501).
[9]He notes that it can be employed in such a manner, though that is not the main point (21).

a rich range of configurations, associations, and significations. Certainly central is the concern that exile should not be detached from its historical and geopolitical origins, or from its existence as an ongoing lived reality for Israel, by viewing it as but an example, type, or metaphor. Yet, at the same time and in certain ways, Wright also recognizes the conceptual, metaphorical, and symbolic significance of "exile." Indeed, he insists that the combination of key exile-related texts such as Deuteronomy 27–30 and Daniel 9, regularly taken up in later sources, requires that "exile" be viewed "as the best controlling metaphor to characterize this continuing moment in the single, though complex, perceived narrative of a great many Jews, including Pharisees, in the second-Temple period."[10] All this makes wrestling with Wright on "the whole concept" of exile (19) all the more challenging, and contributes to the interaction with his interlocutors on this important issue. It also requires some recognition of the fact that exile functions for Wright within a crucial wider interpretative framework: a continuing and controlling narrative encompassing history, story, and theology.

Exile Within a Continuing and Controlling Narrative

Wright's understanding of Israel's ongoing exile works within a wider complex but coherent narrative (or metanarrative) that he argues is implicit and variously attested in the Old Testament, Second Temple Jewish literature, and the New Testament. For Paul, "Scripture tells a great story, the triple story of God and the world, and humankind, and Israel."[11] This comprises an "outer story" and "framing plot of creator and creation" that operates in relation to three subplots: (1) "the story of the human creatures through whom the creator intended to bring order to the world"; (2) humanity's failure, "the story of Israel as the people called to be the light of the world," and the role of the Torah therein; and (3) "because of Israel's own failure . . . [there is] the story of Jesus, Israel's crucified and risen Messiah."[12]

---

[10]Wright, *Paul and the Faithfulness of God*, 162; this remark is made in responding (at pages 160-62) to the critique by S. M. Bryan in *Jesus and Israel's Traditions of Judgment and Restoration*, SNTSMS 117 (Cambridge: Cambridge University Press, 2002), 12-20.

[11]Wright, *Paul and the Faithfulness of God*, 519.

[12]Ibid., 484-85; see the extensive discussion at 456-537, and also earlier at 108-75. Compare this more elaborate schema with the simplified one in Wright's essay in this volume, 63-72, which will be broadly followed below. Further to the brief discussion in this section on Wright's narrative analysis in relation to Paul's theology, see the broader review and assessment in Joel R.

All this is operative under the plan and agency of a sovereign and righteous God. As more fully focused on Israel it is a single, continuous "great controlling narrative," giving depth and meaning to Israel's life, with high points including "Passover, exodus, freedom, Sinai, covenant, and homecoming" (38). Most of Paul's fellow Jews regarded themselves as living within this narrative, with many during the Second Temple period interpreting it "in terms of the so-called Deuteronomic scheme of sin—exile—restoration" (21): sin leads Israel into exile, renders it subject to Torah's curse (rather than its blessing), which continues under successive and oppressive foreign rule, with the promised restoration envisaged by prophets such as Isaiah and Ezekiel yet to be realized.[13]

Israel's story for Paul reaches its denouement and resolution in the death and resurrection of the faithful Messiah Jesus, who embodies and enacts the return of YHWH to Zion, and thereby defeats evil, brings about a new exodus, the "real return" and end of exile, and covenant life, and ushers in the new age. Paul's gospel concerning Jesus "means what it means within the larger story of Israel, within the story of the whole human race which is larger still, and within the story of the whole world which is the ultimate narrative horizon."[14] Yet it is also the central character Jesus—whose own story is, to shift the rubric slightly, the "play within the play"—in whom the wider narratives are centered, interlock, find their meaning, and are together resolved.[15] The ensuing sending of the Spirit issues in "the newly symbolic world of the people of God," no longer in exile but rather "living under the rule of the one God, as free citizens of his kingdom" (63). In short, and to stress the historical aspect of the exile in all of this, God's plan was always, via this remarkable route, to rescue Adam's children and restore the entire

---

White, "N. T. Wright's Narrative Approach," in *God and the Faithfulness of Paul: A Critical Examination of the Pauline Theology of N. T. Wright*, ed. Christoph Heilig, J. Thomas Hewitt, and Michael F. Bird, WUNT 2.413 (Tübingen: Mohr Siebeck, 2016), 181-204; to which Wright responds in "The Challenge of Dialogue: A Partial and Preliminary Response" 711-68 in the same volume, at 731-33 and 735-36.

[13]On Deuteronomy as a framework for reading Paul, see David Lincicum, *Paul and the Early Jewish Encounter with Deuteronomy*, WUNT 2.228 (Tübingen: Mohr Siebeck, 2010); James M. Scott, "Paul's Use of Deuteronomic Tradition," *Journal of Biblical Literature* 112 (1993): 643-65; and Guy Waters, *The End of Deuteronomy in the Epistles of Paul*, WUNT 2.221 (Tübingen: Mohr Siebeck, 2006).

[14]Wright, *Paul and the Faithfulness of God*, 525.

[15]Citation from ibid., 516; see further, 517-36.

world; and "this entire narrative had to pass through the narrow door of exile, and ultimately of the cross of Jesus. This is not a side issue or a different point. It is the key to everything else" (75).

Among various issues raised by this narrative rendering, and the account of exile therein, three may be briefly noted here. First, the extent to which it is intrinsic to and exhibited in—rather than imposed, inferred, or abstracted from—the many and various texts taken together remains much debated.[16] Second, Wright's reconstruction draws widely on both biblical and extra-biblical materials, so that the resulting structure might be construed as less canonical and more of a "'cultural encyclopedia'—the cultural framework of reference—of Jewish religion and culture in the ancient Mediterranean world."[17] Third, with respect to Pauline studies, there is the live issue as to how Paul's theology should be conceived; whether, for example, in essentially salvation-historical and/or apocalyptic terms. Versions of the latter argue that the apostle's Christ-centered apocalyptic gospel is to be regarded as a transcendent, eschatological, revelatory incursion or invasion of cosmic proportion, and that this constitutes the fundamental reference point for its historical and narrative dimensions.[18] Hence it is this gospel that frames and

---

[16]On Paul, see Martinus C. de Boer, "N. T. Wright's Great Story and Its Relationship to Paul's Gospel," *Journal for the Study of Paul and His Letters* 4, no. 1 (2014): 49-57: "It is evident that the triple narrative has been constructed by Wright from his own careful study of the Scripture (and of Second Temple Judaism), and that it has not been derived from Paul's letters, except second-arily. A nagging question forces itself on the reader: has Wright not imposed his own vision of the Bible's grand narrative on Paul, the always-troublesome and recalcitrant apostle?" (52). See Wright's reply in "Right Standing, Right Understanding, and Wright Misunderstanding: A Response," *Journal for the Study of Paul and His Letters* 4, no. 1 (2014): 87-103 (88-91). Note the more positive overall analysis in Joel R. White, "N. T. Wright's Narrative Approach," extended with particular reference to exile in his "Führt der Messias sein Volk aus dem Exil? Eine kritische Auseinandersetzung mit N. T. Wrights These eines implizites Metanarrativs hinter dem pau-linischen Evangelium," in *Der jüdische Messias Jesus und sein jüdischer Apostel Paulus*, ed. Armin D. Baum, Detlef Häusser, and Emmanuel L. Rehfeld, WUNT 2.425 (Tübingen: Mohr Siebeck, 2016), 227-42. More broadly on Paul and narrative, see Bruce W. Longenecker, ed., *Narrative Dynamics in Paul: A Critical Assessment* (Louisville, KY: Westminster John Knox, 2002).

[17]Richard B. Hays, "Knowing Jesus: Story, History and the Question of Truth," in *Jesus, Paul, and the People of God: A Theological Dialogue with N. T. Wright*, ed. Nicholas Perrin and Richard B. Hays (Downers Grove, IL: InterVarsity Press, 2011), 47, regarding the Gospels.

[18]See Wright's extensive engagement with the wide-ranging and contested matter of Paul and "apocalyptic," an ambiguous term, in his *Paul and His Recent Interpreters: Some Contemporary Debates* (Minneapolis: Fortress, 2015), part II (133-218); *The Paul Debate: Critical Questions for Understanding the Apostle* (Waco, TX: Baylor University Press, 2015), chap. 3 (41-64); and his remarks in "The Challenge of Dialogue: A Partial and Preliminary Response," in *God and the Faithfulness of Paul*, 711-68, on "Apocalyptic," at 743-54, including interaction with Jörg Frey's

governs Paul's understanding of God in relation to creation, humanity, and Israel,[19] rather than the gospel involving "the insertion of Jesus into the longer narratives of Israel and the world."[20]

Wright's response, operating on its grandest scale in the very structure and content of *Paul and the Faithfulness of God*, is to argue that Paul's interlocking worldview, mindset, and theology together bear a strongly implicit narrative that finds varied and illuminating expression in both the poetic and referential sequence of his letters.[21] Moreover, this narrative is significantly shaped by and consonant with Scripture (and also Second Temple Jewish texts). The "apocalyptic" element of Paul's gospel is to be seen as doing something new and fresh, working transformatively from *within* the historical-narrative dimension. In Wright's reading of Paul, history, narrative, and theology are inextricably interrelated, and salvation history, apocalyptic, and indeed all key theological facets are held together in an essentially covenantal theology.[22] Paul was always "a basically Jewish thinker" and "a Messiah-man" who recognized in the gospel events and announcement

---

essay "Demythologizing Apocalyptic? On N. T. Wright's Paul, Apocalyptic Interpretation, and the Constraints of Construction," 489-531 in the same volume. Note also Samuel V. Adams, *The Reality of God and Historical Method: Apocalyptic Theology in Conversation with N. T. Wright* (Downers Grove, IL: IVP Academic, 2015).

[19]See de Boer, "N. T. Wright's Great Story and Its Relationship to Paul's Gospel," 52-53; see also Francis Watson's comments on Paul's gospel and narrative in his "Is There a Story in These Texts?," in *Narrative Dynamics in Paul: A Critical Assessment*, ed. Bruce W. Longenecker (Louisville, KY: Westminster John Knox, 2002), 231-39, at 232-34; and Wright's interaction with this in *Paul and the Faithfulness of God*, 462-63.

[20]Wright, *Paul and the Faithfulness of God*, 522.

[21]Again, see ibid., 456-537, which opens with a defense of his approach, "Introduction: To Narrate or Not to Narrate," 456-68, and includes a brief discussion of *"poetic sequence* (the order in which material appears in the text itself) and the *referential sequence* (the order in which, if we try to reconstruct the world which the text both presupposes and addresses, this same material, and more besides, will appear)," 463 (italics original), here referencing N. R. Petersen, *Rediscovering Paul: Philemon and the Sociology of Paul's Narrative World* (Philadelphia: Fortress, 1985). Among earlier and briefer discussions along these lines, see his *The New Testament and the People of God*, Christian Origins and the Question of God 1 (Minneapolis: Fortress, 1992), 403-9.

[22]For example, in discussing Rom 5–8, he notes "how the regularly separated elements of Paul's thought, especially 'juridicial' and 'participationist' on the one hand, 'apocalyptic' and 'salvation history' on the other, and also 'transformation' and 'anthropology', are held together within an essentially *covenantal* framework," Wright, *Paul and the Faithfulness of God*, 1013 (italics original). See the earlier discussions at 22-74, especially, 36-45. Similarly, for example, in his concluding comments on "apocalyptic" in *The Paul Debate*: "We cannot say that 'apocalyptic' must be played off against 'covenant theology' . . . [or] that the 'vertical invasion' of the gospel events rules out any sense of ongoing history," 64.

that "a new sort of 'apocalypse' had happened and was happening (the unveiling of Jesus as Messiah)," and that paradoxically "these shocking, tra-
dition-overturning, radically new events were *the things that Israel's God had
promised all along*."[23] Moreover, this is what the Abrahamic covenant always
envisaged and involved: "God's providential ordering of Israel's history,"
which culminates with "the bursting-in of the Messiah upon a Jewish
world."[24]

The power and persuasiveness of Wright's view of exile, functioning
within his account of a continuing and controlling narrative, and together
contributing to his wide-ranging and contested understanding of the Jewish
matrix, Jesus, and Paul himself, is significantly contingent on the extent to
which it makes better sense of more of the crucial elements in play. In the
case of Paul this obviously includes his theology and letters. With this in
mind, and following the fourfold headings in Wright's essay in the present
volume, we now briefly consider aspects of his approach to exile and associated elements in certain select passages in Paul.

EXPLICATING EXILE IN PAUL'S LETTERS

In his essay, Wright argues that Paul "drew on" the continuing exile theme,
and with particular reference to his belief that Jesus had accomplished the
end of exile: "The Creator/covenant God has brought his covenant purpose
for Israel to fruition *in Israel's representative, the Messiah, Jesus. Therefore,
now, a new world has dawned*. The new day promised by the prophets, and
by Moses himself in Deuteronomy, has arrived. For Paul, the period of exile
has ended in Christ" (62, emphasis original). Moreover, this has issued in
"the returned-from-exile people, the people of the new covenant."[25] While
to some degree such elements are discernible, arguably there are also additional dimensions in view, which together suggest that exile operates
within an unfolding divine economy—that is, the plan and providence of
God—whose nature and scope may be the more fully conceived, even as it
ultimately remains beyond our present imagining.[26]

---

[23]Wright, *Paul and the Faithfulness of God*, 1262 (italics original).
[24]Ibid.
[25]Ibid., 502.
[26]See Murray Rae, "Texts in Context: Scripture and the Divine Economy," *Journal of Theological
Interpretation* 1, no. 1 (2007): 23-45, for "a proposal about how to read the Bible on its own terms

Creation and new creation (Rom 8:18-27; Gal 6:14-15; 2 Cor 5:17). Interacting briefly in his essay with a number of pertinent passages in Paul (Rom 8:18-27; Gal 6:14-15; Col 1:23; 2 Cor 5:17), Wright observes that the gospel story implicitly told at its widest level encompasses the entirety of creation and new creation.[27] The whole world is rescued from its current dire condition through the death of Jesus, "the hinge on which the door of world history turns" (64). Those conformed to the crucified and risen Messiah Jesus and enlivened by the Spirit become a new people, a new humanity, who even now participate in the inaugurated if yet to be fully realized new reality, albeit in the midst of present suffering. While there is no explicit mention of exile in Wright's exposition of the texts in question, certain language in Romans 8 does evoke the new exodus experience[28]—e.g., being "led by the Spirit of God" rather than being subject to "a spirit of slavery" (Rom 8:14-15)—and thus to life on the other side of exile, with the promised Spirit attested in Ezekiel (Ezek 36:27), and new covenant status as children and heirs of God and coheirs with Christ (Rom 8:17).[29] Yet we may note that other elements indicate the incomplete and as-yet-unseen ultimate outworking and fullness of God's providence: e.g., the awaited final "revealing of the children of God," the liberation of creation, "the redemption of our bodies," and the hope of glory (Rom 8:18-19, 21, 23-25). In the interim, "the Spirit intercedes for the saints according to the will of God" (Rom 8:27), as does the risen and exalted Christ Jesus "at the right hand of God" (Rom 8:34). And so nothing in life or death, on earth or in the heavenly realm, present or future, indeed anything at all, can separate the suffering saints from their present and final participation in the love of God in Christ Jesus their Lord (Rom 8:35-39). In short, the scope and final realization of all that

---

as witness to and instrument in the saving economy of God," 44. Taking Is 52:13–53:12—with its exilic setting—as a case study, Rae argues a biblical text's meaning is "a function, ultimately, of the role(s) it serves in the divine economy," 40. This includes authorial intention and subsequent reader reception; and it involves historical, narrative, christological, canonical, and ecclesial considerations (38-45).

[27]Compare Wright, *Paul and the Faithfulness of God*, 475-85; also 485-94. Also see his *The Paul Debate* for thought-provoking remarks throughout on new creation and various related aspects of Paul's theological vision, including the dawning of a new and different time, world, and human existence.

[28]On exodus in Romans 8:14-39 and also Galatians, see S. C. Keesmaat, *Paul and His Story: (Re) Interpreting the Exodus Tradition*, JSNTSup181 (Sheffield: Sheffield Academic Press, 1999).

[29]Biblical citations normally follow the NRSV.

is envisaged takes up but also transcends human present experience, earthly and heavenly powers, and reality as currently known.

And all this is under the unfolding governance of God in Jesus and the Spirit (one in aim and activity, Rom 8:9-11). This encompasses God sending his Son (Rom 8:3; cf. Gal 4:4; Phil 2:6-11; Jn 3:16): a preexistent, incarnate, redeeming, risen, exalted, and interceding Jesus, a living Lord present with his people through the indwelling Spirit. Their ultimate glorification will both realize who they are and transfigure them into who they are yet to be. In this wider context "exile" (evident in sin and death), though ended in Jesus' death and resurrection and in Spirit-renovated lives, remains residually in play until the estrangement of humanity and creation is ultimately overcome and they become participants in an inconceivably greater glory.

Wright goes on to note also the new-creation perspective that suddenly emerges into view at Galatians 6:14-15. Here Paul regards the conflicted Galatian believers both as members of the new people of God in Jesus and the Spirit and, in virtue of the world being crucified in the cross of the Messiah, as now located on a much broader horizon (Gal 6:14-15).[30] They are themselves a sign of "a much larger reality," a human new creation. Indeed, a new world has been birthed, and "the landscape itself has decisively changed" (64). Illuminating and expansive though this is, as Wright's evocative use of metaphor intimates, more might be said concerning this radical crucifixion of the world and resulting new creation. Accomplished by God, it includes crucifixion not only of the old person but liberation from "the elemental spirits of the world" (Gal 4:3, 9; cf. Col 2:8, 13-15). Thus it must be allowed that any division now overcome (e.g., that implicit in "neither circumcision nor circumcision is anything," Gal 6:15) extends to include absolutely everything that separates from the love of God (cf. Rom 8:38-39, noted above). Moreover, the broken syntax and compressed exclamation ("—*new creation!*") tries to articulate the "utter discontinuity between the abolished cosmos and the new world."[31] And, while Wright's essay makes no mention

---

[30]See Wright, *Paul and the Faithfulness of God*, 477-78, and also 1143-51. Wright (ibid., 478) cites Richard B. Hays: "A new reality has been brought into being that determines the destiny of the whole creation," in "The Letter to the Galatians: Introduction, Commentary, and Reflections," in *The New Interpreter's Bible*, ed. L. Keck (Nashville, TN: Abingdon Press, 2000), 11:181-348 (344).

[31]Hays, "Letter to the Galatians," 344 (italics original), who adds that here Paul "is claiming that the God who created the world has come to reclaim and transform it," 345.

of exile, the passage may also evoke Isaiah 65:17-25 (cf. Rom 8:19-23), with its postexilic vision of "new heavens and a new earth" (Is 65:17; cf. Rev 21:1).[32] Given the enormity of all that is here briefly in view, Paul rightly observes that there is no room for any human boasting in the face of all that God has done in and through the cross of the Lord Jesus Christ (Gal 6:14).

New creation also makes a rather sudden appearance in the midst of Paul's remarks on his ministry of reconciliation in 2 Corinthians 5:11–6:13: "So if anyone is in Christ, there is a new creation: everything old has passed away; see, everything has become new!" (2 Cor 5:17). Wright locates this remark within Paul's wider discussion correlating the cross, his costly apostolic ministry, and hardships endured for the gospel. He observes that Jesus' death deals with death itself and ushers in new creation, which is now evident in the people of God and is a sign of the new life that is to encompass creation overall. Yet it is to be noted that Paul's remark is more immediately bracketed first by his recognition that believers no longer know Christ "according to the flesh" and then with "all this is from God," who in Christ reconciles the world to himself (2 Cor 5:16, 18).[33] This entails not merely a new perspective but an entirely new understanding, one which arises out of the actualization of a new life, a new order of things. This did not previously exist but has now been brought into being by God's reconciling work in the death and resurrection of Jesus (2 Cor 5:15). And it enables a divinely disclosed, Christ-centered, Spirit-empowered comprehension of what is going on in the world, such that present earthly affliction cannot obscure or obstruct participation now or ultimately so in heavenly/eternal glory (2 Cor 4:16–5:21; cf. Rom 8:18-39).[34]

Israel (Rom 2:17–3:9; Gal 3:6-12; 2 Cor 5:21). The story of Israel is complicated but crucial to understanding Paul's worldview and theology. It is

---

[32]Noted by Hays, "Letter to the Galatians," 345.

[33]Compare, for example, "from God" (2 Cor 5:18) and "God sent his Son" (Gal 4:4, on which see below): God sends, reconciles, renews. And all this is "the grace of God" (2 Cor 6:1).

[34]Among the various striking contrasts in 2 Cor 4:16–5:21, differentiating between what is and what will be: "this slight momentary affliction" and "an eternal weight of glory beyond all measure" (2 Cor 4:17); "what can be seen," which is temporary, and "what cannot be seen," which is eternal (2 Cor 4:18); "the earthly tent," in which we groan (cf. Rom 8:23) and "a building from God, a house not made with hands, eternal in the heavens" (2 Cor 5:1-2); being "at home in the body" and "away from the Lord" (2 Cor 5:6; cf. 5:8); and "everything old has passed away" and "everything has become new!" (2 Cor 5:17).

"the story of God's people, of Abraham's people, as the people *through whom the creator was intending to rescue his creation*."[35] Yet since Israel itself is caught up in the sinful human condition, it is unable to fulfill its vocation as it currently stands. As his essay indicates, Wright discerns the Israel-focused aspect of the problem in passages such as Romans 2:17–3:9 and Galatians 3:6-12; and, focusing on Romans, its solution is seen in God's righteousness (answering Dan 9:16) manifest in a faithful redeeming Messiah Jesus (Rom 3:21-26; cf. Rom 1:16-17), resulting in a single faithful family (Rom 3:27-31) and the realization of the promise to Abraham (Rom 4:1-25).[36] Exile, evoked by the prophetic judgment referenced at Romans 2:24 (Is 52:5; Ezek 36:20), is, metaphorically speaking, where "the single-plan-through-Israel-for-the-world had run into the sand," and also "the massive demonstration, carved in the granite rock of Israel's history" that Israel too needed redemption (66). Yet the great prophets also anticipate a suffering and sin-bearing Servant (Is 52:13–53:12) and a transformed Israel (Ezek 36:24-30), which is now realized in Messiah Jesus and the Spirit, and in a new people of God (Rom 2:25-29). This is "return-from-exile theology" (66).

The Israel-focused problem is also evident in Galatians (e.g., Gal 3:6-12), where the curse (of Deut 28; 30) has placed Israel under condemnation and impeded—"bottled up" (66) and blocked—the Abrahamic promises reaching the Gentiles. This is resolved by Jesus taking the curse on himself, his death redeeming "us" so that "we" (Jews under the Deuteronomic curse) "might receive the promise of the Spirit through faith" (Gal 3:13-14).[37] In this

---

[35]Wright, *Paul and the Faithfulness of God*, 495 (italics original); see further, 495-505.

[36]See further, ibid., 836-51.While not taken up in his essay in this volume, Wright elsewhere addresses the deeply paradoxical outworking of God's plan evident in the "large-scale narrative of Israel" at Rom 9–11 in *Paul and the Faithfulness of God*, briefly at 499-502 (499), and extensively at 1156-1258. Israel's story had taken it through the "long tunnel" of exile (501, cf. 139-63), traced in Rom 9:6–10:13 with reference to Deut 27–30. Paul fuses the stories of Israel and Messiah Jesus, in whom "Israel's covenant story" culminates, issuing in "the returned-from-exile people, the people of the new covenant." Thus the human story is put "back on track" and God's purposes for creation achieved, 502. Note Joel R. White, "Führt der Messias sein Volk aus dem Exil?," 234-40, offering an analysis of Rom 9–11 (and 15:14-20) supportive of Wright's reading of Paul in relation to a metanarrative involving exile. See also N. T. Wright, "The Letter to the Romans: Introduction, Commentary, and Reflections," in *New Interpreter's Bible*, 10:620-99 on Rom 9–11, including 658-70 on exile in Rom 10:5-11.

[37]See N. T. Wright, "Curse and Covenant: Galatians 3.10-14," in *The Climax of the Covenant: Christ and the Law in Pauline Theology* (Edinburgh: T&T Clark, 1991), 137-56. Also Scott J. Hafemann, "Paul and the Exile of Israel in Galatians 3–4," in *Exile: Old Testament, Jewish, and Christian Conceptions*, ed. James M. Scott, JSJSup 56 (Leiden: Brill, 1997), 329-71.

way "the exile is over" (66). And this is accomplished because God "made him to be sin, who knew no sin" (so 2 Cor 5:21), a remark cognate with Jesus' self-giving "for our sins to set us free from the present evil age" (Gal 1:4), and that "Christ died for our sins in accordance with the scriptures" (1 Cor 15:3).[38] In the first instance, texts such as these are to be read in relation to Israel's sin, curse, and continuing exile (rather than to "a dehistoricized atonement-theory," 67), which culminates and ends, and the real return begins, with the death and resurrection of Messiah Jesus (68). That for Paul the story of the Messiah is at the very center of Israel's story and its decline into and deliverance from exile finds its most pointed and compressed expression in Galatians 2:19-21.[39] That, as implied in Galatians 2:21, Israel's Messiah had to die, "indicates that Israel, as defined by Torah, needed to die and to come through to a new sort of life, a life in which the promises would at last be fulfilled" (69). The righteous people of God are now fundamentally defined not by Torah but by their dying and (as implied by "might live to God," Gal 2:19) rising with the faithful Messiah Jesus.

Certainly notable aspects of these key passages in Paul do attest to the "complex narrative structure" (62) of Paul's theology and to the story of Israel—including the Abrahamic covenant, Torah (not least Deuteronomy), the prophets, and exile—culminating in the death and resurrection of Jesus. And Wright's historical and narrative-orientated analysis unearths and explicates this in very important and instructive ways. Yet, as his own further use of metaphorical language may imply, this too points toward and may be taken up into an even greater account of what is envisaged. While his stress on Jesus as Israel's Messiah again affords a strenuous and welcome "ground-up" and "inside-out" account of the outworking of divine redemption (and the incarnation), further reflection is needed on the residual mystery concerning how this happens and, together with the resurrection, on the transcendent dimension entailed.[40] Indeed, Wright's regular recourse to

---

[38]Compare also Paul's indirect affirmation of the resurrection at 1 Cor 15:17: "If Christ has not been raised, your faith is futile and you are still in your sins."

[39]See further Gal 2:19-21 in Wright, *Paul and the Faithfulness of God*, 852-60.

[40]So, for example, while later Christian "atonement theology" (66) in its various forms and uses may be problematic in certain respects and might benefit from Wright's historical approach, arguably it is wrestling—not least via various analogies—with the sheer enormity of Jesus' redemption within the economy of God.

"somehow" language intimates recognition that aspects of Jesus' representative role, atonement, and identity in relation to "God" remain beyond even the most discerning delineations.[41]

With respect to Romans 2:17–3:9, the passage functions within a letter that, above all, attests to the overarching transcendence of God. Thus, for example, while Romans is all about the righteousness of God (e.g., Rom 1:16-17; 3:21-26; 10:1-4) revealed in the gospel, the Creator God remains eternal, the only true object of worship and judge "from heaven" over all things, with the whole of humanity and creation contingent on divine grace and mercy, and awaiting the ultimate outworking of divine glory.[42] To focus this on but one feature of the passage, the opening remarks regarding the Jew who claims to know God by virtue of following and teaching Torah (Rom 2:17-21),[43] bears some correlation with the account of Nicodemus (Jn 3:1-10). He is a teacher of Israel whose incomplete knowledge of Jesus' identity and mission "from God" (Jn 3:2) requires that he be "born from above" and "born of water and Spirit" (Jn 3:3-5; cf. Ezek 36:25-26). Jesus' ensuing remarks concerning "heavenly things," the Son of Man's ascent into and descent from heaven, the Moses/Son of Man typology, and eternal life (Jn 3:11-15), all invoke a transcendent frame of reference and a divinely disclosed understanding.

Paul's argument concerning the Abrahamic promise, Israel, and Torah at Galatians 3:6-12 (extending over Gal 3:13-29) is bracketed by his remarks about his converts' experience of Jesus and the Spirit (Gal 3:1-5; 4:1-7). In Galatians 3:1-5, the Galatians are those characterized by the God-given and Spirit-authenticated gospel "message that elicits faith [*akoēs pisteōs*]"

---

[41]Wright remarks, for example, "Jesus had somehow borne Israel's destiny by himself, was somehow its representative" (62); "Conversely, if somehow Israel's sins were to be dealt with, finished with, and blotted out, then exile could be undone and the people could go free" (67); "My proposal, then, is not that we assume that we know what the word *God* means and somehow manage to fit Jesus into that. Instead, I suggest that we think historically about a young Jew . . . dying on a Roman cross, and that we somehow allow our meaning for the word *God* to be recentered around that point. Place Jesus within his genuine first-century context . . . and all this makes sense" (74-75).

[42]Among many pertinent texts, cf. Rom 1:7, 18-20, 25; 2:5-7; 5:1-2; 8:18-39; 11:33-36; 15:25-27, including doxological elements.

[43]On Rom 2:21-24 (and also Rom 2:25-29), see Wright, *Paul and the Faithfulness of God*, 812-15 and 921-25. See also his "Romans 2.17–3.9: A Hidden Clue to the Meaning of Romans?," in *Pauline Perspectives: Essays on Paul, 1978-2013* (Minneapolis: Fortress, 2013), 489-509; originally published in *Journal for the Study of Paul and His Letters* 1, no. 2 (2012): 1-25.

(Gal 3:2, 5),[44] a phrase that may have echoes of Isaiah 53:1 and the Suffering Servant disfigured in exile.[45] Galatians 4:1-7 further dramatically depicts God in Jesus and the Spirit as operative in the Galatians' lives. Galatians 3:1-5 is itself immediately preceded by Galatians 2:19-21, which, Wright notes, shows that the story of Messiah Jesus' redeeming death is at the heart of Israel's story and situation, and it is conformity thereto that marks out the people of God. Yet the correlation of Galatians 2:19-20 and Galatians 6:14-15 indicates that dying (and rising) with Christ means transference from "the present evil age" (Gal 1:4) to the new age/creation, indicating the "apocalyptic" nature and scope of all that is entailed.[46] Similarly, the correlation of "Christ who lives in me" and "the Son of God, who loved me and gave himself for me" (Gal 2:20) with Paul's remarks regarding his transformative encounter with the risen and exalted Jesus—as God pleased "to reveal his son to [in] me (*apokalypsai ton huion autou en emoi*)" (Gal 1:15-16; cf. also Gal 1:3-4)—further indicates the enormity of the divine drama in view.

Torah (Gal 3:21-25; 4:4-7; Rom 7:1–8:11). Embedded within the Israel story is the third narrative, the story of the Torah, played out in Paul in passages such as Galatians 3:21-25, 4:1-7 and even more extensively in Romans 7:1–8:11.[47] Though a good gift from God to Israel (Rom 7:12), the Torah has "a *deliberately negative purpose*" (69, italics original), says Wright, operative until the redemption achieved by Jesus (himself living "under the law," Gal 4:4). That is, it works as God's agent in an Israel that (like the rest of humanity) remains sinful, and thus serves to place "Israel under a new kind of slavery" (69). Indeed the Torah itself becomes identified as one of "the elemental spirits of the world [*ta stoicheia tou kosmou*]" (Gal 4:3, cf. Gal 4:8-11). It binds Israel "not to God . . . but to Adam" (70) (cf. Rom 5:20; 6:14; 7:1-3), a condition (cf. Rom 7:7-12) wherein the Torah is bound to highlight and condemn sin. Indeed, it can be seen to draw, lure, and focus sin (so Rom 5:20) "onto one place—Israel, and thence to Israel's representative, the

---

[44]On this rendering, and the range of possible translations of this compressed phrase, see Hays, "Letter to the Galatians," 251-52.

[45]Cf. also Is 6:9-10; Rom 10:14-16; 1 Thess 2:13; Acts 23:25-31; and Jn 12:38-43.

[46]Hays, "Letter to the Galatians," on Gal 2:19-21, observes that Paul regards the cross as "a transformative event that has changed the world and incorporated Paul—along with all who receive the gospel—into a new sphere of power," 243.

[47]Among Wright's many notable discussions of Romans 7:1–8:11, see "Letter to the Romans: Introduction, Commentary, and Reflections," 549-90.

Messiah" (71), so that in his death sin can be condemned (Rom 8:3). Thus those once under Torah who "die with the Messiah to the Torah are set free from the bond that binds them to Adam . . . [and are] free for a new life, a life in the risen Christ, a life in the new undying dawn of the new day" (cf. Rom 7:4; 8:3-4) (70).[48]

While not everyone will follow Wright fully through this embedded and intricate narrative understanding of the Torah,[49] and exile further entrenched therein, arguably overall it offers considerable coherency to Paul's wide-ranging and complex remarks on the law, not least at Romans 7:1–8:11.[50] Yet, again, the passages in question involve wider considerations. The argument (story) of Israel and Torah traced through Galatians 3 leads into Galatians 4:1-6. This indicates that the captivity entailed includes enslavement to "the elemental spirits of the world [*ta stoicheia tou kosmou*]" (cf. Gal 4:3, 9) and suggests a cosmic-wide purview and power struggle in play. Israel and the whole of humanity is estranged from God. This situation is overcome "when the fullness of time [*to plērōma tou chronou*] had come" and "God sent his Son" (Gal 4:4). Wright reads this historically and temporally with particular reference to the fulfillment of Abrahamic promises and Israel's rescue from "under the law."[51] Without denying the Israel-specific focus of what is in view—e.g., "born under the law, in order to redeem those who were under the law" (Gal 4:4-5)—the passage fundamentally concerns *God's* decision, timing, and action. And God's sending of the Son is not only a commission to complete the covenant in Messiah Jesus but the incarnation of Jesus, who, together with God sending "the Spirit of his Son" (Gal 4:6), is in service of the plan and providence (economy) of God. The implied Christology is expansive: preexistence, incarnation, earthly life, death, resurrection, exaltation, and living Lord. And the relationship between God the Father (Gal 4:6), the

[48]On Gal 2–4 and Torah, see further Wright, *Paul and the Faithfulness of God*, 851-79.
[49]In which, for example, Torah qua Torah is tied very closely to sin itself in a rather sinister ("luring," 70) fashion.
[50]See also John K. Goodrich, "Sold Under Sin: Echoes of Exile in Romans 7.14-25," *New Testament Studies* 59 (2013): 476-95, on the influence of Is 49–50 on Rom 7:14-25.
[51]Wright, *Paul and the Faithfulness of God*, 876: "*A chronological sequence* in which the coming of the Messiah and the spirit occur at a late stage in a long process" (italics original), dismissing "sudden 'invasion'" approaches (876), and insisting "apocalyptic" cannot be invoked "to rule out the idea of a continuous flow of history, looking back to Abraham," 877.

Son, and the Spirit points towards the Christian affirmation of a triune God. Moreover, the Galatians are participants in all that is in play and heirs to all this entails (Gal 4:7). While no justice can be done here to Romans 7:1–8:11, whose Israel-specific and Torah-focused argument has been explicated by Wright in remarkably instructive ways, arguably God "sending his own Son" (Rom 8:3); the interaction of God, Christ, and Spirit; and the participation therein of those being addressed (at Rom 8:9-12) invites similar evaluation.

Notably various features of what follows in Galatians reinforce the over-arching divine dimension. For example, that the Galatians "have come to know God, or rather to be known by God" (Gal 4:9), itself indicates the priority of God's grace, disclosure, relationship, understanding, etc., in all that has transpired from Abraham to the Galatian believers. The ensuing Hagar and Sarah allegory (Gal 4:21-31) further indicates that the Israel-specific covenantal aspect functions within a transcendent, cosmic-wide, and eschatological scenario, as evident for example in the "present Jerusalem"/"Jerusalem above" (Gal 4:25-26) contrast, the former to be cor-related carefully with "the present evil age" (Gal 1:4).[52] Exile and its ultimate resolution lies in the yet-to-be-fully-realized-and-visualized "Jerusalem above," and the Galatians are even now participating therein.[53]

Humanity (Rom 8:18-24; 2 Cor 3:7–4:6). The fourth interlocking story concerns the Creator God's image-bearing but flawed humanity, who, rescued and renewed through Jesus and the Spirit, may "regain their noble status, their 'glory' (Rom 5:2; 8:17, 21, 30)," and now exercise their calling to be stewards of creation (71). The end of Israel's exile, a condition recapitu-lating the expulsion of Adam and Eve from Eden, also "means that the 'exile' *of the whole human* race has at last been dealt with" (71, italics original). And the return from exile for Israel and the world is accompanied by the return of God's glory to abide within Spirit-indwelt faithful human beings

---

[52]The passage includes a citation of Is 54:1, which opens an oracle promising a barren, exiled Jerusalem that it will be restored (Is 53:1-17). Paul's use of a typological and allegorical reading of Scripture intimates the enormity of all that is already in view, anticipated, and yet to be experienced.

[53]On a theology of "heavenly participation" within the Christian tradition, see Hans Boersma, *Heavenly Participation: The Weaving of a Sacramental Tapestry* (Grand Rapids: Eerdmans, 2011), with brief reference to Paul at, for example, 4-6.

(Rom 8:9-11; 2 Cor 3:7–4:6), long awaited by a creation that itself looks for liberation from its enslavement (Rom 8:21).

What has been suggested already in relation to Wright's account of the creation story—and the subplots involving Israel and Torah—may be applied here too concerning the regained glory of humanity. There is much to be affirmed, yet more may be said and seen. The passages in question indicate that humanity's regained glory is in virtue of the Lord Jesus and the ministry of the life-giving Spirit, who is empowering the people of God. Believers presently experience the recovery of their lost glory, including being made in the image of God, and with this comes new covenant life and its freedom (2 Cor 3:17). This is true even in and through their costly ministry and suffering, on behalf of which the Lord and the Spirit intercede in the heavenly realm (Rom 8:23, 26-27).

They are also, by the power that is the Lord, the Spirit, "being transformed into the same image from one degree of glory to another" (2 Cor 3:18). This entails even now seeing "the glory of Christ, who is the image of God" (2 Cor 4:4), and being given "the light of the knowledge of the glory of God in the face of Jesus Christ" (2 Cor 4:6). All this is a present and powerful glory to which they have access and in which they now participate, and also a sign of their "hope of sharing the glory of God" fully and finally (so Rom 5:2; cf. Rom 8:17, 21, 30). And as to what this will look like, it is glimpsed but not yet fully seen.[54] The nature and final realization of humanity's liberation from Edenic exile and its ultimate glorification, while in continuity with all that is, also remains qualitatively and immeasurably more than can be imagined (Eph 3:14-21).

CONCLUDING COMMENTS

Israel's exile plays a very prominent role within Wright's engaging and extensive contribution to biblical and cognate studies. The term's various referents, dimensions, and limited metaphorical use (as more than just geographic) demands careful attention to all that is (and is not) involved.

---

[54]Cf. Edith M. Humphrey, "Glimpsing the Glory: Paul's Gospel, Righteousness and the Beautiful Feet of N. T. Wright," 161-80, and Wright's "Response to Edith Humphrey," 180-82, in *Jesus, Paul, and the People of God.* Note also Wright's "Whence and Whither Pauline Studies in the Life of the Church?," 262-81, in the same volume.

Wright stresses the actuality of exile for an Israel that continues to experience oppression (metaphorically, "a long night," 79) and awaits God's return and restoration. As such it is not a mere example, type, or metaphor (in a broader sense) but an ongoing, lived reality, whose resolution Paul and the early church believed was achieved in the sending of Messiah Jesus and the Spirit.

For Wright the nature and significance of exile is more fully recognized when located and viewed within a complex but coherent, continuing, and controlling narrative concerning God's "single-plan-through-Israel-for-the-world" (66). As noted, this comprises a triple story (God, world, humankind), with an "outer story" (Creator and creation) and its three subplots (the story of human creatures, Israel and its Torah, and Messiah Jesus). Wright has responded to various concerns about the nature of this narrative: for example, the extent to which it is inherent, abstracted, or imposed on the text; the wide-ranging use of a varied corpus of both biblical and extrabiblical literature; and how to construe Paul's theology in relation thereto, whether in salvation-historical, apocalyptic, or other terms. He argues that the narrative is strongly implicit within and shaped by Scripture, widely attested in Second Temple Jewish literature, and that Paul's letters—and their intertextual engagement with the Old Testament—exemplify this.

Moreover, the narrative indicates an essentially covenantal theology that encompasses the various theological constituents operative in Paul's thought and writings. Herein we see that God's purposes for Israel, humanity, and the world have unfolded and culminated in the dramatic transformation brought about by the "bursting-in" of Messiah Jesus. In all this Wright's cautions regarding any "de-Judaized and decovenantalized readings of Paul" (66) are well taken; his own constructive and creative program is an engaging and important contribution; and the conversation will no doubt long continue.

The extent and explication of exile in Paul's writings remains contested. Here it has been suggested that exile is indeed in play, but not immediately and everywhere apparent. It is a deeper current within interrelated elements such as exodus, covenant, and Torah-focused concerns. And as such Wright's narrative approach is effective in bringing it more fully into view, even if more might be said about how it is worked out in the particularities of issues, contexts, and congregational concerns addressed by Paul's letters. This matter has not been pursued here, but what has been pressed is that exile in those Pauline passages briefly considered could be more fully seen as functioning within the all-compassing economy of God.

Paul acknowledges above all the transcendence and unfolding providence of a gracious God, and the complete contingency of creation and humanity. God is definitively disclosed in Jesus and the Spirit. Wright has done much to delineate the historical, Israel-specific, and Messiah Jesus outworking of this, including its expression in the Spirit-empowered covenant people of God. Of course, as he recognizes, God sending his own Son (Rom 8:3; Gal 4:4) also demands the explication of a high Christology: an eternally preexistent, incarnate, atoning, risen, exalted, and living Lord. Moreover, God sending the Spirit of his Son (Gal 4:6), and the interrelationship and interaction entailed, signifies an inextricably triune God. In virtue of Jesus and the Spirit, Paul's churches are even now participants in all that this triune God is accomplishing in heaven and on earth. Paul reminds them of the cosmic-wide struggle involved, of the heavenly intercession of the Lord Jesus and the Spirit on their behalf, and that they are children of "the Jerusalem above" (cf. Rom 8:26, 34; Gal 4:3, 9, 26). He stresses the transcendent glory that they as the new humanity now experience, wherein they are being transformed, and into which they will ultimately be taken up in yet-to-be-seen ways that are beyond imagining. Exile is fully overcome and restoration finally realized within the eschatological outworking of the economy of God.

CHAPTER NINE

HOW TO WRITE A SYNTHESIS

Wright and the Problem of Continuity in New Testament Theology

TIMO ESKOLA

N. T. WRIGHT UNDOUBTEDLY BELONGS to the most influential New Testament scholars of our time. His studies are innovative, his use of new methods is encouraging, and his books have inspired much research in the field of biblical theology. In what follows, his views will be discussed from the perspective of writing a synthesis, a presentation of an entire New Testament theology, because this is the heart of his project. In his multivolume series called Christian Origins and the Question of God, Wright is constructing an overview of the teaching of the New Testament. The crucial questions focus on his application of his own premises, especially the idea of the continuing exile and restoration eschatology, to the different writings of the New Testament.[1]

A NARRATIVE APPROACH: EXILE AND RESTORATION

As Wright began to plan his huge project on New Testament theology, Bultmannian frustration still governed the field, doubting the sense of any such enterprise. For decades, New Testament theology had been more or less a matter of Pauline theology. As the Third Quest started to change views about the teaching of the historical Jesus, some scholars, probably inspired

---

[1]Wright himself has listed his main publications in the leading article. I only need to refer to his monumental book on Paul, because this is how far his project has proceeded for now.

by these ideas, returned to the issue of biblical theology with renewed interest. The crucial turning point in scholarship was when the hermeneutical stance that guided interpretation of Jewish identity in the Second Temple period changed. Wright revitalized the idea, which some scholars had already suggested, that Israel's exile had never really ended and that such a belief was shared also by many Jewish teachers themselves at that time.

Ideas have histories, and the theory concerning Israel's exilic condition is a fascinating one. It is impossible to understand the new perspective on Jesus without the work of Ben Meyer and E. P. Sanders. Sanders and his Canadian mentor, Meyer, who wrote an innovative monograph *Aims of Jesus* in 1979, developed these new ideas together. In this investigation Meyer wrote about Jesus' relation to the temple and suggested that Jesus' attitude had to do with the belief that the exile was not entirely over yet. Many of Meyer's ideas found a developed formulation in Sanders's work. Sanders, in turn, applied new expertise in Jewish studies to New Testament criticism. Both his *Paul and Palestinian Judaism* and his other studies on Jewish writings prepared the ground for his monograph on Jesus.[2] This is probably why Sanders, in his investigations about the background of Jesus' teaching, emphasizes the essential role the exile still played in the writings of Second Temple Jewish theologians.[3] Following George Nickelsburg's *Jewish Literature Between the Bible and the Mishnah* (noted by Wright in the lead article of the present volume), Sanders reminds us that, according to several Jewish writers of the Second Temple period, Israel's essential institutions had never been fully restored.[4] The question concerning the continuation of the exile was thus a discussion that had remained alive inside Jewish theology itself. Most of the tribes had never returned to Israel. Even the status of the rebuilt Second Temple had been questioned by some Jewish groups. Jewish identity

---

[2]See especially E. P. Sanders, *Jesus and Judaism* (Philadelphia: Fortress, 1985), 77-81. For the subject of exile and restoration as such, the standard monograph has been Peter Ackroyd's *Exile and Restoration: A Study of Hebrew Thought of the Sixth Century BC*, The Old Testament Library (Philadelphia: Westminster, 1968). Later treatments are numerous but cannot be discussed here.

[3]Sanders in fact wished to revitalize Albert Schweitzer's eschatological interpretation of Jesus' message. See Schweitzer's own description in his *The Quest of the Historical Jesus: A Critical Study of Its Progress from Reimarus to Wrede* (Baltimore, MD: Johns Hopkins University Press, 1998), 385-88. For Sanders's reflection on this, see Sanders, *Jesus and Judaism*, 23-24.

[4]Sanders, *Jesus and Judaism*, 79-80; G. W. E. Nickelsburg, *Jewish Literature Between the Bible and the Mishnah: A Historical and Literary Introduction* (London: SCM Press, 1981), 18.

at the time of Jesus was not monolithic. Many Jewish teachers in the Second Temple period still believed that the exile was not over. Therefore Sanders saw this as a theme that Jesus was able to use in his critical proclamation against the present Israel.

This, in short, is the background for Wright's *Jesus and the Victory of God* (1996), where he used the idea of a continuing exile to explain Jesus' teaching. Wright connected the idea with Jesus' proclamation of a renewed eschatological temple. Wright's basic view has been summarized in many different passages in his writings, one of which can be found at the core of his monograph: "One of the main kingdom-themes informing Jesus' retelling of Israel's story was his belief that the real return from exile, and the real return of YHWH to Zion, were happening in and through his own work."[5] Furthermore, following Meyer and Sanders, Wright suggests that "in his work the Temple was being rebuilt."[6]

Wright's claim about the continuation of the exile has been debated but, considering the evidence, it is as certain as a scientific explanation can be. It is true that at that time such views depended on whom you asked. Sadducean circles probably were quite happy with the history of Israel as it was, but many others were not. There are several arguments that prove Wright's point of departure useful. Not all tribes had returned, and Jewish teachers were very much aware of this. Several groups believed that Israel was run by apostates. Moreover, some Jewish writers believed that Israel and even the temple were polluted. If we look at the question from a slightly different angle, the issue becomes even clearer: Who in Jesus' time really believed that the restoration had already started? Practically no Jewish teacher taught that the present Israel was the promised kingdom of restoration. To the contrary, Israel had not been independent since the days of Babylon. Now it lived under Roman rule. If anything, this was a troubled kingdom—not God's kingdom of peace.[7]

---

[5]N. T. Wright, *Jesus and the Victory of God*, Christian Origins and the Question of God 2 (Minneapolis: Fortress, 1997), 428.

[6]Ibid., 434.

[7]Apart from the analyses found in his article in the present volume, Wright also discusses the issue of the continuing exile in *Paul and the Faithfulness of God*, Christian Origins and the Question of God 4 (Minneapolis: Fortress, 2013), 139-62. My own contribution will be presented in *A Narrative Theology of the New Testament: Exploring the Metanarrative of Exile and Restoration*, WUNT 350 (Tübingen: Mohr Siebeck, 2015).

Hence the renewed eschatological hypothesis. Jesus' message can be best explained as a prophetic denunciation of the sins of Israel. Jesus stands in line with Isaiah and Zechariah when he states that the present Israel does not represent the true Israel of the patriarchal time or of the faithful kings. Instead, Israel still suffers under God's wrath. Hence any prophetic warning presented by the great prophets in their own time is valid also in Jesus' time. The Jerusalem temple does not yet serve the joyous gospel that God promised through the prophets. Priests and scribes cannot redeem the people from their guilt. The exile still enslaves the people of Israel. Therefore, a new temple will be built when the promised Messiah enters the eschatological scene.

A WELL-SUPPORTED THEORY

Wright has provided a metanarrative that can be used when a synthesis is written. This is a good point of departure. However, we need to examine the numerous other investigations that have contributed to the explanation. Restoration theology became an important focus of New Testament scholarship around the time of Wright's first publications. David Ravens focused on Luke in his *Luke and the Restoration of Israel* (1995), and James Scott published an edited collection called *Exile: Old Testament, Jewish, and Christian Conceptions* (1997).[8] Some years later Brant Pitre published an extensive dissertation investigating exilic themes in eschatological settings, *Jesus, the Tribulation, and the End of the Exile* (2005). Pitre's contribution in particular has helped to develop the interpretation further. He pointed out that, in Jesus' proclamation, eschatological tribulation was seen as a period that must necessarily arrive before Israel's restoration can take place. John the Baptist's execution was a crucial sign of this tribulation since it proved that fallen Israel still killed its prophets. This elucidates why Jesus,

---

[8]David Ravens, *Luke and the Restoration of Israel*, JSNTSup 119 (Sheffield: Sheffield Academic Press, 1995); James M. Scott, ed., *Exile: Old Testament, Jewish, and Christian Conceptions*, JSJSup 56 (Leiden: Brill, 1997). I am not attempting to present a complete bibliography here. I can only mention some interesting investigations that contribute to the issue. For Pauline interpretation, Scott had already suggested in his early work that restoration eschatology had a crucial role in the interpretation of the apostle's soteriology. James M. Scott, *Paul and the Nations: The Old Testament and Jewish Background of Paul's Mission to the Nations with Special Reference to the Destination of Galatians*, WUNT 84 (Tübingen: Mohr Siebeck, 1995). See also the other collection he edited, James M. Scott, ed., *Restoration: Old Testament, Jewish, and Christian Perspectives*, JSJSup 72 (Leiden: Brill, 2001).

already before Easter, spoke openly about the inevitable death of the Son of Man. And this must be the reason why Jesus sent his disciples like sheep among wolves. Anyone proclaiming God's gospel could be persecuted.[9]

Other features in Jesus' theology can easily be explained in terms of the metanarrative of exile and restoration. As Nicholas Perrin suggests in his *Jesus the Temple,* Jesus believed that the days of restoration would inaugurate a jubilee for Israel. The exile will be over when God sits on his heavenly throne and is allowed to be the King of Israel. This heavenly Lord summons the year of redemption and forgiveness. These features can be seen throughout Jesus' message. This is a gospel for the poor. The blind will see, and slaves will be freed. The year of release has come.[10]

Restoration eschatology has also been explored in the context of temple ideology. Wright himself suggested this and discusses the issue in section two of his article in the present volume. The significance of the subject could be anticipated because the destruction of the first temple was seen as a symbol for the entire exile. In several Old Testament passages prophetic hope takes on the appearance of a new eschatological temple that becomes the center of Israel's final restoration. One of the main treatments of this issue is Gregory Beale's monograph from 2004.[11] Several years later Desmond Alexander wrote a complete New Testament theology on the issue.[12] Wright's own notions are more than welcomed in this discussion. One of Jesus' aims was the building of a temple not made by human hands, a sanctuary that is constructed of living stones.

Furthermore, there are several other features in Jesus' teaching that betray his deep commitment to the restoration gospel. One of the most interesting of these concerns the nature of the Lord's Supper. According to new analyses, it seems evident that Jesus understood the holy meal as a priestly meal of wine and bread. Like the priests in the temple who drink wine and eat the bread of the presence with the high priest, so too does Jesus

---

[9] See Brant Pitre, *Jesus, the Tribulation, and the End of the Exile: Restoration Eschatology and the Origin of the Atonement* (Grand Rapids: Baker, 2005).

[10] See Nicholas Perrin, *Jesus The Temple* (Grand Rapids: Baker, 2010).

[11] Gregory Beale, *The Temple and the Church's Mission: A Biblical Theology of the Dwelling Place of God* (Downers Grove, IL: InterVarsity Press, 2004).

[12] T. Desmond Alexander, *From Eden to the New Jerusalem: An Introduction to Biblical Theology* (Grand Rapids: Kregel, 2008).

offer a sacrificial meal for the new priests of the eschatological temple. Such action was not completely without parallel because, as is well known, the Qumran community understood its holy meal as a priestly meal. Jesus' meal, however, surpasses the eschatological views of Qumran. Now the Suffering Servant sacrifices himself in order to bring release for his people and start Israel's restoration.[13]

Paul: Continuity or Discontinuity?

Up to this point the case for a new, consistent New Testament theology seems to be well grounded and justified. As we move on to Paul, though, things change. Paul's thinking has always been a test case in New Testament theology, and it continues this role. It is easier to find scholars who separate the apostle from Jesus' teaching or who make him a curiosity among the early preachers of the gospel than to find a consistent explanation where Paul is seen as an heir to Jesus' eschatological gospel. Furthermore, Bultmannian New Testament theologies focusing almost completely on Paul did not yet recognize Paul the Jew with a Pharisaic background.[14] The quite famous "new perspective on Paul," influencing most Pauline studies one way or another since the 1980s, did try to make a contribution. Many problems remained unsolved, but a new debate concerning the interpretation of Paul's soteriology arose. The construction of New Testament theology presents scholars with a challenging claim: the new perspective on Paul produces more questions than answers.

Can restoration eschatology and the adopted metanarrative help us with these issues? The answer is not as simple as one would hope. It is proper to ask whether Wright is able to use the narrative of exile and restoration fruitfully when explaining Paul's theology.[15] Difficulties in this discussion

---

[13]I address this element in my *Narrative Theology of the New Testament*, 222-25. When working on the issue I came across Pitre's small book on the Lord's Supper, where he presents quite similar conclusions. See Brant Pitre, *Jesus and the Jewish Roots of the Eucharist: Unlocking the Secrets of the Last Supper* (New York: Doubleday, 2011).

[14]Tübingen theology had started to change the situation, though, and Peter Stuhlmaher's *Biblische Theologie des Neuen Testaments, Bd. 1* (Göttingen: Vandenhoeck & Ruprecht, 1992) presents a consistent picture of the unity between Jesus and Paul. In North America, Sanders made a strong statement concerning the Jewish nature of Paul's soteriology; see *Paul and Palestinian Judaism* (Philadelphia: Fortress, 1977).

[15]For a positive answer to this question, see Cummins's contribution in the present volume.

concern issues that lie in the background, especially in the new perspective and Sanders's theory of covenantal nomism. The fundamental claim behind the covenantal nomism theory is that the covenantal Jewish religion in Jesus' time did not consider itself in any serious trouble or experience events as crises. Instead, as Sanders maintains, Israel's "staying in" was merely a matter of first keeping the covenant and then following the law with a sincere heart. This point of departure has been used to interpret Paul's soteriology. Paul is made a covenantalist who either wants to deny that works of the law were a matter of "getting in" (Sanders) or who abandons purity regulations and other boundary markers as futile works of the law (James Dunn) because true salvation had arrived. In many respects, Wright is an heir of the new perspective. He addresses covenantal theology in his early investigations on Paul. Even though he makes a distinction between strict covenantal nomism and his own view on covenantal theology, he still adopts Sandersian rhetoric against the standard "Lutheran" (see also below) interpretation of Paul and the law.[16]

The basic problem—and an essential one—appears to be that the new paradigm in Jesus studies, which owes much to Sanders himself, is at odds with his covenantal view on Second Temple Judaism. Jesus studies and Pauline studies do not fit together. According to the restoration eschatology Jesus taught, Israel still lives in the exilic condition. Seen from this perspective, Israel is not at all in the situation of "staying in" but, rather, in serious trouble with the "getting in." This observation is not merely in the eye of the beholder. As many analyses have shown, even according to several Jewish observers and writers of that time, Israel's situation was not a matter of staying in the covenant. The covenant had been broken, and these theologians were convinced that only divine intervention could bring reconciliation, forgiveness, and restoration. It is impossible to apply Sanders's categories in such a situation because those staying in the assumed covenant would have been the exiled and cursed Israelites who had not yet reached renewal.

To state this in the context of the present discussion implies simultaneously a transformation of the concepts that are used in this argumentation. Jesus

---

[16]See N. T. Wright, *The Climax of the Covenant: Christ and Law in Pauline Theology* (Edinburgh: T&T Clark, 1991), 150, 156 (also n61).

was never content with proclaiming the benefits of the covenant. In his speeches one encounters the rhetoric of discontinuity. The eschatological tension is extreme: the restoration can become real only after the final period of tribulation, where Israel kills the messengers God sends to it. The relation between sociology and eschatology is entirely different from what Sanders suggested. Paul appears to build on a similar eschatology. He attacks Israel's religious apostasy, in which he himself had taken part in his earlier life. In Paul's theology there is always a contrast between Israel's (or all children of Adam's) exilic condition and their restorative release. This view questions the traditions of Pauline interpretation in the Sandersian vein. A simple covenant-alist interpretation following the premises of the Sandersian school is impos-sible should one want to explain the nature of the discontinuity in Paul's texts.

Do these critical observations hit the mark? What is Wright's relation to Sanders's theory today, and what has he done in his new book on Paul? Even though Wright's views may not be so straightforward as one might expect on the basis of my presentation above, something can be said already here. In his new monumental work he does state that Paul, too, believed in the continu-ation of the exile. Wright focuses more on Jewish literature but, nevertheless, he does apply these ideas in Pauline interpretation. Something is lacking, though. In the first part of the large investigation Wright discusses the issue of the continuing exile for forty pages but, after that, he never mentions Paul's reaction to Israel's crisis. Only when later discussing the crucial "plight" and "solution" debate (inaugurated by Sanders) does Wright finally, toward the end of this particular treatment, turn to the problem of the continuing exile.

I do not mean to say that Wright does not use the idea, quite the contrary. In the passage mentioned above he says that there was a plight for which Christ's atoning death provides a solution. "What is now being offered is the 'solution' to the problem of *Israel's 'exile*,' the ongoing condition from the time of the geographical Babylonian exile to the present."[17] In this respect I do agree with Wright that Paul's theology should be interpreted on the premise that Israel's struggle was its exilic condition.

However, I do wonder why the reality of Israel's crisis is almost hidden in Wright's treatise. The passage above has few parallels in his work. For me,

---

[17]Wright, *Paul and the Faithfulness of God*, 761 (italics his).

the answer is to be found in his covenantal interpretation. Wright does not emphasize the metanarrative of exile and restoration but a much wider covenant narrative instead. The abovementioned passage continues a few lines later: "Thus, near the heart of the complex of elements involved in 'the original plight,' then radicalized and reframed in 'the reimagined plight,' we find the need for fresh divine action, in faithfulness to the covenant and the 'justice' which that involved, to deal with sin and to regenerate the chosen people as a new kind of family altogether."[18]

This is why, in my estimation, Wright remains a covenantalist. When explaining the role of Deuteronomy 30 behind Romans 9–11 (especially Rom 10:5-13) he proposes a covenantal interpretation: "This is all about the fulfillment of Deuteronomy 30 . . .—*covenant renewal and the end of exile.*"[19] For Wright this passage reveals that Paul is here *"telling the Torah's own story of Israel,* from the call of Abraham to the . . . *telos,* the 'goal,' the 'end' in the sense of 'the moment when, with the covenant renewed, Israel would finally be established as God's people.'"[20] This is why Wright, toward the end of his investigation, proposes that "Paul's understanding of Israel's Scriptures should have as its basic framework the *covenant narrative of Israel.*"[21]

Such conclusions create the impression that the main narrative Wright uses when explaining Paul's soteriology is not precisely that of exile and restoration but, instead, the covenant narrative of Israel. This makes the reader wonder whether Wright has in fact changed the governing metanarrative and returned to covenantal nomism. This does not solve traditional problems concerning Pauline interpretation. Instead, it creates a kind of dichotomy in the interpretation. As noted above, it is quite clear that Sanders's idea of covenantal nomism puts trust in continuity. Wright, however, wishes to interpret the covenantal view in terms of the narrative of exile and restoration, where the entire train of thought depends on the ideas of crisis and discontinuity. Is he able to ease the tension that results from combining such incompatible approaches?

---

[18]Ibid., 761.
[19]Ibid., 1164.
[20]Ibid., 1172 (italics his).
[21]Ibid., 1453 (italics his).

Problems in Composing a Synthesis

The quick analysis concerning the consistency of Wright's project, remaining admittedly on the level of a short commentary, has pointed out a tension between the two rather different narratives that are used when painting a picture of the entirety of New Testament theology. In what follows, I will examine how such difficulties could be defined and how they could be addressed to contribute to the writing of New Testament theology in general.

(1) To my understanding, the heart of the problem lies in the sociological nature of Sanders's theory. It seems that Wright has attempted to provide a covenantal answer to the plight and solution debate, but he does this without discussing Sanders's original (sociological) concepts of "staying in" and "getting in." This is how he can maintain an impression of continuity when using the narrative of exile and restoration. Sanders originally assumed that covenant is a perfect concept for describing Israel's situation and condition because there was no real "plight" in the Israelite religious service. When Wright questions his explanation by stating that there was a plight after all, and a severe one that had put the people under God's curse, he can no longer use the concept of covenant to justify the "staying in." The exiled people are not "in," and the covenant itself has been canceled.

(2) But why would the covenant be canceled? At this point, the modern discussion on Pauline soteriology and New Testament theology drifts into a situation where dogmatic convictions start to influence it (and more examples of this will be presented below). Some dogmatic currents depend heavily on the idea of an everlasting covenant, or different covenants, or even dispensations of grace in this world. This, however, is not what Old Testament prophets proclaim. They state that, before the exile, the covenant was broken, and a completely new one is to be anticipated. Israel's restoration cannot be realized in terms of the ancient covenant. Paul too says this in his letters, and other New Testament letters follow suit. When Wright puts so much weight on the concept of covenant he has to mold the concept according to a particular dogmatic view.[22] In his earlier writings Wright

---

[22]I presume that Wright has adopted a particular definition of "covenant." It seems that, for him, covenant is not merely an agreement that can be broken but, rather, a kind of divine decree that cannot be canceled. This is why it is consistent for him to state that salvation is about renewing

explained his view more clearly. He says that, in the Second Temple period, the covenant ("a single story of God") moves forward "battered but essentially unbroken."[23] My question here is that when Wright adopts this view, is he still able to pay enough attention to the aspect that Israel, in its exilic condition, is under God's curse?

(3) All this must be said because the word *covenant* (*diathēkē*) as such is not a common term in Paul or in the New Testament. Instead, it is difficult to find one passage where it would be treated in the way Wright treats it. The word does occur a few times in a neutral sense, but in all the significant passages, it is presented in an opposition where the old covenant is contrasted with the new covenant (2 Cor 3:6-14). Paul even contrasts the new covenant with the old covenant of slavery (Gal 4:24).[24] The very word that Wright relies on represents discontinuity in the New Testament. No New Testament writer claims that salvation means the restoration of the old covenant (see especially Heb 7–10). It just does not seem to be the way early theologians want to express themselves. This detail confirms the view that a Sandersian covenantalist interpretation of Paul's theology is not well supported.

(4) But why should this be a problem? Why can we not think that Wright, when writing New Testament theology, has simply applied an Old Testament theme in order to explain Paul's way of treating restoration eschatology in terms of Deuteronomy 30? I believe that we have reached the watershed in writing a consistent New Testament theology here. My first answer is: yes, Wright can do this. He can take *covenant* to be a general term and claim that Paul's reinterpretation of Deuteronomy 30 in particular is an example of developing a covenantal theme. But having said this, I must list things that one cannot logically do if following this particular course. First, one should not interpret Pauline soteriology in terms of covenantal nomism. I suspect that Wright does. Since he still adopts Sanders's category of "plight" he accepts the problematic covenantalist interpretation of soteriology. Instead of sociological (and related) categories we need eschatological categories for

---

the (old) covenant. I do not think such a view is well attested in the Scriptures, but I do admit that this is precisely where dogmatic commitments start to affect explanations (my own included).

[23]N. T. Wright, *Justification: God's Plan and Paul's Vision* (Downers Grove, IL: IVP Academic, 2009), 96.

[24]The terminology itself derives probably from the words of institution that promote the theology of a new covenant in the Gospels.

interpreting Paul's soteriology. Second, one cannot follow the other elements of the new perspective on Paul, such as the interpretation of the works of the law, justification, participation, and sanctification. Because Wright still does, at least to some extent, he faces the tensions brought up by Sanders's explanation. And third, in my opinion, one should agree to use the biblical term *new covenant*.

(5) The problem with Wright's adherence to the new perspective on Paul is not an easy one. According to the Sandersian view Paul could not have held Jewish nomism to be a problem. Furthermore, Paul could not really have found a proper plight in Jewish religious service. This is why salvation must primarily be seen as participation in the covenant. The essential problem here is that Wright himself has abandoned Sanders's premises. For Wright, there was a plight, and Jews lived in an exilic condition. Paul must have been right in pointing out the works of the law only revealed that the people served God in a den of robbers (if I may use Jesus' expression here). This is why I am afraid that Wright's presentation remains somewhat confused on this issue. He does not explain fully nomism or justification in terms of discontinuity. Simultaneously, however, he is no longer completely Sandersian in his interpretation.

(6) A brief point concerning the "Lutheran" understanding of Paul's theology is also necessary here. Wright has belonged to those opposing the "Lutheran" interpretation, but his premises have already started to change. In order to understand this we need to listen to Wright himself. He describes justification as God's forensic act where God declares believing persons righteous within the covenant. According to Wright, Paul "is drawing on the framework of eschatological, forensic, participatory and covenantal thought," and claims that "in the present time the covenant God declares 'in the right,' 'within the covenant,' all those who hear, believe and obey 'the gospel' of Jesus the Messiah."[25] Did Lutherans understand Paul wrong? Is Paul simply renewing the covenantal nomism that is supposed to direct Jewish thinking— at least at some period in the past? Wright does not seem to believe so.

If we summarize some of Wright's statements, he admits that Jews in the Second Temple period were in trouble. They lived in an exilic state. The only

---

[25]Wright, *Paul and the Faithfulness of God*, 944 (without his italics). I will not start the debate here about how Lutheran the "Lutheran view," rejected by many Sandersian scholars, really is.

divine act that could help them was justification directly from heaven, a forensic justification where sinners are declared righteous on the basis of Christ's atoning death. It is based, as Wright himself states, "on the past achievement of the Messiah's saving death."[26] It seems to be that Wright has basically approached the Lutheran position but maintains the Sandersian discourse. In fact, Wright's presentation sounds like a classical Lutheran understanding of justification. He almost reestablishes the *iustificatio impii*, justification of the ungodly. Compared with the more rigid post-Sandersian anti-Lutheran discourse conducted by Dunn among others, Wright has shown some flexibility and changed sides. Some differences remain, naturally. Everyone familiar with Wright's debate with Piper remembers that Wright separates faith from justification and, therefore, some details in his interpretation are not exactly (standard) Lutheran views. But considering that he underscores the forensic aspect (God *declares* "in the right," as Wright says), he sounds like a Reformation theologian.[27] Wright never claims that justification would be a process parallel to sanctification. Even the aspect of participation unites Wright with modern Lutheranism because today scholars emphasize that a union (Lat. *unio*) with Christ—who is the gift of God—is the gift (Lat. *donum*) of justification, a simultaneous participation in Christ who has been sacrificed for our sins.[28]

(7) My conclusion, therefore, is that Wright has started to move toward the aspect of discontinuity in his understanding of Paul's soteriology. Even though he speaks of the covenant narrative of Israel, he also clings to his idea of Israel's exilic condition. A possible weakness in his synthesis, if I may dare to suggest, is that his dependence on the covenantal interpretation prevents him from making all the conclusions needed. In the future, Wright will need to elaborate on the concept of covenant and clarify the distinctions between the Sandersian view and his own covenantal interpretation. This will be an interesting task because discussion on Paul has proceeded on a level where confessional and dogmatic views are starting to influence biblical scholarship.

---

[26]Ibid., 949 (without his italics).

[27]Ibid., 948 (not his italics). Exact details cannot be worked out in such a short article.

[28]I dare to take this issue up precisely because I am a Lutheran myself. Readers hopefully understand that I am not defending the Lutheran position here but instead simply using Wright's texts in order to argue that he has veered toward that position himself.

FEATURES OF RESTORATION ESCHATOLOGY IN PAUL

After such critical remarks it is important to attempt to describe Paul's teaching more clearly as a theology of discontinuity. What kind of features should be considered if one wishes to avoid the problems described above? Paul shares in Jesus' eschatology in several ways. The aspect of covenant, however, does not have any significant role in Paul's use of exilic themes and restoration hope in his own theology. Instead, there are several other features that need to be listed here. Some of them do appear in Wright's large monograph, but I will focus mainly on issues that have come up in my own investigations of Paul's writings.[29]

It is common knowledge that the apostle speaks about the turn of ages and the fulfillment of the *kairos*. He defines gospel in a way similar to Jesus' definition. At the end of times God will return and establish his kingship in Israel. For Paul, this means Jesus' enthronement in the resurrection. Fulfilling the expectations that find their expression in Psalm 110, for instance, Christ has been raised "at the right hand" of God on the throne of glory. His heavenly coronation has led to the inauguration of the Lord's jubilee and Israel's restoration. For Paul, too, the time he lives in is the time for reconciliation and forgiveness of sins.

It is well known that Paul calls the new community a new temple. It is the place of salvation where the fallen people can find a perfect sacrifice for their sins. Believers are called priests of the new temple. For Paul, the Christian community is the temple where the Holy Spirit has returned. All have been adopted as children, and in the new obedience of faith believers pray to God as the Abba-Father. It is noteworthy that in a crucial passage, 2 Corinthians 6:14-18, often unnoticed by scholars, Paul uses a tradition that focuses on restoration eschatology and is filled with exilic references.

But there is more to it. The above-mentioned elements explain why Paul follows Jesus in questioning the entire religious service of the old covenant. After the exile—and often even before it too—Israel was in a state of infidelity. This is why the temple, mutatis mutandis for Paul as well, has become a den of robbers. If the heart does not have the right orientation, it is useless to repeat "this is the temple of the Lord." The Jews "have a zeal

---

[29]I willingly admit that Wright has now brought some of these views up in his lead article of the present volume.

for God, but it is not enlightened" (Rom 10:2). Israel, who "did strive for
the righteousness that is based on the law, did not succeed in fulfilling that
law" (Rom 9:31). Religious service without true faith is defective: "They
did not strive for it on the basis of faith, but as if it were based on works"
(Rom 9:32). Works of the law, for Paul, cover all religious service, be it
following the festival calendar, divine commandments, or works at the
temple. What was positive becomes negative—precisely because of the
exilic condition of the people. Paul writes like the great prophets, "I do not
delight in the blood of bulls" (Is 1:11).

Paul is a preacher of discontinuity. In several passages he underscores that
he himself, as a Jew, had to submit himself to God's righteousness so that he
could find salvation in Christ.

> We ourselves are Jews by birth and not Gentile sinners; yet we know that a
> person is justified not by the works of the law but through faith in Jesus
> Christ. And we have come to believe in Christ Jesus, so that we might be
> justified by faith in Christ, and not by doing the works of the law, because no
> one will be justified by the works of the law. (Gal 2:15-16)

To my understanding, this is not a "solution to plight" inference but,
instead, restoration eschatology at its best. This is how the principle of
"regarding as loss" enters Paul's theology. A stark distinction needs to be
made. A submission is necessary. In a sense this means conversion, but
it has a wider meaning. When one understands Jesus' original program
perfectly, one needs to reinterpret the entire content of Israel's service to
the Lord. This is why I would be very hesitant to use covenantal language
for interpreting Paul. For him the covenant of slavery was not a way
to restoration.

CONCLUSION

In sum, it is clear that Wright has had an immense impact on New Testament interpretation. He builds on his predecessors, and his contribution
has been essential. His adherence to the new perspective on Paul shows,
however, that when developing New Testament theology, much remains to
be done. New problems arise, and they need new solutions. Wright's synthesis oscillates between continuity (the new perspective on Paul) and

discontinuity (the new narratological approach). He has started to distance himself from Sandersian theory. However, he has not yet fully integrated the elements of continued exile and the extraordinary release achieved by God's restoration that would guide the writing of a synthesis.

PART FOUR

THEOLOGY

CHAPTER TEN

SACRAMENTAL INTERPRETATION

On the Need for Theological Grounding of Narratival History

HANS BOERSMA

CONTINUITY AND DISCONTINUITY WITH THE TRADITION

We are in great need today of open and vigorous, yet constructive, conversation between biblical and dogmatic theology. The excellent symposium that lies behind this book is a hopeful indication that such dialogue is genuinely starting to burgeon.[1] Though in the symposium I questioned some of the basic underlying presuppositions of Wright's paper, his oral response nonetheless stood out to me for its graciousness and generosity. Wright's response to my response at the symposium gives me, in this essay, the opportunity to respond to his response, to which I suspect he will in turn respond at the conclusion of this book. It is like the gift that keeps on giving! This may seem like a complex web of interactions, but I do hope that the central issue under discussion will become clear and also that perhaps we will get beyond some of our disagreements by identifying common ground. It is my intention with this essay to prod Wright—on the basis of such common ground—to the recognition that his insistence on the faithfulness of God requires the sacramental hermeneutical grid that has served much of the Christian tradition.[2]

---

[1]That such dialogue is beginning to develop is particularly clear in Nicholas Perrin and Richard B. Hays, eds., *Jesus, Paul and the People of God: A Theological Dialogue with N. T. Wright* (Downers Grove, IL: IVP Academic, 2011).

[2]I am using the term *sacramental* to denote not just the sacraments of the church (such as baptism and Eucharist) but also to describe an approach to exegesis common in the

In other words, I hope to make clear that Wright's illuminating work regarding the narratival history of Scripture can be sustained only on the basis of a theological grounding in the eternal life of God.

Wright's conviction that many Jews in Second Temple Judaism believed that they were still in exile, as well as his insistence that this belief influenced the New Testament and, in particular, St. Paul, has placed me deeply in his debt. I find myself in a great deal of agreement with regard to his biblical exegesis of Deuteronomy 27–30; Leviticus 26; Daniel 9; Ezra 9; and Nehemiah 9, as well as with much of Wright's description of Jesus Christ's death and resurrection as the culmination of and return from exile, which St. Paul describes particularly in his epistles to the Romans and the Galatians. In short, the general drift of Wright's exegetical exposé, as it ties in with his overall understanding of exile, has my wholehearted and warm agreement. I have shamelessly borrowed from Wright both in my preaching and in my work on atonement theology, and I remain convinced that Wright has a lot to teach us, not only with regard to the historical question of exile but also in connection with the theological areas of justification and soteriology more broadly construed. Thus, while I am not a historian of Second Temple Judaism, I confess I am largely persuaded by Wright's understanding of a continuous story going back to Abraham and moving on to the great day of God's salvation and also by the related notion that the Pharisees, like many other Jews, saw their own time in this narrative as one of continuing exile. I am convinced we can make important theological (and ecumenical) steps forward by taking seriously the challenges that Wright poses, in particular to Protestant theology.

---

premodern period. On this understanding, the text of the Old Testament serves as a "sacrament" in which the New Testament reality of the Christ event is "really present." Put differently, the events described in the Old Testament participate, from the outset, in the new reality that Christ brings. Similar to the way in which the reality (*res*) of grace is mediated through the sacrament (*sacramentum*) of the elements in the Eucharist, so the reality (*res*) of the Christ event is really present and is mediated to us through the sacrament (*sacramentum*) of the Old Testament. Thus, Old Testament events participate sacramentally in the mystery of the New Testament reality of Christ. For further explanation of the sacramental character of exegesis, see Henri de Lubac, *The Four Senses of Scripture*, vol. 2 of *Medieval Exegesis*, trans. E. M. Macierowski (Grand Rapids: Eerdmans, 2000), 19-27; Hans Boersma, *Scripture as Real Presence: Sacramental Exegesis in the Early Church* (Grand Rapids: Baker Academic, 2017); Boersma, *Heavenly Participation: The Weaving of a Sacramental Tapestry* (Grand Rapids: Eerdmans, 2011), 137-53.

Wright's influence on my thinking is evident especially in my 2004 book, *Violence, Hospitality, and the Cross.*[3] It presents an atonement model that is squarely based on the Irenaean framework of Christ's recapitulation of Adam and on Wright's paradigm of Christ's reconstitution of Israel. And while since that time I have changed my views on some significant issues (and while, again, I also need to plead partial ignorance as I am not expert in Second Temple Judaism), I am still inclined to think that Wright is correct with regard to his views on "continuing exile," and that much of the New Testament—the Pauline epistles, in particular—should be read in the light of that background. Furthermore, though the topic is mostly beyond our current discussion, I am also convinced that Wright's understanding of God's righteousness or faithfulness sheds significant new light on the doctrine of justification, and it seems to me that the Reformation doctrine of justification *sola fide* needs a significant overhaul in the light of Wright's reading of the New Testament. (This is not to say that his approach to justification is entirely novel, since several of the church fathers adumbrate his views in important ways.[4] And Wright's views, I think, are more or less compatible with standard Catholic and Orthodox understandings of justification theology.) All of this is simply to say that I have a great deal of respect for and agreement with Wright's position on exile, and that he has not heard me quite right when he comments: "I have been accused, in particular (at the symposium on exile at Trinity Western University where some of this material was presented and discussed) of presenting a novelty: a view of 'exile that nobody in the Christian tradition had thought of before.'"[5]

Now, to be sure, I did charge Wright with "discontinuity." I insisted that his general theological approach (i.e., his attacks on the allegedly other-worldly, individualist, and denarrativized soteriology of the Reformation) show him to be "far more discontinuous" than the Reformers were in relation to the Great Tradition. These admittedly somewhat sharp comments of mine were not entirely unprovoked. I presented them in the context of what I thought was a rather harsh and maladroit attack on the Reformers.

---

[3]Hans Boersma, *Violence, Hospitality, and the Cross: Reappropriating the Atonement Tradition* (Grand Rapids: Baker Academic, 2004).
[4]See Matthew J. Thomas, "Early Perspectives on Works of the Law: A Patristic Study" (DPhil thesis, University of Oxford, 2016).
[5]See N. T. Wright's essay in the present volume, "Yet the Sun Will Rise Again: Reflections on the Exile and Restoration in Second Temple Judaism, Jesus, Paul, and the Church Today," 75.

The opening essay of this book is a model of nuanced scholarship and theological reflection. But the original paper that Wright wrote for the symposium referred unapologetically to the "cheerful, breezy arrogance" of the
Reformers, who disclaimed continuity with the immediate past to go back
to the Bible and the Fathers, analogously—so they thought—to the way in
which Jesus, Paul, and Peter had appealed over the heads of Second Temple
Judaism to Moses and the prophets. For the Reformers, Wright maintained,
the "idea of a continuous narrative" "constituted the main problem," to
which the solution was an individual narrative: "my story with God."

I think such a reading of the Reformers is problematic for two reasons.
First, this sharp denunciation of the Reformers is demonstrably excessive.
After all, they were deeply critical of the allegorizing approach of the preceding tradition, and they are commonly recognized to have focused on
historical categories much more strongly than theologians had previously
tended to do. (In my view, in fact, the Reformers' disregard of the medieval
sacramental and allegorical tradition is itself disproportionate. The move
away from vertical categories such as sacrament, participation, and anagogical interpretation in favor of horizontal categories such as history, narrative, and grammatical-historical exegesis received a significant boost
through the Reformation, and I am not convinced of the altogether
wholesome direction of this horizontal emphasis.)

Second, Wright's own narrative is *far more discontinuous* than that of the
Reformers. Wright not only commonly assails the allegedly otherworldly,
individualist, ahistorical, and denarrativized soteriology of the Reformation,
but he goes well beyond this by rejecting also the traditional "classic Western
heaven-or-hell scheme," a scheme that appears to envelop both Catholics
and Protestants, and that includes many theologians of the pre-Reformation
period, as well. Wright states matter-of-factly that "'salvation' does not mean
what the Western tradition has often taken it to mean (escaping to a disembodied 'heaven')," and in his initial paper he added that Paul's worldview is
"totally different" "from that envisaged in so much Western Christianity,
both catholic and protestant, evangelical and liberal."[6] Though I will continue to try hard to come up with a Western theologian who could possibly

---

[6]Ibid., 79.

serve as a representative of such a skewed view of salvation, I think in the meantime I am justified in maintaining that a word of caution on my part is not entirely out of order. Luther and Calvin may have jumped over most of the previous thousand years of church history as they went back to the Bible and the church fathers. But when Wright accuses them of "cheerful, breezy arrogance" I can only see this as a case of the pot calling the kettle black, seeing that Wright himself wants to jump over the previous *two* thousand years as he tries to recover what Saint Paul *really* said.

My comments about Wright's "discontinuous" views are inspired, therefore, by his own somewhat unpoised depiction of the Reformation (and of most of the rest of the Christian tradition besides). Certainly, Wright is correct when he applauds the Reformers for insisting that "God may well have more light to break out of his holy word."[7] Absolutely! And I am convinced that Wright has been instrumental in some of this. Wright is also correct to insist—with an appeal to Thomas Aquinas—that tradition is "the story of how the church has read Scripture, not a separate 'source.'"[8] If I have learned anything from the twentieth-century Catholic theologian Yves Congar, it is that a two-source theory of revelation—in which oral tradition brings its own doctrinal contents to the table, a view common in much post-Tridentine Catholic thought—must be rejected;[9] and we may be thankful that this approach *is* almost universally rejected today in Catholic thought.[10] But I am not sure why Wright sees the need to issue a warning against this long-outdated, two-source view of revelation. For my part, in my own writing on the role of tradition, I have never come close to it.[11]

---

[7]Ibid., 75. John Stackhouse has kindly pointed out to me that this expression likely originates with John Robinson (1576–1625), one of the Pilgrim fathers, in his farewell speech as he sailed off from Delftshaven.

[8]Ibid.

[9]See Yves Congar, *Tradition and Traditions: The Biblical, Historical, and Theological Evidence for Catholic Teaching on Tradition*, trans. Michael Naseby and Thomas Rainborough (San Diego, CA: Basilica; Needham Heights: Simon & Schuster, 1966).

[10]See the Vatican II document, *Dei Verbum*, no. 9; and also note the comment of Thomas G. Guarino: "Most Catholic theologians accept the phrase *sola scriptura*; they accept as well the claim that the Bible is the *norma normans non normata*, the ultimate touchstone for Christian faith" ("Catholic Reflections on Discerning the Truth of Sacred Scripture," in *Your Word Is Truth: A Project of Evangelicals and Catholics Together*, ed. Charles Colson and Richard John Neuhaus [Grand Rapids: Eerdmans, 2002], 96).

[11]See Hans Boersma, *Nouvelle Théologie and Sacramental Ontology: A Return to Mystery* (Oxford: Oxford University Press, 2009), 191-241; Boersma, *Heavenly Participation*, 120-36.

But several questions remain when Wright suggests that "tradition is . . . the story of how the church has read Scripture." One of them is this: What role does he accord to this "story" of biblical interpretation (i.e., tradition) in his own reading of the Bible? Does this story—or do elements or strands of it—in any way normatively shape his reading of the Scriptures? Or does he, as a modern historian, attempt to read Scripture in complete disregard of the earlier tradition?[12] Wright's paper hardly ever mentions the tradition— especially not "Western" Christianity—in complimentary fashion. The reader of Wright's paper (and, indeed, of his overall theology) has difficulty escaping the impression that he engages the Scriptures as a modern his- torian, his research free from confessional constraints, reaching back past many centuries of benighted biblical interpretation, in order now to unearth for us the true meaning of the Bible. On this understanding, the history of interpretation (i.e., tradition) is at best reduced to the role of presenting interesting illustrations of how people *used* to read the Bible. (And, as such, the historian-interpreter really does not require this "story" of the tradition in any meaningful sense, as it regularly becomes the object of sweeping criticism.) In this approach to the tradition—which has its roots theologi- cally in the Radical Reformation—a gulf opens up between the history of interpretation and contemporary exegesis.

Andrew Louth, in his magnificent book *Discerning the Mystery*, points to the consequences of such a rift between the history of interpretation and interpretation itself (which in his book he describes as a gulf between the history of philosophy and philosophy itself): "The history of the subject is interesting as the tracing of progressive enlightenment: as we look back we see the errors from which man has been delivered by the advance of knowledge."[13] But, Louth then adds, such confidence ironically entails the inevitability of deep self-doubt: "When that confidence is lacking, the picture looks rather different: then we are aware rather of the fact that we

---

[12]Cf. Kevin J. Vanhoozer's comment: "Theology is faith seeking understanding. This involves not only recovering the explicit meaning of the words the biblical authors used, but also a detailed conceptual elaboration of what they imply, and this is often what we get from attending to the history of interpretation that, at its best, is not a move away from but deeper into the text" ("Wrighting the Wrongs of the Reformation? The State of the Union with Christ in St. Paul and Protestant Soteriology," in *Jesus, Paul and the People of God*, 240).

[13]Andrew Louth, *Discerning the Mystery: An Essay on the Nature of Theology* (Oxford: Clarendon Press, 1983), 15.

are just about to pass into history, just about to form part of the flow of the
subject through history."[14] In other words, once the normative character of
tradition (i.e., the church's story of reading the Scriptures) disappears—as it
inevitably does in a strictly historical understanding of exegesis—then even
the most optimistic biblical scholar cannot but fall into bouts of depression:
he will soon be overtaken by the next generation of scholars who, right over
his head, go directly to the "original sources" to do their own historical investigation. And so, when biblical scholars separate Scripture from tradition
they end up making their own work irrelevant.

What is more, this separation means there is an ironic twist in Wright's
warning (with an appeal to Thomas Aquinas) against tradition as a separate
source of revelation. As already said, I agree with the point that Wright
makes here; we should not speak of two separate sources of revelation. But
is it unduly harsh to ask whether perhaps Wright himself is the one who
separates "the story of how the church has read Scripture" from the Scriptures themselves? After all, it seems the only difference between the way he
separates Scripture and tradition and the way many post-Tridentine Catholics did this is that he regards only one of the two separated entities as a
source of revelation.

The Limits of Historical Categories

It will be clear that part of my underlying concern is with Wright's strictly
historical approach to biblical interpretation. Before digging into this issue
a little more deeply, however, I want to make clear that in this polemic, I
engage at the same time in serious self-criticism. As I already intimated, my
2004 book, *Violence, Hospitality, and the Cross*, was deeply indebted to
Wright's approach. And I still stand by most of what I wrote there regarding
atonement theology and exile—in dependence on Wright. Again, my
problem with Wright's approach does not concern what, as a good historian,
he writes about exile or about how it functioned in Second Temple Judaism.
But the problem both with Wright's biblical hermeneutic and with my own
book has to do with the general reduction of theological categories to this-
worldly, historical narratives. In my atonement book, this comes to the fore

---

[14]Ibid.

especially in connection with election (for which I relied particularly on Wright). Wright certainly provides many wonderful exegetical insights in his discussion of election. For Wright, Christ as the new Israel is God's chosen one; in and through Christ, we as the church are likewise God's chosen ones. This approach to predestination deals with the topic in a historical fashion and may seem less bedeviled by the perceived arbitrariness involved in election from eternity, which features prominently in the Thomist and Calvinist traditions. And Wright's approach to election is of course mirrored in the way he deals with exile. Exile, on Wright's reading, becomes the historical exile experienced by Israel and brought to an end in and through Christ's death and resurrection.

All of this is fine, as far as it goes. But the *restriction* of election to historical categories is seriously problematic (as are, therefore, several chapters of my book on atonement theology). It is not so much that what Wright positively writes about election and about exile as historical categories is unbiblical or wrong; it is just that the strict historicizing of these notions is simply inadequate. The limitation of election to the historical realm and the restriction of exile to that of corporate Israel are unduly narrow. This ties in, I think, with Wright's general occlusion of heavenly concerns, of immanent trinitarian doctrine, and of theological metaphysics in general. Wright's relentless critique of "timeless truth," of anything "ahistorical" or "metaphysical," is indicative of his rather modern penchant to separate historical, this-worldly realities of nature from their supernatural, heavenly origin and goal. By limiting ourselves to historical categories we dislodge historical and earthly realities from their eternal, heavenly anchor.[15] Election is just one case in point. By saying that it is a historical act of God, we are not speaking falsehood; we are simply ignoring the follow-up question of the basis of this historical election: How is it anchored in the eternal, divine reality of the Word of God? And it seems to me that, when it comes to divine election, Scripture itself—followed by nearly the entire Christian tradition—does link this historical election to eternity (e.g., Jer 1:5; Eph 1:4, 11; 2 Tim 1:9-10). To be sure, the journey from historical events to eternal mysteries is strewn with obstacles, and we need to navigate our travels with a great deal of

---

[15]For further discussion of the modern separation of heaven and earth (and of the loss of the former), see my book *Heavenly Participation* (Grand Rapids: Eerdmans, 2011).

caution. Some views of double predestination may well be overly rational and too confident in uncovering the mystery of eternal, divine election. Still, the radically historical approach of Wright's theology comes at the cost of neglecting the theological, christological metaphysical grounding of historical events.

Some defense of the broad, ecumenical tradition would seem necessary in view of Wright's off-handed dismissal of it as Docetic and escapist and thus as downplaying the goodness of creation. Unfortunately, there is not the space here to trace the tradition and to analyze the various articulations of the doctrine of creation. I am confident, however, that the Platonic influence on Christianity, which Wright's writings often lament, hardly prevented Christian theologians from affirming strongly the transcendence and freedom of God in the *ex nihilo* act of creation and from insisting that creation was hence a good gift of divine grace. Similarly, the creed's reference to the resurrection of the body makes clear that even the most Platonically inclined among the Fathers—theologians such as St. Gregory of Nyssa—went out of their way to combat the Platonic separation of body and soul and to affirm that the body was God's good creation and was destined for eternity (all of this, of course, hand in hand with a robust insistence on a heavenly future!).[16] Finally, while there is no doubt as to the great significance of individual freedom and salvation—indeed, it seems to me that few questions are as important as the much lampooned "how to be saved" question—hardly anyone in the broad tradition of the church regarded this focus on the individual as clashing with the centrality of baptism, of Eucharist, or of the church itself as the great sacrament of the mystery of what St. Augustine called the *totus Christus*, the eschatological unity of the church's head and members.[17]

Perhaps it is true that contemporary evangelical theology has lost much of this corporate focus, but such recent losses hardly justify broad-sweeping denunciations of Western, Platonized theology. Indeed, is it unreasonable to entreat Wright to approach the tradition of the church—the continuous

---

[16]See Hans Boersma, *Embodiment and Virtue in Gregory of Nyssa: An Anagogical Approach* (Oxford: Oxford University Press, 2013).

[17]For Augustine's *totus Christus* theology, see Jason Byassee, *Praise Seeking Understanding: Reading the Psalms with Augustine* (Grand Rapids: Eerdmans, 2007).

story of its engagement with Scripture—with the same meticulous historical care and attention with which he reads Second Temple Judaism? I am convinced that on a more careful and more charitable reading of the history of doctrine, the repeated caricatures would disappear from his writing, for there is little doubt that the Great Tradition of East and West is united in the affirmation of a robust doctrine of creation, of a deeply held belief in bodily resurrection, and of a corporate view of salvation in which the sacraments play a significant role. Without going into further detail, I simply put forward these few suggestions, in the hope that my comments may urge Wright to a somewhat more congenial portrayal and perhaps even to somewhat of a retrieval of the tradition of the church both East and West.

THE NEED FOR A PARTICIPATORY LINK

In the remainder of this essay, I want to zero in on one aspect of that tradition, which I believe Wright's approach undervalues (though we will see that there are elements in his approach that fit well with it). It is probably clear at this point that I see the problem with Wright's presentation not so much in the historical work that he does, much less in his understanding of exile per se. What is problematic, I think, is the notion that this focus would be irreconcilable with Platonic (or with any kind of metahistorical) categories. The focus on history—on what we may call the *oikonomia* of God's faithful dealings with creation and humanity—seems to me to require recognition of the importance also of *theologia*, of the mystery of the triune God, whose life we are called to join by sharing in the virtues of Christ.[18] In particular, I wonder whether perhaps Wright has written off too quickly much of the Great Tradition, East and West, and whether perhaps at least *some* Platonic categories—in particular the notion of eternal Forms or Ideas—actually *helped* Christians articulate their faith. An emphasis on narrative and on history is all good and well.

---

[18]With regard to the virtues, I have deep appreciation for N. T. Wright's recent book *After You Believe: Why Christian Character Matters* (New York: HarperOne, 2010). Again, however, I think he should have pushed further, by insisting that these virtues are not just modeled on the narrative of Christ's humble life on earth (as if virtue were a matter of external discipleship) but are actually participation in the very life of God. Only such a participatory or sacramental anchoring adequately protects an emphasis on virtue against the charge of moralism.

But when we ask what it is that gives this history its significance, we will either need recourse to an arbitrary act of divine will (as in voluntarism) or to the sacramental notion of "participation."[19] Either the historical exigencies of the created order exist completely separate from the Creator, or they are connected by way of sacramental participation in the eternal Word of God.

Wright squarely focuses on the biblical narrative, on the *oikonomia* of God. As I have already indicated, it seems to me obvious that Scripture does contain such a narrative. Wright, however, links his narratival, economic focus, both here and in his other works, with warnings against Philonic allegorizing, against "otherworldly salvation," against a notion of individual salvation that asks, how can I go to heaven when I die?[20] and against a dualistic, Western, Platonic vision that allegedly comes "with the abolition of the universe of space, time and matter, or the escape of humans from such a wreckage."[21] Wright's focus on the narratival *oikonomia* of God is so distinct that one wonders where the *theologia* is in this approach—the eternal, dare we say "timeless," life of God himself, to which he calls us through the process of justification and deification.

Wright's strict focus on the *oikonomia* leads to an exegetical approach that is purely historical; and in that light, it is hardly surprising that he repeatedly and sharply attacks the broad tradition of "Western orthodoxy." And, indeed, he might well have added "Eastern orthodoxy," since both West *and* East have generally maintained that from the narrative of the *oikonomia* we can learn about the eternal realities of the triune God. The tradition's practices of spiritual (or theological) interpretation of Scripture—based on an integration of nature and the supernatural that is alien to Wright's methodologically natural or historical approach—imply that historical realities such as election and exile carry *deep within themselves* hidden realities that cannot be reduced to "facts on the ground," as Wright calls them. The theology of the tradition (i.e., the story of the

[19]Cf. Matthew Levering, *Participatory Biblical Exegesis: A Theology of Biblical Interpretation* (Notre Dame, IN: University of Notre Dame Press, 2008).
[20]Wright, "Yet the Sun Will Rise Again," 77. Cf. the excellent response to Wright's theology of heaven in Markus Bockmuehl, "Did St. Paul Go to Heaven When He Died?," in Perrin and Hays, eds., *Jesus, Paul and the People of God*, 211-31.
[21]Wright, "Yet the Sun Will Rise Again," 77.

interpretation of Scripture) is replete with contemplation (*theōria*), allegory (*allēgoria*), and anagogy (*anagōgē*)—modes of spiritual interpretation that, in one way or another, characterized both the Antiochian and
the Alexandrian schools of thought, and that, as a result, have come to
shape nearly the entire history of Christian thought. Spiritual interpretation of Scripture, along with the recognition of the vertical or anagogical
focus on heavenly realities and the significance of the individual and his
or her salvation, are the common heritage of East and West as a result of
the church's acknowledgment of the newness of the Christ event.[22] Wright's
opposition to this shared traditional theological heritage shows how it is
that his essay—in which he consistently plays off his narrative, communal
approach to Scripture over against timeless, individualist (and ultimately
Platonic) readings of it in the tradition—works with a radically discontinuous view of history.

This consistent juxtaposition of historical, narrative categories with
what Wright deems to be abstract, timeless truths constitutes my deepest
concern with regard to his project. It implies a disjunction of history and
eternity, of heaven and earth, and of nature and the supernatural. As a
result, Wright finds it difficult roundly to acknowledge a participatory or
sacramental framework, in which the two sides of his disjunctions are
interconnected by means of divine providence. For example, as he expresses his apprehension about the way in which the Deuteronomic notion
of exile is sometimes dealt with, Wright asserts: "To highlight 'exile' in the
way I have done is to see all of history focused on the cross, not flattened
out into a set of general truths that just happened to be exemplified in
Jesus."[23] But the question is why we should feel forced into an either/or
approach: either history or eternity; either the horizontal or the vertical;

---

[22]Henri de Lubac points out that for the premodern tradition, the "many words" (*verba multa*) of
the Old Testament find their point of unity in the "one Word" (*Verbum unum*) of the incarnate
Christ, who as such is the "abbreviated Word" (*Verbum abbreviatum*). In the Christian tradition,
the practice of allegory arises not from slavish following of Philo but from the recognition that
Christ has recapitulated in himself the history of salvation, so that the entire Old Testament is
contained in him and finds its significance in him (*Scripture in the Tradition*, trans. Luke O'Neill
[New York: Herder & Herder–Crossroad, 2000], 182–94). The literature in the field of spiritual
interpretation is fortunately garnering growing interest. For some recent essays, see Hans
Boersma and Matthew Levering, eds., *Heaven on Earth? Theological Interpretation in Ecumenical
Dialogue*, Directions in Modern Theology (Malden, MA: Wiley-Blackwell, 2013).
[23]Wright, "Yet the Sun Will Rise Again," 76.

either narrative or allegory. Wright wants us to do justice to the historical narrative, and I welcome this. But could it be that precisely in order for the narrative to *have* significance at all it must have an anchor beyond itself, must participate sacramentally in eternal realities beyond history? And could it be that precisely this conviction—that history and narrative have significance because of their being anchored in the eternal Word of God— allows us to recognize the faithfulness of God in history and thus allows us properly to value the Old Testament narrative? Indeed, I have become convinced that it is precisely such an intrinsic, participatory link between "this-worldly" or earthly events and "otherworldly" or heavenly realities that has driven so many theologians of East and West to insist that the economy of God is based on the theology of God. It is the sacramental or participatory link between the two that gives God's economic dealings in history their value.

WRIGHT'S OPENNESS TO SACRAMENTAL READING

Despite the sometimes-excessive rhetoric of Wright's discourse, it none- theless does contain elements that fit remarkably well with the participatory or sacramental interpretive strategy that I have just advocated. For example, when he interprets the parable of the prodigal son (Lk 15:11-32) as referring to exile and restoration, he elaborates as follows: "What its God had done for it [i.e., Israel] in the exodus—always the crucial backdrop for Jewish expectation—he would at last do again, even more gloriously. YHWH would finally become king, and would do for Israel, in covenant love, what the prophets had foretold."[24] Though he does not speak of "typology," Wright in fact reads the exodus in some sense typologically, with the his- torical exodus from Egypt serving as type and the exodus from exile in and through Christ's resurrection as antitype. Wright's insistence that in Christ God has acted similarly to and yet "more gloriously" than he did in the historical exodus constitutes a beautiful illustration of the fact that typology functions according to the pattern of the doctrine of analogy: God's actions in Christ are similar to those he performed earlier in history, and yet they are at the same time infinitely dissimilar (cf. Wright's "more gloriously"

---

[24]Ibid., 47.

above), because God's grace in Christ infinitely surpasses anything that came before.[25]

Likewise, when discussing the Pauline theology of exile, Wright quite appropriately insists that Romans 8 "uses exodus language in relation to the whole creation"[26] and correctly observes that "Paul speaks of baptism in 1 Corinthians 10:2 in terms of the crossing of the Red Sea, and . . . echoes this in Romans 6: the slaves (slaves to sin) are freed by sharing the death and resurrection of the Messiah."[27] What Wright seems unaware of is that this reading of the biblical text comes close to traditional typological or allegorical readings of Scripture.[28] It is important to take note of the many connections that Wright posits between various moments within the history of redemption. In his "spiritual reading" of exile (and also of creation, temple, Israel, etc.), historical events find their true essence in the newness of the Christ event. Thus, despite his stringent historical emphasis, Wright's reading of the New Testament often seems typological, and for that reason it often yields exegetical results that are remarkably similar to those of the church fathers and the medieval tradition. Seeing, then, that Wright's exegesis is, in significant ways, similar to the approach of the earlier tradition, it seems to me that we have some common ground here and a basis on which to explore how biblical and dogmatic theology may embark on a fruitful dialogue.

Still, this common ground leads to the question of whether or not Wright grounds the typological similarity between Old and New in a participatory or sacramental fashion. The eminent patristic scholar Charles Kannengiesser observes the following with regard to patristic interpretation:

---

[25]This analogical reading of Scripture is something the twentieth-century Jesuit theologian Jean Daniélou consistently argued for. For him, the element of similarity between Old and New serves to safeguard against the danger of arbitrariness in exegesis, while the element of dissimilarity highlights the newness and greater reality of the Christ event. See Boersma, *Nouvelle Théologie and Sacramental Ontology*, 178-80.

[26]Wright, "Yet the Sun Will Rise Again," 62.

[27]Ibid., 62-63.

[28]Though I cannot elaborate here, I simply observe that I agree with the growing consensus in patristic scholarship that the church fathers did not distinguish between allegory and typology and that there are no essential differences between them. See, for instance, Manlio Simonetti, *Biblical Interpretation in the Early Church: An Historical Introduction to Patristic Exegesis*, ed. Anders Bergquist and Markus Bockmuehl, trans. John A. Hughes (Edinburgh: T&T Clark, 1994), 12, 32n7; Frances M. Young, *Biblical Exegesis and the Formation of Christian Culture* (Peabody, MA: Hendrickson, 2002), 152-57.

The biblical "letter" as understood by patristic interpreters had its own status, originating from a divine source in a supernatural way; therefore it admitted no neutral reading devoid of the appropriate kind of religious faith. For the exegetes of the early church the correct interpretation of the *littera* was in itself a *spiritual* exercise, because for them the materiality of the written text itself was filled with divine mysteries.[29]

Kannengiesser suggests that the biblical text, for the Christian tradition, is sacramental: the materiality of the text itself is "filled" with divine mysteries or sacraments.[30] It is the newness of the Christ event that made the much-maligned Western (as well as Eastern) tradition insist that the historical events of the Old Testament were future sacraments (*futura sacramenta*) that already carried deep within their bosom the ultimate realities of the Christ event (in allegorical readings), of Christian living (in moral or tropological readings), and of the eschatological redemption on the last day (in eschatological or anagogical readings).[31] The question I have is whether, for Wright, the New Testament christological reality (*res*) is already present in the events described in the Old Testament (*sacramentum*).

If the story of redemption is a "continuous story," as Wright repeatedly and eloquently insists, what is it that makes the story continuous, apart from the obvious intertextual narrative references back and forth? The Platonist Christian heritage maintains that it is only when we recognize the vertical or anagogical anchoring of historical particularity that the biblical narrative has any meaning at all. The real question, therefore, is whether Wright sees the return from exile only as a historical *event* or whether he regards this redemption also as a historical *sacrament* whose eternal reality God has made truly present to us in Christ. The sacramental perspective soundly protects history from being reduced to a mere self-referential intertextual flux. For history—and for the Old Testament events—to have genuine meaning, it is not enough to observe the many similarities between Old and New, much less to insist that it is all part of one and the same continuous historical development. History is in need of a metahistorical, christological

---

[29]Charles Kannengiesser, *Handbook of Patristic Exegesis: The Bible in Ancient Christianity* (Leiden: Brill, 2006), 168.

[30]Cf. ibid., 175.

[31]For the notion of *futura sacramenta*, see Henri de Lubac, *Medieval Exegesis: The Four Senses of Scripture*, trans. E. M. Macierowski (Edinburgh: T&T Clark, 2000), 2:94-96.

anchor. In short, it seems to me that Wright *needs* the Platonist Christian emphasis on sacramental participation in order to sustain his desired continuity of the biblical narrative.[32]

Of course, there is an alternative to my proposal, but it would be an immanent and therefore ultimately autonomous sequencing of disconnected historical tidbits, the many intertextual narrative references notwithstanding. And if, on the basis of Christian convictions, one still wants to hold on to a divine basis for this intertextual narratival web, one will then be forced to posit the arbitrary will of a God who no longer has an intrinsic link with the creation that he has made. This means that Wright is much more susceptible to the charge of deism than is the orthodox Western tradition against which he repeatedly and wrongly brings this accusation. I appreciate Wright's recognition of analogous, intertextual echoes between Old and New Testaments. But this acknowledgment of a continuous story and a continuing exile only makes sense within a providential, sacramental theology, which was the traditional matrix of the Platonist-Christian synthesis.

There are places in Wright's exposé where he comes remarkably close to this sacramental view of the Great Tradition and where he moves beyond just noticing historical, intertextual similarities. He comments, for example:

> The temple was not simply a convenient place to meet for worship. It was not even just the "single sanctuary," the one place where the One God was to be worshiped with sacrifice. It was the place above all where the twin halves of the good creation intersected. When you went up to the temple, it was not *as though* you were "in heaven." You were actually there. That was the point. Israel's God did not have to leave heaven in order to come down and dwell in the wilderness tabernacle or the Jerusalem temple.[33]

---

[32]Subsequent to my writing of this essay, the fourth volume of Wright's Christian Origins and the Question of God has appeared. Though I have not had the opportunity to work through it in detail, it appears to contain some interesting shifts in emphasis. Significantly, Wright (in response to Bruce McCormack) explicitly advocates a participatory ontology (*Paul and the Faithfulness of God*, Christian Origins and the Question of God 4 [Minneapolis: Fortress, 2013], 950n488). He even presents a plea for the doctrine of deification (ibid., 1021). Wright happily also comes around to a more positive evaluation of Plato, saying that Paul "might have had some sympathy for Plato's belief that one ought to look through and beyond the material world to the transcendent truths that might be glimpsed there as if behind a veil" (ibid., 1369).

[33]Wright, "Yet the Sun Will Rise Again," 37.

Wright insists that by entering the temple, you actually entered heaven itself. Exactly so, I think, and in line with this, it seems to me right to suggest (as Wright did in his original paper) that the Pharisees were convinced that current temporal conditions could not contain God. That is why they celebrated Sabbath. For the Pharisees, as Wright puts it elsewhere, it was "time for 'messianic time,' for a new *kind* of time, for the same thing to happen to our time and history as happens in space and matter when we go to the temple: an intersection of our world with God's world, of our time with God's time."[34] Somehow, Wright seems to suggest, God's faithfulness meant that time itself had to change so that exile would end.

Part of the broad heritage of the Christian tradition has been the view that in this time-space universe of ours we are still in exile and that this-worldly categories of "time" and "narrative" are insufficient to do justice to the astounding change in conditions that will prevail once heaven and earth will be reunited. Despite his firm insistence on the continuity of time, space, and matter in the hereafter, Wright is not blind to the notion that even matter will have to undergo a significant change so as to be fitted for the resurrection life. His book on the resurrection helpfully speaks of "transphysicality" to describe the resurrection body.[35] The very physicality of the created order dramatically changes when heaven comes down to earth—as it does both in the church (the temple) and in the eschaton (the "templified" new Jerusalem). The very materiality and temporality of the created order—precisely because they are the outflow of eternal divine grace—yearn for a narratival resolution in which time, matter, and space will take on surprising, and hitherto unknown, heavenly dimensions. Heaven is the end of exile. Analogical notions such as "messianic time" and "transphysicality" imply that heaven and earth really do intersect. It is because of this intersection of nature and the supernatural that Wright needs to be more open than he often is to spiritual readings of the biblical text and that he needs to recognize that the intertextual references between Old and New Testaments are grounded in a sacramental or participatory ontology, that is to say, grounded in the eternal Word of God himself (cf. Prov 8:22-31; Jn 1:1-14; Col 1:15-20).

---

[34]Wright, *Paul and the Faithfulness of God*, 178-79.
[35]N. T. Wright, *The Resurrection of the Son of God*, Christian Origins and the Question of God 3 (Minneapolis: Fortress, 2003), 477-78, 606-7, 612, 678-79.

Fortunately, as we have seen, several aspects in Wright's own work appear to suggest he is somewhat open to such an approach. These elements in Wright's project would be an excellent starting point for a discussion about the plausibility of a theological (and, as such, christological) grounding of narratival history.[36]

[36]I express my warm thanks to Markus Bockmuehl, Gerald P. Boersma, James M. Houston, John G. Stackhouse, Matthew J. Thomas, and Jens Zimmermann for their comments on an earlier draft of this essay.

CHAPTER ELEVEN

EXILE AND FIGURAL HISTORY

EPHRAIM RADNER

THIS ESSAY OFFERS A STRAIGHTFORWARD summary exposition of scriptural exile's figural explication within the Christian tradition.[1] But I present it within the context of a discussion of N. T. Wright's historical-critical argument regarding the idea of "ongoing exile" as informing the expectations of first-century Judaism, and hence of Jesus and of Paul's own attitudes regarding the divine promise for Israel's restoration.[2] My point in doing this is twofold. First, I want to expand a bit the reach of the historical-

---

[1]My use of the term *figural* in what follows is deliberately broad. Theologically, it includes what many early Fathers simply called the "spiritual" sense as contrasted with "historical." This comprehends, of course, what came to be explained in the Middle Ages in terms of the three non-literal levels of meaning: allegory (matters of faith), tropology (matters of morals), and anagogy (matters of our final end). It also embraces the later Protestant dyad of typology and allegory. But the term *figural* extends even further than this and also includes what we would describe as "figurative" rhetorical tropes: metaphor, metonymy, etc. Part of the problem in any of these categorizations is that the contrasts are equally vague: "literal" and "historical" are themselves of uncertain reference, with the former including "figurative" readings often (as narratively embedded tropes) and the latter depending on various construals of temporality that have shifted within different cultural settings. Frei's category of "ostensive reference" as a contrast to "figural" may be among the most handy frameworks, even if it too is ultimately inadequate. See his *The Eclipse of Biblical Narrative: A Study in Eighteenth and Nineteenth Century Hermeneutics* (New Haven, CT: Yale University Press, 1974), 76-85, on Anthony Collins. Frei's notion of "ostensive reference" as a "spatio-temporal" "event" does not in itself distinguish a nonfigural referent, since that latter could be that as well; what is at issue is the exclusivity of that event: figural meanings multiply spatio-temporal referents of a single text.

[2]See, in general, his *Jesus and the Victory of God*, Christian Origins and the Question of God 2 (Minneapolis: Fortress, 2010), xvii-xviii; 126-29; 428-30; Wright, *What Saint Paul Really Said: Was Paul of Tarsus the Real Founder of Christianity?* (Grand Rapids: Eerdmans, 1997), 29-35; Wright, "Yet the Sun Will Rise Again: Reflections on the Exile and Restoration in Second Temple Judaism, Jesus, Paul, and the Church Today" (see the lead essay in the present volume).

critical argument itself: the notion of "ongoing exile" has within itself a paradoxical signification even at the time of Jesus. Second, I want to suggest that the figural interpretation of exile not only rightly engages this paradox but also (and therefore) relativizes the historical-critical temporal framework itself. If in fact "ongoing exile," as understood or grasped after first-century Judaism, transcends unitary temporal limits, what are we talking about exactly when we speak about "history"? My hope in making this twofold point is to narrow somewhat the gap in mutual understanding that has, alas, arisen between historical critics and figural exegetes. It is a gap that has unhelpfully made antagonistic two necessary aspects of scriptural reading.

In what follows, then, I will evaluate the *historical* meaning of concepts such as "continuing exile" and "restoration" as exegetically useful tools. Wright believes they are central concepts for understanding the gospel, and they are so because of their historical referentiality, understood in a certain way: investigating and identifying what these terms meant at the time of Jesus tells us what in fact Jesus "was about" and therefore significantly explicates the Christian faith *in* Jesus. While I do not disagree, I will argue that his notion of historical reference itself is too limited, and as such the place that exile and restoration hold within the gospel itself needs significant elaboration. My goal is to see how the concepts of "exile" and "restoration" rightly point beyond first-century Palestinian referents and engage the figural referents of these terms that Christians have consistently identified within the wider biblical text. These figural readings depend on a broader understanding of temporality, within a theological perspective, than historical critics like Wright tend to assume. Ultimately, I believe that this figural understanding of time is itself more "scriptural." And so my conclusion is that, while concepts such as "continuing exile" construed in a historicist manner are indeed useful, they are so only on a limited basis, and only insofar as they find their place in a more supple understanding of the Bible's historical referentiality itself, one that figural reading provides. Understanding how this may be the case is one way, perhaps, to narrow the gap between critical and figural exegesis.

In my discussion, then, I will reverse what is often seen as the normal order of biblical exegesis and begin with the figural sense of the scriptural text, before engaging the literal. In part, I want to enter *in media res* with respect to traditions of interpretation, where in fact figural readings of Scripture often constituted the first-order entry into the text, rather than being the subsequent result of exegetical ascent (or descent) in levels of meaning. So, I will first present the figural approach to scriptural exile and then reflect more broadly on some traditional significations of this referent. One of the key issues is to gauge their historical meaning, that is, the way these traditional figural significations conceptualize history itself as a scrip-turally informed reality. The "literal" in this context, I will show, is often less a "level" of referentiality, as it is bound up with the figural as a unitary reality. Next, I will briefly try to locate these traditional significations within the scriptural text itself, addressing the basic question of whether they have any prima facie plausibility as valid readings of the Bible within its own frame of reference. Since my conclusion is that they *do* have such plausibility, I will then want to assess more broadly what a Christian "theology of exile" might constitute and how it in fact might relate to historical experience. Only from this perspective will I suggest ways in which the concepts of "continuing exile" and "restoration" reliably function as historically referring terms in the way that Wright would have it.

THE FIGURAL CHALLENGE

Let me begin with a classic example of simple figural explication as a way of setting out what has been called the "precritical" challenge. What does the word *exile* refer to in the Bible? In Calvin's view it was a textual term with a multiple range of temporally simultaneous referents—there were *many* historical "exiles" that the Bible referred to when the term appears in Scripture, happening at different times. So, in a famous letter written from Geneva to Jacques de Bourgogne, Monsieur de Falais, whose reformed con-victions had set him at odds with the French authorities, Calvin takes the contemporary political referent as a tool to leverage out several scriptural meanings.[3] First, he calls de Falais to accept *being exiled* from France for sake of his faith. But this exile, similar to the one that Calvin accepted for

---

[3]Cf. Yan Brailowsky, "Mis au ban de la terre promise? La mythographie des exilés religieux sous le règne de Mary Tudor," in *Le bannissement et l'exil en Europe aux XVIe et XVIIe siècles*, ed. Pascal Drouet and Yan Brailowsky (Rennes: Presses Universitaires de Rennes, 2010), 15-30, which offers an overview of sixteenth-century Protestant, especially English, understandings of scriptural exile.

himself, refers to Christ's own "banishment" from France, something implicit in his passion and death. Here is a case where one must follow the Master. But one does so, according to Calvin, in line with Abraham's earlier exile, one in which he "hastened forth without hesitation."

> We have no express revelation commanding us to leave the country; but seeing that we have the commandment to honour God, both in body and soul, wherever we are, what more would we have? It is to us, then, equally that these words are addressed, *Get thee out of thy country and from thy kindred.*[4]

Calvin's appeal to Abraham, on the basis that "we are his children," proved a frequent move in seeking a referent for the experience of contemporary exile.[5] But he also made use of other referents, slightly less paradigmatic and more situational: the Roman Church was the "Babylon" of old, into which one might in fact be carried away in captivity—so be careful! But as a place of idolatry, the Roman Church was also to be fled in bodily suffering, much as the early Christians had demanded flight from the "Babylonian" Rome of the book of Revelation. In such a Rome as this, after all, antichrist had set himself up, in the form of the papacy.[6]

Yet more broadly and perhaps deeply, Calvin could view the scriptural—and hence contemporary—referent of exile as the "world" itself, a place of material limitations and suffering, a place of perverting fleshly satisfactions and unfulfilled spiritual desires, a landscape of passage in contrast to one's true heavenly "home." Here, the "banishment" of Christ takes form in the body of his incarnation itself, something to be suffered for the sake of a final exaltation and reign. "In Christ," the true Christian also lives through such an existential exile, now synonymous (as already in Abraham's case) with the act of "pilgrimage" and wayfaring.[7]

Of course, this is all a familiar application of spiritual—multivalent—signification, much as the Christian tradition had been engaging for

---

[4]John Calvin, *Letters of John Calvin*, ed. Jules Bonnet, trans. David Constable (Edinburgh: Thomas Constable, 1855), 1:374. The letter is dated October 14, 1543.

[5]E.g., ibid., 1:401; 2:121.

[6]E.g., Calvin, *Institutes of the Christian Religion*, IV.2.4 and 12; IV.2.10, 23.

[7]Calvin, *Letters*, 2:208-9; "Even if no necessity compelled you to quit the nest, yet you were no daughter of God, if this earthly life did not seem to you a pilgrimage. But now when the sacrilegious tyranny of Antichrist expels you from it, and God calls you with a loud voice to go forth, let not the condition of your peregrination seem painful to you, till the time when at last he shall bring us all together into his eternal inheritance" (452-53).

centuries. And with respect to the referent of *exile*, Calvin draws on an established and rich legacy of exegesis, beginning at least in the early church, as well as in Rabbinic Judaism. (To what degree it is embedded, as it were, in the scriptural text itself is a question we will raise later.) In what follows, I want to explore this interpretive phenomenon, less as a matter of historical description than as a matter of engaging the historical effect given by the meaning of the scriptural text itself. When Scripture speaks of exile, what are we "meant" to understand by the verbal referent? What do our times, which are given by God, press us into apprehending?

The theological stakes are obviously high in answering this kind of question. N. T. Wright's own influential reading of the meaning of the Christian gospel, founded on Jesus' recorded preaching and Paul's central proclamation, derives from a particular claim regarding the meaning of exile *for* Jesus and Paul, and therefore the meaning of exile's resolution or healing.[8] The claim itself is based on a self-consciously "critical" examination of the Scripture. On a straightforward level, we might wonder whether Jesus' understanding of exile and its overcoming, in scriptural terms, was simply different from Calvin's, and therefore whether Calvin's understanding of the gospel was somehow off-base. This might seem a (methodologically) simple historical problem to address. But what if the traditional and "precritical" reading of exile as holding multiple referents is evangelically valid, that is, what if it properly—in the sense of deriving from the message of Jesus Christ—founds the gospel? How might this inform our *historical* thinking about the meaning of exile in its scriptural enunciation, even in the context of Jesus' own specific teaching and hence "self-understanding"?

THE CHRISTIAN FIGURAL TRADITION OF EXILE

We have already seen some of Calvin's understandings of the scriptural referent for "exile": there is such a thing as a politico-religious exile, in which individuals (such as himself) leave their country and go to live in another. Generally Calvin sees this as a necessity to be borne for the sake of fidelity to the gospel. (As some commentators have pointed out, he was here

---

[8]N. T. Wright, "Theology, History and Jesus: A Response to Maurice Casey and Clive Marsh," *JSNT* 69 (1998): 105-12, which offers a succinct view as to how he views this topic within the context of a critical historian's task.

following an "Athanasian" tradition of defending the Christian acceptance of exile, over against the tradition of Tertullian that argued for the Christian acceptance of martyrdom *in situ*.)[9] "Conscience" and the freedom to worship God faithfully might well demand that one leave one's home. But Calvin places this concrete experience of politico-religious exile within the "reality" of Jesus' own experience of exile, now viewed in various ways: his "exile" from heaven to earth in his incarnation; deriving from this, his passion and death; but upholding this, his own politico-religious exile given in the form of his persecution and arrest, and thereby his being "driven" from the nation of Israel. It is out of this fundamental Christic character and experience of exile that Calvin identifies a number of other specific scriptural exiles: Abraham's, the Jews' exile from Jerusalem, and so on. Likewise, he frames the Christian life as a whole in terms of Christ's exilic-incarnational form: the world in "this life" is a place of exile, cast in terms of a difficult journey or pilgrimage leading back to one's heavenly "home" or "inheritance," and defined in terms of temptations and the assaults of Satan, the latter of which is given historical force especially through the form and action of the Roman Church and its pontiff.

The context of his usage was firmly grounded, from one perspective, in lived experience, that is, in his own exile from France and in that of countless others whom he either knew personally or about whom he had heard. This fact is important to bear in mind, for the same can be said for other scriptural interpreters of the era, especially among Reformed readers of the Bible: to speak, of exile as a "scriptural" referent was to speak of something whose lived contours were familiar. So, for instance, William Tyndale's interest in exile as a theological category was clearly informed by a life whose very shape was bound to his own exilic existence. Yet it was also one that he had to reflect upon theologically in terms of Scripture's own referents. Tyndale's

---

[9]Tertullian's *De fuga in persecutione* is the classic text for the argument that persecution is to be accepted, since (according to Tertullian) its ultimate author is God, who uses it for the good of the suffering Christian and for the unveiling of a clear witness to the gospel. Flight—or, as it were, the acceptance of exile for the sake of one's faith—is by contrast a form simply of cowardice and disobedience. Tertullian deals with scriptural examples of flight by consigning them to a now-overcome dispensation. Athanasius, on the other hand, in his *Apologia de fuga sua*, offers the contrasting position of one who views persecution as inherently satanic, and thus properly resistible, until the point that death is simply unavoidable. His own use of scriptural figures is less dispensationalist than is Tertullian's.

usage is, in his case, more continuous with early church understandings in the tradition of Tertullian, where persecution and martyrdom were seen as specific demands of faithfulness and also finally prizes for it as well. In general, Tyndale does not speak explicitly of "exile," but rather of "captivity," in the terms of Egypt or Babylon. And in this regard, the pope embodies, e.g., Pharaoh, aiming his evil wiles against an Israel that embraces "all" of God's people, including of course the true church. In this, however, the dynamic of oppression is historically extensive, moving throughout the entire scriptural history, where "prophet" and king stand in a kind of primordial struggle, with the pope standing for all the enemies of the truly faithful, subjecting them to "bondage" and "captivity," and finally personifying "the world" itself, who "hateth them [Israel] for their faith and trust which they have in God." It is precisely because the nature of this struggle is thus intrinsic to the world's history as a whole that Tyndale will take the route of Tertullian (despite his own personal flight to the Continent) and urge patience in one's place of witness. Hence, scriptural "exile" as "captivity" is in fact the experience of persecution itself, in all its forms, and such persecution becomes the identifying mark of the true church. Yet even here, one can go further: the church is true insofar as it rightly and honestly lives out the true historical condition of humankind, which *is* a form of exile. "Captivity" is, at its most fundamental, the condition of the sinner bound by Satan. As a result, the scriptural events that recount forms of bondage are but instances that figure sin's domain. Salvation, then, derives from this recognition and the turn to God's grace in Christ for forgiveness and empowered love.[10]

Calvin's "calling out" of his French friends *into* an experienced exile was, in its most pragmatic orientation, a contrasting "Athanasian" response and made use of its own set of scriptural figures. But whether Tyndalian or Calvinistic, what shaped the Christian tradition that each shared in common was a sense that "exile" was something that was intransigently a part of the

---

[10]For the various references to Tyndale above, see respectively his *Obedience of a Christian Man*, *Prologue to Exodus*, *Prologue to Jonas*, and *Parable of the Wicked Mammon*, all found in *The Works of the English Reformers William Tyndale and John Frith*, ed. Thomas Russell (London: Ebenezer Palmer, 1831), 3:343, 17, 58, and passim. The quotation itself is from the *Prologue to Exodus*, 17. While this edition is critically outdated, it is easily accessible and accurately provides the major texts.

Christian existence, something to be grappled with and navigated, including and most especially in its scriptural demarcation. We tend to forget this in our own day, as we imagine exile in terms of an almost ideal form or experience, requiring somehow existential translation for the modern mind. But from the ancient world to the sixteenth century (and obviously beyond) the actual experience of exile was a central part of social life. It is only recently that historians and cultural critics have begun to pay attention to this fact.[11] Banishment and exile, of individuals or of whole groups and peoples, were a regular practice over the centuries, used generally for purposes of political and sometimes simply personal control, display, and vindictiveness. These repeated, remembered, experienced, and often-expected elements of "displacement" were memorialized by great writers (e.g., Ovid, whose attitudes joined with Scripture in informing exilic experience in the Middle Ages), as well as by the folk wisdom of widespread adepts. Popular traditions of the fugitive (e.g., Robin Hood) bumped up with sophisticated literary articulation (e.g., Dante and Cino da Pistoia, or François de Villon), but in both cases these publicized attitudes were bound to actual lives whose pointed details were broadly familiar. Furthermore, exile continued to be something aimed at the center of Christian existence quite specifically in various ways, including within a context of legal expectation and even sanctioned authority.[12] Hence, "excommunication" becomes a form of "exile," or simply the life of disciplined subjection within the Christian church's authoritative structures, sometimes under bishops, sometimes as bishops (e.g., Beckett and Anselm) under the secular arm. The so-called Babylonian Captivity of the papacy in Avignon is a formidable example of how exile becomes a specifically *Christian* ecclesial condition that gathers within its concrete forms, often quite painful, not only the full scriptural weight of

---

[11]In addition to the volume of Drouet and Brailowsky above, see Jan Felix Gaertner, ed., *Writing Exile: The Discourse of Displacement in Greco-Roman Antiquity and Beyond* (Leiden: Brill, 2007), and Laura Napran and Elisabeth Van Houts, eds., *Exile in the Middle Ages* (Turnhout, Belgium: Brepols, 2004). The introductory chapters by Gaertner and Napran respectively provide overviews of the burgeoning literature for these periods. See also the two volumes edited by James M. Scott, *Exile: Old Testament, Jewish, and Christian Conceptions* (Leiden: Brill, 1997), and *Restoration: Old Testament, Jewish & Christian Perspectives* (Leiden: Brill, 2001).

[12]The development of ecclesial laws and canons governing "exclusion" on various grounds follows the ramification of the actual practice of exile. See Elizabeth Vodola, *Excommunication in the Middle Ages* (Berkeley: University of California Press, 1986).

meaning but the expectations of the early Fathers and saints who had already borne these figures.[13]

The fact that the experience of exile not only failed to diminish in the early modern and modern periods but actually expanded its reach, and at least initially did so on the basis of religious realities, is again something we tend to forget. Calvin's own discussion is a specifically religious discussion, but one whose demands are existentially ineluctable, as they continue to be throughout the seventeenth and eighteenth centuries and for many beyond. Catholics, Protestants, dissenters, sectarian trouble-makers, Anabaptists, and so on were driven out of their homes, fled, or were imprisoned and banished by the thousands (and in the case of the French Huguenots, by the hundreds of thousands).[14] The "modern" and contemporary experience of exile, as it has tended to attract commentary, has been more political in its ramifications.[15] One speaks today of a "political refugee" rather than an "exile," although the causal base of each is usually similar, and the contemporary nomenclature tends to stress provisionality over permanence (something with its own existential implications, especially if unreflected by actual outcomes).[16] But one can properly project

---

[13]See Brian Briggs's discussion of the twelfth-century Osbert of Clare, "*Expulsio, Proscriptio, Exilium:* Exile and Friendship in the Writings of Osbert of Clare," in *Exile in the Middle Ages,* 131-44. Osbert's exiles seem to have been due to ecclesiastical conflicts. But Briggs discusses how, in his letters, Osbert made use of an astoundingly broad rhetorical repertoire of exilic figures, whose imaginary purchase was due less to the monk's learning than to their insistent pertinence.

[14]See Christopher D'Addario, *Exile and Journey in Seventeenth-Century Literature* (Cambridge: Cambridge University Press, 1999); Philip Major, ed., *Literatures of Exile in the English Revolution and Its Aftermath, 1640-1690* (Farnham, Surrey: Ashgate, 2010); Bertrand Van Ruymbeke and Randy J. Sparks, eds., *The Huguenots in France and the Atlantic Diaspora* (Columbia: University of South Carolina Press, 2003). For a rather sobering account of the confusing fruit of the exilic experience, religiously and politically, see Abraham Friesen, *In Defense of Privilege: Russian Mennonites and the State Before and During World War I* (Winnepeg, Manitoba: Historical Commission of the US and Canadian Mennonite Brethren Churches, 2006).

[15]Terry Eagleton's *Exiles and Émigrés: Studies in Modern Literature* (London: Chatto & Windus, 1970) was an early examination of modern English writing in this vein. Many other studies have followed, concentrating on different political locales and geographical origins: e.g., David Bevan, *Literature and Exile* (Amsterdam: Rodopi, 1990); Sophia A. McClennan, *The Dialectics of Exile: Nation, Time, Language, and Space in Hispanic Literatures* (Purdue, IN: Purdue University Press, 2004); John Neubauer and Borbála Zsuzsanna Török, eds., *The Exile and Return of Writers from East-Central Europe: A Compendium* (Berlin: de Gruyter, 2009), etc.

[16]According to Refugees International (basing their numbers on UN statistics) there were over 65 million displaced persons in the world in 2015, the largest number on record. See www .refugeesinternational.org/currentwork, accessed January 22, 2017.

backwards the considerations of contemporary "exilic" writers in their response to experiential constraints, reading the tropes of their self-understanding within the traditional stream of religious figuralism, and discover how the meaning of their philosophies and political science in particular have taken on peculiar nuances in ways inexplicable except from within this tradition.[17]

These concrete experiences, furthermore, were only fragmentary—if often overwhelming—elements of a larger picture of human existence, where material, social, and geographical instability were constant features of most people's lives. Again, modern Westerners tend to forget this perennial element of our race's heritage. Philosophical judgments about this fact were in any case long in play, from a range of antique visions regarding the fleeting character of human life to developed metaphysics of material alienation. Plotinus's famous framework of *exitus-reditus* (the increasingly burdensome departure of being from its source of oneness, and its eventual return into unity) was given a common conceptual stamp at the celebrated end of his *Enneads*: "This is the life of gods and of the godlike and blessed among men, liberation from the alien that besets us here, a life taking no pleasure in the things of earth, the passing of solitary to solitary."[18] The standard MacKenna translation just quoted colors the Greek perhaps too strikingly, but Plotinus's vision is clear enough: the things of this earth are "other" ("alien") to the truly "godlike" human being, and divinity consists of "liberation" from their grip and literally "fleeing" to the One.[19] It was this framework that simply fit into the widespread categories already in use, politically, economically, and religiously for some time: "flight" or "exile" from the world of useless passions and besetting suffering, and searching instead for some kind of union with that which lasts. Even in the late twentieth century, Kolakowski can affirm that "exile is the permanent human

---

[17]The more nihilistic strand of thinking, e.g., by Emil Cioran, can only be grasped from within this specifically European and Christian stream of exilic perspective. See also Leszek Kolakowski, "In Praise of Exile," in his *Modernity on Endless Trial* (Chicago: University of Chicago Press, 1997), 55-59. Kolakowski is explicit in trying to relocate contemporary exilic consciousness within a more traditional scriptural context.

[18]Plotinus, *Enneads*, trans. Stephen MacKenna, 2nd ed. by B. S. Page (London: Faber and Faber, 1956), 625.

[19]Cf. the Greek text in Plotinus, *Ennead* VI:6-9, trans. A. H. Armstrong (Cambridge, MA: Harvard University Press, 1988), 344.

condition."[20] But as permanent, its alternative—redemption or release—is obviously located elsewhere than in the "world" itself. This is, in fact, Tyndale's claim about "the world" (in a certain Johannine and perhaps Pauline reading of the matter) and Calvin's too.

But they were well established long before. Origen had his own Christian version of the Plotinian paradigm of exile, driven by a sophisticated scriptural ascetic. Figurally, it was given in the sin of Adam and Eve and their expulsion from Paradise, into a world of mortality, suffering, and sinful debasement. But it was this reality that the historical narratives of the Bible, and indeed therefore their historical weight as temporal experiences, signified.[21]

> Therefore, when you hear of the captivity of the people, believe that it did indeed happen according to the historical narrative, but then go on to understand that story as a sign of something else. Following that sign you will discover the mystery. You, if you call yourself a believer, when you experience peace—Christ indeed is our peace—inhabit Jerusalem. If you then sin, God's visitation leaves you, and you are handed over captive to Nebuchadnezzar, and so led captive into Babylon. When then your soul is troubled by vices and disturbances, you are taken into Babylon. . . . Adam was indeed in Paradise, but the serpent caused his captivity, and brought it about that he was expelled from Jerusalem or Paradise, and entered into this place of tears.[22]

Jesus, then, the Son from heaven, "descends into corruption," into the place of "captivity" that is Ezekiel's, the human prophets', and ours. But because we are made one with him, Jesus can say to us "Come out!"—out of Babylon, out of captivity, out of the "storms of life," out of the fallen world, out of sin—and rise into forgiveness, sinlessness, immortality, and glory. The "world" is a place of purgation's "hot wind"; Jesus is the means by which we reach the pacific cool of heaven.

The purgative character of the world, at least for the believer, was taken up robustly by the ascetic vocation of the monastic movement. Hence, exile is increasingly filled by Christian writers with a paradoxical value, and just as "discipline comes from the Lord" (Heb 12:3-11), suffering is granted a divine purpose whose end lies beyond this life. Jerome, for instance, can call

---

[20]Kolakowski, "In Praise of Exile," 59.
[21]See Joseph Trigg, "Origen, *Homily I on Ezekiel*," in *Ascetic Behavior in Greco-Roman Antiquity: A Sourcebook*, ed. Vincent L. Wimbush (Minneapolis: Fortress, 1990), 45-67.
[22]Ibid., 52.

exile a "crown" for the Christian, turning political oppression on its head as a prize. But he goes on to point out that the life of the monk more particularly is itself a kind of positive exile: "Is not every monk an exile from his country? Is he not an exile from the whole world?" The public authorities have no power over one whose retreat into the ever-present Christ releases him from the landscape of physical arrest and banishment.[23] And this is only because there is no difference between such political exile and daily existence itself. Human life, in its bare form, is intrinsically captive. So Chrysostom expresses himself on the Christian life, whose sojourn in this world is one of the "foreigner" (*xenos*—as used in Heb 11:13, and then joined conceptually to Heb 13:13-14) from heaven.[24] As the Latin, and finally Vulgate translation of Hebrews 11:13 made use of the term *peregrinus*, the "pilgrim" figure took wing, classicized in the West by Augustine and Gregory.[25] We are all sojourners on earth within this mortal life, and the Christian "alien" is particular in that his or her eyes are rightly cast upon the true *patria* in heaven. By the Middle Ages, devotionally upheld by a complicated network of geographical pilgrimage routes, this consciousness moved far beyond monastic vocation[26] and became a standard lens for popular self-understanding. Books treating human life as a pilgrimage

---

[23]Jerome, *Letter* 82.10 to Theophilus of Alexandria (*NPNF*[2] 26:172).

[24]John Chrysostom, *Homilies on Matthew*, in PL 58:548. Chrysostom's own embodied fate in an exiled death was more than fitting to his exegesis.

[25]Irenaeus was in fact one of the first to stress this theme. See Emmanuel Lanne, "La 'xeniteia' d'Abraham dans l'oeurvre d'Irénée. Aux origines monastiques de la thème de la 'peregrinatio,'" *Irenikon* 47, no. 2 (1974): 163-87. Augustine uses the *peregrinus* image frequently. In the *Confessions*, for instance, in 3.6, 9.13 (the pilgrimage of earth away from the eternal Jerusalem), 10.5. The *City of God*, of course, is replete with examples, especially where the city of God is itself described as an "earthly pilgrim": 1.35, 15.1, 18.54, etc. See M. A. Claussen, "'Peregrinatio' and 'Peregrini' in Augustine's 'City of God,'" *Traditio* 46 (1991): 33-75. Further, see Augustine's commentaries on the Psalms, 38.21, 49.22, 64.2, 119.6-9, etc. On Augustine and his role in the Western tradition here, see Manuela Brito-Martins, "The Concept of *Peregrination* in Saint Augustine and Its Influences," in *Exile in the Middle Ages*, 83-94. For other patristic discussion, see Wendy Pullan, "Ambiguity as a Central Condition of Early Christian Pilgrimage," in *Pilgrimage in Graeco-Roman and Early Christian Antiquity: Seeing the Gods*, ed. Jaś Elsner and Ian Rutherford (Oxford: Oxford University Press, 2006), 387-410. Gregory provided the foundation for the medieval tradition of "spiritual pilgrimage," often spoken of in terms of early "exile," yet specifically colored by a range of affective elements, such as "desire" and "yearning" for heaven. See his *Moralia* 18 (PL 76:63). For an extensive treatment of the tradition here, see F. C. Gardiner, *The Pilgrimage of Desire: A Study of Theme and Genre in Medieval Literature* (Leiden: Brill, 1971).

[26]See the standard analysis by Jean Leclercq, "Monachisme et peregrination du IXe au XIIe siècle," *Studia Monastica* III (1969): 33-52.

proliferated, often in multiple translations, and in fact successfully migrated into the epoch of printing, as well as crossing the Catholic-Protestant frontier into the seventeenth century. From Guillaume de Digulleville to John Bunyan, mutations of the Augustinian outlook shaped a comprehensive cultural interpretation of human life.[27] And it did so, in large part, because it "fit" the felt ordering of human existence.

We can take Bede's summary of the threefold meaning of Psalm 136 (137)—"By the waters of Babylon"—as a crystallization of this entire outlook in terms of its explicit scriptural referents. There are three "captivities" to which Babylon refers, he writes: there is first, of course, the captivity of the Jews at the hands of the Babylonians themselves; there is, second, the captivity of the human race in sin, brought by Adam's fall and expulsion from Paradise; and there is, third, the captivity into which the devil would ensnare the church's members during their earthly pilgrimage.[28] "Captivity," more generally, can be rendered as "the world," just as "Jerusalem" can be rendered as Christ's salvation and as heaven.[29] The *Glossa* takes this further, and, as with the tradition as a whole, ramifies captivity's reach in terms of a range of assaults—"carnality," "cupidity," and so on.[30] But the range of referents is clear and relatively stable. As the tradition reads "captivity" or "exile," Christian writers also bring into referential coincidence various scriptural figures:[31] besides Babylon, we have Abraham and his own exile from Ur; the Egypt of

---

[27]For references to studies of Digulleville's three popular "pilgrimage" poems (translated a century later into English by John Lydgate, and then one of the earliest books printed in England), see Maureen Boulton, "Digulleville's *Pèlerinage de Jésus* Christ: A Poem of Courtly Devotion," in *The Vernacular Spirit: Essays on Medieval Religious Literature*, ed. Renate Blumenfeld-Kosinski, Duncan Roberston, and Nancy Warren (New York: Palgrave Macmillan, 2002), 125-44. More broadly, see Dee Dyas, *Pilgrimage in English Literature, 700–1500* (Cambridge: Boydell and Brewer, 2001). For an overview that covers material from the early church to the seventeenth century, see Juergen Hahn, *The Origins of the Baroque Concept of* Peregrinatio (Chapel Hill: University of North Carolina Press, 1973).

[28]Certain ecclesiological elements conformed to as well as made possible some of these distinctions, for instance, the common view that there were different levels or even referents for "the church's members" in this regard, e.g., the perfect, the imperfect, and the evil, to which aspects of "captivity" might apply differently. See Marcia L. Colish's discussion of medieval psalm exegesis in her *Peter Lombard* (Leiden: Brill, 1994), 1:162-88, esp. 172.

[29]The discussion by Bede on Ps 136/7 (or probably a much later follower) is found in *PL* 93:1093-94.

[30]For the *Glossa*, see *PL*, 113:344 and 1056-58 on Ps 136/37 in particular.

[31]In fact, the Vulgate rarely uses the word *exilium*, and hence *captivitas* came to be seen as equivalent (though sometimes the distinction was played upon). See C. P. Lewis, "Gruffudd ap Cynan and the Reality and Representation of Exile," in *Exile in the Middle Ages*, 45-46.

Pharaoh; there is also David, especially in the Psalmic location of his laments—flight from Saul and exile in Philistia; flight from Jerusalem, and so on; the prophets as a group become figures of exile, whether before or after the key moment of Babylonian captivity, for they struggle with Israel's sinful leadership and are always, as it were, standing "outside the camp" in their truthful witness. Moving to the New Testament, figures such as John exiled at Patmos and his own visions in the Apocalypse are commonly taken up; as is Paul in his final journey, and so on.[32] Overarching all of these is the dual figure of Adam and Christ, each exiled in their own way, yet with the latter carrying through the former's restoration precisely through his own subjection to captivity's fundamental grasp in sin and death. It is in this movement that the Christian is caught within the world, neither wholly free nor yet wholly imprisoned. Hence the notion of progression, the journey and pilgrimage *toward* freedom, the "Jerusalem above," somehow already spiritually touched.

A Scriptural Figural Tradition?

Where do these referents for captivity and exile stand in terms of a scriptural textual tradition in itself? Part of Wright's own project, along with others, has been to found the notion of a "continuing exile," even after the nominal "return" from Babylon, within biblical texts themselves, such as Daniel and Ezra. And he has done that well, it seems to me.[33] Likewise, he has insisted, again rightly, that intertestamental texts raise the exilic demand into an eschatological pitch (something I will return to shortly). He also notes that Israel-as-expelled-Adam was already rooted in Jewish tradition in the intertestamental period. If nothing else, this leads one to assume at least the potential resonance of such thinking regarding the figural reach of the exilic condition within the intentionality of New Testament writers, including Jesus himself. But even without such specific exegetical (and to some extent difficult-to-date) resolutions on hand, one cannot escape the fundamental exilic projection into the full range of scriptural figure by the canonical Psalms themselves, whose superscriptions alone demand a

---

[32]These common figures can be gleaned from the various discussions in Napran and Van Houts, whose wide scope of focus, from Viking to Italian culture, nonetheless maintains a consistent set of exilic scriptural texts as they are applied to contemporary experience.

[33]Wright, "Yet the Sun Will Rise Again."

multireferential application: chronological exclusivity is rejected in favor of a historical simultaneity that must include, by definition, the "now." This, after all, lies at the base of Jesus' own usage of the Psalms to indicate his place within them.[34]

It is, of course, this drawing together of Jesus and David, and through this David and a host of other realities, from Adam through the exodus and beyond, that makes of exile, as in Psalm 136/7, a referentially multivalent reality. When Jesus speaks of a future destruction for Jerusalem, he does so in terms of this Psalm (cf. Lk 19:43-44). But he also places his own disciples (along with himself) within this turmoil. Many of the discipleship sayings are in fact cast in exilic terms, as are the end-time sayings: Luke 9, for instance, is filled with references to the impoverishment of wandering and homelessness, while the final age is to be one of flight from home and land (Lk 21:21), just as the disciple must be like "Lot's wife" (Lk 17:32). The Johannine translation of some of these elements into the language of the "world" and its sufferings (cf. Jn 16:33) does not, for all that, eliminate the specific chronological aspects of divine demand and historical crisis (Jn 15:19; Rev 7:14). Existence and crisis are conflated and take the form of the persecuted Christ (Acts 14:22; 1 Thess 3:4; 2 Tim 3:12). Specific notations of exile (e.g., Mt 10:23; cf. Ps 105:12-13) are located within the general vocation of a discipleship whose normalcy is defined in the terms of the Last Days (Mt 10:5-43), and these in the specific form of Jesus himself (cf. Jn 15:20). Paul's and the other letter writers' diasporal (Gal 6:16; Jas 1:1; 1 Pet 1:1; Heb 13:14) and two-age discussions (e.g., 2 Cor 4:18–5:2; Phil 3:2-21) are inseparable from this framework, and they are founded on elements of spiritual expectation already embedded in the Psalms especially (cf. Ps 73:25).

These texts and their scripturally networked meanings provide a fairly straightforward basis for the Christian tradition's appropriation of their intersecting referents. The movement from historical *exilium* (or *captivitas*) to existential *peregrinatio* becomes not only a fluid possibility but a permanent connection: "this world" is a world of "exile" in which we "make our way"—both in terms of endurance but also perhaps progress—to something "better," to "Jerusalem, our home," the divine *patria* or *civitas vera* who is

---

[34]Most famously in his cry of dereliction from the cross (Ps 22:1) and self-commendation (Ps 35:5).

God's own self. And the way to this goal is the way of Jesus himself, in him and after him, as patient disciple. The stable meaning of this vision is given in its multitraditional and cross-denominational popularity, from monastic outlooks to nineteenth-century (and beyond) American Protestant spirituality. "Jesus, my all, to heav'n is gone . . . I'm on my journey home";[35] "I feel like, I feel like I'm on my journey home";[36] "I'm a pilgrim and a stranger, rough and thorny is the road";[37] "O who will come and go with me?":

> O who will come and go with me,
> I am on my journey home;
> I'm bound fair Canaan's land to see,
> I am on my journey home.
> O come and go with me,
> O come and go with me,
> O come and go with me,
> For I'm on my journey home.
> Farewell vain world, I'm going home,
> I am on my journey home;
> My Savior smiles and bids me come,
> I am on my journey home.
> Sweet angels beckon me away,
> I am on my journey home;
> To sing God's praise in endless day,
> I am on my journey home.[38]

---

[35]Text by John Cennick (a young acquaintance of Wesley), originally in *Sacred Hymns for the Use of Religious Societies, 1743; frequently reprinted, with the chorus, in America, e.g. Southern Harmony* no. 11; *Baptist Harmony* no. 70.

[36]The verses, beginning "When I Can Read My Title Clear," are by Isaac Watts (included in Richard Allen's 1801 Hymnal for the African Methodist church), by the famous chorus and tune derived from nineteenth-century America. See Howard W. Odum, "Religious Folk-Songs of the Southern Negroes," *American Journal of Religious Psychology and Education* 3 (1909): 265-365 (originally published as Odum's doctoral dissertation at Clark University), where Odum provides a range of examples from African American hymnody that fall squarely into the *exilium-peregrinatio* scheme, and that drifted between black and white spiritual in their adaptations.

[37]Text by Mary Hamlin Maxwell; this hymn became popular within the Salvation Army at the turn of the twentieth century.

[38]Stith Mead, ed., *General Selection of the Newest and Most Admired Hymns and Spiritual Songs Now in Use* (Richmond, VA: Seaton Grantland, 1807), no. 89.

What is crucial to grasp is the way this stable tradition finds its vital taproot, not simply in a congenial and long-lived devotional style but in the very referential exactitude of the Scripture's description of exilic existence as it is in fact historically located in the ongoing lives of Christians.[39] That is part of the insistence of African American theologians, whose rejection of the compensatory theory of "slave religion" in favor of its scriptural fidelity has done so much to revitalize the proper recognition each reality's nature—the Scripture's inherent meaning and power, and its just appropriation by African American Christians.[40]

All this is not just an interesting piece of intellectual or devotional history. It must, if only as a matter of usage, raise the question, to what does the scriptural referent of exile actually refer? If *actually* is taken in a strict historical sense, it is nonetheless just this historically inescapable experience of "ongoing exile" in the lives of those reading the Bible that cannot be avoided in a first-order way. It is an experience whose formal similarities with the shape of first-century exile provide a consistent standard for judging referentiality as a scriptural category. One can note simply the perspective of Jewish readers of the text, for whom *exile* can only refer to a *sequence* of realities and does so in fact: not only to the tense prolongation of Babylon's captivity through Roman hands—the purported "intended" meaning of the term at the time of Jesus— but also the already recognized expectation, only budding or fully formed, of a captivity whose breadth stretched backwards and forwards more mysteriously. It was, and remains, a reach that would include the temple's destruction, further dispersion, Christian and Muslim oppression and persecution, and most recently a conflagration of unimagined magnitude in the Holocaust.

---

[39]See Kiri Miller, *Traveling Home: Sacred Harp Singing and American Pluralism* (Champaign: University of Illinois Press, 2008), 201-7, with its attempt to restate the central Christian tradition of exile and pilgrimage in a modern psychocultural dress, something whose postmodern self-referentiality must still bow to the assertive and explicit practice of this spirituality.

[40]The theological seriousness of the "spiritual," in its lived context, was emphasized in the early twentieth century by critics such as James Weldon Johnson. More recently, see James Cone, *The Spiritual and the Blues: An Interpretation* (Maryknoll, NY: Orbis, 1991). For a discussion that touches more acutely on the topic of this essay, see Cheryl Sanders, *Saints in Exile: The Holiness-Pentecostal Experience in African American Religion and Culture* (New York: Oxford University Press, 1999). Michael Stone-Richards, in *Logics of Separation: Exile and Transcendence in Aesthetic Modernity* (New York: Peter Lang, 2011), draws together African American and African, as well as modern European authors such as Paul Celan, in a contemporary revision of exilic consciousness (see above).

Indeed, that there *is* a historical question of the moral relationship between the Jews and the Christian church—a question whose answer has
been ominously given in terms of a profound Christian culpability that
cannot help but resonate with the words of Romans 11:21—must touch on
any interpretive claim regarding this or that "historical" meaning attached
to "ongoing exile" and "return from exile." The classic observances of the fast
day of Tisha B'av (the "ninth day of the month of Av"), lamenting the destruction of the two temples, and later the mourning of other Jewish ca-
lamities, has, for all its debated significance as a holiday, long pointed to a
chronological notion of "expectation" that obviously has extended far
beyond the first century, and historically speaking well ought to. And if this
is so, for the reader of the Scripture seeking the proper referent of *exile*, there
remains a real question: To which Jews are we asked to listen in order to
ascertain correct scriptural "intentionality"? If the referent of "Israel" is already scripturally extended beyond the spatial-temporal location we identify
as Babylon in the sixth century BCE, how far shall this go?

There is also the issue of the church's experiential outcome when taken as
the fruit of a corporate entity: How does the church relate to "exile," not only
under Rome—the book of Revelation's initial historical locale—nor only
under a range of experiences in the East and Near East, but under diverse
Christian governing groups, and then within non-Western political and cultural alienations after especially the sixteenth century? In all this, individual
Christian lives, in their many particulars, have moved to recast the character
of exile in a temporally extended or at least multilayered simultaneity with
respect to scriptural descriptions, so that formal frameworks of referential
interpretation like Bede's made common sense.

Part of both Jewish and Christian extensions of reference is bound up
with the simple but inescapable theological and moral demands of theodicy:
if the Scripture is somehow true in its reference, then its referents cannot be
limited to chronologies of signification that exclude a clear relationship to
the present. If "exile" is truly dealt with in the Scriptures—"restoration"—
then that truth must somehow include the historical exiles of the present.
These demands have been properly tethered to renewed and repeated scriptural discernment, with the result that scriptural reality resolves exile in
different ways: exile, for instance, may refer to a discipled participation in

the cross; or to an ascetic denial and yearning; or to some transtemporal pneumatic embrace; or an agonistic resistance to evil; to penitence; to the long practice of prayer. Paradoxically, from a Christian perspective, such referents *also* signify some true aspect of a *restoration from* exile, insofar as they are bound, in their enactment, to Christ Jesus.[41]

For on a scriptural level all of these resolutions of signification have been given through their enfigured realization: here is where we return to the specific question of scriptural reference. If the resolution is given "in Christ" somehow, then the character of "exile" itself encloses the standard referents of exile as "now," as still true in the same way as "Jesus is raised" or "Jesus is Lord" demands a rethinking of the life and nature of Jesus of Nazareth. Adam, Abraham, David and Saul, Jewish Babylon, Psalm 137, etc., must now be determined by a character that is chronologically complex, for "He is the God of the living" (see Mk 12:27). Their resolution as referents is given in their ongoing life. Jerusalem as true home is expected because inhabited by various kings in David's line, to be sure; but this is so because it is, in a first-order way, lived as Jesus, Jerusalem's Lord, whose own exile "outside the camp" becomes, however oddly, the fullest expression of its restoration. Since all find their home in him, exile and return are coincident in Christ.

The coincidence here is important. For the temporal framework presup-posed by these resolutions does not correspond neatly, let alone exhaus-tively, to the serial chronological scheme that expectation and fulfillment—along with its assumed phenomenologically identified experienced referents—might indicate. From a temporal standpoint, these resolutions

---

[41]N. T. Wright, in his more popularly oriented *Evil and the Justice of God* (Downers Grove, IL: InterVarsity Press, 2009), properly links the scriptural thematic of exile to theodicy (46-63) but is less clear about the properly figural reach of such a thematic into the character of restoration itself. He prefers, instead, to lay these links out on a still fairly strict serial chronological basis, as if what can prove to be the case in Old Testament terms—a figural exile that is broached for theodicy reasons by Israel—must no longer apply when it comes to Jesus himself (95-96). He goes further in engaging the cross's "extended" temporal role in Paul's ministry in something like "Redemption from the New Perspective? Towards a Multi-Layered Pauline Theology of the Cross" in *Redemption*, ed. S. T. Davis et al. (Oxford: Oxford University Press, 2006), 69-100, especially 94-98. But even here, there is a commitment to maintaining a commonsense past-present-future schema in a rather rigid, if not always illuminating, way, where "anticipation" (i.e., of restoration's "full" accomplishment) as a temporal category bears more weight than it can with clarity. I am not here arguing that "figural time" provides a *better* theodicy, in the sense of more morally realistic, than serial chronology, but such an argument could probably be made. More to the present point, I am arguing that theodicy probably requires both.

point rather to a certain kind of simultaneity and historical extension (or distention), such that, at least in this kind of case, sequential and mutually discrete (and exclusive) events cannot properly identify a given scriptural referent at all. They can only provide an often-limited perspective upon it. From a scriptural perspective, that is, what we learn from the text—its referents—are not fundamentally single narratives, but rather, in Jacob Neusner's phrase, narratives that act as "paradigms," whose forms actually found temporality's very nature in a primary fashion and provide coherence to what could otherwise appear as only random experiential surd.[42] In a specifically Christian sense, it is the formative emergence of these paradigms—let us say, for instance, Adam and Abraham and Paul and John—within the experience of this or that individual and the church especially, that discloses the single temporal character that is Christ Jesus' own life. History consistently looks like Jesus, even as that one narrative is ordered by its appropriated narrative figures.

This is, in fact, a standard way of understanding "figural time," as it upholds a certain way of reading the Bible. It does not contradict the kind of claims N. T. Wright might make about a "single narrative drama" that informs the whole of the world's time, nor of the accumulating expectations that inform the religious orientations of first-century Jews such as Paul. It can affirm that he was indeed, in his own view, living in the "middle stage" of a single overarching Deuteronomistic narrative of which we are a part encompassing sin, exile, and restoration.[43] That middle term is simply temporally extended. But how far? And in what directions? Within figural time, "extension" itself becomes part of the practice of phenomenal referentiality. Furthermore, Jesus as the Restorer does not somehow undercut or bring to an "end" such temporal extensions but rather simply complicates them in on himself yet more fully. "We had hoped that he was the one who was going to redeem Israel" (Lk 24:21 NIV). The Restorer reengages the middle stage in one sense, his resurrection underlining its experiential form. But more importantly, the Restorer is, as Wright has argued, granted his prophetic

---

[42]For an accessible entrée into Neusner's notion of temporal "paradigm," see his *The Theology of the Oral Torah: Revealing the Justice of God* (Montreal and Kingston, Canada: McGill-Queen's University Press, 1999), 6, 241-79.

[43]Wright, "Yet the Sun Will Rise Again," 21.

leverage within the coming of the eschaton, and thus, "eschatological time" takes over the dynamics of the grand narrative itself. And this is precisely where chronological sequence as an arbiter of referentiality breaks down, and where the historian's task trembles before the facts of God.

CRITICAL REALISM AND ITS PROBATIVE LIMITS

Wright's own approach to the historian's task, which would uncover to some fair extent the meaning of a historical text such as the Bible's, is governed by what he calls a "critical realism."[44] A critical realist will interpret a text according to the ongoing testing and adjustment of perspectives brought by reader, author(s), and cultural context, but also with the assumption of a stable and objective meaning to the text whose critical engagement must properly constrain interpretive directions and conclusions. These, finally, properly find their expression in the narrative forms by which textual meaning is always articulated in human terms.

> [Critical realism] is a way of describing the process of "knowing" that acknowledges the *reality of the thing known, as something other than the knower* (hence "realism"), while also fully acknowledging that the only access we have to this reality lies along the spiraling path of *appropriate dialogue or conversation between the knower and the thing known* (hence "critical"). This path leads to critical reflection on the products of our enquiry into "reality," so that our assertions about "reality" acknowledge their own provisionality.[45]

> A critical-realist reading of a text will recognize, and take fully into account, the perspective and context of the reader. But such a reading will still insist that, within the story or stories that seem to make sense of the whole of reality, there exists, as essentially other than and different from the reader, texts that can be read, that have a life and a set of appropriate meanings not only potentially independent of their author but also potentially independent of their reader; and that the deepest level of meaning consists in the stories, and ultimately the worldviews, which the texts thus articulate.[46]

---

[44]See N. T. Wright, *The New Testament and the People of God*, Christian Origins and the Question of God 1 (Minneapolis: Fortress, 1992), 32-46. A lucid presentation of this topic is given by Robert Stewart, "N. T. Wright's Hermeneutic: Part 1. Critical Realism," *The Churchman* 117, no. 2 (2003): 153-76. References to some of the informing and parallel philosophical categories at work in critical realism are usefully provided.

[45]Wright, *New Testament and the People of God*, 35.

[46]Ibid., 66.

Wright's version of critical realism is in fact an approach that is widely pursued in a practical way. Biblical commentators share varying degrees of worry over whether the approach implies a "purely" perspectival view of knowledge or even more fundamental skepticism. But most practitioners of the critical study of the past, in whatever field, employ some form of the "method," if that is what it is, if only because it is obvious that the past needs to be "studied," in part precisely because its form is somehow "missing" elements that must be hypothesized in order to be apprehended; and these hypotheses are ordered by a range of assumptions that are to be tested in concert with the evidence as one attempts to engage it.[47] At one clear end of the spectrum, one can observe how archaeologists, given a very limited collection of artifacts, must create contexts for them ("stories" or "narratives") whose shape can only be "critically"—that is, arguably on the basis of persuasive but rarely definitive evidence—theorized in order to elucidate the meaning of their contents.[48] But even here, precisely because the critical concerns are brought to bear on found objects and actual locations, there are parameters to skepticism, as well as immovable prods to potential truthful explanation. And as the evidence becomes more extensive, as artifacts proliferate, the critical edge becomes finer, as do the promises (and pitfalls) of understanding.

Most practicing historians do in fact subscribe to such a general method. Even a delicately attuned phenomenologist such as Paul Ricoeur, whose concern with historical understanding proved a lifelong intellectual project, affirmed its fundamental and unavoidable soundness.[49] Indeed, as a

---

[47]See Wright, *New Testament and the People of God*, 42, which presents just such a standard critical process in terms of "question, hypothesis, testing of hypothesis."

[48]The self-understanding of "interpretive" or "post-processual" archeology has been consciously driven by this critical edge. For a well-ordered example of this, see Julian Thomas, *Understanding the Neolithic*, rev. ed. (New York: Routledge, 2002); more relevant perhaps to biblical parallels, see Susan Alcock's *Archaeologies of the Greek Past: Landscape, Monuments, and Memories* (Cambridge: Cambridge University Press, 2002). The slide off the realist spectrum, however, can perhaps be seen in something like Barbara Bender, Sue Hamilton, and Christopher Tilley, *Stone Worlds: Narrative and Reflexivity in Landscape Archaeology* (Walnut Creek, CA: Left Coast Press, 2005), where the constraints of artifact and its ambiguously defined location dissolve into almost complete interpretive *jouissance*.

[49]See Paul Ricoeur, "Philosophies critiques de l'histoire: Recherche, explication, écriture," in *Philosophical Problems Today*, ed. G. Fløistad (Dordrecht: Kluwer Academic Publishers, 1994), 1:139-201; also, Ricoeur's *The Reality of the Historical Past* (Milwaukee: Marquette University Press, 1984).

phenomenologist, Ricoeur sought to describe what is taking place when we perceive the world and encounter it. To that extent, Wright's critical realism is common sense, almost by definition: this *is* what is going on when, not just a person of higher consciousness, but any normal person—the "we" of the common reader—perceives and comes to knowledge. And with this articulation of common sense comes, as with Wright, an assertion that what is common sense is embedded in what is in fact the case, what is "true." Not in a way that is exact in its expression; our common sense is always "more or less" true and thus must be critically examined to gauge its place within this continuum of probabilities. Still, Wright seems to think that this ongoing critical practice is good enough.

But is this actually enough? It is precisely the "more or less" of reality that opens up what metaphysically—the truly true—remains a chasm of ignorance within our daily and pragmatically compelling common actions. There is always something "missing" in our accounts of the past, let alone our simple apprehension or knowledge of it, even as we move in the direction of filling out our accounts. Indeed, "accounting" itself can never represent the past except analogically, that is, as some kind of human narrative, cognitively incommensurable with the *bruta facta*, whatever they may be. This is not to say that such narratives are untethered to reality. One need not embrace the skepticism of Oakeshott on this matter.[50] Narratives themselves can be readjusted in order to take account of facts that arise anew. But Ricoeur and Oakeshott both demonstrate how, at best, this readjustment is not something straightforward or commonsense in the least: it involves a morally complex engagement with the reality of death and of "dead things," of disappearance, ignorance, fear, hope, and so on. Historians engage this challenge less as pure historians than as those who simply must live as human beings, before the demands of a present whose connection to something we call "the past" is mysterious yet inescapable. Ricoeur, in my mind, rightly acknowledges this ongoing stage of historical inquiry as primarily moral. Just so, theodicy as a historiographical discipline drives theological renewal.[51]

---

[50]Among his several essays on the topic, see Michael Oakeshott, "The Activity of Being an Historian," in *Rationalism in Politics* (London: Methuen, 1962), 137-67.

[51]Paul Ricoeur, *Memory, History, Forgetting* (Chicago: University of Chicago Press, 2004), 350-70, on history and disappearance, and the way that remembering and forgetting, as a historical practice, is driven by the facing or avoiding of death. The book as a whole gathers together many

The point is, even a commonsense "critical realism" must *open up* a realm of mystery about the past and its actual status as "real" in relation to the present and cannot narrow that gap except to the degree that it seeks to ignore "history" altogether. When Scripture refers to something in "the past," this is itself to raise a question about the nature of our relationship with God, in any and every aspect: How are we made by God and toward God that we can be ordered toward a "knowledge" of something that lies outside the immediacy of our experience? Indeed, is this even possible? Is this not, in fact, something analogous to our relationship with our creation and our death, boundary realities that defy clear reference? From a theological point of view, just as it intersects with common sense, we must wonder whether "the past" to which Scripture refers is not simply a divine mode of the present, whose nature exceeds comprehension even as its moral demands can never be evaded. And this question, raised and answered if only cautiously and uncertainly, is precisely what lies behind the straightforward figural reading of something like "exile" that we have been examining.

If, for instance, we look at how Wright himself deals with a traditionally understood figural discussion within Scripture, we see some of this "opening up" language being used. In a case such as that of 1 Corinthians 10:1-14, where Paul's use of the exodus-church figure is presented in the language of historical event rooted in the actuality of Christ's transhistorical existence, Wright chooses to use an array of historically allusive but also historically specific terms at once: the exodus is "like" the Christian church's experience in Paul's day; there is an "analogy" at work; Paul's usage of the figure aims at making a certain "point"; aspects of the comparison are "unnatural"; but the Corinthians are actually located (historically?) in the "same drama"; the literal idea of the Rock following the Israelites is nonetheless "fanciful." Some of these terms indicate an ill-defined area of reality that can somehow encompass diverse historical moments and understandings (e.g., the same drama, or an analogy), but others seem to resist such an embrace (likeness, the real point, fancifulness).[52]

The seeming inexactitude of these terms taken together, however, is surely inevitable in this case. For the question of "what happened" or "what does

---

of Ricoeur's themes around the moral demand of a certain kind of remembering and historical practice.

[52]N. T. Wright, *Paul for Everyone: 1 Corinthians* (London: SPCK, 2004), 121-25.

this (present event/experience) mean" as it is related to the past has always been seen, in certain respects, to be nonstraightforward. Consider, for instance, the category of "the forgiveness of sins," especially in the scriptural language of "wiping away" or "being no more": largely because the character of these disappearing actions of the past is given in relation to God, their status as actions and now as past actions is governed by a divine reality that in itself surpasses humanly temporal definitions. One may wish to speak in terms of "analogical" description here, but even so, this only underscores the historical mystery involved in "forgiving sins" from the side of God. Likewise, the existence of the dead, in terms of their relationship to temporal sequence and its unidirectional "flow," must raise, but without ever being able to resolve in commonsense historical terms, a profound question regarding the nature of past and present. If God is the "God of the living" (Mk 12:27), precisely in his relationship with those who seem to be "dead" in historical terms, then the "past" cannot be accessible to the present *only* as the past. When dealing with these kinds of examples, we are thrust into an area of exegesis that must make use of more commonly accepted figural categories (if rarely applied as contemporary currency), such as that between the "earthly" and "heavenly" temples (e.g., Ex 25:40; Ezek 40–48; Heb 8:5; 9:23; Rev 4–5; 14; 21–22; etc.), where some kind of articulated historical form is proposed whose actual temporal, though not necessarily spatial, character is displaced. To speak of "simultaneity" in this case is itself only an analogical term, and certainly a misleading one if taken in terms of historical sequence. The kinds of claims made about temporal chronology in a book such as Jubilees, for instance—which provides a Jewish framework for figural referentiality culturally close to Jesus' period—are too uncertain to sustain clear historical categories of any kind.[53] But "simultaneity" as a divine "mode" of creative referentiality is one that, I think, appropriately indicates the direction historical thinking must take if it is to make sense of scriptural signification.

---

[53]James M. Scott's treatment of the book of Jubilees in this regard, in his *On Earth as in Heaven: The Restoration of Sacred Time and Sacred Space in the Book of Jubilees* (Leiden: Brill, 2005), is more interested in the chronological framework of the book's vision; but his detailed discussion of the heaven-earth mirroring axis of this vision offers a solid approach to the figural exegetical claim. This kind of axis goes beyond an explanation of extended exile in terms of "extended metaphor" (e.g., as argued in Martien A. Halvorson-Taylor, *Enduring Exile: The Metaphorization of Exile in the Hebrew Bible* [Leiden: Brill, 2011]).

Broadly speaking, a careful critical realism will allow these elements to pry apart the exhaustive character of serial chronology, in this case, in its application to scriptural referents; that is, it will encourage a critique of such chronology on the basis of data that do not fit its contours.

That critique has been explored most self-consciously (and, perhaps, still most fully) by Augustine and some of the tradition he inaugurated (e.g., Wycliffe). What does it mean for God to "create" something in which time itself is invented out of a divine will that is both logically and ontologically prior to it? Although he never systematized his thoughts on this, Augustine at various points indicated that the very reality of a divine Word who creates must somehow include within his (i.e., Christ's) own self the referents of all historical particulars, something that founds the figural exegetical enterprise as central to scriptural historical understanding.[54] These kinds of reflections, for Augustine and others, have rightly made exegetical notions of "ongoing exile," for instance, temporally dense but also chronologically mysterious and opaque. They have reshuffled temporal identities, with respect to referents such as "exile" and "restoration," making such reshuffling a constant of their referencing altogether. Exile and restoration, from a temporal perspective, are indeed elements that not only can but must coexist in a fundamental existential and moral simultaneity, whose precise explication remains a challenge.[55]

Theologically, a number of elements come to bear in such conclusions, as their conditions: obviously aspects of divine transcendence and creation are

---

[54]Augustine's concerns with time have been treated extensively and continue to engage interest. For the current general argument, see his *De Genesi ad litteram* (*Literal Meaning of Genesis*), bk V. (e.g., chaps. 30-45 especially), and the *Confessions*, book XIII, 34-38. More broadly on the philosophical aspects of this, see Richard Sorabji, *Time, Creation, and the Continuum: Theories in Antiquity and the Early Middle Ages* (Ithaca, NY: Cornell University Press, 1983), which remains the most thorough and serious synoptic treatment of Augustine's (among others) inherited arguments and concerns in this regard.

[55]I have used the term *existential* loosely thus far, standing in for historical, personal, and social experiences whose actual significance could well overlap with the kind of sociological-political concerns we find in a treatment of exile such as Daniel L. Smith-Christopher's *A Biblical Theology of Exile* (Minneapolis: Fortress, 2002): "experience," on Smith-Christopher's model, instigates social "responses" (e.g., by Israel or Judaism) that may turn to biblical tropes in order to form adjustive meanings for otherwise cognitively difficult situations. At issue in the present essay, however, is the character of these tropes as "divinely given," and if so, as given by the divine agent of final restoration. What is "existential," then, must also refer to the way that human experience is scripturally founded in a prior way that necessarily raises the question of temporal sequence.

primary. But so too is the priority of the scriptural text as a divinely creative agent in the articulation of temporality itself (this, at least, touches on the ideas of a "heavenly Torah" in Judaism and Wycliffe's scriptural "ideas"):[56] the Word and its "words" are logically prior to historicality as it is experienced in any commonsense way. (Here, obviously, the Christian theologian—and historian!—must go further than the atheistic phenomenologist.) It is not so much that exile and restoration are temporally simultaneous realities as that they are comprehended together in the metaphysically prior reality of the Word, the living Christ. Therefore, Christ's reality founds the history of exile and restoration both, and their relation to him "in time" is secondary to his originating and exhaustive comprehension of their very being at any temporal moment. We do not look to history to find Christ; but at Christ, to find history in its divinely constructed form.

But this also means that in the history we have, we *do* find Christ. Here, the theodicy character of much Christian exile literature gathers an inevitable theological demand: whatever "restoration from exile" might mean—what *Jesus* means when he speaks in these scriptural terms—must cohere with the divine justice that orders the events of human suffering *in* exile, even within the church's redeemed life. If the words of Christ are divine words, then their meaning must explicate the fact that the freedom brought by Christ is one that takes place within the existential experience of *continued* exile itself. This is where the question of scriptural reference becomes so specific. In this case, the *peregrinatio* theme (or better, the various historical instantiations of *peregrination*)—Abraham perhaps, or John the Baptist, or Paul's journeys, or Hebrews 11, or simply Adam and Eve's expulsion—provides the primary figural limits to the words of Jesus. In the same way his own divine life of incarnate pilgrimage and expulsion (Jn 1 and Heb 13) must tether the semantics of his restorationist discourse and its resurrection focus. And it is just this semantic constraint that will therefore provide a new energy to the historical challenges of Jewish Israel's "ongoing exile" as well, in particular as it has been shaped by the reality of vicitimization at specifically Christian hands. If the witnesses of Christ, who themselves recorded the words of Jesus in their integrity and order are yet to be

---

[56]On Wycliffe, a good place to start is Ian Christopher Levy, "John Wyclif's Neoplatonic View of Scripture in Its Christological Context," *Medieval Philosophy and Theology* 11 (2003): 227-40.

"true" witnesses of the promises Jesus offered, then their own ethical denial of this or that implied referent must be taken into account in evaluating the "intent" of the words themselves. To say, that is, that "this is what Jesus meant when he spoke of exile and restoration," is useful and true only to the extent that it coheres with the historical outcome of the words themselves. Scripture and the Christian tradition (the latter often despite itself) in fact offer lines of interpretation that permit the articulation of such coherence. But these lines do not necessarily follow the clear path of the semantic contextual reconstructions of the historical critic, nor should they.

Figural History

Wright has long insisted that the Christian gospel—and the Scriptures that articulate it—is concerned with "flesh and blood" referentiality, as opposed to abstracted religious categories: Jesus, his death on a cross and resurrection, are "real" in the sense of having existentially temporal foundations.[57] It is this reality that grants their power for temporal beings like ourselves. Hence the historical critic's role is, for the church's practical witness as much as for the truth's sake, essential in uncovering and buttressing this kind of reference. Surely Wright is correct in this insistence. And his defense of the centrality of the historian's contribution to evangelical witness is thus also well founded. But such concerns become evangelically limiting if they are satisfied by the identification only of punctiliar temporal reference within the scriptural text. For one thing, the "flesh and blood" target of historical criticism must itself uncover the moral ambiguities of such reference. Naming "exile" and "restoration" as "just this" or "just that" in historical terms, from a scriptural (that is, in Christian terms, theologically substantive) perspective, is to invite the objections of historical contradiction: "ongoing exile" is seemingly never overcome in a historically precise way. That is Calvin's tacit assumption because it is his explicit experience. And if this contradiction is ignored in favor of such limited temporal

---

[57]See Wright, *Evil and the Justice of God*, 94, 116, etc. The fact that one prominent secular investigator of the theoretical physical basis for what might be viewed as a figurally ordered history, the physicist Julian Barbour, calls the actual universe of time's experience "Platonia," may well confirm Wright's worries. See Julian Barbour, *The End of Time: The Next Revolution in Physics* (Oxford: Oxford University Press, 2001). Yet such a worry, nonetheless, emerges from a confusion of "flesh and blood" with a particular definition of temporality, and so begs the question.

reference, "exile" itself therefore threatens to become a theologically irrelevant category in scriptural terms.

In this case, I have suggested that theodicy represents, in part, a wedge in historical criticism's scriptural application, but also perhaps a prod: the ramification of historical reference that figuration assumes is itself the product of historical criticism's inherent moral force. Second, however, the historical-critical enterprise must always face into its own incapacities in the face of a reality—of "history" understood simply as a temporal set—that is resistant to definition and comprehension. Here, Wright's treatment of the resurrection offers a kind of parable: one can walk to the edge of the tomb and confront its empty confines, but at this point a threshold of understanding is encountered that defies the categories of temporally referential precision.[58] It is not so much that the figural exegetical approach "takes over" at this point—faith picking up where science leaves off—as this approach orders scriptural referentiality *in congruence* with this reality of such a threshold existing at all, given the truth of God's creative being. The referents of temporal experience themselves emerge across this threshold as coextensive gifts of God's own self "in Christ." That is a discovery that, once made, historical experience itself confirms, over and over. And once made, as Calvin, or Origen, or Augustine and so many others did, it reasserts itself within the continual and repeated reading of the Scriptures, again and again. Exile and restoration are both aspects of the form of the one Lord, Jesus Christ, Son of David, of Abraham, of Adam, and "son of God" (Mt 1:1 and Lk 3:38).

---

[58]See N. T. Wright, "Christian Origins and the Resurrection of Jesus: The Resurrection of Jesus as a Historical Problem," *Sewanee Theological Review* 41, no. 2 (1998): 1-13.

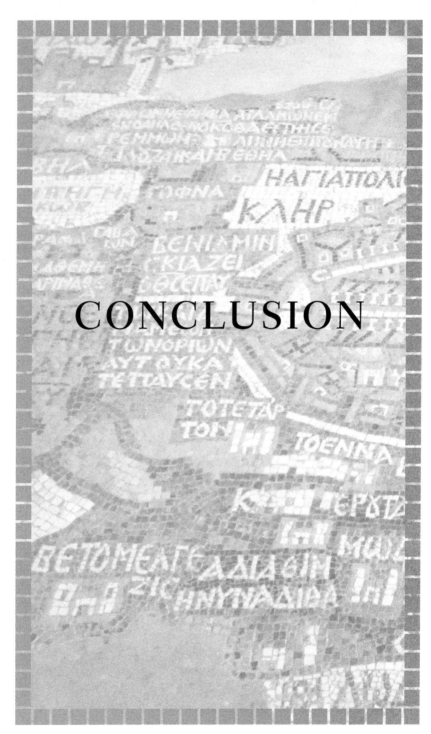

CONCLUSION

RESPONDING TO *EXILE*

N. T. WRIGHT

I AM EXTREMELY GRATEFUL TO THE EDITOR and the contributors for this fascinating collection of essays. I have mixed memories of the conference, back in 2010, at which this dialogue began: Hans Boersma recalls me saying some unguarded things about the Reformers, and I recall him saying some—to me—astonishing things about how one should do theology. But more of that anon. I am delighted that slowly but surely the issue of exile in the Second Temple Jewish world, and the impact of that way of looking at things on Jesus and the early Christians, is firmly back on the scholarly agenda. This, we should perhaps say, represents a significantly new moment in the discussion of early Christianity. Nobody that I am aware of in the 1970s or even the 1980s was looking at things this way. Even when Ed Sanders wrote energetically about "restoration eschatology" in relation particularly to Jesus, he was not, I think, referring to the specific theme we are discussing here, though his proposals can certainly be mapped on to this larger theme, and profitably so.[1] All credit to Odil Steck, whose work stands behind so much of this discussion, and to James Scott, who has labored mightily to bring it to this point.[2]

In the long gestation of the present collection, several other things have happened. In particular, I have found myself making the basic case yet one more time, in the second (and scene-setting) chapter of *Paul and the Faithfulness of God*.[3] My opening essay in the present volume draws freely on that

---

[1]E. P. Sanders, *Jesus and Judaism* (London: SCM Press, 1985).
[2]See the notes to the opening chapter.
[3]N. T. Wright, *Paul and the Faithfulness of God* (London: SPCK, 2013).

treatment, and though there is no doubt more that could be said I would hope that future discussions would engage with the material set out there, and the arguments that I have advanced against those who still resist the whole notion. The essays presented here approach things, for the most part, in what seems to me a much healthier mode than some previous treatments, probing from different angles rather than either straightforwardly affirming what I have said or rejecting it out of hand. Some misunderstandings remain, and I shall do my best in what follows to clarify the relevant issues. In particular, the responses from the two colleagues in systematic theology—for which I am grateful, since I too believe in the importance of dialogue between our disciplines—raise none the less some disturbing questions about whether it is even possible for theologians to hear what biblical specialists are saying. And perhaps vice versa.

The material falls naturally into three areas: biblical and Jewish studies, New Testament studies, and systematic theology. The weight rightly falls on the first of these, with six essays as opposed to three on the New Testament and two on theology. In each category I shall make some general remarks followed by specific comments on the individual papers.

BIBLICAL AND JEWISH STUDIES

The case for a "continuing exile" understanding of Second Temple Jewish thought rests on a variety of evidence, and I am grateful that Philip Alexander has insisted not only on written texts but also on the actual events of the period, especially times of war and revolution; and also on the necessity to understand the deep motivations of those who engaged in this kind of activity by invoking such categories as *ideology* or *worldview*. This is, after all, what historians characteristically do, trying to understand why things happened as they did and answering that question in terms of the way people thought, what they believed, what they were hoping for—in other words, the implicit narratives they believed themselves to be living in. Many historians at the present time, looking back a century or so, are trying to understand why the First World War happened and why it took the course it did; and, like Alexander, they are using all available sources to reconstruct the implicit narratives of the key agents, the stories they told themselves about the way the world was and the role of their own nation within that world and those stories.[4] Thus, however much we agree with Brueggemann and Kiefer, in this volume, that there were undoubtedly many Jews in the first century who saw things differently, we still have to explain the large-scale revolutions and wars, and the various other movements that swirled this way and that, in the period from the Maccabees to Bar-Kokhba. It is indeed highly likely that many Jews living in the ancient homeland would have preferred to continue with their present less-than-satisfactory existence rather than risk everything for an eschatological vision they may not have understood or shared. And it is certainly likely that many Jews in the period who lived elsewhere, whether still in Babylonia or in the Mediterranean diaspora, did not share the eschatological urgency of those who clung to the Deuteronomic narrative or looked back to Daniel 9 and prayed for the moment of ultimate renewal, the ultimate Jubilee. I doubt whether too many dispersed Jewish communities actually saw themselves in the idealistic way that they were seen by writers from Philo to some rabbis (and indeed some much more recent Jewish writings such as the very interesting 1869 Philadelphia Conference quoted by Philip Alexander) as signs of a coming day when, through the Jewish people, the one God would reveal himself to all the world. But since there are passages in Scripture, not least the Psalms and Isaiah, that hint at exactly this kind of thing, we should not be surprised to find some evidence pointing in that direction. Though I may not have made this clear in my early attempts to discuss this whole question, my point was never that *all* first-century Jews believed themselves to be in exile in the sense of the "extended exile" of Daniel 9; merely that a significant number of Jews living in the ancestral homeland saw things this way, and that this understanding of the ongoing biblical story, and of the need for a resolution, did indeed drive eschatological expectations of the sort that would then be encoded in a claim about the kingdom of God.

That, indeed, is the overall point that constitutes my main response to Walter Brueggemann and Jörn Kiefer. I fully take Brueggemann's point that the texts we possess may well not represent a "popular" position and may well mask considerably more diversity on the ground. (I hope, by the way,

---

[4]A fine example is Margaret MacMillan, *The War That Ended Peace: How Europe Abandoned Peace for the First World War* (London: Profile Books, 2013), especially chap. 9: "What Were They Thinking? Hopes, Fears, Ideas, and Unspoken Assumptions."

that the second chapter of *Paul and the Faithfulness of God* will refute any charge of being "selective"; I have tried to present a full range of evidence.) But I think Philip Alexander's study of actual popular uprisings and the like gives at least a partial answer to this: whatever texts we have, plenty of people joined in these mass movements, not because some great leader forced them into doing so but because there really was, as Josephus says, a sense that scriptural promises might now at last be coming to fulfillment. I do not see in these essays any reference to Roger Beckwith's studies on calendar and chronology, but they remain important; they first alerted me to the ways in which different groups were reading Daniel 9—and hence to the fact that Daniel 9, with its prediction of a greatly elongated "exile," remained important as a text that could drive not only speculation but also real social and political events.[5] The actual movements indicate that even if such texts were "intensely didactic" and were "great paradigmatic narratives sponsored by the elites," that teaching, and that narrative, had borne fruit in the imagination and actions of a great many in the first century. Of course, there may equally well have been many Jews, both in Palestine and further afield, who were relatively content with their lot. I persist in regarding the Sadducees in this way, suspicious of any new-fangled doctrines such as resurrection that might encourage people to believe that a new era, the "age to come," really was on the way. Undoubtedly many did take seriously the command in Jeremiah 29:1-9 to settle down in Babylon and "seek the welfare of the city." But there is no reason to suppose that they all thereby forgot what the next five verses in Jeremiah were about, namely, the promise of return to the land. The point is not so much, as Brueggemann says, that the biblical texts in question are few in number; the point is, how are those texts being read in the first century, and what biblical echoes would be awoken by someone going about announcing that now was the time for God to become king?

A particular question is raised by Brueggemann's challenge on the metaphorical meaning of exile. Of course at one level the word *exile*, as applied to people living in Jerusalem, must be metaphorical. This is important for several reasons, not least the way in which some theologians have seized on the point in order to say that since it is metaphorical it can be a metaphor

---

[5]See R. T. Beckwith, *Calendar and Chronology, Jewish and Christian: Biblical, Intertestamental and Patristic Studies* (Leiden: Brill, 1996), incorporating earlier articles.

for other things as well. The question is not whether "exile" is a metaphor, but what this metaphor is referring to and what it is saying about it. My point is meant to ward off the kind of interpretation proposed in the present volume by Ephraim Radner, in which exile is simply an idea that might be used to interpret, for instance, the present state of human beings in general, "exiled" from their true home in heaven (see below). The explicit dehistoricization is the problem. The point is that from Daniel 9 onwards many Jews in a variety of traditions, visible in some texts and in some popular movements, saw their Bible in terms of a long narrative in search of a conclusion, a conclusion that would indeed involve the land, generating a hope that was certainly not "disinterested" and which did indeed constitute a claim. Claim and counterclaim is what we see in the events of 66–70 CE, and if in that same first century someone else was announcing God's kingdom, alluding to Daniel from time to time, and saying (among many other things) that the meek would inherit the land, then it looks as though that person and his followers must be understood within that same complex and contested world.

A similar point must be made about the temple. I would not argue that all first-century Jews were equally interested in the temple and its symbolic importance for the present life of God's people and for their future hope. But granted the way in which the temple theme assumes great importance in the New Testament, going back it seems to Jesus himself, it makes sense to try to understand how that theme would actually play out, what implicit narratives it would carry. This is not a matter of subsuming everything to the temple, but is rather an attempt to think Jewishly about God, God's presence, and God's purpose. For too long modern Protestantism has downplayed the temple; but if we are to understand first-century God-language—let alone kingdom-of-God language!—we need at least to see how the grammar worked. Thus I am perfectly happy to concede Brueggemann's point that many in the Second Temple period had no desire for a return, though his final hermeneutical flourish about today's Christians who should not be looking for "flight to a more perfect home," but rather ought to "remain, and to remain faithful" tells me that he, like the systematicians, has not actually grasped the central point that I have been trying to make. I am *not* saying that exile becomes a paradigm for some kind of true spirituality, such that today's Christians should construe their own situation that way. (They might, for all sorts of reasons, such as those of Calvin in Geneva; but that is quite beside the point.) I am saying that the New Testament as a whole (whether we take Matthew's genealogy, or Paul's retelling of Israel's story in Romans 9–10, climaxing with the Messiah's inauguration of the "return" spoken of in Deuteronomy 30, or any one of a number of other options) insists that the long biblical story has reached its messianic moment, its end-of-exile moment, in the events concerning Jesus of Nazareth. In fact, once this point is fully grasped, the application that Brueggemann desires comes through all the more strongly, since from the resurrection onwards what we have is precisely the challenge to "remain, and to remain faithful," since Jesus possesses all authority not only in "heaven" but also "on earth" (Mt 28:18).

Thus while it is clear, as Kiefer indicates, that many Jewish groups made a virtue out of diaspora, and saw it not as divine punishment but as divine opportunity, the phenomenon to which I have tried to draw attention concerns the significant number of Jewish groups, again as evidenced in the large-scale movements of the period, for whom the present state of affairs was deeply unsatisfactory and who mapped that dissatisfaction on the covenantal narrative of Deuteronomy 27–32 and the promises of Daniel 9. It is true that one cannot speak simply of *the* exile, since the Hebrew Scriptures are full of exiles and returns (the most obvious being the sojourn in Egypt, or indeed Jacob's fourteen years with Laban). The somewhat ambiguous verse Ezekiel 11:16 needs to be read in the context of the book as a whole, in which the divine glory abandons the temple but promises eventually to return; this verse is, in fact, *part of* that promise of return (set in the context of a polemic against those who had *not* gone to Babylon), not some kind of validation of permanent diaspora. Thus I thoroughly agree that the ending of Chronicles, and the placing of the books of Chronicles at the close of the nascent canon, was a way of indicating that the story was not yet over and that "true restoration" (Kiefer's phrase) was still awaited. My point is simply that anyone reading the Hebrew canon as we now have it—without wishing to get into the questions of when anybody saw it as a *canon*!—would see the whole thing, from Genesis to Chronicles, in the same way as some at least (including Josephus) saw the Torah from Genesis to Deuteronomy: a long story still in search of an ending. I do not think it will do to cite Josephus,

Nehemiah, or Daniel as an indication that those who wrote or edited their stories were looking for salvation *within* exile rather than *from* it. Esther 3:8 and Daniel 6:13 (not Dan 6:14, as in Kiefer) do indeed show that Jews in exile could still worship their own God, but the context in both cases indicates dangerous local hostility to their doing so, and Daniel in particular is looking toward Jerusalem (Dan 6:10). Only by taking selected highlights from the book could anyone imagine that Daniel and his friends were settling into a happy, long-term accommodation with Babylon. For Kiefer to cite Deuteronomy 4:27 to demonstrate that Judean exiles "were able to find YHWH," as part of an argument that "the Hebrew Bible does not theologically disparage Israel's existence in exile," is extraordinary given the paragraph in which that verse comes (Deut 4:25-31, anticipating the fuller statement in Deuteronomy 27–30). There, exile is explicitly a punishment for idolatry, and the idea that the exiles will reach out and find YHWH while in exile is not so that they can then happily stay there, but precisely so that he will remember his covenant—which, in the larger context of the book, must mean that he will restore his people to the land promised to the patriarchs. Exile and diaspora do not, indeed, mean the end of the story with God. Kiefer is obviously right to stress that for many Jews living outside the land there was no sense either of punishment or of a theologically urgent need to return. But, as I said before, when we find on the one hand large-scale movements in the first century for which the only serious explanation is an upsurge of scripturally fueled eschatological expectations, and when we find on the other hand a kingdom-of-God movement claiming that "the time is fulfilled," we are right to look to the exile-and-restoration paradigm of Deuteronomy and Daniel as the framework within which such movements make best sense. If someone says, "This is the moment you've all been waiting for" when nobody has been waiting for anything, such a preacher is unlikely to find many hearers.

Thus I am happy to welcome the remarkably detailed study of Robert Hiebert about the ways in which, beyond what might have been there in the parent text, the Septuagint highlights exilic meanings and also the promise of a restoration "predicated upon the forgiveness of sins." Hiebert has, it seems to me, added very considerably to the weight of the argument I and others have put forward. My only question about his essay is whether

4 Maccabees 17:22 will quite bear the weight that some writers are now trying to put on it, that is, of providing a possible parallel for the meaning required for *hilastērion* in Romans 3:25.[6] I have discussed this in a forthcoming article. But Hiebert thereby raises the right question, as also does Robert Kugler: Granted an extended exile (Kugler completely accepts my basic point), how is that exile to come to an end?

To address this question, however, Kugler poses a sharp antithesis: Is the end of exile "the work of God," or is it "the result of renewed human righteousness"? Granted that "righteousness" is mentioned in Daniel 9—God's righteousness on the one hand, i.e., his faithfulness both to the promise to punish sinful Israel and to the promise to restore Israel in the end, and the people's righteousness, or rather the lack thereof, on the other hand—it seems stretching the point to smuggle that language back into Deuteronomy 30, where it is not mentioned, and then to make it thematic. Kugler seems to be translating the themes of the relevant texts into the language of later dogmatics, as for instance when he speaks (despite 1QS!) of a "return on the basis of the covenanters' righteousness" and of "the effectual character of their own righteousness." This looks more like part of an attempt to prove that Second Temple Jews were guilty of what the sixteenth-century Reformers saw as "works-righteousness" than an actual study of the way Jewish minds worked in the relevant period. Nor do I find it helpful to refer to God's "pride," though I take it that Kugler means by this the reputation of YHWH among the nations, as for instance in Exodus 32:12. The attempt to prise apart the divine purpose and action from the human purpose and action is not, I think, so easily managed in relation to biblical or postbiblical texts (sometimes it is quite clear; at other times it is not). His eventual distinction of three possibilities (human righteousness precipitating divine action, God determining the timing and nature of exile's end, and God's acting alone) strikes me as thoroughly artificial. When he admits that the three views can "overlap in single works," this impression is confirmed. When he says that I "seem to favor" the picture of exile's end offered in Deuteronomy 30, this is because (1) I find the last chapters of Deuteronomy playing a very significant role in many Second Temple accounts, and (2) I

---

[6]See, e.g., J. J. Williams, *Christ Died for Our Sins: Representation and Substitution in Romans and the Jewish Martyrological Background* (Eugene, OR: Pickwick Publications, 2015).

find Deuteronomy 30 placed at the crucial point in Paul's own telling of the story (Rom 10). And when Kugler declares that ideas he finds incompatible are held together not only in Jewish texts but in a book such as 1 Peter, I think we can agree with his earlier statement that "a hallmark of ancient ethnic groups was their openness to a diversity of views on matters inessential to a group's identity." This is, I think, notoriously true of the questions he is discussing, namely the interplay of divine sovereignty and human responsibility. I suspect that the "seemingly mutually exclusive theological notions" he finds in 1 Peter are just that: seemingly—to those schooled in various comparatively modern systems of thought. These questions, though interesting in themselves, and certainly deserving of more detailed study, are ultimately beside the point for the present volume, where Kugler simply acknowledges the main contention: even though we may find it hard to say how different Jewish groups envisaged the ultimate end of exile being accomplished, many such groups did indeed presuppose the belief that exile was ongoing and that sooner or later it would come to an end.

The essay by Dorothy Peters provides a welcome historical thickening to these somewhat abstract theological discussions, though in terms of the overall argument of the present book it simply reinforces the main point. The question of balance between divine and human activity in bringing exile to an end had more to do, in this period, with the question of whether and at what stage loyal Jews would be required to engage in actual violence. Would they, like the Israelites at the Red Sea, simply "stand still and see the salvation of YHWH"? Or would they have to engage in terrorist activity, like the Sicarii, or more organized military operations, like the Maccabees, Bar-Kokhba, and many besides? These too are fascinating questions deserving of more study. The questions raised by Robert Kugler could profitably be mapped on to them for a complete picture to emerge. But they, too, simply undergird the point I have been making all along: many Second Temple Jews regarded the present state of affairs in terms of the Deuteronomic narrative of exile and return, and were concerned to act appropriately at the single, unrepeatable moment when redemption would occur. It is that sense of a single moment that constitutes the main point to be made over against the systematic theologians' attempts to generalize, to turn exile into a theological motif and thereby to avoid the challenge of history. But more of that anon.

The final paper on the biblical and Jewish context of exile is that of Philip Alexander, which to my mind—with no disrespect to the other contributors!— I regard as unquestionably the most important piece in this book. Students of the New Testament could learn a lot from studying it and following up the many important references in the notes. He is obviously right, it seems to me, to draw attention to the way in which many Jewish groups of the period thought, planned, prayed, and acted in relation to what people today might call an "ideology" but they would have called Torah, or something like it (focused, as he says, on Deuteronomy). He provides a fascinating brief account of the various movements from the Maccabees to the Herods, showing that whatever differences there were between the various groups they were differences *within* an assumed paradigm in which national sovereignty was the goal, present exile the problem, and, increasingly, an expected Messiah was the solution, at least for some. So too with his account of the first war with Rome.[7] He rightly stresses that the rebels were longing for freedom in *their* sense as opposed to the normal Roman one. So too with the later revolts, culminating in Bar Kokhba. Alexander's discussion of the rabbinic period is most suggestive: the disasters of the wars had led to a rejection of messianic nationalism. The "translation" of the longing for the return of the Shekinah to an actual temple in Jerusalem into the promise that the Shekinah would abide with a group, or even an individual, studying Torah is especially telling, not least in relation to Alexander's subsequent discussion of Jesus. Alexander's discussion of the fraught questions surrounding the varieties of contemporary Zionism, though necessarily brief, is evocative and suggestive. So, too, are the final two paragraphs on Jesus, though here I think Alexander could perhaps have gone much further, granted all that he says earlier in his essay. I agree that for Jesus the theme of the renewed heart appears central—in line, arguably, with the very

---

[7]My one question to Alexander would be whether, as he suggests, Martin Goodman's book *The Ruling Class of Judea: The Origins of the Jewish Revolt Against Rome, A. D. 66–70* (Cambridge: Cambridge University Press, 1987) supports him here: Goodman argues, against Josephus's blaming the "Fourth Philosophy" for the war, that it was actually the Sadducean hierarchy who were most to blame. See my discussion in *The New Testament and the People of God* (Minneapolis: Fortress, 1992), 178-79.

passage in Deuteronomy 30 that we have seen to be so important, and also with its various developments in Jeremiah and elsewhere. That by itself would indicate, within the frame of reference we have all been studying, that Jesus himself was invoking the "new covenant" theme. The parallel, then, with the rabbis is only apparent; where, for them, the internalization of Torah was a way of avoiding apocalyptic eschatology, for Jesus it was a sign that he believed he was inaugurating it in his own kingdom-of-God work, and then, yes, ultimately in his death and what would follow. He believed that he was bringing the prophecies of Isaiah, Jeremiah, Daniel, and the others to their appointed destination. This was how the long story would reach its destination. To Klausner and others it may indeed have appeared as though Jesus were lacking in the normal savvy wisdom or shrewd planning associated with politics. But this did not mean that his vision was purely spiritual or internal only. The Sermon on the Mount is a real agenda for real public living, replete with danger precisely because it enjoins a new way of being human, a way that, to be sure, Jesus' followers would have to work out later, but in which, as in John 16, they would call the world to account. Thus I am not sure that for Jesus "everything begins in the heart of the individual": I think for him that everything begins with his own powerful kingdom work, producing a proposed and shocking "return from exile" in line with Isaiah 52 and other passages. The transformed heart is one of the necessary by-products, the inner and transforming sign of the outer and world-changing divine action.

New Testament Studies

The New Testament is represented here by the essays of Scot McKnight, Tony Cummins, and Timo Eskola. I am in considerable agreement with the first two, less so with the third, but in each case there are interesting points to raise.

McKnight is absolutely right to make the substantive connection between "the age to come" and "return from exile," though only in the period up to the Bar Kokhba revolt. As Philip Alexander shows, the rabbis turned sharply away from the kind of "end-of-exile" ambitions connected with renewed national sovereignty and possible messianism, but they did not stop hoping for the "age to come." (This is an important point over against those who have supposed that any sense of the "two ages" means we are in the presence of something called "apocalyptic.") They merely detached it from the large narrative of Scripture; indeed, though they remained massively shaped by Israel's story, and by the smaller stories within it, they seem to many observers to have lost or deliberately abandon the sense of a single great story arriving at its divinely intended goal. (Again, it is wearisome but necessary to insist that this has nothing to do with "progressive revelation" or a Hegelian sense of "development," and everything to do with the dark and complex narrative encoded in dozens of scriptural and postscriptural passages.)

I agree with McKnight, too, that what he calls the C-F-R-C story, as regularly understood in Western Christianity, is in danger of reducing the story of Jesus to the story of "how we get saved," often within an otherworldly or Platonic sense of "salvation." I confess that I am not so sanguine about his proposed A-B-A' scheme. It is clever, and it is important to note the sharp rejection of the monarchic proposal in 1 Samuel 8. But, at least on a surface reading of the Torah and Former Prophets, it does appear that monarchy is not an unmixed evil. The book of Judges complains bitterly that there was no king in Israel, so everyone did as they pleased. Deuteronomy 17 gives permission for the appointment of a king, and issues regulations. Whatever we may say about David and Solomon in other respects, David was "the man after God's own heart," and Solomon was the proverbially wise king. I am not prepared to jettison, as some want to do, the monarchic traditions from the Psalter and Isaiah—and that, I should add (knowing that Walter Brueggemann, among others, will be reading this!) has nothing to do with my being British, or indeed an Anglican. The present-day British monarchy, after all, has very little in common with ancient monarchies. For that one would do better to look, say, to the power wielded by an American president; there are good reasons why political theorists two hundred years ago saw the presidency in terms of elected monarchy, as in some European countries. Despite the obvious and long-lasting failures in the post-Solomonic monarchies, the Psalms keep recalling the original ideal, to which indeed the figure of Adam himself in Genesis 1–2 may be linked, as Psalm 8 probably indicates. The fact that the kings did not match up to the noble vision of Psalm 72 does not mean that the psalm was wrong or hopelessly idealistic. The institution of the monarchy may have been a broken and damaged signpost to God's eventual purpose, but it was such a signpost none the less. I do not think that, in a world where the Psalms continued to be sung, "YHWH the King became a distant memory." I think, rather, that this noble theme was constantly before the people, functioning both as critique and as hope.

This, however, is really a quibble. We both agree that Jesus' announcement of the kingdom of God, and his embodiment of that new reality, belongs on the map of ancient Israelite and Jewish eschatology in which the messianic moment would arrive to put an end to the prolonged (and sin-caused) exile. That is what matters.

In the same way, I am quite prepared to agree with Tony Cummins that the theme of exile may be "both less and more significant in Paul" than I have suggested. I think that, like some other themes, it has been subsumed for Paul under the massive and central point that the Messiah "died for our sins in accordance with the Bible"—granted that, of course, "in accordance with the Bible" does not mean "as I can show with two or three proof-texts" but rather "in accordance with the entire flow of the narrative." In that narrative, and in both Jesus and Paul, I totally agree of course that exile should not be "detached from its historical and geopolitical origins," and should not be seen "as but an example, type, or metaphor" (granted what I said earlier about metaphor). Much of what follows is Cummins's own elegant summary and exposition of my views, and of course he gets it right. I fully admit that I find myself at certain points saying "somehow" ("Jesus had *somehow* borne Israel's destiny," and so forth). There are points in theology and exegesis where we can see that two things are regarded by the writer as inextricably bound up together but where it is not clear, or not to us, what precisely has to be presupposed for this to be self-evident in the first century but still puzzling in the twenty-first. In such circumstances, I think it is better to say "somehow" and to leave that as a challenge to others to figure it out more fully, than to back off and leave the point unmade. Ultimately, Cummins's own proposal—that exile in the relevant Pauline passages "could be more fully seen as functioning within the all-compassing economy of God"—is what I tried to argue in *Paul and the Faithfulness of God* chapter seven, and I am grateful to Tony for thematizing it in this way.

With Timo Eskola I am not so sure. I confess that, despite his sending me a copy some months before I had to write this paper, I have been so busy that I have still not read his own obviously important book *A Narrative Theology of the New Testament*.[8] From a quick glance there is a great deal there with which I need, and want, to engage. But some points in his lively essay in the present volume must be taken up, however briefly.

First, I am of course glad that Eskola, like most of the contributors here, is in full support of my basic contention about the ongoing exile. I do not think, however, that this theme is found in either Sanders or Meyer (and, by the way, I do not think Meyer was a "mentor" to Sanders: they were colleagues at McMaster University for several years).[9] They both insisted strongly on "restoration eschatology," but neither of them linked this to the sense of ongoing exile drawn from Daniel 9 and interpreted—as is Daniel 9 itself—in the light of Deuteronomy 27–32. More importantly, perhaps, Eskola's paper hinges on what seems to me a completely false dichotomy. He seems to think that in studying Paul we have to choose between the theme of exile and restoration on the one hand and the theme of the covenant narrative on the other, and that "new perspective" writers, among whom he naturally numbers me, are committed to the covenant narrative and hence are inclined to soft-pedal exile and restoration. For him, new perspective implies continuity between Judaism and the church, whereas exile and restoration would imply discontinuity.

This, however, is very unhelpful. For a start, there are as many versions of the "new perspective" as there are scholars writing under that broad headline. Ed Sanders, Jimmy Dunn, and I—not to mention Richard Hays, Bruce Longenecker, and a host of others—never thought of ourselves as a group; we never formed a seminar at SBL or SNTS; and we have always had many serious disagreements and divergences among ourselves. At many points some of us line up with quite different paradigms. The "new perspective" has meant many things to many people, and the myth of its supposed unity is only really kept alive by those who know in their bones that whatever it means, they are against it. I have written about this recently elsewhere.[10] I never "abandoned" Sanders's premises because I never shared them in the first

---

[8]Timo Eskola, *A Narrative Theology of the New Testament: Exploring the Metanarrative of Exile and Restoration*, WUNT 350 (Tübingen: Mohr Siebeck, 2015).

[9]On Meyer, and his relationship to Sanders, see my preface to the second edition of his wonderful book *The Aims of Jesus* (San Jose, CA: Pickwick Publications, 2002).

[10]See Wright, *Paul and His Recent Interpreters* (London: SPCK, 2015), chaps. 3 and 4.

place; nor do I adopt Sanders's category of "plight," except in the general sense that that is a useful word to pinpoint certain issues, issues indeed where I have argued explicitly and at length for a different view from that of Sanders. And so on.

All this comes to a head when Eskola suggests that if we stress "exile and restoration" then "the covenant has been canceled." Not so: as in Daniel 9 (and indeed, once more, Deuteronomy), exile is precisely to be seen as *covenantal punishment*, and restoration is *covenantal restoration*. I was amused to be told that "dogmatic convictions start to influence" modern discussions of Paul, as though that were not always the case, back to F. C. Baur and beyond. What has influenced me more than anything else in my interpretation of Paul is my growing understanding of the various hopes and aspirations of Second Temple Jews and the way they drew on their Scriptures to articulate them. This has nothing to do with being pro- or anti-Luther, or indeed pro- or anti-Sanders, and it certainly does not mean that I have tried to combine Luther and Sanders in some fresh way, let alone that I have "changed sides." These are anachronistic boxes into which to force either Paul or my exposition of him. Eskola has not, I think, grasped what I have tried to make central: that, for Paul, it was Jesus as Israel's Messiah, more specifically Jesus as the *crucified and risen* Messiah, in whom simultaneously the covenant with Israel had been fulfilled and refocused. I have tried to suggest that the discontinuity that is visible all through ("I through the Law died to the Law, so that I might live to God," and so on) is held by Paul within a larger continuity that is, in fact, the whole argument of Romans 9–11: "The word of God has not failed." Israel's God has done (Paul argues) what he always said he would do. It is just that Israel, Paul's old self included, had not rightly understood just what that would mean. I look forward to closer acquaintance with Eskola's stimulating work and hope that with these misunderstandings cleared up we will find our way to greater convergence.

SYSTEMATIC THEOLOGY

"We are in great need today," writes Hans Boersma, "of open and vigorous, yet constructive, conversation between biblical and dogmatic theology." I totally agree. If there is anything I can do to set that forward, I would like to try. But I fear the essays by Boersma himself, and by Ephraim Radner, are simply further instantiations of the problem, at least in one of its forms. There are of course many varieties of "biblical studies," as indeed of dogmatic or systematic theology, and the particular conversation that I might be able to have with Boersma and Radner is by no means necessarily typical of wider conversations across other, superficially similar, fault lines. But it would be good to think that the present opportunity might at least start such a conversation.

For that to happen, however, we must first face a problem: these two essayists seem not to have heard what is actually being said. Hans Boersma sees the point about the continuous narrative, but accuses me repeatedly of offering a form of reductionism, even of deism. (I was more amused than affronted by that, seeing that I have spent much of my adult life opposing the deist influence in biblical studies.) He suggests, over and over, that I am forgetting, or squeezing out, the supernatural in the quest for the historical. Ephraim Radner goes one further, appearing not to notice that the whole point of the continuing exile, and its claimed resolution in Jesus, is precisely *not* because "exile" is a helpful and evocative theme that resonates (for instance) with Calvin's exile in Geneva. Here we have to be careful, because in the Old Testament it is undoubtedly the case, as I have argued in various places, that Israel's exile from the Promised Land was seen as the large-scale historical instantiation of the exile of Adam and Eve from the garden. Radner's discussion of Bede is pertinent to this point: in reading Psalm 137 (136 in LXX and Vulgate) we can indeed see, behind the actual historical exile in Babylon, the expulsion of Adam from Paradise and also the threat of a diabolical captivity awaiting Christians who sin. The first "echo" is clearly envisaged within Scripture itself, the second a natural and justifiable ongoing homiletic application. What is not clear from this is whether Bede recognized—let alone whether Radner recognizes!—that the Second Temple Jews I have cited saw the Babylonian exile still continuing, albeit under other pagan empires, right up to the first century, and that they interpreted their eschatological hopes, and launched their revolutionary movements, in relation to the ultimate undoing of that continuing exile. In particular, it is not clear from all this whether Radner at least recognizes the point I have been making, that Jesus himself, and his first followers, claimed that this long-awaited moment had come about through his own kingdom work and death.

Radner does speak of Jesus' own exile in submitting "to captivity's fundamental grasp in sin and death." What is not clear, however, is whether he
sees that Jesus' resurrection is thus the launch of the ultimate postexilic
existence, in which what matters is not an escape from earth to heaven but
the explosive in-breaking of heaven's life into earthly reality, starting with
the body of Jesus but aiming at the entire creation. How we label the various
echoes and allusions (typology, allegory, or whatever) is not so important.
What matters is *how the relevant texts would be understood in the first century*,
both by Second Temple Jews in general and then by the early Christians as
they saw everything afresh in the light of Jesus and the Spirit. When we link
the exile from Eden with the exile to Babylon—they are of course linked in
the narrative of Genesis by the sequence of thought which runs up to
Genesis 11!—then we do indeed have the exile resonating back to the human
plight in general. *But the human plight is not that we are exiled from "heaven"
and need to return there.* That suggestion, central to Ephraim Radner's paper,
represents I think a denial of the very heart of Scripture and also, I would
suggest, of the first article of the Creed. In Scripture from start to finish we
are taught that heaven and earth belong together; that the Creator's purpose
always was to bring together all things in heaven and on earth in the Messiah
(Eph 1:10); that the final scene, as in Revelation 21, will not be saved souls
going up to heaven but the new Jerusalem coming down from heaven to
earth, in fulfillment (we must suppose) of the crucial petition in the Lord's
Prayer, that God's kingdom would come "on earth as in heaven." I have been
arguing this point in many places for many years, and I did not expect to
have to repeat it here—though the remarkable misunderstandings to which
I have been subjected on the way indicates that, as with these two essays,
people still find it hard to grasp.

At the heart of it all, and central to the biblical and early Christian vision
of exile and restoration, is not a world of Platonic forms that we must invoke
to help the biblical writers say what they really ought to have said but the
Jewish world in which the temple symbolized the promise of that ultimate
coming together of heaven and earth. The original creation was good and
is to be redeemed, and is indeed to be flooded with the divine presence and
power "as the waters cover the sea." The original creation was a kind of
temple, with heaven and earth held together; conversely, the wilderness

tabernacle and then Solomon's temple were seen as microcosmic, the "little world" in which heaven and earth came together dangerously but power-fully, *anticipating the day when heaven and earth would be one forever.* That is why the strand in exilic thought in which, as in Ezekiel, YHWH has abandoned the Jerusalem temple but will one day not only restore it but reinhabit it is so important, and refutes directly the suggestion of Boersma that I am reducing things to a one-dimensional history. Start again, if you will, with Isaiah 52:7-12: when the exile is over, Israel's God will return in power and victory, demonstrating in action that he is the King. (This, of course, is the immediate and highly paradoxical prelude to the fourth Servant Song, reminding us that when the Gospels join the themes of kingdom and cross they are resonating with this same combination of ideas.) Granted the extent to which I have labored this point in my works over many years,[11] it seems hard to be accused of reductionism (Boersma ought to hear what some of my secular biblical studies colleagues accuse me of!). Boersma seems not to realize that this is for me the center of every-thing, focused of course on Jesus himself.

Let me make this more precise. Boersma accuses me of caricaturing the theology of the Reformers by insisting, particularly, that they retained the medieval framework in which "going to heaven" was the assumed goal (with the main question being, "Will you have to go to purgatory first?"). When I read his paper I was at a loss: where should I start to find examples of the kind of thing I was meaning? Then I read Ephraim Radner's paper and he kindly provided me with what I needed. Calvin, he says, "frames the Christian life as a whole in terms of Christ's exilic-incarnational form: the world in 'this life' is a place of exile, cast in terms of a difficult journey or pilgrimage leading back to one's heavenly 'home' or 'inheritance.'" I do not know how typical this is of Calvin or of the Reformers as a whole, but it is exactly the sort of thing I was referring to. In Israel's Scriptures the "inheri-tance" was the Promised Land, extended in Psalm 2 and elsewhere to the entire world. In the New Testament *this is not "spiritualized" but extended further:* for Paul in Romans 8, the "inheritance" is the entire cosmos, the whole creation. Nowhere in the New Testament does anybody suggest that

---

[11]Particularly in Wright, *Surprised by Hope: Rethinking Heaven, Resurrection and the Mission of the Church* (London: SPCK, 2007).

"heaven" is the "inheritance" to which the Christian is going; when Boersma says that "heaven is the end of exile" he is merely exemplifying the unbiblical view of far too many Western Christians. The early Christians (as opposed to the gnostics!) were, after all, creational and new-creational thinkers. The incarnation was not, for Paul or John or the other early Christians, a *faute de mieux*, something that the Creator undertook with reluctance. In John 1; Colossians 1; and Hebrews 1 it is presented as the glorious goal for which all creation had been waiting. To be sure, the fact that, following human sin, incarnation now had to include the horror, shame, and agony of the cross means that the whole story takes on the aspect of an incipient tragedy. But incarnation itself, as many in the great tradition have insisted, was in view from the start; or, to put it the other way, the creation of humans in the divine image was itself a statement of intent, the composer writing a solo part designed ultimately for himself to play. And it is within this frame of reference, rather than any incipient Platonic understanding, that we find the rich sacramental thought and practice of the early church, which Boersma supposes I have lost sight of.

Radner goes so far as to invoke Plotinus, suggesting that his vision of liberation from the grip of "the things of earth" is what lies behind Tyndale and Calvin and that John and Paul see "the world" in the same way. "We are all sojourners on earth within this mortal life," writes Radner, "and the Christian 'alien' is particular in that his or her eyes are rightly cast upon the true *patria* in heaven." This, however much it is backed up with medieval and other references, is exactly what I am arguing against. To say it again: according to Paul in Romans 8 (picking up from Rom 4:13, where Abraham is promised "the world"), the Christian's "inheritance" is the renewed creation. According to Jesus himself, it is God's kingdom *on earth* as in heaven, in fact with heaven and earth joined together completely and forever. When Radner announces that he is going to argue that my "notion of historical reference itself is too limited," I wonder whether perhaps he means that the gospel is not after all about certain events that happened once for all *sub Pontio Pilato*.

The biblical fusion of heaven and earth, intended from the beginning, anticipated in the wilderness tabernacle and the Jerusalem temple, realized in Jesus and inaugurated in human lives through the Spirit, offers the biblical, Jewish, and early Christian answer to Boersma's repeated accusation that I am moving away from vertical categories and replacing them with horizontal ones. It is precisely this false dichotomy that I am objecting to—particularly when the supposedly "vertical" categories are first privileged over the "horizontal" ones and then, as in so much Western theology, allowed to replace them altogether and indeed being congratulated for doing so. Boersma says he is concerned with my "strictly historical" approach; to which I reply that if, as the New Testament declares, the living God has revealed himself fully and finally within history, any step away from history must be a step toward idolatry. This does not of course mean, as he fears, "the general reduction of theological categories to this-worldly, historical narratives," because the Bible's own "theological categories" concern the God who is both utterly transcendent over the world *and* determined to dwell in the midst of his people, with the glorious presence in the temple a true anticipation of the promised ultimate dwelling in the whole world (as, for instance, in Ps 72:19). All this is spelled out at considerable length in my various works, which is why I find it so surprising to be accused of "restricting" election to "historical categories," or indulging in a "strict historicizing" of election and exile, and ultimately of a "general occlusion of heavenly concerns, of immanent trinitarian doctrine, and of theological metaphysics in general." I would respectfully request Boersma to reread *Paul and the Faithfulness of God* chapter nine and think again about such extraordinary charges. My insistence on understanding the Jewish and early Christian beliefs about God within their own historical context rather than that of philosophically minded people half a millennium or more later has nothing whatever to do with "a modern penchant to separate historical, this-worldly realities of nature from their supernatural, heavenly original and goal," and everything to do with my belief that Jesus of Nazareth and he alone is "the image of the invisible God," that he and he alone has revealed who this God is and what he has done and is doing, and that it is the theologians' flight from history (aided and abetted by much modern piety) that has done the real damage. "By limiting ourselves to historical categories," writes Boersma, "we dislodge historical and earthly realities from their eternal, heavenly anchor." This is exactly the wrong way round. According to the Bible itself, if we ignore historical reality—including such realities as the extended exile and its dramatic resolution in Jesus and the Spirit!—we dislodge theological and spiritual realities from their creational, historical anchor. Boersma asks me how historical election is "anchored in the eternal, divine reality of the Word of God"; but in the Bible the Word becomes *flesh*, the first-century Jewish flesh of Jesus of Nazareth, and he and he alone unveils the God whom no one has ever seen (Jn 1:14, 18). Of course, that means that as we read John's Gospel we are supposed to recall the truths of the prologue all the way through. But the point again and again is that the divine glory is revealed in the human story of Jesus, supremely in his crucifixion. Again, I think a fresh reading of chapter thirteen of *Jesus and the Victory of God*, or chapter nine of *Paul and the Faithfulness of God*, might show Boersma how far from the mark he is in accusing me of "neglecting the theological, christological metaphysical grounding of historical events"—except that I would dispute the word "grounding." My fear is that too many systematicians have neglected, and have even poured scorn on, the historical grounding of the biblical view of God, Jesus, and the heaven/earth reality encapsulated in the temple and in Jesus himself.

Boersma and Radner both eventually show their hands: they ultimately invoke Plato, not the Bible. The "sacramental" or "participatory" reality for which Boersma pleads finds its true scriptural grounding, once again, in the temple theology that runs from Genesis to Revelation and that the New Testament sees coming into specific and powerful focus in Jesus and the Spirit. Though this would undoubtedly be an oversimplification, it really does appear from their work that the church brought in Platonic categories to try to do the job that the ancient Jewish worldview did with that temple theology—without, it seems, realizing that, whereas the temple theology held heaven and earth together, the Platonic substitution forced them apart. Since I have argued for this strong and biblical holding together it is strange to be accused by Boersma of a "methodologically natural or historical approach" to which such an integration would be "alien." Throughout my career I have argued for (and, as a priest, have tried to practice) a "participatory or sacramental framework"—though it is true that since I do not find the Platonic notion of "eternity" in the Bible (what I find is "the age to come," which is rather different)—I would not phrase that integration in terms of "history and eternity" but in terms of "earth and heaven." Nor would I want to play off "narrative" and "allegory" against each other, though I worry about what happens when "allegory" forgets that what matters (to say it yet again) is God's kingdom coming on earth as in heaven. There is, after all, allegory and allegory: there are repeating patterns, but the point of that repetition, and of our highlighting it, is not so that we can escape from the actual concrete historical message then and now, but so that we can understand the significance, including the full theological, christological, and pneumatological significance, of the actual events in which we ourselves are called to participate. Thus I am perfectly happy to think in terms of "typology" or "allegory." I am not, as Boersma suggests, "unaware" of them (!); they are after all categories that the biblical writers themselves explicitly evoke. But it must be clear that the types and the allegories illuminate and give theological depth to the ultimate heaven-and-earth reality of God's kingdom. The literal sense remains the anchor.

Boerma's question to me, "whether . . . the New Testament christological reality (*res*) is already present in the events described in the Old Testament (*sacramentum*)" can only be answered with "yes and no." Of course the Christian reader of Israel's Scriptures recognizes the full reality that we see in Jesus when contemplating the heaven-and-earth reality of Genesis 1–2, the human "image-bearing" vocation, the exodus events (Jesus himself, after all, chose Passover as the moment to bring his kingdom-work to its terrifying conclusion), the tabernacle and the sacrificial system, as well as the promises to David, the building—and destroying, and rebuilding!—of the temple, the psalms of suffering and vindication, the promise that YHWH will return to Zion through the suffering of the Servant, and much, much more. But these are all signposts, pointing forward within the history of Israel (which encapsulates and focuses the history of creation and of the human race), not to an otherworldly, non-spatio-temporal reality (the "vertical" on which Boersma wishes I would concentrate) but to the heaven-and-earth reality of the kingdom of God, inaugurated by Jesus on earth as in heaven and awaiting its final consummation when the heavenly city comes to earth at last. If, as he says, "the Platonist Christian heritage maintains that it is only when we recognize the vertical or anagogical anchoring of historical particularity that the biblical narrative has any meaning at all," then this invites the riposte that the *biblical* Christian heritage maintains that it is only when we recognize that the Creator's intention was to flood all creation with his powerful and healing presence, and that this eventual goal was realized, close up and personally, in Jesus, and is being implemented through the Spirit, that the Platonic vision can be redeemed from its anticreational tendency and allowed to serve as a broken signpost pointing to a reality to which the biblical symbol of the temple will point much more accurately. As Schweitzer said, why then would the gardener take a leaky bucket to a far-off tap when there is a fresh and flowing stream near at hand? The answer can only be that combination of philosophical dualism and anti-Jewish instinct that has bedeviled the Christian tradition and from which the Bible itself, seen of course sacramentally as the vessel of God's own powerful self-revelation, could (and, please God, will) free us at last. The suggestion that I have reduced history "to a merely self-referential intertextual flux" is absurd; nor have I proposed a "continuous historical development." The "desired continuity of the biblical narrative" is secured, not by introducing a "Platonic Christian emphasis on sacramental participation" but by paying attention, as I have tried to do throughout my work, to the *ancient Israelite, Jewish, and early Christian* emphasis on sacramental participation for which the temple is the primary symbol. I have not, as Boersma suggests, shifted to this emphasis in my recent work on Paul, though I have expounded at much more length—to the frustration of some!—the emphasis on a *Jewish* "participatory ontology" that was already there in my earlier writing. Yes, I did say that Paul might have had some sympathy for Plato's belief in glimpsing truths behind the veil of the material world, but Boersma naturally misses out the rest of the sentence he quotes, which concludes, "but [Paul] would have had none at all for the way some of his contemporaries were interpreting the Platonic tradition to the effect that the material world was essentially a bad place from which one ought to long to escape"—pretty much what Radner says explicitly, in line (to my surprise) with Calvin.[12] Yes, heaven and earth really do intersect, and the biblical and authentically Christian affirmation of that— which I have spent many years trying to articulate—achieves its goal in a way that Platonism can only look at from afar. It may be that one should therefore cast Platonism in the role of Moses, gazing from the top of Pisgah at the Promised Land. But if Joshua had found some of his troops wanting to go

---

[12]See *Paul and the Faithfulness of God*, 1369. For the Platonic position see, e.g., Plutarch, *On Exile*.

back to Pisgah, because the view from there was so splendid, rather than going in to possess the land, he would have had sharp words for them. "Spiritual readings of the biblical text" are all very well. What we need in tomorrow's church and world are (among other things) biblical rereadings of human philosophies. Paul declared that he took all human thought captive—exiled, one might say, from its natural habitat!—to obey the Messiah. That would be—to paraphrase Boersma's final sentence—an excellent starting point for a discussion about the plausibility of a historical, Jewish, Jesus-centered and kingdom-focused grounding of theology.

My response to Ephraim Radner will by now be predictable, but something further must still be said. First, I want to put some critical distance between a full-orbed "history" and the idea of a "historical-critical argument." The phrase "historical-critical" belongs within a problematic context in modern Western scholarship, being sometimes (not always) employed to denote a would-be "historical" exercise designed from the outset to undermine traditional ways of reading Scripture. Sometimes this was done in order to undermine traditional Christianity; sometimes, as with Bultmann and others, it was done in order to direct attention away from a historical focus (lest anyone should try to base their faith on history and so turn it into a "work") and to focus instead on the existential or experiential reality of Christian existence. Ironically, Radner's distancing of himself from what he sees me doing (which I would describe as "history" rather than "historical-critical") masks the fact that his own proposals remind me again and again of none other than Bultmann himself. His opening move away from "history" and toward "figural exegesis" needs further exploration: as I have said, allegory and type are evident in Scripture itself, so that (ironically again, perhaps) to recognize and expound them as such is actually to pay attention to the "literal" sense of the passages concerned. And of course the Bible, like most great writing, abounds in metaphor and metonymy, and when it uses those figures of speech they are the primary meaning of the text—in that sense, however ironically, they are the "literal" sense, that which the writers themselves may be presumed to have intended. My fundamental concern, of course, is that when systematicians refer to the historical analysis of something like "continuing exile" as "historicism," what they are really objecting to is the major biblical theme of God's kingdom embracing earth as well as heaven. I hope I am wrong, but this is what I see writ large in Radner's paper.

So when Radner moves at once to Calvin's exposition of "exile" in terms of his own exile from France to Geneva I find myself wanting to say, "Why did you change the subject?" This is simply avoiding the question: Does the New Testament, or does it not, envisage the "redemption" accomplished in Jesus as the fulfillment of the hope of Israel? And if that hope of Israel was for something to *happen* in real space and time—the arrival of God's kingdom, no less—then either that happened or it did not, and if it *did* happen it was hugely important, not to be reduced to an example of a pattern of which Calvin's own exile fifteen hundred years later might be simply another example. And when (as discussed above) Radner cites Calvin's further suggestion that "the world itself" is a place of exile in contrast to our heavenly home, I am shocked that Calvin turns out to have been so thoroughly Platonist. Perhaps this is one of the reasons why he never wrote a commentary on the book of Revelation, since its ending is such an uncompromising statement of the opposite view. When Radner then suggests that if "the traditional and 'precritical' reading of exile as holding multiple referents is evangelically valid," and expounds his own question by saying "What if it properly—in the sense of deriving from the message of Jesus Christ—founds the gospel?" it becomes clear: he really is now advocating something quite close to Bultmann. Jesus is removed from his historical context, his eschatological context, his apocalyptic context, his *Jewish* context, and instead of announcing the one-off message of God's kingdom arriving on earth as in heaven he is made to articulate a generalized message that might be applied to this or that personal situation.

This brings into focus the central question at issue between me and at least these two systematicians. Can they any longer give an account of the *ephapax* of the gospel, the "once-for-all" achievement of Jesus? Have they left themselves anything to say about the way in which God sent his son "when the time had fully come" (Gal 4:4)? What sense can they give to Jesus' own foundational announcement that "the time is fulfilled" (Mk 1:15)? Do they give any importance to the fact that, in the New Testament itself, what matters is not a set of timeless truths or the possibility of ongoing spiritual or sacramental experiences, all washed down with subtle figural readings of

Israel's Scriptures, but the belief that in and through Israel's Messiah *something had happened as a result of which the world was a different place*? After all, in the great tradition the literal sense was always given priority; one can no doubt use the Bible, especially in preaching, in any number of evocative ways that can loosely be formalized in terms of allegory and other figural readings, and as Radner points out even the headings for the Psalms point in this direction. But the use that Radner in particular describes is a rather sharp example of the kind of excess to which the nonliteral readings can be put, against which the Reformers reacted sharply with their insistence on the "literal sense." For the Reformers that mattered not simply because of the strange teachings to which the other supposed senses had given apparent free rein, but also because the Reformers rightly saw that the thing that mattered above all—the reason why the Bible mattered above all!—was that the events concerning Jesus, particularly his death and resurrection, were one-off, unique, and unrepeatable, events through which the living God was inaugurating his saving rule on earth as in heaven. That too was of course polemical in the sixteenth century: Jesus died only once, so any suggestion of his being resacrificed in every Mass would be a blasphemous nonsense. But here, as in so many other ways (though not, as Barth saw, in their eschatology), the Reformers were highlighting the central point of the Scriptures. "The time is fulfilled, and the kingdom of God is at hand": if all that Jesus meant was "I am showing you a new and better way to escape earth and get to heaven," then not only his first-century hearers but also the four Evangelists appear to have radically misunderstood what he was about. Radner's citation of normal escapist eschatology may be "a stable tradition," but its root is precisely not in "the very referential exactitude of the Scripture's description of exilic existence." The scriptural roots tell the story of Israel longing for the Creator God to become king on earth as in heaven, and of Jesus and his first followers celebrating the fact that this had come to pass. To use an apparently "stable tradition" of interpretation to argue for the exact opposite is the kind of hermeneutical error, supplanting the clear teaching of Scripture itself by traditions that undermined it, against which not only the Reformers but also Jesus himself spoke words of sharp rebuke. The fact that the Babylonian "exile" was explicitly extended, in Daniel 9 and the many Second Temple writings that develop the idea, is no excuse for "extending" it in a different direction altogether, implying that the Creator and covenant God has given up on his purposes for creation and Israel altogether.

When Radner then argues that history can only take us so far, and that figural exegesis will be needed to get us the rest of the way on our projected journey, he is raising several questions that go beyond the possibilities of this present essay and indeed volume. But, while I am very much aware of the limitations of "history" as an exercise, it seems to me central and essential to the Christian faith that what happened in and through Jesus not only happened in history but that it launched a new and ongoing reality, again within history (and again, to anticipate Hans Boersma's likely reaction, within a history that is not closed against, but rather open to, the strange, elusive but powerful, divine presence). The question, once again, concerns the kingdom of God. To insist on this is not to become "evangelically limiting," or to ignore subsequent experience "in favor of such limited temporal reference," but to insist on the one-off events of Jesus' death and resurrection as the defining and paradigmatic events of the new creation in which God will do for the whole creation what he did for Jesus at Easter. The earth *shall* be filled with the knowledge and glory of YHWH as the waters cover the sea. God's plan was to sum up, in the Messiah, all things in heaven and on earth. That is the reality toward which the extended exile is pointing. To exchange it for some version of Platonism, however firmly rooted in some aspects of the Christian tradition, may not be such an obvious mistake as throwing the Bible away altogether. It may appear that allegory, or figural readings, are actually (as used to be said) rescuing the Bible for the church. I believe it remains important, for central gospel-related reasons, that the Bible itself should rescue the church from the dangers of which unfettered Platonic allegorical or figural exegesis are symptomatic. When Paul summed up the gospel, he did not say "Jesus died for our sins in accordance with Platonic philosophy (with a few biblical footnotes thrown in)." He said, "The Messiah died for our sins in accordance with the Bible." The Bible—Paul's Bible—told the story of how the Creator God was rescuing his image-bearing humans, and thereby his entire creation, from idolatry, sin, and death; in other words (it is all there in 1 Cor 15) how the one true God was establishing his kingship on earth as in heaven. Paul believed, as Jesus himself had claimed, that this project had now been decisively launched. One does not repeat a decisive moment; to do so is to question whether it was decisive after all. One implements it. Figural readings may well be helpful in tracking and encouraging that implementation. But if they pull away from the once-for-allness of the gospel events, complaining that such a notion of historical reference is too limited, they are cutting off the branch on which they ought to be sitting.

CONCLUSION

These eleven essays, in their different ways, have done what academic conversation ought to do: that is, they have compelled me to think through once more what exactly I have been wanting to say, and (I hope) how to say it more sharply. My claim is not that "all Jews believed they were still in exile." Clearly that was not the case. Many, however, did think like that, and—this is the point—*Jesus and the early Christians picked up this belief, and the hope for "redemption" that it produced, and claimed that this "redemption" was now happening.* Jesus' announcement of God's kingdom belongs within this hope, not some other, as the obvious passages such as Isaiah 52 and Daniel 7 make clear; this also brings with it the full meaning of "forgiveness of sins" (since, according to the prophets, exile was the result of Israel's sins), and perhaps above all of "the return of YHWH to Zion." These themes, I have suggested, interpreted in this way, are at the heart of New Testament soteriology, Christology, and pneumatology, and to take them out of this context, out of the Israel-narrative within which they make the sense they make, and to place them into a different narrative, especially if that different narrative has to do with an escape from the world of space, time, and matter, is to falsify them, to invent a new, hybrid philosophy or religion. The church has not been immune to this danger. The role of serious historical research into Christian origins is not to provide a few biblical footnotes to theories and arguments arrived at on other grounds or expressed within other worldviews. It is to remind the church that everything we are called to say about God, about Jesus, about the Spirit, about salvation, and about the Creator's plan to sum up all things in heaven and on earth in the Messiah is to be found *in nuce* in the early Christian writings themselves, interpreted within the terms of Israel's Scriptures. Rather to my surprise, I have found myself defending two of the Reformers' principal watchwords: *solus Christus* on the one hand, *sola Scriptura* on the other.

CONTRIBUTORS

Philip S. Alexander is emeritus professor of post-biblical Jewish literature at the University of Manchester, a fellow of the British Academy, and the former president of the Oxford Centre for Hebrew and Jewish Studies (1992–1995). He began his career as a classicist, then switched to the study of Hebrew and Semitic languages, but has retained a fundamental interest in the problem of how to contextualize Rabbinic Judaism in the Greco-Roman world of late antiquity. He is currently collaborating with his wife, Professor Loveday Alexander, on a commentary on Hebrews for the International Critical Commentary Series.

Hans Boersma is the J. I. Packer Professor of Theology at Regent College in Vancouver, Canada. His interests are in patristic theology, twentieth-century Catholic thought, and spiritual interpretation of Scripture. Boersma is the author of a number of books, including *Scripture as Real Presence: Sacramental Exegesis in the Early Church* (Baker Academic, 2017), *Sacramental Preaching: Sermons on the Hidden Presence of Christ* (Baker Academic, 2016), and *Heavenly Participation: The Weaving of a Sacramental Tapestry* (Eerdmans, 2011).

Walter Brueggemann is William Marcellus McPheeters Professor Emeritus at Columbia Theological Seminary. He has written numerous books on the Old Testament and most recently published *Money and Possessions* (Westminster John Knox, 2016) and *God, Neighbor, Empire* (Baylor University Press, 2016).

S. A. (Tony) Cummins is professor of religious studies at Trinity Western University. He teaches and writes in New Testament studies and theology, with particular interests in Jesus and the Gospels, Paul, and theological exegesis.

Timo Eskola is a New Testament scholar at the Theological Institute of Finland. He also works as a Privatdozent at the University of Helsinki, Finland. His latest monograph is *A Narrative Theology of the New Testament: Exploring the Metanarrative of Exile and Restoration* (Mohr Siebeck, 2015).

Robert J. V. Hiebert is professor of Old Testament at the Graduate School of Theological Studies of Trinity Western University and director of the John William Wevers Institute for Septuagint Studies in Langley, British Columbia, Canada. He is the author and editor of books and articles on a range of subjects in the areas of textual criticism and exegesis of the Septuagint and of Hebrew and Syriac biblical texts. He is preparing the critical edition of 4 Maccabees for the Göttingen Septuaginta series and a commentary on Genesis for the forthcoming Society of Biblical Literature Commentary on the Septuagint series, for which he also serves as a joint-editor-in-chief.

Jörn Kiefer has been a Lutheran pastor in Bergen auf Rügen, Germany, since 2003. He studied Protestant theology and Jewish studies in Rostock, Berlin, and Jerusalem. His dissertation at the University of Greifswald under Thomas Willi was published as *Exil und Diaspora: Begrifflichkeit und Deutungen im antiken Judentum und in der hebräischen Bibel* (Evangelische Verlagsanstalt, 2005). His forthcoming *Habilitationsschrift* is on "Gut und Böse in der Hebräischen Bibel."

Robert Kugler is Paul S. Wright Professor of Christian Studies at Lewis and Clark College. He is the recipient of an American Council of Learned Societies Fellowship for 2016 and 2017. Kugler has authored books and articles on topics in the Hebrew Bible, the Dead Sea Scrolls, Jewish pseudepigrapha, and Jewish documentary texts from Hellenistic Egypt.

Scot McKnight is the Julius R. Mantey Professor of New Testament at Northern Seminary. He is the author of more than fifty books, including *A New Vision for Israel* (Eerdmans, 1999), *The King Jesus Gospel* (Zondervan, 2011), and *Kingdom Conspiracy* (Brazos Press, 2014).

Dorothy M. Peters is adjunct professor at Trinity Western University and research associate of the Dead Sea Scrolls Institute at TWU. She is the author of *Noah Traditions in the Dead Sea Scrolls: Conversations and Controversies of Antiquity* (Society of Biblical Literature, 2008) and numerous articles and essays.

Ephraim Radner is professor of historical theology at Wycliffe College, University of Toronto. His two most recent books are *A Time to Keep: Theology, Mortality, and the Shape of a Human Life* (Baylor University Press, 2016) and *Time and the Word: Figural Reading of the Christian Scriptures* (Eerdmans, 2016).

James M. Scott is professor of religious studies at Trinity Western University. He has authored or edited several books that are relevant to the subject at hand: *Exile: Old Testament, Jewish, and Christian Conceptions* (Brill, 1997), *Restoration: Old Testament, Jewish, and Christian Conceptions* (Brill, 2001), and *On Earth as in Heaven: The Restoration of Sacred Space and Sacred Time in the Book of Jubilees* (Brill, 2004). His latest book is *Bacchius Iudaeus: A Denarius Commemorating Pompey's Victory over Judea* (Vandenhoeck & Ruprecht, 2015).

N. T. (Tom) Wright is research professor of New Testament and early Christianity at the University of St. Andrews. He took a "double first" in classics and theology from Oxford University, where he wrote his DPhil on Paul and was later awarded the DD. He also holds honorary DDs from twelve other institutions. He has worked in both the academy and the church and has published over eighty books. The latest in his multivolume series on Christian Origins and the Question of God is *Paul and the Faithfulness of God* (Fortress, 2013).

SCRIPTURE INDEX

New Testament

Finding the Textbook You Need

The IVP Academic Textbook Selector
is an online tool for instantly finding the IVP books
suitable for over 250 courses across 24 disciplines.

---

ivpacademic.com

LINE-INC.

Creating Inspiring Places for People

Frame Publishers, Amsterdam

CONTENTS

Cover photo by Tetsuya Ito

P002 - P009 : The recent office of LINE-INC., on the third floor of THE WORKS, completed in 2014 in Meguro, Tokyo.

LINE-INC. is an interior design company established in 2002.
Director Takao Katsuta leads a team of 12 in the daily design
and production of space. During our 12 years in operation,
we have created approximately 800 spaces such as shops,
restaurants, bars, cafes, salons, offices, galleries and residences
ranging from casual styles to places of luxury.
When asked, 'What is a LINE-INC. space like?' it is difficult
for us to articulate a concrete characteristic because the space,
materials and style change drastically depending on the
particular project. Each design is something we create together
with the client. We make 'Places for People', meaning we
imagine the people who will visit and use the space and come as
close to their ideal as possible. As a result, the spaces we create
are completely different to one another.
We are very pleased to have this opportunity to introduce our
work to the readers of this book. We hope they see the effort that
went into each project, enjoy the stories behind the details and
feel the atmosphere of the spaces through reading this book.

THE WORKS and Its Design Process

Type: Restaurant & Cafe / Community Lounge(1F+2F),
        LINE-INC. Office(3F), Shared Office(4F+5F)
Open: November 2014
Location: Meguro-ku, Tokyo, Japan
Floor area: 277m²(1F), 308m²(2F), 300m²(3F), 499m²(4F), 486m²(5F)
Contractor: DECOR / REM
Lighting Designer: Endo Lighting / ModuleX

Completed at the end of 2014, 'THE WORKS' is one of LINE-INC.'s
most recent projects. We renovated and renewed an old, forgotten
building in its entirety.
The first floor is a restaurant, the second floor an event space and
the third to fifth floors are shared office spaces. We decided to rent
the third floor and move in ourselves, so we put a lot of personal
thought into how the work space should be. We considered what type
of office space would be suitable for many people to spend the bulk
of their time. The ideal office should inspire, with a good balance
of tension and relaxation. For example, people that work can take
a break on a comfortable sofa in one of the communal areas or, to
switch things up, have a meeting in the cafe on the first floor. If the
meeting goes well, they may have lunch there and host events on the
second floor.
We hope that the people working here will meet and spend their time
with a variety of people who gather at this building. We hope the
place becomes a location of community.

THINGS GO BETTER AFTER CO

COFFEE
TO GO

Between Maple and Chestnut

Teer Wellenbach

J'ai perdu ma tête

Peter Granser

Oculus Ken Schles

Letters to a Daughter

JAPAN

PIÉ MAN SON

LIND

The Workers coffee / bar

Length of stay

In the design phase of each of our projects, the first thing we consider is how long the client will spend in the space. This determines the appropriate approach for us to take. From the shortest to the longest lengths of stay, the projects we have been involved in are gallery shows, retail stores, salons, cafes, bars and restaurants, offices and homes. The essence of the space should fit the type of space; stronger impressions are effective for gallery spaces, while for homes, more subtle characteristics are warranted.

Materials

Trends in materials are a harsh reality. What is popular today soon becomes old. When thinking about popular trends in the past, people may say, "Remember when that was popular?" What we strive for is a design space that is still relevant in 10 years. That is why we choose to use materials that age beautifully such as iron, wood, stone and other organic materials. How we use and combine these materials will reflect the feel of the times in any case, but never feels outdated. For every project, we get samples of all the materials we would like to use and discuss them with the clients. We strive to choose the materials that will properly suit the function of the space design.

At the site

To progress smoothly and efficiently, we draw as many specific details as possible on the blueprint. At the same time, retaining flexibility at the construction site is important. Our strength lies in our ability to express style in the finishing touches, such as the finish of the mortar or stucco, how the iron is rusted, or how much wax is left on the wood. These details demonstrate our care for the overall atmosphere. In order to realise the nuances we strive for, we often work on site with the carpenters.

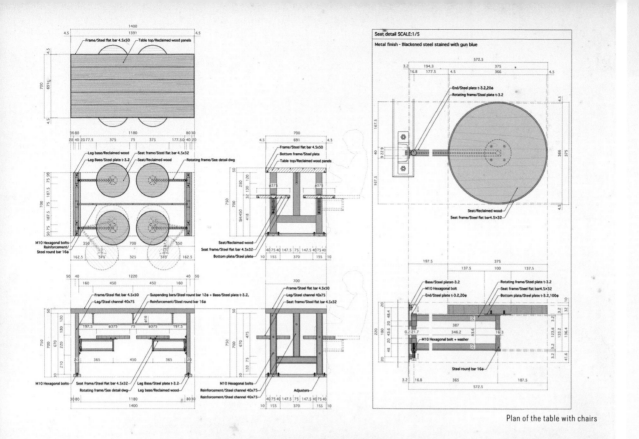

Seat detail SCALE:1/5
Metal finish - Blackened steel stained with gun blue

Plan of the table with chairs

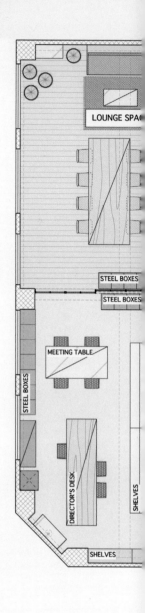

LOUNGE SPACE

STEEL BOXES

STEEL BOXES

MEETING TABLE

STEEL BOXES

DIRECTOR'S DESK

SHELVES

SHELVES

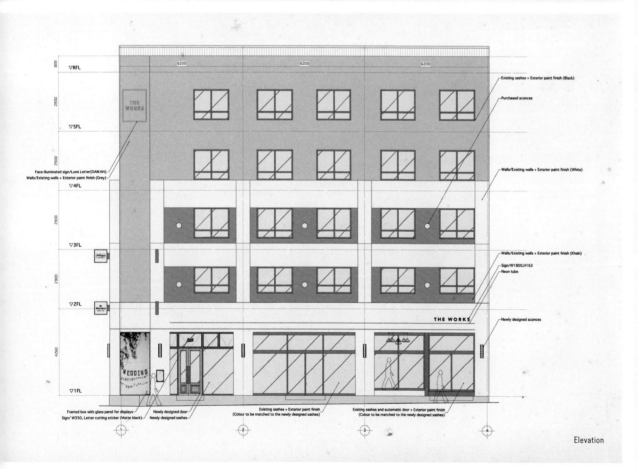

Elevation

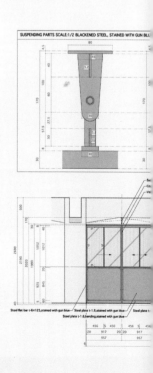

SUSPENDING PARTS SCALE:1/2 BLACKENED STEEL, STAINED WITH GUN BLUE

Planning

Spaces that can be experienced and discovered in several ways are most appealing. For example, a retail shop where you can see all the products upon entering will probably make you feel like leaving immediately. If you can simulate how people will spend time and move within a space, and how they will experience the light, air flow and sounds in a variety of situations, you can come up with a plan that will incorporate multifaceted layers and changes.

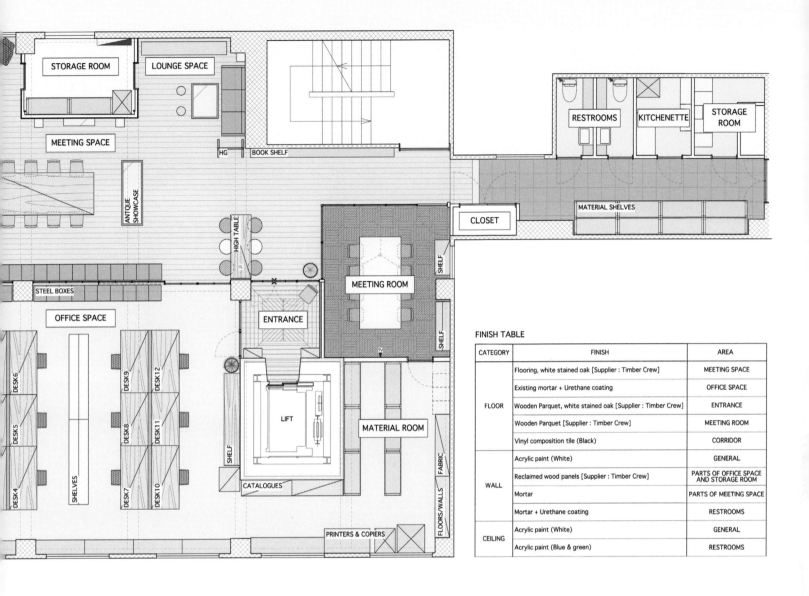

STORAGE ROOM	LOUNGE SPACE

MEETING SPACE

RESTROOMS KITCHENETTE STORAGE ROOM

MATERIAL SHELVES

ANTIQUE SHOWCASE

HG BOOK SHELF

CLOSET

SHELF

HIGH TABLE

MEETING ROOM

STEEL BOXES

OFFICE SPACE

ENTRANCE

SHELF

DESK6 DESK9 DESK12
DESK5 DESK8 DESK11

LIFT

MATERIAL ROOM

SHELVES

SHELF

FABRIC

DESK4 DESK7 DESK10

CATALOGUES

FLOORS/WALLS

PRINTERS & COPIERS

FINISH TABLE

CATEGORY	FINISH	AREA
FLOOR	Flooring, white stained oak [Supplier : Timber Crew]	MEETING SPACE
	Existing mortar + Urethane coating	OFFICE SPACE
	Wooden Parquet, white stained oak [Supplier : Timber Crew]	ENTRANCE
	Wooden Parquet [Supplier : Timber Crew]	MEETING ROOM
	Vinyl composition tile (Black)	CORRIDOR
WALL	Acrylic paint (White)	GENERAL
	Reclaimed wood panels [Supplier : Timber Crew]	PARTS OF OFFICE SPACE AND STORAGE ROOM
	Mortar	PARTS OF MEETING SPACE
	Mortar + Urethane coating	RESTROOMS
CEILING	Acrylic paint (White)	GENERAL
	Acrylic paint (Blue & green)	RESTROOMS

Plan of the office of LINE-INC. on the third floor

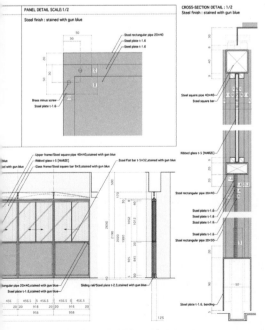

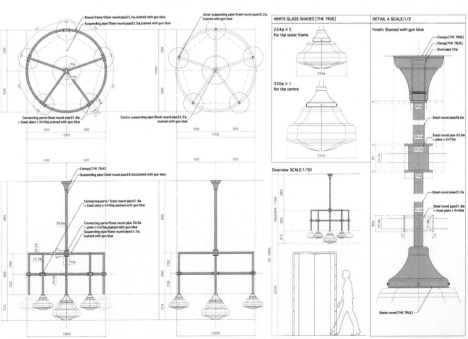

Left: Detail plan of the sliding door / Right: Detail plan of the lamp

THE WORKS

Collaboration

We consider each project a collaboration with our client.
Even when we are asked to be responsible for every aspect
of the project, which is not uncommon, we often make new
discoveries and come up with fun ideas and functional ways
of thinking through conversations with our clients. These
conversations greatly affect the design, so we consider
chatting with the clients an important part of the design
process and therefore make time to meet with them.

PLACES TO BUY

CA4LA
Onitsuka Tiger
BEAMS
NUMBER(N)INE
ARTS&SCIENCE
J.I
mother
The SECRETCLOSET
24karats SURF
nano·universe
FRAPBOIS
Adam et Ropé
ACTUS

The most common projects we undertake are for retail shops. Of course, what we strive for changes according to the brand, so we communicate with each client and explore the brand identity, which we project into the design of the space.

The location and environment of the store are also important. For example, some shops are open to the street, while others are housed inside large commercial buildings. The design process must take into account the first impression of the location and the final atmosphere of the completed space. What we mean by 'completed space', of course, is the shop with all its products in place. It doesn't mean much if the space looks impressive when only the construction is complete. This is why, during the design stage, we discuss in detail how our client would like to display their products, on which shelf or rack, how much or how many, and even what will be on the hangers. We design a lot of shelves for many shops, but never without knowing how they will be used.

When designing for retail shops, the amount and overall balance of the products is an important element, not just the space or furniture. We may ask the client to reduce the number of products displayed to give a higher-end feel or increase the volume of products to give a more lively, energetic feel.

PLACES TO BUY 1
CA4LA

2005—

CA4LA Omotesando
CA4LA Ginza
CA4LA Nishinomiya Gardens
CA4LA Horie
CA4LA Grand Front Osaka

'CA4LA' is pronounced, 'kashira,' meaning 'head' in Japanese. As the name implies, CA4LA is a specialty hat store that also makes their own hats. We have designed all of the CA4LA stores, more than 20 throughout Japan, as well as their main office and factory. When designing stores or interiors for CA4LA, we keep their brand concept in mind: 'If it's not fun, it's not a hat' and design every shop to be fun and joyful places to visit.
Another thing we try to express through each of the stores is the tradition of hats, and the air of authenticity and elegance.
With these two elements as the foundation, we came up with a different design theme for each store that suits each location and its target customers.

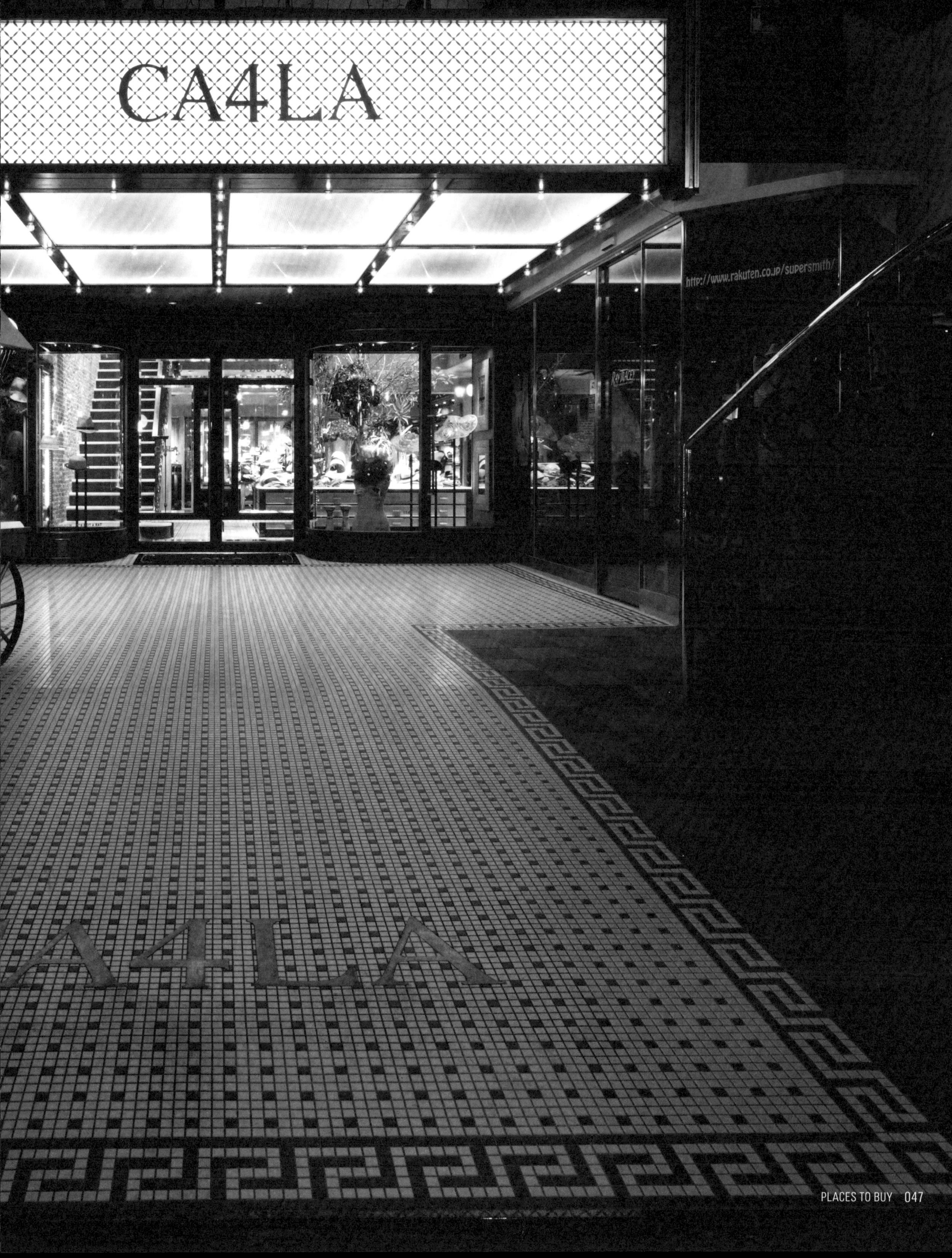
CA4LA
http://www.rakuten.co.jp/supersmith/
CA4LA

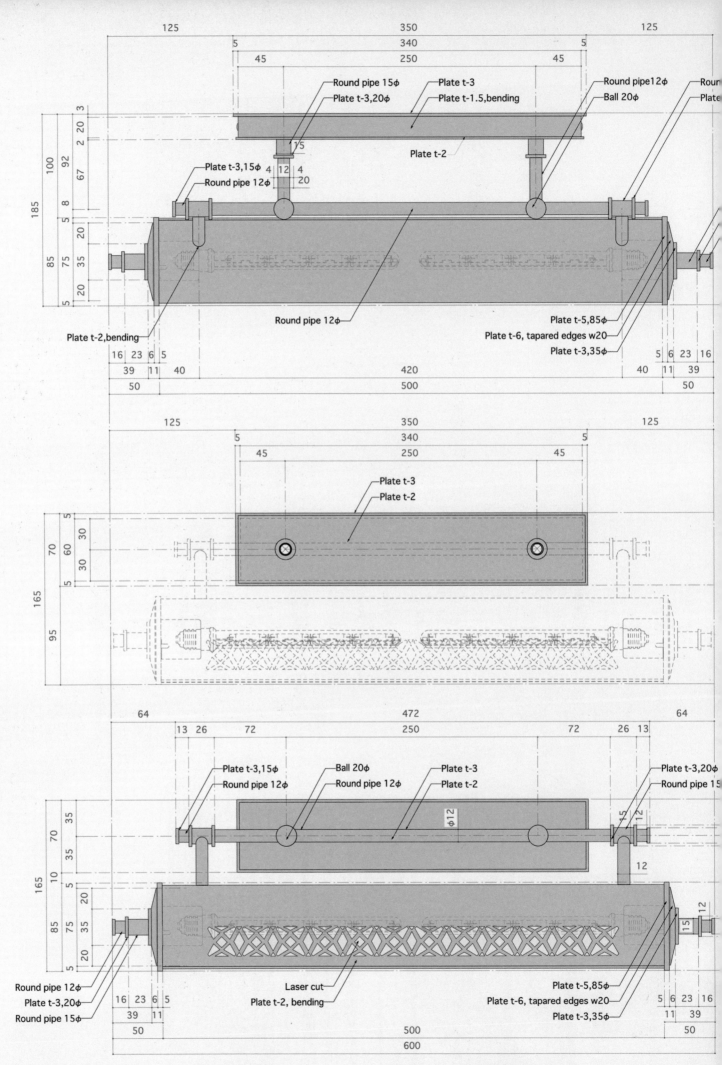

Round pipe 15φ Plate t-3
Plate t-3,20φ Plate t-1.5,bending
Round pipe12φ Roun
Ball 20φ Plate

Plate t-2

Plate t-3,15φ
Round pipe 12φ

Plate t-2,bending

Round pipe 12φ

Plate t-5,85φ
Plate t-6, tapared edges w20
Plate t-3,35φ

Plate t-3
Plate t-2

Plate t-3,15φ Ball 20φ Plate t-3
Round pipe 12φ Round pipe 12φ Plate t-2

Plate t-3,20φ
Round pipe 1

φ12

Round pipe 12φ
Plate t-3,20φ
Round pipe 15φ

Laser cut
Plate t-2, bending

Plate t-5,85φ
Plate t-6, tapared edges w20
Plate t-3,35φ

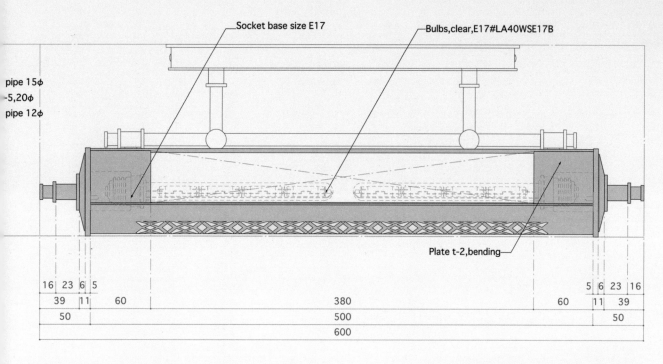

Socket base size E17

Bulbs,clear,E17#LA40WSE17B

pipe 15φ
-5,20φ
pipe 12φ

Plate t-2,bending

16 23 6 5   5 6 23 16
39 11 60   60 11 39
50   500   50
        600

Metal finish - steel, antique brass plating

Laser cut design detail scale 1 / 1

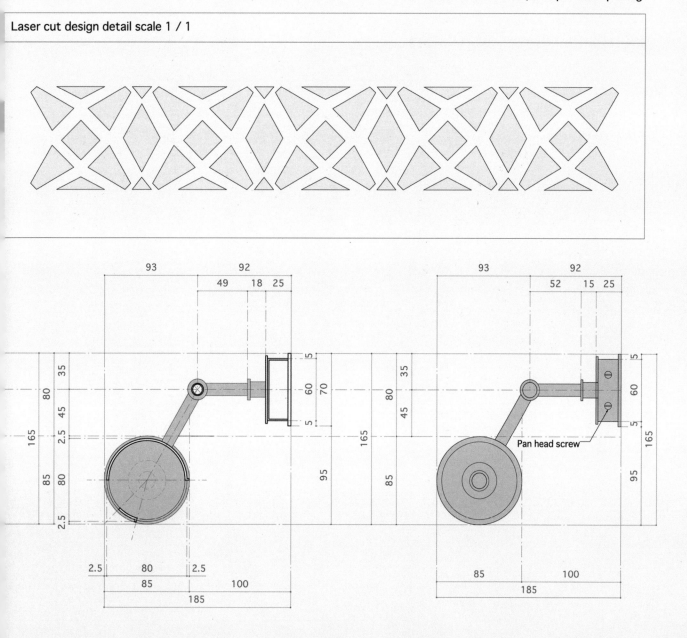

Pan head screw

IT IS NOT FUN, IT'S NOT A HAT

P040 - P054:

CA4LA Omotesando (2013)

Type: Apparel retailer
Open: June 2013
Location: Shibuya-ku, Tokyo, Japan
Floor area: 175m²(1F), 128m²(2F)
Contractor: D.BRAIN
Lighting Designer: LIME DESIGN

The largest CA4LA flagship store which opened in 2013 in
a location where many fashion conscious people pass by. The
theme was 'A Museum of Hats'. We created a space exuding
high-end vintage.

THIS PAGE:

CA4LA Omotesando (2009)

Type: Apparel retailer
Open: December 2009
Location: Shibuya-ku, Tokyo, Japan
Floor area: 113m²(1F), 52m²(2F)
Contractor: D.BRAIN
Lighting Designer: ENDO Lighting

This is the storefront of CA4LA Omotesando before it moved to a different location shown bn P040 - P054. As the ceiling was very high and the hats were hung along the entire wall of the long narrow space, the shop gave a strong impression.

THIS PAGE:

CA4LA Ginza

Type: Apparel retailer
Open: June 2013
Location: Chuo-ku, Tokyo, Japan
Floor area: 81m²
Contractor: D.BRAIN
Lighting Designer: LIME DESIGN

To suit the location where many high-end shops line the streets, the Ginza CA4LA is the most luxurious. We achieved this by using luscious wood and black mirrors. Because the area attracts many tourists, we added a touch of traditional Japan into the design by accentuating the floor with graphics and using exclusively designed lights.

THE OPPOSITE PAGE:

CA4LA Nishinomiya Gardens

Type: Apparel retailer
Open: March 2014
Location: Nishinomiya, Hyogo, Japan
Floor area: 92m²
Contractor: D.BRAIN
Lighting Designer: LIME DESIGN

The theme for this location is 'Merry-go-Round', which is represented by the mirrored pillar in the centre of the shop. Because many family shoppers visit this shop, we hope they can enjoy choosing hats around this pillar.

THIS PAGE:

CA4LA Horie

Type: Apparel retailer
Open: October 2005
Location: Osaka-shi, Osaka, Japan
Floor area: 172m²
Contractor: D.BRAIN
Lighting Designer: Takeshi Obana / JAPAN LIGHTING

The theme of this shop is that of a world where
dinosaurs roam. Horie attracts many young
adults with creative minds, so we wanted to
express something unusual for them. We strived
to create a dark space where time has stopped.
The displays and racks are decorated with
antiques, which the client collected on their
travels around London, Paris and Japan.

THIS PAGE:

CA4LA Grand Front Osaka

Type: Apparel retailer
Open: April 2013
Location: Osaka-shi, Osaka, Japan
Floor area: 53m²
Contractor: D.BRAIN
Lighting Designer: ENDO Lighting

The theme of a modern and classic library represents the sophisticated, intelligent feel associated with its target customers. We installed a modern black mirror on the ceiling to create a feeling of space, and a classic patterned floor.

Onitsuka Tiger

2012 —

Onitsuka Tiger Marunouchi
Onitsuka Tiger Omotesando

Born in Japan, Onitsuka Tiger is an apparel and shoe brand that combines fashion and sport in a very original way. Their sport-inspired shoes are unique and highly fashionable with a strong global presence. In order to break the Japanese stereotype and express their true brand identity, they renewed their shop's concept and opened their flagship store in Omotesando. As Japanese people living in modern times are different from the days of sliding paper doors, tatami mats and kimonos, we were able to suggest a new design concept with modern Japan as the central component. We paid attention to details that are easily overlooked, finding beauty in indirect things. We believe this aesthetic design component is more appropriate for modern Japan.

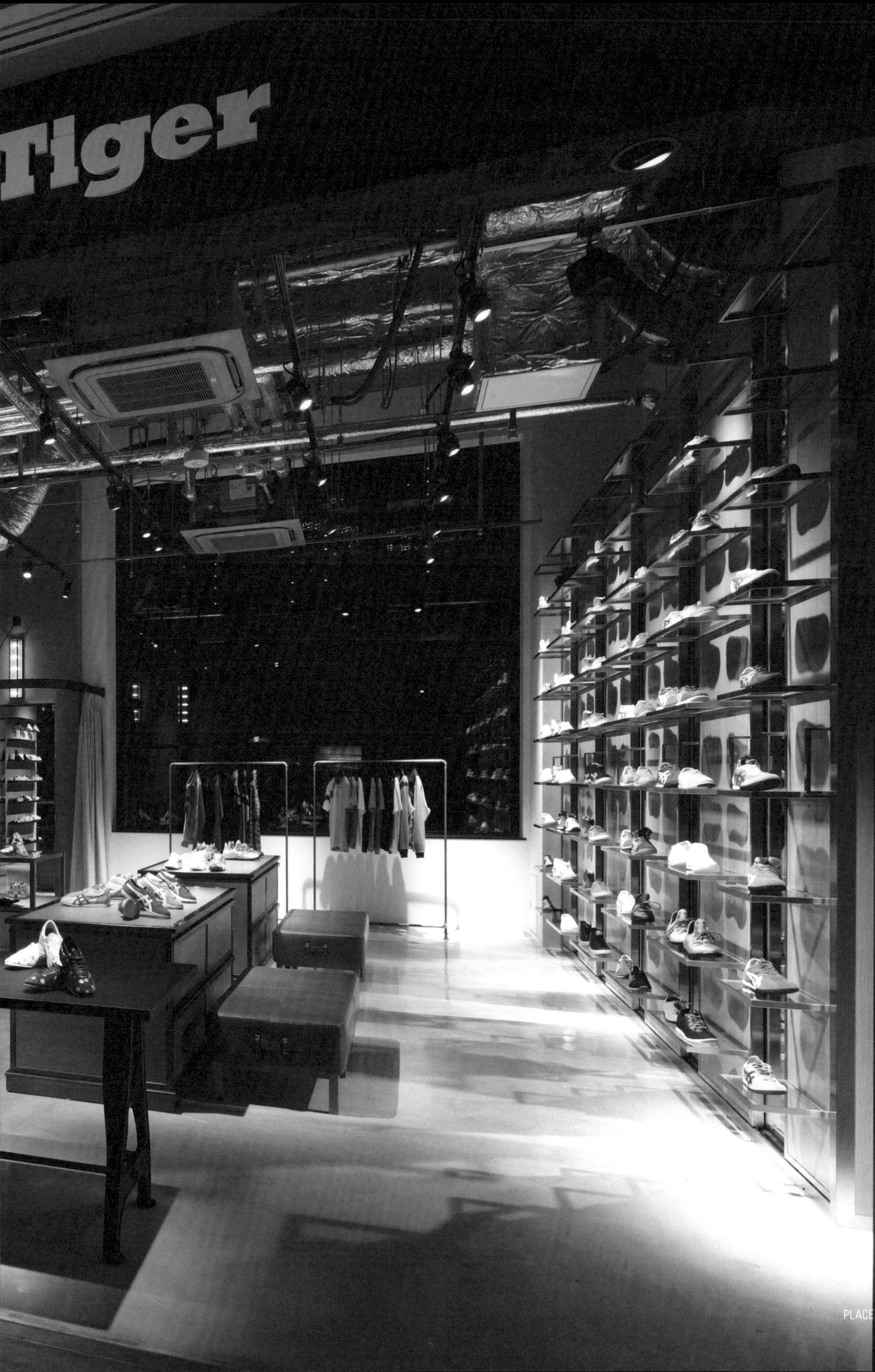
Tiger

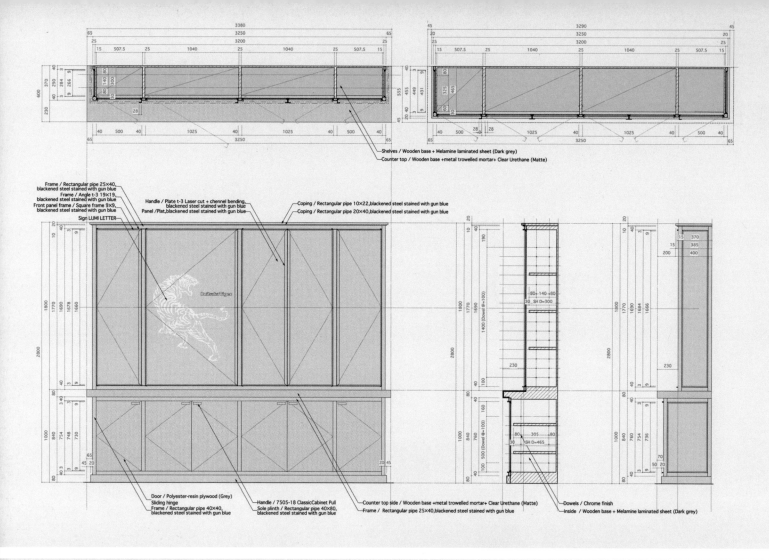

Shelves / Wooden base + Melamine laminated sheet (Dark grey)
Counter top / Wooden base + metal trowelled mortar + Clear Urethane (Matte)

Frame / Rectangular pipe 25×40, blackened steel stained with gun blue
Frame / Angle t-3 19×19, blackened steel stained with gun blue
Front panel frame / Square frame 9×9, blackened steel stained with gun blue
Sign LUMI LETTER

Handle / Plate t-3 Laser cut + chennel bending, blackened steel stained with gun blue
Panel / Plat, blackened steel stained with gun blue

Coping / Rectangular pipe 10×22, blackened steel stained with gun blue
Coping / Rectangular pipe 20×40, blackened steel stained with gun blue

Door / Polyester-resin plywood (Grey)
Sliding hinge
Frame / Rectangular pipe 40×40, blackened steel stained with gun blue
Sole plinth / Rectangular pipe 40×80, blackened steel stained with gun blue

Handle / 7505-18 ClassicCabinet Pull

Counter top side / Wooden base + metal trowelled mortar + Clear Urethane (Matte)
Frame / Rectangular pipe 25×40, blackened steel stained with gun blue

Dowels / Chrome finish
Inside / Wooden base + Melamine laminated sheet (Dark grey)

Top: Detail plan of the counter / Bottom: Detail plan of the curtain rail

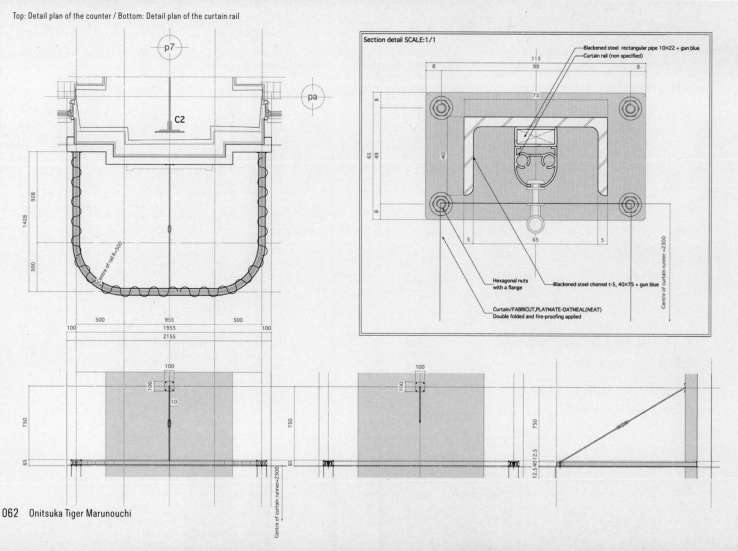

p7

C2

pa

Section detail SCALE:1/1

Blackened steel rectangular pipe 10×22 + gun blue
Curtain rail (non specified)

Hexagonal nuts with a flange

Blackened steel channel t-5, 40×75 + gun blue

Curtain/FABRICUT, PLAYMATE-OATMEAL(NEAT)
Double folded and fire-proofing applied

Centre of curtain runner =2300

P060 - P065

Onitsuka Tiger Marunouchi

Type: Apparel retailer
Open: March 2013
Location: Chiyoda-ku, Tokyo, Japan
Floor area: 85m²
Contractor: ALEN'S CRAFT
Lighting Designer: USHIO SPAX

This Onitsuka Tiger concept store was designed with three keywords in mind: craftsmanship, modern Japan and minimal design. Normally, having big windows covering the entire wall means there is less space to display the products. However, as the classic and beautiful building of Tokyo station can be seen from the shop, we asked our clients to reduce the amount of display items slightly to incorporate the existing windows into our design.

Onitsuka Tiger Omotesando

Type: Apparel retailer
Open: April 2012
Location: Shibuya-ku, Tokyo, Japan
Floor area: 133m²(1F), 131m²(2F)
Contractor: SOGO DESIGN
Lighting Designer: USHIO SPAX

The black wall we use in the interiors and exteriors in all store locations is created by embossing larch plywood panels, also known as Tiger Ply, onto mortared walls and coating them with specially blended black paint containing Japanese 'Sumi' ink. It looks like a simple black wall from afar, but on closer inspection, the grain resembling tiger stripes is visible. The flooring of the first floor is a Japanese type of bamboo, patterned in a European herringbone style. The ceiling of the second floor, which can easily be seen from the outside, is made with louvers in a pattern similar to the soles of shoes. The louvers are an aesthetic part of the design but they also serve as a place from which to hang products.

BEAMS NAGOYA
BEAMS SHIZUOKA
BEAMS TIME

BEAMS was founded in 1976 as the first fashion department store in Japan. They introduced American West Coast casual fashion at a time when it was still rare in Japan. They quickly gained popularity, opening stores across Japan and in other Asian countries soon after their launch. It is still a well-known brand among people of various generations in Asia.

We have produced many interior designs for this brand, but chose a different design for every store as this is the concept that BEAMS requested.

For example, BEAMS HARAJUKU, situated at the location of the first BEAMS store, is a flagship store for menswear. Therefore, we wanted to make it very 'BEAMS-like': a store to become a Harajuku landmark. We suggested shimmering light bulbs for the ceiling of the entrance to gently light the entrance and give the feeling of a porte-cochere of old style American hotels. This was so well received, it now also graces the front of the nearby International Gallery BEAMS and every store in the neighbourhood associated with BEAMS, thus making the cityscape more beautiful.

P072 - P075:

BEAMS HARAJUKU

Type: Apparel retailer
Open: September 2004
Location: Shibuya-ku, Tokyo, Japan
Floor area: 125m²(1F), 125m²(2F)
Contractor: D.BRAIN
Lighting Designer: Shinji Yamaguchi / On & Off

With good old America as the theme, we used aged wood on the first floor for warmth, and mortar on the second floor to look rather cool, which we combined with brick pillars. We also revealed the staircase, which was previously hidden from view, and painted its steel parts to make it look old. The light from the original stained glass above the stairs also adds a touch of history to the space.

THIS SPREAD:

International Gallery BEAMS

Type: Apparel retailer
Open: May 2005
Location: Shibuya-ku, Tokyo, Japan
Floor area: 440m²(B1F), 121m²(1F)
Contractor: D.BRAIN
Lighting Designer: Shinji Yamaguchi / On & Off

This is the most creative of the BEAMS shops. The theme of the shop, as the name implies, is a gallery. For the interior of its women's floor, we were conscious of accentuating the beauty of the lines of the space and emphasising the gallery-like feel. We asked the brand to purposefully refrain from playing any music in the store.

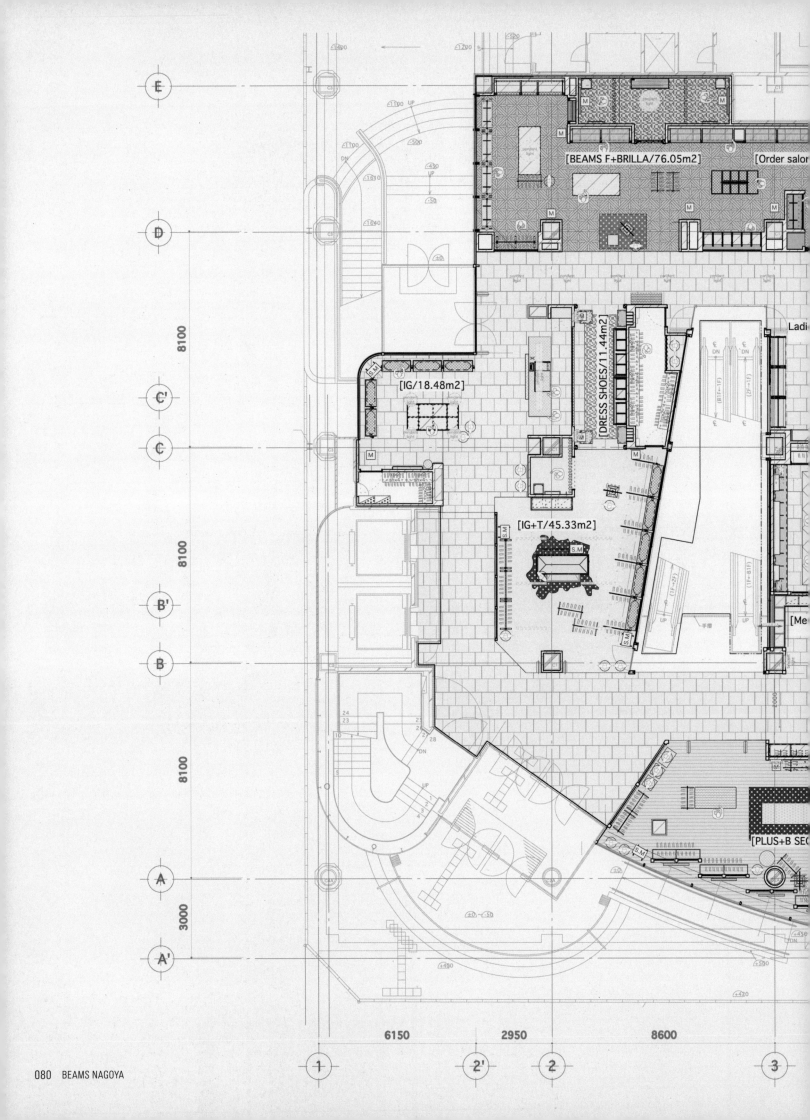

[BEAMS F+BRILLA/76.05m2]   [Order salon

[IG/18.48m2]

[DRESS SHOES/11.44m2]

Ladi

[IG+T/45.33m2]

[Me

[PLUS+B SE

E

D

8100

C'

C

8100

B'

B

8100

A

3000

A'

6150   2950   8600

1   2'   2   3

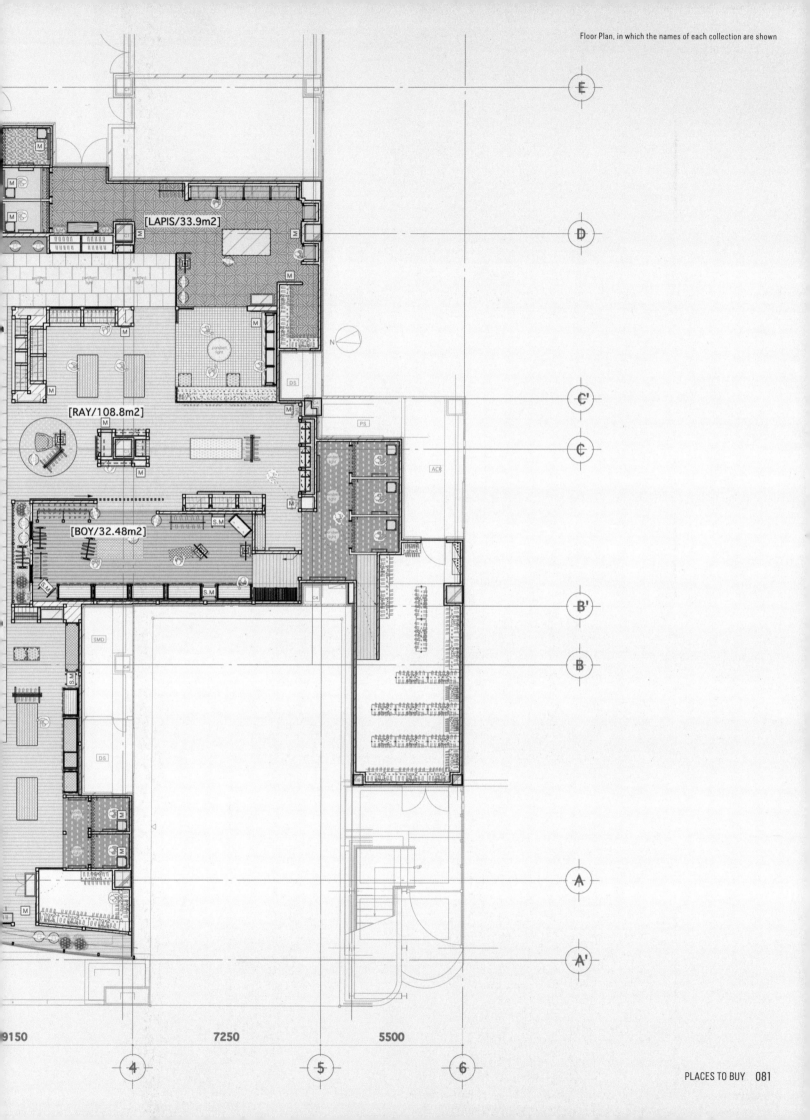

[LAPIS/33.9m2]

[RAY/108.8m2]

[BOY/32.48m2]

E

D

C'

C

B'

B

A

A'

9150

7250

5500

4

5

6

P079 · P083:

BEAMS NAGOYA

Type: Apparel retailer
Open: October 2012
Location: Nagoya-shi, Aichi, Japan
Floor area: 789m²
Contractor: NOMURA
Lighting Designer: USHIO SPAX

The shop with the largest space on one floor only, of all the
BEAMS stores. It occupies the entire floor of a department
store, so we designed its plan like a maze, matching
the interior to each collection so that customers flow
subconsciously from one collection to the next by walking
through the space.

THIS SPREAD:

BEAMS SHIZUOKA

Type: Apparel retailer
Open: October 2010
Location: Shizuoka-shi, Shizuoka, Japan
Floor area: 354m²
Contractor: SPACE
Lighting Designer: USHIO SPAX

When designing any retail shop, the location of the cash desk is important. In this Shizuoka store, an impressive cash desk was placed in the middle of the shop to divide the men's and women's sections. For the ceiling lights, light bulbs were inserted into half spheres to give the appearance of successive, indirect lighting.

THIS SPREAD:

BEAMS TIME

Type: Apparel retailer
Open: March 2006
Location: Shibuya-ku, Tokyo, Japan
Floor area: 456m²
Contractor: NOMURA
Lighting Designer: Shinji Yamaguchi / On & Off

This shop was part of a large project to open five BEAMS
stores at the same time in Shibuya. Like the other stores in
the project, this shop – covering two floors – also has a large
floor space. Stacking Okinawan Ryukyu blocks on the exterior
wall greatly changed the impression of this location. To make
the wall less heavy at the top, we used brick-moulded styrene.

NUMBER(N)INE

2003 —

NUNBER(N)INE Ebisu
NUNBER(N)INE New York

As designer of this brand from 1996 to 2009,
Takahiro Miyashita mixed high-fashion with
a rock sensibility and had a huge following,
especially among young people.
We designed their Ebisu and New York
locations during the same period. Our theme
became 'Design that isn't Designed'. We
wanted the place to look like it had always
been there, and unlike other projects, we
did not design or make any of the furniture,
displays or racks. Instead, we found most
of the items in New York antique shops.
At the time, this was an unusual and
ground-breaking approach to designing a
shop in Japan. The brand itself suddenly
ended production in 2009, but the place
remains close to our hearts as a project that
dramatically changed our ideas about design.

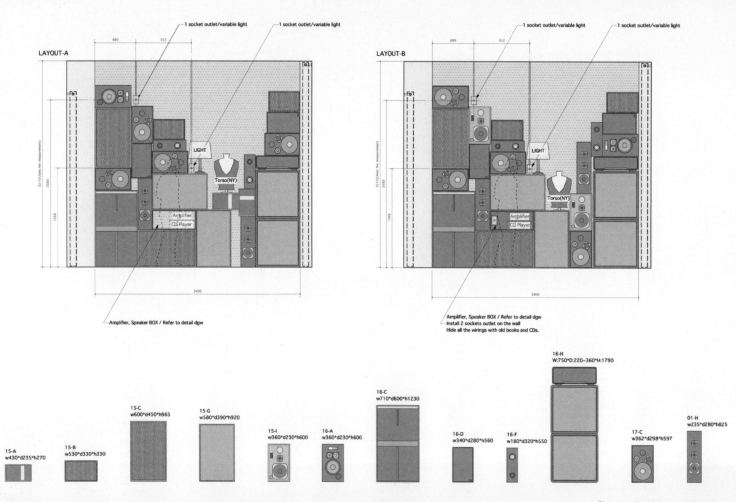

LAYOUT-A

1 socket outlet/variable light   1 socket outlet/variable light

LIGHT

Torso(NY)

Amplifier
CD Player

Amplifier, Speaker BOX / Refer to detail dgw

LAYOUT-B

1 socket outlet/variable light   1 socket outlet/variable light

LIGHT

Torso(NY)

Amplifier
CD Player

Amplifier, Speaker BOX / Refer to detail dgw
Install 2 sockets outlet on the wall
Hide all the wirings with old books and CDs.

15-A
w430*d235*h270

15-B
w530*d330*h330

15-C
w600*d450*h965

15-G
w580*d390*h920

15-I
w360*d230*h600

16-A
w360*d230*h600

16-C
w710*d600*h1230

16-D
w340*d280*h560

16-F
w180*d320*h550

16-H
W:750*D:220~360*H:1790

17-C
w362*d298*h597

01-H
w235*d280*h825

Elevation plan of the stacked speakers

P068 - P091

NUMBER(N)INE Ebisu

Type: Apparel retailer
Open: May 2003
Location: Shibuya-ku, Tokyo, Japan
Floor area: 98m²(B1F), 96m²(1F)
Contractor: D.BRAIN
Lighting Designer: LINE-INC.

The design for this store, which has one floor in the basement and another on the first floor, was influenced by the method in which customers enter the store. The entrance is not on street level, so customers must descend the dimly lit stairs leading underground to reach a large antique door that opens to the store. From the basement, customers go up another set of stairs to the ground level, and they leave the store from the first floor. Both floors remain dark during the day to enable the style and aesthetics of the brand to be experienced as they should be.

NUMBER(N)INE New York

Type: Apparel retailer
Open: September 2003
Location: New York, USA
Floor area: 293m²
Lighting Designer: Shinji Yamaguchi / On & Off

The antique tin panels that line the ceiling, the counter made
of piled up old books and the antique speakers that appear to
be randomly placed were experimented with using multiple
combinations and positions to achieve the best effect. We made
image data of every antique part purchased and tried many
different scenarios. Every detail may seem to have been made
by chance, but in fact, they were all deeply considered. This is
the approach of a 'design that isn't designed'.

PLACES TO BUY 5
ARTS&SCIENCE

2004 –

ARTS&SCIENCE is the brand founded in
2003 by stylist Sonya Park. It suggests a
lifestyle based on original apparel as the
focus. The shop, located on a fashion street
in Aoyama, Tokyo, is their second store.
The ceiling is very low and the space is
very small for a shop, but we developed
these characteristics to create a place that
feels like one has been personally invited
into Sonya's home. We rounded the edges of
every pillar and beam to create a soft, gentle
feel. The furniture in the shop is almost all
selected by Sonya herself. We succeeded in
creating a space that is intimate yet leaves
a strong impression of Sonya's exceptional
sense of style.

P096 - P099:

ARTS&SCIENCE

Type: Apparel retailer
Open: December 2004
Location: Minato-ku, Tokyo, Japan
Floor area: 49m²(1F), 57m²(2F)
Contractor: D.BRAIN
Lighting Designer: LINE-INC.

We pieced together the stained glass by the entrance, which decorates and highlights the facade, in multiple ways until we got it right. The panels are from Sonya's personal collection.

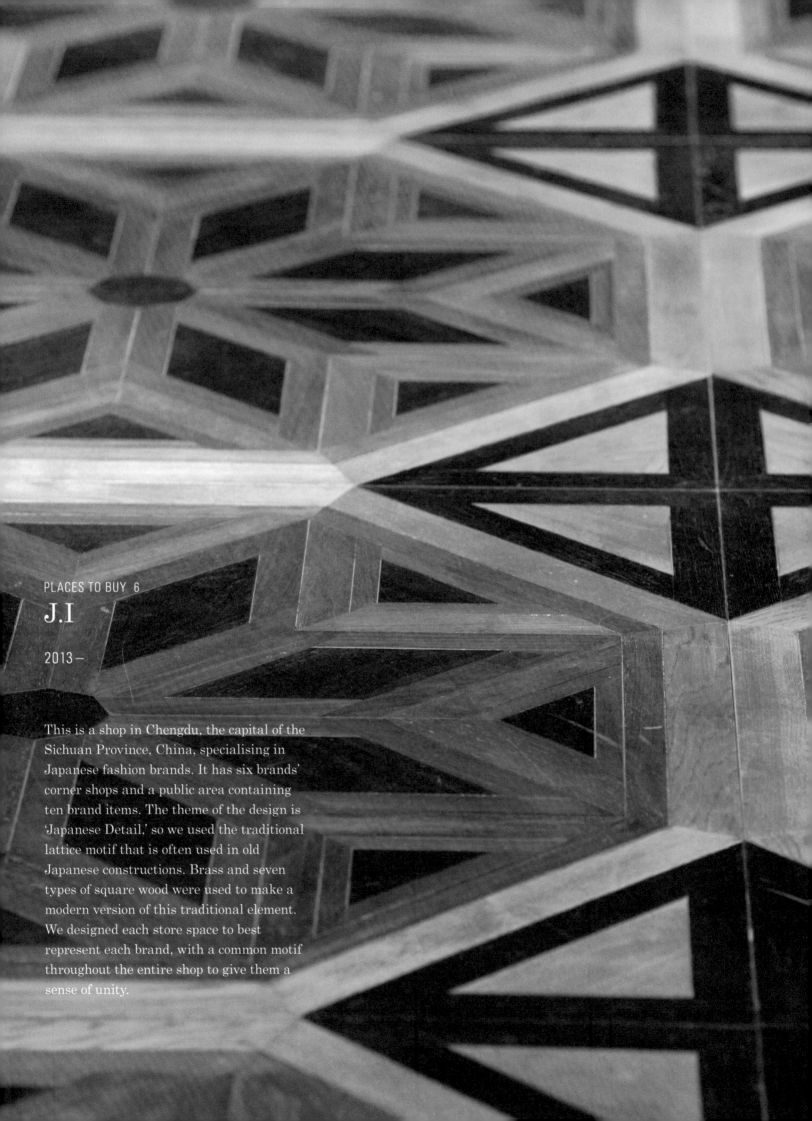

J.I

2013—

This is a shop in Chengdu, the capital of the
Sichuan Province, China, specialising in
Japanese fashion brands. It has six brands'
corner shops and a public area containing
ten brand items. The theme of the design is
'Japanese Detail,' so we used the traditional
lattice motif that is often used in old
Japanese constructions. Brass and seven
types of square wood were used to make a
modern version of this traditional element.
We designed each store space to best
represent each brand, with a common motif
throughout the entire shop to give them a
sense of unity.

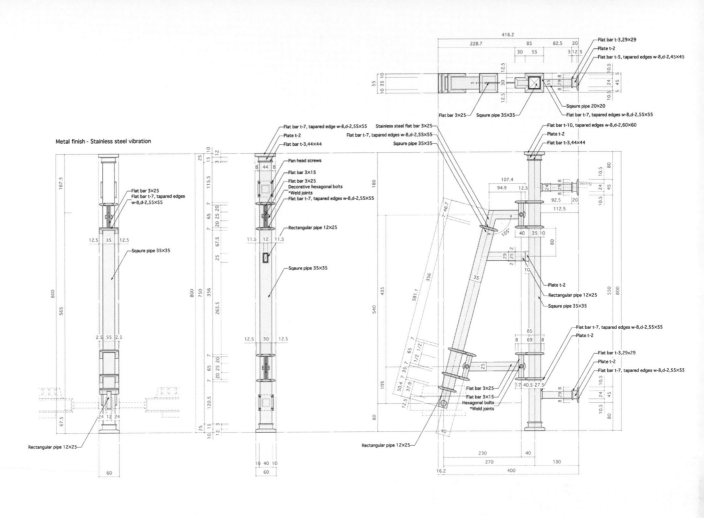

Metal finish - Stainless steel vibration

Flat bar t-7, tapared edge w-8,d-2,55×55
Plate t-2
Flat bar t-3,44×44
Pan head screws
Flat bar 3×15
Flat bar 3×25
Decorative hexagonal bolts
*Weld joints
Flat bar t-7, tapared edges w-8,d-2,55×55

Flat bar 3×25
Flat bar t-7, tapared edges w-8,d-2,55×55
Sqaure pipe 35×35

Rectangular pipe 12×25
Sqaure pipe 35×35

Rectangular pipe 12×25

Flat bar t-7, tapared edges w-8,d-2,55×55
Stainless steel flat bar 3×25
Flat bar t-7, tapared edges w-8,d-2,55×55
Sqaure pipe 35×35

Flat bar t-3,29×29
Plate t-2
Flat bar t-5, tapared edges w-8,d-2,45×45

Flat bar 3×25
Sqaure pipe 35×35
Sqaure pipe 20×20
Flat bar t-7, tapared edges w-8,d-2,55×55

Flat bar t-10, tapared edges w-8,d-2,60×60
Plate t-2
Flat bar t-3,44×44

Wiring

Plate t-2
Rectangular pipe 12×25
Sqaure pipe 35×35

Flat bar t-7, tapared edges w-8,d-2,55×55
Plate t-2

Flat bar t-3,29×29
Plate t-2
Flat bar t-7, tapared edges w-8,d-2,55×55

Flat bar 3×25
Flat bar 3×15
Hexagonal bolts
*Weld joints

Rectangular pipe 12×25

Section detail of bracket

Pipe joint parts A

Pipe joint parts B

Stainless steel Round pipe 32φ, vibration finish

150

R50

32

32

32

Flange/Plate t-10
Hexagonal bolts

21
80 38 32
3 3
21

65

Flange/Plate t-10
Stainless steel Round pipe 38φ, vibration finish

10
40 30

Stainless steel Round pipe 32φ, vibration finish
Engraved sign
Flange/Plate t-40

10 15
40 10
15

White Mountaineering®   te Mountaineering®   te Mountaineering®   Mountaineering®

32   32   32   32

Stainless steel Round pipe 32φ, vibration finish
Pipe joint parts A

Pipe joint parts B

38
32

32

32

32

38   38   38

Stainless steel Round pipe 32φ, vibration finish

Detail of the hanging pipe

P100 - P105:

J.I

Type: Apparel retailer
Open: May 2013
Location: Chengdu, China
Floor area: 556m²
Lighting Designer: USHIO SPAX

We designed the flooring of the White Mountaineering section to remind visitors of traditional Japanese wooden mosaics. To appreciate the natural colours of the wood, such as teak, oak, walnut and rosewood, we kept the staining process to a minimum. Because a special technique was required to assemble those materials and form the complicated pattern, all the processes were executed in Japan and the finished products were delivered to the site in Chengdu, China.

mother

2009–

The designer, eri, produces the fashion brand, mother. The brand creates clothing that has a silkiness and brightness reminiscent of the Belle Epoque of the 1920s and orientalism. Her unique fashion has a following of young women.

The flagship store is located in Nakameguro, Tokyo. The project was to renovate a small, two-storey wooden house. Old wood structures have a wonderful aged texture created only by the passing of time, which we accentuated in our design. We exposed the original pillars and beams, and repainted the walls white for contrast. The wallpaper and curtains were chosen in collaboration with the designer. The space accentuates the brand's exotic mood and the feel of uniquely amalgamated cultures.

Type: Apparel retailer
Open: July 2009
Location: Meguro-ku, Tokyo, Japan
Floor area: 57m²(1F), 44m²(2F)
Contractor: EIKOSHA
Lighting Designer: USHIO SPAX

The mirrors covering the entire wall not only give the illusion of space but also the possibility of another world expanding on the other side.

The SECRETCLOSET

2014 —

Keiko Onose launched the brand The
SECRETCLOSET in 2007. Having produced
their interiors from the beginning, we
imagine an independent woman being able
to shop in the store as if visiting the house of
a close friend who knows her heart's desires
very well. For the interior of the shop, we were
inspired by Onose's living room in her flat
in London. With no frills, the space perhaps
seems too pristine to enter at first glance, but
we think this style is most appropriate for this
brand, as it allows each customer to take their
time choosing the items most suited to them.
We accentuated the luxurious textures, and
we purposely did not incorporate too many
displays, wanting instead to subtly show the
brand's philosophy.

P110 - P113:

The SECRETCLOSET Marunouchi

Type: Specialty store
Open: November 2014
Location: Chiyoda-ku, Tokyo, Japan
Floor area: 55m²
Contractor: SOGO DESIGN
Lighting Designer: ModuleX

Symmetrical spaces give a clean and proper energy, but if the vibe is too tense the shop is not welcoming for guests. To rectify this, we placed a large sofa and rug to balance the tension with a relaxing atmosphere. Like music, lighting and the smell of the space, we think the service of the staff is an important part of the interior. Here, the staff welcome the customers with gentle smiles.

24karats SURF

2010 —

This is a Japanese casual wear brand based in Hawaii. Since we wanted to make a shop where both tourists and locals feel comfortable, we created a space with a balanced and relaxed look and feel. We mostly used local materials, but the flooring – which we gave an aged finish – and the functional furniture were made in Japan and shipped to Hawaii. To precisely realise the intricate nuances of these details, it was necessary to work closely with the craftsmen in Japan. At the construction site, we functioned as carpenters and showed the local workers – who were unsure of how to proceed with the finishes – what we had in mind. The ability to participate in the build is one of our strengths.

24karats SURF

Type: Apparel retailer
Open: November 2010
Location: Hawaii, USA
Floor area: 158m²
Contractor: Hawaii Project Design
Lighting Designer: USHIO SPAX

We flew craftsmen from Japan to Honolulu for the final finishes because the nuances were crucial when adding the aging effects to parts of the interior.

nano·universe

1999 —

nano·universe Ground Floor
nano·universe Ginza
nano·universe Yokohama
nano·universe Tokyo

nano·universe is a brand that feels like a traditional European brand. Their first store, nano·universe Ground Floor, opened in 1999. This was the first retail shop that Katsuta produced with his former company, EXIT METAL WORK SUPPLY, before starting LINE-INC. As the shop was located in the basement and the storefront very narrow, it was hard for pedestrians to notice it from the street. Our solution was to build a three dimensional entrance wall to catch the eye of passers-by. This was an idea we came up with while arranging samples for the store space below. This wall leaves a strong impression and draws customers into the basement. Katsuta worked on the following project, nano·universe Tokyo, with his current company LINE-INC.
From this store on, the shop design for this brand became a combination of two opposing styles: trendy and classical.

THIS SPREAD:

nano·universe Ground Floor

Type: Apparel retailer
Open: April 1999
Location: Shibuya-ku, Tokyo, Japan
Floor area: 170m²
Contractor: ALPHA STUDIO
Lighting Designer: Hiroe Tanita / MAXRAY

The first shop of the brand was split across two buildings. We broke down the wall of the front building, where the basement entrance is located, and connected it to the basement of the building at the back.

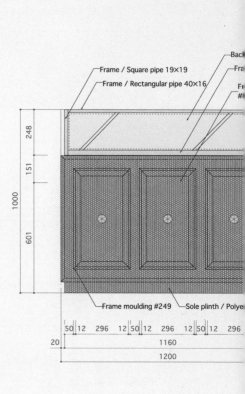

Frame / Square pipe 19×19
Frame / Rectangular pipe 40×16
Back
Fra
Fr
#

248
151
1000
601

Frame moulding #249
Sole plinth / Polye

50 12 296 12 50 12 296 12 50 12 296
20
1160
1200

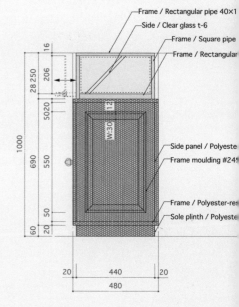

Frame / Rectangular pipe 40×1
Side / Clear glass t-6
Frame / Square pipe
Frame / Rectangular

16
28 250 206
5020 12
W.30
1000
690 550

Side panel / Polyeste
Frame moulding #24

50
60 20

Frame / Polyester-res
Sole plinth / Polyeste

20 440 20
480

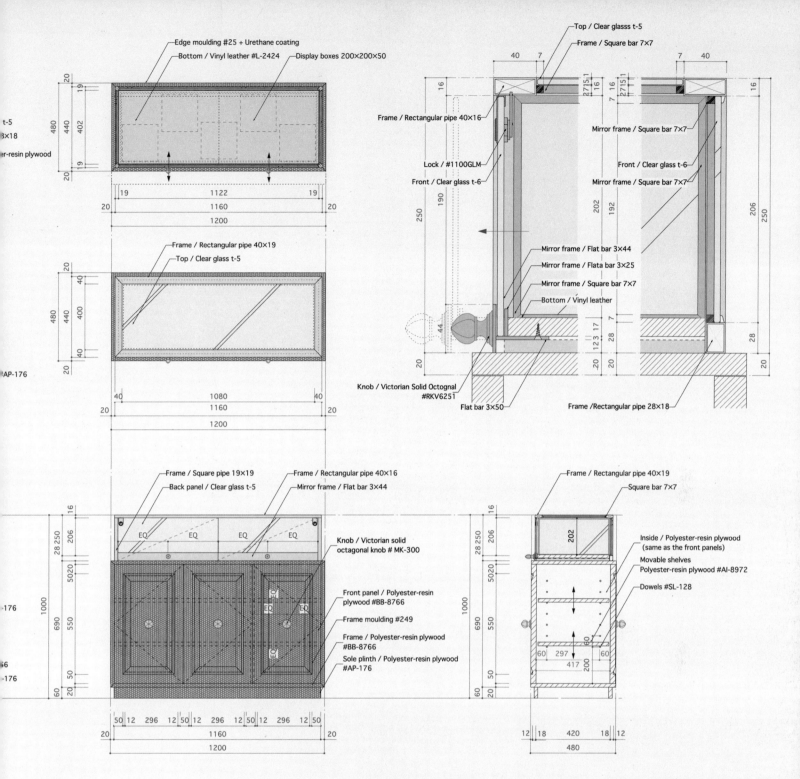

Edge moulding #25 + Urethane coating
Bottom / Vinyl leather #L-2424 — Display boxes 200×200×50

Top / Clear glasss t-5
Frame / Square bar 7×7

t-5
3×18
er-resin plywood

Frame / Rectangular pipe 40×16

Mirror frame / Square bar 7×7

Lock / #1100GLM
Front / Clear glass t-6

Front / Clear glass t-6
Mirror frame / Square bar 7×7

Frame / Rectangular pipe 40×19
Top / Clear glass t-5

Mirror frame / Flat bar 3×44
Mirror frame / Flata bar 3×25
Mirror frame / Square bar 7×7
Bottom / Vinyl leather

AP-176

Knob / Victorian Solid Octognal #RKV6251
Flat bar 3×50

Frame /Rectangular pipe 28×18

Frame / Square pipe 19×19 — Frame / Rectangular pipe 40×16
Back panel / Clear glass t-5 — Mirror frame / Flat bar 3×44

Frame / Rectangular pipe 40×19
Square bar 7×7

EQ   EQ   EQ   EQ

Knob / Victorian solid octagonal knob # MK-300

Inside / Polyester-resin plywood (same as the front panels)
Movable shelves Polyester-resin plywood #AI-8972

-176

Front panel / Polyester-resin plywood #BB-8766
Frame moulding #249
Frame / Polyester-resin plywood #BB-8766
Sole plinth / Polyester-resin plywood #AP-176

Dowels #SL-128

6
-176

Elevation of the store furniture

P120 - P122

nano·universe Ginza

Type: Apparel retailer
Open: April 2007
Location: Chuo-ku, Tokyo, Japan
Floor area: 152m²
Contractor: D.BRAIN
Lighting Designer: Shinji Yamaguchi / On & Off

This shop combines two opposing styles: classic and trendy.
After walking through a modern walkway of reflective glass,
one comes to a display corner with old books in red covers.

nano·universe Yokohama

Type: Apparel retailer
Open: November 2003
Location: Yokohama-shi, Kanagawa, Japan
Floor area: 292m²
Contractor: D.BRAIN
Lighting designer: Takayoshi Murai / JAPAN LIGHTING

By using raised floors of different levels and partitions, the varying ceiling heights changed the intimacy of each zone, creating a dynamic space as a whole. We also created a method of indirect lighting by cutting out squares in the ceiling.

nano·universe Tokyo

Type: Apparel retailer
Open: October 2002
Location: Shibuya-ku, Tokyo, Japan
Floor area: 194m²(1F), 265m²(2F)
Contractor: D.BRAIN
Lighting Designer: Osamu Wakai / DAIKO ELECTRIC

More than 10 years have passed since construction of the flagship store was completed. The shop continues to evolve and has become a landmark of Shibuya, Tokyo.

FRAPBOIS

2003—

FRAPBOIS Nagoya
FRAPBOIS Osaka
FRAPBOIS Kyoto

Designer Eri Utsugi started this brand in
2001. We worked with her for the launch and
have since designed about ten of her stores.
Eri has a truly attractive personality and
magnetically draws in those around her.
Even at work, it becomes hard
to distinguish what is the discussion and
what we are just chattering about. The
fashion that she creates uses original
textiles and has a unique imbalance, which
elevated FRAPBIOS to be one of Japan's
most favoured brands. Meetings with her
are always a back and forth between her
humorous ideas and ours. Every meeting is
full of laughter, and those conversations are
effecting the desgin of each store.

P127 - P129:

FRAPBOIS Nagoya

Type: Apparel retailer
Open: March 2004
Location: Nagoya-shi, Aichi, Japan
Floor area: 161m²
Contractor: EIKOSHA
Lighting Designer: Osamu Wakai / DAIKO ELECTRIC

There are four antique doors at the entrance, but as part of its playful design, only one of the doors will let you enter the store. The corridor with its illuminated floor symbolises a path to the future. This long and narrow corridor lets customers enter the store from the rear of the building.

FRAPBOIS Osaka

Type: Apparel retailer
Open: February 2004
Location: Osaka-shi, Osaka, Japan
Floor area: 161m²
Contractor: WITH
Lighting Designer: Osamu Wakai / DAIKO ELECTRIC

This shop comprises two stories of an old wooden building. On the first floor we used the existing reclaimed wood, and on the second floor we had the wood painted white. As a result, even with the same materials, the two spaces have completely different characters. The two floors are linked by a well-lit stairway, as if leading to the future.

THIS SPREAD

FRAPBOIS Kyoto

Type: Apparel retailer
Open: March 2003
Location: Nakagyo-ku, Kyoto, Japan
Floor area: 90m²+21m²(Terrace)
Contractor: WITH
Lighting Designer: Osamu Wakai / DAIKO ELECTRIC

The theme for this store, located in a building that we also designed, is 'Factory'. Since it was a time when most of the retail shops were very neatly designed, it took a lot of courage to go with a concept completely in the other direction.

Adam et Ropé

2010–

Shibuya Parco Adam et Ropé
Mark Is Minatomirai Adam et Ropé

Adam et Ropé is a fashion shop that began
in 1990 with imports from around the world
and original items. The diverse stock and the
location attract a diverse clientele. We have
been flexible with the interior according to
the shops' locations.
Shibuya Parco Adam et Ropé features items
for both ladies and men, and another specific
brand is sold in a shop-in-shop format. We
completed the store as one while maintaining
a diversity of design, materials and eras.
Mark Is Minatomirai Adam et Ropé is
located in Yokohama, so we put the locality
into consideration. The space opening to the
street gives an impression of fresh sincerity,
which we extended by creating a simple and
minimal interior.

Shibuya Parco Adam et Ropé

Type: Apparel retailer
Open: March 2010
Location: Shibuya-ku, Tokyo, Japan
Floor area: 282m²
Contractor: D.BRAIN
Lighting Designer: Shinji Yamaguchi / On & Off

The challenge we faced when designing this shop was how to incorporate United Bamboo in the shop-in-shop style, as it held a different aesthetic from Adam et Ropé's. We successfully created a surprise for customers by allocating the United Bamboo section at the rear of the shop, thus giving both brands the same floor pattern.

Mark Is Minatomirai Adam et Ropé

Type: Apparel retailer
Open: June 2013
Location: Yokohama-shi, Kanagawa, Japan
Floor area: 210m²
Contractor: ALEN'S CRAFT
Lighting Designer: USHIO SPAX

To suggest an ideal lifestyle through fashion is one of this brand's concepts. At the Yokohama location, which is a city by the sea, the locality was well considered while designing. The outcome is an open, very simple design using materials and colours resembling the nearby ocean.

PLACE TO BUY 13
ACTUS

2013 —

ACTUS Minatomirai
ACTUS Umeda

This interior shop emulates a Scandinavian design and offers both casual and high-end collections. Since ACTUS Minatomirai sells not only furniture but lots of other products such as children's items, plants and miscellaneous goods, we decided to make clear distinctions between the interior design of the different sections in the shop to make it seem as though there were multiple shops inside one large one. However, we were careful not to close off the individual spaces with walls, and instead changed the materials for the floor and the ceiling to create different atmospheres for each space. On the other hand, ACTUS Umeda is located in a long and narrow space, with sunlight only at the back of the shop. To overcome this, we used pendant lights to zone off the space into sections.

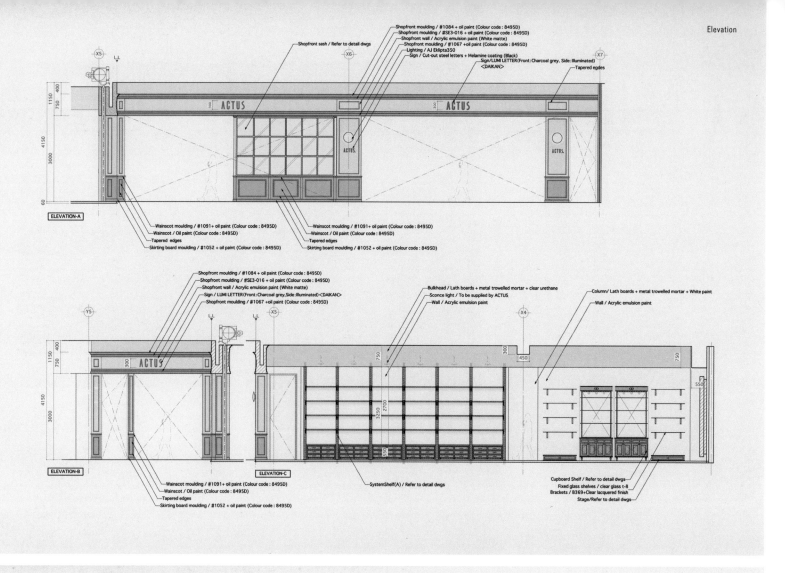

ELEVATION-A

Shopfront sash / Refer to detail dwgs
Shopfront moulding / #1084 + oil paint (Colour code : 8495D)
Shopfront moulding / #SE3-016 + oil paint (Colour code : 8495D)
Shopfront wall / Acrylic emulsion paint (White matte)
Shopfront moulding / #1067 +oil paint (Colour code : 8495D)
Lighting / AJ Eklipta350
Sign / Cut-out steel letters (Black)
Sign/LUMI LETTER(Front:Charcoal grey. Side : Illuminated)
<DAIKAN>
Tapered egdes

Wainscot moulding / #1091+ oil paint (Colour code : 8495D)
Wainscot / Oil paint (Colour code : 8495D)
Tapered edges
Skirting board moulding / #1052 + oil paint (Colour code : 8495D)
Wainscot moulding / #1091+ oil paint (Colour code : 8495D)
Wainscot / Oil paint (Colour code : 8495D)
Tapered edges
Skirting board moulding / #1052 + oil paint (Colour code : 8495D)

Shopfront moulding / #1084 + oil paint (Colour code : 8495D)
Shopfront moulding / #SE3-016 + oil paint (Colour code : 8495D)
Shopfront wall / Acrylic emulsion paint (White matte)
Sign / LUMI LETTER (Front : Charcoal grey, Side : Illuminated) <DAIKAN>
Shopfront moulding / #1067 +oil paint (Colour code : 8495D)
Bulkhead / Lath boards + metal trowelled mortar + clear urethane
Sconce light / To be supplied by ACTUS
Wall / Acrylic emulsion paint
Column/ Lath boards + metal trowelled mortar + White paint
Wall / Acrylic emulsion paint

ELEVATION-B   **ELEVATION-C**

Wainscot moulding / #1091+ oil paint (Colour code : 8495D)
Wainscot / Oil paint (Colour code : 8495D)
Tapered edges
Skirting board moulding / #1052 + oil paint (Colour code : 8495D)
SystemShelf(A) / Refer to detail dwgs
Cupboard Shelf / Refer to detail dwgs
Fixed glass shelves / clear glass t-8
Brackets / 8369+Clear lacquered finish
Stage/Refer to detail dwgs

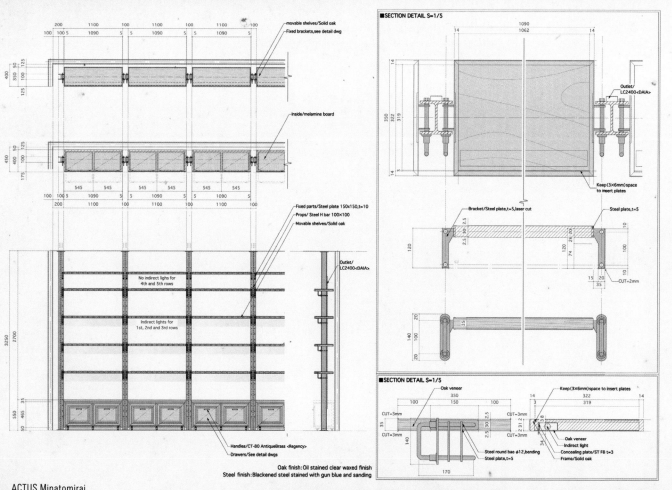

movable shelves/Solid oak
Fixed brackets,see detail dwg
inside/melamine board
Fixed parts/Steel plate 150x150,t=10
Props/ Steel H bar 100×100
Movable shelves/Solid oak
Outlet/ LC2400<DAIA>
No indirect lighs for 4th and 5th rows
Indirect lights for 1st, 2nd and 3rd rows
Handles/CT-80 AntiqueBrass <Regency>
Drawers/See detail dwgs
Oak finish:Oil stained clear waxed finish
Steel finish:Blackened steel stained with gun blue and sanding

■SECTION DETAIL S=1/5
Outlet/ LC2400<DAIA>
Keep(3×6mm)space to insert plates
Bracket/Steel plate t=5,laser cut
Steel plate,t=5
CUT=2mm

■SECTION DETAIL S=1/5
Oak veneer
Keep(3×6mm)space to insert plates
CUT=3mm
Concealing plate/ST FB t=3
Frame/Solid oak
Steel round bae φ12, bending
Steel plate,t=5
Oak veneer
Indirect light

P140 - P143:

ACTUS Minatomirai

Type: Interior Shop
Open: June 2013
Location: Yokohama-shi, Kanagawa, Japan
Floor area: 878m²
Contractor: ZYCC CORPORATION
Lighting Designer: Kenji Ito

In this store we wanted to make an area selling items for children. What we came up with were the playful small houses where children can fully enjoy themselves.

THIS SPREAD:

ACTUS Umeda

Type: Interior Shop
Open: April 2013
Location: Osaka-shi, Osaka, Japan
Floor area: 878m²
Contractor: ZYCC CORPORATION
Lighting Designer: Kenji Ito

The cafe at the back of the shop, with its clean impression, is surrounded by tall glass windows. The open kitchen in the middle adds to the shop's energy and vitality.

PLACES TO EAT

Going to a restaurant is like going on a small vacation. It's not only about being able to make the trip, but also the view on the way there, the smell of the flowers or the ocean, and the unexpected encounters, which all shape the impression of the trip. Similarly, the food and interior design don't tell you everything about the restaurant. For example, the music and the volume it is played, the staff and their uniforms, and the service and lighting all need to be satisfying for the customer before one can truly say it is a 'well-designed' restaurant.

When thinking about a restaurant, we envision sitting at every seat to see what the customers will see and understand how they will experience their meal. We consider and simulate everything. There shouldn't be a single seat in which a guest feels disappointed by their experience. In other words, if we feel confident that the customers can enjoy their meals in every seat of our plan, then 80% of the design is complete.

Often overlooked when designing a restaurant are the toilets. Even when guests go to the toilet, it must be a continuation of their experience. It should not be a moment when they come back to reality.

It is important that guests have an overall positive experience and want to come back another time. For that, the interior design cannot be the only impression that stays in the customers' minds. All the elements must work in harmony toward the same goal. To achieve this, we have many meetings and discussions with the owners and within our team.

PLACES TO EAT 1
daylight kitchen

2006 –

With this cafe we strived to create a forest sanctuary discovered in the middle of a busy city. The cafe is located at the entrance of a school for chefs and patissiers, so the cafe is also a place where the students of the school can try the recipes and techniques they have learned as the actual shop staff. We used familiar materials such as unfinished pine and iron, being careful not to make the place too fancy because we wanted the guests to feel relaxed on entering the space.
We used much wood for the interior because we wanted the atmosphere of the cafe to develop as time passed. Ten years on since its opening, the cafe has developed more character as the wood has aged, almost like a real forest.

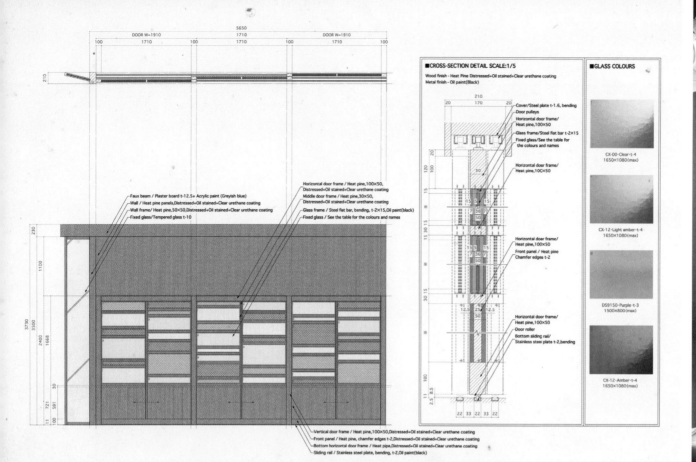

5650

DOOR W=1910 · DOOR W=1910

100 1710 100 1710 100 1710 100

210

■CROSS-SECTION DETAIL SCALE:1/5

Wood finish - Heat Pine Distressed+Oil stained+Clear urethane coating
Metal finish - Oil paint(Black)

210
20 170 20

Cover/Steel plate t-1.6, bending
Door pulleys
Horizontal door frame/
Heat pine,100×50
Glass frame/Steel flat bar t-2×15
Fixed glass/See the table for
the colours and names

Horizontal door frame/
Heat pine,10C×50

Horizontal door frame/
Heat pine,100×50
Front panel / Heat pine
Chamfer edges t-2

Horizontal door frame/
Heat pine,100×50
Door roller
Bottom sliding rail/
Stainless steel plate t-2,bending

22 33 22 33 22

■GLASS COLOURS

CX-00-Clear-t-4
1650×1080(max)

CX-12-Light amber-t-4
1650×1080(max)

DS9150-Purple-t-3
1500×800(max)

CX-12-Amber-t-4
1650×1080(max)

Faux beam / Plaster board t-12.5+ Acrylic paint (Greyish blue)
Wall / Heat pine panels,50×50,Distressed+Oil stained+Clear urethane coating
Wall frame/ Heat pine,50×50,Distressed+Oil stained+Clear urethane coating
Fixed glass/Tempered glass t-10

Horizontal door frame / Heat pine,100×50,
Distressed+Oil stained+Clear urethane coating
Middle door frame / Heat pine,30×50,
Distressed+Oil stained+Clear urethane coating
Glass frame / Steel flat bar, bending, t-2×15,Oil paint(black)
Fixed glass / See the table for the colours and names

230
1100
3730 3500
2400 1668
30
721 591
11 100

Vertical door frame / Heat pine,100×50,Distressed+Oil stained+Clear urethane coating
Front panel / Heat pine, chamfer edges t-2,Distressed+Oil stained+Clear urethane coating
Bottom horizontal door frame / Heat pipe,Distressed+Oil stained+Clear urethane coating
Sliding rail / Stainless steel plate, bending, t-2,Oil paint(black)

Detail plan of the coloured-glass sliding door

P148 - P159

daylight kitchen

Type: Restaurant & Cafe
Open: July 2006
Location: Shibuya-ku, Tokyo, Japan
Floor area: 146m²
Contractor: SHIMIZU KENSETSU
Lighting Designer: Takayoshi Murai / JAPAN LIGHTING

With seven large sliding windows, there is no separation
between the luscious plants outside and the indoors. It feels
as though one is wrapped in green.

LADIES & GENTLEMEN

2012 –

Inside the famous Isetan department store
in Shinjuku is a trendy fashion floor. On this
floor is a bistro/cafe that is divided into three
areas: a bar area reminiscent of a 1950s
diner, a dining area with impressive royal
blue chairs and a lounge area filled with
books. The flooring with its original pattern
and the ceiling made with reclaimed wood
unify these three areas. Guests can choose
their preferred area according to their needs
or moods.
The method of taking many elements and
combining them into a unique mix is a
current trend in Tokyo. It is perhaps a 'Tokyo
mode' that is interpreted, created and found
nowhere else.

LADIES & GENTLEMEN

Food menu produce
Takemasa Kinoshita

BISTRO CAFE

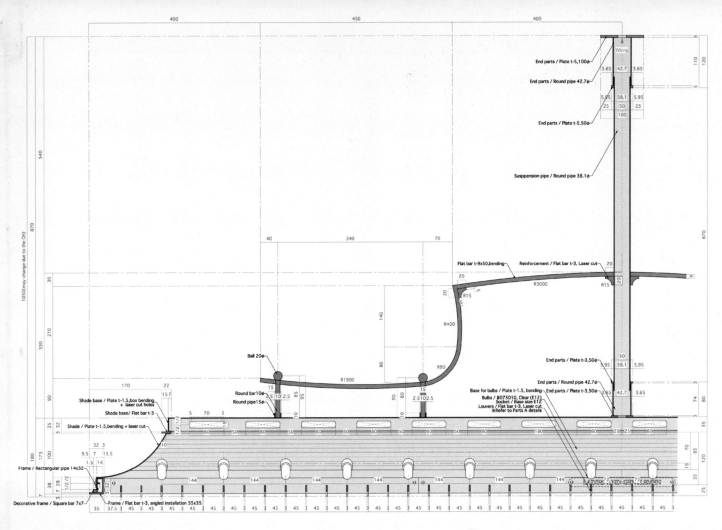

Detail plan of the pendant lamp

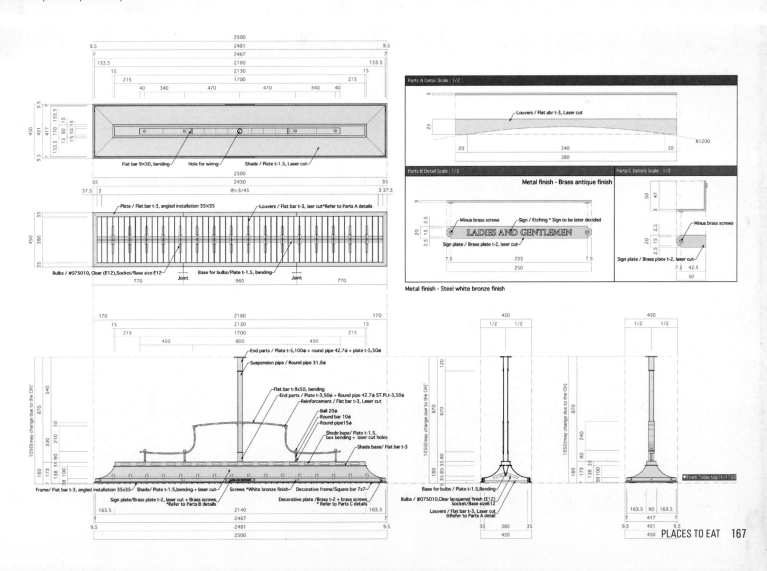

P160 - P169:

LADIES & GENTLEMEN

Type: Restaurant & Cafe
Open: December 2012
Location: Shinjuku-ku, Tokyo, Japan
Floor area: 130m²
Contractor: PLUS 8
Lighting Designer: Kenji Ito

Every piece of furniture including the tables, chairs, sofa, lights and display units were custom-made for this space. Like this project, we design furniture and displays for most of our projects.

The Courtyard Kitchen

2014 —

Shunkado, one of the largest confectioners in Japan, opened a family park called nicoe in Hamamatsu. The large green landscape is home to several buildings and attractions. One of them, The Courtyard Kitchen is a buffet style restaurant. We were faced with the question of how best to shape this restaurant for many families with young children. We designed a large hexagon-shaped kitchen in the middle, as if it was a stage. People can enjoy seeing their meals and desserts being made on the stage, as if they were watching a live show. Because the ceiling is high, we randomly suspended light bulbs so that the soft light could illuminate the entire space. The outside walls are made entirely of glass, drawing people from the surrounding park into this building.

LIFE IS LIKE A BOX OF
WHAT YOU'RE GON

SAID, AND SO,
LAD ANNIVERSARY.

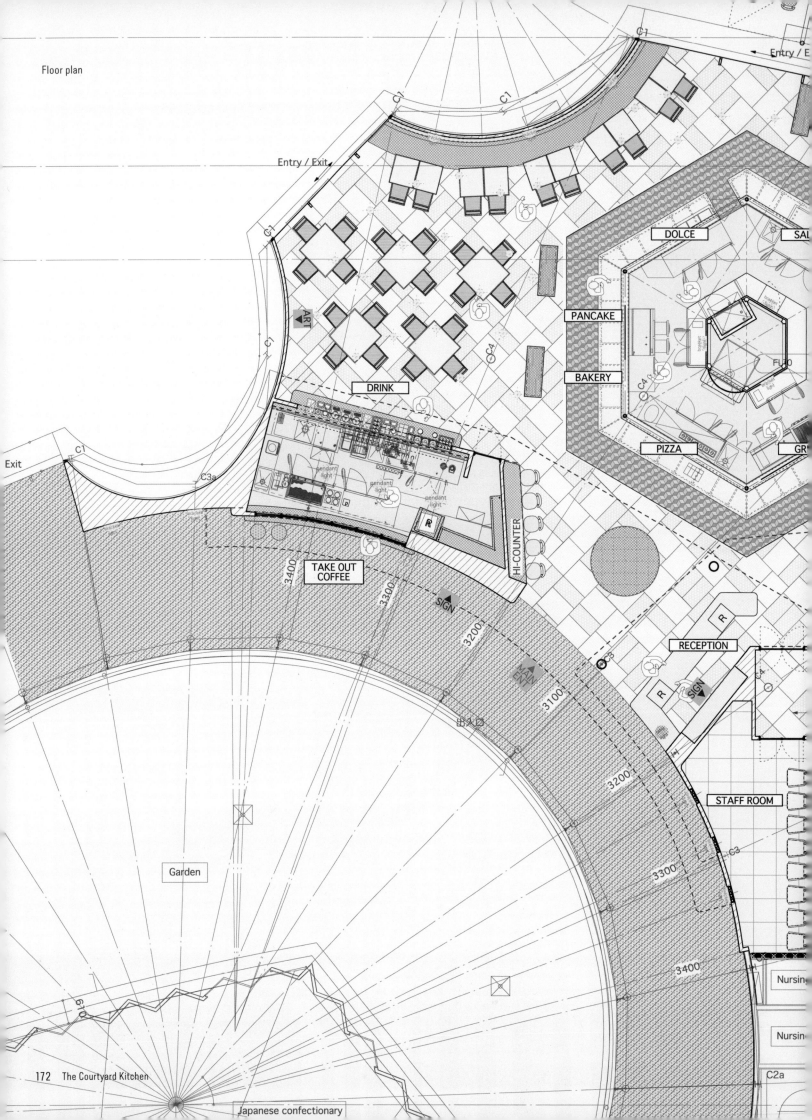

Floor plan

Entry / Exit

C1

C1

C1

C1

C1

Exit

C3a

ART

DRINK

C4

TAKE OUT
COFFEE

pendant
light

pendant
light

pendant
light

P

R

HI-COUNTER

3400

3300

SIGN

3200

MAIN
ENT

3100

3200

3300

3400

Garden

Entry / E

C1

DOLCE

SAL

PANCAKE

BAKERY

C4

PIZZA

GR

breakfast
light

FU

R

RECEPTION

R

SIGN

C4

STAFF ROOM

C3

Nursin

Nursin

C2a

C2a

172   The Courtyard Kitchen

Japanese confectionary

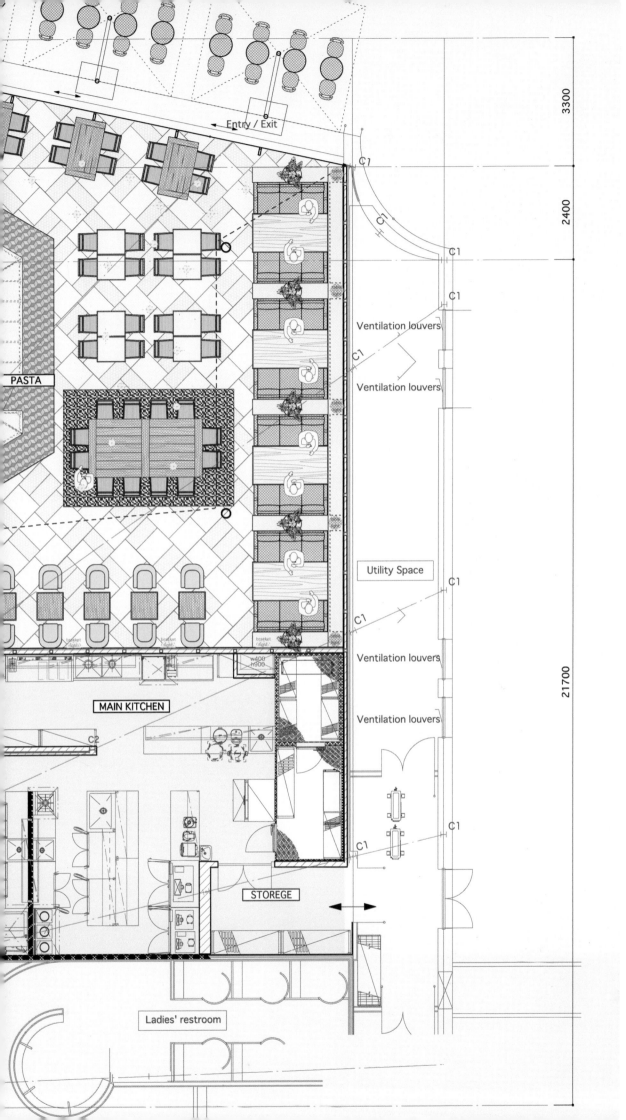

PASTA

Entry / Exit

3300

2400

C1

C1

C1

C1

Ventilation louvers

C1

Ventilation louvers

C1

Utility Space

C1

21700

Ventilation louvers

MAIN KITCHEN

C2

Ventilation louvers

C1

C1

STOREGE

Ladies' restroom

P170 · P175:

The Courtyard Kitchen

Type: Restaurant & Cafe
Open: July 2014
Location: Hamamatsu-shi, Shizuoka, Japan
Floor area: 518m²
Contractor: TANSEISHA
Lighting Designer : Kenji Ito

Lighting is an important element in determining the impression of a space. We consider the subtle nuances of its colours to create an ideal space. With this space, our goal was to emulate a soft and pleasant atmosphere.

KOEDO LOUNGE

2014 —

The word 'Koedo' means 'small Edo (old name of Tokyo)'. The streets of Kawagoe, a historical town often referred to as 'Koedo', are lined with old storehouses and merchant houses. The owner of KOEDO LOUNGE, who was born and raised in Kawagoe, contacted us requesting us to make the most attractive lounge in the town. The place has a lounge area with sofas to relax in, booths to comfortably enjoy meals or tea, a bar area where people can easily come in alone and even a karaoke room where a large group can party without worrying about others. By making areas in different styles, everybody of any age can enjoy themselves in this lounge. On one wall we displayed photos of Kawagoe from which guests can sense the seasons of this area. At first glance it may not be obvious, but by gazing at the walls, guests may recognise the scenery from the town. We hope that this lounge becomes a place where people of all ages gather and is loved by the city in which it belongs.

MEMBER'S ROOM

P176 - P181:

KOEDO LOUNGE

Type: Restaurant & Cafe
Open: June 2014
Location: Kawagoe-shi, Saitama, Japan
Floor area: 140m²
Contractor: WACT
Lighting Designer: ModuleX

The long Chesterfield sofa that lines one entirety wall is
custom-made. To be able to eat comfortably while sitting on it,
we made the seating harder than a normal sofa, with a depth
that is closer in size to a dining room chair.

diage

2006 –

In downtown Shanghai, one can find old buildings with a strong European influence called 'Lao fang zi' that were built during the French occupation. The design of diage involved converting one of these buildings after it had been abandoned for a long time. We transformed it into a restaurant, apparel shop and gallery space. Because of the building's age, the blueprints did not exist, so we started the project by taking precise measurements of the site and drawing the blueprints ourselves. The Chinese government sets very detailed building restrictions for historical buildings in China which we had to adhere to reach completion. This was a memorable project.

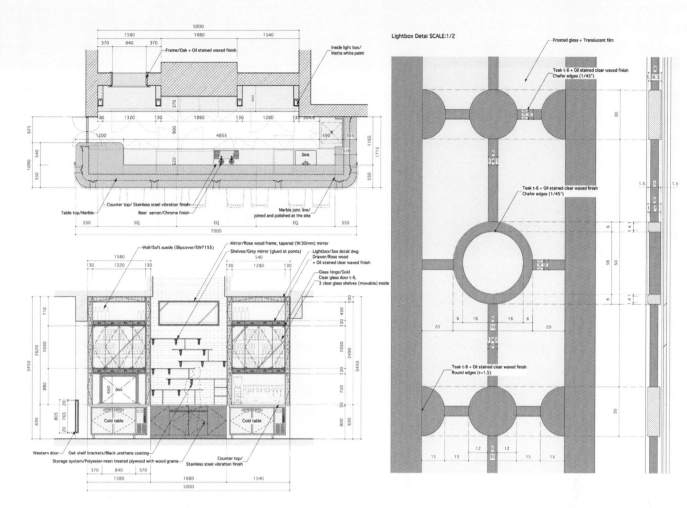

Lightbox Detai SCALE:1/2

Plan of the counter / Detail plan

P182 - P187:

diage

Type: Restaurant & Cafe, Apparel & Gallery
Open: June 2006
Location: Shanghai, China
Floor area: 379m²(1F), 379m²(2F)
Contractor: Shanghai Sunny Industrial
Lighting Designer: Shinji Yamaguchi / On & Off

The variety of materials and the details used in this project are remarkable compared to all our other projects. We incorporated wood, stone, iron, tiles, brick, leather, carpets, cloth, glass, cushions and screws with different decorations. The list is never-ending. We also encountered difficulties maintaining Japanese standards and quality in a foreign country.

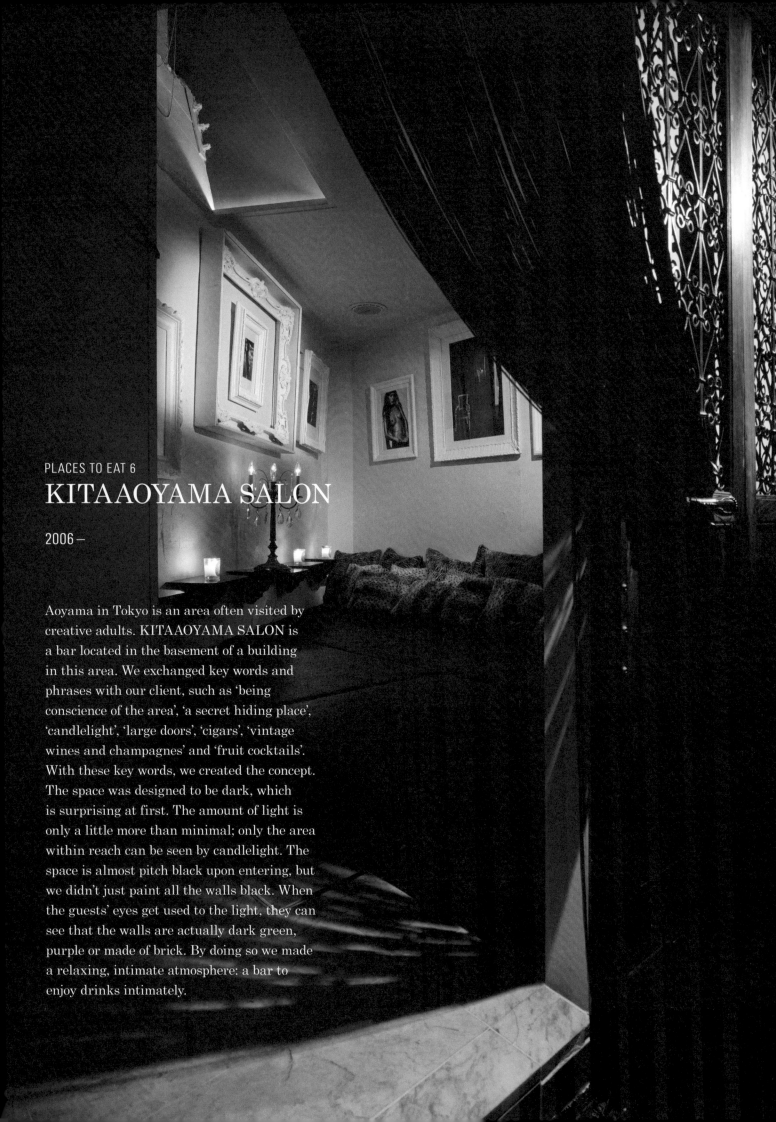

KITAAOYAMA SALON

2006 –

Aoyama in Tokyo is an area often visited by
creative adults. KITAAOYAMA SALON is
a bar located in the basement of a building
in this area. We exchanged key words and
phrases with our client, such as 'being
conscience of the area', 'a secret hiding place',
'candlelight', 'large doors', 'cigars', 'vintage
wines and champagnes' and 'fruit cocktails'.
With these key words, we created the concept.
The space was designed to be dark, which
is surprising at first. The amount of light is
only a little more than minimal; only the area
within reach can be seen by candlelight. The
space is almost pitch black upon entering, but
we didn't just paint all the walls black. When
the guests' eyes get used to the light, they can
see that the walls are actually dark green,
purple or made of brick. By doing so we made
a relaxing, intimate atmosphere: a bar to
enjoy drinks intimately.

KITAAOYAMA SALON

Type: Bar
Open: July 2006
Location: Minato-ku, Tokyo, Japan
Floor area: 63m²(B1F), 6m²(1F)
Contractor: D.BRAIN
Lighting Designer: Shinji Yamaguchi / On & Off

We ultimately wanted guests to experience an escape from the ordinary. We tried to create a space where, the moment the guests left the bar, they would question whether it had been part of their dreams or was in fact a reality.

bills

2008—

bills Shichirigahama
bills Odaiba

bills is an all-day casual dining restaurant,
which has been praised for its famous 'world's
No.1 breakfast', was first opened in Sydney,
Australia, by the world-famous restauranteur
Bill Granger.
A new company, a merge of SUNNY SIDE
UP Inc. and TRANSIT GENERAL OFFICE
Inc. was established for the operation and
public relations of the restaurant. We started
the project by visiting Sydney to gain a
physical and emotional understanding of
Bill's environment. By spending time on
the land with the beautiful blue sky and
ocean, and getting to know Bill's charming
personality, we understood what sort of space
we were expected to create for his restaurant
in Japan. We have designed four of the
Japanese locations.

P192-P194

bills Shichirigahama

Type: Restaurant & Cafe
Open: March 2008
Location: Kamakura-shi, Kanagawa, Japan
Floor area: 316m²
Contractor: PLUS 8
Lighting Designer: USHIO SPAX

Surrounded by the ocean and nature, Shichirigahama bears a resemblance to Sydney. Despite being only an hour away from Tokyo, the place provides a relaxing and laid-back atmosphere. With these factors in mind, we placed importance on the ocean breeze and sunlight when designing the interior for this restaurant's very first Japanese location. It quickly gained popularity and created a breakfast trend in Japan.

bills Odaiba

Type: Restaurant & Cafe
Open: July 2011
Location: Minato-ku, Tokyo, Japan
Floor area: 564m²
Contractor: PLUS 8
Lighting Designer: USHIO SPAX

This is the third location for bills in Japan. Offering a view of Tokyo Bay and Rainbow Bridge, Odaiba is often visited by families and couples. The space, designed to resemble the home of Bill Granger, divides this huge 564m² space into two sections. One section resembles a living room while the other is an open, relaxing dining room, allowing customers to enjoy different atmospheres under the same roof.

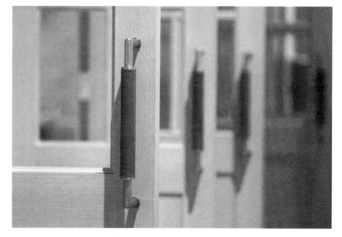

PLACES TO GET PAMPERED

comomavi
THE OVERSEA
F organics
THE SURREY
SIGN & SEAL

We have produced many hair salons, beauty parlours where people can relax, get pampered and be transformed, as well as wedding venues to have the celebration of one's dreams. We strive to create a space where each visitor feels comfortable, as we do with places like shops, restaurants and offices. It is important not to dismiss the people that work there. For example, at a hair salon, we consider the hairstylist's wishes. What type of plan will allow their work to go smoothly? Where should the hairdryers and other tools be placed? How should the lighting plan be designed to make their work easier? Finding the best answers to these questions leads to better customer service, as the input from the people who work there lines up with the needs of the customer.

We take into account the needs of both the staff and the customers and we try to see the space through their eyes. To love and care for every perception when creating a space is something that should not be forgotten.

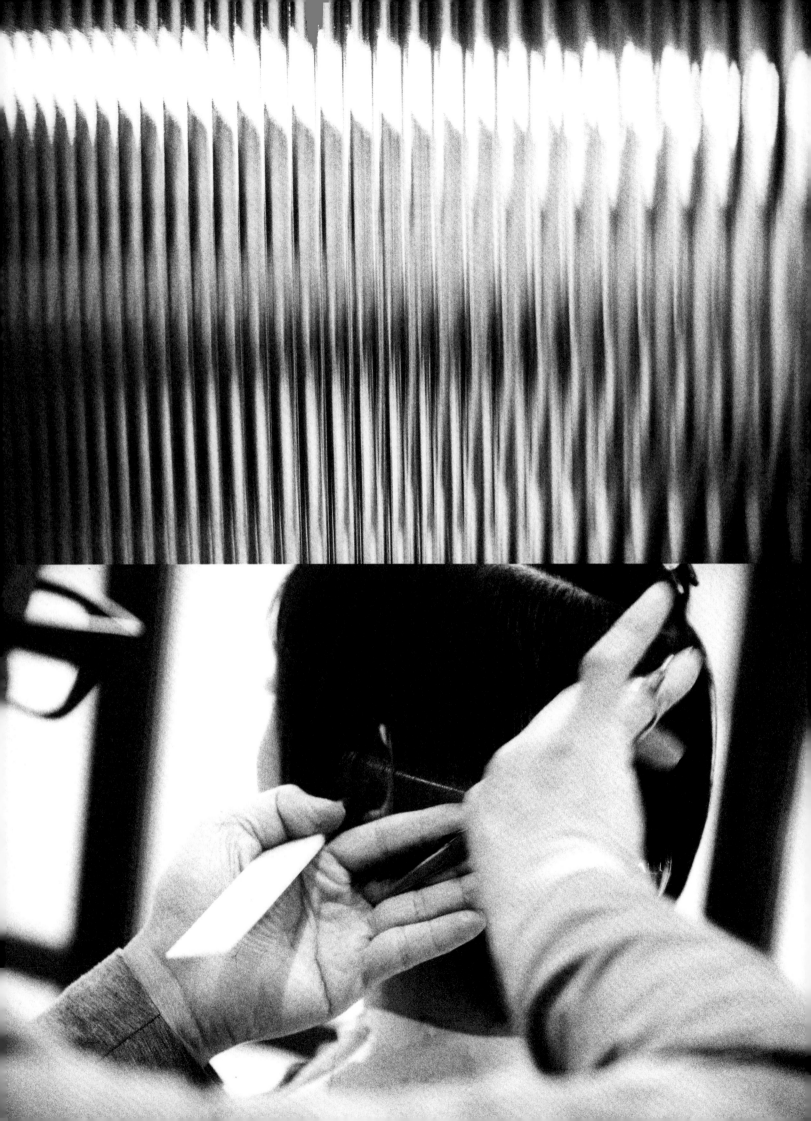

comomavi

2013 –

The name of the hair salon 'comomavi',
located in Omotesando, Tokyo, is derived
from four words: cool, fashionable, maniac
(meaning fanatical in Japanese) and vintage.
It is a place to experience and discover
attractive styles that reflect these four words,
so we created the interior with that in mind.
When the door of the elevator opens, the
guests first come to the counter. From there,
they walk down a narrow corridor to the
waiting area and salon space. The walkway
acts as a shield from the view of the building
next door, but also shows just a little of the
atmosphere of the hair cutting area.
Walking through the walkway builds up
excitement, as guests get closer to the salon.
The two bathrooms at this location are
luxurious. Because of the short duration of
the customers' stay in the salon, we wanted
them to feel as if they had entered a rich and
luxurious world.

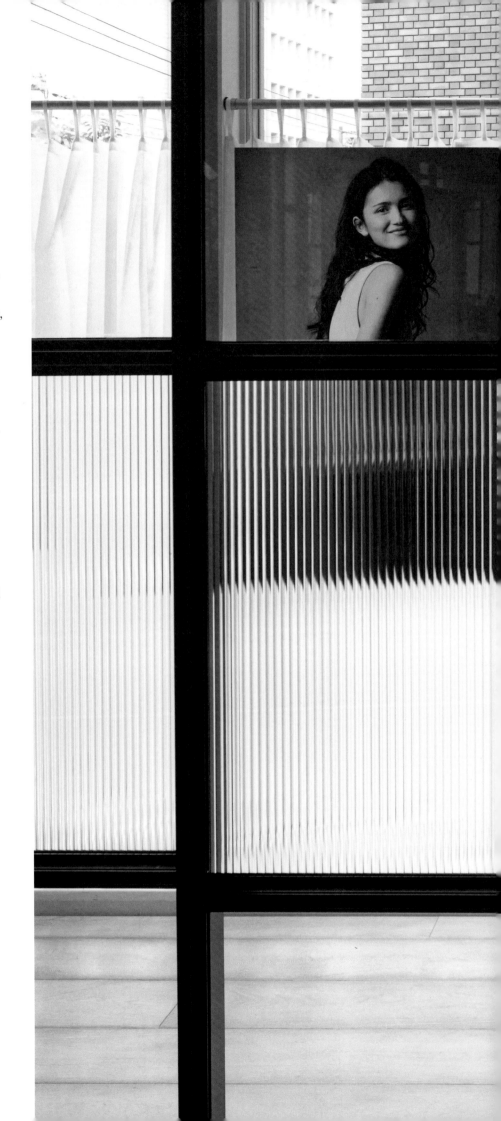

P198 - P209:

comomavi

Type: Beauty salon
Open: May 2013
Location: Minato-ku, Tokyo, Japan
Floor area: 188m²
Contractor: ALPHA STUDIO
Lighting Designer: USHIO SPAX

The comfortable shampoo space and the bright and lively cutting area are connected by a narrow hallway. At the shampooing area, where the chairs become fully horizontal, we replaced all the lighting fixtures that would shine directly into the eyes of those lied down with indirect lighting.

THE OVERSEA

2008—

THE OVERSEA is the Tokyo location of
a popular New York hair salon run by a
Japanese hairstylist. Situated in the basement,
we considered many ways to make the space
efficient without being claustrophobic. Instead
of placing the seating along the walls, we
decided to place it in the middle of the space,
facing each other with mirrors in between.
The stylists work around the island of mirrors
and chairs.

Having everything along the wall may seem
like it would make the space look bigger, but by
having the seats in the middle, the movement
of the people becomes smoother. Sometimes
doing the opposite of an initial thought can
create new, enriching spaces. We incorporated
tin panels into the ceiling and decorated the
walls to look like randomly piled bricks, to
give a New York feel.

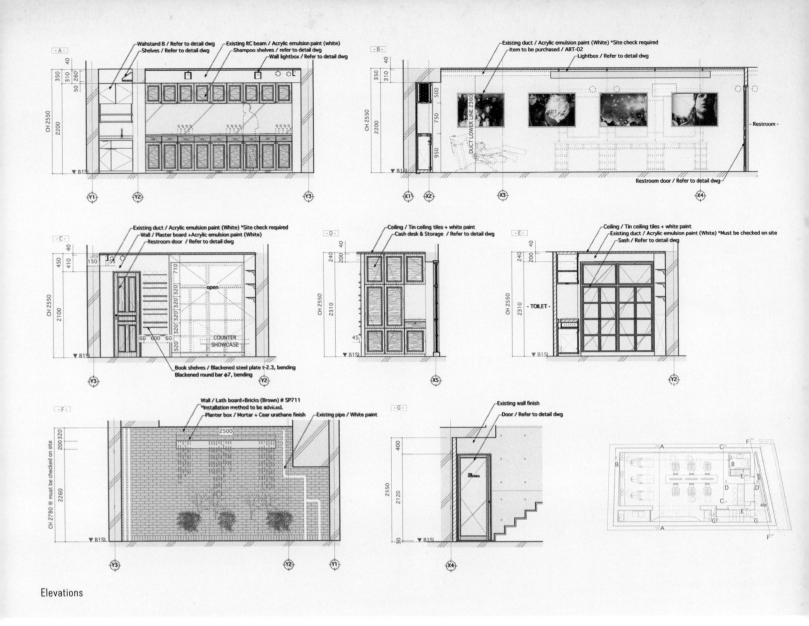

Elevations

P210 - P213:

THE OVERSEA

Type: Beauty salon
Open: May 2008
Location: Minato-ku, Tokyo, Japan
Floor area: 54m²
Contractor: PLUS 8
Lighting Designer: USHIO SPAX

We thought it would be more beautiful if there weren't any spotlights on the tin panelled ceiling. Therefore, we made mirror-finished metal boxes and hung them from the ceiling. The spotlights are hidden in these boxes, so one might not immediately notice where the light is coming from.

F organics

2014 –

F organics is the flagship store for an organic
cosmetics brand based in Japan. The first
floor houses the shop, and the second floor
is their beauty parlour. The building is a
Japanese style house, so we kept the original
details such as the beams, pillars and the
outer wood panelling as intact as possible and
reinforced the building for improved strength.
The brand envisions their main customer to
be a sensitive and sexy woman, with an inner
strength. Based on that image, we chose black
and white as the theme colours. We chose a
sofa made of cotton and applied white paint
lightly onto all the wood. This allowed the
grain to show through and gave it a feeling of
softness. We also chose a black steel material
– the thinnest possible – to symbolise inner
strength. The steel is used for items such as
the shelves and window frames. This contrast
allows customers to feel the brand concept
through the entire space.

P214 - P217:

F organics DAIKANYAMA

Type: Cosmetics store, Salon and Spa
Open: April 2014
Location: Shibuya-ku, Tokyo, Japan
Floor area: 51m²(1F), 40m²(2F)
Contractor: Smile Design
Lighting Designer: ModuleX

When renovating an old building, the important decisions to make are what to keep and what to add. We draw everything out beforehand, but we believe the most precious inspirations are those we come up with while on site.

THE SURREY

2013 —

Japan's wedding industry is oddly restrictive; the hotels or wedding venues have dress rental businesses and gift services under contract so if you don't require their services there is an extra fee to 'bring your own'. THE SURREY does not fancy those norms, so it is possible to purchase stylish wedding items the couple would love. On the first floor, customers can find a gift shop, while the second floor is dedicated to dresses and accessories.
We wanted this place to be pure and of the highest quality without being too extravagant. When creating a simple space, our skills can be best seen in the details. For example, we pay attention to the details of the handrails on the staircase and the ends of display racks. Customers may not notice each small thing, but we believe the accumulated attention to detail adds up to exude an elegance.

THE SURREY

P218 - P221:

THE SURREY Aoyama

Type: Wedding items and dress shop
Open: May 2013
Location: Minato-ku, Tokyo, Japan
Floor area: 66m²(1F), 90m²(2F)
Contractor: PLUS 8
Lighting Designer: USHIO SPAX

Do we first deliberate the details and construct the whole
or do we build the whole and then proceed with the details?
It seems that either way would lead to the same outcome,
but we find that changing the order of our work changes the
final design. This space followed the latter method.

SIGN & SEAL

2013 –

SIGN & SEAL is a Japanese jewellery brand designed and produced in-house. The majority of their products are engagement and wedding rings. To allow the stars of the shop – the jewellery – to shine the brightest, we designed the interior of the shop to take a supporting role with a monotone and simple look made of the highest quality materials. We wanted the space to serve as a place where the couple could take photos with their newly completed rings. We decorated a wall with sola flowers made of tree bark. This textured wall adds a depth to what would be simply a white space. Even when photos are taken with a colour film, the pictures look classy as though they were taken in black and white.

SIGNATURE LINE

S-04

SIGNATURE LINE

S-05

N°

P222 - P225:

SIGN & SEAL

Type: Jewellery shop
Open: February 2013
Location: Chuou-ku, Tokyo, Japan
Floor area: 54m²
Contractor: PLUS 8
Lighting Designer: USHIO SPAX

The greyish walls and ceiling were achieved with diluted white paint on mortar. The grey and whiteness vary according to the amount of water used in the paint on that area. When deciding special finishings, we always work on site with the painters to adjust the final touches.

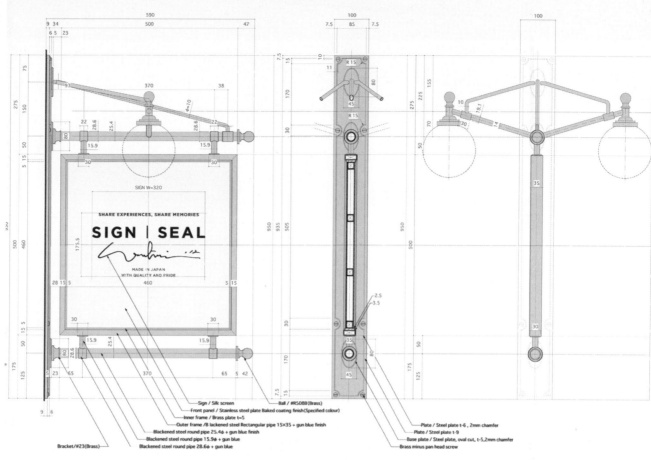

SHARE EXPERIENCES, SHARE MEMORIES

SIGN | SEAL

MADE IN JAPAN
WITH QUALITY AND PRIDE

Sign / Silk screen
Ball / #R5088(Brass)
Front panel / Stainless steel plate Baked coating finish(Specified colour)
Inner frame / Brass plate t=5
Outer frame /B lackened steel Rectangular pipe 15×35 + gun blue finish
Blackened steel round pipe 25.4φ + gun blue finish
Bracket/#23(Brass)
Blackened steel round pipe 15.9φ + gun blue
Blackened steel round pipe 28.6φ + gun blue

Plate / Steel plate t-6 , 2mm chamfer
Plate / Steel plate t-9
Base plate / Steel plate, oval cut, t-5,2mm chamfer
Brass minus pan head screw

Detail plan of the sign

PLACES TO WORK

TRANSIT GENERAL OFFICE
CHC Office
UNITED ARROWS LTD. Pressroom

The thinking that workplaces should foremost be functional for improved efficiency unfortunately still prevails in Japan.
However, as most people spend as much time, or perhaps even more time, at the office than at home, if the place was designed based on efficiency and function, would it really be possible to work well there? If all the chairs and desks were the same, if the meeting room contained only a large table, and if the space for breaks had only a sofa to sit on, would people still want to go to work every day? We hope to design offices that differ from the norm, designed from the perspective of the people that work there. Our goal is to interpret each company and produce a space where employees can work efficiently, take refreshing breaks and truly enjoy their time at the office.

TRANSIT GENERAL OFFICE

2012–

TRANSIT GENERAL OFFICE is a consulting, production and management firm in the fashion, architecture, design, music, art and food industries. Our project was to build their main office which contains shared offices within. They are, so to speak, trendsetters who convey information of cultures to a variety of people. So we looked at a similar company – a newspaper office – as a source of inspiration. Shared offices are filled with creative people, thus we aimed to give the public space a roomy feel. What stands out is the 200m² lounge area with a large Chesterfield sofa and other seating. It stimulates creativity by encouraging conversation among the people who enter.

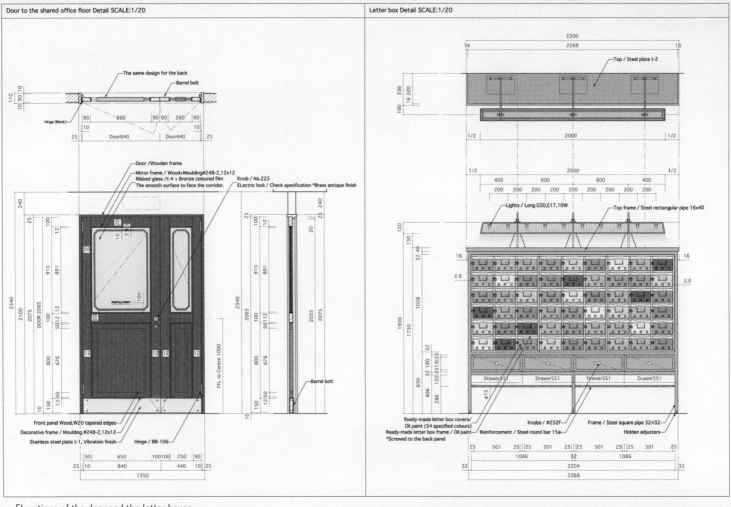

| Door to the shared office floor Detail SCALE:1/20 | Letter box Detail SCALE:1/20 |

Door to the shared office floor Detail:

The same design for the back
Barrel bolt
Hinge (Black)
Door /Wooden frame
Mirror frame / Wood+Moulding#248-2,12x12
Ribbed glass /t-4 + Bronze coloured film
The smooth surface to face the corridor.
Knob / No.225
ELectric lock / Check specification *Brass antique finish
PORTAL POINT
FFL to Centre 1000
Barrel bolt
Front panel Wood,W20 tapered edges
Decorative frame / Moulding #248-2,12x12
Stainless steel plate t-1, Vibration finish
Hinge / BB-106

Letter box Detail:

Top / Steel plate t-2
Lights / Long G30,E17,10W
Top frame / Steel rectangular pipe 16x40
Drawer551   Drawer551   Drawer551   Drawer551
Ready-made letter box covers/
Oil paint (54 specified colours)
Ready-made letter box frame / Oil paint
*Screwed to the back panel
Knobs / #232F
Reinforcement / Steel round bar 15φ
Frame / Steel square pipe 32×32
Hidden adjusters

Elevations of the door and the letter boxes

TRANSIT GENERAL OFFICE

Type: Office
Open: March 2012
Location: Minato-ku, Tokyo, Japan
Floor area: 244m²
Contractor: PLUS 8
Lighting Designer: USHIO SPAX

We used furniture with a variety of designs – designer items, antiques and originals – all from different time periods. People can choose their spot in the office according to the time of day or their topic of discussion. The Tokyoesque graphics on the wall are by fantasista utamaro, a popular artist of animation graphics.

CHC Office

2008 –

For the office of an IT firm, we designed
the space to feel digital and a little tense,
but with a clear and open feeling. When one
comes out of the elevator they are greeted by
a long hallway illuminated by red LED lights.
Along this hallway are meeting rooms and
office spaces behind glass walls. This layout
allows the staff and guests to be aware of
one another. The presence of the glass walls
between these rooms and hallway creates a
comfortable tension for a workplace.

CHC Office

Type: Office
Open: March 2008
Location: Shibuya-ku, Tokyo, Japan
Floor area: 163m²
Contractor: PLUS 8
Lighting Designer: USHIO SPAX

The art pieces by Gerhard Richter and Wolfgang Tillmans add a visual accent to the simple walls.

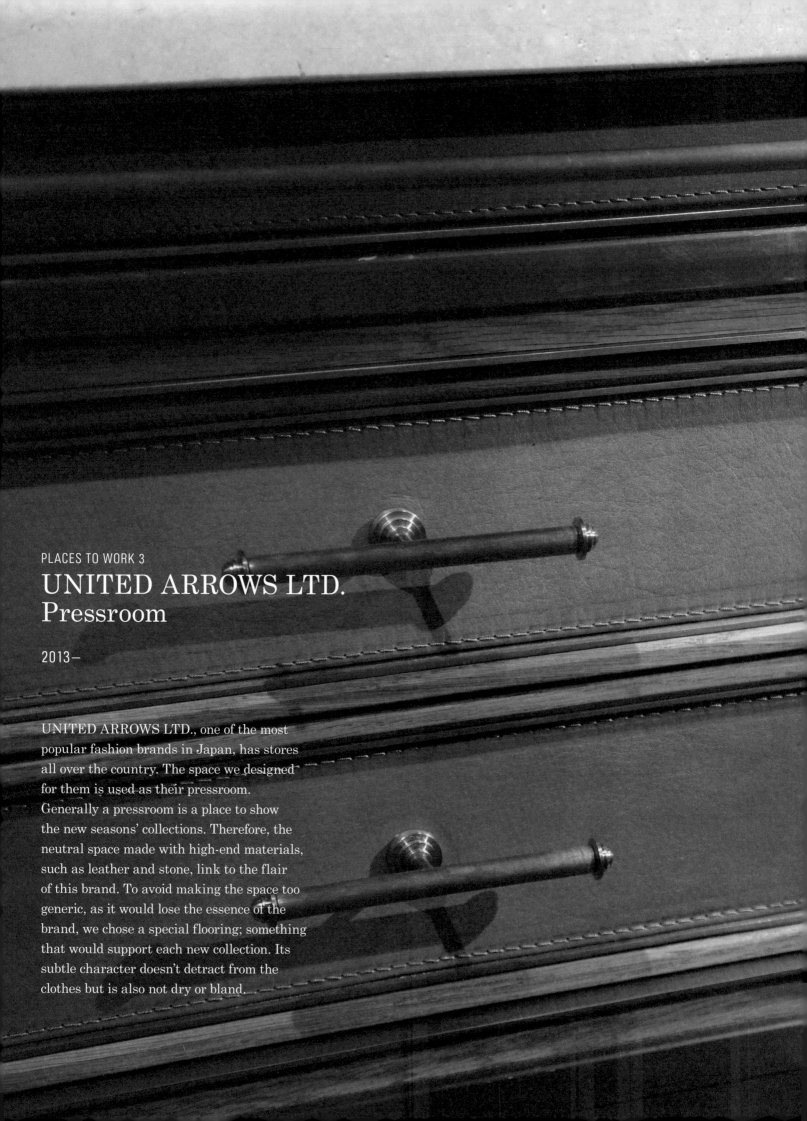

PLACES TO WORK 3
UNITED ARROWS LTD.
Pressroom

2013–

UNITED ARROWS LTD., one of the most
popular fashion brands in Japan, has stores
all over the country. The space we designed
for them is used as their pressroom.
Generally a pressroom is a place to show
the new seasons' collections. Therefore, the
neutral space made with high-end materials,
such as leather and stone, link to the flair
of this brand. To avoid making the space too
generic, as it would lose the essence of the
brand, we chose a special flooring; something
that would support each new collection. Its
subtle character doesn't detract from the
clothes but is also not dry or bland.

P238 - P241:

UNITED ARROWS LTD. Pressroom

Type: Office and Showroom
Open: August 2013
Location: Minato-ku, Tokyo, Japan
Floor area: 257m²
Contractor: DECOR
Lighting Designer: USHIO SPAX

We custom designed the door handles and the knobs on the drawers for this project. We prefer not to use mass produced items, even for the minor details, and we wanted to get the smallest detail just right including the colour of the stitching on the drawers. Perhaps the difference between good and bad design is in the tenacity in the final stages.

PLACES TO SHOW

Lloyd's Antiques Exhibition
YAMAHA Booth, TOKYO MOTOR SHOW

We accept inquiries to design gallery shows and
exhibitions. Our longstanding company motto is to
design a space that doesn't become outdated after
10 years. Therefore, our designs are not too
influenced by trends and we use materials that age
gracefully. With that as our basis, we insert clever
accents to add character to the spaces.
As show places are only designed to last a few days
or months and leave without a trace, it may seem to
differ from our motto fundamentally. But, even if it
no longer physically exists, we hope to leave a
strong impression in people's minds.
We design 'Places to Show' with that as our goal.
We hope that if an attendee is asked what the show
space was like, they can remember and tell you
without hesitation. However, the design shouldn't
detract from the main concept or product. First, we
find out what will be on show and fully understand
the concept of it so that the whole booth can help
tell the story.

Lloyd's Antiques Exhibition

2007 –

Lloyd's Antiques, which was launched in
1988, is a well-known antique interior shop
in Japan. In 2007, we designed their
exhibition held at their flagship store in
Aoyama. We pitched for the theme 'cutting
edge', a fashion show of furniture.
After walking through large black curtains,
the guests come to a long, glass showcase
resembling a runway. The furniture
purchased especially for this show was
displayed on the 'runway' and each item was
lit with a spotlight to give the illusion it was
floating. Visitors were served champagne and
taken 'into the show' in silence and with the
scent of aroma candles. It was an exhibition
for visitors to experience the fashionable
aspect of the brand using all five senses.

Lloyd's Antiques Exhibition

Type: Exhibition
Open: October 2007
Location: Shibuya-ku, Tokyo, Japan
Floor Area: 789m²
Contractor: D.BRAIN
Lighting Designer: Shinji Yamaguchi / On & Off

We decorated one of the areas above the glass runway with one hundred bare hanging light bulbs. We strived to leave a strong impression by making it completely different from a usual store.

YAMAHA asked us to design their exhibition booth for the TOKYO MOTOR SHOW four times. The first time was our first design for a booth at an international trade event in any industry. Lacking a little confidence, we decided to approach it in the same we always approach our work and our doubts gradually subsided. We designed a counter at which to greet guests, followed by an ideal space for people to flow through.

The theme of 'The Art of Engineering' formed the basis of each year's design to which we linked the main theme of each year's concept.

YAMAHA Booth,
The 37th TOKYO MOTOR SHOW

Type: Exhibition
Open: October 2003
Location: Japan
Floor area: 893m²
Contractor: MURAYAMA
Lighting Designer: Yasushi Kuramoto / AIR POWER SUPPLY
Space Composer: Junji Tanigawa

The booth was a completely closed design, which was unusual for a booth at the motor show. The guests were greeted at the large counter at the front, as if visiting a shop. The horizontal, illuminated lines, stood out between the wide black lines of the black mirrors, giving the impression that the motorcycles were moving.

YAMAHA Booth,
The 39th TOKYO MOTOR SHOW

Type: Exhibition
Open: October 2005
Location: Japan
Floor area: 851m²
Contractor: MURAYAMA
Lighting Designer: Yasunori Ito / I's Complex
Space Composer: Junji Tanigawa

This was a semi-open style purely white booth with an unconventional shaped stage to express the fluidity, speed and stability of the motorcycle. The part protruding from the booth was actually in the territory of the booth. We gave the illusion of it protruding by covering the surrounding part with carpet.

YAMAHA Booth,
The 40ᵗʰ TOKYO MOTOR SHOW

Type: Exhibition
Open: October 2007
Location: Japan
Floor area: 851m²
Contractor: MURAYAMA
Lighting Designer: Yasunori Ito / I's Complex
Space Composer: Junji Tanigawa

For our third YAMAHA booth, we designed a completely
open style booth with the image of being above the clouds.
The main attraction of the exhibition was an electric
motorcycle, so we decided to express a runway to the future.

THIS SPREAD:

YAMAHA Booth,
The 41st TOKYO MOTOR SHOW

Type: Exhibition
Open: October 2009
Location: Japan
Floor area: 695m²
Contractor: MURAYAMA
Lighting Designer: AIR POWER SUPPLY
Space Composer: Junji Tanigawa

This open style booth, with its impressive ceiling, contained a shining block that emitted light all directions. The block rose up from the circular stage in the centre. This was a metaphor for the possibilities of the motorcycle.

Chronological Overview of Selected Projects

Works of Katsuta, LINE-INC.'s Director,

from EXIT METAL WORK SUPPLY Period   As LINE-INC.

1999-2001   2002-2014

- T6M Daikanyama	- X-RAY Shichirigahama Atelier	- BEAMS STREET UMEDA
- HERE WE ARE marble	- High tension Low-Bolt	- JILL by JILLSTUART LUCUA Osaka
- NUMBER(N)INE Nagoya	- LOWRYS FARM Sannomiya	- CA4LA LUCUA Osaka
- social studies Harajuku	- Josiane Laure Omotesando	- Kiwasylphy LUCUA Osaka
- nulv by EYE HEART	- Restrict abx Fujii Daimaru	- LUCUA Osaka Adam et Ropé
- N.S Morioka	- KEL cafe Soga	- furfur LUCUA Osaka
- FRAPBOIS Nakameguro	- Sendai PARCO	- BEAMS UMEDA
- NUMBER(N)INE Minamiaoyama	- CA4LA Sendai	- broadcast bo beijing Sanlitun Village
- You Xian Aoyama	- JILL by JILLSTUART Shibuya	- LOWRYS FARM HEP FIVE
- GUADELOPE	- CA4LA Kyoto	- LOWRYS FARM LUMINE Yokohama
- WORLD STYLE Shibuya	- PINCEAU Ikebukuro PARCO	- JILL by JILLSTUART Kanazawa FORUS
- WASABI BISTRO	- Salon de Balcony Shibuya PARCO	- CA4LA Shinjuku LUMINE EST
- OZOC	- PINCEAU united bamboo Osaka E-MA	- collect point CANAL CITY Hakata
- ARTS&SCIENCE Daikanyama	- collect point AEON MALL Okazaki	- 10 mois AOYAMA
- LANTIKI centraaaaal TOKYO	- KASUMICHO SALON Nishiazabu	- LUMINE Yurakucho Adam et Ropé
- Rockets	- 5cm Macao	- CA4LA Ikebukuro PARCO
- RUPERT	- Design Tshirts Store graniph Harajuku	- BEAMS KITASENJU
- Lady's Levi's Store Tokyo	- Tennoji MIO Adam et Ropé	- Cosme Kitchen LUMINE Yokohama
- FRAPBOIS Hakata	- Sannomiya OPA Adam et Ropé	- BLISS POINT AEON LakeTown
- KEL	- O house	- Fujii Daimaru Adam et Ropé
- FRAPBOIS Aoyama	- Balcony Namba PARKS	HOMME / FEMME
- Edition Ikebukuro PARCO	- BEACON Cafe Shinonome	- Jewel Changes Nagoya MATSUZAKAYA
- fukuoka visionary arts	- SHEL	- CA4LA Fujii Daimaru
- CA4LA Karuizawa	- collect point Harajuku	- LOAVES Tokyu Plaza Omotesando / Harajuku
- SANTOSPIRITO	- Sushi Ichigo	- MELROSE claire LACHIC
- CA4LA Harajuku	- J house	- bills Omotesando
- CA4LA Daikanyama	- macher	- Tokyo SOLAMACHI Le Magasin
- Balcony Daikanyama	- CA4LA JOINUS TheDIAMOND	- CA4LA Tokyo Skytree Town SOLAMACHI
- actuel Hankyu Umeda	- SOLARIA PLAZA	- The SECRETCLOSET FUTAKOTAMAGAWA
- UNTITLED MEN Fujii Daimaru	ASSEMBLAGE Adam et Ropé	- BLISS POINT AEON MALL Miyazaki
- nano-universe Nagoya	- Hiroshima PARCO Adam et Ropé	- Ciaopanic Kyoto Teramachi
- CA4LA Shibuya	- HOUSE of JILLSTUART LUMINE Kitasenju	- MERCURYDUO Utsunomiya PARCO
- Design Tshirts Store graniph Nakameguro	- furfur Shibuya PARCO	- Shinjuku LUMINE Adam et Ropé
- Garibaldi	- n°11 LUMINE Shinjuku	- Salon de Balcony KITTE
- mellow beauté azabujuban	- JILL by JILLSTUART	- Sapporo STELLAR PLACE
- RUPERT Tennoji MIO	Shinsaibashi DAIMARU	ASSEMBLAGE Adam et Ropé
- NUMBER(N)INE Isetan Shinjuku	- JILLSTUART LUMINE Shinjuku	- LIVE LOVE LAUGH Yokohama
- RAGEBLUE Minamihorie	- collect point Shinsaibashi	- JET Roppongi
- CA4LA Sapporo	- R.P.T Fukuoka PARCO	- BEBE
- BEAMS PLUS SHIBUYA	- Sapporo PARCO Adam et Ropé	- J.M Chengdu China
- CA4LA London	- LUMINE Shinjuku	- LE JUN / Café de Ropé La mer
- StompStamp Roppongi Hills	ASSEMBLAGE Adam et Ropé	AEON MALL Makuhari New City
- allureville Flags	- bills Yokohama	- anyFAM AEON MALL Makuhari New City
- CA4LA Fukuoka	- Jewel Changes LUMINE Shinjuku	- LUMINE Ikebukuro Le Magasin
- nano-universe Namba	- Haute Hippie Minami-Aoyama	- ViS LUMINE EST
- Mano nella Mano Ginza Velviakan	- CA4LA FACTORY	- ViS LaLaport TOKYO-BAY
- BEAMS SHINMARUNOUCHI	- BEAMS HONG KONG	- SHARE PARK CAFE
- CA4LA Marunouchi	- mad HECTIC STORE Harajuku	LaLaport TOKYO-BAY
- TWIGGY	- THE PARLOR Isetan Shinjuku	- Salon de Balcony Shibuya PARCO
- The SECRETCLOSET JINGUMAE	- collect point Shinjuku	- BEAMS STREET YOKOHAMA
- TOKYO SWEETS FACTORY	- BEAMS HAKATA	- Biople by Cosme Kitchen JOINUS
- PAPER CHEST Minamihorie	- CA4LA Amu Plaza Hakata	The DIAMOND
- BEAMS NIIGATA	- ARCHIPELAGO	- CA4LA Kichijoji KIRARINA
- CA4LA Kobe	UNITED ARROWS LTD. HAKATA	- GOOD MEALS SHOP
- Weave Toshi	- HOUSE of JILLSTUART	- BROOKLYN MUSEUM
- BAD HABITS Yurakucho MARUI	Futako Tamagawa RISE	- Cosme Kitchen Shinsaibashi OPA
- PAUL & JOE Omotesando	- Village de Biotop Adam et Ropé	- Organic Burger Kitchen Shinsaibashi OPA
- FRAPBOIS Yurakucho MARUI	Futako Tamagawa RISE	- Ciaopanic HEPFIVE
- adonis green Okayama	- moussy Shinsaibashi OPA	- TAKEO KIKUCHI Hankyu Men's Osaka
- LOWRYS FARM PACIFICO Yokohama	- CAFFERA DAIMARU Umeda	- Tenerita LACIC
- nemo Bakery & Café	- SHARE HOUSE JR Nagoya TAKASHIMAYA	- Organic Market Kitchen
- Hollywood Wife Daikanyama	- CA4LA Harajuku	- Fukuoka PARCO Adam et Ropé
- TOP GEAR	- LOAVES Shibuya	- Dainipponichi Fukuoka PARCO
- CA4LA Umeda	- STAR JEWELRY DAIMARU Umeda	- HAND BAKES Musashikosugi
- Metro Hat	- STAR JEWELRY Amu Plaza Hakata	- Cosme Kitchen Grand Tree Musashikosugi
- CRAMP Nagoya	- Namba CITY Adam et Ropé	- Wafflish Waffle Omotesando Shop

Works of Katsuta, LINE-INC.'s Director,

1999 - 2001 | from EXIT METAL WORK SUPPLY Period

1999

T6M Daikanyama

Type : Apparel retailer
Open : November 1999
Location : Shibuya-ku, Tokyo, Japan
Floor area : 52m²(1F), 52m²(2F)
Contractor : ALPHA STUDIO
Lighting Designer : Hiroe Tanita / MAXRAY

2000

HERE WE ARE marble

Type : Restaurant & Cafe
Open : February 2000
Location : Suginami-ku, Tokyo, Japan
Floor area : 89m²
Contractor : IMPACT
Lighting Designer : Hiroe Tanita / MAXRAY

NUMBER(N)INE Nagoya

Type : Apparel retailer
Open : September 2000
Location : Nagoya-shi, Aichi, Japan
Floor area : 118m²
Contractor : I.D.A.
Lighting Designer : Hiroe Tanita / MAXRAY

2001

social studies Harajuku

Type : Apparel retailer
Open : January 2001
Location : Shibuya-ku, Tokyo, Japan
Floor area : 42m²
Contractor : ALPHA STUDIO
Lighting Designer : Hiroe Tanita / MAXRAY

nulv by EYE HEART

Type : Apparel store & Cafe
Open : March 2001
Location : Yokohama-shi, Kanagawa, Japan
Floor area : 264m²
Contractor : DIREC
Lighting Designer : Hiroe Tanita / MAXRAY

N.S Morioka

Type : Apparel retailer
Open : May 2001
Location : Morioka-shi, Iwate, Japan
Floor area : 68m²
Contractor : Marui
Lighting Designer : Hiroe Tanita / MAXRAY

2001

FRAPBOIS Nakameguro

Type : Apparel retailer
Open : December 2001
Location : Meguro-ku, Tokyo, Japan
Floor area : 39m²(1F), 26m²(2F)
Contractor : EIKOSHA
Lighting Designer : Hiroe Tanita/ MAXRAY

2002 - 2014 | AS LINE-INC.

2002

NUMBER(N)INE Minamiaoyama

Type : Exhibition
Open : April 2002
Location : Minato-ku, Tokyo, Japan
Contractor : D.BRAIN
Lighting Designer : LINE-INC.

You Xian Aoyama

Type : Restaurant
Open : April 2002
Location : Minato-ku, Tokyo, Japan
Floor area : 243m²
Contractor : D.BRAIN
Lighting Designer : Kenji Ito / MAXRAY

GUADELOPE

Type : Office
Open : July 2002
Location : Shibuya-ku, Tokyo, Japan
Floor area : 42m²
Contractor : ALPHA STUDIO
Lighting Designer : LINE-INC.

WORLD STYLE Shibuya

Type : Apparel retailer
Open : September 2002
Location : Shibuya-ku, Tokyo, Japan
Floor area : 22m²
Contractor : D.BRAIN
Lighting Designer : Shinji Yamaguchi / On & Off

WASABI BISTRO

Type : Restaurant
Open : November 2002
Location : Kawasaki-shi, Kanagawa, Japan
Floor area : 42m²(2F), 108m²(3F), 90m²(4F),
Contractor : D.BRAIN
Lighting Designer : Shinji Yamaguchi / On & Off

2003

OZOC

Type : Exhibition
Open : January 2003
Location : Minato-ku, Tokyo, Japan
Floor area : 210m²
Contractor : FLEX SP
Lighting Designer : LITE UP SYSTEMS

ARTS&SCIENCE Daikanyama

Type : Apparel retailer
Open : May 2003
Location : Shibuya-ku, Tokyo, Japan
Floor area : 25m²
Contractor : D.BRAIN
Lighting Designer : LINE-INC.
Photo : Higashi Ishida

LANTIKI centraaaaal TOKYO

Type : Apparel retailer
Open : August 2003
Location : Shibuya-ku, Tokyo, Japan
Floor area : 135m²
Contractor : D.BRAIN
Lighting Designer : Osamu Wakai / DAIKO ELECTRIC

Rockets

Type : Hair salon
Open : August 2003
Location : Shibuya-ku, Tokyo, Japan
Floor area : 74m²
Contractor : D.BRAIN
Lighting Designer : Takayoshi Murai / JAPAN LIGHTING

RUPERT

Type : Apparel retailer
Open : September 2003
Location : Osaka-shi, Osaka, Japan
Floor area : 91m²
Contractor : Tanseisha
Lighting Designer : Takayoshi Murai / JAPAN LIGHTING

Lady's Levi's Store Tokyo

Type : Apparel retailer
Open : October 2003
Location : Shibuya-ku, Tokyo, Japan
Floor area : 29m²(1F), 29m²(2F),
Contractor : D.BRAIN
Lighting Designer : Takayoshi Murai / JAPAN LIGHTING

FRAPBOIS Hakata

Type : Apparel retailer
Open : November 2003
Location : Fukuoka-shi, Fukuoka, Japan
Floor area : 119m²(1F), 81m²(2F)
Contractor : WITH
Lighting designer : Osamu Wakai / DAIKO ELECTRIC

KEL

Type : Restaurant & Cafe
Open : January 2004
Location : Koutou-ku, Tokyo, Japan
Floor area : 282m²
Contractor : WITH
Lighting Designer : Takayoshi Murai / JAPAN LIGHTING

FRAPBOIS Aoyama

Type : Apparel retailer
Open : March 2004
Location : Minato-ku, Tokyo, Japan
Floor area : 124m²
Contractor : WITH
Lighting Designer : Osamu Wakai / DAIKO ELECTRIC

Edition Ikebukuro PARCO

Type : Apparel retailer
Open : March 2004
Location : Toshima-ku, Tokyo, Japan
Floor area : 272m²
Contractor : NISSHO INTER LIFE
Lighting Designer : Shinji Yamaguchi / On & Off

fukuoka visionary arts

Type : Technical college
Open : April 2004
Location : Hakata-ku, Fukuoka, Japan
Contractor : SHIMIZU KENSETSU
Lighting Designer : Takayoshi Murai / JAPAN LIGHTING

CA4LA Karuizawa

Type : Apparel retailer
Open : April 2004
Location : Karuizawa, Nagano, Japan
Floor area : 121m²
Contractor : D.BRAIN
Lighting Designer : Takayoshi Murai / JAPAN LIGHTING

SANTOSPIRITO

Type : Restaurant
Open : July 2004
Location : Meguro-ku, Tokyo, Japan
Floor area : 138m²
Contractor : D.BRAIN
Lighting Designer : Shinji Yamaguchi / On & Off

CA4LA Harajuku

Type : Apparel retailer
Open : July 2004
Location : Shibuya-ku, Tokyo, Japan
Floor area : 121m²
Contractor : D.BRAIN
Lighting Designer : Takayoshi Murai / JAPAN LIGHTING

2004

CA4LA Daikanyama

Type : Apparel retailer
Open : September 2004
Location : Shibuya-ku, Tokyo, Japan
Floor area : 96m²
Contractor : D.BRAIN
Lighting Designer : Takayoshi Murai / JAPAN LIGHTING

Balcony Daikanyama

Type : Apparel retailer
Open : October 2004
Location : Shibuya-ku, Tokyo, Japan
Floor area : 51m²(1F), 40m²(2F)
Contractor : D.BRAIN
Lighting Designer : Takayoshi Murai / JAPAN LIGHTING

2005

actuel Hankyu Umeda

Type : Apparel retailer
Open : February 2005
Location : Osaka-shi, Osaka, Japan
Floor area : 126m²
Contractor : D.BRAIN
Lighting Designer : Shinji Yamaguchi / On & Off

UNTITLED MEN Fujii Daimaru

Type : Apparel retailer
Open : March 2005
Location : Shimogyo-ku, Kyoto, Japan
Floor area : 90m²
Contractor : TANSEISHA
Lighting Designer : 1LUX

nano·universe Nagoya

Type : Apparel retailer
Open : March 2005
Location : Nagoya-shi, Aichi, Japan
Floor area : 303m²
Contractor : D.BRAIN
Lighting Designer : Shinji Yamaguchi / On & Off

CA4LA Shibuya

Type : Apparel retailer
Open : May 2005
Location : Shibuya-ku, Tokyo, Japan
Floor area : 89m²(1F), 116m²(2F)
Contractor : ASK PLANNING CENTER
Lighting Designer : Takeshi Obana / JAPAN LIGHTING

Design Tshirts Store graniph Nakameguro

Type : Apparel retailer
Open : September 2005
Location : Meguro-ku, Tokyo, Japan
Floor area : 78m²
Contractor : ALPHA STUDIO
Lighting Designer : Takayoshi Murai / JAPAN LIGHTING

2006

Garibaldi

Type : Restaurant & Cafe
Open : December 2005
Location : Shinagawa-ku, Tokyo, Japan
Floor area : 109m²
Contractor : Kotaro Ushizaki
Lighting Designer : Takayoshi Murai / JAPAN LIGHTING

mellow beauté azabujuban

Type : Studio & Beauty salon
Open : January 2006
Location : Minato-ku, Tokyo, Japan
Floor area : 194m²
Contractor : NITTEKU
Lighting Designer : Takayoshi Murai / JAPAN LIGHTING

RUPERT Tennoji MIO

Type : Apparel retailer
Open : January 2006
Location : Osaka-shi, Osaka, Japan
Floor area : 40m²
Contractor : WILLE
Lighting Designer : Takayoshi Murai / JAPAN LIGHTING

NUMBER(N)INE Isetan Shinjuku

Type : Apparel retailer
Open : February 2006
Location : Shinjuku-ku, Tokyo, Japan
Floor area : 37m²
Contractor : D.BRAIN
Lighting Designer : Shinji Yamaguchi / On & Off

RAGEBLUE Minamihorie

Type : Apparel retailer
Open : February 2006
Location : Osaka-shi, Osaka, Japan
Floor area : 213m²
Contractor : SPACE
Lighting Designer : Shinji Yamaguchi / On & Off

CA4LA Sapporo

Type : Apparel retailer
Open : March 2006
Location : Sapporo-shi, Hokkaido, JAPAN
Floor area : 118m²
Contractor : D.BRAIN
Lighting Designer : Takeshi Obana / JAPAN LIGHTING

BEAMS PLUS SHIBUYA

Type : Apparel retailer
Open : March 2006
Location : Shibuya-ku, Tokyo, Japan
Floor area : 61m²(1F), 64m²(2F)
Contractor : NOMURA
Lighting Designer : Shinji Yamaguchi / On & Off

2006

CA4LA London

Type : Apparel retailer
Open : February 2006
Location : London, UK
Floor area : 50m²(1F), 37m²(2F)
Contractor : Office Sekkei London Office
Lighting Designer : Takayoshi Murai / JAPAN LIGHTING

StompStamp Roppongi Hills

Type : Apparel retailer
Open : September 2006
Location : Minato-ku, Tokyo, Japan
Floor area : 159m²
Contractor : D.BRAIN
Lighting Designer : Shinji Yamaguchi / On & Off

allureville Flags

Type : Apparel retailer
Open : September 2006
Location : Shinjuku-ku, Tokyo, Japan
Floor area : 251m²
Contractor : Hi.To.D
Lighting Designer : Shinji Yamaguchi / On & Off

CA4LA Fukuoka

Type : Apparel retailer
Open : December 2006
Location : Fukuoka-shi, Fukuoka, Japan
Floor area : 56m²(1F), 53m²(2F), 53m²(3F)
Contractor : D.BRAIN
Lighting Designer : Takayoshi Murai / JAPAN LIGHTING

2007

nano·universe Namba

Type : Apparel retailer
Open : April 2007
Location : Osaka-shi, Osaka, Japan
Floor area : 253m²
Contractor : SEMBA CORPORATION
Lighting Designer : Shinji Yamaguchi / On & Off

Mano nella Mano Ginza Velviakan

Type : Apparel retailer
Open : April 2007
Location : Chuo-ku, Tokyo, Japan
Floor area : 225m²
Contractor : Hi.To.D
Lighting Designer : JAPAN LIGHTING

BEAMS SHINMARUNOUCHI

Type : Apparel retailer
Open : April 2007
Location : Chiyoda-ku, Tokyo, Japan
Floor area : 423m²
Contractor : D.BRAIN
Lighting Designer : Shinji Yamaguchi / On & Off

2007

CA4LA Marunouchi

Type : Apparel retailer
Open : April 2007
Location : Chiyoda-ku, Tokyo, Japan
Floor area : 78m²
Contractor : D.BRAIN
Lighting Designer : JAPAN LIGHTING

TWIGGY

Type : Beauty salon
Open : July 2007
Location : Shibuya-ku, Tokyo, Japan
Floor area : 133m²(B1F), 75m²(1F)
Contractor : D.BRAIN
Lighting Designer : Shinji Yamaguchi / On & Off

The SECRETCLOSET JINGUMAE

Type : Specialty store
Open : July 2007
Location : Shibuya-ku, Tokyo, Japan
Floor area : 62m²
Contractor : D.BRAIN
Lighting Designer : Shinji Yamaguchi / On & Off

TOKYO SWEETS FACTORY

Type : Restaurant & Cafe
Open : July 2007
Location : Setagaya-ku, Tokyo, Japan
Floor area : 107m²
Contractor : PLUS 8
Lighting Designer : JAPAN LIGHTING

PAPER CHEST Minamihorie

Type : Apparel retailer
Open : September 2007
Location : Osaka-shi, Osaka, Japan
Floor area : 232m²
Contractor : ALEN'S CRAFT
Lighting Designer : USHIO SPAX

BEAMS NIIGATA

Type : Apparel retailer
Open : September 2007
Location : Niigata-shi, Niigata, Japan
Floor area : 680m²
Contractor : D.BRAIN
Lighting Designer : USHIO SPAX

CA4LA Kobe

Type : Apparel retailer
Open : September 2007
Location : Kobe-shi, Hyogo, Japan
Floor area : 164m²
Contractor : D.BRAIN
Lighting Designer : ENDO-Lighting

Weave Toshi

Type : Showroom & Office
Open : October 2007
Location : Shibuya-ku, Tokyo, Japan
Floor area : 108m²
Contractor : D.BRAIN
Lighting Designer : ENDO-Lighting

BAD HABITS Yurakucho MARUI

Type : Apparel retailer
Open : October 2007
Location : Chiyoda-ku, Tokyo, Japan
Floor area : 63m²
Contractor : WILLE
Lighting Designer : USHIO SPAX

PAUL & JOE Omotesando

Type : Apparel retailer
Open : October 2007
Location : Shibuya-ku, Tokyo, Japan
Floor area : 93m²(B1F), 143m²(1F)
Contractor : D.BRAIN
Lighting Designer : Shinji Yamaguchi / On & Off

FRAPBOIS Yurakucho MARUI

Type : Apparel retailer
Open : October 2007
Location : Chiyoda-ku, Tokyo, Japan
Floor area : 67m²
Contractor : WITH
Lighting Designer : JAPAN LIGHTING

adonis green Okayama

Type : Apparel retailer
Open : October 2007
Location : Okayama-shi, Okayama, Japan
Floor area : 152m²
Contractor : WILLE
Lighting Designer : USHIO SPAX

LOWRYS FARM PACIFICO Yokohama

Type : Apparel retailer
Open : November 2007
Location : Yokohama-shi, Kanagawa, Japan
Floor area : 158m²
Contractor : Taisho Kogei
Lighting Designer : Shinji Yamaguchi / On & Off

nemo Bakery & Café

Type : Restraurant & Cafe
Open : December 2007
Location : Shinagawa-ku, Tokyo, Japan
Floor area : 142m²
Contractor : Frontier INTERNATIONAL
Lighting Designer : USHIO SPAX

2008

Hollywood Wife Daikanyama

Type : Apparel retailer
Open : January 2008
Location : Shibuya-ku, Tokyo, Japan
Floor area : 32m²
Contractor : ALEN'S CRAFT
Lighting Designer : USHIO SPAX

TOP GEAR

Type : Showroom & Office
Open : March 2008
Location : Taito-ku, Tokyo, Japan
Floor area : 97m²
Contractor : ALPHA STUDIO
Lighting Designer : USHIO SPAX

CA4LA Umeda

Type : Apparel retailer
Open : March 2008
Location : Osaka-shi, Osaka, Japan
Floor area : 90m²
Contractor : D.BRAIN
Lighting Designer : ENDO-Lighting

Metro Hat

Type : Public space
Open : April 2008
Location : Minato-ku, Tokyo, Japan
Floor area : 592m²
Contractor : NOMURA
Lighting Designer : Shinji Yamaguchi / On & Off

CRAMP Nagoya

Type : Apparel retailer
Open : May 2008
Location : Nagoya-shi, Aichi, Japan
Floor area : 97m²
Contractor : I.D.A.
Lighting Designer : USHIO SPAX

X-RAY Shichirigahama Atelier

Type : Photo studio
Open : May 2008
Location : Kamakura-shi, Kanagawa, Japan
Floor area : 149m²(1F), 91m²(2F)
Contractor : WITH
Lighting Designer : JAPAN LIGHTING

High tenstion Low-Bolt

Type : Restaurant & Bar
Open : June 2008
Location : Meguro-ku, Tokyo, Japan
Floor area : 101m²
Contractor : ALPHA STUDIO
Lighting Designer : USHIO SPAX

LOWRYS FARM Sannomiya

Type : Apparel retailer
Open : June 2008
Location : Kobe-shi, Hyogo, Japan
Floor area : 191m²
Contractor : Taisho Kogei
Lighting Designer : Shinji Yamaguchi / On & Off

Josiane Laure Omotesando

Type : Beauty salon
Open : August 2008
Location : Shibuya-ku, Tokyo, Japan
Floor area : 92m²
Contractor : PLUS 8
Lighting Designer : USHIO SPAX

Restrict abx Fujii Daimaru

Type : Apparel retailer
Open : September 2008
Location : Shimogyo-ku, Kyoto, Japan
Floor area : 96m²
Contractor : SOGO DESIGN
Lighting Designer : USHIO SPAX

KEL cafe Soga

Type : Restaurant & Cafe
Open : July 2008
Location : Chiba-shi, Chiba, Japan
Floor area : 251m²
Contractor : WITH
Lighting Designer : JAPAN LIGHTING

Sendai PARCO

Type : Public space
Open : August 2008
Location : Sendai-shi, Miyagi, Japan
Contractor : NITTO SOGYO
Lighting Designer : ENDO-Lighting+Shinji Yamaguchi / On & Off

CA4LA Sendai

Type : Apparel retailer
Open : August 2008
Location : Sendai-shi, Miyagi, Japan
Floor area : 83m²
Contractor : D.BRAIN
Lighting Designer : ENDO-Lighting

JILL by JILLSTUART Shibuya

Type : Apparel retailer
Open : August 2008
Location : Shibuya-ku, Tokyo, Japan
Floor area : 125m²(1F), 125m²(2F)
Contractor : MESSE
Lighting Designer : USHIO SPAX

CA4LA Kyoto

Type : Apparel retailer
Open : September 2008
Location : Shimogyo-ku, Kyoto, Japan
Floor area : 91m²
Contractor : D.BRAIN
Lighting Designer : ENDO-Lighting

PINCEAU Ikebukuro PARCO

Type : Apparel retailer
Open : September 2008
Location : Toshima-ku, Tokyo, Japan
Floor area : 45m²
Contractor : TANSEISHA
Lighting Designer : USHIO SPAX

Salon de Balcony Shibuya PARCO

Type : Apparel retailer
Open : September 2008
Location : Shibuya-ku, Tokyo, Japan
Floor area : 67m²
Contractor : EIKOSHA
Lighting Designer : USHIO SPAX

PINCEAU united bamboo Osaka E-MA

Type : Apparel retailer
Open : October 2008
Location : Osaka-shi, Osaka, Japan
Floor area : 122m²
Contractor : SOGO DESIGN
Lighting Designer : USHIO SPAX

collect point AEON MALL Okazaki

Type : Apparel retailer
Open : November 2008
Location : Okazaki-shi, Aichi, Japan
Floor area : 369m²
Contractor : Taisho Kogei
Lighting Designer : Shinji Yamaguchi / On & Off

KASUMICHO SALON Nishiazabu

Type : Lounge & Restaurant
Open : December 2008
Location : Minato-ku, Tokyo, Japan
Floor area : 196m²
Contractor : PLUS 8
Lighting Designer : Shinji Yamaguchi / On & Off

5cm Macao

Type : Apparel retailer
Open : August 2008
Location : Macau, China
Floor area : 150m²
Lighting Designer : Shinji Yamaguchi / On & Off

2009

Design Tshirts Store graniph Harajuku

Type : Apparel retailer
Open : February 2009
Location : Shibuya-ku, Tokyo, Japan
Floor area : 309m²
Contractor : ALPHA STUDIO
Lighting Designer : USHIO SPAX

Tennoji MIO Adam et Ropé

Type : Apparel retailer
Open : February 2009
Location : Osaka-shi, Osaka, Japan
Floor area : 115m²
Contractor : ALEN'S CRAFT
Lighting Designer : USHIO SPAX

Sannomiya OPA Adam et Ropé

Type : Apparel retailer
Open : March 2009
Location : Kobe-shi, Hyogo, Japan
Floor area : 113m²
Contractor : ALEN'S CRAFT
Lighting Designer : USHIO SPAX

O house

Type : Residence
Open : March 2009
Location : Tokyo, Japan
Floor area : 94m²
Contractor : TAISEI CORPORATION
Lighting Designer : USHIO SPAX

Balcony Namba PARKS

Type : Apparel retailer
Open : March 2009
Location : Osaka-shi, Osaka, Japan
Floor area : 102m²
Contractor : EIKOSHA
Lighting Designer : USHIO SPAX

BEACON Cafe Shinonome

Type : Restaurant & Cafe
Open : March 2009
Location : Koto-ku, Tokyo, Japan
Floor area : 129m²
Contractor : TAISEI CORPORATION
Lighting Designer : Shinji Yamaguchi / On & Off

SHEL

Type : Beauty salon
Open : April 2009
Location : Shizuoka-shi, Shizuoka, Japan
Floor area : 141m²
Contractor : Takai Kensetsu
Lighting Designer : USHIO SPAX

collect point Harajuku

Type : Apparel retailer
Open : April 2009
Location : Shibuya-ku, Tokyo, Japan
Floor area : 529m²(1F), 557m²(2F)
Contractor : Taisho Kogei
Lighting Designer : Shinji Yamaguchi / On & Off

Sushi Ichigo

Type : Restaurant
Open : May 2009
Location : Setagaya-ku, Tokyo, Japan
Floor area : 33m²
Contractor : ALPHA STUDIO
Lighting Designer : USHIO SPAX

J house

Type : Residence
Open : June 2009
Location : Tokyo, Japan
Floor area : 93m²
Contractor : D.BRAIN
Lighting Designer : USHIO SPAX

macher

Type : Apparel retailer
Open : August 2009
Location : Shibuya-ku, Tokyo, Japan
Floor area : 24m²
Contractor : ALPHA STUDIO
Lighting Designer : USHIO SPAX

CA4LA JOINUS TheDIAMOND

Type : Apparel retailer
Open : August 2009
Location : Yokohama-shi, Kanagawa, Japan
Floor area : 94m²
Contractor : D.BRAIN
Lighting Designer : ENDO-Lighting

SOLARIA PLAZA
ASSEMBLAGE Adam et Ropé

Type : Apparel retailer
Open : September 2009
Location : Fukuoka-shi, Fukuoka, Japan
Floor area : 91m²
Contractor : ALEN'S CRAFT
Lighting Designer : Shinji Yamaguchi / On & Off

Hiroshima PARCO Adam et Ropé

Type : Apparel retailer
Open : September 2009
Location : Hiroshima-shi, Hiroshima, Japan
Floor area : 115m²
Contractor : ALEN'S CRAFT
Lighting Designer : Shinji Yamaguchi / On & Off

2009

HOUSE of JILLSTUART
LUMINE Kitasenju

Type : Apparel retailer
Open : October 2009
Location : Adachi-ku, Tokyo, Japan
Floor area : 262m²
Contractor : MESSE
Lighting Designer : USHIO SPAX

furfur Shibuya PARCO

Type : Apparel retailer
Open : October 2009
Location : Shibuya-ku, Tokyo, Japan
Floor area : 62m²
Contractor : ALEN'S CRAFT
Lighting Designer : USHIO SPAX

n°11 LUMINE Shinjuku

Type : Apparel retailer
Open : November 2009
Location : Shinjuku-ku, Tokyo, Japan
Floor area : 66m²
Contractor : ALEN'S CRAFT
Lighting Designer : USHIO SPAX

JILL by JILLSTUART
Shinsaibashi DAIMARU

Type : Apparel retailer
Open : November 2009
Location : Osaka-shi, Osaka, Japan
Floor area : 118m²
Contractor : SOGO DESIGN
Lighting Designer : USHIO SPAX

2010

JILLSTUART LUMINE Shinjuku

Type : Apparel retailer
Open : February 2010
Location : Shinjuku-ku, Tokyo, Japan
Floor area : 90m²
Contractor : MESSE
Lighting Designer : USHIO SPAX

collect point Shinsaibashi

Type : Apparel retailer
Open : February 2010
Location : Osaka-shi, Osaka, Japan
Floor area : 308m²(1F), 293m²(2F)
Contractor : Taisho Kogei
Lighting Designer : Shinji Yamaguchi / On & Off

R.P.T Fukuoka PARCO

Type : Apparel retailer
Open : March 2010
Location : Fukuoka-shi, Fukuoka, Japan
Floor area : 106m²
Contractor : SOGO DESIGN
Lighting Designer : USHIO SPAX

2010

Sapporo PARCO Adam et Ropé

Type : Apparel retailer
Open : March 2010
Location : Sapporo-shi, Hokkaido, Japan
Floor area : 192m²
Contractor : SOGO DESIGN
Lighting Designer : Shinji Yamaguchi / On & Off

LUMINE Shinjuku ASSEMBLAGE Adam et Ropé

Type : Apparel retailer
Open : March 2010
Location : Shinjuku-ku, Tokyo, Japan
Floor area : 76m²
Contractor : ALEN'S CRAFT
Lighting Designer : Shinji Yamaguchi / On & Off

bills Yokohama

Type : Restaurant & Cafe
Open : March 2010
Location : Yokohama-shi, Kanagawa, Japan
Floor area : 347m²
Contractor : PLUS 8
Lighting Designer : USHIO SPAX

Jewel Changes LUMINE Shinjuku

Type : Apparel retailer
Open : August 2010
Location : Shinjuku-ku, Tokyo, Japan
Floor area : 187m²
Contractor : DECOR
Lighting Designer : USHIO SPAX

Haute Hippie Minami-Aoyama

Type : Apparel retailer
Open : August 2010
Location : Minato-ku, Tokyo, Japan
Floor area : 86m²
Contractor : NOMURA
Lighting Designer : USHIO SPAX

CA4LA FACTORY

Type : Factory
Open : September 2010
Location : Nishinomiya-shi, Hyogo, Japan
Floor area : 180m²
Contractor : D.BRAIN
Lighting Designer : ENDO-Lighting

BEAMS HONG KONG

Type : Apparel retailer
Open : September 2010
Location : Kowloon, Hong Kong
Floor area : 219m²
Contractor : SOGO DESIGN
Lighting Designer : USHIO SPAX

2010

mad HECTIC STORE Harajuku

Type : Apparel retailer
Open : September 2010
Location : Shibuya-ku, Tokyo, Japan
Floor area : 66m²(1F), 66m²(2F)
Contractor : SPACE
Lighting Designer : USHIO SPAX

THE PARLOR Isetan Shinjuku

Type : Exhibition
Open : October 2010
Location : Shinjuku-ku, Tokyo, Japan
Floor area : 81m²(1F), 57m²(2F), 120m²(RF)
Contractor : MARI-ART
Lighting Designer : Air Brain Company

collect point Shinjuku

Type : Apparel retailer
Open : November 2010
Location : Shinjuku-ku, Tokyo, Japan
Floor area : 308m²(1F), 653m²(2F)
Contractor : SPACE
Lighting Designer : DAIKO ELECTRIC

2011

BEAMS HAKATA

Type : Apparel retailer
Open : March 2011
Location : Fukuoka-shi, Fukuoka, Japan
Floor area : 458m²
Contractor : SOGO DESIGN
Lighting Designer : USHIO SPAX

CA4LA Amu Plaza Hakata

Type : Apparel retailer
Open : March 2011
Location : Fukuoka-shi, Fukuoka, Japan
Floor area : 79m²
Contractor : D.BRAIN
Lighting Designer : ENDO-Lighting

ARCHIPELAGO
UNITED ARROWS LTD. HAKATA

Type : Apparel retailer
Open : March 2011
Location : Fukuoka-shi, Fukuoka, Japan
Floor area : 229m²
Contractor : DECOR
Lighting Designer : USHIO SPAX

HOUSE of JILLSTUART
Futako Tamagawa RISE

Type : Apparel store, Restaurant & Cafe
Open : March 2011
Location : Setagaya-ku, Tokyo, Japan
Floor area : 198m²(Store), 110m²(Cafe)
Contractor : NOMURA
Lighting Designer : USHIO SPAX

Village de Biotop Adam et Ropé Futako Tamagawa RISE

Type : Apparel retailer
Open : March 2011
Location : Setagaya-ku, Tokyo, Japan
Floor area : 251m²
Contractor : NOMURA
Lighting Designer : Shinji Yamaguchi / On & Off

moussy Shinsaibashi OPA

Type : Apparel retailer
Open : March 2011
Location : Osaka-shi, Osaka, Japan
Floor area : 153m²
Contractor : TANSEISHA
Lighting Designer : USHIO SPAX

CAFFERA DAIMARU Umeda

Type : Restaurant & Cafe
Open : March 2011
Location : Osaka-shi, Osaka, Japan
Floor area : 201m²
Contractor : Taisho Kogei
Lighting Designer : Shinji Yamaguchi / On & Off

SHARE HOUSE JR Nagoya TAKASHIMAYA

Type : Apparel retailer
Open : March 2011
Location : Nagoya-shi, Aichi, Japan
Floor area : 66m²
Contractor : EIKOSHA
Lighting Designer : USHIO SPAX

CA4LA Harajuku

Type : Apparel retailer
Open : March 2011
Location : Shibuya-ku, Tokyo, Japan
Floor area : 41m²(1F), 41m²(2F)
Contractor : D.BRAIN
Lighting Designer : ENDO-Lighting

LOAVES Shibuya

Type : Apparel retailer
Open : March 2011
Location : Shibuya-ku, Tokyo, Japan
Floor area : 108m²(B1F), 112m²(1F), 111m²(2,3F)
Contractor : MESSE
Lighting Designer : USHIO SPAX

STAR JEWELRY DAIMARU Umeda

Type : Jewellery store
Open : March 2011
Location : Osaka-shi, Osaka, Japan
Floor area : 71m²
Contractor : NOMURA
Lighting Designer : MAXRAY

STAR JEWELRY Amu Plaza Hakata

Type : Jewellery store
Open : March 2011
Location : Fukuoka-shi, Fukuoka, Japan
Floor area : 57m²
Contractor : Yoshichu Mannequin
Lighting Designer : USHIO SPAX

Namba CITY Adam et Ropé

Type : Apparel retailer
Open : April 2011
Location : Osaka-shi, Osaka, Japan
Floor area : 249m²
Contractor : ALEN'S CRAFT
Lighting Designer : Shinji Yamaguchi / On & Off

BEAMS STREET UMEDA

Type : Apparel retailer
Open : April 2011
Location : Osaka-shi, Osaka, Japan
Floor area : 464m²
Contractor : SOGO DESIGN
Lighting Designer : USHIO SPAX

JILL by JILLSTUART LUCUA Osaka

Type : Apparel retailer
Open : May 2011
Location : Osaka-shi, Osaka, Japan
Floor area : 142m²
Contractor : SEMBA CORPORATION
Lighting Designer : USHIO SPAX

CA4LA LUCUA Osaka

Type : Apparel retailer
Open : May 2011
Location : Osaka-shi, Osaka, Japan
Floor area : 47m²
Contractor : D.BRAIN
Lighting Designer : ENDO-Lighting

Kiwasylphy LUCUA Osaka

Type : Apparel retailer
Open : May 2011
Location : Osaka-shi, Osaka, Japan
Floor area : 68m²
Contractor : SEMBA CORPORATION
Lighting Designer : ENDO-Lighting

LUCUA Osaka Adam et Ropé

Type : Apparel retailer
Open : May 2011
Location : Osaka-shi, Osaka, Japan
Floor area : 132m²
Contractor : ALEN'S CRAFT
Lighting Designer : Shinji Yamaguchi / On & Off

2011

furfur LUCUA Osaka

Type : Apparel retailer
Open : May 2011
Location : Osaka-shi, Osaka, Japan
Floor area : 62m²
Contractor : NOMURA
Lighting Designer : USHIO SPAX

BEAMS UMEDA

Type : Apparel retailer
Open : May 2011
Location : Osaka-shi, Osaka, Japan
Floor area : 521m²
Contractor : TANSEISHA
Lighting Designer : USHIO SPAX

broadcast bo beijing Sanlitun Village

Type : Apparel retailer
Open : June 2011
Location : Beijing, China
Floor area : 124m²
Contractor : BEIJING TANSEI
Lighting Designer : Shinji Yamaguchi / On & Off

LOWRYS FARM HEP FIVE

Type : Apparel retailer
Open : August 2011
Location : Osaka-shi, Osaka, Japan
Floor area : 232m²
Contractor : SOGO DESIGN
Lighting Designer : DAIKO ELECTRIC

LOWRYS FARM LUMINE Yokohama

Type : Apparel retailer
Open : August 2011
Location : Yokohama-shi, Kanagawa, Japan
Floor area : 135m²
Contractor : SPACE
Lighting Designer : DAIKO ELECTRIC

JILL by JILLSTUART Kanazawa FORUS

Type : Apparel retailer
Open : September 2011
Location : Kanazawa-shi, Ishikawa, Japan
Floor area : 103m²
Contractor : SOGO DESIGN
Lighting Designer : USHIO SPAX

CA4LA Shinjuku LUMINE EST

Type : Apparel retailer
Open : September 2011
Location : Shinjuku-ku, Tokyo, Japan
Floor area : 77m²
Contractor : D.BRAIN
Lighting Designer : ENDO-Lighting

2011

collect point CANAL CITY Hakata

Type : Apparel retailer
Open : September 2011
Location : Fukuoka-shi, Fukuoka, Japan
Floor area : 544m²(2F), 864m²(3F)
Contractor : SOGO DESIGN
Lighting Designer : DAIKO ELECTRIC

10 mois AOYAMA

Type : Apparel retailer
Open : September 2011
Location : Minato-ku, Tokyo, Japan
Floor area : 119m²
Contractor : D.BRAIN
Lighting Designer : USHIO SPAX

LUMINE Yurakucho Adam et Ropé

Type : Apparel retailer
Open : October 2011
Location : Chiyoda-ku, Tokyo, Japan
Floor area : 307m²
Contractor : SOGO DESIGN
Lighting Designer : USHIO SPAX

CA4LA Ikebukuro PARCO

Type : Apparel retailer
Open : October 2011
Location : Toshima-ku, Tokyo, Japan
Floor area : 66m²
Contractor : D.BRAIN
Lighting Designer : ENDO-Lighting

BEAMS KITASENJU

Type : Apparel retailer
Open : November 2011
Location : Adachi-ku, Tokyo, Japan
Floor area : 322m²
Contractor : D.BRAIN
Lighting Designer : USHIO SPAX

2012

Cosme Kitchen LUMINE Yokohama

Type : Cosmetics store
Open : February 2012
Location : Yokohama-shi, Kanagawa, Japan
Floor area : 75m²
Contractor : SPACE
Lighting Designer : USHIO SPAX

BLISS POINT AEON LakeTown

Type : Apparel retailer
Open : March 2012
Location : Koshigaya-shi, Saitama, Japan
Floor area : 333m²
Contractor : SOGO DESIGN
Lighting Designer : DAIKO ELECTRIC

Fujii Daimaru
Adam et Ropé HOMME / FEMME

Type : Apparel retailer
Open : March 2012
Location : Shimogyo-ku, Kyoto, Japan
Floor area : 73m²(HOMME), 148m²(FEMME)
Contractor : SOGO DESIGN
Lighting Designer : USHIO SPAX

Jewel Changes Nagoya MATSUZAKAYA

Type : Apparel retailer
Open : March 2012
Location : Nagoya-shi, Aichi, Japan
Floor area : 117m²
Contractor : Nitten
Lighting Designer : USHIO SPAX

CA4LA Fujii Daimaru

Type : Apparel retailer
Open : March 2012
Location : Shimogyo-ku, Kyoto, Japan
Floor area : 77m²
Contractor : D.BRAIN
Lighting Designer : ENDO-Lighting

LOAVES
Tokyu Plaza Omotesando / Harajuku

Type : Apparel retailer
Open : April 2012
Location : Shibuya-ku, Tokyo, Japan
Floor area : 199m²
Contractor : SOGO DESIGN
Lighting Designer : USHIO SPAX

MELROSE claire LACHIC

Type : Apparel retailer
Open : April 2012
Location : Nagoya-shi, Aichi, Japan
Floor area : 97m²
Contractor : ALEN'S CRAFT
Lighting Designer : USHIO SPAX

bills Omotesando

Type : Restaurant & Cafe
Open : April 2012
Location : Shibuya-ku, Tokyo, Japan
Floor area : 335m²
Contractor : SOGO DESIGN
Lighting Designer : USHIO SPAX

Tokyo SOLAMACHI Le Magasin

Type : Apparel retailer
Open : May 2012
Location : Sumida-ku, Tokyo, Japan
Floor area : 94m²
Contractor : SPACE
Lighting Designer : USHIO SPAX

2012

CA4LA
Tokyo Skytree Town SOLAMACHI

Type : Apparel retailer
Open : May 2012
Location : Sumida-ku, Tokyo, Japan
Floor area : 76m²
Contractor : D.BRAIN
Lighting Designer : ENDO-Lighting

The SECRETCLOSET
FUTAKOTAMAGAWA

Type : Specialty store
Open : August 2012
Location : Setagaya-ku, Tokyo, Japan
Floor area : 99m²
Contractor : D.BRAIN
Lighting Designer : USHIO SPAX

BLISS POINT AEON MALL Miyazaki

Type : Apparel retailer
Open : August 2012
Location : Miyazaki-shi, Miyazaki, Japan
Floor area : 1,260m²
Contractor : SOGO DESIGN
Lighting Designer : DAIKO ELECTRIC

Ciaopanic Kyoto Teramachi

Type : Apparel retailer
Open : September 2012
Location : Chukyo-ku, Kyoto, Japan
Floor area : 209m²(1F), 143m²(2F)
Contractor : ZYCC CORPORATION
Lighting Designer : ENDO-Lighting

MERCURYDUO Utsunomiya PARCO

Type : Apparel retailer
Open : September 2012
Location : Utsunomiya-shi, Tochigi, JAPAN
Floor area : 84m²
Contractor : THE BLUE WORKS
Lighting Designer : USHIO SPAX

2013

LUMINE Shinjuku Adam et Ropé

Type : Apparel retailer
Open : March 2013
Location :Shinjuku-ku, Tokyo, Japan
Floor area : 71m²(HOMME), 90m²(FEMME)
Contractor : ALEN'S CRAFT
Lighting Designer : USHIO SPAX

Salon de Balcony KITTE

Type : Apparel retailer
Open : March 2013
Location : Chiyoda-ku, Tokyo, Japan
Floor area : 159m²
Contractor : ALEN'S CRAFT INC.
Lighting Designer : USHIO SPAX

2013

Sapporo STELLAR PLACE
ASSEMBLAGE Adam et Ropé

Type : Apparel retailer
Open : March 2013
Location : Sapporo-shi, Hokkaido, JAPAN
Floor area : 170m²
Contractor : AZABU SPACE FACTORY
Lighting Designer : USHIO SPAX

LIVE LOVE LAUGH Yokohama

Type : Wedding salon
Open : April 2013
Location : Yokohama-shi, Kanagawa, Japan
Floor area : 330m²(1F), 144m²(8F)
Contractor : ZYCC CORPORATION
Lighting Designer : USHIO SPAX

JET Roppongi

Type : Apparel retailer
Open : April 2013
Location : Minato-ku, Tokyo, Japan
Floor area : 41m²
Contractor : Virise
Lighting Designer : L-GROW

BEBE

Type : Beauty salon
Open : November 2013
Location : Minato-ku, Tokyo, Japan
Floor area : 110m²
Contractor : ALPHA STUDIO
Lighting Designer : ModuleX

J.M Chengdu China

Type : Apparel retailer
Open : November 2013
Location : Chengdu, China
Floor area : 43m²
Lighting Designer : ModuleX

LE JUN / Café de Ropé La mer
AEON MALL Makuhari New City

Type : Apparel retailer, Cafe, Restaurant
Open : December 2013
Location : Chiba-shi, Chiba, Japan
Floor area : 376m²(Store), 208m²(Cafe)
Contractor : NOMURA
Lighting Designer : ModuleX

anyFAM
AEON MALL Makuhari New City

Type : Apparel retailer
Open : December 2013
Location : Chiba-shi, Chiba, Japan
Floor area : 231m²
Contractor : ONWARD CREATIVE CENTER
Lighting Designer : ENDO-Lighting

LUMINE Ikebukuro
Le Magasin

Type : Apparel retailer
Open : February 2014
Location : Toshima-ku, Tokyo, Japan
Floor area : 33m²
Contractor : AIM CREATE
Lighting Designer : ModuleX
Photo : Ittoku Kawasaki

ViS LUMINE EST

Type : Apparel retailer
Open : March 2014
Location : Shinjuku-ku, Tokyo, Japan
Floor area : 127m²
Contractor : ALEN'S CRAFT
Lighting Designer : ENDO-Lighting

ViS LaLaport TOKYO-BAY

Type : Apparel retailer
Open : March 2014
Location : Funabashi-shi, Chiba, Japan
Floor area : 165m²
Contractor : ALEN'S CRAFT
Lighting Designer : ENDO-Lighting

SHARE PARK CAFE
LaLaport TOKYO-BAY

Type : Restaurant & Cafe
Open : March 2014
Location : Funabashi-shi, Chiba, Japan
Floor area : 23m²
Contractor : NOMURA
Lighting Designer : L-GROW

Salon de Balcony Shibuya PARCO

Type : Apparel retailer
Open : March 2014
Location : Shibuya-ku, Tokyo, Japan
Floor area : 119m²
Contractor : Smile Design
Lighting Designer : ModuleX

BEAMS STREET YOKOHAMA

Type : Apparel retailer
Open : April 2014
Location : Yokohama-shi, Kanagawa, Japan
Floor area : 342m²
Contractor : NOMURA
Lighting Designer : ModuleX

Biople by Cosme Kitchen
JOINUS TheDIAMOND

Type : Cosmetics store
Open : April 2014
Location : Yokohama-shi, Kanagawa, Japan
Floor area : 124m²
Contractor : Co-lab design
Lighting Designer : ModuleX

2014

CA4LA Kichijoji KIRARINA

Type : Apparel retailer
Open : April 2014
Location : Musashino-shi, Tokyo, Japan
Floor area : 58m²
Contractor : D.BRAIN
Lighting Designer : ENDO-Lighting

GOOD MEALS SHOP

Type : Restaurant & Cafe
Open : May 2014
Location : Shibuya-ku, Tokyo, Japan
Floor area : 58m²(2F), 60m²(3F)
Contractor : DECTOR
Lighting Designer : ModuleX

BROOKLYN MUSEUM

Type : Apparel retailer
Open : September 2014
Location : Shibuya-ku, Tokyo, Japan
Floor area : 123m²
Contractor : MESSE
Lighting Designer : ModuleX

Cosme Kitchen Shinsaibashi OPA

Type : Cosmetic store
Open : September 2014
Location : Osaka-shi, Osaka, Japan
Floor area : 98m²
Contractor : SMILEDESIGN
Lighting Designer : ModuleX

Organic Burger Kitchen Shinsaibashi OPA

Type : Restaurant & Cafe
Open : September 2014
Location : Osaka-shi, Osaka, Japan
Floor area : 94m²
Contractor : SMILEDESIGN
Lighting Designer : LIME DESIGN

Ciaopanic HEPFIVE

Type : Apparel retailer
Open : September 2014
Location : Osaka-shi, Osaka, Japan
Floor area : 342m²
Contractor : HANKYU KENSOU
Lighting Designer : ENDO-Lighting

TAKEO KIKUCHI Hankyu Men's Osaka

Type : Apparel retailer
Open : September 2014
Location : Osaka-shi, Osaka, Japan
Floor area : 113m²
Contractor : SOGO DESIGN
Lighting Designer : 1Lux

2014

Tenerita LACIC

Type : Goods and fabric store
Open : September 2014
Location : Nagoya-shi, Aichi, Japan
Floor area : 49m²
Contractor : D.BRAIN
Lighting Designer : ModuleX

Organic Market Kitchen

Type : Restaurant & Cafe
Open : November 2014
Location : Nagoya-shi, Aichi, Japan
Floor area : 320m²
Contractor : EIKOSHA
Lighting Designer : LIME DESIGN

Fukuoka PARCO Adam et Ropé

Type : Apparel retailer
Open : November 2014
Location : Fukuoka-shi, Fukuoka, Japan
Floor area : 221m²
Contractor : MORE LIFE UP
Lighting Designer : ModuleX

Dainipponichi Fukuoka PARCO

Type : Apparel retailer
Open : November 2014
Location : Fukuoka-shi, Fukuoka, Japan
Floor area : 97m²
Contractor : SEMBA CORPORATION
Lighting Designer : ModuleX

HAND BAKES Musashikosugi

Type : Restaurant & Cafe
Open : November 2014
Location : Kawasaki-shi, Kanagawa, Japan
Floor area : 125m²
Contractor : Hakusensha
Lighting Designer : ModuleX

Cosme Kitchen
Grand Tree Musashikosugi

Type : Cosmetic store
Open : November 2014
Location : Kawasaki-shi, Kanagawa, Japan
Floor area : 127m²
Contractor : Co-lab design
Lighting Designer : ModuleX

Wafflish Waffle Omotesando Shop

Type : Apparel retailer
Open : November 2014
Location : Shibuya-ku, Tokyo, Japan
Floor area : 95m²
Contractor : DECOR CO
Lighting Designer : ModuleX

One line is the start of every design.

— LINE-INC.

Construction site of 'The WORKS', 2014.

As of 2015, works of LINE-INC. count up to some 800.
Having had the first project in Tokyo, our operation is spreading all over Japan, Asia, Europe and the USA.

LINE-INC. BACKYARD

1992 - 2001
EXIT METAL WORK SUPPLY

Before LINE-INC.

LINE-INC. was founded in 2002 by Takao Katsuta, and in telling its story it is necessary to discuss the 6 years he spent prior to that.

EXIT METAL WORK SUPPLY began in 1996 with Kaoru Shimizu at the centre. The other members were Takahisa Suematsu, Norito Takahashi, Takuya Kikkojin and, of course, Katsuta. Their average age at the time was 23. They were all aspiring designers, but their first purchase was a welder machine and a beaten-up old truck.

They had a studio where they could not only design but also build metal furniture. Their activities, that they make things by themselves, were unusual at the time and attracted a lot of media attention. Their work in furniture design eventually grew into interior design. Each of the members of EXIT continues to be successful in their genres, and their bond is as strong as ever. Perhaps the reason Katsuta and the staff of LINE-INC. continue to visit the construction sites and talk directly with carpenters, and even help with the construction themselves at times, can be attributed to his experience at EXIT.

2002-2014
Higashiyama Office

First Office of LINE-INC.

Two floors of an old building in Nakameguro area became LINE-INC.'s first office. The main working area was placed on the upper floor, while the floor below became more flexible space in which a variety of sofas, large tables, chairs, books and other decorations were arranged. As time went by, this floor became like a showcase of our design preferences. Even though we have moved out, this place still acts as our annex studio that is used for various events, such as shooting photos and movies.

Who We Are

Led by its director Takao Katsuta, LINE-INC. has created more than 800 spaces all over the world.

Designers:
Front row, left to right
> Yoshitaka Okuma
> Aya Shinohara
> Takao Katsuta
> (Director, Born on 1972 in Shizuoka, Japan)
> Takumi Furukawa
> Nao Katashima

Back row, left to right
> Naohide Inagaki
> Naomichi Ishikawa
> Mizuki Sakamoto
> Takashi Mori
> Takashi Masutani
> Yu Fukuda
> Minoru Oda

Former Staff:
> Kazuya Sasaki
> Kiyono Fujisawa
> Yasuhiko Nakano
> Mika Ito
> Daisuke Funakoshi
> Tomomi Omori
> Reiko Oku
> Ikki Shimoda
> Keiko Yamashita
> Tomokatsu Kusumoto
> Akiko Asano
> Kana Honda
> Ayase Hattori

2015 -
'THE WORKS' Office

Where We Are Now

On completion of 'THE WORKS', we moved to this new location. It is close to our first office, but it is a lot more spacious. Currently, this place feels quite new, but its character will develop with time.

LINE-INC.

Creating Inspiring Places for People

Publisher:
Frame Publishers

Authors:
Takao Katsuta (LINE-INC.), Sawako Akune

Editors:
Sawako Akune, Takahiro Shibata

Art direction and graphic design:
Nobuo Sekiguchi (PLUG-IN GRAPHIC)

Photography:
Kozo Takayama, Tetsuya Ito, Higashi Ishida (P096 - P099)

Translation:
Hitomi Thompson, Sawako Akune

Proofreading:
Uni-edit

Production:
Aya Shinohara (LINE-INC.), Nao Katashima,
Kumiko Hoshino (PLUG-IN GRAPHIC),
Jessica Shortreed (PLUG-IN GRAPHIC)

Trade distribution USA and Canada
Consortium Book Sales & Distribution, LLC.
34 Thirteenth Avenue NE, Suite 101,
Minneapolis, MN 55413-1007
United States
T +1 612 746 2600
T +1 800 283 3572 (orders)
F +1 612 746 2606

Trade distribution Benelux
Frame Publishers
Laan der Hesperiden 68
1076 DX Amsterdam
the Netherlands
distribution@frameweb.com
frameweb.com

Trade distribution rest of world
Thames & Hudson Ltd
181A High Holborn
London WC1V 7QX
United Kingdom
T +44 20 7845 5000
F +44 20 7845 5050

ISBN: 978-94-91727-43-6

Printed on acid-free paper produced from chlorine-free pulp. TCF ∞
Printed in the Netherlands
987654321

LINE-INC.

3F / THE WORKS
3-18-3 Aobadai, Meguro-ku, Tokyo, 153-0042 Japan

T +81-(0)3-6452-5593
F +81-(0)3-6452-5594
line@line-inc.co.jp

http://www.line-inc.co.jp